Handbook of Social Network Technologies and Applications

Borko Furht
Editor

Handbook of Social Network Technologies and Applications

 Springer

Editor
Borko Furht
Florida Atlantic University
Dept. of Comp. & Elect. Engin. and Comp. Sci.
Glades Road 777
33431 Boca Raton Florida
USA
borko@cse.fau.edu

ISBN 978-1-4419-7141-8   e-ISBN 978-1-4419-7142-5
DOI 10.1007/978-1-4419-7142-5
Springer New York Dordrecht Heidelberg London

Printed on acid-free paper

Springer is part of Springer Science+Business Media (www.springer.com)

To my first granddaughter Sophia Rolleri, who is the cutest in the world.

Preface

Social networking is a concept that has been around for a long time; however, with the explosion of the Internet, social networking has become a tool for connecting people and allowing their communications in the ways that was previously impossible. Furthermore, the recent development of Web 2.0 has provided for many new applications such as Myspace, Facebook, Linkedin, and many others.

The objective of this Handbook is to provide comprehensive guidelines on the current and future trends in social network technologies and applications. This Handbook is a carefully edited book – contributors are 82 worldwide experts in the field of social networks and their applications. The Handbook Advisory Board, comprised of 11 researchers and practitioners from academia and industry, helped in reshaping the Handbook and selecting the right topics and creative and knowledgeable contributors.

The scope of the book includes leading edge social network technologies, infrastructures, and communities; social media analysis, organizations, mining, and search; privacy and security issues in social networks; and visualization and applications of social networks.

The Handbook comprises of five parts, which consist of 31 chapters. The first part on *Social Media Analysis and Organization* includes chapters dealing with structure and dynamics of social networks, qualitative analysis of commercial social networks, and various topics relating to analysis and organization of social media.

The second part on *Social Media Mining and Search* focuses on chapters on detecting and discovering communities in social networks, and mining information from social networks and related topics in social media mining and search.

The third part on *Social Network Infrastructures and Communities* consists of chapters on various issues relating to distributed and decentralized online social networks, accessibility testing of social Websites, and understanding human behavior in social networks and related topics.

The fourth part on *Privacy in Online Social Networks* describes various issues related to security, privacy threats, and intrusion detection in social networks.

The fifth part on *Visualization and Applications of Social Networks* includes chapters on visualization techniques for social networks as well as chapters on several applications.

With the dramatic growth of social networks and their applications, this Handbook can be the definitive resource for persons working in this field as researchers, scientists, programmers, engineers, and users. The book is intended for a wide variety of people including academicians, designers, developers, educators, engineers, practitioners, researchers, and graduate students. This book can also be beneficial for business managers, entrepreneurs, and investors. The book can have a great potential to be adopted as a textbook in current and new courses on Social Networks.

The main features of this Handbook can be summarized as follows:

1. The Handbook describes and evaluates the current state-of-the-art in the field of social networks.
2. It also presents current trends in social media analysis, mining, and search as well social network infrastructures and communities.
3. Contributors to the Handbook are the leading researchers from academia and practitioners from industry.

We would like to thank the authors for their contributions. Without their expertise and effort, this Handbook would never come to fruition. Springer editors and staff also deserve our sincere recognition for their support throughout the project.

Boca Raton, Florida   Borko Furht
2010   Editor-in-Chief

Editor-in-Chief

Borko Furht is a professor and chairman of the Department of Electrical & Computer Engineering and Computer Science at Florida Atlantic University (FAU) in Boca Raton, Florida. He is also director of recently formed NSF-sponsored Industry/University Cooperative Research Center on Advanced Knowledge Enablement. Before joining FAU, he was a vice president of research and a senior director of development at Modcomp (Ft. Lauderdale), a computer company of Daimler Benz, Germany, a professor at University of Miami in Coral Gables, Florida, and a senior researcher in the Institute Boris Kidric-Vinca, Yugoslavia. Professor Furht received Ph.D. degree in electrical and computer engineering from the University of Belgrade. His current research is in multimedia systems, video coding and compression, 3D video and image systems, wireless multimedia, and Internet, cloud computing and social networks. He is presently Principal Investigator and Co-PI of several multiyear, multimillion dollar projects including NSF PIRE project and NSF High-Performance Computing Center. He is the author of numerous books and articles in the areas of multimedia, computer architecture, real-time computing, and operating systems. He is a founder and editor-in-chief of *The Journal of Multimedia Tools and Applications* (Springer). He has received several technical and publishing awards and has consulted for many high-tech companies including IBM, Hewlett-Packard, Xerox, General Electric, JPL, NASA, Honeywell, and RCA. He has also served as a consultant to various colleges and universities. He has given many invited talks, keynote lectures, seminars, and tutorials. He served on the Board of Directors of several high-tech companies.

Contents

Part I Social Media Analysis and Organization

1 **Social Network Analysis: History, Concepts, and Research** 3
Mingxin Zhang

2 **Structure and Dynamics of Social Networks Revealed by
Data Analysis of Actual Communication Services** 23
Masaki Aida and Hideyuki Koto

3 **Analysis of Social Networks by Tensor Decomposition** 45
Sergej Sizov, Steffen Staab, and Thomas Franz

4 **Analyzing the Dynamics of Communication in Online
Social Networks** 59
Munmun De Choudhury, Hari Sundaram, Ajita John,
and Doree Duncan Seligmann

5 **Qualitative Analysis of Commercial Social Network
Profiles** 95
Lester Melendez, Ouri Wolfson, Malek Adjouadi,
and Naphtali Rishe

6 **Analysis of Social Networks Extracted from Log Files** 115
Kateřina Slaninová, Jan Martinovič, Pavla Dráždilová,
Gamila Obadi, and Václav Snášel

7 **Perspectives on Social Network Analysis for Observational
Scientific Data** 147
Lisa Singh, Elisa Jayne Bienenstock, and Janet Mann

8 **Modeling Temporal Variation in Social Network: An
Evolutionary Web Graph Approach** 169
Susanta Mitra and Aditya Bagchi

9   **Churn in Social Networks** 185
     Marcel Karnstedt, Tara Hennessy, Jeffrey Chan, Partha
     Basuchowdhuri, Conor Hayes, and Thorsten Strufe

Part II   Social Media Mining and Search

10   **Discovering Mobile Social Networks
     by Semantic Technologies**...223
     Jason J. Jung, Kwang Sun Choi, and Sung Hyuk Park

11   **Online Identities and Social Networking**...................................241
     Muthucumaru Maheswaran, Bader Ali, Hatice Ozguven,
     and Julien Lord

12   **Detecting Communities in Social Networks** 269
     Tsuyoshi Murata

13   **Concept Discovery in Youtube.com Using Factorization
     Method**...281
     Janice Kwan-Wai Leung and Chun Hung Li

14   **Mining Regional Representative Photos from Consumer-
     Generated Geotagged Photos**..303
     Keiji Yanai and Qiu Bingyu

15   **Collaborative Filtering Based on Choosing a Different
     Number of Neighbors for Each User** 317
     Antonio Hernando, Jesús Bobadilla, and Francisco Serradilla

16   **Discovering Communities from Social
     Networks: Methodologies and Applications** 331
     Bo Yang, Dayou Liu, and Jiming Liu

Part III   Social Network Infrastructures and Communities

17   **Decentralized Online Social Networks** 349
     Anwitaman Datta, Sonja Buchegger, Le-Hung Vu, Thorsten
     Strufe, and Krzysztof Rzadca

18   **Multi-Relational Characterization of Dynamic Social
     Network Communities** 379
     Yu-Ru Lin, Hari Sundaram, and Aisling Kelliher

19   **Accessibility Testing of Social Websites** 409
     Cecilia Sik Lányi

20 **Understanding and Predicting Human Behavior for Social Communities** 427
Jose Simoes and Thomas Magedanz

21 **Associating Human-Centered Concepts with Social Networks Using Fuzzy Sets** 447
Ronald R. Yager

Part IV Privacy in Online Social Networks

22 **Managing Trust in Online Social Networks** 471
Touhid Bhuiyan, Audun Josang, and Yue Xu

23 **Security and Privacy in Online Social Networks**.........................497
Leucio Antonio Cutillo, Mark Manulis, and Thorsten Strufe

24 **Investigation of Key-Player Problem in Terrorist Networks Using Bayes Conditional Probability** 523
D.M. Akbar Hussain

25 **Optimizing Targeting of Intrusion Detection Systems in Social Networks** 549
Rami Puzis, Meytal Tubi, and Yuval Elovici

26 **Security Requirements for Social Networks in Web 2.0**.................569
Eduardo B. Fernandez, Carolina Marin, and Maria M. Larrondo Petrie

Part V Visualisation and Applications of Social Networks

27 **Visualization of Social Networks**...585
Ing-Xiang Chen and Cheng-Zen Yang

28 **Novel Visualizations and Interactions for Social Networks Exploration** 611
Nathalie Henry Riche and Jean-Daniel Fekete

29 **Applications of Social Network Analysis**..................................637
P. Santhi Thilagam

30 **Online Advertising in Social Networks**....................................651
Abraham Bagherjeiran, Rushi P. Bhatt, Rajesh Parekh, and Vineet Chaoji

**31 Social Bookmarking on a Company's Intranet: A Study of
    Technology Adoption and Diffusion** 691
    Nina D. Ziv and Kerry-Ann White

Index 713

Contributors

Malek Adjouadi Florida International University, Miami, FL, USA

Masaki Aida Tokyo Metropolitan University, Tokyo, Japan, maida@sd.tmu.ac.jp

Bader Ali McGill University, Montreal, Canada

Aditya Bagchi Indian Statistical Institute, Kolkata, India

Abraham Bagherjeiran Yahoo! Labs, Santa Clara, CA, USA

Partha Basuchowdhuri Digital Enterprise Research Institute, National University of Ireland, Galway, Ireland

Rushi Bhatt Yahoo! Labs, Bangalore, India

Touhid Bhuiyan Queensland University of Technology, Brisbane, Australia, t.bhuiyan@qut.edu.au

Elisa Bienenstock Georgetown University, Washington, DC, USA

Jesús Bobadilla Universidad Politecnica de Madrid, Madrid, Spain

Sonja Buchegger Royal Institute of Technology (KTH), Stockholm, Sweden, buc@csc.kth.se

Jeffrey Chan Digital Enterprise Research Institute, National University of Ireland, Galway, Ireland

Vineet Chaoji Yahoo! Labs, Bangalore, India

Ing-Xiang Chen Telcordia Applied Research Centre - Taiwan, Telcordia Technologies, Piscataway, NJ 08854, seanchen@research.telcordia.com

Kwang Sun Choi Saltlux, South Korea

Munmun De Choudhury Arizona State University, Tempe, AZ, USA

Leucio-Antonio Cutillo Eurecom, Sophia Antropolis, France

Anwitaman Datta Nanyang Technological University, Singapore

Pavla Drazdilova Technical University of Ostrava, Ostrava-Poruba, Czech Republic

Doree Duncan-Seligmann Avaya Labs, New York, NY, USA

Yuval Elovici Ben-Gurion University of the Negev, Israel, elovici@bgu.ac.il

Jean-Daniel Fekete INRIA, University of Paris-Sud, 91405 Orsay Cedex, France

Eduardo Fernandez Florida Atlantic University, Boca Raton, FL, USA,
ed@cse.fau.edu

Thomas Franz University of Koblenz-Landau, Landau, Germany

Conor Hayes Digital Enterprise Research Institute, National University of Ireland,
Galway, Ireland

Tara Hennessy Digital Enterprise Research Institute, National University
of Ireland, Galway, Ireland

Antonio Hernando Universidad Politecnica de Madrid, Madrid, Spain,
ahernandoe@yahoo.com

D.M. Akbar Hussain Aalborg University, Aalborg, Denmark, akh@es.aau.dk

Ajita John Avaya Labs, Lincroft, NJ, USA

Audun Josang University of Oslo, Oslo, Norway

Jason J. Jung Yeungnam University, Gyeongsan, South Korea,
j2jung@gmail.com

Marcel Karnstedt Digital Enterprise Research Institute, National University
of Ireland, Galway, Ireland

Aisling Kelliher Arizona State University, Tempe, AZ, USA

Hideyuki Koto KDDI R&D Laboratories, Saitama, Japan

Cecilia Sik Lanyi University of Pannonia, Veszprem, Hungary,
lanyi@almos.uni-pannon.hu

Maria Larrondo-Petrie Florida Atlantic University, Boca Raton, FL, USA

Janice Kwan-Wai Leung Hong Kong Baptist University, Hong Kong,
janice@Comp.HKBU.Edu.HK

Chun Hung Li Hong Kong Baptist University, Hong Kong

Yu-Ru Lin Arizona State University, Tempe, AZ, USA

Dayou Liu Jilin University, Changchun, China

Jiming Liu Hong Kong Baptist University, Hong Kong

Julien Lord McGill University, Montreal, Canada

Thomas Magedanz Fraunhofer Fokus, Berlin, Germany

Muthucumaru Maheswaran McGill University, Montreal, Canada,
maheswar@cs.mcgill.ca

Janet Mann Georgetown University, Washington, DC, USA

Mark Manulis TU Darmstadt & CASED, Darmstadt, Germany

Carolina Marin Florida Atlantic University, Boca Raton, FL, USA

Jan Martinovic Technical University of Ostrava, Ostrava, Czech Republic

Laster Melendez Florida International University, Miami, FL, USA

Susanta Mitra Meghnad Saha Institute of Technology, Kolkata, India, susanta_mitra@yahoo.com

Tsuyoshi Murata Tokyo Institute of Technology, Tokyo, Japan, murata@cs.titech.ac.jp

Gamila Obadi Technical University of Ostrava, Ostrava, Czech Republic

Hatice Ozguven McGill University, Montreal, Canada

Rajesh Parekh Yahoo! Labs, Santa Clara, CA, USA, rparekh@yahoo-inc.com

Sung-Hyuk Park KAIST Business School, Seoul, South Korea

Rami Puzis Ben-Gurion University of the Negev, Beersheba, Israel, faramir.p@gmail.com

Bingyu Qiu The University of Electro-Communications, Chofu-shi, Tokyo, Japan

Naphtali Rishe Florida International University, Miami, FL, USA, ndr@acm.org, rishe@cs.fiu.edu

Nathalie Henry Riche Microsoft Research, Redmond, WA, USA, Nathalie.Henry@microsoft.com

Krzysztof Rzadca Nanyang Technological University, Singapore

Francisco Serradilla Universidad Politecnica de Madrid, Madrid, Spain

Jose Simoes Fraunhofer Fokus, Berlin, Germany, jose.simoes@fokus.fraunhofer.de

Lisa Singh Georgetown University, Washington, DC, USA, singh@cs.georgetown.edu

Sergej Sizov University of Koblenz-Landau, Koblenz, Germany, sizov@uni-koblenz.de

Katerina Slaninova Technical University of Ostrava, Ostrava, Czech Republic and
Silesian University of Opava, Opava, Czech Republic, slaninova@opf.slu.cz

Vaclav Snasel Technical University of Ostrava, Ostrava, Czech Republic

Steffen Staab University of Koblenz-Landau, Koblenz, Germany

Thorsten Strufe TU Darmstadt & CASED, Darmstadt, Germany, strufe@cs.tu-darmstadt.de

Hari Sundaram Arizona State University, Tempe, AZ, USA,
Hari.Sundaram@asu.edu

P. Santhi Thilagam National Institute of Technology Karnataka, Surathkal,
Karnataka, India, santhi_soci@yahoo.co.in

Meytal Tubi Ben-Gurion University of the Negev, Beersheba, Israel

Le Hung Vu Ecole Polytechnique Federale de Lausanne (EPFL), Lausanne,
Switzerland

Kerry-Ann White Polytechnic Institute of New York University, New York, NY,
USA

Ouri Wolfson University of Illinois, Chicago, IL, USA

Yue Xu Queensland University of Technology, Brisbane, Queensland, Australia

Ronald R. Yager Iona College, New Rochelle, NY, USA, yager@panix.com

Keiji Yanai The University of Electro-Communications, Chofu-shi, Tokyo, Japan,
yanai@cs.uec.ac.jp

Bo Yang Jilin University, Changchun, China, ybo@jlu.edu.cn

Cheng-Zen Yang Yuan Ze University, Chungli, Taiwan

Mingxin Zhang Wuhan University, Wuhan, China, zhmxintop@yahoo.com.cn

Nina D. Ziv Polytechnic Institute of New York University, New York, NY, USA,
nziv123@gmail.com

Part I
Social Media Analysis and Organization

Chapter 1
Social Network Analysis: History, Concepts, and Research

Mingxin Zhang

1.1 Introduction

Social network analysis (SNA), in essence, is not a formal theory in social science, but rather an approach for investigating social structures, which is why SNA is often referred to as structural analysis [1]. The most important difference between social network analysis and the traditional or classic social research approach is that the contexts of the social actor, or the relationships between actors are the first considerations of the former, while the latter focuses on individual properties. A social network is a group of collaborating, and/or competing individuals or entities that are related to each other. It may be presented as a graph, or a multi-graph; each participant in the collaboration or competition is called an actor and depicted as a node in the graph theory. Valued relations between actors are depicted as links, or ties, either directed or undirected, between the corresponding nodes. Actors can be persons, organizations, or groups – any set of related entities. As such, SNA may be used on different levels, ranging from individuals, web pages, families, small groups, to large organizations, parties, and even to nations.

According to the well known SNA researcher Lin Freeman [2], network analysis is based on the intuitive notion that these patterns are important features of the lives of the individuals or social entities who display them; Network analysts believe that how an individual lives, or social entity depends in large part on how that they are tied into the larger web of social connections/structures. Many believe, moreover, that the success or failure of societies and organizations often depends on the patterning of their internal structure.

With a history of more than 70 years, SNA as an interdisciplinary technique developed under many influences, which come from different fields such as sociology, mathematics and computer science, are becoming increasingly important across many disciplines, including sociology, economics, communication science, and psychology around the world. In the current chapter of this book, the author discusses

M. Zhang (✉)
School of Journalism and Communication, Wuhan University, Wuhan, China
e-mail: zhmxintop@yahoo.com.cn

B. Furht (ed.), *Handbook of Social Network Technologies and Applications*,
DOI 10.1007/978-1-4419-7142-5_1, © Springer Science+Business Media, LLC 2010

the history of social network analysis, including its origin and development, in a brief manner, and discusses definition, features, fundamental concepts and research of social network analysis. In the end of this chapter, the author points out that developing and looking for new techniques and tools that resolve corresponding problems challenging SNS research is urgent.

1.2 Social Network Analysis: Definition and Features

Social network is formally defined as a set of social actors, or nodes, members that are connected by one or more types of relations [3]. Nodes, or network members, are the units that are connected by the relations whose patterns researchers study. The units are most commonly individuals, groups or organizations, but in principle any units that can be connected to other units can be studied as nodes, such as web pages, blogs, emails, instant messages, families, journal articles, neighborhoods, classes, sectors within organizations, positions, or nations [4–6]. Research in a number of academic fields has shown that social networks operate on many levels, from families up to the level of nations, and play a critical role in determining the way problems are solved, organizations are run, and the degree to which individuals succeed in achieving their goals [7].

Traditionally, mainstream social research focus exclusively on the behavior of individuals. This approach neglects the social part or structure of human behavior; the part that is concerned with the ways individuals interact and the influence they have on one another [8]. However, social network analysts, take these parts as the primary building blocks of the social world, they not only collect unique types of data, they begin their analyses from a fundamentally different perspective than that had been not adopted by individualist or attribute-based social science.

In social science, the structural approach, that is based on the study of interaction among social actors is called social network analysis [8]. The relationships that social network analysts study are usually those that link individual human beings, since these social scientists believe that besides individual characteristics, relational links or social structure, are necessary and indispensable to fully understand social phenomena. Specifically, Wetherell et al. describe social network analysis as follows [9, p. 645]:

> Most broadly, social network analysis *(1) conceptualizes social structure as a network with ties connecting members and channelling resources, (2) focuses on the characteristics of ties rather than on the characteristics of the individual members, and (3) views communities as 'personal communities', that is, as networks of individual relations that people foster, maintain, and use in the course of their daily lives.*

Structural approach is not confined to the study of human social relationships. As Freeman pointed out [8], it is present in almost every field of science. For example, Freeman wrote that, molecular chemists examine how various kinds of atoms interact together to form different kinds of molecules, while electrical engineers observe how the interactions of various electronic components – like capacitors and resistors – influence the flow of current through a circuit. And biologists study the ways in which each of the species in an ecosystem interacts with and impinges on each of the others.

There are different types of networks. Generally, network analysts differentiate the following networks:

One Mode Versus Two Mode Networks. The former involve relations among a single set of similar actors, while the latter involve relations among two different sets of actors. An example of two mode network would be the analysis of a network consisting of private, for profit organizations and their links to non-profit agencies in a community [10]. Two mode networks are also used to investigate the relationship between a set of actors and a series of events. For example, although people may not have direct ties to each other, they may attend similar events or activities in a community and in doing so, this sets up opportunities for the formation of "weak ties" [11].

Complete/Whole Versus Ego Networks. Complete/whole or Socio-centric networks consist of the connections among members of a single, bounded community. Relational ties among all of the teachers in a high school is an example of whole network. Ego/Ego-centric or personal networks are referred to as the ties directly connecting the focal actor, or ego to others, or ego's alters in the network, plus ego's views on the ties among his or her alters. If we asked a teacher to nominate the people he/she socializes with outside of school, and then asked that teacher to indicate who in that network socializes with the others nominated, it is a typical ego network.

Social network analysis is the study of structure, because the social network approach is grounded in the intuitive notion that the patterning of social ties in which actors are embedded has important consequences for those actors. This is the most important feature of SNA. Early structural intuitions is seen as come from sociologists including Auguste Comte, Ferdinand Tönnies, Emile Durkheim, Sir Herbert Spencer. Freeman argued [8] that these early sociologists all tried to specify the different kinds of social ties that link individuals in different forms of social collectivities. Thus, since they were all concerned with social linkages, they all shared a structural perspective.

If structural intuition is looked as the driving force of social network analysis, we could say that SNA is grounded in systematic empirical data, especially relational, or network data. Relational data is different with the traditional, attribute, or sector data in that it used to describe and explain the relationship between two or more social actors (individuals i and j, for example), while attribute data describe and explain the relationship between two or more attributes of a single social actor (individuals i or j, for example). Tables 1.1 and 1.2 show relational data and attribute data, respectively.

In the context of relational data, as Table 1.1 shows, researcher explores the structure of all the social actors (i.e., i_1, j_1, i_2, j_2 and other nodes), and the mathematical formula could be represented as $S_{ij} = f(ij)$. However, when dealing with attribute data, researcher investigates correlation, causal, mediated, and other relationships

Table 1.1 Relational data

	i_1	j_1	i_2	j_2	...
i_1	–	S_{j1i1}	S_{i2i1}	S_{j2i1}	S_{*i1}
j_1	S_{i1j1}	–	S_{i2j1}	S_{j2j1}	S_{*j1}
i_2	S_{i1i2}	S_{j1i2}	–	S_{j2i2}	S_{*i2}
j_2	S_{i1j2}	S_{j1j2}	S_{i2j2}	–	S_{*j2}
...	S_{i1*}	S_{j1*}	S_{i2*}	S_{j2*}	–

Table 1.2 Attribute data

Y	x_1	x_1	x_3	x_4	...
1	...	...	...	...	...
2	...	...	...	...	...
3	...	...	...	...	...
...	...	...	...	...	...
N	...	...	...	...	...

between different variables (i.e., dependent and independent variables, Y and x_1, x_2, x_3, x_4 and other variables in Table 1.2). $Y = f(x)$ is mathematical formula in this context.

The third prominent feature of SNA is it draws heavily on graphic imagery. In the field of SNA, researchers use points to represent social actors and lines to represent linkages among them. There are two types of graphs: directed and undirected graphs. Directed graph consists of a set of nodes and a set of links (also called arcs or edges). A link e, is an ordered pair (i, j) representing a connection from node i to node j. Node i is called the initial node of link e, $i = \text{init}(e)$, and node j is called the final node of the link: $j = \text{fin}(e)$. If the direction of a link is not important, or equivalently, if existence of a link between nodes i and j necessarily implies the existence of a link from j to i, we say that this network is an undirected graph. A path from node i to node j is a sequence of distinct links (i, u_1), $(u_1, u_2), \ldots$, (u_k, j). The length of this path is the number of links (here $k + 1$). An undirected graph can be represented by a symmetrical matrix $M = (m_{ij})$, where m_{ij} is equal to 1 if there is an edge between nodes i and j, and m_{ij} is 0 if there is no direct link between nodes i and j.

Table 1.3 shows an imaginary relational data matrix. There is a line connecting node A and node B. It is noticeable that this link is an ordered relation. Here A is the initial node of link, while B is the final node. Using directed graph to describe this data matrix, we will get Fig. 1.1.

However, graph showed in Fig. 1.1 is rather primitive, because it only consists of six nodes and seven links. Figure 1.2 describes a more complex graph in a study of China inter-provincial interactions conducted by Jonathan Zhu [6]. In this context, there are 32 nodes (i.e., provinces) and numerous links between any pair of two nodes. There links describe information and population interactions in China mainland. It is clear that Beijing and Shanghai, the biggest cities in China, occupy the centric position in the graph.

Table 1.3 An imaginary
relational data matrix

	A	B	C	D	E	F
A	–	1	1	0	0	0
B	0	–	1	1	0	0
C	1	1	–	0	0	0
D	0	0	0	–	1	1
E	0	0	0	0	–	1
F	0	0	0	1	1	–

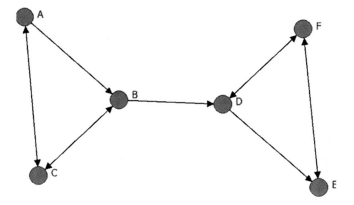

Fig. 1.1 Directed graph of relational data matrix in Table 1.3

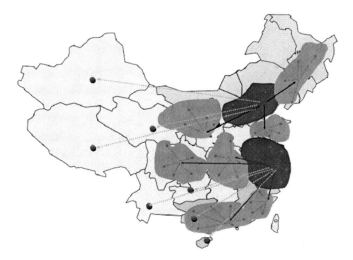

Fig. 1.2 China inter-provincial interactions

Figure 1.3 shows a more complex graph regarding the co-citation network in the research field of media economics [12]. In this graph, it is easy to know that the following documents, such as *Picard_89, Albarran_96, Owen/Wildman_92, Scherer_73/90, Litman_79, Lacy_89,Bagdikian_83/00*, and so on, occupy more

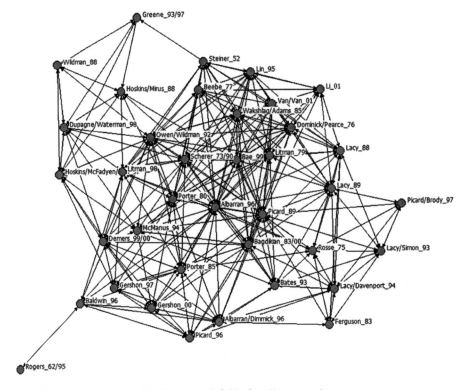

Fig. 1.3 Co-citation network in the research field of media economics

central positions in the network, indicating that they are more important than others. Reflected by the number of ties in the graph, we could see that there are more links point to them.

Freeman argued [8] that unlike many other approaches to social research, network analysis has consistently drawn on various branches of mathematics both to clarify its concepts and to spell out their consequences in precise terms. Thus, the usage of mathematical and/or computational models, is an important feature of SNA. This is the fourth feature of SNA.

1.3 The Development of Social Network Analysis: A Brief History

As stated above, early sociologists in the late 1800s, including Émile Durkheim and Ferdinand Tönnies, are precursors of social network theory. Tönnies argued that social groups can exist as personal and direct social ties that either link individuals who share values and belief or impersonal, formal, and instrumental social links.

Durkheim gave a non-individualistic explanation of social facts arguing that social phenomena arise when interacting individuals constitute a reality that can no longer be accounted for in terms of the properties of individual actors. He distinguished between a traditional society – "mechanical solidarity" – which prevails if individual differences are minimized, and the modern society – "organic solidarity" – that develops out of cooperation between differentiated individuals with independent roles [8]. Georg Simmel, writing at the turn of the twentieth century, was the first scholar to think directly in social network terms. His essays pointed to the nature of network size on interaction and to the likelihood of interaction in ramified, loosely–knit networks rather than groups [13].

Social network as a relatively separate academic concept generated in 1920s–1930s in the research filed of anthropology in Britain. Anthropologist Roger Brown was the first researcher who used the term social network, implying that social structure is similar with a network and that interpersonal communication among individuals resembles relationship between a node and another nesting in the network [14].

One of the line of social network analysis could be traced back to *Sociomery Method* created by social psychologist Jacob Levy Moreno in 1930s, and this method paved the way for quantitative analysis in social network approach. In the 1930s, Moreno pioneered the systematic recording and analysis of social interaction in small groups, especially classrooms and work groups. According to Freeman [8], in Moreno's 1934 book, he used the term "network" in the sense that it is used today. Freeman further pointed out that by 1938, then, the work of Moreno – with the help of Jennings and Lazarsfeld—had displayed all four of the features that define contemporary social network analysis [8].

The second line is a Harvard group led by W. Lloyd Warner and Elton Mayo, which exhibited research effort that focused on the study of social structure in the late 1920s. However, the Harvard effort never "took off" in Freeman's eye, because it never provided a general model for a structural paradigm. As a matter of fact, the efforts at Harvard group are almost never recognized in historical reviews of social network analysis [8].

The 1940s–1960s is called by Freeman as the Dark Ages in the history of the development of SNA. In this period, there was no generally recognized approach to social research that embodied the structural paradigm. Social network analysis was still not identifiable either as a theoretical perspective or as an approach to data collection and analysis [8].

In the 1960s–1970s, a growing number of scholars worked to combine the different tracks and traditions. One large group was centered around Harrison White and his students at Harvard University: Ivan Chase, Bonnie Erickson, Harriet Friedmann, Mark Granovetter, Nancy Howell, Joel Levine, Nicholas Mullins, John Padgett, Michael Schwartz and Barry Wellman. Freeman called it as the Renaissance of SNA at Harvard. The Harvard school published so much important theory and research focused on social networks that social scientists everywhere, regardless of their field, could no longer ignore the idea. By the end of the 1970s, then, social network analysis came to be universally recognized among social scientists.

According to Freeman's statistics, Harrison White group at Harvard University was not the only ones who could lay claim to the social network approach. On the contrary, in the 40-year period from the late 1930s through the late 1970s, there were at least 17 research groups or centers adopted a general social network perspective. Of course, the developments at these groups or centers were not all independent of one another. Those that emerged later undoubtedly drew on the work of at least some of the earlier efforts [8].

Table 1.4 lists some founders and the most prominent researchers of SNA from 1940s through 1970s. However, it can't provide more information regarding the internal structure of these founders and researchers, just like the traditional social research could not discover the interaction patterns of social actors. Figure 1.4 describes the influences of parts of the above founders and researchers. When introducing the basic concepts in the next part of this chapter, we will give more detailed explanations about this figure.

Table 1.4 Noticeable research groups in the development of SNA: 1930s–1970s

Time period	Group leader	Known researchers	University/institution
1930s–1940s	Kurt Lewin, John French, Alex Bavelas	Dorwin Cartwright, Leon Festinger, Duncan Luce	University of Iowa, MIT, University of Michigan
Mid 1940s	Charles P. Loomis	Leo Katz, Charles Proctor, T. N. Bhargava	Michigan State College
Late 1940s	Lévi–Strauss	–	University of Chicago
Early 1950s	Torsten Hägerstrand	–	Lund University
Early 1950s	Nicolas Rashevsky	Walter Pitts, Herbert D. Landahl, Hyman G. Landau, Anatol Rapoport	University of Chicago
Mid 1950s	Paul Lazarsfeld, Robert K. Merton	James S. Coleman, Elihu Katz, Herbert Menzel, Peter Blau, Charles Kadushin	Columbia University
Mid 1950s	Everett M. Rogers	George Barnett, James Danowski, Richard Farace, Peter Monge, Nan Lin, William Richards, Ronald Rice	Iowa State University, Michigan State University
Mid 1950s	Alfred Reginald Radcliffe–Brown, Max Gluckman	John Barnes, John Barnes, J.Clyde Mitchell, Elizabeth Bott, Sigfried Nadel	Manchester University, London School of Economics
Late 1950s	Karl Wolfgang Deutsch, Ithiel de Sola Pool	Fred Kochen	MIT
Late 1950s	Linton C. Freeman, Morris H. Sunshine	Thomas Fararo, Sue Freeman	Syracuse University
Early 1960s	Claude Flament	–	Paris Sorbonne University

(continued)

Table 1.4 (continued)

Time period	Group leader	Known researchers	University/institution
Mid 1960s	Edward O. Laumann	Stephen Berkowitz, Ronald Burt, Joseph Galaskiewicz, Alden Klovdahl, David Knoke, Peter Marsden, Martina Morris, David Prensky, Philip Schumm	University of Michigan
Late 1960s	Peter Blau, James A. Davis	–	University of Chicago
Late 1960s	Robert Mokken	Jac Anthonisse, Frans Stokman	
1960s–1970s	Harrison Colyer White	Peter Bearman, Paul Bernard, Phillip Bonacich, Ronald L. Breiger, Kathleen M. Carley, Ivan Chase, Bonnie Erickson, Claude S. Fischer, Mark Granovetter, Joel Levine, Siegwart M. Lindenberg, Barry Wellman, Christopher Winship	Harvard University

When the concept of social network has been recognized by more and more researchers, more contributions have been made in research methodology: more and more measurement, data collection and analysis technologies were created and developed to understand social construe and relationships better, and these in turn advanced social network research.

In the 1980s, a number of sociologists began to use SNA as analytical technique to examine social and economic phenomena. In mid 1980s, Mark Granovetter, proposed the concept of "embedded-ness", guiding SNA approach into the mainstream social research field again. Granovetter argued that the operation of economics is embedded in social structure, however, the core social structure is individuals' social networks. In early 1980s, Granovetter formulated marketing network theory in his well known article *"Where Do Markets Come From?"* [15].

After 1990s, SNA has been gradually associated with social capital, drawing scholars' attention from the field of sociology, politics, economics, communication science, and other disciplines. Ronald Burt's book *Structural Holes* is representative work of this period. Burt argues that social capital has not relationship with the strength of ties, but with the existence of structural holes. Lin Nan, another well known sociologist who proposed Social-resource theory, studied SNA from the social capital perspective. In the next part of this chapter, when comes to theorization of SNA research design, the author will discuss Burt and Lin more.

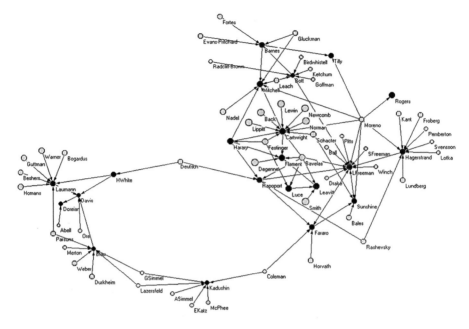

Fig. 1.4 Influences on some founders of SNA [8, p.131]

1.4 Basic Concepts of Social Network Analysis

Social network is formally referred to as a set of social actors, or nodes, members that are connected by one or more types of relations. To understand networks and their participants, researchers should evaluate the location of actors in the network. To measuring location of each node, one should use the concept centrality and other related concepts. Through empirical measurement of a network, one will find various roles and groupings in a network – who are the connectors, mavens, leaders, bridges, isolates? where are the clusters and who is in them? who is in the core of the network? And, who is on the periphery?

In the following of this part, important concepts, such as ties, density, centrality, cliques and other concepts will be explained.

1.4.1 Ties

Ties or links connect two and more nodes in a graph. Many human behaviors, such as advice seeking, information-sharing, and lending money to somebody are directed ties while co-memberships are examples of undirected ties. Directed ties may be reciprocated, as would be the case for two people who visit one another, or they may exist in only one direction as when only one gives emotional support to the other [16]. Both directed and undirected ties can be measured as binary ties that either exist or do not exist within each dyad, or as valued ties that can be stronger or weaker, transmit more or fewer resources, or have more or less frequent contact.

1.4.2 Density

One of the most widely used, and perhaps over-used, concepts in graph theory is that of "density", which describes the general level of linkage among the points in a graph. A "complete" graph is one in which all the points are adjacent to one another: each point is connected directly to every other point. As an attempt to summarize the overall distribution of lines, the concept of density aims to measure how far from this state of completion the graph is [14]. The density of a graph is quantitatively defined as the number of links divided by the number of vertices in a complete graph with the same number of nodes. It is an indicator for the general level of connectedness of the graph.

Density is one of the most basic measures in network analysis and one of the most commonly used notions in social epidemiology. Some network structures are particularly advantageous for certain functions [17]. For example, dense networks are particularly good for coordination of activity among the actors (because everyone knows everyone's business). In the case of Fig. 1.1, results of density measures(ego networks) are shown in Table 1.5.

1.4.3 Path, Length, and Distance

Nodes or actors may be directly connected by a line, or they may be indirectly connected through a sequence of lines. A sequence of lines in a graph is a "walk", and a walk in which each point and each line are distinct is called a path. The concept of the path is, after those of the node and the line, one of the most basic of all graph theoretical concepts. The length of a path is measured by the number of lines which make it up. The distance between two nodes is the length of the shortest path (the "geodesic") which connects them [14].

Table 1.5 Density measures of Fig. 1.1

	Size	Ties	Pairs	Density
A	2.00	2.00	2.00	100.00
B	3.00	2.00	6.00	33.33
C	2.00	1.00	2.00	50.00
D	3.00	2.00	6.00	33.33
E	2.00	2.00	2.00	100.00
F	2.00	1.00	2.00	50.00

Table 1.6 Geodesic
distances of nodes in Fig. 1.1

	A	B	C	D	E	F
A	0	1	1	2	3	2
B	2	0	1	1	2	2
C	1	1	0	2	3	3
D	–	–	–	0	1	1
E	–	–	–	2	0	1
F	–	–	–	1	1	0

As to graph in Fig. 1.1, the average distance (among reachable pairs) is 1.667, distance-based cohesion("compactness") is 0.511 (range 0–1; larger values indicate greater cohesiveness), distance–weighted fragmentation ("breadth") is 0.489. As to every node in Fig. 1.1, the Geodesic Distances are shown in Table 1.6.

1.4.4 Centrality

The measures of centrality identify the most prominent actors, especially the star or the "key" players, that is, those who are extensively involved in relationships with other network members. The most important centrality measures are: degree centrality, closeness centrality and between-ness centrality.

(1) *Degree Centrality.* Degree of a node is the number of direct connections a node has. Degree centrality is the sum of all other actors who are directly connected to ego. It signifies activity or popularity. Lots of ties coming in and lots of ties coming out of an actor would increase degree centrality.

(2) *Between-ness Centrality.* This type of centrality is the number of times a node connects pairs of other nodes, who otherwise would not be able to reach one another. It is a measure of the potential for control as an actor who is high in "between-ness" is able to act as a gatekeeper controlling the flow of resources (information, money, power, e.g.) between the alters that he or she connects. This measurement of centrality is purely structural measure of popularity, efficiency, and power in a network; in other words, the more connected or centralized actor is more popular, efficient, or powerful.

(3) *Closeness Centrality.* Closeness centrality is based on the notion of distance. If an node or actor is close to all others in the network, a distance of no more than one, then it is not dependent on any other to reach everyone in the network. Closeness measures independence or efficiency. With disconnected networks, closeness centrality must be calculated for each component.

Table 1.7 indicated centrality measures of Fig. 1.1. As to complete network, when measuring with *Degree Centrality*, network centralizations are both 4.000% for in-degree and out-degree measures (asymmetric model); when using Freeman *Between-ness Centrality* indicator, un-normalized centralization of the complete

Table 1.7 Centrality measures of Fig. 1.1

	Out-degree	In-degree	In-closeness	Out-closeness	Between-ness
A	2	1	1.500	3.167	0
B	2	2	2.000	3.500	6
C	2	2	2.000	3.167	1
D	2	2	3.500	2.000	6
E	1	2	3.167	1.500	0
F	2	2	3.167	2.000	1

Table 1.8 Two cliques of graph in Fig. 1.1

	Sub-group 1	Sub-group 2
A	1.000	0.000
B	1.000	0.333
C	1.000	0.000
D	0.333	1.000
E	0.000	1.000
F	0.000	1.000

network is 22.00%; when using *Closeness Centrality Measures* (method: Reciprocal Geodesic Distances), the results are both 51.00% for network in-centralization and out-centralization.

1.4.5 Clique

A clique in a graph is a sub-graph in which any node is directly connected to any other node of the sub-graph. There two cliques in the graph of Fig. 1.1, that is, subgroup {A, B, C} and {D, E, F}. Clique proximities analysis shows the probability of clique members that each node is adjacent to, as described in Table 1.8.

1.5 Research of SNA: Design, Theorization, and Data Processing

1.5.1 Designing a Social Network Analysis

Before conducting a SNA study, especially before collecting network data, one must first decide what kinds of networks and what kinds of relations they will study. As stated above, there have two important dimensions along which network data vary: one-mode vs. two-mode networks and complete vs. ego networks. As a general rule, researchers must make these choices at the beginning of study.

Complete/whole networks, taking a bird's eye view of the social structure, focus on all social actors rather than privileging the network surrounding any particular actor. These networks begin from a list of included actors and include data on the presence or absence of relations between every pair of actors. When examining all students and their interpersonal relationship in a class [18], or a network of actors appearing on film or television showing who has co-starred with whom [5], a whole network approach should be applied. Generally, researchers using whole network data frequently analyze more than one relation. When researcher adopts the whole network perspective, he/she will inquire each social actor and all other individuals to collect relational data, then transforming into matrix (i.e., network data). In this situation, emphasis on data analysis is not the nature of each relation type, but structure of relation.

Ego-centric network data, however, focus on the network surrounding one node, or in other words, the single social actor. Data are on nodes that share the chosen relation(s) with the ego and on relations between those nodes. Ego network data can be extracted from whole network data by choosing a focal node and examining only nodes connected to this ego. Ego network data, like whole network data, can also include multiple relations. These relations can be collapsed into single networks, as when ties to people who provide companionship and emotional aid are collapsed into a single support network [19]. Unlike whole network analyses, which commonly focus on one or a small number of networks, ego network analyses typically sample large numbers of egos and their networks. Researchers using ego network approach emphasize the significance of individual's exploitation of his/her social network for social resources. In these researchers' view, individual's social network influences his/her social attitude and behavior.

When studying whole networks, researchers most frequently collect data on a single type of node in networks where every node could conceivably be connected to any other nodes. Most of the networks they analyze are one-mode networks. Two-mode networks, involve relations among two different sets of actors or nodes – typically organizations and organization members, or events and attendees. In these two-mode networks or affiliation networks, relations consist of things such as memberships or attendance at events that cannot exist between nodes of the same type: A person can attend an event or belong to an organization, but a person cannot attend or belong to another event or organization [20].

After deciding what kinds of networks and what kinds of relations under consideration, researchers should decide to how to collect network data. Many methods could be used, including (trace) observation, archives and historical materials analysis, survey, interview, and experiment [21, 22].

When using survey to collect data, the following techniques could be considered in designing questionnaire. (1) Name generators: researchers ask respondents to list the people with whom they share ties, and further ask the types, strength or importance, and other characteristics of these ties. This technique is especially suitable for ego network data. (2) Structurally selecting format: respondents are asked to indicate the people with whom they have relations, however, the number of the people should not larger than a threshold. For example, a probable question may ask respondents that: In recently 6 months, whom do you interact with (you can list five persons at the most)? (3) Indicating characteristics of network members: researchers may ask respondents report democratic, societal, attitudinal, and behavioral properties of their network members. (4) Position generators, which was put forward by Lin Nan and colleagues, ask respondents to list their network members in different social ranks.

Interview as an often used method, also helps SNA researchers to collect ego network data. Researchers could ask respondents' circle of friends, peer relations, and primitive comradeship. This data collection method is also used to study social support network.

1.5.2   Theorization in Social Network Analysis

Theorization is the basic goal of all research fields of social science. As a perspective or a research paradigm, social network analysis takes as its starting point the premise that social life is created primarily and most importantly by relations and the patterns they form, and it provides a way of looking at a problem, but it does not predict what we will see [20]. However, in the stage of research design, scholars should do their best to carry out research with the application of related theories, and aim to extend and modify social theories. In fact, several famous theories have been exactly developed under the social network perspective.

Diffusion of innovations theory, DIT, explores social networks and their role in influencing the spread of new ideas, products, and practices, etc. As Rogers' s book shows, many communication theories, such as the theory of two step flow of communication, heterophily and communication channels, have been integrated in related studies. Taking communication science as an example, in recent years, many research articles examining the impacts of communication networks on the adoption and usage of new information and communication technologies (ICTs) among specific social groups in different cultural contexts [23–25] have been published in top international journals, such as *Information Research, Communication Research, Journal of Computer Mediated Communication*, etc.

Using a network perspective, Mark Granovetter [11] put forward the theory of the "strength-of-weak-ties". Granovetter found in one study that more numerous weak ties can be important in seeking information and innovation. Because cliques have a tendency to have more homogeneous opinions and common traits, individuals in the same cliques would also know more or less what the other members know. To gain new information and opinion, people often look beyond the clique to their other friends and acquaintances. However, Bian Yanjie, a Chinese social scientist, found that in China, personal networks (Guanxi[1]) are used to influence authorities who in

---

[1] Guanxi, used to describe a personal connection between two people in which one is able to prevail upon another to perform a favor or service, or be prevailed upon, is a central concept in Chinese society.

turn assign jobs as favors to their contacts, which is a type of unauthorized activity facilitated by strong ties characterized by trust and obligation. Bian called his theory as Strong Ties [26].

The Small World is other example of theorization of social network research. The idea of small world hypotheses that in a network, most nodes are not neighbors of one another, but most nodes can be reached from every other by a small number of hops or steps. This concept gave rise to the famous phrase "Six Degrees of Separation". In psychologist Stanley Milgram's experiment, a sample of US individuals were asked to reach a particular target person by passing a message along a chain of acquaintances. Result shows that the average length of successful chains turned out to be about five intermediaries or six separation steps.

After 1990s, scholars extend the theorization of social network analysis greatly, among which the most famous were Ronald Burt's theory of Structural Holes and Lin Nan's Social Capital Theory. Burt argue that the weaker connections between groups are holes in the social structure of the market. These holes in social structure create a competitive advantage for an individual whose relationships span the holes. Finally, structural holes are an opportunity to broker the flow of information between people, and control the projects that bring together people from opposite sides of the hole.

As one of the very first scholars to undertake serious research on the social networks foundation of social capital, Lin Nan's studies in recent years produce universal influences around the world. Lin's assumption is that the macro-level social structure is a type of hierarchical structure, which is determined by the allocation of various resources such as wealth, social status, and power [27, 28]. In his famous book *Social Capital: A Theory of Social Structure and Action*, Lin explains the importance of using social connections and social relations in achieving goals. Social capital as resources, accessed through such connections and relations, is critical in achieving goals for individuals, social groups, organizations, and communities. The framework of Lin's social capital research consists of the following elements: social actor's network position, the strength of ties, resources, redound, and otherwise.

1.5.3 SNA Data Processing Tools

As stated above, since network data are different with the traditional attribute data, social network analysts use corresponding techniques to process data collected. Social network analysis software is used to identify, represent, analyze, visualize, or simulate nodes and ties from various types of input data.

At the present, popular social network tools are UCINET, PAJEK, STRUCTURE, NETMINER, STOCNET, and others.

UCINET is developed by Steve Borgatti, Martin Everett and Lin Freeman [29]. The program is distributed by Analytic Technologies. It works in tandem with freeware program called NETDRAW for visualizing networks, which is installed automatically with UCINET. This type of software can process, read and write a multitude of differently formatted text files, as well as Excel files, and handle a maximum of 32,767 nodes (with some exceptions), although practically speaking, many procedures get too slow around 5,000–10,000 nodes. Centrality measures, subgroup identification, role analysis, elementary graph theory, permutation-based statistical analysis, and other SNA measures can be performed on the software.

PAJEK, Slovene word for Spider, is an open source Windows program for analysis and visualization of large networks having some thousands or even millions of vertices. It started development in November 1996, and is implemented in Delphi (Pascal). It is freely available, for noncommercial use, at its homepage: http://vlado.fmf.uni-lj.si/pub/networks/pajek/. The main goals in the design of Pajek are to support abstraction by (recursive) factorization of a large network into several smaller, which can be treated further using more sophisticated methods; to provide the user with some powerful visualization tools; and to implement a selection of efficient algorithms for analysis of large networks.

The program STRUCTURE is a free software package for using multi-locus genotype data to investigate population structure. Its uses include inferring the presence of distinct populations, assigning individuals to populations, studying hybrid zones, identifying migrants and admixed individuals, and estimating population allele frequencies in situations where many individuals are migrants or admixed. It can be applied to most of the commonly-used genetic markers, including SNPs, microsatellites, RFLPs and AFLPs. Furthermore, functions that STRUCTURE provide cannot be found in other social network data processing tools.

NETMINER is an innovative software tool for Exploratory Analysis and Visualization of Network Data. It can be used for general research and teaching in social networks. This tool allows researchers to explore their network data visually and interactively, helps them to detect underlying patterns and structures of the network. Especially, it can be effectively applied to various business fields where network-structural factors have great deal of influences on the performance (e.g., intra and inter-organizational financial Web criminal/intelligence informetric telecommunication distribution transportation networks). Statistically, this program supports many standardized computer methods, including descriptive statistics, ANOVA, correlation, and regression.

1.6 Summary

Social network analysis is the study of social structure. The social network analysts are interested in how the individual is embedded within a structure and how the structure emerges from the micro-relations between individual parts [30]. Hence, the greatest advantage of SNA is that it considers how the communication network structure of a group shapes individuals' cognition, attitude and behavior. As an approach to social research, SNA displays four features: structural intuition, systematic relational data, graphic images and mathematical or computational models [8]. In its more than 70 years of history, social network analysts have developed a number of formal and precise ways of defining terms like "relation", "density", "centrality", "clique" and others, so that they can be applied unambiguously to data on populations of individuals.

Recognizing that "we all connect, like a net we cannot see" [31], social network analysis is more and more popular with researchers from various fields such as sociology, mathematics, computer science, economics, communication science, and psychology around the world. In social sciences, theorization of SNA has been improved obviously in the recent two decades, although it had been criticized before 1980s. However, as new information and communication technologies (e.g., the Internet, mobile phones, digital broadcast, etc.) have made the collection of social network data much easier on a much larger scale at a much lower cost than what conventional methods could offer, problems regarding the analysis and the subsequent interpretation of the resulting data raise. Existing techniques seem to be inadequate to handle new types of social network data that are continuous, dynamic, and multilevel [6]. Thanks to the current situation, developing and looking for new techniques and tools that resolve these problems should become social and engineering scientists research agenda.

References

1. B. Wellman and S. D. Berkowitz (Eds). "Social Structures: A Network Approach." Cambridge: Cambridge University Press, 1988.
2. L. C. Freeman. "What is Social Network Analysis?" Last Update Friday, 08-Feb-2008, Available at: http://www.insna.org/sna/what.html
3. S. Wasserman and K. Faust. "Social Network Analysis: Methods and Applications." Cambridge: Cambridge University Press, 1994.
4. S. A. Boorman and H. C. White. "Social Structure from Multiple Networks. II. Role Structures." American Journal of Sociology, Vol. 81, No. 6, 1976, pp. 1384–1446.
5. D. J. Watts. "Networks, Dynamics, and the Small-World Phenomenon." American Journal of Sociology, Vol. 105, No. 2, 1999, pp. 493–527.
6. J. J. H. Zhu. "Opportunities and Challenges for Network Analysis of Social and Behavioral Data." Seminar Series on Chaos, Control and Complex Networks City University of Hong Kong, Poly U University of Hong Kong & IEEE Hong Kong R&A/CS Joint Chapter, 2007.
7. H. D. White, B. Wellman, and N. Nazer. "Does Citation Reflect Social Structure? Longitudinal Evidence from the 'Globenet' Interdisciplinary Research Group." Journal of the American Society for Information Science and Technology, Vol. 55, No. 2, 2004, pp. 111–126.
8. L. C. Freeman. "The Development of Social Network Analysis: A Study in The Sociology of Science." Canada: Empirical Press Vancouver, 2004.
9. C. Wetherell, A. Plakans, and B. Wellman. "Social Networks, Kinship, and Community in Eastern Europe." Journal of Interdisciplinary History, Vol. 24, No. 1, 1994, pp. 639–663.
10. P. Hawe, C. Webster, and A. Shiell. "A Glossary of Terms for Navigating the Field of Social Network Analysis." Journal of Epidemiology and Community Health, Vol. 58, 2004, pp. 971–975.
11. M. Granovetter. "The Strength of Weak Ties." American Journal of Sociology, Vol. 78, 1973, pp. 1360–1380.
12. M. X. Zhang. "Co-citation Network and the Structure of Paradigms in the Research Field of Media Economics: 1999–2008." Unpublished manuscript, 2011.
13. G. Simmel. "On Individuality and Social Forms." Chicago: University of Chicago Press, 1908/1971.

14. J. Scott. "Social Network Analysis: A Handbook." London: Sage Publications, 1987.
15. M. Granovetter. "Economic Action and Social Structure: The Problem of Embedded-ness." American Journal of Sociology, Vol. 91, No. 3, 1985, pp. 481–493.
16. G. Plickert, R. Côté, and B. Wellman. "It's Not Who You Know. It's How You Know Them: Who Exchanges What with Whom?" Social Networks, Vol. 29, No. 3, 2007, pp. 405–429.
17. J. Liu. "An Introduction to Social Network Analysis (In Chinese)." Beijing: Social Sciences Academic Press, 2004.
18. M. X. Zhang. "Exploring Adolescent Peer Relationships Online and Offline: An Empirical and Social Network Analysis." Proceedings of 2009 WRI International Conference on Communications and Mobile Computing, Vol. 3, 2009, pp. 268–272.
19. B. Wellman. "The Community Question: The Intimate Networks of East Yorkers." American Journal of Sociology, Vol. 84, 1979, pp. 1201–1231.
20. A. Marin and B. Wellman. "Social Network Analysis: An Introduction." In: P. Carrington and J. Scott (Eds). Handbook of Social Network Analysis. London: Sage, 2010.
21. D. Gibson. "Concurrency and Commitment: Network Scheduling and Its Consequences for Diffusion." Journal of Mathematical Sociology, Vol. 29, No. 4, 2005, pp. 295–323.
22. R. Gould. "Insurgent Identities: Class, Community and Protest in Paris from 1848 to the Commune." Chicago: University of Chicago Press, 1995.
23. L. Wei and M. X. Zhang. "The Adoption and Use of Mobile Phone in Rural China: A Case Study of Hubei, China." Telematics and Informatics, Vol. 25, No. 3, 2008, pp. 169–186.
24. L. Wei and M. X. Zhang. "The Impacts of Internet Knowledge on College Students' Intention to Continue to Use the Internet." Information Research, Vol. 13, No. 3, 2008, paper 348. Available at http://InformationR.net/ir/13–3/paper348.html
25. J. J. H. Zhu and Z. He. "Perceived Characteristics, Perceived Needs, and Perceived Popularity: Adoption and Use of the Internet in China." Communication Research, Vol. 29, No. 4, 2002, pp. 466–495.
26. Y. J. Bian. "Bringing Strong Ties Back in: Indirect Ties, Network Bridges, and Job Searches in China." American Sociological Review, Vol. 62, No. 3, 1997, pp. 366–385.
27. N. Lin, K. Cook, and R. Burt (Eds). "Social Capital: Theory and Research." New Brunswick, NJ: Transaction Press, 2001.
28. N. Lin. "Social Capital: A Theory of Social Structure and Action." NewYork: Cambridge University Press, 2001.
29. S. Borgatti, M. Everett, and L. Freeman. "Ucinet for Windows: Software for Social Network Analysis." Harvard, MA: Analytic Technologies, 2002.
30. R. Hanneman. "Introduction to Social Network Methods." 2002, Available at: www.faculty.ucr.edu/,hanneman/
31. R. Mickenberg and J. Dugan. "Taxi Driver Wisdom." San Francisco: Chronicle, 1995.

Chapter 2
Structure and Dynamics of Social Networks Revealed by Data Analysis of Actual Communication Services

Masaki Aida and Hideyuki Koto

2.1 Introduction

Up to now, data of actual communication services obtained from communication networks, such as the volume of traffic and the number of users, has mainly been used to forecast traffic demands and provision network facilities. It can be said that this use focuses on the "quantitative" side of the data. On the other hand, such data can also illuminate several characteristics of the structures of the human society. This chapter introduces a new "qualitative" use of communication network data. We try to extract social information from the data, and investigate the universal structure of social networks that underlie the most popular communication services. Our expectation is that each communication service provides a different window on the universal social network structure. The question is how to access those windows.

A direct technique for examining social network structures is the questionnaire approach. However, its extremely high cost makes it impractical if we target a comprehensive analysis of the universal social network structure. Our solution is to collect and analyze the quantitative data generated by communication services. The contents of communication logs etc. offer views of the individual situations associated with that service. Examples of these situations include interpersonal relationships in an organization and agreements reached between corporations. However, conventional analysis fails to extract complete images of the universal social network structure.

In this chapter, we focus on the power laws that appear in the data of actual communication services. In explaining the reasons that underlie the power laws, we elucidate the whole universal social network structure. Since the power laws examined in this chapter describe the relations present in coarse data, detailed behaviors (e.g., who is communicating with who) of each user cannot be observed. However, we can expect to extract a more nearly universal structure that is independent of the superficial structures present in each data set. Once we develop a universal model of

M. Aida (✉)
Tokyo Metropolitan University, Hino-shi, Tokyo 191-0065, Japan
e-mail: maida@sd.tmu.ac.jp

B. Furht (ed.), *Handbook of Social Network Technologies and Applications*,
DOI 10.1007/978-1-4419-7142-5_2, © Springer Science+Business Media, LLC 2010

social networks, we can better understand the process of service penetration and can find a better activation method that can replace the word-of-mouth communication-based marketing approach, for not only existing services but also future services. In addition, a comprehensive understanding of the universal social network structure could be applied to not only communication services but also more general commodities and services such as business and marketing strategies.

We explain here why we focus on power laws. We know that certain types of distributions (e.g., normal, Poisson, etc.) originate from randomness. Differing from these distributions, power laws can be assumed to have deterministic causes. Therefore, investigation of the reason of power laws is not disturbed by randomized effect, and the cause of power laws is connected to other phenomena.

Our approach is summarized as follows. We analyze three different data sets: the volume of traffic in the initial stage of NTT DoCoMo's i-mode service [3], the logs of NTT DoCoMo's voice traffic, and the number of mixi users [9]. Hereafter, we call these data sets as Service I, II, and III, respectively. Service I is the first Internet access service offered over cellular phone terminals, Service II is a cellular phone service, and Service III is the largest social networking service (SNS) in Japan. By combining these analyses we obtain three results with regard to the social networks that underlie specific communication services. The first is the degree distribution of social networks, the second is the topological rules of social networks, and the last is user dynamics with regard to the actions needed to join a communication service. The first result was verified through a cross-check using different data; the logs of voice traffic presented by KDDI's cellular phone service [11]. We call this data set as Service IV.

The rest of this chapter is organized as follows: Section 2.2 provides a conceptual image of the methods available for analyzing social networks. Section 2.3 analyzes, according to [1, 2], the data of the cellular phone service (Service I and II) to derive partial information on the social network structure. The partial information so obtained cannot completely determine the model of social networks and there is an undetermined parameter in the model. Section 2.4 analyzes data on SNS (Service III) users to supplement the partial information obtained in Sect. 2.3. The combined use of both results enables us to determine the value of the parameter in the social network model. The result is a social network model that is self-consistent with the data observed from different services (Service I, II, and III). In Sect. 2.5, we verify the validity of our social network model by using the traffic logs of a cellular phone service that were not analyzed in earlier sections (Service IV). Section 2.6 concludes our discussion with a brief summary.

2.2 Analysis Strategy

We use graph $G(V, E)$ to represent the relationship of people exchanging information, where V is a set of nodes (people) and E is a set of links (information exchanges) between nodes. We call $G(V, E)$ the social network.

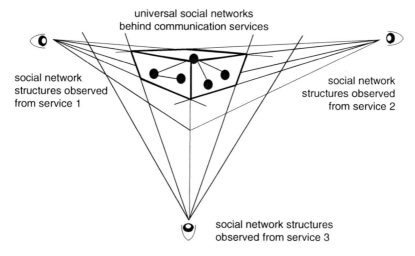

Fig. 2.1 The relationship between the universal social network and images obtained from specific communication services

The global structure of $G(V, E)$ cannot, unfortunately, be observed directly although the object of our interest is to clarify the structure of $G(V, E)$. Our solution is to adopt the approach of investigating the structure of $G(V, E)$ indirectly; we analyze specific communication services, such as cellular phone and SNS. Our purpose is not to investigate the specific services themselves, but to use them to elucidate the structure of social network $G(V, E)$.

How then is it possible to extract the universal social network structure? The concept of our approach is illustrated in Fig. 2.1. The network at the center of Fig. 2.1 is the "multi-dimensional" social network, and the three eyes represent three different services that hold partial information of the social network as "contracted" information. Although the "universal" social network at the center of the figure cannot be observed directly, we assume that sets of partial information can be extracted from specific communication services. These partial information sets may allow us to construct the "multi-dimensional" or "universal" social network model by combining them.

2.3 Analysis of Social Networks Based on Traffic Data of Internet Access Service Offered Over Cellular Phones

In this section, we introduce the partial information set created by analyzing the data of the cellular phone service.

2.3.1 Data To Be Analyzed

This subsection analyzes the data that holds the relationship between the number of users and email traffic during the early growth period of Service I; the world's first Internet access service from cellular phone terminals [3]. Since Service I was launched on February 22, 1999, the service has seen an explosive increase in the number of users. In the first one and half years (up to August 2000) the number of users exceeded ten million. The process by which a network service can acquire users at such a dramatic rate offers an interesting window on the structure of social networks and user behavior regarding hot-selling products.

This set of Service I data is useful for understanding social networks because it has the following properties:

- Since the number of Service I users increased explosively within a short period, it can be assumed that the Service I traffic was little affected by external factors such as a change in people's lifestyle.
- Since most cellular phones are exclusively used by their owners, traffic between cellular phones can be regarded as information exchange between people.
- Since most Service I emails are one-to-one communication, it can be assumed that email traffic is closely related to the number of pairs of Service I users who are exchanging information with each other.
- Since the cost of sending an email is far lower than that of talking on the phone, it can be assumed that the volume of email communication is little affected by such external factors as the income level of the individual users.
- Since the early period of the Service I had few problems with unwanted advertising emails sent to users indiscriminately, it can be assumed that almost all traffic arose from existing social networks.

During the early expansion period, 6 months from the beginning of August 1999 to the end of January 2000, the number of Service I users increased almost threefold, from 1,290,000 to 3,740,000. The relationship between the Web traffic (number of Web access attempts) and the number of Service I users during this period can be modeled as:

$$\text{(Web traffic)} \propto n, \tag{2.1}$$

where n is the number of users (chart on the left in Fig. 2.2). This is self-evident as long as the average number of Web access attempts per user is constant. Conversely, the fact that the above relation holds means that people's average usage of the Service I service did not change during this period. In other words, there is no evidence that the earliest subscribers to the Service I were heavier users. Meanwhile, the volume of email traffic (number of email messages) can be modeled as:

$$\text{(Email traffic)} \propto n^{5/3}. \tag{2.2}$$

Thus, a power law applies (chart on the right of Fig. 2.2). If the volume of communication per user remained constant even as n increased, then the volume of email traffic should be proportional to n. The fact that email traffic is proportional to $n^{1+\alpha}$

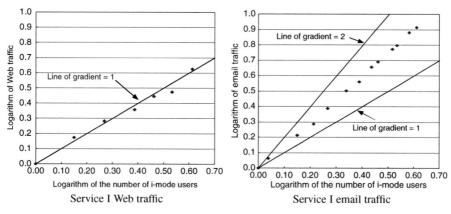

Fig. 2.2 The relationship between the number of users and the volume of Service I traffic for Web and email

($\alpha \simeq 2/3$) suggests that an increase in n results in an increase in the number of Service I users a single user communicates with. Therefore, $\alpha \simeq 2/3$ characterizes the rate of increase in email traffic. This also tells us something about the strength of human relations in social networks.

The following examines the graphical structure of universal social networks $G(V, E)$, involving not only Service I users but also others, using the power law (2.2) identified from the email traffic data described above.

2.3.2 Definition of Symbols and Problem Description

As mentioned in Sect. 2.2, $G(V, E)$ represents the social network, and the number of people in V is N ($|V| = N$). We assume that $G(V, E)$ does not change over time.

We use a rule to select n nodes from V; the subset of these selected nodes is $V_i(n)$ ($n \leq N$). Let $G_i(V_i(n), E_i(n))$ be the subgraph induced by $V_i(n)$ from $G(V, E)$. That is, a node pair is connected by a link in $G_i(V_i(n), E_i(n))$ if and only if the corresponding node pair in $G(V, E)$ is connected by a link. Each element of $V_i(n)$ is an Service I customer and social networks among all Service I customers are represented by $G_i(V_i(n), E_i(n))$ (see Fig. 2.3).

Equation (2.1) indicates that the usage of Service I by individual users did not change even as the number of Service I users increased. Therefore, it can be assumed that the traffic per link between a user and a Web site remained constant. Similarly, we assume that the average email traffic per link is also constant irrespective of the number of Service I users.[1] Thus, the number of links $|E_i(n)|$ becomes,

$$|E_i(n)| = O(n^{1+\alpha}). \tag{2.3}$$

---

[1] The fact that traffic per link is not affected by the number of Service I users, n, has been indirectly confirmed from Service II. See Appendix A for details.

Graph expressing relationships between humans
(potential customers)

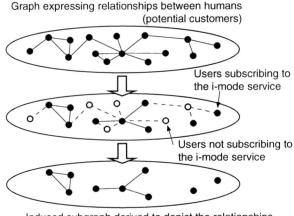

Users subscribing to
the i-mode service

Users not subscribing to
the i-mode service

Induced subgraph derived to depict the relationships
between i-mode users

Fig. 2.3 Example of $G(V, E)$, a graph showing the structure of the social networks, and $G_i(V_i(n), E_i(n))$, the subgraph induced from Service I users

The issue addressed by this paper is not the study of $G_i(V_i(n), E_i(n))$, or social networks established between Service I users, but $G(V, E)$, or universal social networks among both users and non-users of the Service I, as indicated by the traffic data of Service I. Figure 2.3 shows the relation between $G(V, E)$ and $G_i(V_i(n), E_i(n))$. The upper graph, $G(V, E)$, shows universal social networks while the bottom graph is a subgraph, $G_i(V_i(n), E_i(n))$, derived from $G(V, E)$, showing the social networks among Service I users. The number of Service I users and the volume of email traffic correspond to the number of nodes and the number of links, as derived in (2.3), in $G_i(V_i(n), E_i(n))$. The structure of $G(V, E)$ and how people begin to subscribe to the Service I are considered below.

2.3.3 How People Subscribed to the Service I and the Structure of Social Networks

First, we introduce two different schemes for numbering the elements of V, and define three sequences of node degree (the number of links that a node has) based on the numbering.

We call the node with the largest node degree as node 1. Similarly, we call the node with the jth largest node degree as node j. In addition, let the magnitude of node degree of node j be $D(j)$. Next, we introduce another numbering of elements in V according to the time of subscribing to the Service I. Let $D_i(\ell)$ be the node degree of the ℓth earliest subscribed node in $G(V, E)$. Similarly, let $d_i(n, \ell)$ be the degree of the ℓth earliest subscribed node with respect to $G_i(V_i(n), E_i(n))$ when the number of Service I users is n.

Fig. 2.4 Example of $c_i(n)$

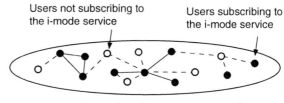

Users not subscribing to the i-mode service

Users subscribing to the i-mode service

the number of i-mode users: $n = 9$

Assume that the degree of Service I user in $G_i(V_i(n), E_i(n))$ can be related to his or her degree in $G(V, E)$ as follows:

$$\sum_{\ell=1}^{n} d_i(n, \ell) = c_i(n) \sum_{\ell=1}^{n} D_i(\ell), \qquad (2.4)$$

where $c_i(n)$ indicates the ratio of the number of Service I user's acquaintances subscribing to the Service I to the total number of acquaintances, given that the number of Service I users is n. That is

$$c_i(n) = \frac{2 \times (\text{total number of links between Service I users})}{\text{total number of Service I users' degrees w.r.t. } G(V, E)}.$$

The function $c_i(n)$ is a monotonically increasing function with $c_i(1) = 0$ and $c_i(N) = 1$. Figure 2.4 shows an example of $c_i(n)$. In this case, $N = 15, n = 9$, and

$$\sum_{\ell=1}^{n} D_i(\ell) = 22, \quad \sum_{\ell=1}^{n} d_i(n, \ell) = 12, \quad c_i(n) = \frac{6}{11}.$$

We assume the following power function as a property of $c(n)$:

$$c_i(n) \propto n^{1-\delta}, \qquad (2.5)$$

where δ is a constant. The validity of the assumption (2.5) is discussed below.

Since $c_i(n)$ will increase as the penetration of the Service I increases, δ sould satisfy $\delta < 1$. Here it is worth to note the relationship between the value of δ and topology of the social networks.

- If $\delta > 0$, since $c_i(n)$ is convex, this inequality indicates that $c_i(n)$ grows rapidly in the early stage of the Service I. In other words, there is something about cluster structures in that earlier subscribers to the Service I are more likely to be acquaintances of each other. If $\delta = 0$, this means that there is no evidence of the above cluster structures. Otherwise, $\delta < 0$ is not realistic because this would mean that later subscribers of the Service I were more likely to be acquaintances of each other.

From (2.3) and (2.4), we can derive

$$\sum_{\ell=1}^{n} D_i(\ell) \propto n^{\alpha+\delta}, \quad (n \ll N). \tag{2.6}$$

If this holds for any n of $n \ll N$, then

$$D_i(\ell) \propto \ell^{\alpha+\delta-1}, \quad (\ell \ll N). \tag{2.7}$$

Here, let us consider three cases identified by the value of $\alpha + \delta - 1$. First, in the case of $\alpha + \delta - 1 < 0$, $D_i(\ell)$ decreases with respect to ℓ. Therefore, $D_i(\ell)$ is the node degree of the ℓth earliest subscribed node in $G(V, E)$, and it is simultaneously the node degree of the ℓth largest magnitude of node degree. This correspondence is not so strict but is valid for accuracy in terms of observations in logarithmic charts. Consequently, if $\alpha + \delta - 1 < 0$, we have

$$D_i(\ell) \simeq D(\ell) \quad \text{(in terms of order)}, \tag{2.8}$$

for $\ell \ll N$. This relation leads to the following results.

- The node degree of social networks $G(V, E)$ obeys Zipf's law where the exponent is $-(1 - \alpha - \delta)$,

$$D(\ell) \propto \ell^{-(1-\alpha-\delta)}, \quad (\ell \ll N). \tag{2.9}$$

- People tend to subscribe to the Service I in the order of decreasing degree in $G(V, E)$. In other words, people with more acquaintances tend to subscribe to the service earlier.

This finding about the who subscribed to the Service I service first can be considered to mirror the tendency generally cited in the marketing area where people with higher sensitivity to information (more acquaintances) are more likely to try something before it becomes known or popular.

Next, in the case of $\alpha + \delta - 1 = 0$, $D_i(\ell)$ is independent of ℓ. It is known that if we construct an induced subgraph by selecting nodes in $G(V, E)$ at random, the number of links in the induced subgraph is proportional to n^2 where the number of selected nodes is n [1]. This is independent of the structure of $G(V, E)$, and means $\alpha = 1$. From (2.2), the number of links should be proportional to $n^{1+\alpha}$ ($\alpha \simeq 2/3$). Therefore, the assumption of $\alpha + \delta - 1 = 0$ contradicts the observed data of the actual service.

Finally, in the case of $\alpha + \delta - 1 > 0$, people tend to subscribe to the Service I in the order of increasing degree in $G(V, E)$. In other words, people with fewer acquaintances tend to subscribe to the service earlier. This result contradicts our personal experience. From the above considerations, we regard the assumption $\alpha + \delta - 1 < 0$ as being valid.

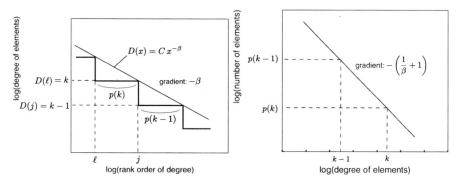

Fig. 2.5 Two points are extracted from data that satisfies Zipf's law (*left*), and they are plotted to give the distribution of degree (*right*)

If the distribution of the degree of nodes in the graph representing social networks follows Zipf's law, social networks can be taken as being scale-free. A scale-free network is a graph in which the distribution of the degree of the nodes follows a power law [6, 7],

$$p(k) \propto k^{-\gamma}, \tag{2.10}$$

where k is the degree of a node, $p(k)$ is the number of nodes with degree k, and $\gamma > 0$ is a constant.

Assume that $D(\ell)$ follows a Zipf distribution with a gradient of $-\beta$ (where $\beta = 1 - \alpha - \delta > 0$) as

$$D(\ell) = C \, \ell^{-\beta}, \tag{2.11}$$

where C is a constant. Consider ℓ and j for which $D(\ell) = k$ and $D(j) = k - 1$, then

$$\ell = C^{1/\beta} \, k^{-1/\beta}, \quad j = C^{1/\beta} \, (k-1)^{-1/\beta}. \tag{2.12}$$

Since $p(k)$ is $j - \ell$ when $D(\ell) = k$,

$$p(k) = C^{1/\beta} \left\{ (k-1)^{-1/\beta} - k^{-1/\beta} \right\}$$

$$\simeq C^{1/\beta} \, k^{-1/\beta} \, \frac{1}{\beta \, k}$$

$$= O(k^{-(1/\beta+1)}). \tag{2.13}$$

Hence, the graph representing social networks is a scale-free graph whose exponent, γ, is

$$\gamma = \frac{1}{\beta} + 1 = \frac{1}{1 - \alpha - \delta} + 1. \tag{2.14}$$

Assumptions

- From Fig. 2.12 in Appendix A, the volume of email traffic is proportional to $|E_i(n)|$.
- From Fig. 2.2, $|E_i(n)| = O(n^{1+\alpha})$, $(\alpha \simeq 2/3)$.
- $c_i(n) \propto n^{1-\delta}$, $(\delta < 1 - \alpha)$.

Results

- The sequence of subscription to the Service I is the sequence of the magnitude of the degree in $G(V, E)$,

$$D_i(\ell) \simeq D(\ell) \quad \text{(in terms order)}$$

  for $\ell \ll N$.

- The degree of nodes obeys Zipf's law:

$$D(\ell) \propto \ell^{-(1-\alpha-\delta)}, \quad (\ell \ll N).$$

- The distribution of the degree of nodes in $G(V, E)$:

$$p(k) = O(k^{-\gamma}), \quad \left(\gamma = \frac{1}{1-\alpha-\delta} + 1\right)$$

Fig. 2.6 The assumptions made in the analysis of service I data and the results

The assumptions made in the above discussion and its results are summarized in Fig. 2.6.

Although the above discussion does not lead to a specific value for δ, δ should satisfy $\alpha + \delta - 1 < 0$. The fact that $\alpha + \delta < 1$ indeed holds will be supported along with the assumption of $c_i(n)$ in the next section through an analysis of the Service III.

2.4 Analysis of Social Networks Based on the Number of SNS Users

In this section, we investigate the structure of social networks $G(V, E)$ from a different viewpoint, i.e., data generated by the Service III. In addition, by combining these results with the results of our analysis of Service I data, we clarify the details of the social network model including the verification of our assumption of the power law of $c_i(n)$ and the determination of the value of γ.

2.4.1 Analyzed Data

Service III is Japan's largest social networking service provided by mixi, Inc. [9].

For a person to become a member of Service III, he or she needs to be invited to join by an existing member. Although this is a system where only those invited by

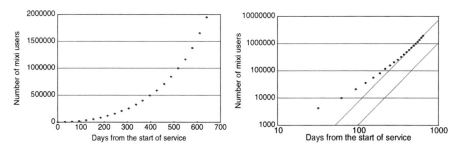

Fig. 2.7 Growth in the number of service Ⅲ users

existing members may join, the number of users is growing rapidly due to the fact that the mechanism of existing members inviting new people to join is functioning well. The Service Ⅲ started in February 2004. The number of users reached one million on August 1, 2005, and two million on December 6, 2005. While it took 17.5 months for the number of users to reach one million, it took only 4 months for the number to grow by another million. Because of the following characteristics of the growth in the number of users, Service Ⅲ data is useful for understanding social networks.

- Since the number of Service Ⅲ users grew explosively over a short period of time, it can be assumed that the process behind its growth was little affected by external factors such as changes in peoples' lifestyles.
- Since a person needs to be invited to join by an existing member, the process of the growth process of its popularity, i.e., number of users, is closely related to links in social networks.

The left chart in Figure 2.7 shows the growth in the number of Service Ⅲ users in the early days of the service after launch with 600 users. The horizontal axis is the number of days elapsed since the start of the service. The vertical axis is the number of Service Ⅲ users. The right chart is a double logarithmic chart. The lines with the gradient of 3 are shown for reference. It was reported that the number of Service Ⅲ users grew exponentially [10]. Excluding the very early days, when the growth depended on the initial conditions, it can be seen that the growth in the number of users was time to the power of three.

2.4.2   Growth in the Number of SNS Users and Social Networks

Let $m(t)$ be the number of Service Ⅲ users at time t, and assume that the following holds:

$$m(t) \propto t^3. \tag{2.15}$$

Then, the rate of growth in the number of Service Ⅲ users, dm/dt, can be expressed as

$$\frac{dm}{dt} \propto t^2. \tag{2.16}$$

Substituting t in (2.15) into (2.16), we get

$$\frac{dm}{dt} \propto m^{2/3}. \tag{2.17}$$

Next, we consider the degree of Service Ⅲ users. We assume that the potential users of the Service Ⅲ service are the same as those of the Service I, i.e., the set of V. In other words, the target customers (including potential customers) are the same for both services, specifically, the targets are people living in Japan. We sort the elements in V according to the sequence of the time of joining the Service Ⅲ service, and let $D_x(\ell)$ be the degree of the ℓth element in $G(V, E)$. Let $d_x(m, \ell)$ be the degree of the ℓth element with respect to the graph consisting of Service Ⅲ users alone (See the middle graph in Fig. 2.8). As in the case of the Service I, function $c_x(m)$ is introduced to relate $d_x(m, \ell)$ to $D_x(\ell)$ as follows:

$$\sum_{\ell=1}^{m} d_x(m, \ell) = c_x(m) \sum_{\ell=1}^{m} D_x(\ell). \tag{2.18}$$

$c_x(m)$ indicates the ratio of the number of Service Ⅲ users' acquaintances subscribing to the Service Ⅲ to the total number of his or her acquaintances, when the number of Service Ⅲ users is m, that is

$$c_x(m) = \frac{2 \times (\text{total number of links between Service Ⅲ users})}{\text{total number of Service Ⅲ users' degrees w.r.t. } G(V, E)}.$$

It is a monotonically increasing function with $c_x(1) = 0$ and $c_x(N) = 1$.

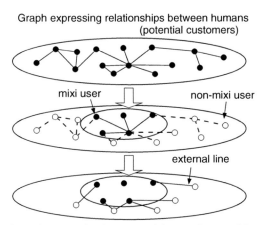

Graph expressing relationships between humans (potential customers)

mixi user   non-mixi user

external line

Fig. 2.8 Example of $G(V, E)$, a graph showing the structure of social networks; the subgraph is for just Service Ⅲ users

subgraph connecting between mixi users & non-mixi users

The upper and middle figures of Fig. 2.8 show social networks $G(V, E)$ and the induced subgraph of $G(V, E)$ (just Service Ⅲ users), respectively. The links that are connected to Service Ⅲ users but do not interconnect Service Ⅲ users in $G(V, E)$ are referred to as external lines (see the figure at the bottom of Fig. 2.8). There are six such lines in this example. The number of external lines can be expressed as

$$\sum_{\ell=1}^{m} D_x(\ell) - \sum_{\ell=1}^{m} d_x(m, \ell) = (1 - c_x(m)) \sum_{\ell=1}^{m} D_x(\ell).$$

Since the expansion of the Service Ⅲ service depends on the invitations made by existing members, it is reasonable to assume that the rate of growth in the number of Service Ⅲ users is proportional to the number of external lines. In other words,

$$\frac{dm}{dt} \propto (1 - c_x(m)) \sum_{\ell=1}^{m} D_x(\ell). \tag{2.19}$$

Therefore, from (2.17)

$$(1 - c_x(m)) \sum_{\ell=1}^{m} D_x(\ell) \propto m^{2/3}. \tag{2.20}$$

Thus, a major difference in analyses made on the Service I and Ⅲ services is the relations being analyzed. The analysis of Service I considered the relations between Service I users, while that of Service Ⅲ considers the relations between Service Ⅲ users and non-Service Ⅲ users. The analysis of the Service I itself cannot illuminate the details of $c_i(n)$, since it only analyzes the relations between users. On the other hand, since the analysis of Service Ⅲ service considers relations between users and non-users, $c_x(m)$ appears in the form of $(1 - c_x(m))$ in (2.20). The analysis of Service Ⅲ, therefore, provides different view of social networks than that of Service I.

Let us consider the region of m such that $c_x(m) \ll 1$. For m in this region, the following holds

$$(1 - c_x(m)) \simeq \text{constant}, \quad (c_x(m) \ll 1) \tag{2.21}$$

on a log scale[2]. We can then extract the behavior of the degree from (2.20) as

$$\sum_{\ell=1}^{m} D_x(\ell) \propto m^{2/3}, \quad (m \ll N), \tag{2.22}$$

where $m \ll N$ means $c_x(m) \ll 1$ since $c_x(m)$ is an increasing function of m. If the extracted behavior of the degree is true for any value of m where $m \ll N$, we get

$$D_x(\ell) \propto \ell^{-1/3}, \quad (\ell \ll N). \tag{2.23}$$

---

[2] The validity of (2.21) is verified in Appendix B.

Therefore, the order of subscribing to the Service Ⅲ follows the order of the magnitude of the degree,

$$D_x(\ell) \simeq D(\ell), \quad \text{(in terms of order)}, \tag{2.24}$$

for $\ell \ll N$ and we have

$$D(\ell) \propto \ell^{-1/3}, \quad (\ell \ll N). \tag{2.25}$$

The characteristics of $D(\ell)$ obtained from the analyses of Services I, Ⅱ, and Ⅲ should be the same since the targets of both analyses are the same social networks $G(V, E)$. Therefore, by comparing (2.25) and (2.9), we find that

$$\alpha + \delta \simeq \frac{2}{3}, \tag{2.26}$$

for $\ell \ll N$. Using $\alpha \simeq 2/3$, we have the following results:

- For $n \ll N$, $c_i(n)$ is a power function expressed as (2.5).
- The value of δ, which could not be determined by the analysis of the Service I alone, can be determined as

$$\delta \simeq 0. \tag{2.27}$$

  Therefore, $c_i(n)$ is a linear function of n.
- δ is such that the inequality, $\alpha + \delta - 1 < 0$, holds.

Moreover, functions $c_i(n)$ and $c_x(m)$ have the same meaning; If we select n nodes (or m nodes) in order of the magnitude of node degree and construct the induced subgraph, both functions represent the ratio of the total number of node degrees in the induced subgraph to the total number of node degrees of selected nodes. Therefore, $c_x(m) \propto m$, and (2.21) is valid for $m \ll N$.

In addition, as mentioned in Sect. 2.3.3, if $\delta > 0$, there are cluster structures, in which earlier subscribers to the Service I are more likely to be acquaintances of each other. The result $\delta \simeq 0$ means that such cluster structures are not observed.

By considering the analyses of the Services I, Ⅱ, and Ⅲ data, we can summarize the properties of the structure of social networks that satisfy both Services I, Ⅱ, and Ⅲ data as follows. They identify a self-consistent model of social networks obtained from different communication services.

- In general, social networks can be expressed as scale-free graphs with degree distribution of $p(k) \propto k^{-\gamma}$, where γ is

$$\gamma = \frac{1}{1 - \alpha - \delta} + 1 \simeq 4. \tag{2.28}$$

That is, the degree distribution of social networks is

$$p(k) \propto k^{-4}. \tag{2.29}$$

- Function $c_i(n)$, which is an indication of the strength of a cluster of n people sorted according to the magnitude of their degrees, is given by

$$c_i(n) \propto n^{1-\delta} \simeq n. \tag{2.30}$$

This means that there are no cluster structures and $c_i(n)$ is proportional to the penetration ratio n/N (i.e., proportional to the number of users n) of Services I.

The assumptions of the above discussion and its results are summarized in Fig. 2.9.

The above properties are useful in constructing a network model that replicates the characteristics of social networks. Using the constructed network model, we can simulate various processes regarding the penetration of communication services, the mechanism of word-of-mouth communication, and various marketing strategies.

Assumptions

- From Fig. 2.7, $m(t) \propto t^3$.
- The growth rate of the number of Service III users is proportional to the number of external lines,

$$\frac{dm}{dt} \propto (1 - c_x(m)) \sum_{\ell=1}^{m} D_x(\ell).$$

- From Fig. 2.13, $c_x(m) \ll 1$ in some region.

Intermediate results

- The sequence of subscription to the Service III follows the order of the magnitude of the degree in $G(V, E)$,

$$D_x(\ell) \simeq D(\ell) \quad \text{(in terms of order)}.$$

- The assumption used in analyzing Service I data,

$$\delta < 1 - \alpha,$$

is verified.

Results

- The distribution of the degree of nodes in $G(V, E)$:

$$p(k) \propto k^{-4}$$

- No cluster structure is present in n people sorted according to the magnitude of their degrees,

$$c_i(n) \propto n^{1-\delta} \simeq n.$$

Fig. 2.9 The assumptions made for analyzing data and the results

2.5   Verification of Degree Distribution of Social Networks

If the social network structure obtained in the previous section is universal and is independent of characteristics of specific services (e.g., Services I, II, and III), the obtained structure should be validated by data of another communication service. In this section, we verify the degree distribution of social networks by using the logs of cellular phone traffic, i.e., data that was not used in the aforementioned analyses.

We collected the logs of Service IV, the voice communication service of a cellular phone network. The procedures used for validation are as follows. First, we constructed a graph describing the social networks linking Service IV users by using Service IV's log data. The method used to construct the graph was simple. A node denotes a user, and two nodes are connected by a link if and only if there is communication between the users in some observation period. Links are differentiated for incoming and outgoing calls so the graph is a directed graph. Link means there is at least one call, i.e., the link remains the same regardless of the number of calls in excess of one. In addition, the link is independent of call holding time. We analyzed the graph describing social networks of Service IV users and investigated the distribution of node degrees evidenced by the graph.

Note that we can only investigate the Service IV users in a certain sub-area of the service. In other words, the analysed data and results are not the universal, or total, social network $G(V, E)$. To verify the social network model by using this data, it is necessary that the graph obtained from Service IV data has the same characteristics as the universal social network $G(V, E)$. In general, it is known that the characteristics of the distribution of node degree are the same in both graphs if the users are selected independently of their node degree. It is natural to assume that the subset of Service IV users to be analyzed is selected independent of the node degree, and the selection of service area to be analyzed is also independent of the node degree. Therefore, if the probability distribution of node degree is $p(k)$, the degree distribution of Service IV users in a certain sub-area of the service is also $p(k)$.

The data analyzed here are logs of voice communication over a cellular phone service at six different switches. We analyzed 12 h logs and counted the number of incoming and outgoing calls for each user ID. The number of unique people calling the user is the node degree of incoming calls. The number of unique people called by the user is the node degree of outgoing calls.

Figures 2.10 and 2.11 show the distribution of node degrees (PDF) of the outgoing and incoming calls for each area, respectively. The horizontal axis denotes degree k and the vertical axis denotes the probability density $p(k)$ for degree k, in log scales. We can recognize that the tail distributions are proportional to k^{-4}. These results verify the scale-free property (2.29) of social networks $G(V, E)$.

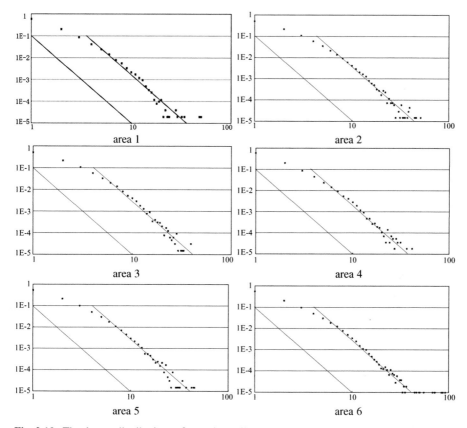

Fig. 2.10 The degree distributions of outgoing calls

2.6 Conclusions

This chapter extracted social information from the data generated by specific communication services, and investigated the universal structure of social networks that uderlie each services. In addition, the structure of social networks was verified. A key point of this research is its use of coarse data for analyzing social networks. The analyses examined the relationship between the volume of traffic and the number of users, and the temporal evolution of the number of users of SNS service. These data do not, of course, describe the behaviors of each user. However, we found the structure of social networks as characterized by the distribution of node degree, topological structure of social networks, and user dynamics.

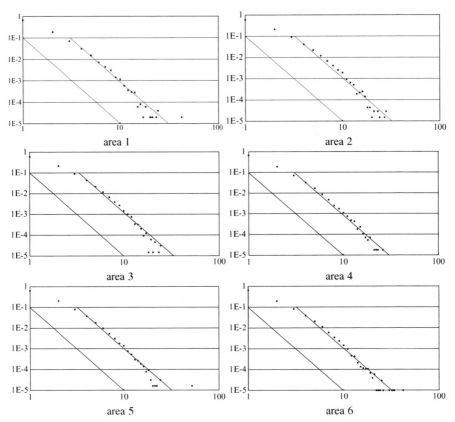

Fig. 2.11 The degree distributions of incoming calls

The features of this work can be summarized as follows.

- Our purpose in analyzing the data of an actual communication service was to extract the structure of the universal social network that is behind the services, not to determine the characteristics of the services themselves.
- The data gathered from a single communication service provides only partial information of the universal social network. By combining the results of data analysis from different communication services, we can extract the detailed structure of social networks.
- We can derive node structures by fitting the data to power laws; note that the data does not describe the detailed behaviors of individual users.
- We cannot verify the analysis results by experiments because we target large-scale social networks. However, we can verify the validity of data analysis from different communication data generated by services that share the common social network.

The characteristics of the social network obtained by the analysis are not characteristics unique to any specific communication service but are universal.

In fact, the obtained model is self-consistent with characteristics of different communication services. Therefore, our findings on social network structure makes it possible to design and engineer some approaches to encourage the penetration of new communication services and information marketing strategies. For example, to improve the speed of the spread when new communication service is introduced, the selecting method of initial users has been studied [12].

Acknowledgements A part of this research was made possible by funds provided by the International Communication Foundation (ICF) (now KDDI Foundation) in its Research Support Program for fiscal year 2005, and by the Grant-in-Aid for Scientific Research (S) No. 18100001 (2006–2010) from the Japan Society for the Promotion of Science.

References

1. M. Aida, K. Ishibashi, H. Miwa, C. Takano, and S. Kuribayashi, "Structure of human relations and user-dynamics revealed by traffic data," *IEICE Transactions on Information and Systems*, vol. E87-D, no. 6, pp. 1454–1460, 2004
2. M. Aida, K. Ishibashi, C. Takano, H. Miwa, K. Muranaka, and A. Miura, "Cluster structures in topology of large-scale social networks revealed by traffic data," *IEEE GLOBECOM 2005*, St. Louis, 2005
3. DoCoMo Net, How the i-mode service is used. http://www.nttdocomo.co.jp/
4. Masaki Aida, Jun Sasaki, "Structural analysis on social networks using the spread process of communication services," *IEICE Tech. Rep.*, IN2006-41, vol. 106, no. 151, pp. 37–42, 2006 (in Japanese)
5. R. Rousseau, "*George Kingsley Zipf: life, idea, his law and informetrics*," Glottometrics, vol. 3 (To Honor G.K. Zipf), pp. 11–18, 2002
6. A.-L. Barabási and R. Albert, "Emergence of scaling in random networks," *Science*, vol. 286, pp. 509–512, 1999
7. R. Albert and A.-L. Barabási, "Statistical mechanics of complex networks," *Rev. Mod. Phys.*, vol. 74, no. 47, 2002
8. Masaki Aida, "Structures of social networks and user-dynamics revealed by power laws, Inspired from phenomenology," *Journal of IEICE*, vol. 91, no. 10, pp. 891–896, 2008 (in Japanese)
9. mixi, Inc. http://mixi.co.jp/
10. K. Yuda, N. Ono, and Y. Fujiwara, "Human network structure in a social networking service," *Transactions of the Information Processing Society of Japan*, vol. 47, no. 3, pp. 865–874, 2006 (in Japanese)
11. au by KDDI, http://www.au.kddi.com/
12. T. Hirano, M. Uwajima, C. Takano, and M. Aida, "Spreading strategy of communication service based on a social network model," *IEICE Tech. Rep.*, IN2008-135, vol. 108, no. 458, pp. 19–24, 2009 (in Japanese)

A Relationship Between the Number of Links and the Volume of Traffic

In order to study the graphic representation of social networks by analyzing Service I traffic, we hypothesized that the observed volume of traffic is proportional to the number of links in the graph. To verify this hypothesis, it is necessary to analyze the communications log data of individual users. The rough data shown in Fig. 2.2 is not sufficient for such verification.

Since detailed communications log data of Service I users during the same period as that used to construct Fig. 2.2 was not available, we attempted to verify the above hypothesis indirectly by using other types of communications log data that were available. We have examined the number of calls between pairs of subscribers (caller ID and callee ID) in the communications log data of a cellular phone voice communication service provided by a certain provider (different from Service IV). The log data was for 1 day in September 2004.

First, we assumed that a link between a pair exists only when there was a communications record for the pair in the one-day log data, and we developed a graph expressing the communications relations between user IDs. In order to eliminate calls that did not arise from social networks, such as calls promoting certain products, a pair was considered to be personal communication only when calls were originated by both parties, each calling the other at least once. From the graph so developed, nodes were sorted according to the number of degree to generate subgraphs. The subgraphs are generated by selecting nodes in accordance with the sorted sequential order of their degree and it becomes the subgraph induced by the selected nodes. We then examined the relationship between the number of links in the induced subgraphs and the total number of calls on links. The result is shown in the left chart in Fig. 2.12. The right chart in Fig. 2.12 shows the results of the induced subgraphs generated by randomly selecting the nodes.

Both results show that the number of calls is proportional to the number of links. Although, in general, the number of calls per link varies greatly from link to link, these results indicate that such a variation does not affect our hypothesis. In other words, the effect of the average values is dominant. These results indirectly verify that the volume of traffic is proportional to the number of links in social networks.

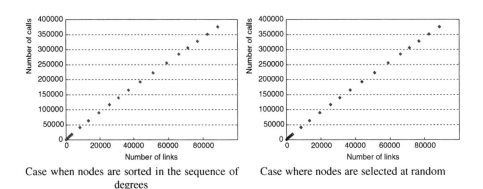

Case when nodes are sorted in the sequence of degrees   Case where nodes are selected at random

Fig. 2.12 Relationship between the actual number of calls and the number of links in induced subgraphs

B   Behavior of $1 - c_x(m)$

Let us examine the behavior of $1 - c_x(m)$ by defining a specific function for $c_x(m)$. If we choose the simplest form that satisfies $c_x(m) \propto m^{1-\delta}$, $c_x(1) = 0$, and $c_x(N) = 1$, then

$$c_x(m) = \left(\frac{m-1}{N-1} \right)^{1-\delta} . \tag{2.31}$$

For example, Fig. 2.13 shows the behavior of $c_x(m)$ and $1 - c_x(m)$ for different values of m for the case where the number of potential users, N, is 60,000,000, for δ is set as 0.0 and 0.5, respectively.

Since the range of the number of subscribers, m for Service Ⅲ (and n for Service I), being considered in this paper is, at most, in the order of several million, we can confirm that the equation, $(1 - c_x(m)) \simeq$ constant, holds on a log scale.

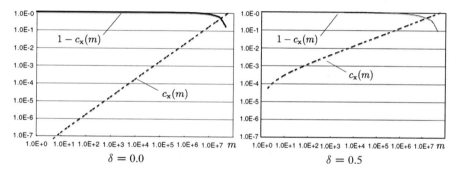

$$\delta = 0.0 \qquad\qquad\qquad\qquad \delta = 0.5$$

Fig. 2.13 Examples of behavior of $1 - c_x(m)$.

Chapter 3
Analysis of Social Networks by Tensor Decomposition

Sergej Sizov, Steffen Staab, and Thomas Franz

3.1 Motivation, or Who Follows Whom

Authority ranking is a crucial component for a wide range of Social Web applications, such as thematically focused, faceted browsing or contact recommendations. Online communities (such as Twitter or Facebook) provide very limited statistics about user relations, such as the number of contacts in the users' contact list, the number of registered observers for user postings (coined "followers" on Twitter), etc. Although these counts appropriately reflect the overall users' centrality/popularity in the social community, their interpretation in a more focused context becomes very difficult. As a realistic example for this problem, we may consider two real and quite popular users in the Twitter community: *timberners_lee* (20K followers) and *parishilton* (1.7 Mio followers). In early 2010, both users have commented the launch of the novel Apple iPad technology – at the same time – by following postings (tweets), as shown in Fig. 3.1.

From the purely calculational perspective, we could draw the conclusion that the user *parishilton* is a stronger twitter authority in the sense of the topic "new technologies" than *timberners_lee*. However, deeper analysis of postings from both users immediately shows the opposite. While contributions of *timberners_lee* are clearly focused on novel research/technology aspects (like Web Science, Linked Open Data, Semantic Web), the user *parishilton* is rather devoted to themes like "celebrities," "lifestyle" or "my person."

The need for better, explicit contextualization of contributions led to various, platform-specific mechanisms, and self-organizing, emerging vocabulary extensions. The best-known form of simple content contextualization is tagging, i.e., use of short text snippets (or particular terms) for content annotation – widely known from social cites like Flickr, YouTube, Bibsonomy, and others. In the previously discussed Twitter community, a similar approach with so-called hashtags (context-indicative, characteristic words within textual content, marked by a preceding hash

S. Sizov (✉)
University of Koblenz-Landau, WeST – Institute for Web Science and Technologies
e-mail: sizov@uni-koblenz.de

B. Furht (ed.), *Handbook of Social Network Technologies and Applications*,
DOI 10.1007/978-1-4419-7142-5_3, © Springer Science+Business Media, LLC 2010

timberners_lee	*parishilton*
Following: 59	Following: 272
Followers: 20.692	Followers: 1.709.116
RT @janl: Apple:	I Love my new I-Pad.
"Preparing your web content for iPad:	So much fun!
2. Use W3C standard web technologies." #w3c	Technology rocks!
9:46 AM Mar 21st via TweetDeck	about 2 h ago via UberTwitter

Fig. 3.1 Real postings of sample users on Twitter

sign) became quite popular. For instance, the term #*w3c* in the running text from Fig. 3.1 is such a hashtag. In this particular case, the community established the practice to use #*w3c* for indicating posting relatedness to the W3C consortium – this is a characteristic example of emergent semantics in modern social networks [10].

The baseline scenario for lightweight contextualization of user *relations* may be organized in a quite analogous manner. In particular, we may assume that some users of the social network explicitly indicate their interest on some topic (say one hashtag h). In the following, we will refer to such group of users as a h-candidate set. Authority ranking for h-candidate sets can be quite similar to the "unfocused" global setting discussed before and based on "contextualized" lists of followers. From the conceptual perspective, this approach can be seen as a special case of collaborative voting "focused" on h. In fact, we can restrict the scope of follower-lists and virtually remove all user entries that are *not* explicitly found in the h-candidate set (i.e., appear "irrelevant" in the context of h). In other words, we simply reduce the follower lists to contacts from the h-candidate set itself. The resulting cardinalities of reduced follower lists give a natural ranking for contact recommendations (whom-to-follow) in the context of the considered hashtag h.

For the discussed Twitter scenario, this functionality is really offered by an external service provider wefollow.com. During registration, users are requested to specify keywords of interest (i.e., hashtags, in our terminology) as well as their account information (ensuring access to the list of followed users from their Twitter account) to the portal provider. Subsequently, "keyword subscribers" can access a ranked list of contact recommendations (i.e., whom-to-follow sugges-tions). Although the exact organization of wefollow.com is not public, the generated list of recommendations can be reproduced with extremely high accuracy using h-candidate sets. Table 3.1 shows the top-20 recommendations regarding keyword *semanticweb* by wefollow.com and by collaborative voting (in the latter case, the h-candidate set of Twitter users is identical to the list of wefollow.com subscribers for *semanticweb*). Our collaborative voting implementation uses proprietary Twitter API for collecting further publicly available user information, such as follower lists. Minor differences in rank positions can be explained by the fact that Twitter profiles of few wefollow.com subscribers for *semanticweb*), namely 6 out of 242, were *not* open to public, i.e., corresponding lists of followed users were not accessible to our test application.

Table 3.1 Simple strategies for to-follow recommendations, $h = $ #*semanticweb*

POS	WeFollow recommends	h-set recommends	#followers: total	in h-set	H-set recommends	#followers: total	in H-set
1	tommyh	PaulMiller	2,215	82	timberners_lee	20,694	252
2	jahendler	jahendler	909	76	timoreilly	1,428,425	200
3	ivan_herman	tommyh	738	76	jahendler	910	185
4	PaulMiller	ivan_herman	680	69	LeeFeigenbaum	273	176
5	opencalais	opencalais	1,797	68	danbri	1,781	160
6	danja	danja	1,313	59	kidehen	1,806	159
7	CaptSolo	juansequeda	988	57	ivan_herman	680	153
8	juansequeda	CaptSolo	1,224	52	PaulMiller	2,216	150
9	sclopit	gothwin	685	50	tommyh	737	142
10	gothwin	robocrunch	3,679	49	novaspivack	7,896	139
11	robocrunch	alexiskold	4,321	48	johnbreslin	1,933	128
12	kristathomas	kristathomas	1,499	48	w3c	10,672	128
13	kendall	kendall	1,694	45	mimasnews	198	127
14	bobdc	andraz	2,065	44	iand	1,094	123
15	phclouin	sclopit	513	42	rww	1,045,511	123
16	brown2020	cjmconnors	466	39	terraces	632	119
17	alexiskold	gkob	399	37	mhausenblas	449	118
18	andraz	dorait	2,541	35	opencalais	1,799	112
19	cjmconnors	phclouin	266	35	ldodds	621	110
20	ontoligent	openamplify	1,387	34	semanticnews	843	102

The apparent drawback of the proposed strategy is its limitation to proactive users that exploit the new service and explicitly "subscribe" for selected hashtags of interest. Unsubscribed users are not part of the h-candidate set and thus cannot be recommended, disregarding their (real) importance in the context of h. This limitation can be avoided with alternate strategies of constructing the candidate set. In particular, we can consider "active" users in the sense of h (e.g., by finding h in their recent postings). In the following, we will refer to a group of candidates that actively used the desired hashtag h within a certain timeframe (e.g., 4 weeks) as a H-candidate set. In practice, the H-candidate set can be directly obtained by keyword-based search (for h as query) through the common API of many social platforms. The second part of Fig. 3.1 demonstrates corresponding follow-recommendations for the hashtag $h = $ #*semanticweb* on Twitter. It can be observed that the the the H-candidate set provides substantially higher recall by including highly relevant users in the field of $h = $ #*semanticweb* that have no explicit registration at wefollow.com.

From the conceptual perspective, the introduced strategies allow for mapping user relations in common Social Web applications onto graph structures, where nodes represent users and edges correspond to relations that link users to each other. Consequently, graph-based authority ranking algorithms known from Web retrieval, such as PageRank [7], HITS [17] or SALSA [20], can be adopted for the Social Web setting, too. Instead of ratings for Web pages they will then output ratings for users in a social environment, with respect to one or more criteria, e.g., hub and authority scores in HITS. These scores reflect the centrality/importance of particular users in the social network and thus can be exploited for relevance estimation, e.g., in contact/follower recommendation scenarios.

Two important observations can be made about the authority ranking for social graphs. On one hand, the computational models of standard algorithms for Web analysis only consider structural information, i.e., the connectivity of graph nodes. Additional link semantics, e.g., knowledge about different types of relations, is not used. On the other hand, there are many cases of overlapping, redundant, and conflicting vocabulary describing similar problems. Therefore, we may expect redundancies like the co-existence of different hashtags/themes with highly similar (or coherent) meaning, such as $h_1 = $ #semanticweb, $h_2 = $ #RDF and $h_3 = $ #ontology. Common authority ranking algorithms provide no support for finding such groups of semantically coherent items.

3.2 The Social Web as a Tensor

This section introduces the advanced TweetRank approach for authority ranking in Social Web communities. In doing so, we refine the formal notion of social graphs and tensors, introduce tensor factorization for faceted authority ranking, and show realistic examples of framework outputs.

3.2.1 The TweetRank Model

We define a Social Web graph as a graph $G = (V, L, E, linkType)$ where V is the set of users in the community, L is the set of literals (e.g., hashtags), and E is the set of relations between users in V. Additionally, the function $linkType : E \rightarrow L$ returns the annotation from L that relates two users. Following our Twitter application scenario introduced in previous section, Fig. 3.2a shows an (over)simplified Social Web graph that contains five users (Alice $= $ A, Bob $= $ B, Chris $= $ C, Don $= $ D, Elly $= $ E), two hashtag-like literals (*lifestyle* $= $ L, *semanticweb* $= $ S) and ten relations of two different types: *follow-lifestyle* and *follow-semanticweb*. The precise semantics of such links remains application-specific; in our sample case we assume that user X links to user Y by edge of type Z iff a) X follows Y (in the common sense of Twitter) and b) both X and Y have recently used the hashtag Z in their own postings/tweets. For instance, the graph expresses that Alex follows Bob regarding *lifestyle*.

We represent Social Web graphs by a 3-dimensional tensor **T** where each of its slices represents an adjacency matrix for one relation type from L. Figure 3.2b illustrates the tensor resulting from the transformation of the sample graph shown

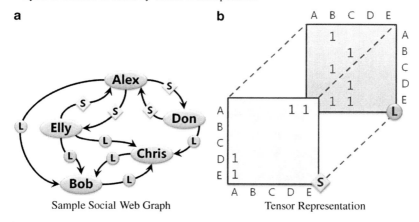

Fig. 3.2 Modeling example

in Fig. 3.2a. The first adjacency matrix $\mathbf{T}$ $(:, :, 1)$[1] models linkage by the property *semanticweb*. An entry >0 corresponds to the existence of a link by this property, empty entries are considered as zeroes. The second matrix $\mathbf{T}$ $(:, :, 2)$ models links by the property *lifestyle*. For instance, the fact that Alex follows Bob regarding *lifestyle* results in $\mathbf{T}$ $(1, 2, 2) = 1$ in tensor representation.

3.2.2 PARAFAC for Authority Ranking

The Social Web graph can be described by an adjacency matrix. For a network graph matrix M the well known authority ranking methods like HITS [17] can be applied. HITS defines the authority ranking problem through mutual reinforcement between so-called hub and authority scores of graph nodes (community users, in our case). The authority (relevance) score of each node is defined as the sum of hub scores of its predecessors. Analogously, the hub (connectivity) score of each node is defined as a sum of the authority scores of its successors. By applying the singular value decomposition (SVD) to the adjacency matrix, we obtain hub and authority scores of graph nodes for each singular value of M, which can be interpreted as rankings regarding different themes or latent topics of interest. Formally, by this method, some arbitrary matrix $M \in \mathbf{R}^{k \times l}$ is splitted into three matrices $U \in \mathbf{R}^{k \times m}$, $S \in \mathbf{R}^{m \times m}$, $V \in \mathbf{R}^{l \times m}$. U and V represent the outlinks and inlinks with respect to the principal factor contained in S. Corresponding to our notation, M can be written as sum of rank-one-matrices by $M = \sum_{k=1}^{m} S^k \cdot U^k \circ V^k$. This 2-way decomposition yields authority and hub scores (cf. Fig. 3.3a) [18].

---

[1] Throughout this chapter we use the common Matlab-notation for addressing entries in tensors and vectors.

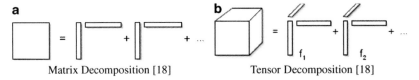

Fig. 3.3 (a) Matrix decomposition (b) Tensor decomposition

Modeling several link types by separate matrices results in very sparse and not connected matrices. Instead, the tensor model applied by TweetRank enables the representation of all adjacency matrices including information about the connections between link types. Tensor decomposition methods like PARAFAC can then detect further hidden dependencies.

These methods are regarded as higher-order equivalents to matrix decompositions. The PARAFAC tensor decomposition has the advantage of robustness and computational efficiency. These advantages are due to its uniqueness up to scaling and permutation of the produced component matrices [14]. By PARAFAC input tensors are transformed to so called Kruskal tensors, a sum of rank-one-tensors. Consequently, in TweetRank we derive authority and hub scores for particular latent aspects (topics) of the analyzed data from particular rank-one-tensors of the decomposition. In the context of this chapter we focus on three-mode-tensors that represent connectivity between graph nodes (users) together with semantics of user relations.

Formally, a tensor $\mathbf{T} \in \mathbf{R}^{k \times l \times m}$ is decomposed by n-Rank-PARAFAC into components matrices $U_1 \in \mathbf{R}^{k \times n}$, $U_2 \in \mathbf{R}^{l \times n}$, $U_3 \in \mathbf{R}^{m \times n}$ and n principal factors (pf) λ_i in descending order. Via these $\mathbf{T}$ can be written as a Kruskal tensor by $\mathbf{T} \approx \sum_{k=1}^{n} \lambda_k \cdot U_1^k \circ U_2^k \circ U_3^k$ where λ_k denotes the kth principal factor, U_i^k the kth column of U_i and $\circ$ the outer product [18]. U_i yields the ratio of the ith dimension to the principal factors. So, similar to SVD, PARAFAC derives hidden dependencies related to the pfs and expresses the dimensions of the tensor by relations to the pfs. Depending on the number of pfs PARAFAC decomposition can be loss-free. For a third-mode-tensor $\mathbf{T} \in \mathbf{R}^{k \times l \times m}$ a weak upper bound for this rank is known: $rank(\mathbf{T}) \leq \min\{kl, lm, km\}$ [18]. There is no proper way for estimating the optimal number of pfs for an appropriate decomposition but several indicators like residue analysis or core consistency exist [2]. The PARAFAC decomposition of a tensor derives authority and hub scores plus additional scores for the relevance of link types (cf. Fig. 3.3b). The tensor $\mathbf{T}$ in Sect. 3.2.1 combines information about who follows whom with our explanations of the follow-links. So the PARAFAC decomposition would yield U_1 with subject-pf relation, U_2 with object-pf relation and U_3 with property-pf relation. In other words U_1 keeps the hub scores as relevance of the users to the pfs, U_2 the authorities scores as relevance of the users to the pfs and U_3 scores of the relevance of literals (hashtags) to the pfs. In line with HITS the largest entry of U_1^1 corresponds to the best hub for the first pf and the largest entry of U_2^1 to the best authority.

Table 3.2 PARAFAC vs. HITS results

PARAFAC				HITS		indegree	
Score	Hashtag	Score	User	Score	User	Degree	User
Group 1				0.62	Chris	3	Bob
1.00	lifestyle	0.71	Bob	0.56	Bob	3	Chris
–	–	0.70	Chris	0.50	Alex	2	Alex
Group 2				0.16	Don	1	Don
1.00	semanticweb	0.70	Don	0.16	Elly	1	Elly
0.001	lifestyle	0.70	Alex				
–	–	0.10	Elly				

3.2.3 Ranking Example

Applying the above factorization and analysis to the graph illustrated by Fig. 3.2 yields the results shown by the first four columns of Table 3.2. Two groups are identified, one where the hashtag *lifestyle* has a high score, and one where *semanticweb* is scored highly. The authoritative resources for each group differ from each other. Bob and Chris have high scores with respect to *lifestyle*. Don and Alex are the top authorities with respect to *semanticweb*. The application of HITS results in the ranking shown by column 5 and 6. The HITS ranking corresponds to a ranking based on the indegrees of the resources. Notably, the rankings produced by the PARAFAC analysis are different from the HITS/indegree results as they provide rankings with respect to different knowledge aspects in the data.

3.3 Implementation

Having introduced the theoretical background behind TweetRank, we present the implementation into an applicable system in Java.[2] We describe the three core components of the TweetRank architecture, which encapsulate a 3-step process, namely (1) the collection of data and its transformation to a tensor model, (2) data pre-processing, and (3) analysis.

3.3.1 Data Collection and Transformation

The first process step for the ranking of Social Web data is its collection. The objective of this stem is to construct the graph of semantic relations between relevant

---

[2] The framework implementation is available as public domain open source package: http://west. uni-koblenz.de/Research.

users of the platform $G = (V, L, E, linkType)$ (cf. Sect. 3.2.1). For many Social Web platforms, gathering of relevant data for constructing the candidate set of users V can be directly implemented on top of existing platform-specific API functions. For instance, Twitter API support is available for all major programming languages (including Java). This API can be used by an arbitrary account holder of the platform, with certain performance limitations (in terms of the hourly request rate). Large-scale access to API functions can be granted upon individual request.

The process of data collection starts with specifying custom terms(s) of interest. These terms are forwarded to the platform-specific API function for keyword-based search, which returns matching postings together with metadata (usually including author ID). The author IDs are then extracted and added to V. Subsequently, predecessors and successors of these "root" users – in terms of content related relations – are also retrieved and added to V. This step is usually supported by platform API functions for user profile details. For instance, Twitter API provides explicit functions for finding predecessors and successors of the given user: a followers-list (i.e., users that observe postings of the given person) and a following-list (other users that are monitored by the given person). Further expansion of V can be achieved by traversing following-relations and follower-relations transitively, up to a certain maximum depth (i.e., finding successors of successors, etc.).

In the next step, for each user from $u \in V$ a number of his recent postings is retrieved. In Twitter API this functionality is explicitly offered as part of the comprehensive search support. Each posting is then decomposed into terms $t \in L$. For constructing edges in E, we assume that user $u_1 \in U$ links to user $u_2 \in U$ by edge $e \in E$ labeled $linkType(e) = t \in L$, if a) u_1 is known to be a predecessor of u_2 in the platform sense (e.g., in terms of Twitter, u_1 follows u_2) and both u_1 and u_2 have frequently used term t in their postings retrieved so far. In the particular Twitter case, a common practice of lightweight content annotation is the use of hashtags. For this reason, we add the preceding hash sign to all the terms of interest before sending the initial query to Twitter, and do not consider non-hashtag terms in returned postings. Finally, the graph is transformed into the tensor representation for factorization analysis.

Important tuning parameters of the framework include the number of necessary postings for userlist initialization, the maximum number of predecessors/successors to be considered for each user, the number of recent postings per user to be processed, and filtering criteria for removing potentially irrelevant users and terms. For Twitter we instantiated our framework with the following settings (empirically estimated in series of comparative experiments): 300 users for the intitial "seed set," up to 500 direct predecessors/successors per user (dropping down by randomly removing superfluous entries, when necessary), 100 recent postings per user to analyze, each hashtag $t \in L$ should be used by at least ten different users, each user $u \in V$ should use at least three hashtags from L in his postings.

A further pre-processing step is the weighting of collected user relations to further remedy the negative effects of domination. We amplify relations based on their hashtag frequency so that statements with less frequent (i.e., selective) hashtags are amplified stronger than more common relations. As an effect, the adjacency indicators in the tensor have the following property:

$$
\mathbf{T}(x, y, z) =
\begin{cases}
1 + log\frac{\alpha}{links(z)}, & x, y \in V, \\
& links(z) = |\{e \in E\,|linkType(e) = z\}|, \\
& \alpha = links(x)\,|\forall t \in L, links(x) \geq links(t) \\
0, & \text{else}
\end{cases}
$$

The value α denotes the number of relations in which the most dominant hashtag participates. The function $links(t)$ ($links : L \rightarrow \mathbb{N}_0$) returns the number of relations in E induced by hashtag $t \in L$.

We remark that the implemented pre-processing steps are valuable for generating ranking analyses in general. Notably, simple methods for authority ranking, e.g., the counting of inlink scores per resource and predicate, benefit more from such pre-processing than more complex methods like PARAFAC.

3.3.2 Analysis

The analysis step implements the PARAFAC decomposition of the tensor, as modeled and created by the previous process steps. We have integrated existing software packages [4] for this purpose. As indicated in Sect. 3.2.2, the number of factors for the PARAFAC decomposition is crucial for the quality of the results of the analysis. The determination of the optimal number of factors is a case of open research. However, heuristics for determining a suitable number of factors have been published, e.g., the core consistency diagnostic (CORCONDIA) [2]. The factor determination applied in TweetRank builds upon such research.

The result of the analysis is a Kruskal (cf. Sect. 3.2.2) tensor [18] that approximates the original tensor. As illustrated in Fig. 3.4, the resulting vectors for the first (row), second (column), and third dimension are represented by three matrices. The columns of each of the matrices correspond to the scores calculated for the different factors $pf_1 \ldots pf_n$. Analogue to the SVD, entries in the column vectors correspond to authority scores, i.e., indicating the relevance of a resource with respect to its

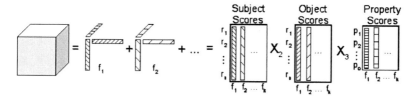

Fig. 3.4 Result of the analysis

in-degree. Entries in the row vectors correspond to hub scores, i.e., indicating the relevance of a resource with respect to its out-degree. We refer to [17] for a thorough analysis of the correspondence between SVD and its interpretation for link analysis. Entries of the vectors in the third dimension indicate the relevance of a term with respect to the hub and authority users. Based on this notion, we interpret hub scores as indicative for the relevance of a user as a "follower" (i.e., observer of other users). Vice versa, authority scores indicate the relevance of a user as subject of observation (whom-to-follow recommendations). As we modeled posting terms by the third dimension, their relevance for particular factors can be looked up in the vectors of the third dimension.

3.3.3 Use Case Example

To demonstrate the functionality of the framework presented so far, we consider the request *semanticweb* from our run-through Twitter scenario. We initiate the construction of the thematically focused social graph by sending to Twitter the keyword-based search request $q = \#semanticweb$. After the expansion step (adding predecessors and successors, downloading postings from all users collected so far) and common preprocessing as described before, we obtain a social graph $G = (V, L, E, linkType)$ with $|V| = 1{,}323$ users, $|L| = 175$ hashtags, and $|E| = 17{,}190$ user relations.

Subsequently, the tensor decomposition with $f = 15$ PARAFAC factors provides user authority, user hub, and hashtag relevance scores for each factor. Table 3.3 shows most relevant top-5 hashtags and users for some factors of this decomposition (ordered by hashtag relevance and user authority, respectively).

Some important observations can be made about the results shown in Fig. 3.3. First, the authority scoring in the prevalent factor "semanticweb" is closely related to results produced by simpler ranking mechanisms (e.g., H-candidate set recommendation as discussed in Sect. 3.1). The results are entirely based on recent user postings and current user relations, so any side effects of long-term user profiling (such as temporary user activity in a certain topic, but long time before) will have no influence on current contact recommendations. Beyond the mainstream factor (say *semanticweb core*) the decomposition captures a number of second-order themes related to *semanticweb* and reflected in Twitter postings, such as *web tools, multimedia, security & privacy, social media*, or *programming*. In this sense, the diversity and structuring of recommendation results are substantially increased. As a result, the user can better identify the actual target (sub-)topic of his personal interest related to *semanticweb*, and then follow best-scored users in the context of this particular, thematically focused theme.

Table 3.3 TweetRank results for query "semanticweb" on Twitter

Score	Hashtag	Score	User	Score	Hashtag	Score	User
Factor 1 ("semanticweb")				Factor 4 ("programming")			
0.147	semantics	0.238	timberners_lee	0.111	programming	0.183	cjmconnors
0.125	business	0.143	PEPublishing	0.053	analytics	0.178	DublinCore
0.106	lod	0.142	jahendler	0.047	semantic	0.108	spirinet
0.091	semweb	0.138	timoreilly	0.046	microdata	0.098	AskAaronLee
0.054	semanticweb	0.097	semanticnews	0.040	startups	0.096	GeoffWigz
Factor 2 ("web tools")				Factor 5 ("securiry&privacy")			
0.266	java	0.419	SCMagazine	0.163	security	0.285	BLSocSci
0.251	php	0.143	HTML5watcher	0.130	web20	0.278	socialwendy
0.220	http	0.128	opencalais	0.083	privacy	0.162	pedantic_web
0.214	joomla	0.102	hadoop	0.067	apps	0.154	drthinkmore
0.199	javascript	0.097	LSIstorage	0.054	china	0.136	linuxhoundhost
Factor 3 ("multimedia")				Factor 6 ("social media")			
0.049	music	0.265	Beyond15	0.212	foaf	0.484	jwolfnbaa
0.044	video	0.185	junglejar	0.172	socialmedia	0.165	rdfQuery
0.032	semweb	0.172	CSS3	0.118	facebook	0.130	CreativeCustoms
0.023	iphone	0.134	davidstack	0.109	rdfa	0.078	websciencetrust
0.021	innovation	0.125	emtacl	0.054	webscience	0.064	virtualrooms

3.4 Related Work

From the conceptual perspective, two topics can be seen as closely related to our
TweetRank approach: authority ranking for Web contents and graph-based relevance
ranking for semi-structured data. This section gives a short overview of these areas
and distinguishes TweetRank from other existing solutions.

3.4.1 Rating Web Pages

PageRank [7], HITS [17] and SALSA [20] are prominent algorithms for ranking
Web pages based on link analysis. PageRank builds upon a model of a random
walk among Web pages, where the stationary probability of passing through a certain page is interpreted as measure of its importance. HITS is based on the notion
of a mutual re-enforcement between importance (authority) and connectivity (hub)
scores of Web pages. SALSA can be seen as a more complex hybrid solution that
integrates ideas of PageRank and HITS by combination of both link traversing directions (i.e., forward and backward) for constructing graph models. The conceptual
generalization for this kind of methods is given in [12]. Unlike TweetRank, this
family of methods provides no natural mechanisms for expressing and exploiting
semantics of links/relations.

The contextualization of graph models can be achieved through different customizations of the mentioned models. Possible adaptations include various custom weightings of graph edges (e.g., based on appearance of particular terms in Web documents [22, 24], content classification [11, 15], structural properties like in-domain vs. out-domain linking [6], etc.) or joint probabilistic modeling for content and connectivity of Web pages [9]. In contrast to TweetRank, these solutions are designed for the Web setting and do not introduce distinguished link semantics. The solution presented in [19] uses for Web authority ranking the higher-order representation of the hyperlink graph by labeling the graph edges with the anchor text of the hyperlinks. This method is closely related to TweetRank, but addresses a fully different problem setting (links and anchors in the Web graph vs. user relations in Social Web).

Another kind of contextualization for authority ranking models can be observed in the area of search personalization. For instance, Eirinaki and Vazirgiannis present a modification of the PageRank algorithm to compute personalized recommendations of Web pages given a path of visited pages [13]. Their approach requires access to web server logs that provide statistics about the paths browsed by other users. BrowseRank [21] is a further example of a page ranking approach that requires to collect statistics on user behavior such as the time spent on a web page. The generalized algorithm for personalized authority ranking is described in [16].

Our TweetRank approach is designed for a different scenario of context-oriented contact recommendation in Social Web environments. The presented approach is conceptually more general and does not rely on user profiles and query logs. As when browsing the Web, detailed statistical information about prior user interactions is often not available through proprietary APIs of Social Web portals (especially for privacy protection reasons). However, this information can be easily integrated with TweetRank, if necessary.

3.4.2 Rating (Semi-)Structured Data

ObjectRank [5] adds authority transfer weights for different types of links to the PageRank algorithm. Such weights influence the *random walk* of prospective users and are to be assigned by domain experts. Beagle++ [8] is an extension for the Beagle desktop search engine that applies ObjectRank to RDF meta data about desktop objects to improve their ranking in desktop search scenarios. TweetRank also considers the semantics of relations, however, it is an approach for computing ranks for users and user groups on-the-fly, as an answer to a hashtag-based query. It does not rely on manually assigned link weights, and is based on the generalized HITS algorithm instead of PageRank.

Anyanwu and Sheth present a framework for query answering with respect to so called semantic associations [3]. A semantic association represents semantic similarity between paths connecting different resources in an RDF model. Aleman-Meza et al. [1] presented and evaluated methods for ranking semantic associations. As a continued work of [3], the presented methods target the identification of similar resources to apply it in scenarios like terror-prevention. Their approach involves ranking criteria considering graph structure, and user context. User context is defined statically by selecting ontology concepts that are considered as representative for a user's context. Ramakrishnan et al. present heuristics for weighting graph patterns connecting two nodes in a graph considering the differences of edges given by RDF graphs that include schema information encoded as RDFS ontologies [23]. Prior approaches on graph pattern analysis presented methods assuming that only one type of edge exists. Next to a presentation of the heuristics, they present an evaluation of them targeting the question which heuristic results in higher quality patterns.

3.5   Conclusion

In this chapter we presented TweetRank, a novel approach for authority ranking in Social Web communities. Conceptually, TweetRank is a correspondent to authority ranking methods known from Web retrieval, such as PageRank or HITS. Our approach exploits the novel representational model for social graphs, based on 3-dimensional tensors. This allows us to exploit in the natural way the available semantics of user relations. By applying the PARAFAC tensor decomposition we identify authoritative sources in the social network as well as groups of semantically coherent terms of interest. Therefore, TweetRank can be seen as a next step towards efficient and effective search/recommendation technology for the Social Web.

References

1. Boanerges Aleman-Meza, Christian Halaschek-Wiener, Ismailcem B. Arpinar, Cartic Ramakrishnan, and Amit P. Sheth. Ranking complex relationships on the semantic web. *IEEE Internet Computing*, 9(3):37–44, 2005
2. Claus A. Andersson and Rasmus Bro. The n-way toolbox for matlab. *Chemometrics and Intelligent Laboratory Systems*, 52(1):1–4, 2000
3. Kemafor Anyanwu and Amit P. Sheth. The p operator: Discovering and ranking associations on the semantic web. *SIGMOD Record*, 31(4):42–47, 2002
4. Brett W. Bader and Tamara G. Kolda. Algorithm 862: MATLAB tensor classes for fast algorithm prototyping. *ACM Transactions on Mathematical Software*, 32(4):635–653, 2006
5. Andrey Balmin, Vagelis Hristidis, and Yannis Papakonstantinou. Objectrank: Authority-based keyword search in databases. In *VLDB*, pages 564–575, 2004
6. Krishna Bharat and Monika Rauch Henzinger. Improved Algorithms for Topic Distillation in a Hyperlinked Environment. In *21st Annual International ACM SIGIR Conference, Melbourne, Australia*, pages 104–111, 1998
7. S. Brin and L. Page. The anatomy of a large-scale hypertextual web search engine. In *Seventh International World-Wide Web Conference (WWW 1998)*, 1998
8. Paul Alexandru Chirita, Stefania Ghita, Wolfgang Nejdl, and Raluca Paiu. Beagle++ : Semantically enhanced searching and ranking on the desktop. In *ESWC*, 2006

9. David A. Cohn and Thomas Hofmann. The missing link – a probabilistic model of document content and hypertext connectivity. In *13th Conference on Advances in Neural Information Processing Systems (NIPS), Denver, USA*, pages 430–436, 2000
10. Klaas Dellschaft and Steffen Staab. An epistemic dynamic model for tagging systems. In *19th ACM Conference on Hypertext and Hypermedia (Hypertext 2008), Pittsburgh, USA*, pages 71–80, 2008
11. Michelangelo Diligenti, Marco Gori, and Marco Maggini. Web Page Scoring Systems for Horizontal and Vertical Search. In *11th International World Wide Web Conference (WWW), Honolulu, USA*, pages 508–516, 2002
12. Chris H. Q. Ding, Xiaofeng He, Parry Husbands, Hongyuan Zha, and Horst D. Simon. PageRank, HITS and a Unified Framework for Link Analysis. In *25th Annual International ACM SIGIR Conference on Research and Development in Information Retrieval, Tampere, Finland*, pages 353–354, 2002
13. Magdalini Eirinaki and Michalis Vazirgiannis. Usage-based pagerank for web personalization. *Data Mining, IEEE International Conference on*, pages 130–137, 2005
14. Richard A. Harshman and Margaret E. Lundy. Parafac: Parallel factor analysis. *Computational Statistics and Data Analysis*, 18(1):39–72, 1994
15. Taher H. Haveliwala. Topic-sensitive PageRank. In *11th International World Wide Web Conference (WWW), Honolulu, USA*, pages 517–526, 2002
16. Glen Jeh and Jennifer Widom. Scaling Personalized Web Search. In *12th International World Wide Web Conference (WWW), Budapest, Hungary*, pages 271–279, 2003
17. Jon M. Kleinberg. Authoritative sources in a hyperlinked environment. *J. ACM*, 46(5):604–632, 1999
18. Tamara G. Kolda and Brett W. Bader. Tensor decompositions and applications. *SIAM Review*, 51(3), 2009 (to appear)
19. Tamara G. Kolda, Brett W. Bader, and Joseph P. Kenny. Higher-Order Web Link Analysis Using Multilinear Algebra. In *5th IEEE International Conference on Data Mining (ICDM), Houston, USA*, pages 242–249, 2005
20. Ronny Lempel and Shlomo Moran. SALSA: the Stochastic Approach for Link-Structure Analysis. *ACM Transactions on Information Systems (TOIS)*, 19(2):131–160, 2001
21. Yu-Ting Liu, Bin Gao, Tie-Yan Liu, Ying Zhang, Zhiming Ma, Shuyuan He, and Hang Li. Browserank: letting web users vote for page importance. In *SIGIR*, pages 451–458, 2008
22. Davood Rafiei and Alberto O. Mendelzon. What is this Page known for? Computing Web Page Reputations. *Computer Networks*, 33(1–6):823–835, 2000
23. Cartic Ramakrishnan, William H. Milnor, Matthew Perry, and Amit P. Sheth. Discovering informative connection subgraphs in multi-relational graphs. *SIGKDD Explor. Newsl.*, 7(2):56–63, 2005
24. Matthew Richardson and Pedro Domingos. The Intelligent surfer: Probabilistic Combination of Link and Content Information in PageRank. In *14th Conference on Advances in Neural Information Processing Systems (NIPS), Vancouver, Canada*, pages 1441–1448, 2001

Chapter 4
Analyzing the Dynamics of Communication in Online Social Networks

Munmun De Choudhury, Hari Sundaram, Ajita John, and Doree Duncan Seligmann

4.1 Introduction

During the past decade, the advent of the "social Web" has provided considerable leeway to a rich rubric of platforms that promote communication among users on shared spaces. These interpersonal interactions often take place in the pretext of either a shared media e.g., an image (Flickr), a video (YouTube), a "blog"/"microblog" (Twitter); or are built across social ties that reflect human relationships in the physical world (Facebook). The resultant impact of the rapid proliferation of these social websites has been widespread. Individuals today, can express their opinions on personal blogs as well as can share media objects to engage themselves in discussion. Right from shopping a new car, to getting suggestions on investment, searching for the next holiday destination or even planning their next meal out, people have started to rely heavily on opinions expressed online or social resources that can provide them with useful insights into the diversely available set of options. Moreover, personal experiences as well as thoughts and opinions on external events also manifest themselves through "memes," "online chatter" or variegated "voting" mechanisms in several peoples blogs and social profiles. As a positive outcome of all these interactional affordances provided by the online social media and social network sites, a broad podium of opportunities and ample scope have begun to emerge to the social network analysis community. Instead of focusing on longitudinal studies of relatively small groups such as participant observation [16, 31] and surveys [8], researchers today can study social processes such as information diffusion or community emergence at *very large scales*. This is because electronic social data can be collected at comparatively low cost of acquisition and resource maintenance, can span over diverse populations and be acquired over extended time periods. The result is that study of social processes on a scale of million nodes, that would have been barely possible a few years back, is now looming a lot of interest currently [20, 22].

M. De Choudhury (✉)
Arizona State University, Tempe, AZ, USA
e-mail: munmun@asu.edu

B. Furht (ed.), *Handbook of Social Network Technologies and Applications*,
DOI 10.1007/978-1-4419-7142-5_4, © Springer Science+Business Media, LLC 2010

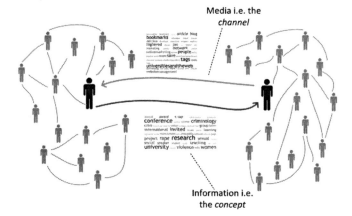

Fig. 4.1 Illustration of the two key organizing ideas that embody online interpersonal communication processes: namely, the information or concept that is the content of communication and the channel or the media via which communication takes place

Our broad goal is to study how such online communication today is reshaping and restructuring our understanding of different social processes. Communication is the process by which participating individuals create and share information with one another in order to reach a mutual understanding [6]. Typically communication involves a form of a *channel*, or a media by means of which information, in the form of *concepts* get transmitted from one individual to another. An illustrative example that describes the key ideas in the online communication process is shown in Fig. 4.1. Note, mass media channels are more effective in creating knowledge of innovations [5], whereas channels promoting social engagement are more effective in forming and changing attitudes toward a new concept, and thus in influencing the decision to adopt or reject a new concept or information.[1]

It, thus, goes without saying that communication is central to the evolution of social systems. To support this empirical finding, over the years, numerous studies on online social communication processes have indicated that studying properties of the associated social system, i.e., the network structure and dynamics can be useful pointers in determining the outcome of many important social and economic relationships [1, 2]. Despite the fundamental importance laid on the understanding of these structures and their temporal behavior in many social and economic settings [8–10, 20, 21], the development of characterization tools, foundational theoretical models as well as insightful observational studies on large-scale social communication datasets is still in its infancy. This is because communication patterns on online social platforms are significantly distinct from their physical world counterpart – consequently often invalidating the methods, tools and studies designed to cater to longitudinal ethnographic studies on observed physical world

---

[1] Also referred to in popular culture as a "meme."

interactions. This distinction can be viewed on several aspects relating to the nature of the online communication process itself: such as inexpensive reach to a global audience, volatility of content and easy accessibility of publishing information content online. The outcome of these differences is that today there is an ardent necessity to develop robust computational frameworks to characterize, model and conduct observational studies on online communication processes prevalent, rather pervasively, on the online domain.

The contributions of this chapter are also motivated from the potential ability of online communication patterns in addressing multi-faceted sociological, behavioral as well as societal problems. For example, the patterns of social engagement, reflected via the networks play a fundamental role in determining how concepts or information are exchanged. Such information may be as simple as an invitation to a party, or as consequential as information about job opportunities, literacy, consumer products, disease containment and so on. Additionally, understanding the evolution of groups and communities can lend us meaningful insights into the ways in which concepts form and aggregate, opinions develop as well as ties are made and broken, or even how the decisions of individuals contribute to impact on external temporal occurrences. Finally, studies of shared user-generated media content manifested via the communication channel can enable us re-think about the ways in which our communication patterns affect our social memberships or our observed behavior on online platforms.

In the light of the above observations, the following two parts summarize our key research investigations:

- *Rich Media Communication Patterns.* This part investigates rich media communication patterns, i.e., the characteristics of the emergent communication, centered around the *channel* or the shared media artifact. The primary research question we address here is: what are the characteristics of conversations centered around shared rich media artifacts?
- *Information Diffusion.* This part instruments the characterization of the *concept*, or the information or meme, involved in the social communication process. Our central idea encompasses the following question: how do we model user communication behavior that affects the diffusion of information in a social network and what is the impact of user characteristics, such as individual attributes in this diffusion process?

The rest of the chapter is organized as follows. In Sect. 4.2, we present the major characteristics of online communication dynamics. Next two sections deal with the methods that help us study rich media communication patterns (Sect. 4.3) and impact of communication properties on diffusion processes (Sect. 4.4). They also present some experimental studies conducted on large-scale datasets to evaluate our proposed methods of communication analysis. Finally we conclude in Sect. 4.5 with a summary of the contributions and future research opportunities.

4.2 Characteristics of Online Communication

We present key characteristics of the online communication process. First we present a background survey of the different aspects of online communication. Next we discuss the different forms of communication affordances that are provided by different online social spaces today and discuss an overview of prior work on the different modalities.

4.2.1 Background

There are several ways in which online social media has revolutionized our means and manner of social communication today: naturally making a huge impact on the characteristics of the social systems that encompass them. We discuss some of the characteristics of this widespread change in the communication process as follows:

1. *Reach.* Social media communication technologies provide scale and enable anyone to reach a global audience.
2. *Accessibility.* Social media communication tools are generally available to anyone at little or no cost, converting every individual participant in the online social interaction into a publisher and broadcaster of information content on their own.
3. *Usability.* Most social media do not, or in some cases reinvent skills, so anyone can operate the means of content production and subsequent communication, eliminating most times the need for specialized skills and training.
4. *Recency.* Social media communication can be capable of virtually instantaneous responses; only the participants determining any delay in response; making the communication process extremely reciprocative, with low lags in responses.
5. *Permanence.* unlike industrial media communication, which once created, cannot be altered (e.g., once a magazine article is printed and distributed changes cannot be made to that same article), social media communication is extremely volatile over time, because it can be altered almost instantaneously by comments, editing, voting and so on.

These key characteristics of online social communication have posed novel challenges on the study of social systems in general. To highlight some of the key statistics of different social sites available on the Web today, we compiled Table 4.1. The natural question that arises is that: how are online social communication patterns today affecting our social lives and our collective behavior? As is obvious from the statistics, traditional tools to understand social interactions in physical spaces or over industrial media or even prior work involving longitudinal studies of groups of individuals are therefore often only partially capable of characterizing, modeling and observing the modern online communication of today.

Table 4.1 Some social media statistics

Social media type	Key statistics
YouTube	139M users; US$200M [Forbes]
Flickr	3.6B images; 50M users
Facebook	350M active users; 1B pieces of content shared each week
MySpace	110M monthly active users; 14B comments on the site
Digg	3M unique users; $40M
Engadget	1,887,887 monthly visitors
Huffington Post	8.9M visitors
Live Journal	19,128,882 accounts

In this chapter, we therefore identify two key components that subsume these diverse characteristics of the online social communication process on social media today. These two components are manifested as below:

1. The entity or the concept (e.g., information, or 'meme').
2. The channel or the media (e.g., textual, audio, video or image-based interactive channel).

4.2.2 Communication Modes in Social Networks

We discuss several different communication modes popularly existent in social networks and social media sites today. These diverse modalities of communication allow users to engage in interaction often spanning a commonly situated interest, shared activities or artifacts, geographical, ethnic or gender-based co-location, or even dialogue on external news events. In this chapter, we have focused on the following forms of communication among users, that are likely to promote social interaction:

1. *Messages.* Social websites such as MySpace feature an ability to users to post short messages on their friends' profiles. A similar feature on Facebook allows users to post content on another user's "Wall." These messages are typically short and viewable publicly to the common set of friends to both the users; providing evidences of interaction via communication.
2. *Blog Comments/Replies.* Commenting and replying capability provided by different blogging websites, such as Engadget, Huffington Post, Slashdot, Mashable or MetaFilter provide substantial evidence of back and forth communication among sets of users, often relating to the topic of the blog post. Note, replies are usually shown as an indented block in response to the particular comment in question.
3. *Conversations around Shared Media Artifact.* Many social websites allow users to share media artifacts with their local network or set of contacts. For example, on Flickr a user can upload a photo that is viewable via a feed to her contacts; while YouTube allows users to upload videos emcompassing different topical categories. Both these kinds of media sharing allow rich communication activity

centered around the media elements via comments. These comments often take a conversational structure, involving considerable back and forth dialogue among users.

4. *Social Actions.* A different kind of a communication modality provided by certain social sites such as Digg or del.icio.us involves participation in a variety of social actions by users. For example, Digg allows users to vote (or rate) on shared articles, typically news, via a social action called "digging." Another example is the "like" feature provided by Facebook on user statuses, photos, videos and shared links. Such social action often acts as a proxy for communication activity, because first, it is publicly observable, and second it allows social interaction among the users.

5. *Micro-blogging.* Finally, we define a communication modality based on microblogging activity of users, e.g., as provided by Twitter. The micro-blogging feature, specifically called "tweeting" on Twitter, often takes conversational form, since tweets can be directed to a particular user as well. Moreover, Twitter allows the "RT" or re-tweet feature, allowing users to propagate information from one user to another. Hence micro-blogging activity can be considered as an active interactional medium.

4.2.3   Prior Work on Communication Modalities

In this section we will survey some prior work on the above presented communication modalities.

Conversations. Social networks evolve centered around communication artifacts. The conversational structure by dint of which several social processes unfold, such as diffusion of innovation and cultural bias, discovery of experts or evolution of groups, is valuable because it lends insights into the nature of the network at multi-grained temporal and topological levels and helps us understand networks as an emergent property of social interaction.

Comments and messaging structure in blogs and shared social spaces have been used to understand dialogue based conversational behavior among individuals [34] as well as in the context of summarization of social activity on the online platform or to understand the descriptive nature of web comments [32]. Some prior work have also deployed conversational nature of comments to understand social network structure as well as in statistical analysis of networks [15]. There has also been considerable work on analyzing discussions or comments in blogs [28] as well as utilizing such communication for prediction of its consequences like user behavior, sales, stock market activity etc.

Prior research has also discovered value in using social interactional data to understand and in certain cases predict external behavioral phenomena [11]. There has been considerable work on analyzing social network characteristics in blogs [20] as well as utilizing such communication for prediction of its consequences like user behavior, sales, stock market activity etc [3, 17]. In [17] Gruhl et al. attempt to determine if blog data exhibit any recognizable pattern prior to spikes in the ranking of the sales of books on Amazon.com. Adar et al. in [3] present a framework for modeling and predicting user behavior on the web. They created a model for several sets of user behavior and used it to automatically compare the reaction of a user population on one medium e.g., search engines, blogs etc to the reactions on another.

Social Actions. The participation of individual users in online social spaces is one of the most noted features in the recent explosive growth of popular online communities ranging from picture and video sharing (Flickr.com and YouTube.com) and collective music recommendation (Last.fm) to news voting (Digg.com) and social bookmarking (del.icio.us). However in contrast to traditional communities, these sites do not feature direct communication or conversational mechanisms to its members. This has given rise to an interesting pattern of social action based interaction among users. The users' involvement and their contribution through non-message-based interactions, e.g., digging or social bookmarking have become a major force behind the success of these social spaces. Studying this new type of user interactional modality is crucial to understanding the dynamics of online social communities and community monetization.

Social actions [12] performed on shared spaces often promote rich communication dynamics among individuals. In prior work, authors have discussed how the voting i.e., digging activity on Digg impacts the discovery of novel information [37]. Researchers [35] have also examined the evolution of activity between users in the Facebook social network to capture the notion of how social links can grow stronger or weaker over time. Their experiments reveal that links in the activity network on Facebook tend to come and go rapidly over time, and the strength of ties exhibits a general decreasing trend of activity as the social network link ages. Social actions revealed via third party applications as featured by Facebook have also lent interesting insights into the social characteristics of online user behavior.

In this chapter, we organize our approach based on these two different modalities of online communication, i.e., conversations and social actions. We utilize the former to study the dynamic characterization of the media channel that embodies online communication. While the latter is used to study the diffusion properties of the concept or the unit of information that is transmitted in a network via the communication process. This is presented in the following two sections.

4.3   Rich Media Communication Patterns

An interesting emergent property of large-scale user-generated content on social media sites is that these shared media content seem to generate rich dialogue of communication centered round shared media objects, e.g., YouTube, Flickr etc. Hence apart from impact of communication on the dynamics of the individuals' actions, roles and the community in general, there are additional challenges on how to characterize such "conversations," understanding the relationship of the conversations to social engagement i.e., the community under consideration, as well as studying the observed user behavior responsible for publishing and participation of the content.

Today, there is significant user participation on rich media social networking websites such as YouTube and Flickr. Users can create (e.g., upload photo on Flickr), and consume media (e.g., watch a video on YouTube). These websites also allow for significant communication between the users – such as comments by one user on a media uploaded by another. These comments reveal a rich dialogue structure (user A comments on the upload, user B comments on the upload, A comments in response to B's comment, B responds to A's comment etc.) between users, where the discussion is often about themes unrelated to the original video. In this section, the sequence of comments on a media object is referred to as a conversation. Note the theme of the conversation is latent and depends on the content of the conversation.

The fundamental idea explored in this section is that analysis of communication activity is crucial to understanding repeated visits to a rich media social networking site. People return to a video post that they have already seen and post further comments (say in YouTube) in response to the communication activity, rather than to watch the video again. Thus it is the content of the communication activity itself that the people want to read (or see, if the response to a video post is another video, as is possible in the case of YouTube). Furthermore, these rich media sites have notification mechanisms that alert users of new comments on a video post/image upload promoting this communication activity.

We denote the communication property that causes people to further participate in a conversation as its "interestingness." While the meaning of the term "interestingness" is subjective, we decided to use it to express an intuitive property of the communication phenomena that we frequently observe on rich media networks. Our goal is to determine a real scalar value corresponding to each conversation in an objective manner that serves as a measure of interestingness. Modeling the user subjectivity is beyond the scope of this section.

What causes a conversation to be interesting to prompt a user to participate? We conjecture that people will participate in conversations when (a) they find the conversation theme interesting (what the previous users are talking about) (b) see comments by people that are well known in the community, or people that they know directly comment (these people are interesting to the user) or (c) observe an engaging dialogue between two or more people (an absorbing back and forth between two people). Intuitively, interesting conversations have an engaging theme, with interesting people. Example of an interesting conversation from YouTube is shown in Fig. 4.2.

A conversation that is deemed interesting must be consequential [13] – i.e., it must impact the social network itself. Intuitively, there should be three consequences (a) the people who find themselves in an interesting conversation, should tend to co-participate in future conversations (i.e., they will seek out other interesting people that they've engaged with) (b) people who participated in the current interesting

Fig. 4.2 Example of an interesting conversation from YouTube. Note it involves back-and-forth dialogue between participants as well as evolving themes over time

conversation are likely to seek out other conversations with themes similar to the current conversation and finally (c) the conversation theme, if engaging, should slowly proliferate to other conversations.

There are several reasons why measuring interestingness of a conversation is of value. First, it can be used to rank and filter both blog posts and rich media, particularly when there are multiple sites on which the same media content is posted, guiding users to the most interesting conversation. For example, the same news story may be posted on several blogs, our measures can be used to identify those sites where the postings and commentary is of greatest interest. It can also be used to increase efficiency. Rich media sites, can manage resources based on changing interestingness measures (e.g., and cache those videos that are becoming more interesting), and optimize retrieval for the dominant themes of the conversations. Besides, differentiated advertising prices for ads placed alongside videos can be based on their associated conversational interestingness.

4.3.1 Problem Formulation

4.3.1.1 Definitions

Conversation. We define a conversation in online social media (e.g., an image, a video or a blog post) as a temporally ordered sequence of comments posted by individuals whom we call "participants." In this section, the content of the conversations are represented as a stemmed and stop-word eliminated bag-of-words.

Conversational Themes. Conversational themes are sets of salient topics associated with conversations at different points in time.

Interestingness of Participants. Interestingness of a participant is a property of her communication activity over different conversations. We propose that an interesting participant can often be characterized by (a) several other participants writing comments after her, (b) participation in a conversation involving other interesting participants, and (c) active participation in "hot" conversational themes.

Interestingness of Conversations. We now define "interestingness" as a dynamic communication property of conversations which is represented as a real nonnegative scalar dependent on (a) the evolutionary conversational themes at a particular point of time, and (b) the communication properties of its participants. It is important to note here that "interestingness" of a conversation is necessarily subjective and often depends upon context of the participant. We acknowledge that alternate definitions of interestingness are also possible.

Conversations used in this section are the temporal sequence of comments associated with media elements (videos) in the highly popular media sharing site YouTube. However our model can be generalized to any domain with observable threaded communication. Now we formalize our problem based on the following data model.

4.3.1.2 Data Model

Our data model comprises the tuple C, P having the following two inter-related entities: a set of conversations, C on shared media elements; and a set of participants P in these conversations. Each conversation is represented with a set of comments, such that each comment that belongs to a conversation is associated with a unique participant, a timestamp and some textual content (bag-of-words).

We now discuss the notations. We assume that there are N participants, M conversations, K conversation themes and Q time slices. Using the relationship between the entities in the tuple C, P from the above data model, we construct the following matrices for every time slice $q, 1 \leq q \leq Q$:

- $\mathbf{P_F}^{(q)} \in \mathbb{R}^{N \times N}$: Participant-follower matrix, where $\mathbf{P_F}^{(q)}(i, j)$ is the probability that at time slice q, participant j comments following participant i on the conversations in which i had commented at any time slice from 1 to $(q - 1)$.

- $\mathbf{P_L}^{(q)} \in \mathbb{R}^{N \times N}$: Participant-leader matrix, where $\mathbf{P_L}^{(q)}(i, j)$ is the probability that in time slice q, participant i comments following participant j on the conversations in which j had commented in any time slice from 1 to $(q - 1)$. Note, both $\mathbf{P_F}^{(q)}$ and $\mathbf{P_L}^{(q)}$ are asymmetric, since communication between participants is directional.
- $\mathbf{P_C}^{(q)} \in \mathbb{R}^{N \times M}$: Participant-conversation matrix, where $\mathbf{P_C}^{(q)}(i, j)$ is the probability that participant i comments on conversation j in time slice q.
- $\mathbf{C_T}^{(q)} \in \mathbb{R}^{M \times K}$: Conversation-theme matrix, where $\mathbf{C_T}^{(q)}(i, j)$ is the probability that conversation i belongs to theme j in time slice q.
- $\mathbf{T_S}^{(q)} \in \mathbb{R}^{K \times 1}$: Theme-strength vector, where $\mathbf{T_S}^{(q)}(i)$ is the strength of theme i in time slice q. Note, $\mathbf{T_S}^{(q)}$ is simply the normalized column sum of $\mathbf{C_T}^{(q)}$.
- $\mathbf{P_T}^{(q)} \in \mathbb{R}^{N \times K}$: Participant-theme matrix, where $\mathbf{P_T}^{(q)}(i, j)$ is the probability that participant i communicates on theme j in time slice q. Note, $\mathbf{P_T}^{(q)} = \mathbf{P_C}^{(q)} \cdot \mathbf{C_T}^{(q)}$.
- $\mathbf{I_P}^{(q)} \in \mathbb{R}^{N \times 1}$: Interestingness of participants vector, where $\mathbf{I_P}^{(q)}(i)$ is the interestingness of participant i in time slice q.
- $\mathbf{I_C}^{(q)} \in \mathbb{R}^{M \times 1}$: Interestingness of conversations vector, where $\mathbf{I_C}^{(q)}(i)$ is the interestingness of conversation i in time slice q.

For simplicity of notation, we denote the i-th row of the above 2-dimensional matrices as $\mathbf{X}(i, :)$.

4.3.1.3   Problem Statement

Now we formally present our problem statement: given a dataset C, P and associated meta-data, we intend to determine the interestingness of the conversations in C, defined as $\mathbf{I_C}^{(q)}$ (a non-negative scalar measure for a conversation) for every time slice q, $1 \leq q \leq Q$. Determining interestingness of conversations involves two key challenges:

1. How to extract the evolutionary conversational themes?
2. How to model the communication properties of the participants through their interestingness?

Further in order to justify interestingness of conversations, we need to address the following challenge: what are the consequences of an interesting conversation?

In the following three sections, we discuss how we address these three challenges through: (a) detecting conversational themes based on a mixture model that incorporates regularization with time indicator, regularization for temporal smoothness and for co-participation; (b) modeling interestingness of participants; and of interestingness of conversations; and using a novel joint optimization framework of interestingness that incorporates temporal smoothness constraints and (c) justifying interestingness by capturing its future consequences.

4.3.2 Conversational Themes

In this section, we discuss the method of detecting conversational themes. We elaborate on our theme model in the following two sub-sections – first a sophisticated mixture model for theme detection incorporating time indicator based, temporal and co-participation based regularization is presented. Second, we discuss parameter estimation of this theme model.

4.3.2.1   Chunk-Based Mixture Model of Themes

Conversations are dynamically growing collections of comments from different participants. Hence, static keyword or tag based assignment of themes to conversations independent of time is not useful. Our model of detecting themes is therefore based on segmentation of conversations into "chunks" per time slice. A chunk is a representation of a conversation at a particular time slice and it comprises a (stemmed and stop-word eliminated) set of comments (bag-of-words) whose posting timestamps lie within the same time slice. Our goal is to associate each chunk (and hence the conversation at that time slice) with a theme distribution. We develop a sophisticated multinomial mixture model representation of chunks over different themes (a modified pLSA [18]) where the theme distributions are (a) regularized with time indicator, (b) smoothed across consecutive time slices, and (c) take into account the prior knowledge of co-participation of individuals in the associated conversations.

Let us assume that a conversation c_i is segmented into Q non-overlapping chunks (or bag-of-words) corresponding to the Q different time slices. Let us represent the chunk corresponding to the i-th conversation at time slice $q(1 \leq q \leq Q)$ as $\lambda_{i,q}$. We further assume that the words in $\lambda_{i,q}$ are generated from K multinomial theme models $\theta_1, \theta_2, \ldots, \theta_K$ whose distributions are hidden to us. Our goal is to determine the log likelihood that can represent our data, incorporating the three regularization techniques mentioned above. Thereafter we can maximize the log likelihood to compute the parameters of the K theme models.

However, before we estimate the parameter of the theme models, we refine our framework by regularizing the themes temporally as well as due to co-participation of participants. This is discussed in the following two sub-sections.

Temporal Regularization. We incorporate temporal characterization of themes in our theme model [27]. We conjecture that a word in the chunk can be attributed either to the textual context of the chunk $\lambda_{i,q}$, or the time slice q – for example, certain words can be highly popular on certain time slices due to related external events. Hence the theme associated with words in a chunk $\lambda_{i,q}$ needs to be regularized with respect to the time slice q. We represent the chunk $\lambda_{i,q}$ at time slice q with the probabilistic mixture model:

$$p(w : \lambda_{i,q}, q) = \sum_{j=1}^{K} p(w, \theta_j | \lambda_{i,q}, q), \qquad (4.1)$$

where w is a word in the chunk $\lambda_{i,q}$ and θ_j is the jth theme. The joint probability on the right hand side can be decomposed as:

$$
\begin{aligned}
p(w, \theta_j | \lambda_{i,q}, q) &= p(w|\theta_j) \cdot p(\theta_j | \lambda_{i,q}, q) \\
&= p(w|\theta_j) \cdot ((1 - \gamma_q) \cdot p(\theta_j | \lambda_{i,q}) + \gamma_q \cdot p(\theta_j | q)),
\end{aligned}
\tag{4.2}
$$

where γ_q is a parameter that regulates the probability of a theme θ_j given the chunk $\lambda_{i,q}$ and the probability of a theme θ_j given the time slice q. Note that since a conversation can alternatively be represented as a set of chunks, the collection of all chunks over all conversations is simply the set of conversations C. Hence the log likelihood of the entire collection of chunks is equivalent to the likelihood of the M conversations in C, given the theme model. Weighting the log likelihood of the model parameters with the occurrence of different words in a chunk, we get the following equation:

$$
L(C) = \log p(C) = \sum_{\lambda_{i,q} \in C} \sum_{w \in \lambda_{i,q}} n(w, \lambda_{i,q}) \cdot \log \sum_{j=1}^{K} p(w, \theta_j | \lambda_{i,q}, q),
\tag{4.3}
$$

where $n(w, \lambda_{i,q})$ is the count of the word w in the chunk $\lambda_{i,q}$ and $p(w, \theta_j | \lambda_{i,q}, q)$ is given by (4.2). However, the theme distributions of two chunks of a conversation across two consecutive time slices should not too divergent from each other. That is, they need to be temporally smooth. For a particular topic θ_j this smoothness is thus based on minimization of the following L^2 distance between its probabilities across every two consecutive time slices:

$$
d_T(j) = \sum_{q=2}^{Q} (p(\theta_j | q) - p(\theta_j | q - 1))^2.
\tag{4.4}
$$

Incorporating this distance in (4.3) we get a new log likelihood function which smoothes all the K theme distributions across consecutive time slices:

$$
\begin{aligned}
L_1(C) = \sum_{\lambda_{i,q} \in C} \sum_{w \in \lambda_{i,q}} n(w, \lambda_{i,q}) \cdot \log \sum_{j=1}^{K} (p(w, \theta_j | \lambda_{i,q}, q) \\
+ \exp(-d_T(j))).
\end{aligned}
\tag{4.5}
$$

Now we discuss how this theme model is further regularized to incorporate prior knowledge about co-participation of individuals in the conversations.

Co-Participation Based Regularization. Our intuition behind this regularization is based on the idea that if several participants comment on a pair of chunks, then their theme distributions are likely to be closer to each other.

To recall, chunks being representations of conversations at a particular time slice, we therefore define a participant co-occurrence graph $G(C, E)$ where each vertex in

C is a conversation c_i and an undirected edge $e_{i,m}$ exists between two conversations c_i and c_m if they share at least one common participant. The edges are also associated with weights $\omega_{i,m}$ which define the fraction of common participants between two conversations. We incorporate participant-based regularization based on this graph by minimizing the distance between the edge weights of two adjacent conversations with respect to their corresponding theme distributions.

The following regularization function ensures that the theme distribution functions of conversations are very close to each other if the edge between them in the participant co-occurrence graph G has a high weight:

$$R(C) = \sum_{c_i,c_m \in C} \sum_{j=1}^{K} (\omega_{i,m} - (1 - (f(\theta_j|c_i) - f(\theta_j|c_m))^2))^2, \qquad (4.6)$$

where $f(\theta_j|c_i)$ is defined as a function of the theme θ_j given the conversation c_i and the L^2 distance between $f(\theta_j|c_i)$ and $f(\theta_j|c_m)$ ensures that the theme distributions of adjacent conversations are similar. Since a conversation is associated with multiple chunks, thus $f(\theta_j|c_i)$ is given as in [26]:

$$f(\theta_j|c_i) = p(\theta_j|c_i) = \sum_{\lambda_{i,q} \in c_i} p(\theta_j|\lambda_{i,q}) \cdot p(\lambda_{i,q}|c_i). \qquad (4.7)$$

Now, using (4.5) and (4.6), we define the final combined optimization function which minimizes the negative of the log likelihood and also minimizes the distance between theme distributions with respect to the edge weights in the participant co-occurrence graph:

$$O(C) = -(1 - \varsigma) \cdot L_1(C) + \varsigma \cdot R(C), \qquad (4.8)$$

where the parameter ς controls the balance between the likelihood using the multinomial theme model and the smoothness of theme distributions over the participant graph. It is easy to note that when $\varsigma = 0$, then the objective function is the temporally regularized log likelihood as in (4.5). When $\varsigma = 1$, then the objective function yields themes which are smoothed over the participant co-occurrence graph. Minimizing $O(C)$ for $0 \le \varsigma \le 1$ would give us the theme models that best fit the collection.

Now to learn the hidden parameters of the theme model in (4.8), we use a different technique of parameter estimation based on the Generalized Expectation Maximization algorithm (GEM [26]). Details of the estimation can be referred to in [13].

4.3.3 Interestingness

In this section we describe our interestingness models and then discuss a method that jointly optimizes the two types of interestingness incorporating temporal smoothness.

4.3.3.1 Interestingness of Participants

We pose the problem of determining the interestingness of a participant at a certain time slice as a simple one-dimensional random walk model where she communicates either based on her past history of communication behavior in the previous time slice, or relies on her independent desire of preference over different themes (random jump). This formulation is described in Fig. 4.3.

We conjecture that the state signifying the past history of communication behavior of a participant i at a certain time slice q, denoted as $\mathbf{A}(q-1)$ comprises the variables: (a) whether she was interesting in the previous time slice, $\mathbf{I_P}^{(q-1)}(i)$, (b) whether her comments in the past impacted other participants to communicate and their interestingness measures, $\mathbf{P_F}^{(q-1)}(i,:) \cdot \mathbf{I_P}^{(q-1)}$,[2] (c) whether she followed several interesting people in conversations at the previous time slice $q-1$, $\mathbf{P_L}^{(q-1)}(i,:) \cdot \mathbf{I_P}^{(q-1)}$, and (d) whether the conversations in which she participated became interesting in the previous time slice $q-1$, $\mathbf{P_C}^{(q-1)}(i;:) \cdot \mathbf{I_C}^{(q1)}$. The independent desire of a participant i to communicate is dependent on her theme distribution and the strength of the themes at the previous time slice $q-1$: $\mathbf{P_T}^{(q-1)}(i,:) \cdot \mathbf{T_S}^{(q-1)}$.

Thus the recurrence relation for the random walk model to determine the interestingness of all participants at time slice q is given as:

$$\mathbf{I_P}^{(q)} = (1-\beta) \cdot \mathbf{A}^{(q-1)} + \beta \cdot (\mathbf{P_T}^{(q-1)} \cdot \mathbf{T_S}^{(q-1)}), \tag{4.9}$$

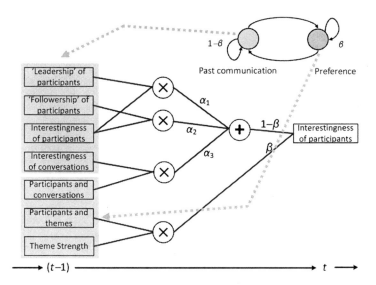

Fig. 4.3 Random walk model for determining interestingness of participants

---

[2] To recall, $\mathbf{X}(i,:)$ is the ith row of the 2-dimensional matrix $\mathbf{X}$.

where,

$$\mathbf{A}^{(q-1)} = \alpha_1 \cdot \mathbf{P_L}^{(q-1)} \cdot \mathbf{I_P}^{(q-1)} + \alpha_2 \cdot \mathbf{P_F}^{(q-1)} \cdot \mathbf{I_P}^{(q-1)} + \alpha_3 \cdot \mathbf{P_C}^{(q-1)} \cdot \mathbf{I_C}^{(q1)}. \quad (4.10)$$

Here α_1, α_2 and α_3 are weights that determine mutual relationship between the variables of the past history of communication state $\mathbf{A}^{(q-1)}$, and β the transition parameter of the random walk that balances the impact of past history and the random jump state involving participant's independent desire to communicate. In this paper, β is empirically set to be 0.5.

4.3.3.2 Interestingness of Conversations

Similar to interestingness of participants, we pose the problem of determining the interestingness of a conversation as a random walk where a conversation can become interesting based on two states as shown in Fig. 4.4. Hence to determine the interestingness of a conversation i at time slice q, we conjecture that it depends on whether the participants in conversation i became interesting at $q - 1$, given as, $\mathbf{P_C}^{(q-1)}(i, :)^t \cdot \mathbf{I_P}^{(q-1)}$, or whether the conversations belonging to the strong themes in $q-1$ became interesting, which is given as, $diag(\mathbf{C_T}^{(q-1)}(i, :) \cdot \mathbf{T_S}^{(q-1)}) \cdot \mathbf{I_C}^{(q-1)}$. Thus the recurrence relation of interestingness of all conversations at time slice q is:

$$\mathbf{I_C}^{(q)} = \psi \cdot \mathbf{P_C}^{(q-1)^t} \cdot \mathbf{I_P}^{(q-1)} + (1 - \psi) \cdot diag(\mathbf{C_T}^{(q-1)} \cdot \mathbf{T_S}^{(q-1)}) \cdot \mathbf{I_C}^{(q-1)}, \quad (4.11)$$

where ψ is the transition parameter of the random walk that balances the impact of interestingness due to participants and due to themes. Clearly, when $\psi = 1$,

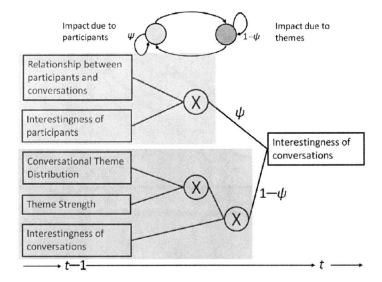

Fig. 4.4 Random walk model for determining interestingness of conversations

the interestingness of conversation depends solely on the interestingness of the participants at $q - 1$; and when $\psi = 1$, the interestingness depends on the theme strengths in the previous time slice $q - 1$.

4.3.3.3 Joint Optimization of Interestingness

We observe that the measures of interestingness of participants and of conversations described in previous sections involve several free (unknown) parameters. In order to determine optimal values of interestingness, we need to learn the weights α_1, α_2 and α_3 in (4.10) and the transition probability for the conversations in (4.11). Moreover, the optimal measures of interestingness should ensure that the variations in their values are smooth over time. Hence we present a novel joint optimization framework, which maximizes the two interestingness measures for optimal $(\alpha_1, \alpha_2, \alpha_3, \psi)$ and also incorporates temporal smoothness.

The joint optimization framework is based on the idea that the optimal parameters in the two interestingness equations are those which maximize the interestingness of participants and of conversations jointly. Let us denote the set of the parameters to be optimized as the vector, $\mathbf{X} = [\alpha_1, \alpha_2, \alpha_3, \psi]$. We can therefore represent $\mathbf{I_P}$ and $\mathbf{I_C}$ as functions of $\mathbf{X}$. We define the following objective function $g(\mathbf{X})$ to estimate $\mathbf{X}$ by maximizing $g(\mathbf{X})$:

$$g(\mathbf{X}) = \rho \cdot \|\mathbf{I_P}(\mathbf{X})\|^2 + (1 - \rho) \cdot \|\mathbf{I_C}(\mathbf{X})\|^2, \tag{4.12}$$

s.t. $0 \leq \psi 1, \alpha_1, \alpha_2, \alpha_3 \geq 0, \mathbf{I_P} \geq 0, \mathbf{I_C} \geq 0, \alpha_1 + \alpha_2 + \alpha_3 = 1$.

In the above function, ρ is an empirically set parameter to balance the impact of each interestingness measure in the joint optimization. Now to incorporate temporal smoothness of interestingness in the above objective function, we define a L^2 norm distance between the two interestingness measures across all consecutive time slices q and $q - 1$:

$$
\begin{aligned}
d_P &= \textstyle\sum_{q=2}^{Q} (\|\mathbf{I_P}^{(q)}(\mathbf{X})\|^2 - \|\mathbf{I_P}^{(q-1)}(\mathbf{X})\|^2), \\
d_C &= \textstyle\sum_{q=2}^{Q} (\|\mathbf{I_C}^{(q)}(\mathbf{X})\|^2 - \|\mathbf{I_C}^{(q-1)}(\mathbf{X})\|^2).
\end{aligned}
\tag{4.13}
$$

We need to minimize these two distance functions to incorporate temporal smoothness. Hence we modify our objective function,

$$g_1(\mathbf{X}) = \rho \cdot \|\mathbf{I_P}(\mathbf{X})\|^2 + (1 - \rho) \cdot \|\mathbf{I_C}(\mathbf{X})\|^2 + \exp(-d_P) + \exp(d_C), \tag{4.14}$$

where $0 \leq \psi 1, \alpha_1, \alpha_2, \alpha_3 \geq 0, \mathbf{I_P} \geq 0, \mathbf{I_C} \geq 0, \alpha_1 + \alpha_2 + \alpha_3 = 1$.

Maximizing the above function $g_1(\mathbf{X})$ for optimal $\mathbf{X}$ is equivalent to minimizing $-g_1(\mathbf{X})$. Thus this minimization problem can be reduced to a convex optimization form because (a) the inequality constraint functions are also convex, and (b) the equality constraint is affine. The convergence of this optimization function is skipped due to space limit.

Now, the minimum value of $-g_1(\mathbf{X})$ corresponds to an optimal $\mathbf{X}^*$ and hence we can easily compute the optimal interestingness measures $\mathbf{I_P}^*$ and $\mathbf{I_C}^*$ for the optimal $\mathbf{X}^*$. Given our framework for determining interestingness of conversations, we now discuss the measures of consequence of interestingness followed by extensive experimental results.

4.3.4 Consequences of Interestingness

An interesting conversation is likely to have consequences. These include the (commenting) activity of the participants, their cohesiveness in communication and an effect on the interestingness of the themes. It is important to note here that the consequence is generally felt at a future point of time; that is, it is associated with a certain time lag (say, δ days) with respect to the time slice a conversation becomes interesting (say, q). Hence we ask the following three questions related to the future consequences of an interesting conversation:

Activity. Do the participants in an interesting conversation i at time q take part in other conversations relating to similar themes at a future time, $q + \delta$ We define this as follows,

$$Act^{q+\delta}(i) = \frac{1}{\varphi_{i,q+\delta}} \sum_{k=1}^{|\varphi_{i,q+\delta}|} \sum_{j=1}^{|P_{i,q}|} \mathbf{P_C}^{(q+\delta)}(j,k), \qquad (4.15)$$

where $P_{i,q}$ is the set of participants on conversation i at time slice q, and $\varphi_{i,q+\delta}$ is the set of conversations m such that, $m \in \varphi_{i,q+\delta}$ if the KL-divergence of the theme distribution of m at time $q + \delta$ from that of i at q is less than an empirically set threshold: $D(C_T^{(q)}(i,:)||C_T^{(q+\delta)}(m,:)) \leq \varepsilon$.

Cohesiveness. Do the participants in an interesting conversation i at time q exhibit cohesiveness in communication (co-participate) in other conversations at a future time slice, $q + \delta$ In order to define cohesiveness, we first define co-participation of two participants, j and k as,

$$O^{(q+\delta)}(j;k) = \frac{\mathbf{P_P}^{(q+\delta)}(j,k)}{\mathbf{P_C}^{(q+\delta)}(j,k)}, \qquad (4.16)$$

where $\mathbf{P_P}^{(q+\delta)}(j,k)$ is defined as the participant-participant matrix of co-participation constructed as, $P_C^{(q+\delta)} \cdot (P_C^{(q+\delta)})^t$. Hence the cohesiveness in communication at time $q + \delta$ between participants in a conversation i is defined as,

$$Co^{(q+\delta)}(i) = \frac{1}{|P_{i,q}|} \sum_{j=1}^{P_{i,q}} \sum_{k=1}^{|P_{i,q}|} O^{(q+\delta)}(j;k). \qquad (4.17)$$

Thematic Interestingness. Do other conversations having similar theme distribution as the interesting conversation c_i (at time q), also become interesting at a future time slice $q + \delta$ We define this consequence as thematic interestingness and it is given by,

$$TInt^{(q+delta)}(i) = \frac{1}{\varphi_{i,q+delta}} \sum_{j=1}^{|\varphi_{i,q+delta}|} I_C^{(q+\delta)}(j). \qquad (4.18)$$

To summarize, we have developed a method to characterize interestingness of conversations based on the themes, and the interestingness property of the participants. We have jointly optimized the two types of interestingness to get optimal interestingness of conversations. And finally we have discussed three metrics which account for the consequential impact of interesting conversations. Now we would discuss the experimental results on this model.

4.3.5   Experimental Studies

The experiments performed to test our model are based on a dataset from the largest video-sharing site, YouTube, which serves as a rich source of online conversations associated with shared media elements. We crawled a total set of 132,348 videos involving 8,867,284 unique participants and 89,026,652 comments over a period of 15 weeks from June 20, 2008 to September 26, 2008. Now we discuss the results of experiments conducted to test our framework. First we present the results on the interestingness of participants, followed by that of conversations.

The results of interestingness of the participants of conversations are shown in a visualization in Fig. 4.5. We have visualized a set of 45 participants over the period of 15 weeks by pooling the top three most interesting participants from each week. The participants are shown column-wise in the visualization with decreasing mean number of comments written from left to right. The intensity of the red block represents the degree of interestingness of a participant at a particular time slice. The figure also shows plots of the comment distribution and the interestingness distributions for the participants at each time slice.

In order to analyze the dynamics of interestingness, we also qualitatively observe its association with a set of external events collected from The New York Times, related to Politics. The events along with their dates are shown in Table 4.2.

From the results of interestingness of participants, we observe that interestingness closely follows the number of comments on weeks which are not associated with significant external events (weeks 1–4, 6–10). Whereas on other weeks, especially the last three weeks 13, 14 and 15, we observe that there are several political happenings and as a result the interestingness distribution of participants does not

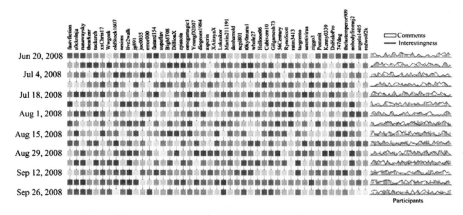

Fig. 4.5 Interestingness of 45 participants from YouTube, ordered by decreasing number of comments from *left* to *right*, is visualized. Interestingness is less affected by number of comments during periods of several external events

Table 4.2 Political events in the time period of analysis

Date	Event
Jul 23'08	Obama makes trip to the Europe and Middle East
Aug 29'08	Alaska Governor Sarah Palin is selected by McCain as his choice for the Republican VP candidate
Sep 1'08	2008 Republican National Convention convenes in Minneapolis-St.Paul, Minnesota
Sep 15'08	Lehman Brothers goes bankrupt, Merrill Lynch is dissolved
Sep 24'08	President Bush addresses the nation on the financial crisis

seem to follow well the comment distribution. Hence we conclude that during periods of significant external events, participants can become interesting despite writing fewer comments – high interestingness can instead be explained due to their preference for the conversational theme which reflects the external event.

The results of the dynamics of interestingness of conversations are shown in Fig. 4.6. We conceive a similar visualization as Fig. 4.5 presented previously. Conversations are shown column-wise and time row-wise (15 weeks). A set of 45 conversations are pooled based on the top three most interesting conversations at each week. From left to right, the conversations are shown with respect to decreasing number of comments. We also show a temporal plot of the mean interestingness per week in order to understand the relationship of interestingness to external happening from Table 4.2.

From the visualization in Fig. 4.6, we observe that the mean interestingness of conversations increase significantly during weeks 11–15. This is explained when we observe the association with large number of political happening in the said period (Table 4.2). Hence we conclude that conversations in general become more interesting when there are significant events in the external world – an artifact that online conversations are reflective of chatter about external happenings.

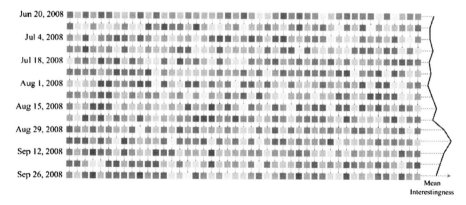

Fig. 4.6 Interestingness of 45 conversations from YouTube, ordered by decreasing number of comments from *left* to *right*, is visualized. Mean interestingness of conversations increases during periods of several external events

In closing for this problem, note that today there is significant online chatter, discussion and thoughts that are expressed over shared rich media artifacts, e.g., photos, videos etc, often reflecting public sentiment on socio-political events. While different media sites can provide coverage over the same information content with variable degrees of associated chatter, it becomes imperative to determine suitable methods and techniques to identify which media sources are likely to provide information that can be deemed to be "interesting" to a certain user. Suppose a user Alice is interested in identifying "interesting" media sources dissipating information on public sentiments regarding the recent elections in Iran back in 2009. To serve Alice's needs, we need to be able to characterize chatter or conversations that emerge centered around rich media artifacts, that she would find useful. We believe the proposed framework can serve the needful to tackle the modern day information needs on the social Web.

Nevertheless, it goes without saying that human communication activity, manifested via such "conversations" involves mutual exchange of information, and the pretext of any social interaction among a set of individuals is a reflection of how our behavior, actions and knowledge can be modified, refined, shared or amplified based on the information that flows from one individual to another. Thus, over several decades, the structure of social groups, society in general and the relationships among individuals in these societies have been shaped to a great extent by the *flow of information* in them. Diffusion is hence the process by which a piece of information, an idea or an innovation flows through certain communication channels over time among the individuals in a social system.

The pervasive use of online social media has made the cost involved in propagating a piece of information to a large audience extremely negligible, providing extensive evidences of large-scale social contagion. There are multifaceted personal publishing modalities available to users today, where such large scale social contagion is prevalent: such as weblogs, social networking sites like MySpace and

Facebook as well as microblogging tools such as Twitter. These communication tools are open to frequent widespread observation to millions of users, and thus offer an inexpensive opportunity to capture large volumes of information flows at the individual level. If we want to understand the extent to which ideas are adopted via these communication affordances provided by different online social platforms, it is important to understand the extent to which people are likely to be affected by decisions of their friends and colleagues, or the extent to which "word-of-mouth" effects will take hold via communication. In the following section we propose models of diffusion of information in the light of how similar user attributes, that embody observed "homophily" in networks, affect the overall social process.

4.4 Information Diffusion

The central goal in this section is to investigate the relationship between homophily among users and the social process of information diffusion. By "homophily," we refer to the idea that users in a social system tend to bond more with ones who are "similar" to them than ones who are dissimilar. The homophily principle has been extensively researched in the social sciences over the past few decades [7, 24, 25]. These studies were predominantly ethnographic and cross-sectional in nature and have revealed that homophily *structures* networks. That is, a person's ego-centric social network is often homogeneous with regard to diverse social, demographic, behavioral, and intra-personal characteristics [24] or revolves around social foci such as co-location or commonly situated activities [14]. Consequently, in the context of physical networks, these works provide evidence that the existence of homophily is likely to impact the information individuals receive and propagate, the communication activities they engage in, and the social roles they form.

Homophilous relationships have also been observed on online media such as Facebook, Twitter, Digg and YouTube. These networks facilitate the sharing and propagation of information among members of their networks. In these networks, homophilous associations can have a significant impact on *very large scale* social phenomena, including group evolution and information diffusion. For example, the popular social networking site Facebook allows users to engage in community activities via homophilous relationships involving common organizational affiliations. Whereas on the fast-growing social media Twitter, several topics such as "#Elections2008," "#MichaelJackson," "Global Warming" etc have historically featured extensive postings (also known as "tweets") due to the common interests of large sets of users in politics, music and environmental issues respectively.

These networks, while diverse in terms of their affordances (i.e., what they allow users to do), share some common features. First, there exists a social action (e.g., posting a tweet on Twitter) within a shared social space (i.e., the action can be observed by all members of the users' contact network), that facilitates a social process (e.g., diffusion of information). Second, these networks expose attributes including location, time of activity and gender to other users. Finally, these networks also reveal these users attributes as well as the communication, to third party users (via the API tools); thus allowing us to study the impact of a specific attribute on information diffusion within these networks.

The study of the impact of homophily on information diffusion can be valuable in several contexts. Today, due to the plethora of diverse retail products available online to customers, advertising is moving from the traditional "word-of-mouth" model, to models that exploit interactions among individuals on social networks. To this effect, previously, some studies have provided useful insights that social relationships impact the adoption of innovations and products [19]. Moreover there has been theoretical and empirical evidence in prior work [36] that indicates that individuals have been able to transmit information through a network (via messages) in a sufficiently small number of steps, due to homophily along recognizable personal identities. Hence a viral marketer attempting to advertise a new product could benefit from considering specific sets of users on a social space who are *homophilous* with respect to their interest in similar products or features. Other contexts in which understanding the role of homophily in information diffusion can be important, include, disaster mitigation during crisis situations, understanding social roles of users and in leveraging distributed social search.

4.4.1 Preliminaries

4.4.1.1 Social Graph Model

We define our social graph model as a directed graph $G(V, E)$,[3] such that V is the set of users and $e_{ij} \in E$ if and only if user u_i and u_j are "friends" of each other (bi-directional contacts). Let us further suppose that each user $u_i \in V$ can perform a set of "social actions," $\mathcal{O} = \{O_1, O_2, \ldots\}$, e.g., posting a tweet, uploading a photo on Flickr or writing on somebody's Facebook Wall. Let the users in V also be associated with a set of attributes $\mathcal{A} = \{a_k\}$ (e.g., location or organizational affiliation) that are responsible for homophily. Corresponding to each value υ defined over an attribute $a_k \in \mathcal{A}$, we construct a social graph $G(a_k = \upsilon)$ such that it consists of the users in G with the particular value of the attribute, while an edge exists between two users in $G(a_k)$ if there is an edge between them in G.[4] E.g., for location, we can define sets of social graphs over users from Europe, Asia etc.

In this section, our social graph model is based on the social media Twitter. Twitter features a micro-blogging service that allows users to post short content, known as "tweets," often comprising URLs usually encoded via bit.ly, tinyurl, etc. The particular "social action" in this context is the posting of a tweet; also popularly

---

[3] Henceforth referred to as the baseline social graph G.

[4] For simplicity, we omit specifying the attribute value υ in the rest of the section, and refer to $G(a_k = \upsilon)$ as the "attribute social graph" $G(a_k)$.

called "tweeting". Users can also "follow" other users; hence if user u_i follows u_j, Twitter allows u_i to subscribe to the tweets of u_j via feeds; u_i is then also called a "follower" of u_j. Two users are denoted as "friends" on Twitter if they "follow" each other. Note that, in the context of Twitter, using the bi-directional "friend" link is more useful compared to the uni-directional "follow" link because the former is more likely to be robust to spam—a normal user is less likely to follow a spam-like account. Further, for the particular dataset of Twitter, we have considered a set of four attributes associated with the users:

Location of users, extracted using the timezone attribute of Twitter users. Specifically, the values of location correspond to the different continents, e.g., Asia, Europe and North America.

Information roles of users, we consider three categories of roles: "generators," "mediators" and "receptors." Generators are users who create several posts (or tweets) but few users respond to them (via the @ tag on Twitter, which is typically used with the username to respond to a particular user, e.g., @BillGates). While receptors are those who create fewer posts but receive several posts as responses. Mediators are users who lie between these two categories.

Content creation of users, we use the two content creation roles: "meformer" (users who primarily post content relating to self) and "informer" (users posting content about external happenings) as discussed in [29].

Activity behavior of users, i.e., the distribution of a particular social action over a certain time period. We consider the mean number of posts (tweets) per user over 24 h and compute similarities between pairs of users based on the Kullback-Leibler (KL) divergence measure of comparing across distributions.

4.4.1.2 Attribute Homophily

Attribute homophily [24, 25] is defined as the tendency of users in a social graph to associate and bond with others who are "similar" to them along a certain attribute or contextual dimension e.g., age, gender, race, political view or organizational affiliation. Specifically, a pair of users can be said to be "homophilous" if one of their attributes match in a proportion greater than that in the network of which they are a part. Hence in our context, for a particular value of $a_k \in \mathscr{A}$, the users in the social graph $G(a_k)$ corresponding to that value are homophilous to each other.

4.4.1.3 Topic Diffusion

Diffusion with respect to a particular topic at a certain time is given as the flow of information on the topic from one user to another via the social graph, and based on a particular social action. Specifically,

Definition 4.1. Given two users u_i and u_j in the baseline social graph G such that $e_{ij} \in E$, there is diffusion of information on topic θ from u_j to u_i if u_j performs a particular social action O_r related to θ at a time slice t_{m-1} and is succeeded by u_i in performing the same action on θ at the next time slice t_m, where $t_{m-1} < t_m$.[5]

Further, topic diffusion subject to homophily along the attribute a_k is defined as the diffusion over the attribute social graph $G(a_k)$.

In the context of Twitter, topic diffusion can manifest itself through three types of evidences: (1) users posting tweets using the same URL, (2) users tweeting with the same hashtag (e.g., #MichaelJackson) or a set of common keywords, and (3) users using the re-tweet (RT) symbol. We utilize all these three cases of topic diffusion in this work.

4.4.1.4 Diffusion Series

In order to characterize diffusion, we now define a topology called a *diffusion series*[6] that summarizes diffusion in a social graph for a given topic over a period of time. Formally,

Definition 4.2. A diffusion series $s_N(\theta)$ on topic θ and over time slices t_1 to t_N is defined as a directed acyclic graph where the nodes represent a subset of users in the baseline social graph G, who are involved in a specific social action O_r over θ at any time slice between t_1 and t_N.

Note, in a diffusion series $s_N(\theta)$ a node represents an occurrence of a user u_i creating at least one instance of the social action O_r about θ at a certain time slice t_m such that $t_1 \leq t_m \leq t_N$. Nodes are organized into "slots"; where nodes associated with the same time slice t_m are arranged into the same slot l_m. Hence it is possible that the same user is present at multiple slots in the series if s/he tweets about the same topic θ at different time slices. Additionally, there are edges between nodes across two adjacent slots, indicating that user u_i in slot l_m performs the social action O_r on θ at t_m, after her friend u_j has performed action on the same topic θ at the previous time slice t_{m-1} (i.e., at slot l_{m-1}). There are no edges between nodes at the same slot l_m: a diffusion series $s_N(\theta)$ in this work captures diffusion on topic θ *across* time slices, and does not include possible flow occurring at the same time slice.

For the Twitter dataset, we have chosen the granularity of the time slice t_m to be sufficiently small, i.e., a day to capture the dynamics of diffusion. Thus all the users

---

[5] Since we discuss our problem formulation and methodology for a specific social action, the dependence of different concepts on O_r is omitted in the rest of the section for simplicity.

[6] Note, a diffusion series is similar to a diffusion tree as in [4,23], however we call it a "series" since it is constructed progressively over a period of time and allows a node to have multiple sources of diffusion.

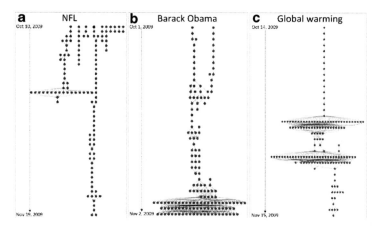

Fig. 4.7 Example of different diffusion series from Twitter on three different topics. The nodes are users involved in diffusion while the edges represent "friend links" connecting two users

at slot l_m tweet about θ on the same day; and two consecutive slots have a time difference of 1 day. Examples of different diffusion series constructed on topics from Twitter have been shown in Fig. 4.7.

Since each topic θ can have multiple disconnected diffusion series $s_N(\theta)$ at any given time slice t_N, we call the family of all diffusion series a *diffusion collection* $\mathscr{S}_N(\theta) = \{s_N(\theta)\}$. Corresponding to each value of the attribute a_k, the diffusion collection over the attribute social graph $G(a_k)$ at t_N is similarly given as $\mathscr{S}_{N;a_k}(\theta) = \{s_{N;a_k}(\theta)\}$.

4.4.2 Problem Statement

Given, (1) a baseline social graph $G(V, E)$; (2) a set of social actions $\mathscr{O} = \{O_1, O_2, \ldots\}$ that can be performed by users in V, and (3) a set of attributes $\mathscr{A} = \{a_k\}$ that are shared by users in V, we perform the following two preliminary steps. First, we construct the attribute social graphs $\{G(a_k)\}$, for all values of $a_k \in \mathscr{A}$. Second, we construct diffusion collections corresponding to G and $\{G(a_k)\}$ for a given topic θ (on which diffusion is to be estimated over time slices t_1 to t_N) and a particular social action O_r: these are given as $\mathscr{S}_N(\theta)$ and $\{\mathscr{S}_{N;a_k}(\theta)\}$ respectively. The technical problem addressed in this section involves the following:

1. *Characterization:* Based on each of the diffusion collections $\mathscr{S}_N(\theta)$ and $\{\mathscr{S}_{N;a_k}(\theta)\}$, we extract diffusion characteristics on θ at time slice t_N given as: $\mathbf{d}_N(\theta)$ and $\{\mathbf{d}_{N;a_k}(\theta)\}$ respectively (Sect. 4.4.3);
2. *Prediction:* We predict the set of users likely to perform the same social action at the next time slice t_{N+1} corresponding to each of the diffusion collections $\mathscr{S}_N(\theta)$ and $\{\mathscr{S}_{N;a_k}(\theta)\}$. This gives the diffusion collections at t_{N+1}: $\hat{\mathscr{S}}_{N+1}(\theta)$ and $\{\hat{\mathscr{S}}_{N+1;a_k}(\theta)\} \forall a_k \in \mathscr{A}$ (Sect. 4.4.4);

3. *Distortion Measurement:* We extract diffusion characteristics at t_{N+1} over the (predicted) diffusion collections, $\hat{\mathscr{S}}_{N+1}(\theta)$ and $\{\hat{\mathscr{S}}_{N+1;a_k}(\theta)\}$, given as, $\hat{\mathbf{d}}_{N+1}(\theta)$ and $\{\hat{\mathbf{d}}_{N+1;a_k}(\theta)\}$ respectively. Now we quantify the impact of attribute homophily on diffusion based on two kinds of distortion measurements on $\hat{\mathbf{d}}_{N+1}(\theta)$ and $\{\hat{\mathbf{d}}_{N+1;a_k}(\theta)\}$. A particular attribute $a_k \in \mathscr{A}$ would have an impact on diffusion if $\hat{\mathbf{d}}_{N+1;a_k}(\theta)$, avergaed over all possible values of a_k: (a) has lower distortion with respect to the actual (i.e., $\mathbf{d}_{N+1}(\theta)$); and (b) can quantify external time series (search, news trends) better, compared to either $\hat{\mathbf{d}}_{N+1}(\theta)$ or $\{\hat{\mathbf{d}}_{N+1;a'_k}(\theta)\}$, where $k' \neq k$ (Sect. 4.4.7).

4.4.3 Characterizing Diffusion

We describe eight different measures for quantifying diffusion characteristics given by the baseline and the attribute social graphs on a certain topic and via a particular social action.

Volume: Volume is a notion of the overall degree of contagion in the social graph. For the diffusion collection $\mathscr{S}_N(\theta)$ over the baseline social graph G, we formally define volume $v_N(\theta)$ with respect to θ and at time slice t_N as the ratio of $n_N(\theta)$ to $\eta_N(\theta)$, where $n_N(\theta)$ is the total number of users (nodes) in the diffusion collection $\mathscr{S}_N(\theta)$, and $\eta_N(\theta)$ is the number of users in the social graph G associated with θ.

Participation: Participation $p_N(\theta)$ at time slice t_N [4] is the ratio of the number of non-leaf nodes in the diffusion collection $\mathscr{S}_N(\theta)$, normalized by $\eta_N(\theta)$.

Dissemination: Dissemination $\delta_N(\theta)$ at time slice t_N is given by the ratio of the number of users in the diffusion collection $\mathscr{S}_N(\theta)$ who do not have a parent node, normalized by $\eta_N(\theta)$. In other words, they are the "seed users" or ones who get involved in the diffusion due to some unobservable external influence, e.g., a news event.

Reach: Reach $r_N(\theta)$ at time slice t_N [23] is defined as the ratio of the mean of the number of slots to the sum of the number of slots in all diffusion series belonging to $\mathscr{S}_N(\theta)$.

Spread: For the diffusion collection $\mathscr{S}_N(\theta)$, spread $s_N(\theta)$ at time slice t_N [23] is defined as the ratio of the maximum number of nodes at any slot in $s_N(\theta) \in \mathscr{S}_N(\theta)$ to $n_N(\theta)$.

Cascade Instances: Cascade instances $c_N(\theta)$ at time slice t_N is defined as the ratio of the number of slots in the diffusion series $s_N(\theta) \in \mathscr{S}_N(\theta)$ where the number of *new* users at a slot l_m (i.e., non-occurring at a previous slot) is greater than that at the previous slot l_{m-1}, to $L_N(\theta)$, the number of slots in $s_N(\theta) \in \mathscr{S}_N(\theta)$.

Collection Size: Collection size $\alpha_N(\theta)$ at time slice t_N is the ratio of the number of diffusion series $s_N(\theta)$ in $\mathscr{S}_N(\theta)$ over topic θ, to the total number of connected components in the social graph G.

Rate: We define rate $\gamma_N(\theta)$ at time slice t_N as the "speed" at which information on θ diffuses in the collection $\mathscr{S}_N(\theta)$. It depends on the difference between the median time of posting of tweets at all consecutive slots l_m and l_{m-1} in the diffusion series $s_N(\theta) \in \mathscr{S}_N(\theta)$. Hence it is given as:

$$\gamma_N(\theta) = 1/(1 + \frac{1}{L_N(\theta)} \sum_{l_{m-1}, l_m \in \mathscr{S}_N(\theta)} (\bar{t}_m(\theta) - \bar{t}_{m-1}(\theta)), \qquad (4.19)$$

where $\bar{t}_m(\theta)$ and $\bar{t}_{m-1}(\theta)$ are measured in seconds and $\bar{t}_m(\theta)$ corresponds to the median time of tweet at slot l_m in $s_N(\theta) \in \mathscr{S}_N(\theta)$.

These diffusion measures thus characterize diffusion at time slice t_N over $\mathscr{S}_N(\theta)$ as the vector: $\mathbf{d}_N(\theta) = [v_N(\theta), p_N(\theta), \delta_N(\theta), r_N(\theta), s_N(\theta), c_N(\theta), \alpha_N(\theta), \gamma_N(\theta)]$. Similarly, we compute the diffusion measures vector over $\{\mathscr{S}_{N;a_k}(\theta)\}$, given by: $\{\mathbf{d}_{N;a_k}(\theta)\}$, corresponding to each value of a_k.

4.4.4 Prediction Framework

In this section we present our method of predicting the users who would be part of the diffusion collections at a future time slice for the baseline and attribute social graphs. Our method comprises the following steps. (1) Given the observed diffusion collections until time slice t_N (i.e., $\mathscr{S}_N(\theta)$ and $\mathscr{S}_{N;a_k}(\theta)$), we first propose a probabilistic framework based on Dynamic Bayesian networks [30] to predict the users likely to perform the social action O_r at the next time slice t_{N+1}. This would yield us users at slot l_{N+1} in the different diffusion series at t_{N+1}. (2) Next, these predicted users give the diffusion collections at t_{N+1}: $\hat{\mathscr{S}}_{N+1}(\theta)$ and $\{\hat{\mathscr{S}}_{N+1;a_k}(\theta)\}$.

We present a Dynamic Bayesian network (DBN) representation of a particular social action by a user over time, that helps us predict the set of users likely to perform the social action at a future time (Fig. 4.8a). Specifically, at any time slice t_N, a given topic θ and a given social action, the DBN captures the relationship between three nodes:

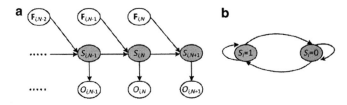

Fig. 4.8 (a) Structure of the Dynamic Bayesian network used for modeling social action of a user u_i. The diagram shows the relationship between environmental features ($\mathbf{F}_{i,N}(\theta)$), hidden states ($S_{i,N}(\theta)$) and the observed action ($O_{i,N}(\theta)$). (b) State transition diagram showing the "vulnerable" ($S_i = 1$) and "indifferent" states ($S_i = 0$) of a user u_i

Environmental Features. That is, the set of contextual variables that effect a user u_i's decision to perform the action on θ at a future time slice t_{N+1} (given by $F_{i,N}(\theta)$). It comprises three different measures: (1) u_i's degree of activity on θ in the past, given as the ratio of the number of posts (or tweets) by u_i on θ, to the total number of posts between t_1 and t_N; (2) mean degree of activity of u_i's friends in the past, given as the ratio of the number of posts by u_i's friends on θ, to the total number of posts by them between t_1 and t_N; and (3) popularity of topic θ at the previous time slice t_N, given as the ratio of the number of posts by all users on θ, to the total number of posts at t_N.

States. That is, latent states $(S_{i,N}(\theta))$ of the user u_i responsible for her involvement in diffusion at t_{N+1}. Our motivation in conceiving the latent states comes from the observation that, in the context of Twitter, a user can tweet on a topic under two kinds of circumstances: first, when she observes her friend doing so already: making her *vulnerable* to diffusion; and second, when her tweeting is *indifferent* to the activities of her friends. Hence the state node at t_{N+1} that impacts u_i's action can have two values as the vulnerable and the indifferent state (Fig. 4.8b).

Observed Action. That is, evidence $(O_{i,N}(\theta))$ of the user u_i performing (or not performing) the action, corresponding values being: $\{1, 0\}$ respectively.

Now we show how to predict the probability of the observed action at t_{N+1} (i.e., $\hat{O}_{i,N+1}(\theta)$) using $F_{i,N}(\theta)$ and $S_{i,N+1}(\theta)$, based on the DBN model. Our goal is to estimate the following expectation[7]:

$$\hat{O}_{i,N+1} = E(O_{i,N+1}|O_{i,N}, F_{i,N}). \tag{4.20}$$

This involves computing $P(O_{i,N+1}|O_{i,N}, F_{i,N})$. This conditional probability can be written as an inference equation using the temporal dependencies given by the DBN and assuming first order Markov property:

$$
\begin{aligned}
P(O_{i,N+1}&|O_{i,N}, F_{i,N}) \\
&= \sum_{S_{i,N+1}} [P(O_{i,N+1}|S_{i,N+1}, O_{i,N}, F_{i,N}).P(S_{i,N+1}|O_{i,N}, F_{i,N})]. \\
&= \sum_{S_{i,N+1}} P(O_{i,N+1}|S_{i,N+1}).P(S_{i,N+1}|S_{i,N}, F_{i,N}). \tag{4.21}
\end{aligned}
$$

Our prediction task thus involves two parts: predicting the probability of the hidden states given the environmental features, $P(S_{i,N+1}|S_{i,N}, F_{i,N})$; and predicting the probability density of the observation nodes given the hidden states, $P(O_{i,N+1}|S_{i,N+1})$, and thereby the expected value of observation nodes $\hat{O}_{i,N+1}$. These two steps are discussed in the following subsections.

---

[7] Without loss of generalization, we omit the topic θ in the variables in this subsection for the sake of simplicity.

4.4.5 Predicting Hidden States

Using Bayes rule, we apply conditional independence between the hidden states and the environmental features at the same time slice (Fig. 4.8a). The probability of the hidden states at t_{N+1} given the environmental features at t_N, i.e., $P(S_{i,N+1}|S_{i,N}, \mathbf{F}_{i,N})$ can be written as:

$$P(S_{i,N+1}|S_{i,N}, \mathbf{F}_{i,N}) \propto P(\mathbf{F}_{i,N}|S_{i,N}) \cdot P(S_{i,N+1}|S_{i,N}). \qquad (4.22)$$

Now, to estimate the probability density of $P(S_{i,N+1}|S_{i,N}, \mathbf{F}_{i,N})$ using (4.22) we assume that the hidden states $S_{i,N+1}$ follows a multinomial distribution over the environmental features $\mathbf{F}_{i,N}$ with parameter $\phi_{i,N}$, and a conjugate Dirichlet prior over the previous state $S_{i,N}$ with parameter $\lambda_{i,N+1}$. The optimal parameters of the pdf of $P(S_{i,N+1}|S_{i,N}, \mathbf{F}_{i,N})$ can now be estimated using MAP:

$$
\begin{aligned}
\mathscr{L}(P(&S_{i,N+1}|S_{i,N}, \mathbf{F}_{i,N})) \\
&= \log(P(\mathbf{F}_{i,N}|S_{i,N})) + \log(P(S_{i,N+1}|S_{i,N})) \\
&= \log \mathbf{multinom}(\mathrm{vec}(\mathbf{F}_{i,N}); \phi_{i,N}) \\
&\quad + \log \mathbf{Dirichlet}(\mathrm{vec}(S_{i,N+1}); \lambda_{i,N+1}) \\
&= \log \frac{\sum_{jk} \mathbf{F}_{i,N;jk}!}{\prod_{jk} \mathbf{F}_{i,N;jk}!} \prod_{jk} \phi_{i,N;jk}^{\mathbf{F}_{i,N;jk}} + \log \frac{1}{B(\lambda_{i,N+1})} \prod_{jl} S_{i,N+1}^{S_{i,N;jl}} \\
&= \sum_{jk} \mathbf{F}_{i,N;jk} \cdot \log \phi_{i,N;jk} + \sum_{jl} S_{i,N;jl} \cdot \log S_{i,N+1;jl} + \text{const.} \quad (4.23)
\end{aligned}
$$

where $B(\lambda_{i,N+1})$ is a beta-function with the parameter $\lambda_{i,N+1}$. Maximizing the log likelihood in (4.23) hence yields the optimal parameters for the pdf of $P(S_{i,N+1}|S_{i,N}, \mathbf{F}_{i,N})$.

4.4.6 Predicting Observed Action

To estimate the probability density of the observation nodes given the hidden states, i.e., $P(O_{i,N+1}|S_{i,N+1})$ we adopt a generative model approach and train two discriminative Hidden Markov Models – one corresponding to the class when u_i performs the action, and the other when she does not. Based on observed actions from t_1 to t_N, we learn the parameters of the HMMs using the Baum-Welch algorithm. We then use the emission probability $P(O_{i,N+1}|S_{i,N+1})$ given by the observation-state transition matrix to determine the most likely sequence at t_{N+1} using the Viterbi algorithm. We finally substitute the emission probability $P(O_{i,N+1}|S_{i,N+1})$ from above and $P(S_{i,N+1}|S_{i,N}, \mathbf{F}_{i,N})$ from (4.23) into (4.21) to compute the expectation $E(O_{i,N+1}|O_{i,N}, \mathbf{F}_{i,N})$ and get the estimated observed action of u_i: $\hat{O}_{i,N+1}$ (4.20). The details of this estimation can be found in [33].

We now use the estimated social actions $\hat{O}_{i,N+1}(\theta)$ of all users at time slice t_{N+1} to get a set of users who are likely to involve in the diffusion process at t_{N+1} for both the baseline and the attribute social graphs. Next we use G and $\{G(a_k)\}$ to associate edges between the predicted user set, and the users in each diffusion series corresponding to the diffusion collections at t_N. This gives the diffusion collection t_{N+1}, i.e., $\hat{\mathscr{S}}_{N+1}(\theta)$ and $\{\hat{\mathscr{S}}_{N+1;a_k}(\theta)\}$ (Sect. 4.4.1.4).

4.4.7 Distortion Measurement

We now compute the diffusion feature vectors $\hat{\mathbf{d}}_{N+1}(\theta)$ or $\{\hat{\mathbf{d}}_{N+1;a_k}(\theta)\}$ based on the predicted diffusion collections $\hat{\mathscr{S}}_{N+1}(\theta)$ and $\{\hat{\mathscr{S}}_{N+1;a_k}(\theta)\}$ from Sect. 4.4.4. To quantify the impact of attribute homophily on diffusion at t_{N+1} corresponding to $a_k \in \mathscr{A}$, we define two kinds of distortion measures – (1) saturation measurement, and (2) utility measurement metrics.

Saturation Measurement. We compare distortion between the predicted and actual diffusion characteristics at t_{N+1}. The saturation measurement metric is thus given as $1 - D(\hat{\mathbf{d}}_{N+1}(\theta), \mathbf{d}_{N+1}(\theta))$ and $1 - D(\hat{\mathbf{d}}_{N+1;a_k}(\theta), \mathbf{d}_{N+1}(\theta))$, avergaed over all values of $\forall a_k \in \mathscr{A}$ respectively for the baseline and the attribute social graphs. $\mathbf{d}_{N+1}(\theta)$ gives the actual diffusion characteristics at t_{N+1} and $D(A, B)$ Kolmogorov-Smirnov (KS) statistic, defined as $max(|A - B|)$.

Utility Measurement. We describe two utility measurement metrics for quantifying the relationship between the predicted diffusion characteristics $\hat{\mathbf{d}}_{N+1}(\theta)$ or $\{\hat{\mathbf{d}}_{N+1;a_k}(\theta)\}$ on topic θ, and the trends of same topic θ obtained from external time series. We collect two kinds of external trends: (1) *search trends* – the search volume of θ over t_1 to t_{N+1}[8]; (2) *news trends* – the frequency of archived news articles about θ over same period[9]. The utility measurement metrics are defined as follows:

Search trend measurement: We first compute the cumulative distribution function (CDF) of diffusion volume as $E_{N+1}^D(\theta) = \sum_{m \leq (N+1)} |l_m(\hat{\mathscr{S}}_{N+1}(\theta))|/Q_D$, where $|l_m(\hat{\mathscr{S}}_{N+1}(\theta))|$ is the number of nodes at slot l_m in the collection $\hat{\mathscr{S}}_{N+1}(\theta)$. Q_D is the normalized term and is defined as $\sum_m |l_m(\hat{\mathscr{S}}_{N+1}(\theta))|$. Next, we compute the CDF of search volume as $E_{N+1}^S(\theta) = \sum_{m \leq (N+1)} f_m^S(\theta)/Q_S$, where $f_m^S(\theta)$ is the search volume at t_m, and Q_S is the normalization term. The search trend measurement is defined as $1 - D(E_{N+1}^D(\theta), E_{N+1}^S(\theta))$, where $D(A, B)$ is the KS statistic.

News trend measurement: Similarly, we compute the CDF of news volume as $E_{N+1}^{\dagger\mathcal{N}}(\theta) = \sum_{m \leq (N+1)} f_m^{\dagger\mathcal{N}}(\theta)/Q_{\dagger\mathcal{N}}$, where $f_m^{\mathcal{N}}(\theta)$ is the number of

---

[8] http://www.google.com/intl/en/trends/about.html
[9] http://news.google.com/

archived news articles available from Google News for t_m, and $Q_{\mathcal{N}}$ is the normalization term. The news trend measurement is similarly defined as $1 - D(E_{N+1}^{D}(\theta), E_{N+1}^{\mathcal{N}}(\theta))$.

Using the same method as above, we compute the search and news trend measurement metrics for the attribute social graphs – given as, $1 - D(E_{N+1;a_k}^{D}(\theta), E_{N+1}^{S}(\theta))$ and $1 - D(E_{N+1;a_k}^{D}(\theta), E_{N+1}^{\mathcal{N}}(\theta))$, averaged over all values of $\forall a_k \in \mathcal{A}$ respectively.

4.4.8 Experimental Studies

We present our experimental results in this section that validate the proposed framework of modeling diffusion. We utilize a dataset that is a snowball crawl from Twitter, comprising about 465K users, with 837K edges and 25.3M tweets over a time period between Oct'06 and Nov'09. For our experiments, we focus on a set of 125 randomly chosen "trending topics" that are featured on Twitter over a 3 month period between Sep and Nov 2009. For the ease of analysis, we organize the different trending topics into generalized themes based on the popular open source natural language processing toolkit called "OpenCalais" (http://www.opencalais.com/).

We discuss attribute homophily subject to variations across the different themes, and averaged over time (Oct–Nov 2009). Figure 4.9 shows that there is considerable variation in performance (in terms of saturation and utility measures) over the eight themes.

In the case of saturation measurement, we observe that the location attribute (LOC) yields high saturation measures over themes related to events that are often "local" in nature: e.g., (1) "Sports" comprising topics such as "NBA," "New York Yankees," "Chargers," "Sehwag" and so on – each of them being of interest to users respectively from the US, NYC, San Diego and India; and (2) "Politics" (that includes topics like "Obama," "Tehran" and "Afghanistan") – all of which were associated with important, essentially local happenings during the period of our analysis. Whereas for themes that are of global importance, such as

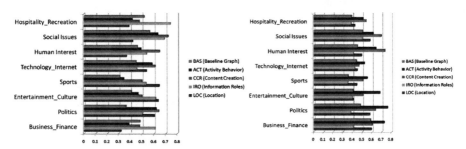

Fig. 4.9 Mean saturation and utility measurement of predicted diffusion characteristics shown across different themes

"Social Issues," including topics like "#BeatCancer," "Swine Flu," "#Stopthevio-lence" and "Unemployment," the results indicate that the attribute, information roles (IRO) yields the best performance – since it is able to capture user interests via their information generation and consumption patterns.

From the results on utility measurement, we observe that for themes associated with current external events (e.g., "Business-Finance," "Politics," "Entertainment-Culture" and "Sports"), the attribute, activity behavior (ACT) yields high utility measures. This is because information diffusing in the network on current hap-penings, are often dependent upon the temporal pattern of activity of the users, i.e., their time of tweeting. For "Human-Interest," "Social Issues" and "Hospitality-Recreation," we observe that the content creation attribute (CCR) yields the best performance in prediction, because it reveals the habitual properties of users in dis-sipating information on current happenings that they are interested in.

From these studies, we interestingly observe that attribute homophily *indeed* im-pacts the diffusion process; however the particular attribute that can best explain the actual diffusion characteristics often depends upon: (1) the metric used to quantify diffusion, and the (2) topic under consideration.

4.5 Summary and Future Work

Our central research goal in this chapter has been to instrument the three organizing principles that characterize our communication processes online: the information or *concept* that is the content of communication, and the *channel* i.e., the media via which communication takes place. We have presented characterization techniques, develop computational models and finally discuss large-scale quantitative observa-tional studies for both of these organizing ideas

Based on all the outcomes of the two research perspectives that we discussed here, we believe that this research can make significant contribution into a better understanding of how we communicate online and how it is redefining our col-lective sociological behavior. Beyond exploring new sociological questions, the collective modeling of automatically measurable interactional data will also enable new applications that can take advantage of knowledge of a person's social context or provide feedback about her social behavior. Communication modeling may also improve the automated prediction and recognition of human behavior in diverse so-cial, economic and organizational settings. For collective behavior modeling, the social network can define dependencies between people's behavior with respect to their communication patterns, and features of the social network may be used to improve prediction and recognition. Additionally, some of the statistical techniques developed in this thesis for analyzing interpersonal communication may find new application to behavior modeling (collective or otherwise) and machine learning.

In the future, we are interested in two different non-trivial problems that can provide us with a deeper and more comprehensive understanding of the online com-munication process. The first of the two problems deals with the idea of evolution of network structure from an ego-centric perspective, in the context of online social spaces that feature multiplex ties. The second problem is geared towards exploring how sociological principles such as homophily (or heterophily) impacts media creation (e.g., uploading a photo on Flickr, or favorting a video on YouTube) on the part of the users. We are interested to study how the observed social interactions among the individuals impact such dynamics. Note, both of the proposed problems consider an observed sociological phenomena prevalent on the social media sites, and attempts to understand it with the help of large-scale quantitative observational studies.

References

1. Lada Adamic and Eytan Adar. How to search a social network. *Social Networks*, 27(3):187–203, 2005
2. Eytan Adar and Lada A. Adamic. Tracking information epidemics in blogspace. In *WI '05: Proceedings of the 2005 IEEE/WIC/ACM International Conference on Web Intelligence*, pages 207–214, 2005. IEEE Computer Society, Washington, DC
3. Eytan Adar, Daniel S. Weld, Brian N. Bershad, and Steven S. Gribble. Why we search: visualizing and predicting user behavior. In *WWW '07: Proceedings of the 16th international conference on World Wide Web*, pages 161–170, 2007. ACM, New York
4. Eytan Bakshy, Brian Karrer, and Lada A. Adamic. Social influence and the diffusion of user-created content. In *EC '09: Proceedings of the tenth ACM conference on Electronic commerce*, pages 325–334, 2009. ACM, New York
5. Frank M. Bass. A new product growth model for consumer durables. *Management Science*, 15:215–227, 1969
6. Charles R. Berger and Richard J. Calabrese. Some explorations in initial interaction and beyond: Toward a developmental theory of interpersonal communication. *Human Communication Research*, 1(2):99–112, 1975
7. Ronald S. Burt. Toward a structural theory of action: Network models of social structure, perception and action. *The American Journal of Sociology*, 90(6):1336–1338, 1982
8. Ronald S. Burt. Structural holes and good ideas. *The American Journal of Sociology*, 110(2):349–399, 2004
9. Robert B. Cialdini and Noah J. Goldstein. Social influence: Compliance and conformity. *Annual Review of Psychology*, 55:591–621, 2004
10. James Coleman. *Foundations of Social Theory*. Belknap Press of Harvard University Press, August 1998
11. Munmun De Choudhury, Hari Sundaram, Ajita John, and Dorée Duncan Seligmann. Can blog communication dynamics be correlated with stock market activity? In *HT '08: Proceedings of the nineteenth ACM conference on Hypertext and hypermedia*, pages 55–60, 2008. ACM, New York
12. Munmun De Choudhury, Hari Sundaram, Ajita John, and Dorée Duncan Seligmann. Social synchrony: Predicting mimicry of user actions in online social media. In *CSE '09: Proceedings of the 2009 International Conference on Computational Science and Engineering*, pages 151–158, 2009. IEEE Computer Society, Washington, DC
13. Munmun De Choudhury, Hari Sundaram, Ajita John, and Dorée Duncan Seligmann. What makes conversations interesting?: themes, participants and consequences of conversations in online social media. In *WWW '09: Proceedings of the 18th international conference on World wide web*, pages 331–340, 2009. ACM, New York
14. Scott L. Feld. The focused organization of social ties. *American Journal of Sociology*, 86(5):1015–1035, 1981

15. Vicenç Gómez, Andreas Kaltenbrunner, and Vicente López. Statistical analysis of the social network and discussion threads in slashdot. In *WWW '08: Proceeding of the 17th international conference on World Wide Web*, pages 645–654, 2008. ACM, New York
16. M. S. Granovetter. The strength of weak ties. *The American Journal of Sociology*, 78(6):1360–1380, 1973
17. Daniel Gruhl, R. Guha, Ravi Kumar, Jasmine Novak, and Andrew Tomkins. The predictive power of online chatter. In *KDD '05: Proceedings of the eleventh ACM SIGKDD international conference on Knowledge discovery in data mining*, pages 78–87, 2005. ACM, New York
18. Thomas Hofmann. Probabilistic latent semantic indexing. In *SIGIR '99: Proceedings of the 22nd annual international ACM SIGIR conference on Research and development in information retrieval*, pages 50–57, 1999. ACM, New York
19. David Kempe, Jon Kleinberg, and Éva Tardos. Maximizing the spread of influence through a social network. In *KDD '03: Proceedings of the ninth ACM SIGKDD international conference on Knowledge discovery and data mining*, pages 137–146, 2003
20. Ravi Kumar, Jasmine Novak, and Andrew Tomkins. Structure and evolution of online social networks. In *KDD '06: Proceedings of the 12th ACM SIGKDD international conference on Knowledge discovery and data mining*, pages 611–617, 2006. ACM, New York
21. Jure Leskovec, Lars Backstrom, Ravi Kumar, and Andrew Tomkins. Microscopic evolution of social networks. In *KDD '08: Proceeding of the 14th ACM SIGKDD international conference on Knowledge discovery and data mining*, pages 462–470, 2008. ACM, New York
22. Jure Leskovec and Eric Horvitz. Planetary-scale views on a large instant-messaging network. In *WWW '08: Proceeding of the 17th international conference on World Wide Web*, pages 915–924, 2008. ACM, New York
23. D. Liben-Nowell and Jon Kleiberg. Tracing information flow on a global scale using internet chain-letter data. *PNAS*, 105(12):4633–4638, 2008
24. Miller Mcpherson, Lynn S. Lovin, and James M. Cook. Birds of a feather: Homophily in social networks. *Annual Review of Sociology*, 27(1):415–444, 2001
25. Miller McPherson and Lynn Smith-Lovin. Homophily in voluntary organizations: Status distance and the composition of face-to-face groups. *American sociological review*, 52(3):370–379, 1987
26. Qiaozhu Mei, Deng Cai, Duo Zhang, and ChengXiang Zhai. Topic modeling with network regularization. In *WWW '08: Proceeding of the 17th international conference on World Wide Web*, pages 101–110, 2008. ACM, New York
27. Qiaozhu Mei, Chao Liu, Hang Su, and ChengXiang Zhai. A probabilistic approach to spatiotemporal theme pattern mining on weblogs. In *WWW '06: Proceedings of the 15th international conference on World Wide Web*, pages 533–542, 2006. ACM, New York
28. Gilad Mishne and Natalie Glance. Leave a reply: An analysis of weblog comments. In *In Third annual workshop on the Weblogging ecosystem*, 2006
29. Chih-Hui Lai Mor Naaman, Jeffrey Boase. Is it really about me? message content in social awareness streams. In *CSCW '10: Proceedings of the 2010 ACM Conference on Computer Supported Cooperative Work*, 2010. ACM, New York
30. Kevin Murphy. *Dynamic Bayesian Networks: Representation, Inference and Learning*. PhD thesis, UC Berkeley, Computer Science Division, July 2002
31. Theodore Mead Newcomb. *The acquaintance process*. Holt, Rinehart and Winston, New York, 1961
32. Martin Potthast. Measuring the descriptiveness of web comments. In *SIGIR '09: Proceedings of the 32nd international ACM SIGIR conference on Research and development in information retrieval*, pages 724–725, 2009. ACM, New York
33. Lawrence R. Rabiner. A tutorial on hidden markov models and selected applications in speech recognition. pages 267–296, 1990
34. Anne Schuth, Maarten Marx, and Maarten de Rijke. Extracting the discussion structure in comments on news-articles. In *WIDM '07: Proceedings of the 9th annual ACM international workshop on Web information and data management*, pages 97–104, 2007. ACM, New York

35. Bimal Viswanath, Alan Mislove, Meeyoung Cha, and Krishna P. Gummadi. On the evolution of user interaction in facebook. In *WOSN '09: Proceedings of the 2nd ACM workshop on Online social networks*, pages 37–42, 2009. ACM, New York
36. D. J. Watts, P. S. Dodds, and M. E. J. Newman. Identity and search in social networks. *Science*, 296(5571):1302–1305, 2002
37. Fang Wu and Bernardo A. Huberman. Popularity, novelty and attention. In *EC '08: Proceedings of the 9th ACM conference on Electronic commerce*, pages 240–245, 2008. ACM, New York

Chapter 5
Qualitative Analysis of Commercial Social Network Profiles

Lester Melendez, Ouri Wolfson, Malek Adjouadi, and Naphtali Rishe

5.1 Introduction

Social-networking sites have become an integral part of many users' daily internet routine. Commercial enterprises have been quick to recognize this and are subsequently creating profiles for many of their products and services. Commercial enterprises use social network profiles to target and interact with potential customers as well as to provide a gateway for users of the product or service to interact with each other. Many commercial enterprises use the statistics from their product or service's social network profile to tout the popularity and success of the product or service being showcased. They will use statistics such as number of friends, number of daily visits, number of interactions, and other similar measurements to quantify their claims. These statistics are often not a clear indication of the true popularity and success of the product. In this chapter the term product is used to refer to any tangible or intangible product, service, celebrity, personality, film, book, or other entity produced by a commercial enterprise.

Social network profiles are complex entities that require one to use heuristics in addition to traditional statistics in order to assess the success and popularity of the product showcased in the profile. For example, a product's profile may have one million friends; using only quantitative analysis, this would lead one to believe that the product showcased has achieved a great deal of success. Using heuristic techniques one can sift through subsets of the profile's friend list and take into account things such as, the number of friends that are not other commercial profiles which interact at least bi-weekly with the profile being analyzed. This will yield a new measurement that may be orders of magnitude lower than the initial one million friends claimed. Thus, showing the success of the product was not as

N. Rishe (✉)
NSF Industry/University Cooperative Research Center, Florida International University,
University Park, ECS-243, Miami, FL 33199, USA
e-mail: rishe@cs.fiu.edu; ndr@acm.org

B. Furht (ed.), *Handbook of Social Network Technologies and Applications*,
DOI 10.1007/978-1-4419-7142-5_5, © Springer Science+Business Media, LLC 2010

great as initially thought when applying only quantitative analysis. Heuristic based qualitative analysis of commercial social network profiles is vital to understanding the impact, popularity, success, and reach of a product or service.

As with many academic avenues, there are outliers and caveats that do not fit neatly into the methods proposed; such instances are out of the scope of this chapter. This chapter will discuss some general methods used in traditional quantitative analysis of commercial social network profiles and introduce heuristics that will facilitate more accurate qualitative analysis in most cases. These heuristics have been developed with the help of partners in the music and entertainment industry.

5.2 What Is a Commercial Social Network Profile?

The social network profiles that the average user will sign up for are standard personal profiles. These profiles are designed for an individual user to use as their own public billboard. Standard personal profiles contain the features an everyday private citizen is likely to require. In addition to a standard personal profile many external social-networking sites, such as MySpace, offer their users the option of specialized profiles [1]. Specialized profiles are created with additional functionality – which is geared to accommodate the needs of a specific domain. These profiles may have additional features not available in standard personal profiles, while still maintaining most of the features that come with standard personal profiles. Commercial enterprises see these additional features as an opportunity to showcase their product in a dynamic and vibrant manner. Often, commercial enterprises will sign up for an account with a social-networking site and create a personal or specialized profile for the sole purpose of furthering their product's success. The resulting profile is considered a commercial social network profile. It is important to distinguish commercial social network profiles from fan or imposter profiles.

Fan profiles, similar to fansites, fanpages [2], and tribute pages, are personal or specialized social network profiles created and maintained by supporters of a product for the purposes of paying homage. At times, fan profiles may be inadvertently confused with commercial social network profiles due to the level of devotion of the individual or group maintaining the profile. The content may be so involved and of such high quality that it is difficult to determine whether the profile is commercial or not. Imposter profiles pose a similar problem such that they are personal or specialized social network profiles created with the explicit purpose of falsely identifying themselves as a commercial social network profile. Imposter profiles often times are nearly identical in design and content to the commercial social network profile they are impersonating. It is difficult to determine the difference between the profile types mentioned without qualitative analysis.

Heuristic 1 provides a straight forward rule for determining whether or not a profile is commercial.

Heuristic 1:

- A social network profile created and maintained by a commercial enterprise for the sole purpose of furthering their product's success is considered a commercial social network profile (CSNP).

5.2.1 Reciprocal Identification

Application of heuristic 1 requires a qualitative analysis of the profile in question. Introduced here is a generic approach that can be applied across different social-networking sites.

An efficient and effective method for the application of heuristic 1 is reciprocal identification. Reciprocal identification (RI) is the presence of a direct hyperlink from the official website of the product or commercial enterprise to the corresponding CSNP. RI establishes the CSNP and the commercial enterprise's recognition of the relationship between the two.

RI can be detected by analyzing the hyperlink structure of the product or commercial enterprise's official website. Many times, it is necessary to spider the hypertext of the product or commercial enterprise's website in order to establish RI. It can be inferred that the profile is likely a CSNP if RI is found to exist.

The presence of RI can be established using automated scripts or manual inspection. An example application of heuristic 1 using RI is depicted below in Fig. 5.1.

Profile in Question:
   http://www.myspace.com/falloutboy
Official Website of Commercial Enterprise:
   http://www.falloutboyrock.com
Source Excerpt from:
   http://www.falloutboyrock.com

```
<a class="footer_link" id="foot_ms"
href="http://www.myspace.com/falloutboy"
target="_blank"> </a>
```

Result: RI is present because a direct link to the CSNP in question exists on the commercial enterprise's official website thus; http://www.myspace.com/falloutboy is a CSNP.

Fig. 5.1 Application of heuristic 1 using RI

5.2.2   Types of Commercial Social Network Profiles

One can categorize most social network profiles as commercial or non-commercial using heuristic 1 at a coarse-grain level. A fine-grain analysis shows that there are various subtypes of CSNPs. This chapter introduces five major types of CSNPs: music, film, television, public figures, and events. Determining which subtype a CSNP falls into requires a simple logical determination as to what product is being highlighted; the design of CSNPs makes this easy to determine.

5.2.2.1   Music

The music industry has been keen on using social-networking as a tool to expand the reach of their products; namely, performing artists. Market demand has made it almost certain that all music CSNPs are specialized profiles. Most social networks offer special functionality to accommodate the demands of music industry CSNPs.

As with most CSNPs, music industry CSNPs can be identified easily by commonsense qualitative observation of the CSNP itself [3]. Additionally, they share common content traits that can assist an inexperienced individual in identifying a profile as a music industry CSNP.

Examples of common content traits for music industry CSNPs are:

- Embedded multimedia player containing a sampling of the artist's music
- Hyperlinks for purchasing the artist's music
- Listing of artists upcoming tour itinerary
- Banners advertising the artist's upcoming featured appearances in media
- Banners advertising the artist's sponsors
- Links to promotional materials (banners, icons, wallpapers, etc.)

The facility provided by music industry CSNPs to present users with such a wide array of content, allows them to serve as stand-alone entities capable of negating the need for an official website if the commercial enterprise behind it so desires; though this is rarely the case. Generally, music industry CSNPs have a lifespan slightly greater than that of the artist they were created to promote. Once the artist becomes inactive, the CSNP may fall into disrepair and eventually be discarded by the commercial enterprise that created it.

5.2.2.2   Films

The motion picture industry has also found a use for CSNPs; these too are usually specialized profiles. Motion picture studios may create a CSNP for one of their upcoming releases [4]. These CSNPs are geared more towards fan-to-fan interaction. Many times the CSNP's main attraction is a forum where fans of the movie can interact with each other pre- and post-premier. The content offered is usually limited to trailers of the movie, content recycled from the official website, and links to the official website. Motion picture CSNPs are used more as tools to funnel potential customers to the official website and establish a social network presence than to serve as a stand-alone attraction. This kind of CSNP has a relatively short lifespan. They rarely remain useful long after the theatrical or DVD release of the film it was created for.

5.2.2.3 Television

Television CSNPs are CSNPs built around products produced by the network and cable television industries. Similar to film CSNPs, they are used primarily to steer fans and potential fans towards the official website. Largely community based, these CSNPs rely on continuous fan-to-fan interaction and fan-to-product interaction to produce a return on their promotional investment; more specifically, creating a cult following and producing higher ratings [5]. Unlike film CSNPs, the lifespan of these profiles is expected to run long after the debut of the product; all the way through to the product's finale.

5.2.2.4 Public Figures

Public figures from television, fashion, sports, politics, and other avenues are known to use standard personal profiles to increase their visibility and to serve as a public relations tool. It is common for personalities to have a CSNP on all of the top social-networking sites [6]. Public figure CSNPs come in all shapes and sizes. Some are the public figure's primary internet presence serving as a means for press releases, media requests, appearance announcements, and more; while other public figures use their CSNP as nothing but a place holder to prevent squatters from creating imposter sites.

5.2.2.5 Events

CSNPs promoting upcoming events are now commonplace [7]. The commercial enterprises behind events such as the Super Bowl, the Vans Warped Tour, and the American Cancer Society's Relay for Life have all left their footprint on the social-networking world. These profiles are the shortest lived of the five subtypes of CSNPs as they are of little to no use once the event is over. They can be either standard personal profiles or specialized profiles. These CNSPs rely almost entirely on participant interaction. The sites have a narrow demographic as the reach of the event is generally confined to a small geographic area. Annual events may, at times, reuse the previous year's CSNP; updating it as necessary.

5.3 Quantitative Analysis of CSNPs

Quantitative analysis is the preferred method by which commercial enterprises evaluate the success of their CSNPs. They use statistics such as the number potential customers connected to the CSNP, customer interactions with the profile, and profile visits as selling points when touting the overall success of the product associated with that particular CSNP. It is important to have a fundamental understanding of some of the more commonly used measurements in order to grasp the importance of using a qualitative approach when analyzing CSNPs.

5.3.1 Connections

Profiles within a social network are often referred to as nodes within the technical community. Each node in a social network has a set of nodes that it is connected to via a social relationship. The nature of this connection, or relationship, is dependent upon the kind of social network. Some examples of connections are friendship, membership in an organization, ancestral ties, and geographic location. One of the more widely used types of connections is friendship.

For the examples in this chapter, it is safe to assume that friendship is the type of connection being used. If two nodes are connected to each other via a friendship relationship, it is said that they are friends. The set of all of a profile's friends is colloquially known as a friend list. In the realm of quantitative analysis, the size of a CSNP's friend list is a prime indicator of its success. Quantitatively, the conclusion can be drawn that the more friends a profile has, the more expansive its reach, and thus, greater its success.

For clarity, in the following scenario, the profile initiating the connection request is known as the "friender" and the profile receiving the connection request is known as the "friendee"; the connection request itself is referred to as a "friend request" and exists on the same social network. There are two ways for a profile's friend list to grow. The first is for the CSNP to act as the friender and initiate a connection with a potential customer, the friendee, by sending a friend request. This request asks permission to add the friendee to the friender's friend list and as a result adds the friender to the friendee's friend list. The friendee, the potential customer, now has the ability to accept or decline the friend request. There are various methods by which commercial enterprises go about initiating friend requests. Many times these friend requesting methods will skew quantitative analysis which will be discussed in greater detail in a later section.

The second is a customer initiated friend request. The potential customer submits a friend request to the CSNP. The CSNP's administrator then decides whether or not to accept the request. Once the request is accepted, the CSNP and the potential customer are friends and are present in each other's friend list. Once the potential customer and the CSNP are on each other's friend list, they are able to interact.

5.3.2   Interactions

By definition, social interaction is an interaction between two or more members of a social group [8]. Analogously, nodes within a social network can interact as well. Generally, the only requirement is that they are friends. Social networks offer a variety of ways in which their nodes can interact with one another. Interactions between nodes are singular one way events; meaning that one node is the sender and one node is the recipient of the interaction. Interactions are also either related or unrelated. Related interactions are interactions that are conducted in response to another interaction. An example of related interactions could be a private message thread in a user's inbox or series of comments made on two profile's main pages. The following is a sample transcript of four related interactions between a band's CSNP and the personal profile of a fan. The type of interaction being illustrated is a wall comment, also known simply as a comment.

(1) **Band CSNP:** Hi there, are you coming to our performance tonight?
(2) **Fan's Profile:** OMG! Yes! It's going to be awesome!
(3) **Band CSNP:** That's great to hear = Will you be bringing friends?
(4) **Fan's Profile:** Of course, my best friend Jane and her sister are coming too.

Interaction (1) triggers, or directly causes, interactions (2), (3), and (4) to be performed and thus all four interactions are considered related. Conversely, the following example shows three unrelated interactions.

(1) **Band CSNP:** We have a new song up! Come check it out!
(2) **Fan's Profile:** Hey, my friend says she went to HS with your singer.
(3) **Band CSNP:** Don't forget, we have new t-shirts for sale!

A brief semantic analysis of the contents of these comments shows no discernible connection. None of the comments show any signs of having triggered the other and thus are considered unrelated.

Commercial enterprises place a lot of stock in the number of overall interactions associated with their CSNP. Quantitatively, it is inferred that the more interactions a CSNP has, the more interest its product has generated and thus the more successful it is. Examples of interactions may be related to the CSNP's main profile page, blog entries, status updates, pictures, videos, bulletin boards, and could even just be generic e-props, such as "kudos" or "likes".

The most popular type of interaction between social network friends is known as the wall, or profile comment [9]. The profile comment is simply a plain text or HTML snippet that the sending friend can leave on the receiving friend's main profile page. This snippet is displayed on a virtual corkboard of sorts on the receiving friend's main profile page. There are variations of comments implemented throughout the social-networking world; such as comments specific to pictures and videos. Though the most prevalent, comments are only one of countless interaction types.

Social networks offer many more novel interactions allowing friends to rank each other's pictures, videos, and blogs; send e-gifts, survey results, event invitations, birthday reminders, and more.

5.3.3 Hit Counters

As with their official websites, commercial enterprises find it beneficial to add hit counters to their CSNPs. Hit counters allow commercial enterprises to assess the traffic on their CSNP. Hit counters need not be limited to tracking the number of visitors who view the CSNP's main profile page. There can be specialized counters attached to specific blogs, videos, pictures, bulletin board posts, and just about any other element of a profile. Many social networks will provide users with options for attaching built in counters to various elements on the profile.

In the case of music profiles, social-networking sites such as MySpace and Facebook provide commercial users with the ability to keep track of fine grain statistics such as how many visitors to their profile listen to the music on their profile's embedded music player. Quantitative analysis takes into account the number hits a profile receives and simply put, it says that the more hits a profile has the more successful it is.

5.3.4 Updates

The number of updates made on a CSNP is not often used in quantitative analysis; but, nonetheless it is important as it will be used to cover qualitative analysis later in the chapter. The number of updates during a period of time can show whether a product has been abandoned by its commercial enterprise or whether it is being backed by an active marketing campaign. Updates are elements such as blog entries, status changes, tweets, bulletins, and others; and can trigger interactions as well. The number of interactions triggered by each update can also be a telltale sign of a product's success.

5.4 Qualitative Analysis of CSNPs

Quantitative analysis leaves much to be desired in the way of accurately assessing the success of a CSNP. The number of friends, interactions, hits, and updates can easily be skewed by any number of factors; such as spam, profile hacks, and automated scripts. Intentionally or unintentionally, the actions of the commercial enterprise behind the CSNP can greatly affect the accuracy of quantitative analysis. Many times commercial enterprises look to artificially influence their CSNP's stats in order to back up their claims of success. Additionally, the popularity of social networks has created a spam epidemic. The number of businesses that were targets for spam, phishing and malware via social networking sites increased dramatically, with spam showing the sharpest rise from 33.4% in April 2009 to 57% in December 2009. This highlights a surge in exploitation of such sites by spammers [10]. This creates the need to sift through any statistics skewed by spam and internal actions in order to arrive at a valid conclusion regarding a CSNP's success.

In order to discern between valid and skewed statistics it is necessary to understand just what factors can skew a CSNP's stats. The following sections will introduce heuristics that can be applied to raw quantitative data to produce an accurate picture of a CSNP's success. The heuristics introduced can be applied together or separately and the more of these heuristics are applied concurrently, the more accurate the results. It is up to the individual performing the analysis to decide what heuristics should be applied to suit their needs.

5.4.1 Connections

The size of a profile's friend list has long been the preferred measure of a CSNP's popularity. A clear application of this principle can be found in the music industry. Record labels, management firms, and concert promoters rely heavily on this measurement alone to validate their claims that the performing artist they are backing is genuinely notable and successful. Their reasoning is that each friend on the CNPS's friend list equates to one devoted fan. This trend is not limited to the music industry; film, television, public figure, and event profiles suffer from the same reliance on friend list size and the assumption that one friend equals one devoted fan as a measure of popularity and success.

5.4.1.1 Valid Connections

Obtaining an accurate count of the number of friends a CSNP is connected to goes further than simply looking at the size of its friend list. Qualitatively perusing the average CSNP's friend list, it doesn't take long to notice the abundance of unrelated CSNPs and spam profiles within the list. Spam profiles are CSNPs disguised as personal profiles. Telling spam profiles apart from personal profiles is a topic onto its own and thus beyond the scope of this chapter. Suffice to say that common-sense observation should allow an individual with intermediate knowledge of social networks to discern between a genuine personal profile and spam profile. It is imperative to understand the importance of the need to categorize connections as valid and invalid.

Take into consideration a situation where a CSNP promoting a performing artist has one million friends. Qualitative analysis has helped us determine that 9,99,000 of those friends are other performing artists and spam profiles. Under quantitative analysis, it can be touted that this CSNP has achieved significant market reach and overall success due to the fact that its friend list contains one million friends. Qualitatively evaluating the friend list and counting only those friends that are not other CSNPs or spam profiles shows that the performing artist has a rather paltry following and not anywhere near as pervasive in the market as quantitative analysis showed. Heuristic two defines a simple way to determine whether a member of a CSNP's friend list should be considered valid for purposes of analysis.

Heuristic 2:

- Only those friends on a CSNP's friend list that are not CSNPs or spam profiles should be considered valid friends.

5.4.1.2 Connection Initiation

In addition to determining the number of valid connections in a friend list, it is helpful to examine the source of the valid connection. As mentioned earlier, there are only two ways to add friends to a friend list. A CSNP can send a friend request to a personal profile or the personal profile can send a friend request to the CSNP. Though a connection may be valid; its source, when looked at qualitatively, can yield more information as to the weight that should be given to it.

A connection initiated by a CSNP to a personal profile for purposes of product promotion shows a proactive effort on the CSNP's part to grow their customer base. On the other hand, a connection initiated by a personal profile towards a CSNP shows an unprovoked overt act by an individual in support of the product associated with the CSNP. This is a clear indication of the individual's true support of the CSNP's product.

Heuristic 3:

- A connection request initiated by a personal profile to a CSNP demonstrates an individual's proactive support for the product associated with the CSNP and thus carries more weight than a CSNP initiated connection request.

5.4.1.3 Connection Demographics

Incorporating demographic information in the analysis of personal profiles is difficult to achieve due to the absence of information verification mechanisms. The owner of a personal profile could claim to be a 50-year-old Asian female in Los Angeles and could, in reality, be a 20-year-old white male in New York. This makes it very difficult to apply any sort of demographic based heuristic to CSNP analysis. If it were possible to verify the user information pertaining to each friend in a CSNP's friend list; it would be prudent to introduce a heuristic to our quantitative analysis. This heuristic would give greater weight to those profiles that fall within the target demographic, as defined by the commercial enterprise behind the CSNP. Demographic information can include age, gender, location, musical tastes, buying patterns, education, yearly income, and more.

In order to fully understand the importance of incorporating a demographic-based heuristic into CSNP analysis, picture a pop–rock band with a CSNP. Their tour manager is trying to plot their tour route. Without the aid of a demographic-based heuristic, CSNP analysis serves no purpose for his situation. If it was possible to verify even a fraction of the demographic information in a profile, the tour manager would be able to analyze his band's friend list to a level of detail that would be of great use to him. For instance, if the geographic location of each friend in the band's friend list became verifiable; the tour manger would be able to create a map overlay and visualize the areas on a map with the highest concentration of the band's friends. This would help him plan a tour route that stopped at locations with high concentrations of the band's friends; thus increasing the chances for a good turnout at each performance.

In the event that further research yields a reliable means for demographic information verification pertaining to standard personal profiles, heuristic 4 will be introduced.

Heuristic 4:

- If a friend's demographic information conforms to a set of specified desirable parameters it, indicates the friend will be more likely to actively support the CSNP's product.

5.4.1.4   Friend Stacking

Friend stacking is a deceptive technique by which CSNPs gain a large number of friends even before they have officially announced the profile to the public [11]. One of the approaches often seen begins with a seemingly legitimate profile for a charitable cause; such as the search for a missing child. In reality it's actually a commercial enterprise behind the site. Automated scripts begin sending thousands of friend requests as part of a coordinated social network spam campaign. The good hearted nature of many social network users causes them to accept the friend request in order to help the charitable effort.

Once enough of the requests have been accepted, the commercial enterprise changes the content of the profile and turns it into a CSNP. Now they have a CSNP that is launched with several thousand friends already present in the CSNP's friend list. This creates the appearance of a sweeping phenomenon that people cannot wait to be a part of. After the CSNP's launch the automated scripts continue to send friend requests; this time without the pretext of the charitable cause. The fact that the friendees see a request from a CSNP with several thousand friends makes it more likely that they will accept the friend request as opposed to seeing a request from a CSNP with a very low number of friends. Friend stacking takes advantage of mob mentality by creating the impression that their CSNP's product already has a devoted following. Taking this into account, it is reasonable to infer that the results of any analysis performed on a CSNP that has benefited from friend stacking is, at minimum, skewed.

Heuristic 5:

- If friend stacking was used at anytime during the lifetime of a CSNP, any conclusions obtained through analysis will be skewed; unless it is possible to identify and remove all connections made through friend stacking.

5.4.1.5 Div Overlaying

A less complicated alternative to friend stacking is a technique known as Div Overlaying. Simply put, an HTML div element with a z-index greater than that of any other element in the profile is positioned over the CSNP's friend list. The content of this div is indiscernible from the real friend list except for the fact that the text indicating the number of friends has been modified [11]. The aim is to deceive the average user into thinking that the CSNP has a greater number of friends than it actually has. Since the content of the div overlay is nothing more than standard HTML, the CSNP's administrator can choose to display any number they wish. They can even periodically increment the number so as to give the illusion of legitimate increases in friend list size.

A straight forward way to determine whether a CSNP is employing Div Overlaying is to select the option to view the complete list of the CSNP's friends. This will show the true number of friends as the use of Div Overlaying is, more often than not, limited to the main profile page. Div overlaying is not a technique that can be used on all social networks; though it is one of the most popular hacks used on MySpace personal and specialized profiles alike. The use of Div Overlaying extends far beyond merely changing the apparent size of a friend list. Div Overlaying has been used to replace entire profile main mages. Examples can be found on every other CSNP throughout MySpace and other popular social networks.

Heuristic 6:

- When conducting analysis that takes into account the size of a friend list, a check for the use of Div Overlaying must be performed in order to insure the accuracy of the friend list size.

5.4.2 Interactions

As with connections, quantitative analysis of interactions based simply on raw numbers can be very misleading. Qualitative factors must be weighed-in if accurate analysis is to be achieved; most notably the type, source, and content of the interactions.

5.4.2.1 Interaction Type, Source, and Content

Interaction types can be wall posts, comments, picture ratings, bulletin board replies, e-props, and any other interaction defined within a social network. The significance, or weight, given to each type of interaction will be determined by nature of the analysis being conducted. For instance, if analysis is being performed in hopes of determining the impact a particular bulletin board entry has had on the overall CSNP then, emphasis will be placed on bulletin board replies.

The source of an interaction is determined by identifying the origin of the interaction. For an unrelated CSNP to personal profile interaction the source is the CSNP, as the interaction was initiated by the CSNP. When it comes to related interactions, the source of each subsequent interaction is the same as the source of the first interaction of the series of related interactions.

Content is a factor that is difficult to evaluate yet very valuable for analysis. The content of an interaction needs to be semantically analyzed in order to assign a proper weight to it. These three key factors should be considered concurrently in order to yield the most accurate analysis possible. To demonstrate this, consider the following two unrelated interactions and the analysis that follows.

Interaction *A*

Social Network	Facebook
Type	Wall Post on Bob's Personal Profile
Source	Acme Inc.'s CSNP
Content	"Hi! Do you like our product?"

Interaction *B*

Social Network	Facebook
Type	Wall Post on Acme Inc.'s CSNP
Source	Jane's Personal Profile
Content	"I enjoy your product! I use it all the time!"

Note: Both interactions are unrelated to any other interaction

Under strict quantitative analysis, interactions A and B are identical. If qualitative analysis of the three key factors mentioned is incorporated then it is clear that the resulting analysis will indicate a significant difference between the two interactions.

A cursory glance reveals two noticeable differences, the first being that the sources for the interactions are different. Interaction *A* is CSNP to personal profile while interaction *B* is personal profile to CSNP. Secondly, the content is very different. The content of interaction *A* appears to be an attempt by Acme Inc. to solicit feedback from Bob concerning their product and interaction *B* is apparently an unsolicited compliment from Jane to the Acme Inc. regarding their product. As interaction *A* is unrelated to any other interaction, was initiated by the CSNP, and has content intended to trigger one or more related interactions, it is not a genuine social interaction. Interactions such as interaction *A* are said to be part of interaction phishing.

Interaction phishing is an attempt by a CSNP to elicit personal profile to CSNP interactions for the sole purpose of increasing its overall and personal profile to CSNP interaction counts by baiting a personal profile into initiating social interactions. Interaction phishing may occur via CSNP initiated connection requests or CSNP initiated interactions. A personal profile to CSNP interaction that was triggered by a CSNP to personal profile connection request or a CSNP to personal profile interaction is considered to be a result of interaction phishing.

Heuristic 7:

- Interactions resulting from interaction phishing are not genuine social interactions

Unlike the case with interaction A, the source and content of interaction B leads one to conclude that interaction B was an unsolicited attempt by a personal profile to engage a CSNP in social interaction. As interaction B is unrelated to any other interaction, is originated from a personal profile, and its content is clearly indicative of the personal profile's support of the CSNP's product, then it is considered a genuine social interaction and should be weighed appropriately during analysis.

Heuristic 8:

- A personal profile to CSNP interaction between personal profile φ and CSNP γ that is unrelated to any other interaction or related to a series of interactions whose initial source was φ is a genuine social interaction.

Heuristic 9:

- A CSNP to personal profile interaction between personal profile φ and CSNP γ that is either related to a series of interactions whose initial source was φ or initiated by γ as a response to a connection request initiated by φ is a genuine social interaction.

5.4.2.2 Interaction Based Spam

Considerations pertaining to the content of an interaction should be made to account for the spam epidemic that plagues social networks [12]. Social network spam can have many forms; some of which are analogous to those found in email spam [13]. Social network spam includes offers from supposed foreign politicians, real estate deals that are too good to pass up, prescription drugs at prices too low to believe, and more. In addition to these well known forms of spam, social networks fall victim to social network specific spam such as interaction phishing, ballot stuffing, and friend stacking just to name a few. Interaction based spam can greatly skew any kind of quantitative analysis results unless the proper heuristics are applied. The topic of social network spam deserves in depth consideration far beyond the scope of this chapter. This section is limited to the introduction of a couple of heuristics that may help negate or at least lessen the effect that interaction based spam has on the analysis of CSNPs.

Heuristic 10:

- Any unrelated interaction whose sole purpose is to solicit the interaction recipient is considered social network spam.

It is important to note that interaction based spam can originate from either a CSNP or a personal profile. Personal profiles are capable of creating interaction based spam with things such as birthday announcements, links to surveys, holiday tidings, joke links, and countless other things. CSNPs create interaction based spam with a much more specific purpose, to solicit the interaction recipient. Evidence of CSNPs using interaction based spam can be seen throughout each of their friend's profiles. CSNPs are known for initiating random unrelated interactions at specific times, such as product release dates, on their friends' profiles. Some of the more notorious producers of interaction based spam are music CSNPs.

Music CSNPs will often use interactions to announce every single stop on their tour. If a band with a CSNP is playing in New York on January 1, 2010 then they will initiate interactions with as many friends as possible; soliciting their attendance to the performance. Tactics such as this create interaction based spam equivalent to the number of stops on the tour times the number of friends in the CSNP's friend list. As music CSNPs are known to use friend stacking [11] and other techniques to artificially raise the number of friends on their friends list, this can create millions of instances of interaction based spam.

Heuristic 11:

- Any interactions deemed to be social interaction based spam are not genuine social interactions and should be treated accordingly during interaction analysis.

In determining if an interaction is spam it may be useful to apply traditional spam detection heuristics found in email and social spam detection systems [14]. The principle is the same; analyze the content of the interaction and based on the results and determine if it's spam or not. Additionally, it will be necessary to apply social network specific heuristics to obtain a better estimate of the amount of spam in the set of a profile's total interactions.

Heuristic 12:

- When analyzing interaction statistics, generic and social network specific spam heuristics must be developed and applied and any interaction deemed to be spam must be removed from consideration.

As stated earlier, social network spam and the topics it encompasses, such as social network spam detection, deserve separate and in depth attention beyond the scope of this chapter. Suffice to say, a good foundation for the development and application of social network spam detection and management can be found using heuristics 10 and 11.

5.4.2.3   Interaction Frequency and Timing

Two attributes of social network interactions rarely taken into account during analysis are frequency and timing of interactions. That is, when a set of interactions occur and how often they occur over a set period of time. When it comes to CSNPs the frequency and timing of interactions are valuable pieces of information. They help commercial enterprises directly correlate past events to customer reaction and anticipate customer responses to future events. In the case of band's CSNPs, it is useful to see what kind of a reaction the band receives from their social network friends who attended their performance as well as gauge how many friends will be attending the performance to begin with.

For instance, the week leading up to a performance in Chicago a band receives 1,000 genuine interactions and valid connection requests initiated by personal profiles in the Chicago area. This can be taken as an indication that the band can expect a great turnout for their performance in Chicago. The same could not be said if the band received the same 1,000 interactions over the course of the 6 months prior to the show due to the uncertainty large spans of time cause in the entertainment industry. In the week following the band's performance in Chicago, their CSNP receives 1,000 more genuine interactions and valid connection requests from personal profiles in the Chicago area. This can be taken as a clear indication that their performance in Chicago was a great success. On the other hand, if the band had received only 100 genuine interactions and valid connection requests it could be said, with considerably less certainty, that their performance was not as successful as it could have been. In many cases, increases in interaction frequency around a specific time can help tie the jump to a specific event.; while a lack of increases in interaction frequency around a specific time are not as easily tied to a specific event. This is simply because the nature of social network interactions is that users will not always interact. This means that the lack of interaction may be attributed typical user patters as opposed to the lack of interaction being caused by a specific event, such as a performance or product release.

Heuristic 13:

- If there is an increase in the number of genuine personal profile to CSNP interactions and valid personal profile to CSNP connection requests received during the period of time immediately preceding and or following an event, it can be reasonably inferred that the event in question is in part responsible for the increase.

Having interaction frequency and timing does not limit one to tying increases in interactions to events. Knowing the frequency and timing of interactions can also help analysts determine how fresh the success of a CSNP is. Take into consideration a case where as CSNP has 1,00,000 valid connections and over its lifetime has participated in 2,00,000 genuine social interactions. At first, it seems as though the CSNP is currently enjoying the heights of success. Now consider additional information has come to light. The latest interaction occurred 6 months ago and in the 2 years preceding that latest interaction, the interaction frequency was six interactions per week.

Heuristic 14:

- When assessing a CSNP's current level of success based on genuine interactions and valid connections, it is necessary to evaluate the frequency of each as compared to the average frequency over the lifetime of the CSNP. If the recent frequency is slightly less than, equal to, or greater than the average overall frequency then the CSNP's success can be considered current.

With this information and the application of heuristic 14, it can be ascertained that in the past two and a half years there have only been 624 interactions that involved this CSNP. One can now infer that the bulk of this CSNP's success happened over two and a half years ago; clearly a sign that this CSNP's best days are behind it. A far cry from the results obtained without the use of heuristic 14.

5.4.2.4 Interaction Uniqueness

Uniqueness of interactions is a brief yet important topic. When analyzing a CSNP one must look at the breakdown of the personal profiles interacting with it. If it is found that any personal profiles take part in a much greater percentage of interactions than average, the value of those interactions must be weighed accordingly. A case might exist where a CSNP has 1,000 genuine interactions but, all of those interactions come from a single source. That should not be evaluated the same as a CSNP with 1,000 interactions that each come from a unique source.
Heuristic 15:

- For every personal profile α in the set of all personal profiles that have been identified as a source of a genuine interaction between itself and the CSNP being analyzed, the number of interactions per α should be within one standard deviation of the total number of interactions divided by the number of unique sources. Otherwise it is considered an outlier and removed from the analytical process.

5.5 Technical Notes

In obtaining the necessary quantitative and qualitative data for this research various approaches were undertaken. In order to develop the heuristics introduced in this chapter it was necessary to have the ability to crawl numerous social network profiles and extract pertinent information from each one. This task was accomplished thanks to tools and methods introduced to the authors by their industrial partners at IBM Almaden Research Center and Barcelona Supercomputing Center (BSC).

Two of the more vital tools were a social network crawler and profile information extractor. Both were developed using IBM and BSC methods; such as SystemT [15] and MapReduce [16]. The social network crawler would retrieve a random sampling of social network profiles and store the results in a series of data files containing the raw HTML of each profile. The profile information extractor would then process these files and using a set of regular expressions, return an organized dataset that allowed us study the results and from there, create the heuristics introduced in this chapter.

In addition, various other scripts in combination with manual methods were used to achieve as accurate a picture as possible of the intricacies behind CSNPs. This chapter will attempt to paint for the reader that very same picture.

5.6 Summary

The furious pace at which social networks and CSNPs are evolving makes it imperative to continually monitor industry trends. The heuristics introduced here are presented in a generic manner to make it easy to adapt them to the inevitable changes in the world of social networks. Much work is left to be done in order to fully understand the impact of CSNPs. A fusion of marketing, sociology, and computer science research is necessary in order to paint a detailed picture of the effects CSNPs have on industry and society.

Acknowledgement This research was supported in part by NSF grants IIS-0837716, CNS-0821345, HRD-0833093, IIP-0829576, IIP-0931517, DGE-0549489, IIS-0957394, IIS-0847680, CNS-0837556 and CNS-0426125. IBM Almaden Research Center and Barcelona Supercomputing Center have contributed to the methodology used and to the first author's training under the NSF PIRE award 0730065.

References

1. "Signup For MySpace, Now with Free Music." Signup for Myspace, Now with Free Music. MySpace.com. Web. 18 Mar. 2010. http://signups.myspace.com/index.cfm?fuseaction=signup
2. "Fansite – " Wikipedia, the Free Encyclopedia. Wikimedia Foundation, Inc. Web. 18 Mar. 2010. http://en.wikipedia.org/wiki/Fanpage
3. "The Drive Home Only Adds REAL People =) on MySpace Music – Free Streaming MP3s, Pictures & Music Downloads." The Drive Home Only Adds REAL People =) on MySpace Music – Free Streaming MP3s, Pictures & Music Downloads. Drive Home Music Inc. Web. 18 Mar. 2010. http://www.myspace.com/drivehomemusic
4. "Twilight Saga New Moon Official MySpace Profile." Twilight Saga New Moon Official Myspace Profile. Summit Entertainment LLC. Web. 18 Mar. 2010. http://www.myspace.com/twilight
5. "MySpace – It's Always Sunny in Philidelphia – Only on FX!" It's Always Sunny in Philidelphia – Only on FX! FX Networks LLC. Web. 18 Mar. 2010. http://www.myspace.com/sunnyfx
6. "Dane Cook on MySpace Comedy – Comic Clips, Funny Videos & Jokes." Dane Cook on MySpace Comedy. Web. 18 Mar. 2010. http://www.myspace.com/danecook
7. Vans Warped Tour 2010. Vans. Web. 18 Mar. 2010. http://www.myspace.com/warpedtour
8. "Social Relation" Wikipedia, the Free Encyclopedia. Wikimedia Foundation, Inc. Web. 18 Mar. 2010. http://en.wikipedia.org/wiki/Social_interaction
9. Melendez, Lester A. Crawl of 1000 MySpace Profiles to Gather Interaction Statistics. 10 Mar. 2010. Raw data. Florida Internaitonal University, Miami
10. "Two Thirds of Businesses Fear That Social Networking Endangers Corporate Security, Sophos Research Reveals." Antivirus | Security Software | Data Protection | Encryption Software for Businesses – Sophos. Sophos Plc. Web. 18 Mar. 2010. http://www.sophos.com/pressoffice/news/articles/2009/04/social-networking.html
11. "Cori Yarckin on MySpace Music – Free Streaming MP3s, Pictures & Music Downloads." Cori Yarckin on MySpace Music. See Why Records. Web. 18 Mar. 2010. http://www.myspace.com/coriyarckin
12. "Malware and Spam Rise 70% on Social Networks, Security Report Reveals." Antivirus | Security Software | Data Protection | Encryption Software for Businesses – Sophos. Sophos Plc. Web. 18 Mar. 2010. http://www.sophos.com/pressoffice/news/articles/2010/02/security-report-2010.html
13. "LOVE SHE WROTE on MySpace Music – Free Streaming MP3s, Pictures & Music Downloads." Love She Wrote on MySpace Music. Web. 18 Mar. 2010.http://www.myspace.com/loveshewrote
14. Benjamin, M., Cattuto, C., and Menczer, F. 2009. Social Spam Detection. Proceedings of the 5th International Workshop on Adversarial Information Retrieval on the Web. ACM International Conference Proceeding Series, Spain, Madrid. New York: ACM Press, 41–48

15. Krishnamurthy, R., Li, Y., Raghavan, S., Reiss, F., Vaithyanathan, S., and Zhu, H. 2009. SystemT: A System for Declarative Information Extraction. SIGMOD Record, 37:4, 7–13
16. Dean, J. and Ghemawat, S. 2008. MapReduce: Simplified Data Processing on Large Clusters. Communications of the ACM Archive, 51:1, 107–113

Chapter 6
Analysis of Social Networks Extracted from Log Files

Kateřina Slaninová, Jan Martinovič, Pavla Dráždilová, Gamila Obadi, and Václav Snášel

6.1 Introduction

Modern applications like information, enterprise, e-commerce systems as well as monitoring applications, web applications and other systems generate huge amounts of data collections. These data collections are stored in various forms, from text-based data sources like logs (pure text), through HTML, XML and other formats to semi-structured data sources like multimedia sources (images, audio or video files etc.), and maintained in databases, data warehouse, or simply in data or log files.

A log file is a simple text file generated by a device, software, application, or a system, and consists of messages represented by the records of the activities provided. The log typically consists of information about originator, activity, event (or process instance), and mostly also have a timestamp (date and time when the activity was provided), originator (performer), and other data.

Though the log files are rich in information, quantifiable and scalable, researchers still argue about their credibility. The authors in [35] and [46] reported a number of limitations of the data stored in web log files, which – if not interpreted precisely – make the results obtained by analyzing this data misleading. Some of these limitations are:

- The log entries do not include any demographic data about the user,
- The IP address recorded in the web log file does not represent the identity of the user, it is the IP address of the host machine that the user was connected while accessing the website,

K. Slaninová (✉)
Department of Computer Science, FEECS, VŠB – Technical University of Ostrava, Ostrava, Czech Republic
e-mail: slaninova@opf.slu.cz

B. Furht (ed.), *Handbook of Social Network Technologies and Applications*,
DOI 10.1007/978-1-4419-7142-5_6, © Springer Science+Business Media, LLC 2010

- The log files record only request transactions; there are other tools used on the web servers, but they are not recorded on the log files (such as Macromedia Flash, Java applets),
- The average time viewed statistic does not accurately measures the time spent by the user on the web page.

Making generally, we should keep in mind the limitations in other spheres of log mining applications as well. Regardless of their limitations, log files have been used extensively by data miners and researchers. A number of studies have been conducted to gather information about the visitors of e-commerce web sites, explore the behavior of elearning students, detect web sites security threats, etc.

One of the log file attributes is the originator of the provided activity. The originator may be a person or a device or software, which depends on type of the log. In the case of the person, we can, using this information, derive social networks on the basis of similar attributes of persons and, in consequence, we can construct models that explain some aspects of persons' behavior [108]. The second part of the chapter shortly describes the basic aspects of social network analysis with relation to the log files.

The main problem, which researchers solve in data collection and data preprocessing while working with log files, is the large amount of obtained data. The third part of this chapter is dedicated to log file analysis and data mining methods frequently used for large data collections.

Besides, the chapter is concluded by a case study, which describes the development and visualization of a synthetic social network based on the relationship between the students with similar study behavior in an elearning management system recorded in the log files.

6.2 Social Networks

A social network (SN) is a set of people or groups of people with similar pattern of contacts or interactions such as friendship, co-working, or information exchange [85]. The world wide web, citation networks, human activity on the internet (email exchange, consumer behavior in e-commerce), physical and biochemical networks are some examples of social networks. Social networks are usually visualized by graphs, where nodes represent individuals or groups and lines represent relations among them. Mathematicians and some computer scientists usually describe these networks by means of graph theory [73]. These graphs can be directed or undirected, depending on the type of the relation between the linked nodes. Weights can be assigned to the links (edges) between the nodes to designate different interaction strengths.

Recently, these graphs are widely used for the network visualization. As an example of social network vizualizers we can mention software, like NetDraw, Vizster, NodeXL, NetMiner, ORA, Pajek, NetVis, SocNetV and many others [27]. The development and the fundamental methods of the social network visualization were published by Freeman [42]. However, other visualization algorithms and methods applicable to large-scale networks were proposed, see Sect. 6.2.2.

6.2.1 Social Network Analysis

Social network analysis (SNA) is a collection of methods, techniques and tools that aim to analyze the social structures and relational aspects of these structures in a social network [94]. Actors and their actions are viewed as autonomous units, relations between actors can be viewed as channels for transfer or flow of resources (e.g., information, material, or other). Network models conceptualize the structure as lasting patterns of relations among actors. The unit of analysis can be the individual or the group, or subgroup of individuals with a certain level of the linkages among them [111].

The study of social networks is a quite old discipline. Many studies oriented to the analysis of social networks have been provided, where the datasets used in these studies were obtained by using questionnaires. In contrast to the previous SNA research, contemporary provided, and more structured approaches, are based on the automated way of research. In the late 1990s, the development of new information and communication technologies (such as internet, cellular phones) enabled the researches to construct large-scale networks using the data collections stored in e-mail logs, phone records, information system logs or web search engines.

The amount of data required to describe even small social networks from the log files can be quite large; the analysis of such data collections is often very complicated. This process can be simplified by using mathematical and graphical tools, which makes the study of the graph theory one of the fundamental pillars of discrete mathematics.

6.2.2 Discovering Structure of Networks

SNA methods of the large-scale social networks facilitate the better understanding of the network structure and provide useful information for addressing the main aspects of SNA: the sources and distribution of power. The power of an individual node is an attribute which depends on its relations with other nodes. The social structure then may be seen as the visualization of the appropriate level of power as a result of variations in the patterns of ties among nodes.

Discovering the basic characteristics of the network (graph) consists of various metrics [94, 111], like size and density, all types of centralities (degree, betweenness, closeness, eigenvector), clustering coefficient, path analysis (reachability, reciprocity, transitivity and distance), flow, cohesion and influence, and other useful information obtained by various types of analysis like small-world phenomenon, finding of clustering coefficient, connected components or community structures.

6.2.2.1   Finding Communities in Social Networks

Finding communities is an important aspect in discovering the complex structure of social networks. A community is defined as a group of nodes within the network such that connections between them are more dense than the nodes in other communities (the rest of the network) [85]. Community structure can be defined using modules (classes, groups or clusters etc.) and generally is intended for mapping the network using hierarchies, often complicated. Hierarchical partitioning process then can produce a tree or dendrogram (in social sciences), which can represent the network structure (see Sect. 6.4). Networks with overlapping structures have more complicated structures, but several mining methods were developed to solve this problem yet [34].

In real-world networks natural hierarchical networks can be found in committee networks (typically presented by US House of Representatives), departmental organization of large companies or institutions, etc. With the growing development of information and communication technologies communities are detected in many spheres, for example VoIP networks [18, 31], identification of communities in the web social networks [109] or phone social networking [31]. These communities can be used to study the dynamic processes in the network more effeciently, and to solve some of the web problems such as new generation search engines, content filtering, automatic classification or the automatic realization of ontologies etc.

6.2.2.2   Finding Patterns in Social Networks

Finding patterns is another process used in the data mining to describe the structure of network. Patterns can be defined as structures that make statements only about restricted regions of the space spanned by the variables of the data [49].

These structures might represent Web pages that are all about the same topic or people that socialize together. The discovery of pattern structures in complex networks is an essential and challenging task in many disciplines, including business, social science, engineering, and biology. Therefore researchers have a great interest in this subject and have been approached it differently through data mining methods, social network analysis, etc. This diversity is not limited to the techniques used to implement this task, but it is also applied to its applications.

Data mining techniques are used widely to discover different patterns in data. The authors of [53] provided an overview about the usage of frequent pattern mining techniques for discovering different types of patterns in Web logs. While in [72] the authors applied different clustering algorithm to detect crimes patterns, and some data mining tools were used in [4] to solve the intrusion detection problem.

SNA is a common method for patterns discovery and has been used in various studies. The authors in [63] used some SNA metrics to study the interaction patterns of students in Elearning online communities. Discovering patterns from email datasets is another topic researches are interested in. In [18] the authors described a multi-stage spam filter based on trust and reputation for detecting the spam behavior of the call in Voice over Internet Protocol (VoIP).

6.3   SNA from Log Files

Modern applications like information, enterprise, e-commerce systems as well as monitoring applications, web applications and other systems generate huge amount of data collections. These data collections are sorted in various forms, from text-based data sources like logs (pure text), through HTML, XML and other formats to semi-structured data sources like multimedia sources (images, audio or video files etc.). These collections of data are maintained in databases, data warehouse, or simply in data or log files.

Log file analysis has been enjoying a growing attention in every area of human activities. This domain is very interesting neither for the research area, nor for the software developers in the commercial sphere. There are various disciplines considered to analyzing the data sources for achieving worthy information, often represented as knowledge. Obtained information (or knowledge) is often used for management, maintenance, improvement of the systems being produced these data sources, or for other purposes like discovering of the network structure and the structure of social networks. When the log file records include information about persons who originate the recorded actions (events), it is possible to discover a social network using SNA.

6.3.1   Log File Analysis

Log analysis is a data mining process oriented to the analysis of computer-generated records (also called audit trail records, event logs or transaction logs) [107]. Log analysis is provided for various reasons, for example system security, compliance with audit or regulation of processes, system trouble shooting, social network analysis, etc.

A log file is a simple text file generated by a device, software, application, or a system, and consisted on messages represented by the record of the activities provided. The log typically consists on information of activity, event (or process instance), and mostly also of a timestamp, originator (performer), and other data. The performer can be recorded as a person or a device; it depends on the type of the log file.

Table 6.1 Example of log file recorded by the Moodle elearning system

"Course";"Date and Time";"IP address";"Full Name";"Action";"Information"
"OPF-ZS-08/09-PRA/E006M-E";16.9.2008 16:05:49;"78.45.26.150";1;"forum view forum";"1224
"OPF-ZS-08/09-PRA/E006M-E";16.9.2008 16:05:57;"78.45.26.150";1;"resource view";"13772
"OPF-ZS-08/09-PRA/E006M-E";16.9.2008 16:07:39;"78.45.26.150";1;"resource view";"13773
"OPF-ZS-08/09-PRA/E006M-E";16.9.2008 16:08:07;"78.45.26.150";1;"course view";"Criminal Law"

For example, a typical *web log* is stored by web server software to record the activities of visitors on a web site. This log file has a standardized format and include the following information: IP address of the client accessing the web page, user's name, date and time of request, resource requested, size in bytes of the data returned to the client and URL that referred the client to the resource. However, the logs that store web activities can contain additional information, which depends on the system or application making the records.

The following Table 6.1 shows an example of an event log file from a Learning management system Moodle, which was used in the case study. Student's full names are replaced by numbers to achieve data anonymization. Detailed description is provided in Sect. 6.6.

Wide-spread is analysis of system data collections in the commercial sphere. Business information systems like ERP, CRM, B2B systems, call center applications and others, record the transactions and other information in a systematic way to the files called event logs. These types of information systems and software applications become more complex and are obliged to cooperate with the heterogeneous software and the hardware components. The data mining and analysis is oriented to easier monitoring, management and maintenance of such systems, or to discovering the structure of network.

Exploring information from these log collections is generally integrated to *process mining*, which refers to methods for distilling a structured process description from a set of real executions. Data collections in log files consist of various types of information. Beside typical information like event, type of event, device or time when event was performed, we can find the information of the person who initiated the event (activity). Using this information, social networks can be derived on the basis of similar attributes of persons and, in consequence, we can construct models that explain some aspects of persons' behavior. Aalst et al. [108] define event log as follows: Let A be a set of activities (also referred as tasks) and P as set of performers (resources, persons). $E = A \times P$ is the set of (possible) events (combinations of an activity and performer). $C = E^*$ is the set of possible event sequences (describing the case). $L \in \beta(C)$ is an event log. $\beta(C)$ is the set of all multi/sets over C.

Large, mostly time-dependent data collections, generated from real-world applications, are often used by large groups of originators (devices, users). Moreover, this type of information is recorded often continuously and the storage of such large data collections (in active memory, in databases, on in log files) is time and space consuming. The main problem, which researchers solve within the data collection process and the data preprocessing, is manipulation with the large amount of obtained data from logs and their clear and understandable visualization and interpretation.

This evokes the need of mathematical tools usage and the development of data reduction algorithms specialized to the large-scale network manipulation and visualization. SNA, and extraction of the social networks from the log files, requires the usage of data mining methods, focused on such areas like data clustering or pattern mining. The next section is oriented to significant algorithms, which researchers widely use in SNA for the extraction and analysis of the network structures and their visualization, with relation to graph partitioning and the data reduction aspect.

6.4   Data Mining Methods Related to SNA and Log Mining

The typical definition of data mining is the analysis of (often large) observational data sets to find unsuspected relationships and to summarize the data in novel ways that are both understandable and useful to the data owner [49]. Data mining is commonly a multistage process of extracting previously unanticipated knowledge from large data collections, and applying the results to decision making [5]. Data mining tools detect patterns from the data and infer associations and rules from them. The extracted information may then be applied to prediction or classification models by identifying the relations within the data records or between data collections. Those patterns, in SNA, can be represented as patterns of groups (or communities) in social network structure and can then guide the network visualization and the study of network evolution. This type of information can be valuable in the decision making process and forecast the effects of those decisions. Data mining is a complex process which consists of a number of phases. These basic phases was described by Schuman [93] as: Collection of data, Data preprocessing, Data analysis, Data visualization and Data interpretation.

Network structure analysis and graph partitioning are essential data mining tasks, in this section the most significant methods used to mine log files will be reviewed. Some of these techniques have a time or space complexity of $O\left(m^2\right)$, or higher (where m represents number of objects). Since log analysis involves studying large data sets, cluster analysis techniques can be applied to find the most representative cluster prototypes. Depending on the type and accuracy of analysis, the results can be used for further SNA of original (often large) data collections. In context of SNA, cluster analysis methods can be used for finding the nearest neighbors in community analysis as well.

6.4.1 Clustering Techniques

*Cluster analysis*is the process of separating objects, with the same or similar properties, into groups that are created based on specific issues. These groups of objects are called *clusters* [55]. Clustering is applied in various research areas, like biology (genetic engineering, neural networks), information retrieval (web pages, text documents, terms, search engines), climate (patterns in the atmosphere and ocean), psycholgy and medicine (types of depression, spatial and temporal distribution of disease), business (customer segmentation, viral marketing, product recommendation) and others. In SNA we can think the term cluster as a group of persons with similar attributes (based on their interaction) or with similar behavior.

The process within which the ideal cluster partitioning for sets of objects is searched, and within which there are mutually similar objects, is called *clustering* [54, 82]. The cluster is then formed mutually by a set with similar objects.

In an ideal situation, the clustering procedure should accomplish two goals: correctness and effectiveness [33, 82]. The criteria for correctness follow:

- Methods should remain stable while collections grow or, in other words, distribution into clusters should not drastically change with the addition of new objects,
- Small errors in object descriptions should be carried over as small changes in cluster distributions into clusters,
- A method should not be dependent on its initial object ordering.

Conventional cluster distribution methods [6, 43, 54] can be divided in two main categories:

- Partitional methods – The goal is to employ a partition that best maintains clustering criteria.
- Hierarchical methods – The goal of this methods is to create a cluster hierarchy (tree cluster). The methods are based on matrix similarities in objects.

In real-world social networks the structure is not clear and transparent. One node (object), member of one community, can simultaneously belong to more then one community (group, cluster). The membership depends on the intensity of relations between the members, or – in other words, on the set threshold level. From this point of view we can distinguish other groups of clustering methods:

- Exclusive clustering – methods, which can create the network structure with nonoverlapping clusters
- Non-exclusive clustering – methods, which create the network structure with overlapping clusters; one node can belong to more than one cluster
- Fuzzy clustering – clusters are treated as fuzzy sets; every object has assigned the weight, represented its membership in each cluster of the network. This approach is not suitable for multiclass situations, due to the constraint that the sum of all weights for each object must equal 1.

Sets of clustering algorithms being used and developed today are too large. A similar view can be found in publications such as [43, 54].

Due to the fact that most clustering methods work with mutual similarities between clusters, it is necessary to convey this similarity by using *cluster similarity partitioning coefficient*.

Let us have a twin cluster $c_i, c_j \in \{c_1, c_2, \ldots, c_l\}$, where l is the amount of all calculated clusters. Then, similarity coefficient $sim(c_i, c_j)$ fulfills these conditions:

$$sim(c_i, c_j) \geq 0 \tag{6.1}$$

$$sim(c_i, c_j) = sim(c_j, c_i) \tag{6.2}$$

$$sim(c_i, c_i) = max_{sim}, \tag{6.3}$$

where max_{sim} is the maximum value of similarity coefficient. Similarity between clusters is defined the same as the similarity between two objects.

6.4.1.1   Partitional Clustering

Partitional clustering is the method for division of the set of data objects into non-overlapping subsets [6]. The subsets (groups) are obtained on the basis of measure of similarity between the vertices. The number of clusters is predefined (assigned as k); the goal is to separate the nodes (objects) in k clusters while maximizing/minimizing the cost function based on similarity measure and/or from nodes to centroids. The most popular partitional technique is *k-means clustering*, where the cost function is the total intra-cluster distance, or squared error function

$$\sum_{i=1}^{k} \sum_{x_j \in S_i} \|x_j - c_i\|^2, \tag{6.4}$$

where S_i is the subset of objects of the i-th cluster and c_i is its centroid. Extensions of k-means clustering to graphs have been proposed by many researchers [51, 86].

Similar clustering technique, based on overlapping structures is *fuzzy k-means clustering*. The method is based on the principle, that objects may belong to more than one cluster. This clustering method is widely used in pattern recognition [7]. The associated cost function

$$J_m = \sum_{t=1}^{n} \sum_{j=1}^{k} u_{i,j}^m \|x_i - c_j\|^2, \tag{6.5}$$

where u_{ij} is the membership matrix, which represents the degree of i object's membership with position x_i in cluster j, m is a real number >1 and C_j is the center of cluster j

$$c_j = \frac{\sum_{t=1}^{n} u_{i,j}^m x_i}{\sum_{t=1}^{n} u_{ij}^m} \tag{6.6}$$

The sum of the all object's memberships is equal to 1. The membership $u_{i,j}$ then represent the distance from the object i to the center of the cluster j.

The limitation of partitional clustering is that the number of clusters must be specified before clustering, it can not be derived automatically. This limitation is solved using other methods like neural network clustering, when the results of clustering does not depend on starting conditions. Centers of clusters are found automatically using neuron-like procedure [69].

Other large group of applications represents *Multidimensional Scaling Techniques*, such as singular value decomposition and principal component analysis [43].

Experts agree that singular value decomposition (SVD) is one of the most important instruments used in linear algebra. Additional information relevant to SVD can be found in [32, 45]. The basic theorem can be provided as:

Theorem 6.1. *Any $m \times n$ matrix A, with $m \geq n$, may be factorized as*

$$A = U \Sigma V^T, \tag{6.7}$$

where $U \in R^{m \times m}$ and $V \in R^{n \times n}$ are orthogonal, and $\Sigma \in R^{m \times n}$ is diagonal,

$$\Sigma = diag(\sigma_1, \sigma_2, \ldots, \sigma_n), \tag{6.8}$$

$$\sigma_1 \geq \sigma_2 \geq \cdots \geq \sigma_n \geq 0. \tag{6.9}$$

The columns of U and V are called singular vectors and the diagonal elements σ_i singular values. The SVD appears in various other scientific fields under different names. In statistical and data analysis, the singular vectors are closely related to principal components, and in image processing the SVD goes by the name Karhunen-Loewe expansion. Let us consider the following notation for designating singular values: $\sigma_i(A) =$ the ith largest singular value of A.

SVD serves as a very useful tool when searching for the approximation matrix A using B with a lower rank. Informally, it can be stated that SVD enables us to reduce dimensions within which we solve problems. Another effect of this reduction is the elimination of static. Formally, these ideas may be formulated by the following statement:

Theorem 6.2. *Assume that matrix $A = R^{m \times n}$ has $rank(A) = r > k$. The matrix approximation problem*

$$min_{rank(Z)=k} |A - Z|_2 \tag{6.10}$$

has the solution

$$Z = A_k = U_k \Sigma_k V_k^T, \tag{6.11}$$

where $U_k = (u_1, \ldots u_k)$, $V_k = (v_1, \ldots, v_k)$, and $\Sigma = diag(\sigma_1, \sigma_2, \ldots, \sigma_k)$. The minimum is:

$$|A - A_k|_2 = \sigma_{k+1}(A). \tag{6.12}$$

However, standard decomposition method like SVD do not preserve sparsity. This has led to the development of other methods, CUR and CMD. These methods seek a nonorthogonal basis by sampling the columns an/or rows of the sparse matrix. Traditional versions of these methods are time and memory consuming, as they produce overcomplete bases. In [101] the authors proposed a collection of Colibri methods which deal with these challenges. They developed algorithms for both static and dynamic large-scale graphs with significant space and time savings as compared to traditional CUR and CMD methods.

Another well known clustering method is *Principal component analysis*. This technique is widely used in many applications, for example face recognition or image compression [56]. This clustering method is used for finding patterns in data of high dimension, that enable to express their similarities and dissimilarities. CMD method for pattern mining in the large sparse graphs is presented in [100].

6.4.1.2 Hierarchical Clustering

Hierarchical clustering methods are used in networks, where clusters consist of subclusters. The whole structure is then organized as a tree. The goal of this method is to create a cluster hierarchy (in sociology also called dendrogram). The main principle of the method is based on the definition of a similarity measure between objects (vertices), on which basis is constructed matrix of similarity. The similarity matrix C can be described as follows for the object collection n:

$$C = \begin{pmatrix} sim_{11} & sim_{12} & \cdots & sim_{1n} \\ sim_{21} & sim_{22} & \cdots & sim_{2n} \\ \vdots & \vdots & \ddots & \vdots \\ sim_{n1} & sim_{n2} & \cdots & sim_{nn}, \end{pmatrix} \qquad (6.13)$$

where ith row answers the ith object and jth column answers the jth object.

A hierarchy of partitions for requisite objects is formed by identifying groups of vertices with high similarity. During calculations, a cluster surface is formed.

Hierarchical clustering techniques can be divided in two categories:

- Agglomerative algorithms – clusters are iteratively merged if their similarity is sufficiently high,
- Divisive algorithms – clusters are iteratively split by removing edges connecting vertices with low similarity.

Agglomerative hierarchal clustering methods mainly belong to the sequential agglomerative hierarchical no-overlapping (SAHN) method. It holds true that two clusters formed with this method do not contain the same object [25]. These methods differ in the way in which their similarity matrix is initially calculated (point 4 following Algorithm 1). These methods usually have $O(n^2)$ for memory space complexity and $O(n^3)$ for time complexity, where n is the number of data points. This conversion is derived from Lance-Williams' formula for matrix conversions [25]:

$$prox[t, (p, q)] = \alpha_p \, prox[t, p] + \alpha_q \, prox[t, q] + \beta \, prox[p, q]$$
$$+ \gamma \, |prox[t, p] - prox[t, q]|, \tag{6.14}$$

where $prox[t, (p, q)]$ determines cluster similarity c_t and cluster $c_{(pq)}$ is formed by clusters c_p joined with cluster c_q. Value parameters α_p, α_q, β and γ define various cluster SAHN methods. We list some of these methods in the Table 6.2. Algorithm 1 describe calculations for hierarchal agglomerative clustering. In the following paragraphs N_i is the number of objects in a cluster c_i.

The results of the aforementioned algorithm differ in accordance to the similarity matrix conversion method used. Today, other specialized hierarchical clustering methods exist. Thanks to these new methods, we can reduce time and memory complexity and work with large objects collections more effectively. Some of these new methods include [43]: SLINK, Single-link algorithm based on minimum spanning tree, CLINK, BIRCH, CURE, or others [17].

Algorithm 6.1 Hierarchal agglomerative clustering

---

1. We form an object similarity matrix.
2. When clustering begins, each object represents one cluster. In other words, we have as many clusters as we have objects. Gradually, as each individual cluster is joined, clusters dwindle away until we are left with one cluster.
3. We locate the two most similar clusters p and q and identify this similarity as $prox_s[p, q]$.
4. We reduce the amount of joined clusters p and q. We identify the new cluster as t (replaces row and column q) and recalculates the similarity ($prox_s[t, r]$) of the newly formed cluster t to other clusters r. Further, we identify $prox_t[p, q]$ as the similarity to which p and q clusters have been joined. This similarity is equal to $prox_s[p, q]$ in most methods. Then we delete the row and column corresponding to cluster p from the similarity matrix.
5. We repeat the previous two steps until only one cluster remains.

Table 6.2 SAHN matrix similarity conversion methods

SAHN method	α_p	α_q	β	γ
Single link	$\frac{1}{2}$	$\frac{1}{2}$	0	$-\frac{1}{2}$
Complete link	$\frac{1}{2}$	$\frac{1}{2}$	0	$\frac{1}{2}$
Centroid method	$\frac{N_p}{N_p+N_q}$	$\frac{N_q}{N_p+N_q}$	$\frac{-N_p N_q}{(N_p+N_q)^2}$	0
Ward's method	$\frac{N_p+N_t}{N_p+N_q+N_t}$	$\frac{N_q+N_t}{N_p+N_q+N_t}$	$\frac{-N_t}{N_p+N_q+N_t}$	0
Median method	$\frac{1}{2}$	$\frac{1}{2}$	$-\frac{1}{4}$	0

The *divisive techniques* are based on contradictory procedure. The methods start with the full graph and divide it to smaller parts to find communities [43, 43]. To this group of methods belong spectral methods, described below.

Spectral clustering algorithms cluster a set of data points using the similarity matrix that is derived from the data. It uses the second eigenvector of a graph's Laplacian to define a semi-optimal cut of a weighted undirected graph in which nodes correspond to objects and edges represent the distance (similarity) between the objects. The idea of finding partitions of graphs by using the eigenvectors of their Laplacians can be traced back to 1970s to Fiedler [39], Donath [24]. Fiedler associated the second-smallest eigenvalue of the Laplacian of a graph with its connectivity and suggested partitioning by splitting vertices according to their value in the corresponding eigenvector. Thus, this eigenvalue is called Fiedler value and the corresponding vector is called the Fiedler vector. According to Fiedler, the graphs's Laplacian has the following spectral properties:

- All eigenvalues are non-negative.
- If the graph is divided into g components, there are g zero eigenvalues.
- Eigenvector components act like coordinates to represent nodes in space.
- The Fiedler vector has both positive and negative components, their sum must be zero.
- If the network is connected, but there are two groups of nodes weakly linked to each other, they can be identified from Fiedler vector. Where the positive components are assigned to one group and the negative components are assigned to the other.

Spectral clustering has been studied and applied to solve many problems. In [57] Kannan et al. developed a natural bicriteria measure for assessing the quality of clustering. Cheng et al. [15] showed how to use spectral algorithm studied in [57]. A practical implementation of the clustering algorithm is presented in [14]. In [23] Ding et al. proposed a new graph partition method based on the min–max clustering principle: the similarity between two subgraphs (cut set) is minimized, while the similarity within each subgraph (summation of similarity between all pairs of nodes within a subgraph) is maximized. Shi and Malik [95] treated image segmentation as a graph partitioning problem and proposed a global criterion, the normalized cut, for segmenting this graph. They showed that an efficient computational technique based on a generalized eigenvalue problem can be used to optimize this criterion. A recursive algorithm was used in [20], Dasgupta et al. analyzed the second eigenvector technique of spectral partitioning on the planted partition random graph model, by constructing a recursive algorithm. Spectral clustering was used in [13] for extracting communities from the Enron graph.

This method was generalized by considering different quality functions [41, 88], using more eigenvectors [88, 110], decreasing the global quality to subdivide the communities [88, 114]. The resolution parameter that allows to examine the network's community structure at different mesoscopic scales was included in [2, 87].

There are other data clustering methods, applicable to the social networks, and to general data structures, that we can not discussed due to the space limitation. For

---

Algorithm 6.2 Graph Partitioning Using Fiedler Vector [20]

---
1. Find all connected components in graph.
2. Create Laplacian matrix of component $L = D - P'$. $P' = P - I$, where P is the adjacency matrix with weights, I is unity matrix and D is the diagonal matrix with $d_{ii} = \sum_j p_{ij}$.
3. Find the eigenvector corresponding to the second smallest eigenvalue of L.
4. Divide the component based on the sorted eigenvector.
5. Recurse on the obtained components (back to step 2).

---

example we can mention Modularity based methods [9], like greedy techniques, simulated annealing, extremal optimization and other optimization strategies. The *Centrality-Based algorithms* for community detection, methods based on statistical inference (Bayesian inference, block modeling), and others [84].

6.4.2 Discovering of Network Evolution

Discovering of network evolution with relation to SNA is mostly oriented to the analysis of dynamic communities. Researchers investigate lifetime aspects, related to how communities form, evolve and die, using the concepts like birth, growth, contraction, merger with other communities, split, death, etc. One of the first studies dedicated to network evolution was presented by Hopcroft et al. [52]. The authors analyzed several snapshots of the citation graph induced by the NEC CiteSeer Database using hierarchical clustering method for identification of the natural communities (which were conceptually similar to the stable communities), and which history was followed. Systematic analysis of dynamic communities was realized by Palla et al. [78], where evolution of graph of phone calls and collaboration network was presented. The analysis was oriented to the evolution of overlapping communities (see Sect. 6.4.3). Dynamic relationship between vertices and communities were presented in [3]. The authors distinguished the events involving communities (Continue, k-Merge, k-Split, Form and Dissolve) and events involving vertices (Appear, Disappear, Join and Leave). On the basis of these events, the measures for the definition of community behavior were proposed: stability index, sociability index, populatiry index and influence index.

Dynamic communities can be investigated using methods of information compression [99], or by monitoring the community of a given node (node-centric perspective) at different times [38]. Other works based on evolutionary clustering were proposed in [12, 67, 68].

Change and deviation detection, also called as sequential analysis and sequence discovery [30], is oriented to discovering the most significant changes in data sets or relationships based on time. Resolution parameters related to time scales of dynamical processes unfolded on a network are described in works like [64, 83, 87, 90].

6.4.3   Finding Overlapping Communities

In real-world networks the social structure is not so clear and transparent. One node (object), member of one community, can simultaneously belong to more then one community (group, cluster). The membership depends on the set threshold level, which defines the groups (clusters) of members with appropriate intensity of relations between them.

Overlapping communities are groups of nodes in the network structures with overlapping clusters. One node can belong to more than one cluster. Among the most used techniques for finding overlapping communities we can mention Clique percolation method (PCM) [22, 79]. The communities are created from k-cliques, which can be considered as complete sub-graphs of k nodes. Two cliques are adjacent in the case if they share $k - 1$ nodes. The maximal union of k-cliques which can be reached from each other through a series of adjacent k-cliques defines a community (k-clique template). The k-clique communities of a network are then the sub-graphs that can be explored by moving a k-clique template by relocation one of its nodes and keeping its other $k - 1$ nodes fixed. This definition allows overlaps between the communities.

The extension of the basic concept of PCM to the weighted, directed and bipartite graphs was proposed in [36] and to the sequential clique percolation algorithm [61].

6.5   Application of SNA

With the growing interest of SNA application in many spheres, various mining methods are applied in many domains like software engineering, system management, web analysis, information retrieval and others etc. In this section the authors were concerned only on significant spheres of SNA application with relation to log files' analysis.

6.5.1   Web Mining

Among main fields of web mining research we can include such areas like web searching, and information retrieval from the World Wide Web, scientific collaboration networks and citation networks, web applications and online social networks applications, etc.

Many researchers propose algorithms to define community structure in complex networks using web information, for example [44, 60, 74, 85, 102]. As the internet rapidly grows, these algorithms were redefined for the large-scale networks [17, 109]. These methods were used for the analysis of various types of social groups and weighted networks.

Recently, many researchers focus on the analysis of social communities growing on the web and Internet world. We can observe the occurrence and great expansion of various social bookmarking systems based on recommendation and sharing of various types of information like URLs (del.icio.us), multimedia files - photos, videos etc. (Flickr, YouTube), music, blogs etc. (MySpace, LiveJournal, citation webs). The structure behind these social systems (sometimes called folksonomies) can be represented as a collection of users, tags and resource nodes. These collections of data can be viewed using graphs or visualization software and can be analyzed with orientation to structural properties to show the growth and exploration of social networks.

Pattern match query in large graphs using distance-join operation in Facebook network analysis is presented in [117]. Extension of Principal component analysis to a large-scale social network is presented in [62]. Algorithm was tested using data logs from LiveJournal social network. Another novel approach, the graph clustering algorithm SA-Cluster, based on structural and attribute similarities through a unified distance measure is proposed, for example, in [115]. Authors provided the proposed algorithm on DBLP data collection.

Many works concerned to the extraction of social interactions from the web were proposed. Analysis of topological characteristics of the tripartite hyper graph of queries, users and bookmarks on a large snapshot of del.icio.us web site and on query logs of two large search engines is described in [59].

Data mining of log files available from search engines is another research area. Recommendation of related queries for search engine users using past queries stored in large-scale web access logs and web page archives is presented for example in [66]. Method for weighted social networks construction based on information on the web and search engines such as Google is described in [65]. Modern search engines have integrated social bookmarking services, individual search history information, or statistics of search activities (Google [103], Google Trends [104], Yahoo Buzz [106], Ask IQ [105], and others). This research area is closely linked to recommended system application mentioned below.

6.5.2 Phone Social Networks

With the increasing amount of people using mobile phones the point of research view also turned to this domains. For example the information achievement of social network obtained from call logs is presented in [81]. In this work is proposed an end-to-end system for inferring social networks based on call logs using kernel-based naiive Bayesian learning. The relation between interaction strengths and the networks local structure of mobile communication networks was studied in [77].

Recent development of telephone technologies has provided users the internet connection with the possibility of easy connection to the online social networks. This turn the object of research area to this sphere as well. Similarity management an algorithm for effective finding of friends in a newly joined network using phonebook-centric social networks is described in [31].

Dynamics aspects of mobile phone networks are investigated in [50].

6.5.3   Mail Logs, Server Logs

Social networks can be created by analyzing the history of e-mail traffic recorded by e-mail servers to mail logs as well. The analysis of user's e-mail interactions with relation of social networks has been developed since 10 years. Nardi et al. developed one of the first social network tools called ContactMap [71]. Other examples of similar tools can be Buddy Graph and MetaSight. From mail log analysis can be obtained meaningful business (or organizational) patterns as a valuable issue for further analysis as well as described in many works [37, 40, 71, 76].

Graph theoretical and spectral analysis techniques were, for example, applied to Enron email data set to discover structures within the organisation [13].

In general, the discovered knowledge or any unexpected rules are likely to be imprecise or incomplete, which requires a framework with soft computing techniques like rough sets or fuzzy sets. In [21] is presented a rough approximation-based clustering to cluster web transactions from web access logs.

In [96] Shi use a rough k-means clustering method to group web access patterns. Thus a web access pattern is transformed as a fuzzy web access pattern, which is a fuzzy vector that are composed of n fuzzy linguistic variable or 0. In [96] is proposed a modified k-means clustering algorithm based on properties of rough set to group the gained fuzzy web access patterns.

6.5.4   Business Sphere

Business information systems (ERP, SRM, SCM and others) and software applications become more complex and are obliged to cooperate with heterogeneous software and hardware components. The data mining and analysis is oriented to ease the monitoring, management and maintenance of such systems using data from recorded transactions and other information maintained in event logs.

Exploring information from these log collections is generally integrated to process mining, which refers to methods for distilling a structured process description from a set of real executions, see previous Sect. 6.3 with detailed description.

In [80] is presented automatic mining of system log files regarding to new aspects of log data as data complexity, short log messages and temporal characteristics of log data. There are proposed mining methods specialized to automated categorization of messages in system logs, to incorporated temporal information, and visualization tools to evaluate interesting temporal patterns for system management. The problems of comparison of process models and quantification of process equivalence based on observed behavior using genetic process mining is presented, for example, in [70]. Process mining solves many problems. One of the problems is checking whether the explicit business model (or expected process model) is adequate to process a model extracted from an event log. Conformance checking of an expected process model and behavior extracted from real-life event log is described in [91]. Process mining oriented to aspects of organizational setting and interactions among coworkers is called organizational mining. Organizational mining is focused on understanding and improving organizational and social structures. Human behavior is essential for performance of business processes. Techniques developed for discovering organizational models and SN are described in [97]. Discovering social networks from event logs oriented to business process and process mining is widely described in [108].

6.5.5 Education

With rapid development of new internet and computer-based technologies, web-based education, especially elearning, became very popular in education. This is a form of computer-aided instruction that virtually does not depend on the need for a specific location or any special hardware platform [10].

Elearning is a method of education, that utilizes a wide spectrum of technologies, mainly internet or computer-based, in the learning process. Learning management systems (LMS) – also called course management systems (CMS) or virtual learning environment (VLE) systems – provide effective maintenance of particular courses and facilitate communication between educators and students and within the student community. These systems usually support the distribution of study materials to students; content building of courses, preparation of quizzes and assignments, discussions, distance management of classes. In addition, these systems provide a number of collaborative learning tools such as forums, chats, news, file storage etc [26].

Unlike conventional face-to-face education methods, computer and web-based education environments provide storage of large amounts of accessible information. These systems record all the information about students actions and interactions onto log files or databases. Within these records, data about students learning habits can be found including favored reading materials, note taking styles, tests and quizzes, ways of carrying out various tasks, communicating with other students in virtual classes using chat, forum, and etc. Other common data, such as personal information about students and educators (user profiles), student results and user interaction data, is also available in the systems databases. This collected data is essential for analyzing students behavior and can be very useful in providing feedback both to students and educators. For students, this can be achieved through various recommended systems and through course adaptation based on student learning behavior. For teachers, some benefits would include the ability to evaluate the courses and the learning materials, as well as to detect the typical learning behaviors [28].

Regardless of its benefits, the huge amount of information generated by learning management systems makes it too difficult to manage these data collections and to extract useful information from them. To overcome this problem some LMS offer basic reporting tools, but in such large amounts of information the outputs become quite obscure and unclear. In addition, they do not provide specific information of student activities while evaluating the structure and contents of the course and its effectiveness for the learning process [116].

The application of data mining in elearning is an iterative cycle [89]. This thought is based on the fact that creating an eLearning system entails a complicated and demanding process. The course developer (teacher or instructor) must design a course structure and its components in such a way that ensures the suitability for the course specifications , fulfilling student study requirements and providing communication tools during the lessons. Based on data obtained from LMS, student activities during the term may be monitored. At the end of each term, the study results and the course effectively may be evaluated and any necessary improvements may be made. Data mining results are often applied for adapting courses to user profiles and study assessments.

Area of applying SNA using data mining techniques involves the collaborative learning process, in which students create a community for sharing information about different criteria for completing the courses successfully [19].

Many approaches for data analysis in LMS were published. Most of researchers use data mining techniques oriented to various types of statistics [75,116], grouping methods like clustering [47,98] and classification [48,112] often with combination of visualization tools. Detailed summarization of data mining techniques in elearning is described in [11,89].

In Collaborative Learning the students are engaged in an open-ended effort to advance their collective understanding. They are encouraged to rely on each other as sources of information and assistance. In addition, interactions among the students facilitate learning directly by encouraging them to explain the subject matter to each other and revealing in a constructive way the inconsistencies and limitations in their knowledge. This participation which takes place in a meaningful social context enables a group of the students to acquire the skills of the etutor and play his roles when he/she is not available. However, in some elearning systems it is difficult to achieve efficient and effective knowledge sharing due to the following two barriers: (1) the difficulty in finding quality knowledge, and (2) the difficulty in finding trustworthy learning collaborators to interact with.

An important difference between user-generated content and traditional content is the variance in the quality of the content. In social media the distribution of quality has high variance: from very high-quality items to low-quality; this makes the tasks of filtering and ranking in such systems more complex than in other domains. In that case, models of credibility which are used extensively on search engine research and information retrieval can be used in order to evaluate the trustworthiness of the students' knowledge.

Several graph theoretic models of credibility rely strongly on the consideration of the indegree of the node (the sum of the incoming arcs of a node in a directed graph) so as to extract importance and trustworthiness. However, there are social activities (e.g., collaborative authoring) which derive much of their credibility by their productions (e.g., authorship). In that case, the in-degree cannot provide input to evaluate the importance of that entity and therefore an alternative evaluation is needed, which has to consider the outputs of the entity (productions) [58].

PageRank and HITS were the pioneering approaches that introduced Link Analysis Ranking, in which hyperlink structures are used to determine the relative authority of a Web page. PageRank assumes that a node transfers its PageRank values evenly to all the nodes it connects to. A node has high rank if the sum of the ranks of its in-links is high. This covers both the case where a node has many in-links and that where a node has a few highly ranked in-links. This can be clarified by the following example given in c [8, 113]. If B is able to answer A's questions, and C is able to answer B's questions, then C should receive a high authority score, since he is able to answer the questions of someone who himself has some expertise. PageRank provides interesting results when the interactions between users are around one specific subject only. The study in [113] illustrates this by using a PageRank-like algorithm called ExpertiseRank on data from the Java forum, in which the interactions between users are exclusively about Java programming.

The fundamental assumption of HITS is that in a graph there are special nodes that act as hubs. Hubs contain collections of links to authorities (nodes that contain good information). A good hub is a node that points to good authorities, while a good authority is a node pointed to by good hubs [1]. So, askers can act as hubs and best answerers can act as authorities. HITS associates two scores to each node: a hub score and an authority score.

Detailed description of SNA and usage of other data mining techniques in elearning is described in our previous work Computational intelligence methods for data analysis and mining of eLearning activities [26].

6.6   Case Study: Finding Students' Patterns of Behavior in LMS Moodle

In this case study the authors demonstrate the usage of data mining methods to find and visualize a synthetic social network based on the relationship between the students with the similar patterns of study behavior made through the educational process in an elearning social network. The analyzed data collections are stored in the LMS Moodle logs used to support elearning education at Silesian University, Czech Republic.

6.6.1   Dataset Description

The logs consist of records of all events performed by Moodle's users such as communication in forums and chats, reading study materials or blogs, taking tests or quizzes etc. The users of this system are students, tutors, and administrators, but the study was limited to the events performed only by students. Let us define a set of students $s \in S$, set of courses $c \in C$ and term *Event* as a combination of Event prefix $p \in P$ (e.g., course view, resource view, blog view, quiz attempt) and a course c. An event then represents the action performed by student $s \in S$ in certain course c

in LMS. On the basis of this definition, we have obtained *Set of Events* $e_i \in E$, which are represented by pairs $e_i = (p_j, c_k), j \in \{1, \ldots |P|\}, k \in \{1, \ldots |C|\}$ ordered by TimeStamp.

After that we obtained a set of activities $a_j \in A$. An *Activity* is a sequence of events $a_j = \langle e_1, e_2, \ldots, e_n \rangle$, performed by a certain student s in a certain course c during the optimal time period. In our previous experiments we found, that the 30 min time period is the most effective time interval. The findings showed that in shorter time periods (5 min) students were performing only non-study activities, and in longer periods there was not a significant activity difference (that means activities were very similar). For detailed information, see our previous work [29]. Similar conclusion was presented by Zorrilla et al. in [116].

Two matrices were obtained to represent the data: the Student matrix T ($|S| \times |A|$), where each row $(t_{i1}, t_{i2}, \ldots, t_{i|A|})$ represents a subset of activities executed by a student in the Moodle system, and the Matrix of similarity P ($|S| \times |S|$), which is derived from matrix T, and defines students' relationships using their similar activities. The similarity between two students (vectors) was defined by the Cosine measure [92].

$$p_{i,j} = \frac{\sum_{k=1}^{n} t_{ik} t_{jk}}{\sqrt{\sum_{k=1}^{n} t_{ik}^2} \sqrt{\sum_{k=1}^{n} t_{jk}^2}} \tag{6.15}$$

Matrices T and P were very large and sparse, because of the large number of activities performed by the students. Therefore, the visualization of the latent ties between students with similar behavior was very hard and unfeasible.

Then, spectral clustering was used to cluster the collection into a number of smaller groups. Afterwards, spectral clustering was extended by further analysis of the obtained clusters. For each cluster, a level was set to obtain smaller sets of objects in that cluster. Because the most frequent activities in each cluster describe it precisely, activities which are in all clusters, and activities which are less frequent, were excluded. Then merging the reduced activity sets in each cluster defined a set of typical activities for all objects in the selected group.

6.6.2   Experiment and Results

The main objective of the experiment was to find and visualize the synthetic social network based on the relationship between the students with similar patterns of study behavior made through the LMS Moodle. Moreover, the authors attempted to investigate the relationship between the similarity in students' behavior and their grades. For this purpose was developed a supporting tool, which allows the user (researcher, tutor) to define the input data for further analysis, that meets his needs. The input data definition is based on the data collection filtering using several dimension, setting of parameter time period, setting of similarity level for clustering and setting of suitable threshold for network visualization through graph. In the case of dimensions, the user can select groups of students by Course c, Event Prefix (which represents a set of Events e). For detailed analysis of the student's behavior three courses with the highest student enrollment were selected, see Table 6.3. The activities investigated in this study were resources (downloading or reading resources), taking quizzes, and activities in forums. Other activities, such as course enrollment, were not taken into consideration, because they do not play an important role in improving students' performance.

The following figures illustrate the results of the experiment after the application of spectral clustering to the microeconomics course, where Figs. 6.1–6.3 represents the different clusters obtained for the selected activities: resources, quizzes and forums. Nodes represent students and colors represent the different grades obtained at the end of the evaluation process in the course (yellow is A, green is B, red is C and black is F; in the black/white version the light color shade represents A, the dark color represents F).

Obviously, the graphs show, that the students with grades A and B appears together in most of the clusters of the quiz and the resources with a percentage greater than 60%. These two grades reflect high academic performance. While in the forum, the similarity in grades appeared only in the small components, but in the biggest one the students with both high and low performance behave similarly.

Table 6.3 Number of students and activities in the selected courses

	Resource		Forum		Quiz	
	No. of students	No. of activities	No. of students	No. of activities	No. of students	No. of activities
Microeconomics	215	105	210	690	221	63
Quantitative methods	297	214	256	241	368	65
Corporate Economics	394	303	76	138	254	31

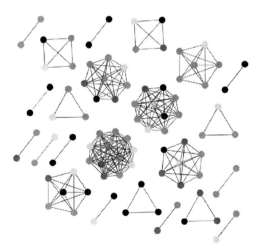

Fig. 6.1 Clusters of the resources activities in the microeconomics course

Fig. 6.2 Clusters of the
quizzes activities in the
microeconomics course

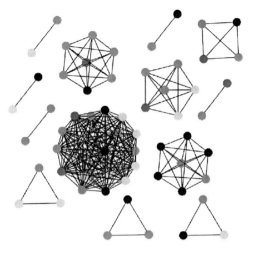

Fig. 6.3 Clusters of the
forums activities in the
microeconomics course

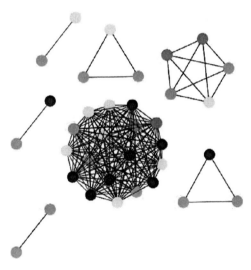

The same procedure was applied to the other courses. The findings showed, that students with the low academic performance appear in most of the clusters, but we can find clusters with the high academic performance as well. Table 6.4 shows the distribution of the grades in the three biggest clusters of the course Corporate Economics, using resources. Regardless of who predominates the clusters, the results of this experiment showed, that the similarity in students behavior led to more than 60% similarity in their academic performance, and in some clusters 80–100% similarty was acheived.

Interaction between students and their peers was suggested by many authors as one of the factors that have an influence on their academic behavior [16]. A test was applied to study the relationship between students position in the network and their

Table 6.4 Grades distribution in three biggest clusters of the course corporate economics, resources

	Grade A	Grade B	Grade C	Grade D
Cluster 1	20%	0%	40%	40%
Cluster 2	0%	25%	50%	25%
Cluster 3	14%	14%	64%	8%

Fig. 6.4 Students degree centrality in the forums of microeconomics

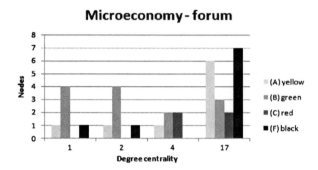

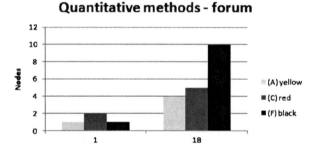

Fig. 6.5 Students degree centrality in the forums of quantitative methods

academic performance. Figures 6.4–6.6 displays students degree centrality in the forums of the three courses, the forums were selected because they are the activities that allows the highest level of interaction between students.

In Fig. 6.4 both students with high academic performance and students with educational difficulties are at the center of the network. both groups participates actively in the course forum, but their grades showed an apparent difference in their performance. However, the students in the other two courses behaved differently. The students with grades C and D were at the center of the graph, they are very active, but maybe they discuss the issues, that are less important to their academic progress. This is one of the limitations of the data extracted from the log files, log files record only request transactions, which depends on the type of the log. The log files used for our experiment did not consist of the content of the topics discussed in the forum. The findings supports the results obtained from the spectral clustering of the forum activities.

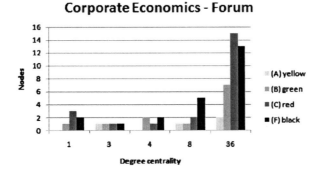

Fig. 6.6 Students degree centrality in the forums of corporate economics

Table 6.5 Number of students with best centrality

	Degree		Closeness		Betweenness	
	A and B	C and D	A and B	C and D	A and B	C and D
Microeconomics	9	9	22	13	21	13
Quantitative methods	4	15	5	18	5	18
Corporate Economics	9	28	16	45	16	45

Unlike degree centrality, closeness centrality measures the number of indirect contacts between students, students with the best centrality are close to many peers. This position could play an important role in improving student's performance, they would have many alternative paths to exchange knowledge with their peers. The findings obtained from the closeness centrality test are presented in the Table 6.5. The students with grades A and B scored the best centrality in the first course, while the students with grades C and D where at the center of the network in the the two other courses.

Betweenness centrality measures the control, that an individual has over the interaction of others, who are not directly connected; again the results obtained from this test showed different effects of students betweenness with relation to their final grades.

6.7   Conclusions

Modern applications and systems continuously record their activities and other types of information in various ways, in databases, data warehouse, or simply in the data log files. This type of information is valuable for further processing using log analysis methods. The obtained information can be used to ease the monitoring, management and maintenance of such systems, or to discover the structure of network generated from the log files. Since record attributes contain information about the person who initiated the monitored activity (event), we can derive social networks based on similar attributes of such persons, and in consequence, we can construct models to explain some aspects of person's behavior. This book chapter is oriented to the analysis of social networks extracted from log files. The authors focused on the significant data mining methods used for SNA through log analysis, various examples of recent research with application in the most significant spheres were presented.

In the last part of the chapter a case study is presented to describe the application of process mining and spectral clustering method for the extraction of the synthetic social network, based on the similar behavioral patterns of groups of students enrolled in an elearning system. For easier visualization of the obtained social network was used graph representation, which described the students' behavioral patterns in elearning system. The suitable visualization required the setting of number of input variables for the selected methods (sequential pattern mining, spectral clustering) like setting of the dimensions (selection of the appropriate course or the students' activities in the course provided in elearning system), similarity measure and threshold for graph visualization. For these purposes was developed specialized software, which enabled input setting more comfortable.

Moreover, the authors attempted to find the relationship between the behavioral study patterns and the students' academic performance in the selected courses. The findings of the experiment showed that similarity in students' behavior led to at least 60% similarity in their final grades. Additionally, the effect of students position in the network on their academic performance was explored. The results obtained from measuring students degree, closeness and betweenness centrality failed to support the notion that student's interaction with his peers could improve his performance. During the implementation of this study we encountered a number of limitations. The first limitation was the small size and homogeneity of the dataset, the second was that all events were given the same importance, better clustering results could be demonstrated if different weights were assigned to the events according to their significance to the academic performance of students.

Nevertheless, developed software can be successfully used as a supporting tool for the tutors managing groups of the students in elearning systems, to discover the significant behavioral patterns of their students. This type of information can be very useful, especially while managing the large groups of students. In the large elearning systems, where are widely used methods of collaborative learning, the tool can be used for finding tutors and as a supporting module of recommended systems. In our future work, we intend to apply a thorough analysis on larger data collections to explore significant patterns of student's behavior more accurately, and to find other factors that might affect students' grades. Moreover, we attempt to test our tool in other spheres like web mining and business process mining.

Acknowledgements The authors acknowledge the support of the following projects: SP/ 2010196 – Machine Intelligence and SGS/24/2010 – The Usage of BI and BPM Systems to Efficiency Management Support.

References

1. Cláudia M. Antunes and Arlindo L. Oliveira. *Grammatical Inference: Algorithms and Applications*, volume 2484, chapter Inference of Sequential Association Rules Guided by Context-Free Grammars, pages 289–293. Springer, Berlin, 2002
2. Alex Arenas, Alberto Fernandez, and Sergio Gomez. Analysis of the structure of complex networks at different resolution levels. *New J. Phys.*, 10, 2008
3. Sitaram Asur, Srinivasan Parthasarathy, and Duygu Ucar. An event-based framework for characterizing the evolutionary behavior of interaction graphs. In *KDD '07: Proceedings of the 13th ACM SIGKDD international conference on Knowledge discovery and data mining*, pages 913–921, NY, 2007. ACM
4. Daniel Barbar, Julia Couto, Sushil Jajodia, Leonard Popyack, and Ningning Wu. Adam: Detecting intrusions by data mining. In *In Proceedings of the IEEE Workshop on Information Assurance and Security*, pages 11–16, 2001
5. G. Benoît. Data mining. *Annual Review of Information Science and Technology*, 36:265–310, 2002
6. P. Berkhin. A survey of clustering data mining techniques. In *Grouping Multidimensional Data*, pages 25–71. Springer, Berlin, 2006
7. James C. Bezdek. *Pattern Recognition with Fuzzy Objective Function Algorithms*. Kluwer, MA, 1981
8. Mohamed Bouguessa, Benoît Dumoulin, and Shengrui Wang. Identifying authoritative actors in question-answering forums: the case of yahoo! answers. In *KDD '08: Proceeding of the 14th ACM SIGKDD International Conference on Knowledge Discovery and Data Mining*, pages 866–874, NY, 2008. ACM
9. Ulrik Brandes, Daniel Delling, Marco Gaertler, Robert G?rke, Martin Hoefer, Zoran Nikoloski, and Dorothea Wagner. On modularity clustering. *IEEE Transactions on Knowledge and Data Engineering*, 20:172–188, 2008
10. Peter Brusilovsky and Christoph Peylo. Adaptive and intelligent web-based educational systems. *Int. J. Artif. Intell. Ed.*, 13(2–4):159–172, 2003
11. F. Castro, A. Vellido, A. Nebot, and F. Mugica. Applying data mining techniques to e-learning problems. *Studies in Computational Intelligence (SCI)*, 62:183–221, 2007
12. Deepayan Chakrabarti, Ravi Kumar, and Andrew Tomkins. Evolutionary clustering. In *KDD '06: Proceedings of the 12th ACM SIGKDD international conference on Knowledge discovery and data mining*, pages 554–560, NY, 2006. ACM
13. Anurat Chapanond, Mukkai S. Krishnamoorthy, and Bülent Yener. Graph theoretic and spectral analysis of enron email data. *Comput. Math. Organ. Theory*, 11(3):265–281, 2005
14. David Cheng, Ravi Kannan, Santosh Vempala, and Grant Wang. On a recursive spectral algorithm for clustering from pairwise similarities. Technical report, MIT, 2003
15. David Cheng, Ravi Kannan, Santosh Vempala, and Grant Wang. A divide-and-merge methodology for clustering. *ACM Trans. Database Syst.*, 31(4):1499–1525, 2006
16. Hichang Cho, Geri Gay, Barry Davidson, and Anthony Ingraffea. Social networks, communication styles, and learning performance in a cscl community. *Computers & Education*, 49(2):309–329, 2007
17. Aaron Clauset, M. E. J. Newman, and Cristopher Moore. Finding community structure in very large networks. *Phys. Rev. E*, 70(6):066111, 2004
18. Ram Dantu and Prakash Kolan. Detecting spam in voip networks. In *SRUTI '05: Proceedings of the Steps to Reducing Unwanted Traffic on the Internet on Steps to Reducing Unwanted Traffic on the Internet Workshop*, page 5, Berkeley, CA, USA, 2005. USENIX Association
19. Thanasis Daradoumis, Alejandra Martinez-Mones, and Fatos Xhafa. A layered framework for evaluating on-line collaborative learning interactions. *International Journal of Human-Computer Studies*, 64(7):622–635, 2006
20. Anirban Dasgupta, John Hopcroft, Ravi Kannan, and Pradipta Mitra. Spectral clustering by recursive partitioning. In *ESA'06: Proceedings of the 14th conference on Annual European Symposium*, pages 256–267. Springer, Berlin, 2006

21. Supriya Kumar De and P. Radha Krishna. Clustering web transactions using rough approximation. *Fuzzy Sets and Systems*, 148(1):131–138, 2004
22. Imre Derényi, Gergely Palla, and Tamás Vicsek. Clique percolation in random networks. *Physical Review Letters*, 94(16), 2005
23. Chris H. Q. Ding, Xiaofeng He, Hongyuan Zha, Ming Gu, and Horst D. Simon. A min-max cut algorithm for graph partitioning and data clustering. In *ICDM '01: Proceedings of the 2001 IEEE International Conference on Data Mining*, pages 107–114, Washington, DC, USA, 2001. IEEE Computer Society
24. W. E. Donath and A. J. Hoffman. Lower bounds for the partitioning of graphs. *IBM J. Res. Dev.*, 17(5):420–425, 1973
25. G. M. Downs and J. M. Barnard. *Reviews in Computational Chemistry*. Wiley, NY, 2003
26. Pavla Dráždilová, Gamila Obadi, Kateřina Slaninová, Shawki Al-Dubaee, Jan Martinovič, and Václav Snášel. Computational intelligence methods for data analysis and mining of eLearning activities. In Xhafa, F., Caballe, S., Abraham, A., Daradoumis, T., Juan Perez, A. A., editors, *Computational Intelligence For Technology Enhanced Learning*, pages 195–224. Springer-Verlag, Heidelberg, 2010
27. Pavla Dráždilová, Gamila Obadi, Kateřina Slaninová, Jan Martinovič, and Václav Snášel. Analysis and visualization of relations in elearning. In *Computational Social Network Analysis*. Springer, London, 2010
28. Pavla Dráždilová, Kateřina Slaninová, Jan Martinovič, Gamila Obadi, and Václav Snášel. Creation of students' activities from learning management system and their analysis. In *CASoN*, pages 155–160, 2009
29. Pavla Drázdilová, Katerina Slaninová, Jan Martinovic, Gamila Obadi, and Václav Snásel. Creation of students' activities from learning management system and their analysis. In *CASoN*, pages 155–160, 2009
30. Margaret H. Dunham. *Data Mining: Introductory and Advanced Topics*. Prentice Hall, NJ, 2003
31. Peter Ekler, Zoltan Ivanfi, and Kristof Aczel. Similarity management in phonebook-centric social networks. In *ICIW '09: Proceedings of the 2009 Fourth International Conference on Internet and Web Applications and Services*, pages 273–279, Washington, DC, 2009. IEEE Computer Society
32. Lars Eldén. *Matrix Methods in Data Mining and Pattern Recognition*. Society for Industrial and Applied Mathematics, Philadelphia, PA, 2007
33. C. Faloutsos. Searching multimedia databases by content. *IEEE Data Eng. Bull.*, 4(18):31–40, 1995
34. Li Ma Fang Wei, Chen Wang and Aoying Zhou. Detecting overlapping community structures in networks with global partition and local expansion. In *Progress in WWW Research and Development*, pages 43–55. Springer, Berlin, 2008
35. K Fansler and R Riegle. A model of online instructional design analytics. In *Proceedings of the 20th Annual Conference on Distance Teaching and Learning*, 2005
36. Illés Farkas, Dániel Ábel, Gergely Palla, and Tamás Vicsek. Weighted network modules. *New Journal of Physics*, 9(6):180, 2007
37. Shelly Farnham, Sean Uberoi Kelly, Will Portnoy, and Jordan L. K. Schwartz. Wallop: Designing social software for co-located social networks. In *HICSS '04: Proceedings of the Proceedings of the 37th Annual Hawaii International Conference on System Sciences (HICSS'04) – Track 4*, page 40107.1, Washington, DC, USA, 2004. IEEE Computer Society
38. Daniel J. Fenn, Mason A. Porter, Mark McDonald, Stacy Williams, Neil F. Johnson, and Nick S. Jones. Dynamic communities in multichannel data: An application to the foreign exchange market during the 2007-2008 credit crisis. *Chaos*, 19, 2009
39. M. Fiedler. Algebraic connectivity of graphs. *Czechoslovak Mathematical Journal*, 23:298–305, 1973
40. Danyel Fisher and Paul Dourish. Social and temporal structures in everyday collaboration. In *CHI '04: Proceedings of the SIGCHI conference on Human factors in computing systems*, pages 551–558, NY, 2004. ACM

41. S. Fortunato. Community detection in graphs. arXiv:0906.0612, 2009
42. L. C. Freeman. *The Development of Social Network Analysis: A Study in the Sociology of Science*. Empirical Press, 2004
43. G. Gan, C. Ma, and J. Wu. Data clustering: Theory, algorithms, and applications. *ASA-SIAM Series on Statistics and Applied Probability*, 20:480, 2007
44. D. Gibson, J. Kleinberg, and P. Raghavan. Inferring web communities from link topology. In *HYPERTEXT '98: Proceedings of the Ninth ACM Conference on Hypertext and Hypermedia: Links, Objects, Time and Space-Structure in Hypermedia Systems*, pages 255–234, 1998
45. Gene H. Golub and Charles F. Van Loan. *Matrix computations (3rd ed.)*. Johns Hopkins University Press, MD, 1996
46. Karl Groves. The limitations of server log files for usability analysis. http://www.boxesandarrows.com/view/the-limitations-of, 2007
47. W. Hämäläinen, T. H. Laine, and E. Sutinen. Data mining in personalizing distance education courses. In *World Conference on Open Learning and Distance Education*, pages 1–11, Hong Kong, 2004
48. W. Hämäläinen and M. Vinni. Comparison of machine learning methods for intelligent tutoring systems. In *Proceedings of the Eighth International Conference in Intelligent Tutoring Systems*, pages 525–534, 2006
49. David J. Hand, Padhraic Smyth, and Heikki Mannila. *Principles of Data Mining*. MIT, MA, 2001
50. Cesar A. Hidalgo and C. Rodriguez-Sickert. The dynamics of a mobile phone network. *Physica A: Statistical Mechanics and its Applications*, 387(12):3017–3024, 2008
51. Adel Hlaoui and Shengrui Wang. A direct approach to graph clustering. In *Neural Networks and Computational Intelligence*, pages 158–163, 2004
52. John Hopcroft, Omar Khan, Brian Kulis, and Bart Selman. Natural communities in large linked networks. In *KDD '03: Proceedings of the ninth ACM SIGKDD international conference on Knowledge discovery and data mining*, pages 541–546, NY, 2003. ACM
53. Renta Ivncsy and Istvn Vajk. Frequent pattern mining in web log data. *Acta Polytechnica Hungarica, Journal of Applied Science at Budapest Tech Hungary, Special Issue on Computational Intelligence*, 3(1):77–90, 2006
54. A. K. Jain, M. N. Murty, and P. J. Flynn. Data clustering: a review. *ACM Comput. Surv.*, 31(3):264–323, 1999
55. Anil K. Jain and Richard C. Dubes. *Algorithms for Clustering Data*. Prentice-Hall, NJ, 1988
56. I.T. Jolliffe. Principal component analysis. In *Springer Series in Statistics*, page 487. Springerlink, NY, 2002
57. Ravi Kannan, Santosh Vempala, and Adrian Vetta. On clusterings: Good, bad and spectral. *J. ACM*, 51(3):497–515, 2004
58. N. Korfiatis, M. Poulos, and G. Bokos. Evaluating authoritative sources using social networks: An insight from wikipedia. *Online Information Review*, 30(3):252–262, 2006
59. Beate Krause, Robert Jäschke, Andreas Hotho, and Gerd Stumme. Logsonomy - social information retrieval with logdata. In *HT '08: Proceedings of the nineteenth ACM conference on Hypertext and hypermedia*, pages 157–166, NY, 2008. ACM
60. R. Kumar, P. Raghavan, S. Rajagopalan, and A. Tomkins. Trawling the web for emerging cyber-communities. In *WWW '99: Proceedings of the Eighth International Conference on World Wide Web*, pages 1481–1493, 1999
61. Jussi M. Kumpula, Mikko Kivelä, Kimmo Kaski, and Jari Saramäki. Sequential algorithm for fast clique percolation. *Phys. Rev. E*, 78(2):026109, 2008
62. Mikls Kurucz, Andrs A. Benczr, and Attila Pereszlnyi. Large-scale principal component analysis on livejournal friends network. In *2nd SNA-KDD Workshop '08 (SNA-KDD'08)*, 2008
63. Laghos and Zaphiris. Sociology of student-centred e-learning communities: A network analysis. In *IADIS international conference*, Dublin, Ireland, July 2006. e-Society
64. R. Lambiotte, J. C. Delvenne, and M. Barahona. Dynamics and modular structure in networks. arXiv:0812.1770, 2008
65. Sang Hoon Lee, Pan-Jun Kim, Yong-Yeol Ahn, and Hawoong Jeong. Googling hidden interactions: Web search engine based weighted network construction, 2007

66. Lin Li, Shingo Otsuka, and Masaru Kitsuregawa. Query recommendation using large-scale web access logs and web page archive. In *DEXA '08: Proceedings of the 19th international conference on Database and Expert Systems Applications*, pages 134–141, Berlin, 2008. Springer

67. Yu-Ru Lin, Yun Chi, Shenghuo Zhu, Hari Sundaram, and Belle L. Tseng. Facetnet: a framework for analyzing communities and their evolutions in dynamic networks. In *WWW '08: Proceeding of the 17th international conference on World Wide Web*, pages 685–694, NY, 2008. ACM

68. Yu-Ru Lin, Yun Chi, Shenghuo Zhu, Hari Sundaram, and Belle L. Tseng. Analyzing communities and their evolutions in dynamic social networks. *ACM Trans. Knowl. Discov. Data*, 3(2):1–31, 2009

69. Leonid B. Litinskii and Dmitry E. Romanov. Neural network clustering based on distances between objects. In *Artificial Neural Networks ICANN 2006*, pages 437–443. Springer, Berlin, 2006

70. Ana Karla Alves De Medeiros, W.M.P. van der Aalst, and A J M M Weijters. Quantifying process equivalence based on observed behavior. *Data Knowledge Engineering*, 64:55–74, 2008

71. Bonnie A. Nardi, Steve Whittaker, Ellen Isaacs, Mike Creech, Jeff Johnson, and John Hainsworth. Integrating communication and information through contactmap. *Commun. ACM*, 45(4):89–95, 2002

72. Shyam Varan Nath. Crime pattern detection using data mining. In *WI-IATW '06: Proceedings of the 2006 IEEE/WIC/ACM International Conference on Web Intelligence and Intelligent Agent Technology*, pages 41–44, Washington, DC, 2006. IEEE Computer Society

73. M. E. J. Newman. The structure and function of complex networks. *SIAM Review*, 45:167–256, 2003

74. M. E. J. Newman and M. Girwan. Finding and evaluating community structure in networks. *Physical Review E*, 69(2):026113, 2004

75. Karthik Nilakant and Antonija Mitrovic. Applications of data mining in constraint-based intelligent tutoring systems. In *Proceeding of the 2005 conference on Artificial Intelligence in Education*, pages 896–898, Amsterdam, 2005. IOS Press

76. H. Ogata, Y. Yano, N. Furugori, and Q. Jin. Computer supported social networking for augmenting cooperation. *Comput. Supported Coop. Work*, 10(2):189–209, 2001

77. J. P. Onnela, J. Saramäki, J. Hyvönen, G. Szabó, D. Lazer, K. Kaski, J. Kertész, and A. L. Barabási. Structure and tie strengths in mobile communication networks. *Proceedings of the National Academy of Sciences*, 104(18):7332–7336, 2006

78. Gergely Palla, Albert-László Barabási, and Tamás Vicsek. Quantifying social group evolution. *Nature*, 446:664–667, 2007

79. Gergely Palla, Imre Derényi, Illés Farkas, and Tamás Vicsek. Uncovering the overlapping community structure of complex networks in nature and society. *Nature*, 435:814–818, 2005

80. Wei Peng, Tao Li, and Sheng Ma. Mining log files for data-driven system management. *SIGKDD Explor. Newsl.*, 7(1):44–51, 2005

81. Santi Phithakkitnukoon and Ram Dantu. Inferring social groups using call logs. In *OTM Workshops*, pages 200–210, 2008

82. J. Pokorný, V. Snášel, and M. Kopecký. *Dokumentografické informační systémy*. Karolinum, 2005

83. Pascal Pons and Matthieu Latapy. Computing communities in large networks using random walks. In pInar Yolum, Tunga Güngör, Fikret Gürgen, and Can Özturan, editors, *Computer and Information Sciences - ISCIS 2005*, volume 3733, chapter 31, pages 284–293. Springer, Berlin, 2005

84. Mason A. Porter, Jukka-Pekka Onnela, and Peter J. Mucha. Communities in networks. *Notices of the American Mathematical Society*, 56:1082–1097, 2009

85. Filippo Radicchi, Claudio Castellano, Federico Cecconi, Vittorio Loreto, and Domenico Parisi. Defining and identifying communities in networks, Feb 2004

86. Matthew J. Rattigan, Marc Maier, and David Jensen. Graph clustering with network structure indices. In *ICML '07: Proceedings of the 24th international conference on Machine learning*, pages 783–790, NY, 2007. ACM
87. Joerg Reichardt and Stefan Bornholdt. Statistical mechanics of community detection, Mar 2006
88. Thomas Richardson, Peter J. Mucha, and Mason A. Porter. Spectral tripartitioning of networks. *Physical Review E*, 80(3):036111–036121, 2009
89. C. Romero and S. Ventura. Educational data mining: A survey from 1995 - 2005. *Expert Systems with Applications*, 33:135–146, 2007
90. Martin Rosvall and Carl T. Bergstrom. Maps of random walks on complex networks reveal community structure. *Proceedings of the National Academy of Sciences*, 105(4):1118–1123, 2008
91. A. Rozinat and W. M. P. van der Aalst. Conformance checking of processes based on monitoring real behavior. *Inf. Syst.*, 33(1):64–95, 2008
92. Gerard Salton and Christopher Buckley. Term-weighting approaches in automatic text retrieval. *Information Processing and Management*, 24(5):513–523, 1988
93. Christoph Schommer. An unified definition of data mining, 2008. http://arxiv.org/PS_cache/arxiv/pdf/0809/0809.2696v1.pdf
94. J. Scott. *Social Network Analysis*. Sage, Newbury Park CA, 1992
95. Jianbo Shi and Jitendra Malik. Normalized cuts and image segmentation. *IEEE Transactions on Pattern Analysis and Machine Intelligence*, 22:888–905, 1997
96. Peilin Shi. Clustering fuzzy web transactions with rough k-means. *Advanced Science and Technology, International e-Conference on*, 0:48–51, 2009
97. Minseok Song and Wil M. P. van der Aalst. Towards comprehensive support for organizational mining. *Decis. Support Syst.*, 46(1):300–317, 2008
98. J. Spacco, T. Winters, and T. Payne. Inferring use cases from unit testing. In *AAAI Workshop on Educational Data Mining*, pages 1–7, New York, 2006
99. Jimeng Sun, Christos Faloutsos, Spiros Papadimitriou, and Philip S. Yu. Graphscope: Parameter-free mining of large time-evolving graphs. In *KDD '07: Proceedings of the 13th ACM SIGKDD international conference on Knowledge discovery and data mining*, pages 687–696, NY, 2007. ACM
100. Jimeng Sun, Yinglian Xie, Hui Zhang, and Christos Faloutsos. Less is more: Sparse graph mining with compact matrix decomposition. *Stat. Anal. Data Min.*, 1(1):6–22, 2008
101. Hanghang Tong, Spiros Papadimitriou, Jimeng Sun, Philip S. Yu, and Christos Faloutsos. Colibri: Fast mining of large static and dynamic graphs. In *KDD '08*, Las Vegas, 2008
102. M. Toyoda and M. Kitsuregawa. Cerating a web community chart for navigating related communities. In *HYPERTEXT '01: Proceedings of the Twelfth ACM Conference on Hypertext and Hypermedia*, pages 103–112, 2001
103. URL. http://www.google.com, 12. April 2009
104. URL. http://www.google.com/trends, 12. April 2009
105. URL. http://sp.ask.com/en/docs/iq/iq.shtml, 12. April 2009
106. URL. http://buzz.yahoo.com/, 2010
107. W. M. P. van der Aalst, B. F. van Dongen, J. Herbst, L. Maruster, G. Schimm, and A. J. M. M. Weijters. Workflow mining: a survey of issues and approaches. *Data Knowl. Eng.*, 47(2):237–267, 2003
108. Wil M. P. Van Der Aalst, Hajo A. Reijers, and Minseok Song. Discovering social networks from event logs. *Comput. Supported Coop. Work*, 14(6):549–593, 2005
109. Ken Wakita and Toshiyuki Tsurumi. Finding community structure in mega-scale social networks. In *Proceedings of the 18th International Conference on World Wide Web WWW 09*, page 1275. ACM Press, 2007
110. Gaoxia Wang, Yi Shen, and Ming Ouyang. A vector partitioning approach to detecting community structure in complex networks. *Comput. Math. Appl.*, 55(12):2746–2752, 2008
111. S. Wasserman and K. Faust. *Social Network Analysis*. Cambridge University Press, Cambridge, 1994

112. Michael V. Yudelson, Olga Medvedeva, Elizabeth Legowski, Melissa Castine, Drazen Jukic, and Rebecca S. Crowley. Mining student learning data to develop high level pedagogic strategy in a medical its. In *Proceedings of AAAI Workshop on Educational Data Mining*, pages 1–8, Boston, 2006

113. Jun Zhang, Mark S. Ackerman, and Lada Adamic. Expertise networks in online communities: Structure and algorithms. In *WWW '07: Proceedings of the 16th International Conference on World Wide Web*, pages 221–230, NY, 2007. ACM

114. Y. Zhang, A. Friend, A. Traud, M. Porter, J. Fowler, and P. Mucha. Community structure in congressional cosponsorship networks. *Physica A: Statistical Mechanics and its Applications*, 387:1705–1712, 2008

115. Yang Zhou, Hong Cheng, and Jeffrey Xu Yu. Graph clustering based on structural/attribute similarities. *Proc. VLDB Endow.*, 2(1):718–729, 2009

116. M.E. Zorrilla, E. Menasalvas, D. Marn, E. Mora, and J. Segovia. Web usage mining project for improving web-based learning sites. In *Computer Aided Systems Theory EUROCAST 2005*, volume 3643/2005 of *Lecture Notes in Computer Science*, chapter Web Usage Mining Project for Improving Web-Based Learning Sites. Springer, Berlin, 2005

117. Lei Zou, Lei Chen, and M. Tamer Özsu. Distance-join: pattern match query in a large graph database. *Proc. VLDB Endow.*, 2(1):886–897, 2009

Chapter 7
Perspectives on Social Network Analysis for Observational Scientific Data

Lisa Singh, Elisa Jayne Bienenstock, and Janet Mann

7.1 Introduction

Social network analysis (SNA) is an empirical methodology for formally describing the structure of relationships between observed entities. Historically, the use of social network metrics to identify and distinguish socially relevant information about group structure and the relationships among group members was validated by empirical work on small closed systems. The metrics supported the intuition of researchers who had a deep knowledge of the social context of individuals in a particular social setting. When used for purely descriptive purposes on data sets with explicit boundary conditions [42], the metrics proved to be robust and beneficial. In the last decade, with an increase in popularity and the exponential growth in computational power, the uses of SNA have extended beyond description, and include making inferences about context from network structure. While this is an exciting direction for SNA, a number of questions arise – an important one being: how do we determine when these inferences are reasonable? Even though in some situations reasonable inferences should be possible, many data sets that apply SNA for inferences are incomplete, biased and contain high degrees of uncertainty.

In this chapter, we provide examples of the many types of incompleteness, bias and uncertainty that impact the quality of social network data. Our approach is to leverage the insights and experience of observational behavioral scientists familiar with the challenges of making inference when data are not complete, and suggest avenues for extending these to relational data questions. Rather than discuss data collection challenges generally, this paper is focused on one example, a 25 year longitudinal study of wild dolphins, which includes numerous examples of incompleteness, uncertainty and bias, but which also provides ample data to develop and test techniques for compensating for these problems and improving the quality of inferences drawn about network structure. While our longterm goal is to develop computational approaches to compensate for different data quality issues that arise,

L. Singh (✉)
Georgetown University, Washington, DC 20057, USA
e-mail: singh@cs.georgetown.edu

B. Furht (ed.), *Handbook of Social Network Technologies and Applications*,
DOI 10.1007/978-1-4419-7142-5_7, © Springer Science+Business Media, LLC 2010

this chapter is a conceptual look at data quality issues that arise during scientific observations and their impact on social network analysis. The focus of our discussion is on observational scientific networks; however, the problems identified here exist in many other domains including online social networks, cell phone networks, covert networks, and disease transmission networks.

This chapter is organized as follows. In the next section, we introduce definitions and background describing the missing data problems. In Sects. 7.3–7.5, we provide examples of each of these problems in the context of a large bottlenose dolphin data set and present recommendations for improving data quality for SNA. Section 7.6 briefly describes some open areas of research for computer scientists. Conclusions are presented in Sect. 7.7.

7.2   Definitions and Background

There is a misconception that SNA is a statistical method [24]. Descriptive statistics and SNA are similar as they provide metrics to characterize patterns in observed data. They differ with regard to their ability to generalize and provide inference beyond the sample measured. Inferential statistics allows researchers to generalize beyond the data observed provided the data meet certain criteria. One principle assumption is that observations are independent, an assumption at odds with the purpose of social network analysis, which is to capture the dependencies between observations. As a result, direct application of classical statistics may lead to incorrect inferences. While approaches for building statistical models for interrelated entities do exist [43], a consensus approach that adequately considers the interrelated population or addresses inference has yet to emerge. A second assumption is that the data sampled represent the population. Statistical solutions address random error, not systematic bias. There is no recognized methodology used to identify or correct for sampling choices that result in samples with bias, which is often the case with social network data. Therefore, it is important to understand how robust SNA metrics are to different types of data incompleteness, uncertainty, and bias for both descriptive and predictive models.

Observational scientists, particularly those that collect field data are familiar with a range of methodological issues concerning imperfect data. While field data are considered to have high ecological or external validity compared to experimental approaches, the degree of external validity can be undermined by sampling or data collection bias. Observational scientists are limited, as observations cannot be universal or persistent. Researchers must make choices about how to sample their subjects efficiently and sufficiently to learn about their behaviors. There are fundamental sources of limitations that must be addressed. While other data quality factors exist, this paper focuses on three: completeness, certainty, and bias.

Our discussion applies to different types of social networks, e.g., one-mode, two-mode, multi-relation, etc. For ease of exposition, we focus on one-mode networks, where the graph $G = (V, E)$. Formally, our network G contains a set of vertices

$V = \{v_1, v_2, ... v_n\}$, where n is the number of vertices in the network, and a set of edges between vertices in V: $E = \{e_{ij} = (v_i, v_j) : v_i \text{ and } v_j \in V\}$. Each vertex may be associated with a set of attributes, while each edge is associated with a set of relationship types and features about those relationships.

Observational scientists collect data and assign observed events to V and E. The challenge for the social network researcher is to get sufficient data to adequately represent the population of individuals (V) and evidence of relationships between these individuals (E) such that the metrics calculated on the available data represents the true population under investigation.

7.2.1 Completeness

An observational scientist monitors a subject for an interval of time. Example subjects include dolphins, humans, or genomes. Each monitoring period can be viewed as a sampling period consisting of a number of observations. Monitoring periods may include one or more events. Depending on the sampling protocol, events could include the behavior, movements, or interactions of one or more subjects. In an open system, observational scientists can only monitor a subset of the entire population and a subset of the relationships. Having relational information about an entire population is an optimal situation for applying social network analysis.

> The social network population is **known** if V contains every entity of the population within the network. The social network connectivity is **known** if E contains every relationship of the entities in the population within the network. If both V and E are **known**, the social network, G is considered to be *structurally complete*. Otherwise, we say that G is structurally incomplete. G' is a single sample or subgraph of G. We refer to the set of samples we have of G as $S(G) = \{G_i' | G_i' \subset G\}$.

In other words, if all the individuals in a population are known and all the relationships between the individuals are known, we consider the network derived from the population to be structurally complete. This is sometimes the case in closed systems, but never the case in open systems. Open system challenges differ because of (1) the accessibility of the subjects (monitoring the subject 24 h a day may not be possible); (2) the flow of individuals in and out of the observation area; and (3) the sampling approach chosen.

7.2.2 Certainty

In many contexts during an observation, there are distinct types of uncertainties that can arise. We begin by describing uncertainty in the context of social network graph topology. We then consider it in the context of data quality during data collection and redefine some general measures to make them applicable to social networks.

Social network uncertainty: An observer may be uncertain about the number of subjects in a group. For instance, in animal behavioral studies the group members may be moving so rapidly that only a range can be certain, e.g., there were between 15 and 20 dolphins in the group. Or there may be ambiguity about subject identity such that the same individual is counted more than once. This case corresponds to one individual with multiple identities on a social networking site. In relation to SNA, this certainty maps to *node existence certainty*. Related to this is *node identity certainty*, where researchers are uncertain about the identities of the individuals in the group, e.g., there are ten howler monkeys but only six can be clearly identified. A third type of certainty concerns whether or not two animals have an association between them. This corresponds to *edge existence certainty*. Another type of uncertainty is related to attributes of edges or nodes. *Node attribute certainty* focuses on certainty of any node feature, e.g., sex, individual behavior, etc. *Edge attribute certainty* maps to uncertainty related to features about associations, e.g., association behavior (the animals are playing). All of these types of certainty directly influence the overall reliability of the data for both descriptive and predictive tasks. Further, as more observations of the same nodes, edges, and attribute are taken, each individual observation is further validated and the overall certainty of those observed values increases. In this way, as sample size increases, certainty and data reliability also increases.

Data quality and uncertainty: Singh et al. [37] present the following quality measures associated with data collection: observation certainty, observation detail consistency, researcher vocabulary confidence and data stability. We redefine the first three in the context of social networks. Observational certainty is defined as the degree of confidence in the measurement itself [37]. In the context of social networks, it is the probability that both of the individuals and a mutual behavior were observed.

> For each observation event, OE, the certainty of the event is the probability that the event occurred, $p(OE)$. If a social network G' is built for individuals observed during OE, then each node, v_i, and each edge, e_{ij} has a probability of occurrence that represents the certainty of the individuals and relationships in G' respectively, $p(v_i)$, $p(v_j)$, and $p(e_{ij})$.

Knowing whether or not an event occurred and who participated in the event are necessary for accurate inference. If a researcher is making inferences and is not identifying the uncertain components of the network, the results of SNA may be misleading. If too much uncertainty exists in the observation, the inferences based on SNA are unreliable. Therefore, it is important to identify degrees of certainty of data during data collection. Doing so improves the overall understanding about the quality of the data and the accuracy of the resulting inferences.

When conducting statistical analysis on traditional observation data, the potential for uncertainty and error exist for the individual and the behavior observed. However, we see from the previous definitions that the potential for uncertainty and error is higher in social network data because error can also occur when measuring the relationship data. Sources of observational uncertainty for SNA include intermittent or poor observation conditions, distance between subjects, indistinguishable characteristics of subjects, ambiguous behaviors, and behaviors that are not mutually exclusive.

Differences in depth of data collection across researchers are relevant for both completeness and certainty. We refer to this as observation detail consistency. Here we ask if two different scientists are recording the same level of detail during an observation? For example, if one scientist records a red bird and another records a male, undersized cardinal eating a juniper berry, the observation detail consistency will be low. In the context of SNA, the observational detail corresponds to the attribute values associated with each vertex or edge in the network. The larger the number of known attribute values, the higher the observation detail. More precisely, given a set of researchers, observation detail consistency $=1$ when every researcher records the same level of detail during observation event OE. It is 0 when every researcher records a different level of detail during the same observation event.

Another quality concern involves identification of a common frame of reference or a consistent language interpretation across researchers in a group. For example, one researcher may look at a rabbit and suggest that it is large. Another researcher looking at the same rabbit may classify it as medium-sized. Singh et al. [37] refer to consistent interpretation among data collectors as researcher vocabulary consistency.

7.2.3 Bias

Bias is present when the likelihood of observation or collection of behavioral data is correlated in some way with a variable of interest to the researcher. This is especially insidious, as it is impossible to measure correlations when data are missing. This unrepresentative sample can result from sampling bias and observer bias, differences in collection criteria among researchers on a project, or different combination of all three.

A recent study illustrates this point: The classically maligned species, the spotted hyena, until recently, was reputed to be a lowly scavenger and kleptoparasite, stealing the prey from the nobler lion. Recent research [41] included nocturnal observations which revealed that the spotted hyenas were the masterful hunters, and it was lions who stole the majority of kills. Though by morning, researchers (and tourists) found lions feeding on the wildebeest while the rightful owners circled.

Daytime sampling was sufficient for answering research questions related to daytime behavior. However, the data sample was insufficient for making more general inferences. If the researcher makes inferences based on incomplete data, then these inferences are biased toward the collected data. For this analysis, data collected only during the day was biased as it could never reveal the nocturnal behavior if it differed from daytime activities, and until observed, these differences could not be measured or accounted for. We pause to point out that this example also highlights limitations with classical statistics. Even though classical statistics methods control for random errors, observational bias is not addressed.

Observer bias is generally defined as the tendency to bias observational or other data toward unconscious or even conscious expectations. Although inter-observer reliability can ameliorate this tendency, it is not uncommon for multiple observers to have the same expectations or implicit hypotheses and hence, the same biases. Most insidious is when observers have the same expectation and thus agree on the outcome without realizing the source of agreement. Even when experimenters or observers are blind to the hypothesis, they often have an implicit premise. Observer bias can also occur because some subjects or behaviors are more obvious or easier to observe or classify than others. Some subjects are more distinctive in appearance (e.g., bottlenose dolphins with mangled dorsal fins), or in behavior (e.g., active socializing more obvious than resting). It is common for observers to, for example, classify a group as "socializing" when only a minority are doing so (see also Altmann 1974 [2], Mann 1999 [28]). Attention is naturally drawn to the socializing individuals and it might appear as if most of the group is involved.

Observational scientists are aware of possible biases inherent in many of their design decisions [14], like observing subjects at specific times or based out of specific locations, and have developed strategies to compensate or control for these. In Sect. 7.5, we present some of their techniques with those used in other communities.

7.3 Dolphin Societies

We now describe the wild dolphin case that will be considered in the remainder of the chapter. After describing data set and its relevance to human societies, we consider the different challenges described earlier and provides concrete examples to highlight the pitfalls of different observational approaches and present some potential remedies that are important for SNA.

7.3.1 Shark Bay Data Collection

Researchers have monitored Indian Ocean bottlenose dolphins in Shark Bay, Australia since 1984. This site offers unparalleled conditions for the study of dolphin behavior: clear, shallow water, a high dolphin density, and relatively low human-related disturbance. All researchers use systematic protocols for monitoring individual dolphins and contribute information on identification, births, deaths, weaning, scars, ranging, behavior, association, and basic ecological data. Among the 1,200+ individuals studied since 1984, 95% are recognizable by dorsal fin features. Over 500 calves have been tracked from birth. These data have been collected using standard quantitative sampling techniques including point, scan, and continuous sampling [28], and include structured values, textual descriptions, photos, and geospatial data. The complementary sampling strategies are important for SNA since it provides a way to use triangulation to improve the confidence of the SNA and inferences based on the SNA [2].

The Shark Bay data set includes extensive survey data (14,000 records) and more intensive focal follow data (2,800 h). Brief (5–10 min) surveys include records on location, behavior, associates, habitat, photographic information, and physical data. They present a "snapshot" of association and behavior. Focal follows (1–9 h per follow) provide detailed minute-to-minute behavioral information including group composition, activity, location, and specific social interactions using standard quantitative sampling techniques. These focal data provide a detailed depiction of dynamic individual behavior across four generations.

7.3.2 Fission Fussion Societies

Most dolphin societies are characterized by extreme fission-fusion dynamics where spatial and temporal stability of groups is low [3]. Bottlenose dolphins, like humans, change their associations over the course of minutes to years, but maintain stable relationships within this fluid structure. In fact, one could easily argue that bottlenose dolphins exhibit greater similarity in social structure to humans than most other primates [11]. Like modern humans, dolphins live in large unbounded complex societies in which individuals maintain short and long-term bonds spanning more than 30 years, and have multi-level alliance structures (alliances of alliances, e.g., [11]). They also exhibit similarly slow life-histories such as prolonged maternal care, late age of maturity, and long-lifespan [29].

From a social network perspective it is important to understand when particular individuals associate with others. For instance, activity budgets have obvious implications for social interactions, and in a fission-fusion species, on the degree of sociability. As an example, foraging is inversely related to sociability [18, 19]. Work on dolphin social structures is in its infancy. However, dolphin social structure seems to be amenable to both ego-network and group-level SNA methods (e.g., see Lusseau et al. [27] and Stanton and Mann [19]).

7.3.3 Advantages and Disadvantages of Non-Human Studies

One of the advantages of studying non-human animals is that they can be observed in their natural habitat for long periods compared to humans. Even so, observers have numerous practical and logistical limitations, and cannot view or monitor their subjects 100% of the time. Some have recommended the use of small cameras or other recording technology, but because of the difficulty of using these devices, particularly with bottlenose dolphins, even data collected in this way would produce incomplete, biased networks.

Given the difficulty of tagging, more traditional, human intensive methods are still used to study dolphins, all of which require the researcher to make decisions during observation. It is incumbent on the researcher to identify the uncertainties and biases introduced and attempt to reduce them.

Finally, when observing animals with low travel costs and long distance communication, it is difficult to determine boundaries of groups. Many different criteria used to define bottlenose dolphin groups ranging from the most conservative 10 m chain rule [17, 38] to all dolphins estimated to be within 100 m radius of the boat/observer [34] to all individuals within sight moving in the same general direction, interacting or engaged in similar activities [13]. The group ranging decision has a large impact on the SNA structure since conservative approaches may miss associations, while less conservative approaches may include erroneous associations. Further, since different researchers use different methods for defining groups, comparisons across sites may not always be possible. For the Shark Bay Dolphin Research project, researchers use the 10 m chain rule.

7.4 Completeness of Network-Sampling Subjects and Collecting Enough Data

One primary challenge of an observational researcher is to observe a large range of behaviors and events. Since researchers of open systems cannot view all the subjects all the time, they must learn as much as possible using only a limited window on their subjects. Many factors have to be considered when collecting data including cost and safety of the researchers.

In this section we begin by looking at different sampling options for social network data. We then compare network measures computed on dolphin data illustrating how different sampling approaches can lead to different outcomes for two social network measures, degree and clustering coefficient. Finally, we discuss sample size and present some recommendations related to completeness of a social network.

7.4.1 Sampling Options

When considering sampling, there are initial questions that must be answered: (1) what sampling approach should one use when collecting observational scientific data for SNA; (2) how does one know that the social network built from the sample is a good structural representation to the actual social network; and (3) how does one know enough data has been collected for the analysis?

A number of researchers have begun working on methodologies for sampling for social network data. Different types of samples include convenience/opportunistic samples, simple random samples, systematic samples, stratified random samples, and cluster random samples, and snowball sampling designs [21, 35]. It is difficult for researchers who observe animals to obtain a completely random sample. Convenience or stratified random samples (based on location or sex for strata) are more readily available. Snowball sampling, is a network focused approach of building a sample network by selecting seed nodes, collecting data on the social network of the seed nodes and then iteratively adding their associates to the data sample [21]. Snowball sampling can be either breadth first or depth first. In both cases, members are added to the sample until the network sample is determined to be sufficient, either because it achieves a pre-specified size or because no new network members are identified. In observational research, because of the high cost associated with keeping track of all the subjects during a snowball sample, quasi-snowball sampling can be a more realistic approach. It limits the number of individuals followed at each stage.

As was mentioned in the last section, the Shark Bay project uses multiple approaches for sampling subjects, focal sampling (a quasi-snowball sampling approach), general survey sampling (a convenience random sample), and transect sampling (a systematic random sample). Surveys (or sightings) are assessments of a group's or individual's status, typically including demographic, ecological and behavioral data. These can by opportunistic (based on group or individual encounters) or systematic (e.g., transect surveys, searching along a particular pre-defined route). Focal sampling or follows are systematic sampling periods on an individual or in some cases a pair (see Mann 1999 [28], Altmann 1974 [2]). These have less locational bias but might reduce the variance in the data as there is a greater cost to focusing so intently on a pair of individual. For focal follows, dolphin pairs are selected using a randomized list order. As the season progresses, dolphins that have been followed the least, i.e., the fewest hours, are selected to maintain similar observation durations for the different dolphin pairs.

7.4.2 Sampling Methods Comparison

Each sampling approach has its strengths and weaknesses and is associated with particular biases. In the context of SNA, previous work demonstrated on synthetic data that social network metrics were robust to missing or erroneous data [9,15]. In other words, even when some data are missing, some important features of the network can still be ascertained, e.g., actors with high centrality or high betweenness. These approaches were focused on data missing due to error, not bias. Stanton et al. [39] conducted an analysis that compared different social network measures when different sampling strategies were used for sampling the same dolphins in Shark Bay. Table 7.1 shows some of the results in [39] along with some other statistics about the social network for quasi-snowball sampled data and random point sampled data.

Table 7.1 Comparing quasi-snowball and random point sampling

Sampling method	Nbr of nodes	Mean normalized degree	Mean clustering coefficient
Random point	1,000+	33	0.654
Quasi-snowball	200+	22	0.653

Notice the large different in number of nodes and degree. We see that while the mean clustering coefficient is similar, using both complementary approaches give the researcher an opportunity to better approximate the ground truth.

7.4.3 Amount of Data per Subject Necessary

Although scientists are often concerned with power or effect size in order to conduct their analysis, they rarely consider how much data per subject is needed. The former typically concerns itself with the number of subjects to include in an analysis or when planning an experimental study, not the amount of data per subject.

There are a number of ways to approach this problem. One is to subsample the entire dataset and analyze it according to these amounts (hours per subject or observations per subject) and see when the outcome variable no longer changes or is no longer correlated with the amount of data. For example, we examined how much focal data are needed per subject before the number of associates is no longer correlated with hours of observation. For the Shark Bay dolphins, the answer was 10 h. That is, we needed to observe dolphin calves for 10 h or more before we could be confident that we captured most of their network. However, the same was not true for their mothers. Only when we sampled 16 h or more on mothers was the relationship not significant.

Most dolphin and whale studies use far less data than this. Table 7.2 shows the variation in network size, degree and clustering coefficient for the focal follow dolphins [39]. It highlights the fact that 10–50 min is not sufficient to accurately determine the network of a dolphin or to eliminate the correlation between amount of data and dolphin degree.

Few have examined how much observation time is needed (samples per subject) to adequately capture the size (degree), density or other characteristics of weighted or unweighted networks. This obviously depends on within-individual variation. In societies characterized by fission-fusion, such as bottlenose dolphins and humans, such variation across different temporal and spatial scales can be substantial.

Table 7.2 Comparing quasi-snowball amount of data

Number of minutes observed	Network size	Mean normalized degree	Mean clustering coefficient
≥10 min	184	33	0.674
≥30 min	157	20	0.665
≥50 min	144	22	0.653

7.4.4 Recommendations

Make sure you have enough data

Having limited amounts of data can severely impact the quality of the social network. One way to verify whether the amount of data is "enough" is to use a smaller sample with lots of data (as a kind of ground-truth) and compare that sample to a larger sample with less data. If the resulting properties are similar, the sample size is reasonable. The assumption here is that having more data about a small set of subjects is a more reliable, higher quality set of data than the overall data set. If that is not the case, this approach will not lead to a valid analysis. Another approach is to weight data by the amount so that subjects with more data do not count more in the analysis. This is a variation of stratified sampling. Finally, one can also statistically control for the amount of data so that it is a factor in the analysis. Traditional ways of estimating necessary sample size are power analysis, information model comparisons, effect size statistics and Bayesian statistics. It is important to mention that while having more data increases the completeness and certainty of the data, it does not necessarily reduce the amount of bias in the sample. Other strategies presented in the next section need to be considered for that.

7.5 Identifying Uncertainties and Biases

As previously discussed, there are multiple layers of certainty and different types of bias. Understanding how confident an observer is about the individual or behavior seen is important for understanding the level of reliability and amount of bias associated with an analysis. Using the Shark Bay data, this section presents a few examples of uncertainty and bias that occur during field research. We focus on problems that have direct implications for accurate SNA.

7.5.1 Uncertain Subjects and Behaviors

Figure 7.1 shows a group of dolphins seen in a survey observation. The gray nodes represent dolphins the researchers are very familiar with an so they have high node identity certainty. The white represents dolphins with moderate node identity certainty. In other words, the researchers code some level of uncertainty in the identity of these nodes. Finally, though the researchers are certain that three more dolphins are present, these can not be identified. The node identity certainty of those three nodes is zero.

There are a few observations this small example highlights. First, maintaining only the certain information would reduce the group size by more than 30%. Second, assuming all the uncertain identities are certain, may lead to conclusions that may

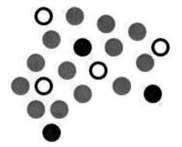

Fig. 7.1 Dolphins present in a single observation – *gray* node = high node identity certainty, *white* nodes = moderate node identity certainty, *black* nodes = no node identity certainty

or may not be accurate. Finally, keeping track of multiple layers of uncertainty provides more information than maintaining only one level. In other words, it is still informative to know that 19 dolphins are in this group even if the identities of three of them are unknown.

Capturing this level of certainty is also important for attributes and interactions. In this dolphin data set, every interaction and behavior is marked with a certainty level – high, moderate and low. This information can not only be used to understand scientific findings, it can also be used to see how well new researchers are being trained. Using the data, one can determine if there are certain subject behaviors that are difficult for new researchers to capture with high certainty and develop new training approaches or new methodologies for identifying these behaviors.

7.5.2 Observers Reliability and Consistency

A number of observer factors can lead to uncertainty and bias in samples. These include observer experience, fatigue, interest or focus, and how behavior or groups are defined. Between observer reliability can sometimes be assessed by using both live coding or videotaped data to compare consistency. This is complicated by a number of factors, including different vantage points for live observations (e.g., on a boat), and that observers may be more vigilant and thus concurrent in their coding when they themselves are being monitored. In addition, observers vary in their experience and it would be difficult for a new field observer to measure up to one with a decade or more of experience.

There are ways around these particular problems. Instead of a single observer, multiple observers can be present to help determine behavior categories. Photographing and videotaping can help verify individuals and behaviors. One can also statistically compare across observers to see what biases they may have introduced into sampling. For example, in the course of analyzing adult female sighting records, it became obvious that one observer at our field site never sighted a dolphin commonly seen by others. The dolphin's dorsal fin was not terribly distinct, so the researcher's team failed to identify her correctly. Researchers were able to go back through the unidentified dolphins in his film records and fill in the missing records.

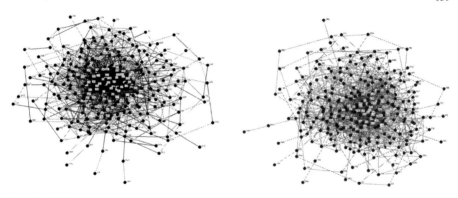

Fig. 7.2 Different views of the sample network by different researchers. The *left* network is one researcher's view. The *right* network is another researcher's view

In other cases, the sampling error cannot be eliminated, but can be accounted for statistically or analyzed at another level. For example, some observers might be adequate for distinguishing between foraging and socializing, but cannot correctly identify behavior subtypes (type of foraging or type of socializing). One can either collapse those data into larger categories, or create confidence intervals around the subtypes.

Figure 7.2 shows a dolphin social network generated using over 10 years of survey data from two different, experienced researchers on the Shark Bay Research Project. These networks contains only relationships that were viewed at least five times by the researchers. On the surface, the structure of the two networks seems very similar. However, the actual dolphins in the network vary considerably. The second observer did not capture 72% of the relationships captured by the first observer. The first observer did not capture 59% of the relationships captured by the second. More specifically, of the 1,145 relationships in the left network, 819 of those relationships were not identified by the second researcher (right network). Similarly, of the 789 relationships observed by the second researcher (right network), 463 were not observed by the first researcher (left network).

There were only 326 associations that were observed by both researchers. Figure 7.3 illustrates the common network found by both researchers. Notice the large difference in density between the network in Fig. 7.3 and the other two networks in Fig. 7.2. So why is there such a discrepancy? Ultimately, each researcher has certain biases or questions of interest that drive their observations. In this case, one researcher favors larger groups and tended to ignore smaller groups. Also, one of these researchers was very interested in mothers and calves, while the other was interested in male alliances. Their different observation preferences and research objectives may have contributed to the biases in the data collection.

Fig. 7.3 A network
representing the common
view of the two researchers,
i.e., the associations both
researchers observed

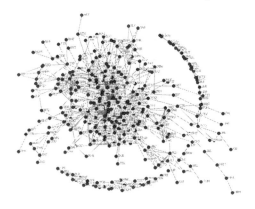

7.5.3 Time and Behavioral Sampling

One fundamental difference between humans and dolphins is that humans are
mostly diurnal while dolphins and whales are cathemeral, active for periods of the
day and night. At present, most data on dolphins was collected during the day, so
researchers can only characterize dolphin diurnal behavior. One reason for a preference for daytime observations is that it is easier for human researchers to see during
the day. However, being limited by visual access to our subjects can, as discussed
earlier, lead to mischaracterizations of species (e.g., spotted hyenas) or of specific
individuals.

As an example, one very sociable female named Square (for the notch in her fin)
spent only 3% of her day hunting, while 30% is the average for all adult females. Her
foraging budget was tiny but stable over a 12 year period. One evening researchers
followed her from 4 p.m. to 10 p.m., and, sure enough, as soon as the sun set, she
hunted for several hours on her own, completely uncharacteristic of her sociable
and restful daytime behavior. Here is a case where her day behavior differs from her
night time behavior. Since foraging and socialization have an inverse relationship,
her day time social network is likely to be different from her night time network.

7.5.4 Depth and Association Sampling

Fortunately, dolphins do not change their associates at depth. That is, one can account for associates because their diving bouts are brief, allowing observers to
monitor group members spatially. This is not true for sperm whales, who stay
submerged for an hour or more and can travel many kilometers during one dive.
Although sperm whales live in stable matrilineal units and tend to disperse temporarily during foraging bouts, it would be difficult to determine associations during
foraging. In sum, association data collected for some species are more likely to be
biased by activity than others. It depends on the temporal scale of sampling. In

studies of killer whales, the definitions of group or pod differs depending on the researcher, making comparisons difficult even within the same population. For example, some studies used the visual range of observers and an assessment of acting coordinated as a definition for "group" [4,5], while others define associates as those in the same photographic frame in at least 50% of the photos over several years. Those associations are used to define pod membership [7]. It would be difficult to determine relative bond strength for killer whales with such disparate methods for defining associations.

One area where depth does have an impact when studying marine mammals is hunting. Marine mammals typically hunt at depth, out of the observers' view. It is easier for humans to observe behaviors that occur near the ocean surface, although clearly much of what dolphins do occurs below the surface. Recording only what happens at the surface is a recognized source of bias. Some researchers try to mitigate this by inferring behavior: although the animals are out of view during a dive, if the observer is confident that the behavior is foraging, then it can be recorded as such. Because the behavior is not seen, to reduce the possible bias the information can be annotated with additional information about the degree of confidence or certainty of each behavior and the quality of the observation (at/near surface, subsurface). Direction changes, the type of dive and observations of prey catches can also be used to help the observer confirm the behavior that occurred mostly out of view.

7.5.5 Hidden Behaviors or Social Encounters

Some behaviors or social encounters are harder to detect because they are only performed when the animal is "cryptic." Dolphins and whales do not "hide" from research observers while foraging or performing other behaviors. However, observers must concern themselves that some behaviors may occur out of view because the animals are hiding from conspecifics, predators or prey. In many primate species, subadult or subordinate males only attempt to mate with females out of view from adults or more dominant males. The consequences of mating in the open can be severe for both sexes. Focal sampling is one of the best ways to address this problem because the observer stays with the individual focal animal regardless of where the animal goes. Even though this method usually works and provides information on a broad range of behaviors, the potential for observational bias persists as observers are more likely to lose their focal when the focal is trying to avoid conspecifics. In Shark Bay, females often avoid adult males and try to do so quietly. Researchers will sometimes follow a focal female and the entire group will dive and seemingly disappear when a group of males is nearby.

7.5.6 Observers Can Affect the Behaviors They Monitor

Most field researchers take years to habituate their population to human presence. This is particularly difficult if the population has been subject to hunting or poaching. In addition, their presence could affect predation rates. Cheetah are known to inhibit hunting in the presence of humans. Vehicles and boat engines make noise that could interfere with communication and can attract or repel predators or prey. Many contraptions that we consider essential for research, such as cameras, make sounds or reflect light that can be disturbing to others.

In Shark Bay, the dolphins became habituated initially through benign interaction with fishers and tourists, and subsequently, by researchers themselves. We use small boats with quiet 4-stroke engines. We check the noise levels underwater (snapping shrimp are much louder than our boats) and we never enter the water with the dolphins. How do we know they are habituated? They show very high tolerance of our presence. They engage in intimate behaviors very close to the boat (nursing, petting, social play), and we often hang back for periods to be certain their movements are not dictated by our presence.

Sometimes a new behavior occurs because of the presence of humans. At many field sites, one behavior, bow-riding, occurs because we are there. Although we discourage it during any sampling periods, there are times we encourage this behavior because dolphins often turn belly-up during bow-rides, which allows us to determine their sex and even age by degree of speckling [38]. Of concern is that some individuals might avoid an approaching boat or vehicle long before sampling begins. In fission-fusion societies this is more likely than in stable groups. Our main strategy for reducing this type of bias is to try and assess group size and behavior from hundreds of meters away. We can usually determine if animals have left or if they change their general behavior before we begin sampling. If the departed animals continue to be evasive, we note this and try and determine identity by photos taken at a distance. In our experience, even these dolphins become habituated to our boats quickly by associating with other habituated animals.

7.5.7 Recommendations

Improve observation certainty and consistency through standardization

The more detailed the recording of the subject and the event, the closer the observation is to reality. Accurately measuring the discrepancy between the observation and reality is a difficult problem. One way to decrease the discrepancy is to develop surveys that specify the minimum amount of information needed from the observation. Because the survey is created by research participants, it is considered a reasonable approximation of reality and represents a meaningful set of data as perceived by a group of scientists. While it cannot be considered a complete reflection of reality, it does identify important features and helps standardize the level of detail across researchers.

If researchers have developed a survey, one approach to measuring the amount of consistency is to have each researcher use the survey to capture measurements about the same event. Then these surveys can be compared to improve observation certainty for newer researchers and observation detail consistency for all observers.

Mark your biases

If researchers are aware of biases, they can devise sampling and observational design strategies to mitigate these. One important initial step is to identify all the sources of uncertainty and bias that are apparent. For each measurement that has uncertainty, an attribute can be added to the data set identifying the level of confidence in the measurement. Subjective measurements can also be separated from more standard measurements. For example, observation location should be a separate attribute, not placed in a large notes field. A similar strategy can be employed to minimize biases. By marking uncertainty and bias, a researcher can better control for these issues during analysis.

Minimize observer bias

There are several ways to minimize observer bias. First, good quantitative sampling techniques are fundamental. In sampling group behavior, explicit scan sampling, where the behavior of each individual is accounted for (or a randomized subset), is essential. Second, in addition to a clear systematic sampling regimen, a detailed, explicit ethogram is also needed. The ethogram defines each behavior in as much detail as possible while explaining what behaviors cannot co-occur. Third, if behaviors or individuals are ambiguous, record the data and also record a certainty level of the data. It is important to allow for all possible permutations of uncertainty in the data coding. By allowing observers to code for uncertainty, more accurate coding is likely to occur. It will discourage observers from being either overconfident in their coding, or neglecting to report what they do know. Finally, there is no substitute for making implicit hypotheses as explicit as possible. After all, the job of the scientist is to undermine the hypothesis, rather than prove it.

Compensate for bias

As with any comparative network analysis, having a reliable ground truth is important for the analysis. Using multiple sampling techniques and finding common parts of the network across samples can help identify a more accurate ground truth. More importantly, triangulation is an important strategy for identifying and adjusting for discrepancies and biases in one or more of the samples.

7.6 Computational Approaches to Improve Data Quality for Social Network Analysis

This chapter has identified different issues that can arise during (1) data collection and (2) application of social network analysis on incomplete, uncertain or biased data. Now we briefly describe a number of contributions that computer scientists can make to help improve the quality of the data and the resulting analysis conducted by social scientists and other researchers.

Develop interactive approaches for data exploration of social networks

Because there are so many factors associated with data exploration, new ways of interacting with data need to be devised. With decades of effort, improved technologies for remote tracking, and heightened concern for disappearing species, the next generation of biologists is measuring more features on larger populations. Novel approaches for data exploration are necessary to better understand different population dynamics. Interactive visualizations can be used to find outliers, highlight uncertainties, and detect possible biases.

Visual analysis of social networks is an integral component of the social network field. Tools fall into two categories, those that have sophisticated statistical analysis using matrix operations and those that focus on interactive visualization of uni-mode networks and multi-mode, heterogeneous networks. Various toolkits have been developed to help programmers create interactive visualizations themselves. The most robust include JUNG [33], Prefuse [23], and GUESS [1]. While tools for heterogeneous networks are emerging [25, 36], a need still exists to develop more tools that incorporate context specific graph visualizations, switch between different granularities of data, handle large data sets, and incorporate sophisticated longitudinal visual analytics.

Develop algorithms that consider uncertain data

Many traditional data mining algorithms ignore uncertainty in attribute and relational data. Developing approaches for clustering, community detection, and anomaly detection that consider the certainty of the attribute and relationships during analysis will result in more accurate approaches for attaining inductive knowledge about social structures. One approach is to represent the uncertainty as probabilities and build probabilistic models for each of the mentioned tasks for networked data.

Use reliable attribute and relational data to determine missing data

Different imputation strategies exist for traditional sampled attribute data. These need to be extended to handle missing data in relational data. One approach for doing this would consider multiple subsamples of the original sample and create a ground truth distribution of the entire sample based on the distribution of these subsamples. This ground truth could then be used to help with imputation of missing values.

Predict structural properties of networks

Newman [31] surveyed approaches for analyzing structural properties of networks. Much of the work has been descriptive in nature, but recently there has been more work which uses structural properties for prediction. Within this category, a number of papers focus on the spread of influence through the network [8, 12, 26]. These papers attempt to identify the most influential nodes in the network. While these approaches are an important start, much work remains to accurately infer structural properties, particularly in the presence of bias.

Identify changing dynamics of social networks

While static network analysis is important for understanding network ambiguity, information transmission, network pruning and the network as a whole, it is also important to consider the evolution of network relations over time. To date methods for this typically involve comparing the structures of static social networks at multiple time points (e.g., GEE regression models).

In hidden community identification, researchers attempt to identify subsets of actors that are densely connected to each other, but less densely connected to others. These densely connected regions are called communities. Communities are found using different measures for cohesion and modularity [20,22,32,40]. Other previous research has focused on community detection [32], extraction of unknown community structures [10], simplifying network topology through K-cores [30], and block modeling [6].

The majority of community detection work focused on static networks and constrained the problem to allow an actor to belong to only a single community. Computer scientists have recently begun analyzing the dynamics of social networks, communities and groups [16,40]. Currently, many of the models make assumptions that limit overlapping group membership and make strict assumptions about the changing dynamics of the participants in the network. The models also ignore sample size. This is a concern since in dynamic analysis, samples at each time point must be large enough for analysis. In a static analysis, there may be 100 observations of an animal. However, in a dynamic one, there may be time periods with only one or two observations. The variation of sample size at different times makes the network less stable. Techniques to compensate for this need to be proposed. We also need to develop strategies to handle the volume of data when multiple relations are combined, community overlap exists and the dynamics of these groups and communities are changing.

Of course many of the mentioned computational challenges are further challenged by the volume of network data that exists. Scalable algorithms and approximation heuristics will need to be considered as data sizes grow.

7.7 Final Thoughts

In this paper, we bring together some techniques and lessons learned from different empirical traditions, social science, animal behavior, and computer science. Our goal was to present issues related to uncertainty, sampling, data quality and SNA that exist across disciplines. Ultimately, limitations in our ability to observe and collect data on social interactions can have a significant impact on our understanding of social structures. By taking the time to understand what is missing, we have a more clear view of what is known.

Acknowledgement This work was funded by the Office of Naval Research under grant number #10230702 and the National Science Foundation under grant numbers #0941487 and #0918308.

References

1. E. Adar. Guess: a language and interface for graph exploration. In *SIGCHI conference on Human Factors in computing systems*, 2006
2. J. Altmann. Observational study of behaviour: sampling methods. *Behaviour*, 49:227–267, 1974
3. F. Aureli, C. Schaffner, C. Boesch, and et al. Fission-fusion dynamics: new research frameworks. *Current Anthropology*, 48:627–654, 2008
4. R. Baird and L. Dill. Ecological and social determinants of group size in transient killer whales. *Behavioural Ecology*, 7:408–416, 1996
5. R. Baird and H. Whitehead. Social organization of mammal-eating killer whales: group stability and dispersal patterns. *Canadian Journal of Zoology*, 78:2096–2015, 2000
6. V. Batageli. Notes on blockmodeling. *Social Networks*, 19:143–155, 1997
7. M. Bigg, P. Olesiuk, G. Ellis, and J. Ford. Social organization and genealogy of killer whales (orcinus orca) in the coastal waters of british columbia and washington state. *Reports to the International Whaling Commission, Special Issue*, 12:383–405, 1990
8. M. Boguna and R. Pastor-Satorras. Epidemic spreading in correlated complex networks. *Physical Review*, E 66 4, 2002
9. Borgatti, Carley, and Krackhardt. Robustness of centrality measures under conditions of imperfect data. *Social Networks*, 28:124–136, 2006
10. D. Cai, Z. Shao, X. He, X. Yan, and J. Han. Community mining from multi-relational networks. *In Proceedings of the 9th European Conference on Principles and Practice of Knowledge Discovery in Databases*, 2005
11. R. Connor, R. Wells, J. Mann, and A. Read. The bottlenose dolphin, Tursiops sp.: social relationships in a fission-fusion society. In J. Mann, R. Connor, P. Tyack, and H. Whitehead (Eds.), *Cetacean Societies: field studies of dolphins and whales*, pages 91–126, 2000. The University of Chicago Press, Chicago
12. P. Domingos and M. Richardson. Mining the network value of customers. *In Proceedings of the 7th ACM SIGKDD International Conference on Knowledge Discovery and Data Mining*, pages 57–66, 2001

13. R.W.E.C.G. Owen and S. Hofmann. Ranging and association patterns of paired and unpaired adult male atlantic bottlenose dolphins. *Canadian Journal of Zoology*, 80:2072–2089, 2002

14. D. Franks, R. James, J. Noble, and G. Ruxton. A foundation for developing methodology for social network sampling. *Behavioral Ecology and Sociobiology*, 63:1079–1088, 2009

15. Frantz and Carley. Relating network topology to the robustness of centrality measures. Technical Report CASOS Technical Report CMU-ISRI-05-117, Carnegie Mellon University, 2005

16. L. Friedland and D. Jensen. Finding tribes: identifying close-knit individuals from employment patterns. In *KDD*, 2007

17. S. Gero, L. Bejder, H. Whitehead, J. Mann, and R. Connor. Behaviorally specific preferred associations in bottlenose dolphins, Tursiops sp. *Canadian Journal of Zoology*, 83:1566–1573, 2005

18. Q. Gibson and J. Mann. The size, composition, and function of wild bottlenose dolphin (Tursiops sp.) mother-calf groups in shark bay, australia. *Animal Behaviour*, 76:389–405, 2008

19. Q. Gibson and J. Mann. Early social development in wild bottlenose dolphins: sex differences, individual variation, and maternal influence. *Animal Behaviour*, 76:375–387, 2008

20. M. Girvan and M.E.J. Newman. Community structure in social and biological networks. *PNAS*, 99(12):7821–7826, 2002

21. L. Goodman. Snowball sampling. *Annals of Mathematical Statistics*, 32:148–170, 1961

22. Habiba, T.Y. Berger-Wolf, Y. Yu, and J. Saia. Finding spread blockers in dynamic networks. In *SNA-KDD*, 2008

23. J. Heer, S.K. Card, and J.A. Landay. prefuse: a toolkit for interactive information visualization. In *SIGCHI conference on Human factors in computing systems*, pages 421–430, 2005. ACM Press, NY

24. R. James, D. Croft, and J. Krause. Potential banana skins in animal social network analysis. *Behavioral Ecology and Sociobiology*, 63:989–997, 2009

25. H. Kang, L. Getoor, and L. Singh. Visual analysis of dynamic group membership in temporal social networks. *SIGKDD Explorations Newsletter*, 9(2):13–21, 2007

26. D. Kempe, J. Kleinberg, and E. Tardos. Maximizing the spread of influence through a social network. In *KDD '03: Proceedings of the ninth ACM SIGKDD international conference on Knowledge discovery and data mining*, pages 137–146, 2003

27. D. Lusseau, B. Wilson, P. Hammond, K. Grellier, J. Durban, K. Parsons, and et al. Quantifying the influence of sociality on population structure in bottlenose dolphins. *Journal of Animal Ecology*, 75:14–24, 2006

28. J. Mann. Behavioral sampling methods for cetaceans: a review and critique. *Marine Mammal Science*, 15:102–122, 1999

29. J. Mann, R.C. Connor, L.M. Barre, and M.R. Heithaus. Female reproductive success in bottlenose dolphins (Tursiops sp.): life history, habitat, provisioning, and group size effects. *Behavioral Ecology*, 11:210–219, 2000

30. J. Moody and D.R. White. Structural cohesion and embeddedness: a hierarchical concept of social groups. *American Sociological Review*, 68(1):103–127, 2003

31. M. Newman. The structure and function of complex networks. *SIAM Review*, 45:167–256, 2003

32. M. Newman. Detecting community structure in networks. *The European Physical Journal B*, 38:321–330, 2004

33. J. O'Madadhain, D. Fisher, S. White, and Y. Boey. The JUNG (Java Universal Network/Graph) Framework, Technical Report UCI-ICS, 03–17

34. E. Quintana-Rizzo and R. Wells. Resighting and association patterns of bottlenose dolphins (tursiops truncatus) in the cedar keys, florida: insights into social organization. *Canadian Journal of Zoology*, 79:447–456, 2001

35. M. Salganik and D. Heckathorn. Sampling and estimation in hidden populations using respondent-driven sampling. *Sociological Methodology*, 34:193–239, 2004

36. L. Singh, M. Beard, L. Getoor, and M.B. Blake. Visual mining of multi-modal social networks at different abstraction levels. In *Proceedings of the 11th International Conference Information Visualization*, pages 672–679, 2007

37. L. Singh, G. Nelson, J. Mann, A.K. Coakes, E. Krzyszczyk, and E. Herman. Data cleansing and transformation of observational scientific data. In *In the ACM SIGMOD Workshop on Information Quality in Information Systems(IQIS)*, 2006
38. R. Smolker, A. Richards, R. Connors, and J. Pepper. Sex differences in patterns of association among indian ocean bottlenose dolphins. *Behaviour*, 123:38–69, 1992
39. M. Stanton, J. Mann, Q. Gibson, B. Sargeant, L. Bejder, and L. Singh. How much does method matter? a comparison of social networks of bottlenose dolphins (Tursiops sp.) in shark bay, australia. In *18th Biennial Conference on the Biology of Marine Mammals*, 2009
40. C. Tantipathananandh, T. Berger-Wolf, and D. Kempe. A framework for community identification in dynamic social networks. In *KDD*, 2007
41. M. Trinkel and G. Kastberger. Competitive interactions between spotted hyenas and lions in the etosha national. *African Journal of Ecology*, 43:220–224, 2005
42. A. Wasserman and K. Faust. *Social network analysis: methods and applications*. Cambridge University Press, Cambridge, 1994
43. S. Wassermann and P. Pattison. Logit models and logistic regressions for social networks: I. An introduction to markov graphs and p*. *Psychometrika*, 61:401–425, 1996

Chapter 8
Modeling Temporal Variation in Social Network: An Evolutionary Web Graph Approach

Susanta Mitra and Aditya Bagchi

8.1 Introduction

A social network is a social structure between actors (individuals, organization or other social entities) and indicates the ways in which they are connected through various social relationships like friendships, kinships, professional, academic etc. Usually, a social network represents a social community, like a club and its members or a city and its citizens etc. or a research group communicating over Internet. In seventies Leinhardt [1] first proposed the idea of representing a social community by a digraph. Later, this idea became popular among other research workers like, network designers, web-service application developers and e-learning modelers. It gave rise to a rapid proliferation of research work in the area of social network analysis. Some of the notable structural properties of a social network are connectedness between actors, reachability between a source and a target actor, reciprocity or pair-wise connection between actors with bi-directional links, centrality of actors or the important actors having high degree or more connections and finally the division of actors into sub-structures or cliques or strongly-connected components. The cycles present in a social network may even be nested [2, 3]. The formal definition of these structural properties will be provided in Sect. 8.2.1. The division of actors into cliques or sub-groups can be a very important factor for understanding a social structure, particularly the degree of cohesiveness in a community. The number, size, and connections among the sub-groups in a network are useful in understanding how the network, as a whole, is likely to behave.

Social scientists, through the analysis of a social network, focus attention on how solidarity and connection of large social structures can be built out of smaller groups. To build a useful understanding of a social network, a complete and rigorous description of a pattern of social relationships is a necessary starting point.

S. Mitra (✉)
Meghnad Saha Institute of Technology (Techno India Group), East Kolkata Township, Kolkata-700107, India
e-mail: susantamit@gmail.com; susanta_mitra@yahoo.com

B. Furht (ed.), *Handbook of Social Network Technologies and Applications*,   169
DOI 10.1007/978-1-4419-7142-5_8, © Springer Science+Business Media, LLC 2010

This pattern of relationships between the actors can be better understood through mathematical or formal representation like graphs. Therefore, a social network is represented as a directed graph or digraph. In this graph, each member of a social community (people or other entities embedded in a social context) is considered as a node and communication (collaboration, interaction or influence) from one member of the community to another member is represented by a directed edge. A graph representing a social network has certain basic structural properties, which distinguishes it from other type of networks or graphs. This type of graph is meant to study the nature of a real life social community and its structural changes over time. It may even be used for structural comparison between two social networks that in turn represents comparison between two social communities.

In order to understand the social properties and behavior of a community, social scientists analyze the corresponding digraph. The number of nodes in a social network can be very small representing a circle of friends or very large representing a Web community. This graphical representation is useful for the study and analysis of a social network. When a new member joins a social community like, a new immigrant to a village or a new member to a club, he/she may not have any connection with any other member of the community. When mapped as nodes of a graph, this type of new members to a social community would give rise to *isolated nodes*. The percentage of isolated nodes in a community is an important parameter of study for a social scientist. Moreover, all members of a community may not have contact with all other members. As a result, the community may form separate sub-groups. Members within a sub-group will have connection among themselves whereas members of two different sub-groups will remain isolated from each other. When mapped on to the graph representing a social network, these sub-groups would give rise to isolated sub-graphs. In addition, each social network will also have some node related information depending on the application area or the type of social community the network is representing [4]. For example, in a Web community, each node may represent a web page containing data relevant for each such page.

Discussions made so far indicate that social scientists make rigorous computation on the node-based and structural information of a graph representing a social network. For each such computation, entire graph related data, both node-based and structural, need to be accessed. Since a social network may give rise to a graph of thousands of nodes and edges, accessing the entire graph each time will contribute significantly on the overall time of computation. Moreover, some social network related applications try to search for interesting patterns on the existing data (both node-based and structural) [5]. Such social network related applications are quite common in web-based mining [6]. Overall computation time can be reduced to a great extent if the structure-based and node-based selection and searching can be done efficiently. In order to make it effective, the relevant information for both nodes and links along with common built-in structures like sub-graphs, cycles, paths etc. may be computed and stored apriori. If any application needs a particular type of computation quite often, such information can also be pre-computed and stored.

In short, instead of starting from raw node and edge related data for each type of analysis, some storage and selective retrieval facility should be provided for social network applications involving large graphs.

8.1.1 Temporal Variation of a Social Network

A social network changes over time. Since a social network involves a social community, new members keep joining and leaving the community. As a result, number of nodes, edges and their interconnections in the corresponding graph also change over time. The models proposed so far for the growth of social networks [7–9] are based on stochastic processes or are predictive in nature. One of the well known growth models of social networks proposed by Barabasi and Albert [10] is based on *preferential attachment*. It considers that during growth, vertices of high degree (in-degree or out-degree) are likely to have more number of new edges than the vertices of low degree. This inclination towards popularity (centrality) or "rich get richer" behavior is typically observed in Web-based social networks. However, this model has certain limitations when applied on a referral network [8]. Moreover, though earlier models on social network have discussed a lot on the concept of 'community structure', there was hardly any in depth study on the temporal changes in community structures due to evolution. These changes can be associated with formation, dissolution, growth, shrink, merger and split of social communities.

8.2 Web as a Social Network

World-Wide-Web (*WWW*) or just Web, as it is popularly known, is a rich and voluminous source of information. The diverse and distributed nature of Web has given rise to variety of research into the Web's link structure ranging from graph-theoretic studies (connectivity, reachability etc.) to community mining (like, discovering strongly connected structural components). Recently, Web has played a major role in the formation of communities (*Cyber-communities or Web communities*) where members or people from different parts of the globe can join the community for common interest. For example, members of a professional institution forming a group like a special interest group (SIG) of ACM. Similarly, news groups, research groups may form Web communities. The number of communities in the Web is increasing dramatically with time. This community formation is a powerful socializing aspect of the Web that has made a tremendous influence on human society. Thus Web has become a good source of social networks. Structural similarities with a social network help in studying different sociological behaviors of a Web community through applications of graph theory and social network analysis. These similarities lead towards a progress in knowledge representation and management on the Web [11].

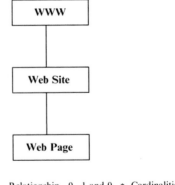

Fig. 8.1 Hierarchy of web objects in UML

8.2.1 Concept of Web Graph

Web can be viewed as a hierarchy of Web objects as represented in Fig. 8.1. The
WWW can be considered as a set of Web sites and a Web site as a set of Web pages.
These Web sites form a directed graph with Web pages as nodes and hyperlinks
between the Web pages as directed edges. Directed graph, thus induced by the hyperlinks between the Web pages is known as the *Web graph*. The formal definition
of Web graph is provided here.

8.2.1.1 Definition

A Web graph is defined as a directed graph G (N, E) where N is the set of Web
nodes, indicating corresponding Web pages, and $E \subseteq \{(u, v)|u, v \subseteq N\}$ is the set
of edges, indicating corresponding hyperlinks, where each edge is associated with
an ordered pair of Web nodes.

Given a Web node i of G, $ind(i)$ denote the set of Web nodes pointing to i or the
indegree of i and $outd(i)$ is the set of Web nodes that i points to or the *outdegree* of
i. Moreover, $I(i) = |ind(i)|$ and $O(I) = |outd(i)|$ denote the cardinalities of $ind(i)$
and $outd(i)$, respectively.

For any two Web nodes i, j $\in$ N, a hyperlink from i to j can be denoted as i $\rightarrow$ j. So,
a Web graph G, like any other graph, can be represented by means of an adjacency
matrix $A = (|N| \times |N|)$, where $A(i, j) = 1$ if and only if i $\rightarrow$ j, and 0 otherwise.
Incidentally for a Web graph, number of nodes is so high that it becomes difficult to
get computational facility for storing and manipulating the corresponding adjacency
matrix. So a considerable effort goes in the compression, storage and corresponding
manipulation of a Web graph.

8.2.1.2 Properties

As explained earlier, a Web community is a social network. So, a Web graph corresponding to a Web community exhibits various properties that are similar to other types of social networks. Some of the important features are:

- *Community Formation:* Web can be seen as sets of communities, connected to or isolated from each other. Each community consists of nodes representing the members of the concerned community with edges connecting them [12]. This property of community formation has been widely adopted in hierarchical models [13, 14] that try to find web communities where the members share some common features. These models are also based on some social measures describing a social network.
- *Evolving:* Web graph is evolving in nature. In other words, it re-shapes its structure over time with the addition or deletion of nodes and links. This evolution reflects the changes in the social structure or the acquaintances and provides an important area of study and research.

A snapshot of a sample social network that covers various properties is shown in Fig. 8.2. Although a few nodes and edges have been considered here, the explanation will soon show that even this small graph covers most of the structural peculiarities of a social network on the Web.

However, in order to understand the properties and graph compression, a novel technique applied in this system in an easier way, another simpler sample social network related to a referral network has also been considered in Fig. 8.3.

Although all the relevant structural components of a Web graph are present in the network of Fig. 8.2, only ISG and isolated nodes are explained referring this figure. For the sake of convenience, the other structural components are explained referring the network of Fig. 8.3.

- *Isolated Subgraph (ISG):* An isolated subgraph is a graph such that, if a graph G(V, E) has two isolated subgraphs G′(V′, E′) and G″(V″, E″), then V′ ⊆ V, V″ ⊆ V but V′∩ V″ = φ and also E′ ⊆ E, E″ ⊆ E but E′∩ E″ = φ.

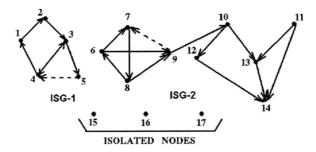

Fig. 8.2 Sample web community

Fig. 8.3 Sample referral
network

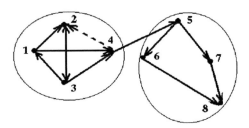

In a community, all members may not have contact with each other, giving rise to isolated subgraphs. The sample social network of Fig. 8.2 has two isolated subgraphs, (1–2–3–4–5) and (6–7–8–9–10–11–12–13–14).

- *Isolated Nodes:* Any node v in a directed graph G(V. E), where $v \in V$, has two properties Ind as the in-degree and Oud as the out-degree. In-degree provides the number of edges incident to v and out-degree is the number of nodes going out of v. A node v is an isolated node, if Ind. $v = 0$ and also Oud. $v = 0$.

In Fig. 8.2, nodes 15, 16 and 17 are the isolated nodes.

As shown in Fig. 8.3, the network initially had four nodes (1, 2, 3, 4). Node 5 is the acquaintance of node 4. So, node 5 joined the net. In turn node 5 brought nodes 6 and 7 and they again brought node 8 in the network. This way the network keeps on growing. It is assumed that at the time of query, Fig. 8.3 shows the current status of the network. It can easily be seen that the referral net of Fig. 8.3 is equivalent to ISG-2 of Fig. 8.2. This network consists of the following structural components:

- *Strongly-Connected-Component (SCC):* A strongly-connected-component is a maximal subgraph of a directed graph such that for every pair of nodes v_1, v_2 in the subgraph, there is a directed path from v_1 to v_2 and also a directed path from v_2 to v_1.

If there exists an operator $R(v_1, v_2)$, such that $R(v_1, v_2) =$ True if node v_2 is reachable from node v_1, i.e. there exists a path from node v_1 to node v_2, then subgraph $G'(V', E')$ of graph G(V, E) is a SCC, if $R(v_1, v_2) =$ True and also $R(v_2, v_1) =$ True, where $(v_1, v_2) \in V'$.

This definition indicates that a reachability operator R will be required, in order to check the existence of paths between any two nodes of a graph. Detail discussion in this regard will be made later.

The sample social network in Fig. 8.3 has two edge-types shown by farm and chain lines. Node sequence (1–2–3) represents a strongly connected component when same edge-types are considered, whereas (1–2–3–4) is a SCC considering both the edge-types.

- *Cycle:* If the sequence of nodes defining a path of a graph, starts and ends at the same node and includes other nodes at most once, then that path is a cycle. If in a graph G(V, E), $(v_0, v_1, \ldots\ldots, v_n)$ be a node sequence defining a path P in G such that $(v_0, v_1, \ldots\ldots, v_n) \in V$ and $v_0 = v_n$, then P is a cycle.

Figure 8.3 shows three cycles; (1–2–3–1), (2–3–4–2) and (2–3–2). Here cycles have been considered irrespective of the variation in edge-types. The cycles may even be nested. Cycle (2–3–2) is nested within the other two cycles, (1–2–3–1) and (2–3–4–2).

- *Reciprocal Edge:* A cycle having only two nodes is a reciprocal edge. So, a reciprocal edge $(v_1, v_2) \in V$ has directed edge from v_1 to v_2 and also from v_2 to v_1. A reciprocal edge is the smallest size cycle.

In Fig. 8.3, (2–3–2) is a reciprocal edge.

- *Hyper-node:* In a nested-cycle structure, the largest or the outermost cycle is defined as a hyper-node. For a graph G(V, E), if there exists a nested cycle structure with a set of cycles such that, $\{C_1 \supseteq C_2 \supseteq \ldots \supseteq C_n)\}$ where C_i is a cycle in G, then C_1 is the hyper-node corresponding to the nested cycle structure. So, a hyper-node represents a SCC.
- *Homogeneous Hyper-node:* If in a hyper-node all the edge-types are same, then it is a homogeneous hyper-node. Let, $\{C_1 \supseteq C_2 \supseteq \ldots \supseteq C_n)\}$ be a nested cycle structure in a graph G(V, E) where, C_i is a cycle in G. Now C_1 will be a homogeneous hyper-node if for any pair of edges, $(v_i, v_j) \in C_1$ and $(v_r, v_s) \in C_1$, (v_i, v_j).edge-type $= (v_r, v_s)$.edge-type.

In Fig. 8.3, (1–2–3) is a homogeneous hyper-node.

- *Heterogeneous Hyper-node:* In a heterogeneous hyper-node all the edge-types need not be same. In Fig. 8.3, (1–2–3–4) is a heterogeneous hyper-node.

Though by definition, a hyper-node is the largest cycle in a nested cycle structure, the hyper-nodes themselves can also be nested. Since in a homogeneous hyper-node all the edges must be of same type, this hyper-node may be nested within another larger cycle formed by edges of different types resulting a heterogeneous hyper-node. So, a homogeneous hyper-node may be nested within a heterogeneous hyper-node. In Fig. 8.3, homogeneous hyper-node (1–2–3) is nested within heterogeneous hyper-node (1–2–3–4).

The directed graph as shown in Fig. 8.3 E be converted to a Directed Acyclic Graph (DAG) through a compression process whereby the hyper-structures are fused to hyper-nodes and the edges are fused to hyper-edges. The compression process includes two types of compression namely, *Homogeneous hyper-node based compression* and *Heterogeneous hyper-node based compression.* The detail of compression process has been discussed elsewhere [15].

8.3 Evolution of Web Graph

It is well known that Web graph is a giant social network that shares many structural properties with other social networks. Hence to understand and explain the evolution of a social network it is better to consider Web graph as a case study. This is also well justified by the fact that change in network is substantial in case of Web where the pages are added to the Web at a very high rate and pages also disappear quite often from the Web. The evolution of Web has been widely studied for quite sometime and has received much attention in the physics literature [16–19]. The studies on the evolution have proved to be challenging due to the complex structure of Web. The evolution pattern of the Web is not fully understood yet and has provided the scope for active research in this area. However, all the proposed models on the evolution of Web graph are based on stochastic processes only and do not attempt to capture the microscopic details of social dynamics through a data model. Evaluation of Web queries for static and dynamic Web was initially proposed by [20]. It is one of the earliest works on dynamic Web graph that have dealt on the computational aspects of dynamic Web queries. However, it has not proposed a formal temporal data model to account for the temporal changes of the structural components of Web graph. Like other social networks, the formation and interaction of communities are also well exhibited by Web graph during evolution. Only a few models [21–23] have considered the same during the study of Web-based social networks. However, none of these models have carried out analysis of the temporal variation of the structures of the communities and their components (pages, hyperlinks) by associating a *valid time* period or interval of existence with each of these dynamic structural objects. Valid time period should also be associated with the hyper-structures and paths as discussed in earlier sections. This approach of analysis can be quite important and valuable for the sociologists and information scientists. An attempt has only been made in [24] to study the dynamic nature of Web graph against a temporal axis, where each edge is labeled with data of its first and last appearance in the Web. However, this approach poses several challenges like; (a) efficient representation of dynamic graphs in secondary memory, (b) application of compression techniques to dynamic Web graph and (c) utilization of timestamps, e.g. valid time, to answer temporal queries on structural evolution of Web graph.

Thus, it is apparent from the above discussion that none of the earlier research efforts have proposed any temporal data model for a dynamic Web graph. This chapter proposes *Dynamic Data Model* to manage temporal changes in the structure of a Web graph representing a social network. With application specific changes, this model may also be adopted for other areas of evolutionary graph (e.g. electrical distribution, biological pathways etc.).

A Web graph representing a social network is a dynamic system that always evolves and re-shapes its structure over time due to the changes in the sociological behavior of its members. However in a data model, such structural changes can only be represented by discrete time instants similar to versioning in standard temporal data models. So between two time instants of study, the graph structure is considered to be constant. Hence, the structure of a Web graph does not remain same at two different time instants. Therefore, the reshaping of the Web structure means that the Web graph at any time point t is different from that at time $t+1$ or $t-1$. This fact, of course demands that the graph needs to be analyzed at several time points to understand the pattern of evolution. The basic mechanism that can explain the dynamic behavior of Web graph is the hyperlinking of Web resources. So, there are four basic processes that characterize the evolution of a Web graph:

- Addition of new nodes (pages)
- Addition of new edges (hyperlinks)
- Removal or deletion of existing nodes
- Removal or deletion of existing edges

In reality, the combination of these four basic processes can produce a complex dynamic behavior of a Web graph due to its evolution over time. When a Web graph is studied in two successive time instants, structural comparison between the two graphs reveals the actual changes that have occurred. It enumerates the number of nodes (pages) and edges (hyperlinks) and also the interconnections among them. Definitely, these changes would also include changes in the hyper-structures and paths, if any.

This study and analysis on the structural evolution of a Web graph can also help in the discovery of compact and densely connected zones of 'information' and 'knowledge'. Moreover, further study on the characteristics and properties of this type of 'Web Knowledge Bases' can bring out many important and interesting information on changes in a Web community structure with respect to pages and links of different time instants i.e., over a period of time. These changes may cause formation, dissolution, growth or merger and decay or split of Web communities [21, 23]. Thus it becomes apparent that collection of structural changes through a set of successive time instants can give rise to a composite structural evolution pattern of a Web community over a long period of time. This fact is well explained and illustrated through the data model and the evolutionary query examples in the subsequent sections. The next sections cover only the structural evolution of Web graph. In other words, change in the content of a page over time, the usual area of study for a temporal data model, has not been considered here. Designing a data model for temporal changes of an evolutionary graph is definitely a new area of study.

8.4 Dynamic Web Graph Model

This section provides the overview and preliminaries of the dynamic data model followed by the detailed description. As discussed earlier, in a social community, different types of social activities may cause changes in social relationship and thus the structure of a Web graph that represents such a community. However, such changes may not happen in the entire graph. It may happen in some portions of a Web graph or in certain sub-graphs of such a graph. In order to study such changes, the temporal evolution process at different parts of a Web-based social network needs to be studied. So, facility for selective retrieval of data would be necessary. Therefore, once again, a data model has to be designed to capture the temporal changes in the Web-based social network. This would help in studying the frequently changing sub-structures leaving the entire graph. To capture these temporal changes in a social network, a dynamic graph data model has been proposed here. This type of analysis may cover situations like,

- Observing social and cultural trends over time for sociological research. For example, the number of accesses to matrimonial or employment sites in a referral network during a time period is a trend indicator for a society.
- Observing structural changes in a society over time (formation of sub-groups, i.e. sub-graphs, dissolution or splitting of such groups etc.) with change in social facilities like communication, financial status, availability of resources etc.

8.4.1 Dynamic Data Model Preliminaries

- *Granularity:* Time granularity provides the domain of the value of time associated with the time stamp for each structural component.
- *Valid Time:* It provides the time stamp for any structural component. It represents a time range through which a structural component exists in a Web graph. It has a Start-time and an End-time.
- *Valid Start-time:* The start-time of a time stamp i.e., Valid time.
- *Valid End-time:* The end-time of a time stamp i.e., Valid time.

Both start-time and end-time will assume values within the domain of granularity defined in an application. For example, if granularity is in terms of year, then a valid time (2001–2005) for a node signifies that the node entered the graph and its associated social network in its version of year 2001 and existed in the graph till its version of year 2005. So, for any valid time, valid end-time > valid start-time within the domain of values of granularity used.

- *Now:* A temporal variable that implicitly represents the current time. So, Now is always associated with the time stamp of the current version.

If a structural component joins and leaves a graph within the same version, its valid start-time = valid end-time. For example, a structural component introduced in 2001 version disappears in 2002 version would have a valid time (2001, 2001).

So, when a new component is introduced in the current version, its valid time, till the next version is created, is (Now, Now).

- *Lifespan:* Lifespan of a structural component in a Web graph is the time interval during which the component is valid. This interval is the difference between a valid start-time when the component first appeared in the graph and a valid end-time after which the component disappeared. If v_e represents the valid end-time and v_s represents the valid start-time of a structural component, then $(v_e - v_s)$ is the lifespan of the component. Accordingly, a member function *lifespan* has been provided to compute time of existence of any object instance of any object type in the temporal version of the object-relational data model as described in Sect. 8.4.2.

Lifespan attribute may be used to compute *lifespan overlapping* between two structural components. It is the intersection of lifespans of the two components. If $[t_i, t_j]$ and $[t_k, t_l]$ be valid time of any two structural components, where $i < j$, $k < l$, $i < k$, $j \geq k$ and $j \leq l$, then $(t_j - t_k)$ is the overlapping lifespan.

Lifespan containment signifies that the valid time of a structural component is within the valid time of another structural component. If $[t_i, t_j]$ and $[t_k, t_l]$ be the valid time of any two structural components, where $i < j$, $k < l$, $i \leq k$, $j \geq l$, then $[t_k, t_l]$ is contained within $[t_i, t_j]$.

- *Query Time Period:* Time interval over which a query has been made. Like valid time, query time will also have a query start-time and query end-time with values in the domain of granularity defined. For example a query, '*Find the number of Web pages related to Indian Internet Banking created since 2003*' will have query time period as [2003, Now].

8.4.2 Temporal Structure-Based Schema

A temporal structure-based schema has been defined in this section to represent the structural evolution of a Web graph representing a social network. This schema admits different type structures. In addition, a temporal attribute valid_time has been provided with each object type to indicate the time of existence of each object instance for each such object type. A member function *lifespan*, as described in Sect. 8.4.1 has also been provided to compute the actual period of existence of each object instance as the difference of its valid_end_time and valid_start_time. A unit named timestamp has been defined to indicate the values of valid_end_time and valid_start_time. The unit of timestamp will depend on the unit of granularity defined for the application modeled. In the experimental schema used in this chapter, it has been marked as a year like, 2001, 2002, etc.

The relevant object types for the temporal structure-based schema are shown below:

Valid_time
(
type: ADT;
valid_start_time: timestamp;
valid_end_time: timestamp;
member functions :
lifespan returns integer;
)
Graph
(
type: ADT;
graph_id: string;
version: timestamp;

ISGs: TABLE OF REF ISG;

isolated_nodes: TABLE OF REF Node;

member functions :

no_of_ISG returns integer,

no_of_isolated_nodes returns integer,

and other member functions;

)

ISG

(

type: ADT;

ISG_id: string;

valid_time: REF Valid_time;

homogeneous_hyper_nodes: TABLE OF REF Homogeneous_hyper_node;

heterogeneous_hyper_nodes: TABLE OF REF Heterogeneous_hyper_node;

hyper_edges: TABLE OF REF Hyper_edge;

nodes: TABLE OF REF Node;

edges: TABLE OF REF Edge;

paths: TABLE OF REF Path;

member functions :

isg_size returns no_of_nodes as integer,

no_of_ heterogeneous_hyper_nodes returns integer,

no_of_ homogeneous_hyper_nodes returns integer,

max_homogeneous_hyper_node_size

returns no_of_nodes as integer,

max_path_length returns no_of_nodes as integer,

and other member functions

)

Homogeneous_hyper_node

(

type: ADT;

homogeneous_hyper_node_id: string;

valid_time: REF Valid_time;

homogeneous_hyper_node_edge_type: string;

//since all edges within a homogeneous_hyper_node are of same type, inclusion of homogeneous_hyper_node_edge_type is useful to process queries searching for homogeneous_ hyper_nodes of specific edge_type//

cycles: TABLE OF REF Cycle;

nodes: TABLE OF REF Node;

edges: TABLE OF REF Edge;

member functions :

homogeneous_hyper_node_size returns no_of_nodes as integer,

and other member functions

)

Heterogeneous_hyper_node

(

type: ADT;

heterogeneous_hyper_node_id: string;

valid_time: REF Valid_time;

homogeneous_hyper_nodes: TABLE OF REF Homogeneous_hyper_node;

hyper_edges: TABLE OF REF Hyper_edge;

cycles: TABLE OF REF Cycle;

nodes: TABLE OF REF Node;

edges: TABLE OF REF Edge;

member functions :

heterogeneous_hyper_node_size returns no_of_nodes as integer,

and other member functions

)

Hyper_edge

(

type: set of edges;

hyper_edge_id: string;

valid_time: REF Valid_time;

start_node: REF Heterogeneous_hyper_node or Homogeneous_hyper_node or Node;

end_node: REF Heterogeneous_hyper_node or Homogeneous_hyper_node or Node;

hyper_edge_type: string;

//since all edges within a hyper-edge are of same type, inclusion of hyper_edge_type
is useful to process queries searching for hyper_edges of specific edge_type//

hyper_edge_members: TABLE OF REF Edge;

member functions :

hyper_edge_size returns no_of_edges as integer,

and other member functions

)

Cycle

(

type: ADT;

cycle_id: string;valid_time: REF Valid_time;

nodes: TABLE OF REF Node;

edges: TABLE OF REF Edge;

member functions :

cycle_size returns no_of_nodes as integer,

and other member functions

)

Path

(

type: sequence_of_nodes;

path_id: string;

valid_time: REF Valid_time;

path_start_node: REF Heterogeneous_hyper_node or Homogeneous_hyper_node or Node;
path_end_node: REF Heterogeneous_hyper_node or Homogeneous_hyper_node or Node; path_edgelist: TABLE OF REF Hyper_edge or Edge;
member functions :
path_length returns no_of_nodes as integer,
//no_of_nodes refers to the total number of heterogeneous_hyper_nodes, homogeneous_hyper_nodes as well as nodes belonging to the path//
and other member functions
)
Edge
(
type: sequence of nodes;
edge_id: string;
valid_time: REF Valid_time;
edge_type: string;
start_node: REF Node;
end_node: REF Node;
//edge is a sequence of nodes of length 2//
)
Node
(
type: object;
node_id: string;
valid_time: REF Valid_time;
in_degree: integer;
out_degree: integer;
node_type: string;
//the system defines four types of nodes; *isolated, source, sink, communicator*//
)

8.5 Conclusion and Future Works

A social network grows over time. Temporal data models developed are the extensions of relational, object-oriented and later, the object-relational models. They could hardly handle graph related data. Dynamic graphs or temporal changes in structure for social network analysis have already been studied but once again, with no effort for data management. A comprehensive object-relational data model has been proposed in this chapter to incorporate the necessary features of a dynamic or evolutionary Web graph represented as a social network. The model covers the possible types of changes that can occur among the structural components due to evolution. It supports efficient evaluation of dynamic or temporal queries on graph structures. Different temporal query operators have been defined for query formulation of queries. The definition of query operators and query examples as well as the detail implementation process of Web graph evolution is beyond the scope of the present chapter. The proposed model is a generic and comprehensive data model for managing the changes in sociological behavior of the Web communities and can bring out the important and interesting information on change in Web community structure over a period of time.

However, a lot of scope for future works exists in this important and challenging area of network evolution. First of all, the model needs to be implemented and thoroughly tested for the current Web Graphs having nodes and edges of order of billions. Novel graph compression techniques based on structures as proposed by the authors in [15] or any other techniques like [25] needs to be applied for efficient data storage and retrieval. Secondly, more efficient query processing systems need to be designed to get the dynamic information on structures as well as their component nodes and edges. Work on complex query processing on static or snapshot data model for a Web graph had already been done by the authors and communicated [26].

It is envisaged that when all the efforts made in this chapter are published, it will provide an impetus to many other research works in the area of social network modeling in particular and on dynamic graph data model in general.

References

1. Leinhardt, S. (1977). Social networks: a developing paradigm. Academic Press, New York.
2. Rao, A.R. and Bandyopadhyay, S. (1987). Measures of reciprocity in a social network. *Sankhya: The Indian Journal of Statistics*, Series A, 49, 141–188.
3. Rao, A.R., Bandyopadhyay, S., Sinha, B.K., Bagchi, A., Jana, R., Chaudhuri, A. and Sen, D. (1998). Changing social relations – social network approach, Technical Report. *Survey Research and Data Analysis Center, Indian Statistical Institute*.
4. Mitra, S., Bagchi, A. and Bandyopadhyay, A.K. (2007). Design of a data model for social network applications. *Journal of Database Management*, 18, 4, 51–79.
5. Chen, L., Gupta, A. and Kurul, E.M. (2005). Efficient algorithms for pattern matching on directed acyclic graphs. *IEEE ICDE*.
6. Chakrabarti, S. (2004). Web mining. Elsevier.
7. Liben-Nowell, D. and Kleinberg, J. (2003). The link prediction problem for social networks. *Proceedings of the ACM CIKM*.
8. Newman, M.E.J. (2003). The structure and function of complex networks. *SIAM Review*, 45, 167–256.
9. Jin, E.M., Grivan, M., and Newman, M.E.J. (2001). The structure of growing social networks. *Physics Review E*, 64, 046132.
10. Barabasi, A. and Albert, R. (1999). Emergence of scaling in random networks. *Science*, 286, 509–512.
11. Kumar, R., Raghavan, P., Rajagopalan, S. and Tomkins, A. (2002). Web and social networks. *IEEE Computer*, 35(11), 32–36.
12. Flake, G.W., Lawrence, S.R., Giles, C.L. and Coetzee, F.M. (2002). Self-organization and identification of web communities. *IEEE Computer*, 35, 66–71.
13. Kleinberg, J.M. (2002). Small world phenomena and the dynamics of information. *Proceedings of the 2001 Neural Information Processing Systems Conference*, MIT Press, Cambridge, MA.

14. Watts, D.J., Dodds, P.S. and Newman, M.E.J. (2002). Identity and search in social networks. *Science*, 296, 1302–1305.
15. Bhanu Teja, C., Mitra, S., Bagchi, A. and Bandyopadhyay, A.K. (2007). Pre-processing and path normalization of a web graph used as a social network. *Journal of Digital Information Management* 5, 5, 262–275.
16. Salathe, M., May, M.R. and Bonhoeffer, S. (2005). The evolution of network topology by selective removal. *Journal of Royal Society Interface*, 2, 533–536.
17. Krapivsky, P.L. and Redner, S. (2002). A statistical physics perspective on web growth. *Computer Networks*, 39, 261–276.
18. Dorogovtsev, S. and Mendes, J. (2002). Evolution of networks. *Advances in Physics*, 51, 1079–1187.
19. Dorogovtsev, S. and Mendes, J. (2000). Scaling behavior of developing and decaying networks. *Europhysics Letter*, 52, 33–39.
20. Mendelzon, A.O. and Milo, T. (1997). Formal models of web queries. *Proceedings of the ACM Database Systems*, 134–143.
21. Tawde, B.V., Oates, T. and Glover, E.J. (2004). Generating web graphs with embedded communities. *Proceedings of the World Wide Web Conference.*
22. Chakrabarti, S., Joshi, M.M., Punera, K. and Pennock, D.M. (2002). The structure of broad topics on the web. *Proceedings of the World Wide Web Conference.*
23. Toyoda, M. and Kitsuregawa, M. (2003). Extracting evolution of web communities from a series of web archives. *Proceedings of the Fourteenth Conference on Hypertext and Hypermedia*, 28–37.
24. Kraft, R., Hastor, E. and Stata, R. (2003). Timelinks: Exploring the link structure of the evolving Web. *Second Workshop on Algorithms and Models for the Web Graph.*
25. Dourisboure, Y., Geraci, F. and Pellegrini, M. (2007). Extraction and classification of dense communities in the web. *Proceedings of the International World Wide Web conference.*
26. Mitra, S., Bagchi, A. and Bandyopadhyay, A.K. (2008). Complex query processing on web graph: A social network perspective. *Journal of Digital Information Management*, 6, 1, 12–20.

Biographies of Authors

Susanta Mitra is a Professor and Head of Department of Computer Science & Engg. and IT at Meghnad Saha Institute of Technology (Techno India Group), Kolkata, India. He has received Ph.D. (Comp. Sc.) from Jadavpur University, Kolkata. His research interests include social networking, Web graph analysis and mining, data modeling, social computing, data structure and algorithm. Prof. Mitra is a Professional Member of Association for Computing Machinery (ACM) and Senior Life Member of Computer Society of India (CSI).

Aditya Bagchi is the Dean of Studies at Indian Statistical Institute, Kolkata, India. Prof. Bagchi received his Ph.D. (Engg.) from Jadavpur University in 1987. He has served as visiting scientist at the San Diego Super Computer Centre, University of California, San Diego, USA and at the Centre for Secure Information Systems, George Mason University, Virginia, USA. He is a Senior member of CSI, member of ACM Sigmod and IEEE Computer Society. His research interests include Access Control and Trust Negotiation algorithms, developing new measures for Association Rule mining and application specific Data Modeling.

Chapter 9
Churn in Social Networks

Marcel Karnstedt, Tara Hennessy, Jeffrey Chan, Partha Basuchowdhuri, Conor Hayes, and Thorsten Strufe

9.1 Introduction

In the past, churn has been identified as an issue across most industry sectors. In its most general sense it refers to the rate of loss of customers from a company's customer base. There is a simple reason for the attention churn attracts: churning customers mean a loss of revenue. Emerging from business spaces like telecommunications (telcom) and broadcast providers, where churn is a major issue, it is also regarded as a crucial problem in many other businesses, such as online games creators, but also online social networks and discussion sites. Companies aim at identifying the risk of churn in its early stages, as it is usually much cheaper to retain a customer than to try to win him or her back. If this risk can be accurately predicted, marketing departments can target customers efficiently with tailored incentives to prevent them from leaving.

Telcom networks, online gaming communities, online communities and discussion forums all have one thing in common: they all can be represented by a network of the social links between people. The links in this social network may be based on calls between customers or explicit and implicit connections extracted from online communities, such as friendship relations, shared activity in popular forums, common contributions to discussion threads and so on. While churn in the telcom sector has been studied extensively, no research has been carried out on the general meaning and consequence of churn in online social networks and communities. This chapter aims at filling this gap. Churn is an important factor for social network providers, as it leads to a loss of social capital and ultimately effects service sustainability. Churn undermines the health and ability of communities to self-govern and self-maintain. The risks to digital social networks arise not only through members stopping their activity, but also through significantly reducing activity. This becomes particularly evident where network services rely upon member activity.

M. Karnstedt (✉)
Digital Enterprise Research Institute (DERI), NUI Galway, Ireland
e-mail: Marcel.Karnstedt@deri.org

B. Furht (ed.), *Handbook of Social Network Technologies and Applications*,
DOI 10.1007/978-1-4419-7142-5_9, © Springer Science+Business Media, LLC 2010

Often, the combination of increasing and decreasing activity (of different customers) is an important indicator for risk. As an example, consider a forum where the popular topic initiators are gradually replaced by spammers. Such a change in the population composition indicates the risk of "losing" the forum, its associated services and revenue model. Therefore, churn analysis should be understood in close relation to analysing activity.

Usually churn prediction is based on pure *feature-based* approaches. This means, key characteristics and features of customers are analysed in order to predict the probability of churning. However, this neglects the importance of social influence between individuals, which can be analysed by examining their social networks. We believe that churn is not only a phenomenon due to individual decisions and profiles, rather it is influenced by external events (e.g., elections or poor reviews for a company) and, more importantly, by community effects. To analyse and understand community effects, a crucial aspect is to understand social roles of single individuals and their influence on the community. Some recent work has identified this issue and argues to replace or extend the feature-based approaches by *influence-based* techniques, mostly by the use of information diffusion models [13, 34]. The idea underlying this approach is that a subscriber is more likely to churn if he is connected to other subscribers that have churned. Thus churn diffuses from subscriber to subscriber, where the degree of influence of the previous churners depends on their importance and social weight. This approach is not only a focus of recent research, it is also receiving attention in the business sector.[1]

Measuring the popularity of an individual in a social network can be examined with social network analysis (SNA) measures such as connectedness, betweenness and centrality. Popularity can also be analysed by measuring the use of the network. For example, in terms of of how many profile visits a subscriber receives. For providers of decentralised online social networks, this can be used to optimise the physical structure of the underlying network. But, with the idea of information diffusion and influence, popularity has an increased importance for churn prediction. Intuitively, popular subscribers that decide to churn have influence on the probability of other customers to churn. We propose to understand popularity as a *meta feature* for churn analysis, which can be used in feature-based and diffusion-based models of prediction.

In this chapter, we summarise the field of churn analysis and prediction with focus on digital social networks. We first discuss the differences between churn in the telcom sector and the emerging sector of digital social networks. We present the reasons and motivations underlying user activity. Then, we discuss appropriate definitions of churn and identify research directions and challenges. The general applicability of a definition proposed by us is analysed on the basis of an empirical study. Finally, we present state-of-the-art approaches for churn prediction and highlight their strengths and weaknesses. We discuss the importance of the underlying

---

[1] http://yro.slashdot.org/story/09/08/01/1946208/IBM-Uses-Call-Detail-Records-To-Identify-Friends.

network structure with reference to observations in recent literature and to the results of our own experiments. We introduce the idea using popularity as an important feature determining influence in social networks. We present a brief analysis of how to determine popularity, where again we highlight the importance of the underlying structural features. Throughout the chapter, we provide implications for further research in order to leverage novel diffusion-based methods for churn prediction by using social roles and popularity, and discuss how to combine these methods with traditional feature-based approaches.

9.2 Understanding Churn in Social Networks

In this section, we focus on what the concept of churn means in digital social networks. Churn has been analysed in a wide range of industries: most widely in the telcom sector [13, 17, 30, 32, 41, 44, 50, 65, 66], but also in the field of retail business [12], banking [69], Internet service providers [31], service industries [53], P2P networks [28] and online games [34]. In its most general sense churn refers to customer loss. In the telcom industry, a subscriber is said to have churned when he leaves one carrier to move to another [33, 49]. Churn rate is defined as the total gross number of subscribers who leave the service in the period divided by the average total customers in the period. The churn rate of a telcom company is a key measure of risk and uncertainty in the marketplace and will be quoted in the company annual report.[2] Annual churn rate may be as high as 40rates tend to be around 2–3 percent.[3] Several studies suggest that retaining existing customers is considerably less expensive than winning new customers [50], and that new customers tend to be less profitable than existing customers [6]. An excerpt from the 2009 Vodafone annual report illustrates uncertainty and risks inherent in not being able to stem customer churn:

> There can be no assurance that the Group will not experience increases in churn rates, particularly as competition intensifies. An increase in churn rates could adversely affect profitability because the Group would experience lower revenue and additional selling costs to replace customers or recapture lost revenue [55].

As such, there is considerable ongoing research focused on extracting features and developing predictive models so that a telcom provider might intervene before a subscriber moves to a competitor. Lifetime value (LTV) analysis is often used to predict the future profitability of a potential churner so that only the most valuable subscribers are targeted for retention [33]. The idea of segmenting contributors in social networks into different value categories based on their predicted value to the community has only begun to be explored [9]. In Sects. 9.6 and 9.7, we begin to develop this idea further.

---

[2] http://www.vodacom.com/reports/ar_2009/pdf/full.pdf, http://www.vodafone.com/annual_report09/downloads/VF_Annual_Report_2009.pdf

[3] http://insidemr.blogspot.com/2006/06/comparison-of-churn-rates.html

9.2.1 Reasons for Churn

Factors contributing to churn have intrinsic and extrinsic features, see Figure 9.1. Intrinsic features relate to inherent qualities of the service/product and/or service provider. For example, Keaveney gives several factors influencing churn in the service industry such as pricing, inconvenience, core service failures, customer service failures and dissatisfaction with provider ethics [35]. In subsequent studies, factors such as these have been decomposed into feature profiles of the customer and customer experience in order to be able to predict churn [1, 33, 49]. Examples of such features include call quality, presence of loyalty points, service usage levels and handset functionality [1]. On the other hand, extrinsic features describe the service in terms of the value it accrues through its social role. This intuition is captured by Metcalfe's "law," which states that the value of a communications network is a function of the number of connected users of the system [3, 46]. Telcom providers that offer discounted calls to the subscribers' family and friends make use of this effect to tie the service to the stability and longevity of a customer's real social network. A related extrinsic function is where the value of a network service is a function of the *opinion* of the customer's social call network. Although there is not a "law" to describe this function, *word-of-mouth* algorithms that combine neighbour preferences to predict the preference of a target user are well established in the domain of on-line recommender systems [18, 27]. Such algorithms explicitly recognise that extrinsic, social features are as important as intrinsic features in determining the perceived value of an object or service. While much research has been carried out on how intrinsic features can be used to predict potential churners, there is comparatively little research on how extrinsic, social features contribute to churn. In Sect. 9.6, we explore this idea in greater detail.

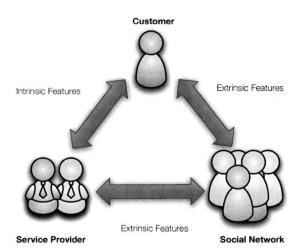

Fig. 9.1 Intrinsic and extrinsic features of churn

Value in Online Communities In this section, we examine the value that subscribers derive from activity in online digital networks. As we will see, such value is tied directly to the social capital of the network. The loss of capital through subscriber loss or significant drop in activity may precipitate spiralling cycles of churn. A key observation of user behavior in online networks is that users, with the exception of spammers, make contributions to online discourse without expecting any immediate return [11, 39]. In sociological discourse, this type of activity is described in terms of the 'gift economy' [58]. In contrast to the commodity or service economy, which is driven by the exchange of good/services for money, economic exchange in the gift economy is defined in terms of an implicit social contract. In a gift transaction, there is an unstated expectation that the benefits of a gift will be reciprocated by the recipient at some reasonable time in the future. A more risky transaction involves 'generalised exchange,' whereby the giver's generosity is reciprocated, not by the recipient, but by someone else in the group. In social networks, this exchange mechanism applies to those contributors who give of their time and expertise but do not appear to receive immediate benefits. However, there is a risk that the group will not assume responsibility for the debt and the contributor will never be reimbursed in kind. In the worst case, if all members of the group never contribute (free-load), no one benefits and the exchange system breaks down. Despite this risk, several motivations for contribution to digital social networks have been proposed [11, 39]. One such is the contributor's expectation of reciprocity under the generalised exchange system. Contributors expect that there will be sufficient payback in terms of information and agreeable social relations from other contributors over time. Another motivation is the contributor's desire to enhance his reputation and prestige by being recognised as a source of valuable information or help. The contributor may also be motivated by trying to have his/her ideas adopted by others in the group. A further motivation concerns the value the contributor places in his attachment to the group or the values represented by the group. Thus, contribution is partly made to sustain the group and the contributor's continuing attachment. For each motivation, the contributor derives value in part from his contribution in a social context. We can hypothesise that churn is an outcome that tends to occur when the expected return drops below a certain threshold–perhaps the cost of contribution. In short, we hypothesise that the contributor's utility function is dependent on the social characteristics of the network.

9.2.2 Churn in Digital Social Networks

As we discussed earlier, the subscriber to an online community is weakly-tied by a non-binding social contract [11]. On the other hand, the telcom subscriber is generally bound by a service contract or by the purchase of advance credit. In general, subscribers have a contract with one telcom provider and tend to break that contract in response to industry-understood 'triggering events,' such as the expiry of the service contract or a poor customer service experience [26]. The main prohibition to customer churn is the switching cost involved in moving to another service provider, such as the loss of loyalty points [37, 43]. Online communities do not have a switching costs. There is a low-entry barrier to join and the contributor may leave without incurring an explicit penalty. More importantly, the contributor may return at any time, and may have simultaneous involvement in several communities. As such, churn is defined by telcom providers in terms of complete loss of custom–the customer has moved to a rival network, while in online communities the notion of churn is less easily defined.

In fact, the ease with which contributors can alter their behavior online suggests that, in contrast to the telcom view, churn is a normative behavior in social networks and that there will always be an an underlying turnover in contributor activity. In P2P networks, churn is defined as the collective effect of the independent join-participate-leave cycles of all peers observed over a given period. Churn in P2P networks effects key design parameters and the resiliency and structure of the overlay network [62]. While this introduces the notion of cyclic join-participate-leave behavior in low entry cost dynamic systems, P2P churn differs from telcom and social network churn because there are no social or contractual ties affecting participation, i.e., peer behavior is independent. In P2P simulation analysis, Herrera and Znati [28] introduced the concept of different classes of peers, some of whose behaviors play a crucial role in the applications that the network can support. Current research in social networks suggests that contributors can be classed according to different roles, and that the presence of roles such as 'popular initiator' or 'supporter' are important for the health and sustainability of the network [9]. Likewise, telcom churn prediction focuses on identifying the profitable subscribers that are about to churn. As such, churn in social networks refers to turnover where there is a net loss of the types of contributors that are needed to maintain the service level of the network. Therefore, churn can be analysed on different levels: per user, per thread, per forum, per community, etc. Unlike in telcom networks where churn is defined in terms of a customer's complete defection, a contributor in a social network may be deemed to be a 'partial defective' if his activity drops significantly below previously established levels of engagement. The overall effect of churn on a social network may be a function of the number of partial defectives who are also high value contributors. By moving from a binary decision (activity stopped or not) to one based on a significant drop in activity, the question of an appropriate churn definition arises. We discuss this in the next section. Moreover, as we show as well, this results in the existence of different types of churn, depending on the significance and duration of drop in activity – and the actual risks and defectives that shall be identified.

9.3 Definitions of Churn in Digital Social Networks

As discussed in Sect. 9.2, the low cost in contributing and in exiting means that online contributors demonstrate behaviour that cannot easily be categorised in terms of binary churn. In this section, we propose an intuitive definition for churn and several variants, while indicating the implications and suitability of different alternatives for several aims and domains. In its most general sense churn is perceived as a significant and sustainable change in the activity of single individuals and/or communities. We argue that no general definition exists that would be the best for each case. Rather, the chosen definition should depend on the application domain and the risks that churn analysis and prediction should indicate. This section is not meant to provide an exhaustive discussion of possible definitions. Rather, its main purpose is to highlight the crucial points for choosing such a definition.

Currently, churn figures highly in research on predicting customer loyalty. Thus, an intuitive definition is a 'partial defective' – customers whose established buying or usage patterns drop significantly, suggesting that they have moved most of their custom elsewhere.

Definition 9.1. Individual Churn: The *previous activity* (PA) window is a time window consisting of time steps t_1 to $t_1 + n - 1$ inclusive, $n \in \mathbb{N}, n \geq 0$. Let $\mu_{PA}(v_i)$ denote the average activity of a user v_i over the previous activity window. The *churn* (C) window is a time window $t_2 = t_1 + n$ to $t_2 + m - 1$ inclusive, $m \in \mathbb{N}, m \geq 0$. Let $\mu_C(v_i)$ denote the average activity of a user v_i over the churn window. A user v_i is considered to have churned during the churn window if:

$$\mu_C(v_i) \leq T(\mathcal{S}) \cdot \mu_{PA}(v_i)$$

$0 \leq T(\mathcal{S}) < 1$ is a threshold factor dependent on the relevant system parameters $\mathcal{S}$.

The definition is more simply stated as:
A user has churned if his or her average activity over a window of m time steps has dropped to less than a fraction T of their average activity in the previous n time steps, where m and n are positive integers and T < 1 is a suitable system-dependent threshold factor.

In Sect. 9.4, we investigate the sensitivity of the above definition to varying parameters n, m and T. Note that it is also possible to define the threshold factor dependent on the user him- or herself, i.e., use v_i as an additional parameter for T. The identification of a suitable threshold factor, the system parameters it depends on and the appropriate past activity presents a particularly interesting problem. Several variants of Definition 9.1 can be differentiated based on these aspects. One alternative is to make churn dependent on whatever constitutes typical activity of the average user in the entire system.

Definition 9.2. Mean activity: Let $a(v_i, t)$ denote the activity of a user v_i at time t, N the total number of time steps in the observations and V denote the set of all users of the network. The mean activity μ_u across all users is defined as:

$$\mu_u = \frac{1}{N \cdot |V|} \sum_{v_i \in V} \sum_{t=1}^{N} a(v_i, t)$$

Based on this mean activity, the following variants of Definition 9.1 are intuitive:

-   **Global Churn:** Replace $\mu_{PA}(v_i)$ in Definition 9.1 by μ_u, use a global threshold factor defined as some function $T(\mu_u, S)$, or both.
-   **Role Churn:** Define separate $\mu_R(r)$ for each existing role r. The definition of $\mu_R(r)$ follows straightforwardly from Definition 9.2 by restricting to only users with role r. Then, replace $\mu_{PA}(v_i)$ in Definition 9.1 by $\mu_R(r)$, use a role threshold factor defined as some function $T(\mu_R(r), S)$, or both.

Roles can be found in a wide range of social networks. For instance, users of forum sites can be classified by the common behaviour roles they play [9]. Some users could play the *popular initiator* role, i.e., tend to initiate many threads and get many replies to their posts. In contrast, other users can play the role of *taciturn*, i.e., have low posting and replying behaviour. The normal and abnormal churning behaviours of the two sets of users are going to be different. Hence, it makes sense to define churn on the basis of the importance of a user, i.e., on the basis of the role they play. Similarly, this can be extended to other levels, dependent on the domain of the system. For instance, for discussion boards, it might be interesting to inspect the typical activity in each forum:

-   **Forum Churn:** Define separate $\mu_F(f)$ for each existing forum f. The definition of $\mu_F(f)$ follows straightforwardly from Definition 9.2 by restricting to only users active in forum f. Then, replace $\mu_{PA}(v_i)$ in Definition 9.1 by $\mu_F(f)$, use a forum threshold factor defined as some function $T(\mu_F(f), S)$, or both.

All the above variants of Definition 9.1 are only examples of how to define churn. Some obvious possibilities to further adapt them, without changing their general meaning, are:

(i) Replace the mean by median.
(ii) Choose other relative thresholds.
(iii) Choose absolute thresholds, i.e., do not include any past activity in the churn definition.
(iv) Require the activity levels to be below the threshold for a continuous span of time, rather than on average.

For certain reasons it might be interesting to identify a user as churner as soon as his activity drops below the threshold for the first time. This can be achieved with Definition 9.1 by setting $m = 1$. As introduced in Sect. 9.2, in social networks different types of churn can occur on different levels. The definition is general and flexible enough to allow several different types of churn and related phenomena to be identified and analysed. Examples of such types for discussion boards are:

-   Detect the emergence of a new forum population: Forum Churn for existing users and increasing activity of other users in the same forum.
-   Detect movement of activity from one forum to another: Forum Churn in one forum and increasing activity of the same users in other forums.
-   Detect the change of the role of an individual user: Role churn of the user while staying above the threshold for another role.

- Churn on different levels of an application can always be mapped to the churn of single individuals: a "dying" discussion thread can be identified if most of the posting users are classified as churners, a "dying" forum is composed of dying threads, etc.

We further investigate the sensitivity of the definition with respect to the included parameters and resulting types of identified churn in Sect. 9.4. Another popular type of churn definition cannot directly be mapped to Definition 9.1. Churn can be defined based on the degree of change in activity, i.e., a point in time when the magnitude of the decreasing rate of change of activity of a user is above some absolute threshold. There are several definitions possible based on a decreasing gradient, where the simplest among them is:

Definition 9.3. Gradient Churn: A user v_i is considered to have churned at time $m, t_1 < m \leq N$ if:

$$-\frac{a(v_i, m) - a(v_i, t_1)}{m - t_1} \geq T(\mathcal{S})$$

where $T(\mathcal{S})$ denotes the threshold associated with this definition.

Simply stated, this definition says:
A user has churned if the absolute slope of his or her decreasing activity over a window of m time steps is above a threshold T, where m is a positive integer and T is a suitable system-dependent threshold.

Again, this definition can be adapted along the dimensions discussed above, i.e., the window size m, absolute and relative thresholds, etc. Other definitions for churn may be based on the ratio between variance and mean of activity, change point detection, etc. However, the discussions presented here highlight the crucial parts in the definition of churn: the applied threshold (factor) T, the window sizes for past activity and churn window as well as the type of past activity used. The right choice is dependent on the domain and the risks that need to be identified. As an example, consider the telcom and online game sectors. To identify likely churners, it is sufficient to identify customers that will drop to an absolute threshold of $T = 0$. The earlier potential churners are required to be identified, the higher this absolute threshold should be. This is based on the observation that usually activity slightly decreases in the months before the decision to churn [34]. The gradient churn definition may be useful to detect churn in any state of the customer lifecycle, rather than only shortly before the churn event. On the other hand, as resources for customer care are usually restricted, providers might want to focus on high-value customers. In this case, applying Role Churn might be the right choice.

A different picture is drawn in social networks that do not imply churning costs for customers, such as discussion boards. Here, risks related to churn materialise in different states and should usually be classified according to the characteristics of the single user, such as his role in a forum. Obviously, relative thresholds for Individual or Role Churn are an intuitive choice in this case. Even if the activity slightly increases after a significant drop, but stays below the critical threshold, this should be understood as an alarming signal in such domains. Whereas in the telcom space it implies that a customer is still active in the network of the operator. In the following section, we present a brief empirical analysis to highlight the effects of different parameters for Definition 9.1 in such social networks.

9.4 Empirical Analysis

Identification of churn in a network will critically depend on whatever constitutes typical behaviour for a user in that network. In this section, we present a basic empirical analysis on two data sets gained from online networks. We indicate the sensitivity of Definition 9.1 from Sect. 9.3 with respect to the choice of the window sizes m and n, and the threshold factor T. We further show that with different parameter combinations it is possible to isolate significantly different types of churn. First, we briefly introduce the two data sets used.

9.4.1 Data Set 1: User Activity in a Discussion Board

The first data set, *Set* 1, consists of the number of posts made per week by individual users in individual forums of the popular Irish forum site *boards.ie*[4] over the course of the year 2006. In the following, we refer to the number of posts vs. time as *activity profile*. On initial inspection of the data the activity profiles for single users in *Set* 1 are very discontinuous and "jagged" (particularly in comparison to *Set* 2, see Sect. 9.4.2). *Set* 1, in its entirety, consists of almost 150,000 activity profiles. However, a large percentage of the users in *Set* 1 make 1–2 posts and never return. These users are of little interest for churn analysis. The loss of regular users is of much greater concern to a service provider. Thus, the data were filtered to isolate users who made an average of at least 10 posts per week. The remaining sample had a size of 300 users. The number of users identified as churners in any window over the course of 2006 was recorded for a range of window sizes and threshold factors. A maximal churn window size m of 26 weeks is a natural choice, as it is half of the total time spanned by the full data set investigated. We applied Definition 9.1 to each activity profile. Selected results of this analysis are shown in Fig. 9.2. The individual figures correspond to different threshold factors. The colour gradient ranges from black, when nobody churns, to white, when all of the sample of 300 are identified as churners.

In Fig. 9.2a it can be seen that when the threshold factor is very low (20%), the condition for churn is quite strong. Thus, for large window sizes m and n very few users are identified as churners. For smaller window sizes more churners are identified. This is due to the nature of the data, as almost all users have a short drop of

---

[4] http://boards.ie

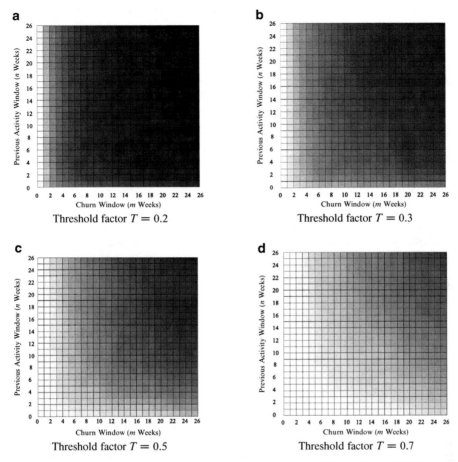

Fig. 9.2 The number of users identified as churners (from black = 0% to white = 100%) is very sensitive to the chosen parameters: previous activity window size n, churn window size m and threshold factor T

activity at some point in time. This explains the white stripe at the far left hand side and shows that such a small window size is not appropriate to identify "real" churn. Along this line the churn window is only one week long, which means that for churn to be identified the user has to be away from the site or has uncharacteristically low activity for only one week. Figure 9.2b shows the same picture for a threshold factor of 30%. Here the condition for churn is weaker, i.e., the drop in activity indicating churn is not as big. Consequently, more churn is identified. In Figs. 9.2c, d it can be seen that as the threshold is raised the conditions for churn become less strict. The number of users identified as churners raises accordingly.

In Sects. 9.2 and 9.3, we mentioned the importance of different types of churn that can occur in social networks. In the following, we present a more detailed analysis using a threshold factor of 20%. Regarding the number of identified churners for different window sizes, it is crucial to understand the relations between parameter values and the according types of identified churn. The threshold factor of 20% represents a rather strict condition and is in-line with an intuitive understanding of churn.

An Approximate Hierarchy. To analyse the effects of parameter choices in more detail, the parameter combinations at A, B, C, D and E in Fig. 9.3 were chosen. They result in significantly contrasting variants of the definition and thus provide insights into the different types of churn that are identified.

As the parameter choices vary from the bottom left of Fig. 9.3 in any positive direction (i.e., as either of the window sizes increases), the criteria for identifying churn becomes stricter. This holds not only along the diagonal, but also, for instance, as we move from parameter combination D to combination A or E. Table 9.1 supports this observation by showing the numbers of users identified as churners for the different parameter combinations. Apparently, the different combinations seem to form a hierarchy, meaning that, for example, all churners identified in A are also identified in D. In fact, this is only an approximate hierarchy, illustrated in Fig. 9.4.

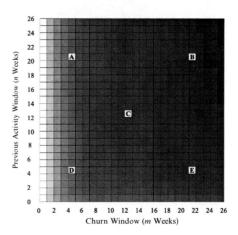

Fig. 9.3 The five parameter sets chosen for further investigation

Table 9.1 Number of churners identified by the different parameter combinations

Parameter set	Previous activity window size n	Churn criteria window size m	No. of churners (out of 300)
A	21	5	130
B	21	21	32
C	13	13	69
D	5	5	137
E	5	21	53

Fig. 9.4 The approximate
hierarchy

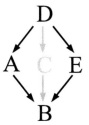

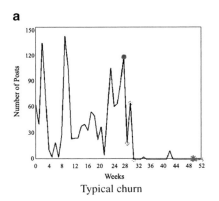

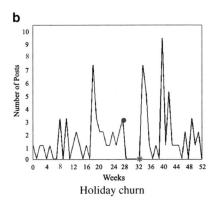

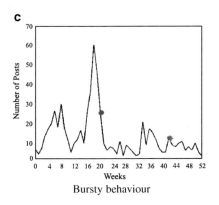

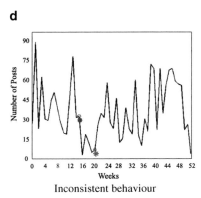

Fig. 9.5 Examples for different types of churn from the approximate hierarchy

Now, the question is what different types of churn are identified by the different parameter combinations. The best way to analyse the differences is by identifying exceptions to the hierarchy. We show examples for these exceptions in Fig. 9.5. In each of the figures, the circles represent the beginning of a churn window in which churn is identified and the stars represent the end of the window. Due to the definition, there may be multiple consecutive churn windows for which churn is detected. The circle and star corresponding to the first churn window are shown in bold.

Typical churn: Churn identified by parameter combination B. Criteria B can be seen as the strictest criteria of all five. It requires that the average activity of the user drops significantly for the longest time, while having been high for an equally long time. The users identified by B are those that we see as *typical churners*. An example is shown in Fig. 9.5a. Out of the 32 churners identified by criteria B, all but 2 are also identified by D and E, all but one are also identified by C and all 32 are identified by A.

Holiday churn: Churn identified by parameter combination A, but not by B or D. We found examples of churn that are identified by parameter combination A, but not by combinations B and D. Such examples might be called *holiday churn*, where a pattern of consistently high activity is interrupted for a short period of 2–4 weeks. Such short drops in activity have to be pronounced enough to significantly affect the average activity when they fall into a short churn window. But, they do not significantly affect the average when they represent only a small part of a much longer churn window. We show an according example activity profile in Fig. 9.5b.

Bursty behaviour: Churn identified by parameter combination E only. E is the parameter combination that refers least to an intuitive understanding of churn. It tends to identify short, uncharacteristically high periods of activity that are preceded by long periods of low or even just average behaviour. This is due to the short previous activity window and the long churn window. We refer to this as *bursty behaviour*. An example, which is identified by E but not by any other combination, is shown in Fig. 9.5c.

Inconsistent behaviour: Churn identified by parameter combination D only. Combination D imposes the least strict criteria for churn. Most users have some uncharacteristically low period of activity for some weeks in the year. Since criteria D has two short windows, it flags a kind of *inconsistent behaviour* as churn, see Fig. 9.5d for an example. By inspecting the amount of churn identified by combination D but not by any other combination, one could try to measure the consistency of users.

Combination C. Combination C, right in the centre of Fig. 9.3, represents a balance between all other combinations. It works well for identifying typical churn, as well as detecting significant periods of churn before recovery. Due to this generality, it is the combination that we use in Sect. 9.6 to analyse network effects for churn.

9.4.2 Data Set 2: Activity in an Online Social Network

The second data set, *Set 2*, is taken from a popular Central-European business-oriented online social network (OSN) and has been used before in [61]. The gathered data are publicly available and delivered automatically through the Web interface of the OSN. Rather than measuring user activity by, for instance, tracing interactions with other users, we could use an explicit activity measure, provided by the OSN operator. This measure does not allow to conclude on session length or exact times of login. But, as simple tests with specially created profiles revealed, represents a reliable indication of the broad frequency of a user's OSN utilisation. It is correlated with each individual user's activity in the previous days and, as a result, never tends to drop off sharply (except in a small percentage of instances where the activity suddenly becomes 0 – this is very likely due to a user's decision to change privacy settings). The activity measure is quantised to multiples of 5 between 5 and 100. In any one day the measure is never observed to change by more than one step. Since the activity measure is slowly varying, the profiles in *Set* 2 are quite smooth. The activity measure was read at 240 intervals over the course of 54 days for a sample of 31,643 users (21,436 male, 10,207 female). The sample has been validated in [61]. The time intervals between each reading were not of consistent duration. As the data gathering was performed on the basis of different random walks, only a random portion of the sample users was measured at each of the 240 steps. On average, 66 activity readings are available for each user over the 54 days. However, since the readings were taken very frequently and the activity measure falls off rather slowly with time, we could reconstruct the activity profiles of all included users. Wherever multiple readings were present for one day, the maximum for that day was taken. If no data were available for a day, the gaps were filled by interpolating between existing values. Because of the short time domain associated with *Set* 2 and the smoothness of the pre-processed activity profiles, we omit a deep analysis and focus on showing that the amount of churn identified is similarly sensitive to the parameters as in the data of *Set* 1.

Definition 9.1 from Sect. 9.3 was applied to each activity profile from a random sample of 3,000 users (we used a random sample for computational reasons). Again, the number of users identified as churners for any window over the course of the 54 days was recorded for a range of window and threshold sizes. Results of this analysis are shown in Fig. 9.6a. The colour gradient ranges from black, when no user is identified as churner, to white, when the maximum of 3,000 users is identified as churners. For the combinations presented, the maximum number of users identified as churners is 380 out of the 3,000. A maximal window size of 27 days is a natural choice, as it is half of the total time spanned by the full dataset investigated. We chose a threshold factor of 50%. Due to the smoothness of the data in *Set* 2, a higher threshold factor is more effective here than for *Set* 1. Figures 9.6b–d show example activity profiles for this threshold factor and previous activity window size $n = 21$ days and churn window size $m = 5$ days. Figure 9.6 shows that, although less data is available than in *Set* 1, the general trends in the sensitivity of the definition to the parameters are the same for both data sets.

Figure 9.6 illustrates that again a variety of different churn types can be identified. Figure 9.6b shows the activity profile of a user who is not identified as a churner for any combination of window sizes. Users like this one, whose average activity over the entire period is greater than 85%, make up almost 40% of the entire data set. In contrast, Fig. 9.6c shows the activity profile of a user who is identified as a churner for a wide range of window sizes. Finally, a potential periodic pattern of activity is illustrated in Fig. 9.6d.

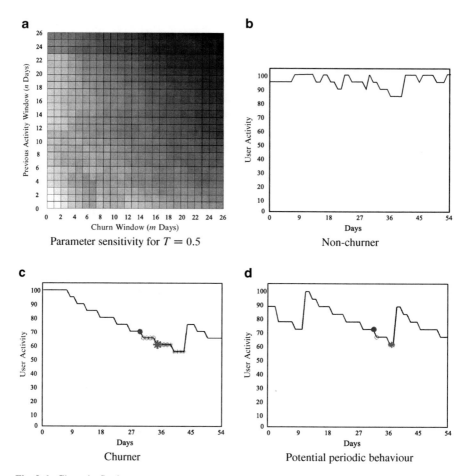

Fig. 9.6 Churn in *Set 2*

9.4.3 Summary

The contrasting nature of the two data sets makes them interesting case studies for the application of the proposed churn definition. By applying Definition 9.1 to *Set* 1, we have shown that the amount and variety of churn identified is highly sensitive to parameter choices. Decreasing the size n of the past activity window increases the sensitivity of the churn detection, i.e., low activity for shorter periods is more often understood as churn. Consequently, increasing n results in detecting more significant churn in an intuitive sense. Increasing the size m of the churn window obviously increases the time until churn is detected as well as the duration of periods of low activity required for indication. Further, we have shown that some interesting types of churn can be isolated by using various combinations of parameters. The data of

Set 1 is better suited to analyse the meaning of the definition and parameters, as it is not as smooth as *Set* 2. However, the similarities in the trends between Figs. 9.2 and 9.6a indicate the same correlations for *Set* 2 as for *Set* 1.

The brief empirical analysis presented here shows that the proposed definition for churn is suited for a wide range of different social networks. Depending on the actual motivation and needs of the analyser, the parameters can be set to detect several different types of churn. The risks and phenomena that can be identified by that range from typical churn, over bursty and (in-)consistent behaviour, to sensitively recognised fluctuations in activity. However, other definitions for churn, as well as data from different kinds of social networks, should be analysed and compared in future work. The presented discussion highlights the importance of the correct understanding and modelling of churn, and the significance of carefully investigating this issue before any meaningful prediction or prevention mechanisms can be developed.

9.5   Models for Churn Prediction

In this section, we briefly summarise the existing state-of-the-art literature on predicting churn. We start with the traditional *feature-based* approaches. Afterwards, we present the few novel approaches based on *social network analysis*.

9.5.1   Feature-Based Approaches

As introduced in Section 9.2, traditionally churn prediction has been approached as a feature-based problem. In this section, we list some concrete techniques and refer to according works. The features of a customer are formed by characteristical data available, such as number of purchased products, number of calls, etc. Feature-based prediction models consist of two parts, *feature selection* and the actual *prediction model*.

During feature selection the most important features of a customer are selected in order to reduce the size of the feature vector. Further, focusing on the most significant features usually increases the accuracy and efficiency of the prediction model [70]. However, feature selection is only used if the number of available features is large enough [6, 12, 49]. Several works discuss feature selection for churn prediction in the telcom sector [49] and other service industries, such as banking [16], Pay-TV [7] and newspapers [12].

[63] suggests two general approaches for feature selection, namely sequential forward selection (SFS) and sequential backward selection (SBS). SFS starts with an empty set and subsequently adds features to it, whereas SBS starts with the complete set of features and eliminates one by one based on a performance test. Several concrete techniques for feature selection are applying clustering techniques, such as k-nearest neighbours (kNN) techniques [14] and self-organising maps (SOM) [65], on the values of feature. Features are chosen based on the quality of the resulting

clusterings. Though, most approaches combine the selection of features with the training step of the actual prediction model. This is the case when building decision trees (or random forests, which basically are multiple decision trees) based on chosen split criteria [8, 14, 52]. [52] applies an induction algorithm to build decision trees. Usually, the best resulting trees, and thus features, are selected using measures like the minimum error rate. Similarly to decision trees, genetic algorithms use fitness functions [14, 63] and neural networks [47, 65] several epochs and hidden layers to select features during the training phase.

Statistical survival analysis has been used to predict churn and is the approach taken in [41]. Ordinal regression has been proposed [22] as an alternative to survival analysis techniques for churn prediction. Latent semantic analysis has also been used to predict churn among insurance policy holders [48]. In this work, the authors highlight the difficulties associated with dealing with time-stamped data. The applicability and suitability of the different approaches varies from one case to another and none of them can be clearly preferred in any of the churn-related industries.

Probably the most popular method for churn prediction (and included feature selection) is logistic regression. It has been applied very successfully in a wide range of works, e.g., [6–8, 12, 49, 51, 53, 57]. The general idea behind it is to create a system of linear equations that combine the available feature values of the training data. Solving the system provides the included coefficients. These represent weighting factors for the different features. For prediction, the gained linear equation is computed based on the features of the user to classify. Logistic regression is a probabilistic classifier, conceptually simple and produces robust results. [7] showed that simple linear regression can outperform sophisticated models like multiple-regression models in special cases. Similar to logistic regression, decision trees (and thus, random forests) are easy to use and provide high accuracy in the classification task [2, 6–8, 12, 17, 49, 57, 69]. One advantage of them is that they are easy to modify during the validation phase, e.g., by pruning nodes with high error-rates. Disadvantages of decision trees are their lack of robustness and suboptimal performance in special cases [7]. A third popular class of prediction models is based on Markov chains [7, 56]. Markov chains represent correlations between successive observations of a random variable. Thus, they are especially effective for evolving populations in rather dynamic systems. Consequently, they are popular if churn data over different time slots is available. On the negative side, the runtime complexity of Markov chains can be very high.

Several alternatives to these traditional approaches have been analysed for churn prediction. One example are neural networks [6, 32, 49, 57, 65, 69]. [2] shows that neural networks can outperform decision trees and logistic regression in the case of the analysed Malaysian wireless provider. Other proposals suggest to apply genetic algorithms [17, 30] and support vector machines (SVM) [12, 69] for the prediction task. In most cases, these alternative approaches may perform as well as the traditional ones, but do not provide a significant increase in accuracy or efficiency. Despite the various approaches for feature selection and churn prediction that can be independently combined, there are also a few systems that process all involved tasks in an automated fashion. Two of them are Data mining by evolutionary learning

(DMEL) [2] and CHAMP (CHurn Analysis, Modeling, and Prediction) [14, 44]. Both support to load raw data and produce churn prediction based on them, without requiring the user to care for feature selection or the actually used prediction model.

Evaluation metrics for binary classifiers (e.g., decision trees) are the well-known measures based on the number of true and false positives and negatives, such as precision, recall and accuracy. Hit ratio (or precision) and lift (also lift ratio) are maybe the two most popular metrics used for evaluating the accuracy of churn prediction models. The hit ratio is measured as the ratio of true positives to true positives plus false positives [13, 32]. Lift measures the improvement of a prediction model compared to a classification based on randomly picking classes and is well used in marketing practice. Hung et al. [32] defined lift as the ratio of hit ratio to the monthly churn rate (i.e., to the number of all churners divided by the number of all customers). Each probabilistic classifier (e.g., logistic regression) can be turned into a binary classifier by introducing a threshold. To evaluate probabilistic classifiers without restricting to a specific threshold, ROC analysis can be used. The ROC graph is built by relating 1-*specificity* on the x-axis to specificity on the y-axis for all possible thresholds, where specificity is the number of true negatives divided by the number of all negatives. [15] showed that the ROC curve is equivalent to the precision-recall curve. The *area under the ROC curve* (AUC) [70] can be used to evaluate a probabilistic classifier and is close to the intuitive understanding of classification quality. It expresses the probability that a randomly picked churner has a higher score than a randomly picked non-churner. Thus, a random classifier has AUC of 0.5, a perfect classifier has AUC 1.0. AUC has the advantage that it is independent from the actual churn rate, in comparison to, for instance, the lift curve (plotted as *Yrate* [8] versus lift, where the Yrate is the number of false and true positives divided by the number of all customers). [8] gives a good overview of the different methods for evaluating churn prediction models and further focuses on the problem of class imbalance. This is a problem if the number of positive cases (churners) is by far below the number of negative cases in the training data. As such, it is particularly crucial for churn prediction. Intuitively, class imbalance can effect the accuracy of the prediction model significantly. [8] discusses several approaches for that problem, such as under-sampling [40] or using specific class ratios (ratio between churners and non-churners) [66]. Similar to [68], one observation is that an equal distribution between both classes is not fruitful, but that otherwise there is no optimal choice for all cases. Further, [8] concludes that advanced sampling techniques do not provide significant improvement and that advanced classification techniques, such as cost-sensitive learners [67] like weighted random forests [10] and boosting [19], should always be compared to logistic regression.

9.5.2   Social Network Analysis for Churn Prediction

As we discuss in Section 9.2, the feature-based approaches are ignoring the social relations in the underlying network. Only recently, some first works consider social network analysis as an alternative or extension to customer churn prediction models solely based on features. [13] models churn in telcom sector as a spread of influence applying the *spreading activation* [60] method. The underlying social networks are created from the call detail records of the customers. Evaluation based on the lift ratio shows that this approach is very promising, as it allows to increase the precision of prediction accuracy significantly. Similarly, [34] models churn for multi-player online games on the basis of the spreading activation model. Churn is represented as a negative influence that propagates from one player to another. In [5], Birke describes a churn prediction model based on the underlying network structure using regression and a diffusion model similar to spreading activation. Hill et al. studied how marketing of a new telcom service was improved by applying a viral marketing process that takes the network structure into consideration [29]. This can be understood as opposite to churn as we define it in this work. All these works are still pioneering and the authors note that the applied diffusion models still require research. Moreover, the common understanding is that the feature-based approaches should probably be enriched by diffusion-based approaches, rather than being replaced. We discuss the use of diffusion models for churn prediction and the combination with feature-based approaches in more detail in the next section.

9.6 Network Effects and Propagation of Churn

As mentioned above, only recently [13, 34] discussed the correlation between the probability of a user to churn and the number of his neighbours that already churned. Both works proposed diffusion models to describe how churn, specifically, churn influence, is propagated between users. Using these models, they were able to increase the accuracy of traditional feature-based prediction methods. We posit that network effects are a crucial factor of churn in social networks and that they are an important component in modelling and predicting churn. To this end, we already highlighted the importance of extrinsic features in Section 9.2. In this section, we provide some details how basic diffusion models were used in the works mentioned above to predict churn and discuss important improvements. Afterwards, we highlight the importance of user roles and how different roles are likely to have different influences on fellow users.

9.6.1 Network Views

Graphs built from social networks are a natural representation of the social influence between people. Vertices represent people and edges can represent a variety of relationships. Examples include friendship links in OSNs, frequent interactions in discussion boards, or similarity in interests. In studying churn, we are interested in how churners influence other people to churn, hence, we are interested in networks that are associated with influences.

In many cases, an explicit network structure exists, e.g., a call graph in the telcom sector or friendship relations in OSNs. However, this explicit network might not be the most appropriate representation for modelling influence between users, or it might be worth analysing different network *views* of the same social network. As an example, consider OSNs, where user-defined friendship relations constitute the explicit network, but other views can be constructed, e.g., on the basis of group membership, blog following, etc. Moreover, other social networks like boards.ie do not always define an explicit network structure. Different influence network views can be built based on connections between users that refer to replies, activity in the same forum or thread, etc.

One useful network view for discussion boards like boards.ie (*Set* 1, cf. Sect. 9.4) is the user-to-user interaction network. It represents the users and the amount of pairwise interaction, in terms of number of posts, number of threads and number of forums two users are involved in. In this section, we want to measure whether there is a network effect for churning based on these interaction networks. The idea is to infer the influence of one user on another by the amount of communication between them. The more communications a user A has with another user B, the more influence user B might have on user A. If user B churns, this will more likely affect user A than some other user who has low communications with A.

In contrast, the users in the business-oriented OSN (*Set* 2, cf. Sect. 9.4) have explicit links between professional associates. Users can see the activities of associates, and in general, a professional network is only valuable to a user if he or she has links to associates of value. If these relatively important associates churn, this might cause a user to churn as well. Therefore, the explicit associate links can be used to model the spread of influence. However, other possible influence paths can be constructed via similarity in features (also known as homophily [45]). The network view here is to link individuals who are similar, such as in hobbies, employment, gender, combinations of individual features, etc.

Based on the different possible network views briefly discussed here, in the following we introduce how diffusion models can be applied on top of these network views. It is important to understand that different network views should be investigated and that different diffusion models (with different extensions and different models for influence) have to be applied.

9.6.2   Diffusion Models

The idea behind diffusion models for churn prediction is that some few key individuals, the churners, may influence other individuals by word-of-mouth effects to churn themselves. These, in turn, influence their neighbours (e.g., friends) in the underlying social network, and so on. Diffusion models have a long history in social sciences [4, 24] and epidemiology [36]. Since that, they have been adopted for a wide range of applications. The basic idea behind modelling churn as a diffusion process is illustrated in Fig. 9.7. The two already influenced nodes (i.e., churners)

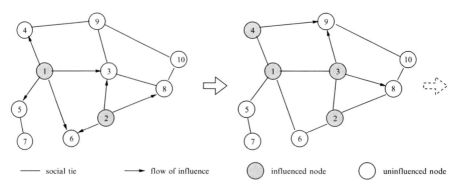

Fig. 9.7 Sketch of an influence diffusion process

1 and 2 have some influence on their neighbours. Consequently, in the next time step some of their neighbours (nodes 3 and 4) are influenced and decide to churn, while some (nodes 5, 6 and 8) stay uninfluenced. This process continues over time, so that nodes 8-10 might become influenced in later time steps. Note that there are models that also allow nodes 5–7 become influenced later on, e.g., in the *spreading activation* (SPA) model the energy (i.e., influence) of an already influenced node can increase over time.

In [29], the authors explored options for improving direct-mail marketing to reach people who might be interested to subscribe to their service. Such target-based marketing can be seen as efforts to initiate activity (as opposite to churn). As resources for such direct marketing initiatives are usually limited, the idea is to identify people who are especially prone to subscribe to their service. The authors observed that this is true for people who have regular communication with the present customers. They developed a multivariate model to predict the people who would be most likely to join their customer base, including network features like degree and connected component size. Thus, this work combines the analysis of *structural* features with a first step of diffusion models – targeting those who are in direct communication with the present customers builds on the assumption that influence diffuses by word-of-mouth over direct relations. [13] applies the SPA model to predict churn based on the idea of social influence in a telcom network. The SPA model is a basic model for information diffusion. Influence is spread by an infected node to its neighbours. The spread takes place in discrete time steps and at any time step the total amount of influence (i.e., energy) over all nodes remains the same. How the influence is spread is modelled using a global spreading factor and a transfer function. The already infected nodes act as seeds from where the spread starts. If the spreading factor is low, the amount of influence transferred is less but the spread takes place quickly. If the spreading factor is high, the spread is more effective in the current neighbourhood of an infected node. Hence, it becomes slow and cannot propagate fast, as it gets "trapped" inside highly connected neighbourhoods. The transfer function depends on the relative weight of the edge between two nodes and signifies what fraction of influence should be transferred from one node to another. At each step, the amount of influence transferred by a node to its neighbour is determined by the product of the spreading factor, the output of the transfer function and the influence remaining in the node at that step. The process terminates under two conditions. Firstly, if the number of the activated nodes remains same for two consecutive steps. Secondly, if the energy transferred by a node at a step is not greater than the *accuracy threshold*. [34] also suggests churn prediction based on the SPA model, but in the area of online games. The authors extend the original model by several parameters based on the features of online gamers. They further model negative influence, include the engagement level of players and develop mechanisms for the exchange of positive and negative influences. [5] uses a model called survival analysis. This is based on the notion of how an infected node infects its neighbours. By that, it is similar to the analysis of virus spreads and viral marketing. Similar to SPA, this is based on the idea of diffusion of information in the underlying network.

SPA can be applied easily to many applications. However, it is a rather simple model for information diffusion. Tuning spreading factor and transfer function to reflect actual influences poses a problem. Some observations that do not adhere to the intuitive understanding of spreading churn influence are:

– churners can collect more energy over time, but actually their influence should not increase
– spread of energy is mainly determined by global factors, rather than by individual relations
– the model does not differentiate between different roles and popularity of individuals, which will result in different influence effects in the network

[13] also states that there are several directions for improving their approach. This involves optimising the SPA parameters, evaluating other diffusion models, focusing on influential individuals for churn prevention, and investigating how social influences can be incorporated. Further, the authors mention the promising idea to combine their approach with decision trees on conventional and structural features. Alternatively, this could be based on link-based classification. We discuss this direction in more detail in Sect. 9.6.3. [34] comes to a similar conclusion. The authors plan to accommodate players engagement versus group engagement into influence propagation, to provide recency-frequency-money (RFM) analysis, and to apply queueing theory for prediction.

We believe that some of the well-known models are better suited to predict churn based on the influence of individuals than the introduced SPA model. In the *linear threshold model* [59] neighbours are only successfully influenced if the influence summed over all seed nodes is larger than a pre-defined threshold. The *independent cascade model* [21] is based on individual cascades between nodes and the *heat diffusion model* [42] works similar to SPA. Further, there exist several extensions of these basic models. [25] provides a broad survey and further pointers to more detailed surveys for most of the traditional models. For an improved churn prediction, these models should be combined with positive and negative influences, e.g., by combining linear thresholds with a sentiment measure. Furthermore, similarity in an

user's and neighbour's features (homophily) and its effect on churn diffusion should
be investigated. In addition, diffusion-based models for predicting churn should take
external circumstances into account. This should include external events (e.g., a new
provider enters the arena with special offers), the importance of providers' pricing
politics and reputation to geographical aspects. A last aspect that up to now did
not receive enough attention is to analyse the "direction" of influence, i.e., is the
influence implicit or is it explicitly initiated by the churner.

As a key observation, the degree of influence and thus the process of diffusion has
to be analysed with respect to the social roles and popularity of the involved individuals. This involves local popularity (influence among the individual's direct friends,
this relates to the strength of social ties [24]) as well as global popularity (with
respect to the whole network, which relates to social roles in the network [9]). Intuitively, popularity and resulting influence are strongly dependent on the underlying
application domain and can therefore not be defined in general. In this light, we
discuss approaches for determining popularity, social roles and according influence
in Sect. 9.7.

9.6.3 Combining Feature-Based Approaches and Diffusion Models

Although recent works successfully predicted churn on the basis of diffusion models, the long history of feature-based approaches for churn prediction shows that
they are also well-suited for that task. In the literature (e.g., [1]), there is the common
agreement that the key to tackle churn is to identify the point at which customers
experience a change of their status, e.g., before they become dissatisfied with the
service and decide to switch to an alternative provider. According data mining
approaches are based on several indicators for predicting customers who are likely to
churn, such as the initial activation period, the number of customer service queries,
price band and the original sales channel. Such approaches were successfully used
to significantly reduce churn rates in telcom industries. However, these numbers
cannot be achieved for all service industries and it is difficult to apply the feature-
based approach in social networks. Reasons for this are the special characteristics of
churn in social networks (cf. Sect. 9.2) and the problem that many required features
are often not available or not trustworthy (e.g., naming a gender on a forum site can
be done by choice and with the intention to cheat).

Intuitively, one should not have to decide between either a feature-based or a
diffusion-based approach. Rather, both ideas should be combined accordingly to

achieve prediction accuracy and efficiency that none of the two approaches could achieve on their own. This idea is also suggested by [13]. After comparing the proposed SPA-based approach with a simple decision tree approach, the authors conclude that a combination of both is the most promising future direction. They suggest a list of features that should be considered for the telcom industry. Apparently, this is only a first list that should be modified and fine-tuned with respect to the prediction accuracy. Feature selection models, as mentioned in Sect. 9.5, can be used to automate this task. To this end, a combination of decision trees with diffusion-based techniques has been identified as most promising. [34] also indicates such a combined approach by using more features to determine player engagement, which shall be used to steer and fine-tune the underlying diffusion process.

To the best of our knowledge, up to now there is no concrete suggestion or proposal of how to exactly combine both worlds. Further research has to analyse the possibilities of using features to adapt the influence of individuals effective in the diffusion process. We propose to focus further research on an enrichment of the *conventional* features by *structural* features (connectivity, degree, triangles, path lengths, etc.). As we show in Sect. 9.7.2, such features are better suited to identify and define social roles, popularity and resulting influence. In a preliminary analysis, [13] found that decision trees combining both types of features perform better than those restricted to conventional features. The authors come to the conclusion that SPA further helps "to learn" the important ties in a network, which cannot be achieved with feature-based approaches only. This goes along with research in the area of *link mining* as a new discipline between link analysis, Web mining, relational learning and graph mining [20]. [20] also suggests to combine the analysis of probabilistic dependencies with the analysis of link structure, resulting in *link-based classification*. Link-based classification uses conventional features of an individual, the links that the individual participates in, as well as features of individuals connected by a path in the network.

An alternative direction worth investigation is the use of an inverse approach, i.e., use information diffusion to adapt (as input for) the feature-based approach. However, this direction seems to be not as obvious. Further, we argue to include a kind of *meta features* and *external features*. Meta features are defined by the combination of several "atomic" features of individuals. That is, several features might not be well-suited as indicators for churn, but still they influence the actual process of diffusion. Classical metrics from the social network analysis, such as local clustering coefficient and betweenness measures, can be understood as meta features on top of structural features. One meta feature on top of structural as well as conventional features is popularity. As we discuss in the following section, popularity of individuals has very strong impact on their local and global influence in the network. Again, this relates to the computation of *aggregate features* as mentioned in [20]. External features relate to external events, such as a general hype due to new players or aggressive advertising, bad reviews, hacking of sites, new alternatives on the market, etc.

9.7 Popularity and Influence in Social Networks

In the previous section, we highlighted the importance of influence that individuals have on their neighbours and other individuals in the network. Intuitively, such influence can be seen in relation to the *popularity* of individuals. The more popular a user is seen by others, the more influence he or she will have on them. We have already briefly discussed the approach of using popularity to model influence in diffusion processes by the means of a meta feature. In this section, we discuss the notion of popularity, its relation to influence and information diffusion as well as approaches for analysing popularity on the basis of the two data sets introduced in Sect. 9.4.

Most service providers provide information about their users by default. Such conventional features include the registration date of the users, their usage frequency, etc. However, the actual notion of popularity and the determining features strongly depend on the kind of social network and application. We posit that in social networks popularity stronger depends on structural features (cf. number of contacts, betweenness) than on conventional features.

9.7.1 Social Roles and Influence in Discussion Boards

In this section, we discuss the roles users play in discussion boards and how these can affect churn. In previous work [9], the authors grouped the common features of users in boards.ie (*Set* 1 from Sect. 9.4), and proposed eight different social roles played by users in boards.ie. These were: joining conversationalists, popular initiators, taciturns, supporters, elitists, popular participates, grunts, and ignored. The roles were determined on the basis of conventional and structural features, where the underlying network was constructed from the reply-to structure (nodes represent users, an edge represents one user replying to another in a forum thread).

We posit that different roles have different amount of influence on other roles. For example, users playing the elitist role might have strong influence on other users playing the same role, but users in all other roles will have little or no influence on the users of the elitist role. Regarding that the roles are determined based on the reply-to structure, the notion of popularity is intuitively an important factor. The more popular a user is, the more post views and replies he or she gets from other users, therefore exerting more influence on him or her fellow users. We indicate the relation between popularity and influence in Fig. 9.8. Similar to preliminary experiments in [13, 34], Fig. 9.8a shows an individual's probability to churn in relation to the number k of the neighbours that already churned. This probability is determined by dividing the number of all current churners that have k churned neighbours by the total number of users that have k churned neighbours. In other words, it is the percentage of all people with k churning neighbours who decided to churn as well. The figure shows this relation for four different reply graphs. The number of replies constitutes the weight of an edge. We averaged the values over all forums and over all analysed time slots. The labels with out refer to the graph based on only

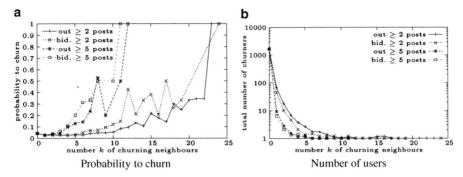

Fig. 9.8 Network effects on the probability to churn

outgoing edges, `bid`. refers to the graph containing only bidirectional edges (thus, it is sparser). To highlight the effects of popularity on influence, we filtered edges by their weight: ≥ 2 contains only edges with a weight larger than 1, ≥ 5 contains only edges with weight larger than 4.

As expected, the churn probability increases with k, which illustrates the existence of network effects (i.e., the more churning neighbours there are, the more likely a user is to churn also). The fact that this probability is 1.0 for some k is because only a few users have that many churning neighbours, and all these users churned as well. To illustrate this, we show the total number of churners with k churned neighbours in Fig. 9.8b. Note that the y axis is shown in log scale. Furthermore, comparing the outgoing edge results for ≥ 2 and ≥ 5 posts in Fig. 9.8a shows that the amount of influence is apparently increasing with the number of replies between users. Intuitively, an increased outgoing edge weight can be interpreted as increased popularity. This means, the more popular the neighbours are, the more likely a user will churn. It demonstrates the validity of determining influence based on popularity, where popularity is determined based on structural features of the graphs. The results provide only first insights into the relation between popularity, influence and diffusion, but highlight the appropriateness of further research in that direction.

In the literature, there are several approaches to measure influence. The popular Pagerank [54] and HITS algorithms [38] are two examples. In these approaches, influential Web pages (or people) are those that receive many in-links from reputable Web pages (or other people) and have fewer out-links. These approaches work well for measuring absolute influence and reputation. However, there are better approaches for measuring relative influence, which should be assumed in the case of roles and churn. One value or measure of influence is hence not appropriate. We propose that we need to examine conditional influence - conditional on the users and possibly features. There has been some recent work in this direction for determining different influence measures for different topics [64] and movies [23], which we plan to explore for determining relative influence of roles.

The crucial point for an appropriate application of diffusion models for churn prediction will be the inclusion of social roles, popularity and the according individual (conditional) influence of users into the used diffusion model. This is not possible in the basic version of the SPA model introduced in Sect. 9.6.2. The main questions that have to be answered are:

1. How should popularity be defined and determined in different social networks?
2. Is the influence of an individual a function of his or her popularity?

In the next section, we briefly investigate an intuitive notion for popularity in OSN and the feasibility of different features to determine it.

9.7.2 Popularity in Online Social Networks

Due to the limitations for *Set* 2 from Sect. 9.4 (explained in that section), and the fact that the relation can be expected to be similar (see also [13, 34]), we omit an analysis of the churn probability in this section. However, the gathered data allows to indicate the importance of an analysis of popularity based on structural features. In the following, we highlight that they are more important than conventional features for this task. To this end, this section indicates one direction of how to combine feature-based churn prediction with diffusion-based approaches.

Social networking services contain a wealth of information. Users voluntarily feed self-descriptive details into the OSN and their utilisation behaviour is completely observable by the OSN provider. Analysing this complex data facilitates understanding of the psychological and sociological properties of online social networks and their users. Identifying key properties of users and their profiles, which allow for the prediction of their popularity, however, is not only interesting for social scientists. Especially system designers and developers of social networking services may capitalise on the extracted knowledge. In case of centralised, server-based systems, the user experience may be enhanced by decreasing service delays of frequently requested profiles. They may prove even more valuable for the development of decentralised designs (cmp. Chap. 17: "Decentralized Online Social Networks"), i.e., for the parametrisation of this entirely different approach to provide social networking services. Being able to predict the popularity may help suggesting necessary availability levels for selected profiles, and they may indicate which profiles can more frequently tolerate temporary inavailabilities without causing a significant deterioration of the service experience. System designers additionally may be able to derive timing constraints for different profiles, and hence be able to decide which profiles need to be presented with very low delay, and be able to identify properties of profiles that may tolerate higher response times.

The same as mentioned for the activity of users (Sect. 9.4.2) holds for the popularity of their profiles. Messages sent to the wall, commenting photos or posts left in guest books indicate at least one profile impression. More detailed information is given by explicit counters of the number of requests to a profile. It consequently allows for the identification of relations between characteristics of profiles and the frequency with which they are viewed. Thus, in the following we refer to the popularity of users by the frequency of profile impressions, i.e., the number of visits to their profile by other users of the OSN.

Features for Determining Popularity. Access to profiles and the full user behaviour for scientific purposes is rather difficult, since, for obvious commercial and privacy reasons, OSN providers are keen on their protection and highly unwilling to disclose them. Some information, however, can be deduced by directly accessing the publicly available profiles through the Web interface of the social networking service. The main purpose of participating in an OSN being to publish information about oneself, the users willingly share quite detailed information on themselves, usually including the list of other users they have contacted. The information that usually is contributed by the users can be grouped into a few categories:

- Identifying data of the person
- Contact details
- Personal interests
- Work experience
- Curriculum vitae (affiliations, educational information)
- Recommendations (or direct comments and messages from other users, left at the wall or guest book)
- The list of friends and contacts

The number of impressions of a profile is usually integrated into the presented profile automatically, without any participation of the user (cmp. Chap. 21: "Security and Privacy Threats in Current Online Social Networks" for a concise list of the data that frequently is published in OSN profiles). The gender, though usually not explicitly stated, can easily be derived from the name, even in an automated fashion.

Relations between Features and Popularity. A previous analysis [61] reveals different relations between selected features and the popularity of profiles, based on data from a large set of monitored profiles. It studies in detail which influence the gender and inclusion of a profile photo have on the popularity and additionally correlates the popularity of profiles with the number of contacts, the number of joined interest groups inside the OSN, and the average activity of the users. The study is divided into two parts. The first part uses Mann-Whitney U tests to analyse non-parametric relationships between classes of users and their corresponding profile popularity. Potential correlations between parametric features of the users and their corresponding profiles are analysed in the second part, using Pearson's correlation coefficient r. In the following, we summarise the main observations of this study, which are collected in Table 9.2.

A first hypothesis stated that the gender of users would have impact on the popularity of their profiles. Profiles of male ($Mdn = 0.039$) and female ($Mdn = 0.041$) users did not experience significantly different popularity (ns). The impact of providing a profile photo has been analysed in the next step. The results supported the hypothesis that profiles including a photo ($Mdn = 0.043$) were significantly more often requested than profiles without a photo ($Mdn = 0.016$, $p < 0.001$, estimated distance $= 0.024$, or one profile impression every second day). Significance and estimated distance where almost identical when testing the subsamples of male and female profiles, including vs. excluding profile pictures.

Table 9.2 Summary of the popularity experiment

Similarity and difference of means of *Popularity* π_{v_i} (rank sum)		
Gender	Male *Mdn* = 0.039 Female *Mdn* = 0.041	*no sign. difference*
Profile Picture	Picture (*Mdn* = 0.043) > No picture (*Mdn* = 0.016) ($p < 0.001$)	
Correlational observations (Pearson's r)		
Accepted contacts	correlation: $r \approx 0.75$ ($p < 0.001$)	
	Male	$0.74 < r < 0.75$	($p < 0.05$)
	Female	$0.81 < r < 0.83$	($p < 0.05$)
Profile alterations	correlation: $r \approx 0.62$ ($p < 0.001$)	
Subscribed groups	correlation: $r \approx 0.37$ ($p < 0.001$)	
	Male	$0.37 < r < 0.4$	($p < 0.05$)
	Female	$0.33 < r < 0.37$	($p < 0.05$)
Average activity	correlation: $r \approx 0.17$ ($p < 0.001$)	
	Male (0.18)	Female (0.16)	*no sign. difference*

A correlational study has been performed in the second part. First, the study examined if the membership duration has an impact on the popularity of the member's profile. With preferential attachment in mind, the correlation between membership duration and the number of contacts was estimated. Testing H_0 that the true correlation between membership duration and the number of contacts was 0 failed ($p < 0.001$), indicating that a correlation indeed exists. Pearson's r was estimated to $r \approx 0.19$, a very slight correlation, with $0.18 < p < 0.20$ to a confidence of 95%.

Since this factor does not seem to have a high influence on the profile popularity, it was further investigated if correlations between popularity and selected features of the profiles could be detected. Investigated were the hypotheses that the popularity of profiles increased in correlation with the activity of the corresponding user, with its degree, and with the number of subscribed interest groups.

The first hypothesis was that profiles of highly active users will experience a generally higher popularity than the profiles of inactive users. Testing the hypothesis that the correlation between activity and popularity is 0 fails ($p < 0.001$). Pearson's product moment correlation is determined to be 0.17, again indicating a very slight correlation between activity of the users and the popularity of their profiles. This correlation is slightly, but not significantly, higher for male users ($0.16 < r < 0.19$ with $p < 0.05$) than for female users ($0.14 < r < 0.18$ with $p < 0.05$). The activity tested in this case was the measure given by the social network provider, which was not very fine-grained and reliable (cf. Sect. 9.4.2). In contrast, using the alteration frequency of profiles (the frequency with which user-maintained details of the profiles had been changed) yielded surprising results. Again, Pearson's test was significant ($p < 0.001$). The product moment correlation between the alteration frequency of a profile and its popularity was estimated to a high 0.62 ($0.61 < r < 0.63$

with $p < 0.025$). This correlation may be caused by the fact that the last five changes to profiles of contacts are presented to the users after logging into the OSN. A constant profile alteration consequently increases the chances of a user to be visible with his contacts.

Modifying the hypothesis, it was studied if a correlation between the degree of a profile (the number of accepted contacts) and its popularity could be found. The hypothesis that the correlation between degree and popularity is 0 fails, too. Pearson's r indicates a quite high correlation between the two variables of $r = 0.75$ ($p < 0.001$). This correlation is significantly higher for profiles of female users ($0.81 < r < 0.83$, $p < 0.05$) compared to male users ($0.74 < r < 0.75$, $p < 0.05$). A final correlational study based on the features of the profiles has been performed to determine the relation between the number of subscribed groups and the popularity of the subscribed users. The results refuse a correlation of 0 between groups and popularity and suggest a correlation of $r = 0.37$. In this case, the correlation is significantly higher for male users ($0.37 < r < 0.4$, $p < 0.05$) compared to female users ($0.33 < r < 0.37$, $p < 0.05$).

Roughly said, intuitive beliefs about profile popularity are abundant. Unverified rumours frequently state that the unfortunate possession of a last name late in the alphabet will inevitably condemn a user's profile to eternal lack of popularity. The simple rationale behind this conjecture is that profiles are usually listed in increasing alphabetical order of the last names. Users in the beginning of that list might plainly enjoy a higher visibility due to the fact that other users start browsing contact lists, which usually contain only ten contacts per presented page. If they do not pursue to the later pages, they hence do not reach users from the end of the alphabetical list. A last analysis reflects this intuitive question of the relation between a user's name and the profile popularity. The tested correlation is very slightly, but not significantly, if determined for the whole group of users ($r = -0.01, ns$). Analysing the *rich club* of profiles with the highest popularity, in contrast, leads to an impressive change of results. Considering the 5% profiles with the highest popularity already yields a correlation of $r \approx -0.09$ ($ns, -0.26 < r < 0.08$ with $p < 0.025$). This correlation gets more significant with increasing "exclusivity" of the rich club: Analysing the top 2‰ of profiles the correlation increases to $r \approx -0.22$ ($ns, -0.47 < r < 0.06$ with $p < 0.025$), for the top 1‰ of profiles to $r \approx -0.29$ ($ns, -0.62 < r < 0.11$ with $p < 0.025$), and for the top 10 users, it finally increases to $r \approx -0.9$, $p < 0.001$ ($-0.98 < r < -0.61$ with $p < 0.025$). Considering the very small samples size, this result of course has to be taken with a grain of salt.

Discussion. Considering the results of the study, certain features can actually indicate the expected popularity of profiles in OSNs. They strongly support correlations between the activity of users, their participation in interest groups, and most importantly the number of accepted contacts of a profile with its popularity. Additionally, they suggest that profiles with pictures will be more frequently viewed than profiles without, while no difference between the profiles and male vs. female users could be determined. As expected, this highlights the importance of combining the right choice of conventional features with structural features in order to meaningfully determine popularity. Next steps should be to analyse different OSN and other types of social networks, and to combine an appropriate classification technique (such as decision trees) with the proposed diffusion-based churn prediction.

9.8 Summary and Conclusion

This chapter dealt with churn in social networks. Research on churn currently enjoys great popularity, since churning customers cause effective loss of revenues at service providers and similarly affected companies. But, the focus usually lies on contractual services like in the telcom sector. The notion of churn, the factors driving it, such as the social costs compared to purely monetary reasons, and the risks in social networks are not well understood nor researched. This chapter aims at filling this gap by reflecting on the specifics of churn in social networks. First, we discussed different notions, reasons and facets of churn. In this context, and as an extension to the traditional understanding, churn was defined as an individual's act of significantly decreasing activity in a social network. The ability to estimate churn behaviour could enable stake-holders to react early, trying to change the potential churner's mind, and churn prediction consequently promises to help companies avert potentially decreasing income. Moreover, in social networks churn is also relating to the health of the underlying communities and its prediction is therefore mandatory for successful (self-)governance.

In this chapter, we have further given an overview of the current research on churn detection and interpretation, including discussions on appropriate definitions of churn. After providing our own suggestion for defining churn, we showed its effectiveness and crucial parameters on the basis of two example social networks. The first data set comprises the activity measures of users in discussion boards (over ten years of data from http://www.boards.ie, from which we took the data for 2006). The second data set contains a random set of over 30,000 user profiles from a predominant central European online social network for professional purposes, which we have gathered using a publicly available interface.

Existing approaches for churn prediction have been introduced. With a look on novel approaches and the intuition of the importance of the underlying social network structure, we discussed required extensions of the traditional approaches by techniques from social network analysis. One focus on this is the introduction of diffusion models, which has also been pointed out in other recent work. Finally, we have presented results of first studies on popularity and churn prediction. We propose that popularity should be regarded as a main factor for modelling the differences in social influence, which is mandatory for a successful application of information diffusion for churn prediction.

The results presented here show that the proposed churn definition is appropriate for identifying a wide range of different churn types that are special for social networks. This enables to detect and predict churn in social networks for a wide range of application domains and potential risks that are of interest. Further, it highlights the crucial factors of understanding and handling churn. We showed that there is a relationship between churn, network effects and influence. Based on the literature review, we proposed to combine traditional feature-based churn prediction with diffusion models. We highlighted possible directions and open issues for this novel field of research in social networks. Finally, we assessed the relationship between popularity, determining the degree of social influence, and features that determine popularity. The results emphasise the need for focusing on structural features and relations as an extension to mining conventional features. Open issues and future research directions resulting from the gained insights and discussions have been highlighted throughout the chapter.

Acknowledgments This work was carried out in part in the CLIQUE Strategic Research Cluster, which is funded by Science Foundation Ireland (SFI) under grant number 08/SRC/I1407, and under partial funding of ETRI and DFG FOR 733 ("QuaP2P").

References

1. J.-H. Ahn, S.-P. Han, and Y.-S. Lee. Customer churn analysis: Churn determinants and mediation effects of partial defection in the korean mobile telecommunications service industry. *Telecommunications Policy*, 30(10–11):552–568, 2006
2. W.-H. Au, K. C. C. Chan, and X. Yao. A novel evolutionary data mining algorithm with applications to churn prediction. *IEEE Trans. Evolutionary Computation*, 7(6):532–545, 2003
3. A. O. B. Briscoe and B. Tilly. Metcalfe's law is wrong, July 2006
4. F. M. Bass. A Dynamic Model of Market Share and Sales Behavior. In *Winter Conference American Marketing Association*, 1963
5. D. Birke. Diffusion on networks: Modelling the spread of innovations and customer churn over social networks. In *GI Jahrestagung (2)*, pages 480–488, 2006
6. W. Buckinx and D. V. den Poel. Customer base analysis: partial defection of behaviourally loyal clients in a non-contractual FMCG retail setting. *European Journal of Operational Research*, 164(1):252–268, 2005
7. J. Burez and D. V. den Poel. CRM at a pay-TV company: Using analytical models to reduce customer attrition by targeted marketing for subscription services. *Expert Syst. Appl*, 32(2):277–288, 2007
8. J. Burez and D. V. den Poel. Handling class imbalance in customer churn prediction. *Expert Syst. Appl*, 36(3):4626–4636, 2009
9. J. Chan, E. M. Daly, and C. Hayes. Decomposing discussion forums and boards using user roles. In *AAAI Conference on Weblogs and Social Media*, pages 215–218, 2010
10. C. Chen, A. Liaw, and L. Breiman. Using Random Forest to Learn Imbalanced Data. Technical report, University of California at Berkley, 2004
11. D. Constant, L. Sproull, and S. Kiesler. The kindness of strangers: The usefulness of electronic weak ties for technical advice. *Organization Science*, 7(2):119–135, 1996
12. K. Coussement and D. V. den Poel. Churn prediction in subscription services: An application of support vector machines while comparing two parameter-selection techniques. *Expert Syst. Appl*, 34(1):313–327, 2008
13. K. Dasgupta, R. Singh, B. Viswanathan, D. Chakraborty, S. Mukherjea, A. A. Nanavati, and A. Joshi. Social ties and their relevance to churn in mobile telecom networks. In *EDBT '08*, pages 668–677, 2008
14. P. Datta, B. M. Masand, D. R. Mani, and B. Li. Automated cellular modeling and prediction on a large scale. *Artif. Intell. Rev.*, 14(6):485–502, 2000

15. J. Davis and M. Goadrich. The relationship between Precision-Recall and ROC curves. In *ICML '06*, pages 233–240, 2006
16. D. V. den Poel and B. Larivière. Customer attrition analysis for financial services using proportional hazard models. *European Journal of Operational Research*, 157(1):196–217, 2004
17. J. Ferreira, M. B. R. Vellasco, M. A. C. Pacheco, and C. R. H. Barbosa. Data mining techniques on the evaluation of wireless churn. In *ESANN*, pages 483–488, 2004
18. Y. Freund, R. Iyer, R. E. Schapire, and Y. Singer. An efficient boosting algorithm for combining preferences. *J. Mach. Learn. Res.*, 4:933–969, 2003
19. J. H. Friedman. Stochastic gradient boosting. *Comput. Stat. Data Anal.*, 38(4):367–378, 2002
20. L. Getoor. Link mining: a new data mining challenge. *SIGKDD Explor. Newsl.*, 5(1):84–89, 2003
21. J. Goldenberg, B. Libai, and E. Muller. Using Complex Systems Analysis to Advance Marketing Theory Development: Modeling Heterogeneity Effects on New Product Growth Through Stochastic Cellular Automata. In *Academy of Marketing Science Review*, 2001
22. S. Gopal, R.K. Meher. Customer churn time prediction in mobile telecommunication industry using ordinal regression. *Lecture Notes in Computer Science*, 884–889(5012):252–268, 2008
23. A. Goyal, F. Bonchi, and L. V. Lakshmanan. Discovering leaders from community actions. In *CIKM '08*, pages 499–508, ACM, NY, 2008
24. M. Granovetter. The Strength of Weak Ties. *American Journal of Sociology*, 78(6):1360–1380, 1973
25. D. Gruhl, R. Guha, D. Liben-Nowell, and A. Tomkins. Information diffusion through blogspace. In *WWW '04*, pages 491–501, 2004
26. A. Gustafsson, M. Johnson, and I. Roos. The effects of customer satisfaction, relationship commitment dimensions, and triggers on customer retention. *Journal of Marketing*, 69(4): 210–218, 2005
27. J. L. Herlocker, J. A. Konstan, A. Borchers, and J. Riedl. An algorithmic framework for performing collaborative filtering. In *SIGIR '99*, pages 230–237, ACM, NY, 1999
28. O. Herrera and T. Znati. Modeling churn in P2P networks. In *Annual Simulation Symposium*, pages 33–40. IEEE Computer Society, 2007
29. S. Hill, F. Provost, and C. Volinsky. Network-based marketing: Identifying likely adopters via consumer networks. *Statistical Science*, 22:2006, 2006
30. B. Huang, B. Buckley, and T. M. Kechadi. Multi-objective feature selection by using NSGA-II for customer churn prediction in telecommunications. *Expert Syst. Appl.*, 37(5):3638–3646, 2010
31. B. Q. Huang, M. T. Kechadi, and B. Buckley. Customer churn prediction for broadband internet services. In *DaWaK*, volume 5691 of *Lecture Notes in Computer Science*, pages 229–243, Springer, Berlin, 2009
32. S.-Y. Hung, D. C. Yen, and H.-Y. Wang. Applying data mining to telecom churn management. *Expert Syst. Appl*, 31(3):515–524, 2006
33. H. Hwang, T. Jung, and E. Suh. An ltv model and customer segmentation based on customer value: a case study on the wireless telecommunication industry. *Expert Syst. Appl.*, 26(2):181–188, 2004
34. J. Kawale, A. Pal, and J. Srivastava. Churn Prediction in MMORPGs: A Social Influence Based Approach. In *CSE '09*, pages 423–428, 2009
35. S. M. Keaveney. Customer switching behavior in service industries: An exploratory study. *The Journal of Marketing*, 59(2):71–82, 1995
36. W. O. Kermack and A. G. McKendrick. A Contribution to the Mathematical Theory of Epidemics. *Proceedings of the Royal Society of London. Series A, Containing Papers of a Mathematical and Physical Character*, 115(772):700–721, 1927
37. M. Kim, M. Park, and D. Jeong. The effects of customer satisfaction and switching barrier on customer loyalty in Korean mobile telecommunication services. *Telecommunications Policy*, 28(2):145–160, 2004
38. J. M. Kleinberg. Authoritative sources in a hyperlinked environment. *J. ACM*, 46(5):604–632, 1999

39. P. Kollock. *The Economies of Online Cooperation: Gifts and Public Goods in Cyberspace.* Routledge, London, 1999
40. C. X. Ling and C. Li. Data Mining for Direct Marketing: Problems and Solutions. In *KDD*, pages 73–79, 1998
41. J. Lu. Predicting customer churn in the telecommunications industry – an application of survival analysis modeling using sas. In *SAS Proceedings, SUGI 27*, pages 114–127, 2002
42. H. Ma, H. Yang, M. R. Lyu, and I. King. Mining social networks using heat diffusion processes for marketing candidates selection. In *CIKM '08*, pages 233–242, 2008
43. J. P. Maicas, Y. Polo, and F. J. Sese. Reducing the level of switching costs in mobile communications: The case of mobile number portability. *Telecommunications Policy*, 33(9):544 – 554, 2009
44. B. M. Masand, P. Datta, D. R. Mani, and B. Li. CHAMP: A prototype for automated cellular churn prediction. *Data Min. Knowl. Discov*, 3(2):219–225, 1999
45. M. McPherson, L. Smith-Lovin, and J. M. Cook. Birds of a Feather: Homophily in Social Networks. *Annual Review of Sociology*, 27:415–444, 2001
46. B. Metcalfe. Metcalfes law: A network becomes more valuable as it reaches more users, 1995
47. A. Meyer-Bäse and R. Watzel. Transformation radial basis neural network for relevant feature selection. *Pattern Recognition Letters*, 19(14):1301–1306, 1998
48. K. Morik and H. Kpcke. Analysing customer churn in insurance data – a case study. In *PKDD '04*, pages 325–336, 2004
49. M. Mozer, R. Wolniewicz, D. Grimes, E. Johnson, and H. Kaushansky. Predicting subscriber dissatisfaction and improving retention in the wireless telecommunications industry. *IEEE Transactions on Neural Networks*, 11(3):690–696, 2000
50. M. Mozer, R. H. Wolniewicz, D. B. Grimes, E. Johnson, and H. Kaushansky. Churn reduction in the wireless industry. In *NIPS*, pages 935–941, 1999
51. T. Mutanen. Customer churn analysis - a case study. Technical report, Helsinki University of Technology, System Analysis Laboratory, 2006
52. K. Ng and H. Liu. Customer retention via data mining. *Artif. Intell. Rev.*, 14(6):569–590, 2000
53. G. Nie, G. Wang, P. Zhang, Y. Tian, and Y. Shi. Finding the hidden pattern of credit card holder's churn: A case of china. In *ICCS '09*, pages 561–569, Springer, Heidelberg, 2009
54. L. Page, S. Brin, R. Motwani, and T. Winograd. The PageRank Citation Ranking: Bringing Order to the Web. Technical report, Stanford, 1998
55. Plc-Vodafone-Group. Vodafone annual report for the year ended 31 March 2009: Principal risk factors and uncertainties, 2009. http://www.vodafone.com/annual_report09/downloads/VF_Annual_Report_2009.pdf
56. A. Prinzie and D. V. den Poel. Investigating purchasing-sequence patterns for financial services using markov, mtd and mtdg models. *European Journal of Operational Research*, 170(3):710–734, 2006
57. J. Qi, Y. Zhang, and H. Shu. Churn prediction with limited information in fixed-line telecommunication. In *Symposium on Communication Systems Networks and Digital Signal Processing*, pages 423–426, Springer, Berlin, 2006
58. H. Rheingold. *The Virtual Community: Homesteading on the Electronic Frontier.* MIT Press, MA, 2000
59. B. Ryan and N. C. Gross. The diffusion of hybrid seed corn in two Iowa communities. *Rural Sociology*, 8(1):15–24, 1943
60. G. Salton and C. Buckley. On the use of spreading activation methods in automatic information. In *SIGIR '88*, pages 147–160, 1988
61. T. Strufe. Profile Popularity in a Business-oriented Online Social Network. In *Social Network Systems, EuroSys*, 2010
62. D. Stutzbach and R. Rejaie. Understanding churn in peer-to-peer networks. In *ACM SIGCOMM conference on Internet measurement*, page 202. ACM, NY, 2006
63. Z. Sun, G. Bebis, and R. Miller. Object detection using feature subset selection. *Pattern Recognition*, 37:2165–2176, 2004
64. J. Tang, J. Sun, C. Wang, and Z. Yang. Social influence analysis in large-scale networks. In *SIGKDD '09*, pages 807–816, 2009

65. C.-F. Tsai and Y.-H. Lu. Customer churn prediction by hybrid neural networks. *Expert Syst. Appl.*, 36(10):12547–12553, 2009
66. C.-P. Wei and I.-T. Chiu. Turning telecommunications call details to churn prediction: a data mining approach. *Expert Syst. Appl*, 23(2):103–112, 2002
67. G. M. Weiss. Mining with rarity: a unifying framework. *SIGKDD Explor. Newsl.*, 6(1):7–19, 2004
68. G. M. Weiss and F. Provost. Learning when training data are costly: the effect of class distribution on tree induction. *J. Artif. Int. Res.*, 19(1):315–354, 2003
69. Y. Xie, X. Li, E. W. T. Ngai, and W. Ying. Customer churn prediction using improved balanced random forests. *Expert Syst. Appl.*, 36(3):5445–5449, 2009
70. L. Yan, R. H. Wolniewicz, and R. Dodier. Predicting customer behavior in telecommunications. *IEEE Intelligent Systems*, 19(2):50–58, 2004

Part II
Social Media Mining and Search

Chapter 10
Discovering Mobile Social Networks by Semantic Technologies

Jason J. Jung, Kwang Sun Choi, and Sung Hyuk Park

10.1 Introduction

Mobile services have been studied to provide useful and relevant contents and information to mobile subscribers anytime and anywhere. Numerous projects have been trying to extract, represent, and reason a variety of contexts detected in mobile environment. The common mission is to recognize meaningful relationships between an user action and a certain combination of contexts, which is regarded as a set of condition-action rules. Consequently, they can predict that if an user is under a condition related to the detected contexts, the consequent rule has to be conducted for him. There are many types of contexts. As shown in Fig. 10.1, such contexts are including not only physical contexts (e.g., spatial and temporal contexts) of environments, but also conceptual contexts (e.g., preferences, mental states and social affinities) of human users. More importantly, there are several context models, e.g., stochastic segment model [28], and ontology-based context model [13], to represent the contexts.

However, because of many uncertainties, it is very difficult for service providers (i.e., telecommunication companies) to be aware of *personal context* at a certain moment and place. The uncertain and unpredictable factors can be dealt with by several *context fusion* approaches [27]. These approaches is to integrate as much contexts as possible. Such approach has been applied in many domains such as location-based systems [3, 20], multiple expert systems [9], image processing by contextual information [22] and information retrieval systems [12, 24].

Thus, we can expect to improve the performance of contextual services provision (i.e., minimizing the error of predicting personal contexts). The important assumption behind these approaches is that contexts on user behaviors are interrelated with each other, i.e., constrained by others. Recently, as referring to the work [23] in social network communities, we have realized that the context of a certain user is strongly depended on those of his acquaintances (e.g., families, colleagues, and

J.J. Jung (✉)
Yeungnam University, Dae-Dong Gyeongsan, Korea, 712-749
e-mail: j2jung@gmail.com

B. Furht (ed.), *Handbook of Social Network Technologies and Applications*,
DOI 10.1007/978-1-4419-7142-5_10, © Springer Science+Business Media, LLC 2010

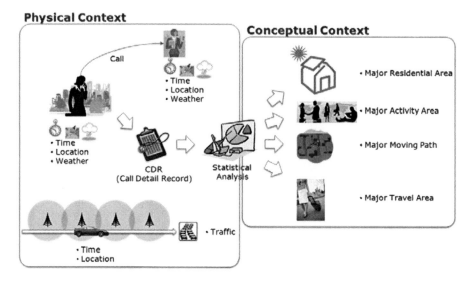

Fig. 10.1 Many types of contexts

	Spatial context	Social affinity context	Integrated context
Table 10.1 An example of contextual dependency of Kim			
Contexts	Spatial context	Social affinity context	Integrated context
Case$_1$	Cafe	Wife	Ctx$_1$
Case$_2$	Cafe	Father	Ctx$_2$
Case$_3$	Hospital	Father	Ctx$_3$

friends). It means that an user can make a different decision and take a different action under same environmental and conceptual contexts, depending on whom he is currently staying with. For example, in Table 10.1, even though Kim is in a cafe (i.e., Case$_1$ and Case$_2$), his context might be different from each other (i.e., Ctx$_1$ and Ctx$_2$), according to whom he is with (e.g., his father or his wife). Sometimes the personal context of a user is significantly influenced by socially-related people, vice versa [5, 11]. Hence, it is referred to as a *social* context in this chapter.

Of course, similar to the previous contexts, this social context is also able to have some dependencies on other contexts. For example, in two cases Case$_2$ and Case$_3$, his personal contexts Ctx$_2$ and Ctx$_3$ are not identical, because the social affinity context might be depended on the spatial context whether they are in "Cafe" or not.

Thereby, in this chapter, we have focused on integrating multiple contexts for generating more meaningful recommendation services. Also, only some basic contextual components will be investigated to implement and evaluate the proposed methods in this chapter. In particular, although we are not going to discuss more in detail, we want to address that during this integration process each individual person will have unique contextual dependency patterns with respect to the cognitive context.

Fig. 10.2 An example of social networks

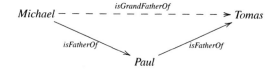

Concerning how to be aware of the social affinity contexts, we have to build a social network among people. Unless we ask users to describe their own social networks, it is difficult to make sure whether two arbitrary users share a social affinity in common. In this study, a data mining tool has been employed to statistically analyze a log dataset and limited profile information. More importantly, a social network ontology is exploited to logically reason a given social network to discover hidden information.

Once we have a social network among people and a social network ontology, we can obtain additional information from logical reasoning process. For example, in Fig. 10.2, a given social network $\mathscr{S}$ is composed of two social relationships

$$\{\langle Michael, isFatherOf, Paul\rangle, \langle Paul, isFatherOf, Tomas\rangle\}. \qquad (10.1)$$

We can extract a new information

$$\{\langle Michael, isGrandFatherOf, Tomas\rangle\} \qquad (10.2)$$

by logical inference of the social network ontology.

Thus, If we have a social network, the personal contexts of the people on the social network can be recognized by considering all possible social contexts.

In this chapter, most importantly, we want to introduce a novel approach to interactive social network discovery method [16]. Basically, interactive problem solving methodologies have been regarded as an efficient way to find better solutions for dealing with very complex problems. For instance, as human users can interact with web search engines (i.e., modify and adjust their query terms over time), they can eventually search for more relevant information from the web. This process is quite similar to the well-known generalization and specialization processes on version spaces [10].

More particularly, as regarding to organizing social networks among mobile subscribers, it is such a difficult and time-wasting task to find out which conditions between two users can be derived from various social relations. Here, we can say that the query terms on web search engines are *contextualized* with the conditions represented as propositional sentence. While the interactions for this query transformation are simply based on human user's intuitions, the proposed interactive systems in this chapter can automatically return statistical results and supplementary information by applying data mining modules to collected usage patterns. The deductive information for a certain social relation is referred to as *social propositions*, and suggested to the human experts for helping generating recommendation services. Hence, as another solution to improve the performance of context-based service, we have been motivated to build a social network among mobile users in this research project.[1]

The remainder of this chapter is organized as follows. In the following Sect. 10.2, we will describe the problem on building social networks from mobile communications. Sections 10.4 and 10.5 will explain the interactive discovery of social networks, show how to provide context-based services by using social networks among mobile users. Section 10.6 will mention some of related work on personalization and building social network between mobile users. Also, we want to discuss some important issues. In Sect. 10.7, we draw a conclusion of this chapter, and address the on-going and future work of this project.

10.2 Contextual Dependency from Social Contexts

Firstly, to establish better personalized services based on personal contexts, we have to take into account *contextual dependency*, i.e., a context can be changed by being influenced on the other contexts. Mainly, we are focusing on social affinity contexts. This assumption is the personal context of a person is depended on others' contexts, if and only if he is socially connected to them. In other words, we can say that the context Cxt_{U_a} is depended on (i.e., able to be changed) Cxt_{U_b}, if user U_a is socially connected with U_b.

The main idea of contextual dependency is to restrict the user activities. In other words, we can more easily predict which actions will be taken by the user under the set of contexts, by extracting contextual dependencies from social affinities. For example, suppose that Michael is a father of Paul (i.e., $\langle$Michael, *isFatherOf*, Paul$\rangle$). When it is Paul's birthday tomorrow, Michael might be trying to buy some present for his son. Thus, we claim that a context (Cxt_{Michael} is depended on the other's context (Cxt_{Paul} = "Birthday") through social affinity (*isFatherOf*).

Thereby, we have to discover an useful social network from a collected dataset. Social networks are generally represented as a graph-structured network.

Definition 10.1 (Social network). A social network $\mathscr{S}$ is defined as

$$\mathscr{S} = \langle \mathscr{V}, \mathscr{R} \rangle \tag{10.3}$$

where $\mathscr{V}$ and $\mathscr{R}$ are a set of participants $\{v_1, \ldots, v_{|\mathscr{V}|}\}$ and a set of relations between the participants, respectively.

---

[1] It is a research project called NICE for delivering personalized information to mobile devices via the social networks. Real customer information has been provided from KT Freetel (KTF), one of the major telecommunication companies in Korea.

In particular, $\mathscr{A}$ is simply represented as an adjacency matrix where

$$\mathscr{R}_{ij} = \begin{cases} 1 \text{ if } n_i \text{ links to } n_j; \\ 0 \text{ otherwise,} \end{cases}$$

and it is not necessarily symmetric, because we want to consider the directionality of the relations. Of course, the links can be weighed for representing the strength of social ties between two users. More importantly, in this work, the social network can contain multiple context together at the same time.

Definition 10.2 (Multiplex social network). A multiplex social network $\mathscr{S}^+$ is defined as

$$\mathscr{S}^+ = \langle \mathscr{V}, \mathscr{R}, \mathscr{C} \rangle \qquad (10.4)$$

where $\mathscr{V}$ and $\mathscr{R}$ are the same components as normal social networks $\mathscr{S}$. Additional component $\mathscr{C}$ is a specified social relation attached to $\mathscr{R}$.

In this chapter we focus on a social network of which two arbitrary nodes are linked with more than an edge. In terms of semantic web, the link between two actors are described with concepts. More importantly, we assume that the concepts applied to label the links by using semantics derived from social network ontology, which will be described in next section. Thus, this semantically multiplex social network $\mathscr{S}$ is represented as

$$\mathscr{S}^+ = \langle \mathscr{V}, \mathscr{R}, \mathscr{L}, \mathscr{C}_{\mathscr{R}} \rangle \qquad (10.5)$$

where $\mathscr{V} = \{v_1, v_2, \ldots, v_{|\mathscr{V}|}\}$ is a set of nodes (i.e., actors participating in $\mathscr{S}$), and $\mathscr{R} \subseteq \mathscr{V} \times \mathscr{V}$ is a set of links (or edges) representing relations between actors. $\mathscr{L}$ is a finite set of labels defined by actors participating in the social network. It can describe the relations $\mathscr{R}$ between actors $\mathscr{V}$. $\mathscr{C}_{\mathscr{R}} \subseteq \mathscr{R} \times \mathscr{L}$ is a set of associating multiple labels attached to each relation $r \in \mathscr{R}$. As a matter of fact, these labels are supposed to be derived with concepts in social network ontologies. Thus, the multiple labels of a relation $r_{ij} \in \mathscr{R}$ between v_i and v_j are represented as a set of triples

$$\{\langle v_i, v_j, c_{ij}^x \rangle | c_{ij}^x \in \mathscr{C}_{\mathscr{R}}, x \in [1, \ldots, X_{ij}]\} \qquad (10.6)$$

where the relation is connected from v_i to v_j, and X_{ij} is the number of concepts labeled to the link r_{ij}. We assume that label c_{ij} is conceptualized by retrieving semantic information from the social network ontologies of v_i or v_j (or somehow, both of them). The direction of links determines which social network ontologies are applied to label. It means that c_{ij} is a semantic substructure of v_i's ontology, because r_{ij} is built by source actor v_i to target actor v_j.

The contextual dependencies from multiplex social networks is found out by the two phases, which is based on divide-and-conquor approach.

10.2.1 Network Separation: Divide

As "divide" step, we separate a given multiplex social network $\mathscr{S}^+$. With respect to concepts c, which is labeling social links $r \in \mathscr{R}$, we can divide $\mathscr{S}$ into a set of sub-networks. A sub-network for a concept c_k is represented as

$$s^{\langle c_k \rangle} = \langle \mathscr{V}_k, \mathscr{R}_k, \mathscr{L}, c_k \rangle \tag{10.7}$$

where $\mathscr{V}_k \subseteq \mathscr{V}, \mathscr{R}_k \subseteq \mathscr{V}_k \times \mathscr{V}_k$. It seems rather simple and trivial, but we have to focus on measuring the similarities between c_k and the other labels to discover the semantically equivalent (or relatively close) concepts on $\mathscr{S}$. Here, we need to exploit semantic alignment function to measure similarity between concepts.

Thus, by using (10.11), (10.7) can be expanded as

$$s^{\langle c_k \rangle} = \{ \langle v_i, v_j, \tilde{c}_k \rangle | r_{ij} = \tilde{c}_k \} \tag{10.8}$$

$$\tilde{c}_k = \{ c_k, c_i | Sim_C(c_k, c_i) \geq \tau_{EQ}, c_i \in \mathscr{C}_\mathscr{R} \} \tag{10.9}$$

where τ_{EQ} is an user-specific threshold value, and the concepts of which similarity with c_k is greater than τ_{EQU} are regarded as semantically equivalent concepts.

10.2.2 Network Superposition: Conquer

For "conquer" step, a set of sub-networks separated in "divide" step should be super-posed reversely. Thereby, we have to combine the local social features (or patterns) $\mathscr{P}(s^{s^{\langle c_k \rangle}})$ discovered from a sub-network with others. The overall social features are formulated as

$$\mathscr{P}(\mathscr{S}) = \bigoplus_k \Phi(s^{\langle c_k \rangle}) \times \mathscr{P}(s^{\langle c_k \rangle}) \tag{10.10}$$

where function $\bigoplus$ can compute the summation of local social patterns of users, as sequentially mapping two sub-networks in the set of sub-networks. After each mapping, we have to conduct normalization. For the overlapped users, we want to make their semantic features reinforced by $\left(\mu \times \frac{|\mathscr{V}_i \cup \mathscr{V}_j|}{|\mathscr{V}_i \cap \mathscr{V}_j|} \right)$.

Additionally, we deploy a coefficient Φ to quantify the membership of sub-networks to the social network $\mathscr{S}$, and $\Phi(s^{\langle c_k \rangle})$ is simply given by $\frac{|\mathscr{V}_k \cap \mathscr{V}|}{|\mathscr{V}_k \cup \mathscr{V}|}$ which expresses simple topological similarity of actors between sub-networks and the original social network as co-occurrence analysis. Obviously, we can make the membership coefficient more elaborated by apply additional social features (e.g., in-degrees, our-degrees, direction of links, and so on).

10.3   Social Network Ontology

More importantly, we have investigated a social network ontology. It is to support the logical inference for finding out the relationships between social affinities from a given multiplex social network.

Basically, this ontology is a term that appears in communities as diverse as philosophy, linguistics and computer science. In computer science, particularly, ontologies are understood as devices that bring a machine-understandable conceptual structure to a certain domain of interest. As such they comprise the logical component (e.g., rules) of the so-called "knowledge base." Currently, ontologies have started to become more popular within the context of the web as they are thought to provide the current web with "meaning" to generate the future "semantic web" [1].

In this work, this ontology can provide semantics to label social affinities on social networks, as shown in Fig. 10.3. More importantly, ontology alignment method is applied to measure the semantic distance (meaning the complementary to similarity) between the corresponding contexts of social affinities. Furthermore, as clustering the equivalent social affinities, consensual ontologies are discovered to support semantic bridging among social network ontologies.

10.3.1   Similarity-Based Ontology Alignment

We exploit the similarity measurement strategy on [7, 15], which defines all possible similarities (e.g., Sim_C, Sim_R, Sim_A) between classes, relationships, attributes, and instances. We need to use only Sim_C. We denote the social network ontologies as $PO = \{po_1, po_2, \ldots, po_N\}$. Given a pair of classes from two different social

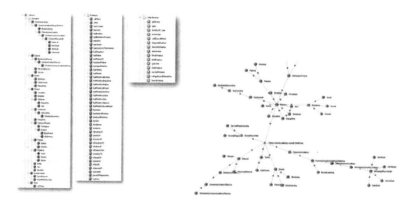

Fig. 10.3 A social network ontology

network ontologies, the similarity measure Sim_C is assigned in $[0, 1]$. The similarity (Sim_C) between $A_i \in po_A$ and $B_j \in po_B$ is defined as

$$Sim_C(A_i, B_j) = \sum_{\mathscr{F} \in \mathscr{N}(C)} \pi_{\mathscr{F}}^{\mathscr{C}} MSim_Y(\mathscr{F}(A_i), \mathscr{F}(B_j)) \tag{10.11}$$

where $\mathscr{N}(C)$ is the set of all relationships in which C participates. The weights $\pi_{\mathscr{F}}^{\mathscr{C}}$ are normalized (i.e., $\sum_{\mathscr{F} \in \mathscr{N}(C)} \pi_{\mathscr{F}}^{\mathscr{C}} = 1$).

In this chapter, hence, we consider three relationships in $\mathscr{N}(C)$, which are the superclass (SUP), the subclass (SUB) and the sibling class (SIB), and (10.11) is extended to

$$\begin{aligned} Sim_C(A_i, B_j) &= \pi_{\mathscr{L}}^{\mathscr{C}} Sim_L(\mathscr{F}(A_i), \mathscr{F}(B_j)) \\ &+ \pi_{\mathscr{SUP}}^{\mathscr{C}} MSim_{\mathscr{SUP}}(\mathscr{SUP}(A_i), \mathscr{SUP}(B_j)) \\ &+ \pi_{\mathscr{SUB}}^{\mathscr{C}} MSim_{\mathscr{SUB}}(\mathscr{SUB}(A_i), \mathscr{SUB}(B_j)) \\ &+ \pi_{\mathscr{SIB}}^{\mathscr{C}} MSim_{\mathscr{SIB}}(\mathscr{SIB}(A_i), \mathscr{SIB}(B_j)). \end{aligned} \tag{10.12}$$

where the set functions $MSim_Y$ is formulated for comparing the two sets of entity collections. According to the characteristics of the sets, it is differently given by two equations

$$MSim_{\mathscr{SUP}, \mathscr{SUB}}(S, S') = \frac{\max_{<c,c'> \in Pairing(S,S')} (Sim_C(c, c'))}{\max(|S|, |S'|)}, \tag{10.13}$$

$$MSim_{\mathscr{SIB}}(S, S') = \frac{1 - \sum_{<c,c'> \in Pairing(S,S')} (Sim_C(c, c'))}{\max(|S|, |S'|)} \tag{10.14}$$

where $Pairing$ is a simple matching function for generating all possible pairs from both sets. These equations express either positive or negative influences on semantic relationships between classes. It means that the more matched super- and subclasses can imply the corresponding classes are more similar, as shown in (10.13). In contrast, the sibling classes (10.14) reflect the negative effect, because they make the semantics dispersed and the degree of similarity decreased.

10.3.2 Consensual Ontology Discovery

Given a set of social network ontologies, we focus on discovering the consensual ontology $\mathscr{CO}$, i.e., a set of the most commonly used concepts, by the follows three steps;

1. Initializing a set of candidate classes $CDT^1 = \{\ldots, \{c_i\}, \ldots\}$,
2. Expanding CDT^{t-1} to $\widetilde{CDT^t} = \{\ldots, \{c_i, \ldots, c_{i+t-1}\}, \ldots\}$ by join operation, and

3. Refining CDT^t by evaluation with user-specific minimum support τ_{SUP} where $\widetilde{CDT}$ and CDT indicate the power sets including the frequent class sets and the candidate class sets, respectively.

The second and third steps are repeated until the constraints such as minimum supports are met ($t = T$). It means that we can finally get the consensual ontology which is composed of T classes.

A candidate class is supposed to be a substructure *semantically induced* from the set of ontologies, and it is represented by

$$cdt_i^t \preceq^\diamond PO_k \iff SemInd(cdt_i^t, PO_k) \geq \zeta \qquad (10.15)$$

where $cdt_i^t \in \widetilde{CDT}^t$ and $PO_k \in \mathscr{PO}$. For testing this induction, matching two ontologies has to be conducted by using the semantic similarity measurement, proposed in [7], rather than simple string-matching, in order to reduce some lexical heterogeneity problems such as synonyms. Hence, based on (10.11), *SemInd* is given by

$$SemInd(o_i, O) = \max \frac{\sum_{(c,c') \in Pairing(o_i, O)} Sim_C(c, c')}{|o_i|}. \qquad (10.16)$$

$SemInd(cdt_i^t, PO_k)$ is assigned into $[0, 1]$. Thus, cdt_i^t of which similarity with a given ontology PO_k is over ζ is regarded as one of semantically induced substructures from PO_k. When $\zeta = 1$, only candidates exactly matched will be chosen without concerning about the semantic heterogeneity.

In order to discover the maximal frequent substructure, we have to repeat these two processes; expansion for generating candidates and refinement. Refinement process of candidates induced from social network ontologies, exactly same as in general data mining, is to compare the frequency of the corresponding substructure candidate with user-specific threshold (e.g., minimum support τ_{SUP}). The candidate cdt_i^t extracted through comparing the similarities measured by *SemInd* with ζ can be counted as the occurrence in the set of social network ontologies $\mathscr{PO}$. Function $Occur^\diamond$ returns 1, if $cdt_i^t \preceq^\diamond PO_k$. Otherwise, it returns 0. Thus, frequency of a candidate is $Freq_{\mathscr{PO}}(cdt_i^t) = \sum_{PO_k \in \mathscr{PO}} Occur^\diamond(cdt_i^t)$, and the support is given by

$$SUP(cdt_i^t) = \frac{Freq_{\mathscr{PO}}(cdt_i^t)}{|\mathscr{PO}|} = \frac{\sum_{PO_k \in \mathscr{PO}} Occur^\diamond(cdt_i^t)}{|\mathscr{PO}|}. \qquad (10.17)$$

Only the candidate set of classes cdt_i^t of which support $SUP(cdt_i^t) \geq \tau_{SUP}$ can be chosen to generate the expanded candidates $\widetilde{CDT}^{t+1}$.

After a set of candidate features CDT^1 is initially selected by

$$CDT^1 = \{cdt_i^1 | SUP(cdt_i^1) \geq \tau_{SUP}\}, \qquad (10.18)$$

we have to expand the set of candidate class sets and refine them where $t \geq 2$. Thus, CDT^t is obtained by

$$CDT^t = refine(\widetilde{CDT^t}) \tag{10.19}$$

$$= refine(expand(CDT^{t-1})) \tag{10.20}$$

where function *refine* is to evaluate $\begin{pmatrix} |CDT^{t-1}| \\ t \end{pmatrix}$ set elements generated by function *expand* where $|CDT^{t-1}|$ is the total number of the single classes in CDT^{t-1}.

By using semantic substructure mining algorithm, the maximal semantic substructures were able to be obtained from a given set of social network ontologies. Then, the consensual ontology $\mathscr{CO}$ is represented as $\{cdt_i^T | cdt_i^T \in CDT^T,$ $SUP(cdt_i^T) \geq \tau_{SUP}\}$ when $\widetilde{CDT}^{T+1}$ is an empty set.

However, we have to realize the problem when the target social network is intermingled with semantically heterogeneous communities. Substructure mining algorithm based on counting simple occurrence (or frequency) analysis is difficult to build more than two consensual ontologies at the same time. Thereby, the social network should be fragmented into the communities (or groups [18]) whose semantic preferences are more cohesive with each other than others. In other words, this is similar to *user clustering* based on the semantic cohesion among users on the social network. Thus, let K the number of communities (user groups) on social network. The best combination of user groups is obtained by maximizing the objective function $F_{SubGroup}(UG_1, \ldots, UG_K)$

$$\max F_{SubGroup} = \max \frac{\sum_{k=1}^{K} Distance(\mathscr{CO}_i, \mathscr{CO}_j)}{K} \tag{10.21}$$

$$= \max \frac{\sum_{k=1}^{K} (1 - Sim_C(c \in \mathscr{CO}_i, c' \in \mathscr{CO}_j))}{K} \tag{10.22}$$

$$\approx \min \frac{\sum_{k=1}^{K} Sim_C(c \in \mathscr{CO}_i, c' \in \mathscr{CO}_j)}{K} \tag{10.23}$$

where $\mathscr{CO}_i = SSM(UG_i)$. Function *Distance* is derived from similarity measure by taking its complement to 1. Through this equation, the underlying communities can be found out. Each time the function *refine* of *SSM* algorithm is finished, this process should be conducted.

10.4 Interactive Discovery of Social Networks

In this chapter, we have investigated interactive discovery process for analyzing a large amount of datasets including usage patterns collected from mobile users. The main goal of this discovery process is to enrich the social propositions from a certain multiplex social network. Main steps for the interactive discovery process is simply composed of the following four steps;

- Step 1: A human expert can input a propositional sentence without any quantitative modifier to the system.
- Step 2: The proposition can be easily translated into a mathematical algebra. In fact, they are just symbols to be compared.
- Step 3: A data mining module can scan the collected dataset to measure the confidence level.
- Step 4: The confidence level of the proposition is shown the human expert.

and repeated the process until finding the best combination of conditions, as shown in Fig. 10.4.

We believe that the social propositions can be discovered (i.e., adjusted and modified) as interacting with the proposed system. For example, suppose that we have to find out the social propositions of a social relation *isFatherOf*. Human experts can assert the following propositional conditions between two users A and B;

- $\mathscr{P}_1$: Both last name is equivalent ($\equiv$).
- $\mathscr{P}_2$: The difference between both ages is more than 20.

The conditions are evaluated, and confidence $\mathscr{L}(\mathscr{P}_1, \equiv)$ and $\mathscr{L}(\mathscr{P}_2, 20)$ are 0.99 and 0.67, respectively. The second condition $\mathscr{P}_2$ might be modified as "The difference between both ages is more than 25," because of $\mathscr{L}(\mathscr{P}_2, 25) = 0.78$.

Now, we want to explain about the whole system architecture for analyzing mobile usage pattern datasets sampled from KTF legacy databases where raw records are stored, as shown in Fig. 10.5. Mainly, it consists of three parts; (1) registration profiles, (2) device (and service) specifications and (3) their calling patterns of over 60 thousand subscribers (mobile users). A set of fields of registration profiles are composed of

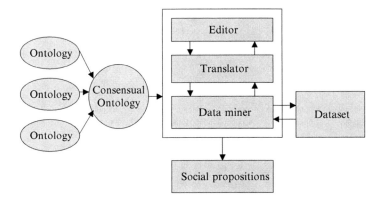

Fig. 10.4 Interactive discovery process for social propositions

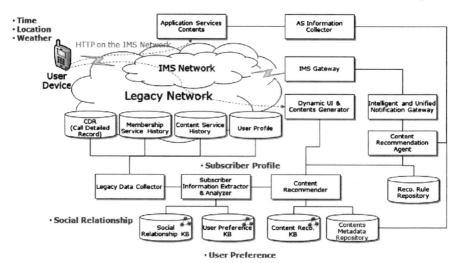

Fig. 10.5 System architecture

1. Name (first name and last name)
2. Social security number (partially encrypted)

   - Date of birth
   - Gender
   - Place of birth

3. Address
4. Job, Hobby, etc. (not provided).

As second part, the information about the devices and services are

1. Phone number
2. Device model

   - Communication protocol types (e.g., 2G, 3G)
   - Bell, sound, color, CDMA, GPS, KBANK types

3. Payment

   - Payment method (e.g., bank transfer, credit card, etc.)
   - Delegated person (e.g., name and social security number)
   - Payment creditability (e.g., history, postpone)

Third kind of information is indicating usage pattern of calling and SMS.

1. Calling

   - Calling number
   - Time of calling
   - Duration of calling

2. SMS

- Receiver number
- Time of Texting
- Types of Texting (e.g., SMS and MMS)

3. Data communication types

- Service types (e.g., CDMA/WCDMA, BREW/WIPI/VOD, DPP, RTSP, etc.)
- Status of Charge (e.g., Start, Stop, Interim-Update, PPP Session Stop, and Accounting-On/-Off)
- Amount of sent/received packets

4. Location

- Scheme (e.g., GPS, CELL, and GPS+CELL)
- Map viewer and map image formats (e.g., BMP, SIS, GML, and CGML)
- Location information (e.g., X, Y, Z coordinations, etc.)

These datasets are applied to predict social relations between mobile users by our heuristics. We have been tried to formalize the scenarios which are easily understandable to people in a common sense. Thus, each scenario can be matched to a set of social relations. Given a certain social relation, we have investigated as many cases as possible. To do so, we have built a decision tree by the following two ways of;

- Interviewing with domain experts in KTF, and
- Machine learning software packages (e.g., clementine and weka).

This process can find out the best orders of fields to verify the scenarios.

Here, we want to give a simple example of social relation *isFatherOf* and *isFamilyWith*, which are the most important social relation in this project. At the first step, by common sense, we can say that n_A is a father of n_B when either P_1 or P_2 in Table 10.2 is satisfied.

During interacting with the proposed data mining module, the real dataset can be analyzed to annotate each proposition with statistical confidence. Thus, the proposition from the first step can be branched to more specific propositions, as shown in Table 10.3.

In addition, this logical expressions can be dynamically updated over time. More importantly, the social relations are semantically represented as concept hierarchy. For example, *isFatherOf* and *isBrotherOf* are subclasses of *isFamilyWith*. Thus,

Table 10.2 Social propositions by common sense about *isFatherOf*

P_1: $(Payment(n_B) = n_A)$
$\wedge(Age(n_A) - Age(n_B) \in [30, 50])$
$\wedge(Lastname(n_B) = Lastname(n_A))$

P_2: $(Location(n_A, AtNight) = Location(n_B, AtNight))$
$\wedge(Age(n_A) - Age(n_B) \in [30, 50])$
$\wedge(Lastname(n_B) = Lastname(n_A))$

Table 10.3 Adjusted social propositions by interactions about *isFatherOf*	P_{1-1}:	$(Payment(n_B) = n_A, 60\%)$ $\wedge(Age(n_A) - Age(n_B) \in [30, 40], 85\%)$ $\wedge(Lastname(n_B) = Lastname(n_A))$
	P_{1-2}:	$(Payment(n_B) = n_A, 60\%)$ $\wedge(Age(n_A) - Age(n_B) \in [40, 50], 60\%)$ $\wedge(Lastname(n_B) = Lastname(n_A))$
	P_2:	$(Location(n_A, AtNight) = Location(n_B, AtNight))$ $\wedge(Age(n_A) - Age(n_B) \in [30, 50])$ $\wedge(Lastname(n_B) = Lastname(n_A))$

when the given information is not clear or enough, we can replace it to one of its superclass relations. (In fact, this issue is planned to work in near future.)

10.5 Context-Based Service

To efficiently support personalized service, various types of information can be applied for modeling a target user's preference. One of well-known approaches, the so-called collaborative filtering [19, 25], is to compare profiles of people. Such profiles are composed of ages, genders, occupation, and so on. Main assumption of this approach is that the more closer profile should be the more like-minded people. It means that two persons whose age are same are more probably interested in the same movie, rather than people who are older (or younger).

However, in real world, current personalized services have not shown efficient performance, people are not satisfied with the services at all. We think that most of the personalization mechanisms are simply trying to find out hierarchical clustering structure (this is very similar to the decision tree) identifying cohesive user groups of which members in the same group might be interested in a common area (e.g., movies and musics) than others [8]. This statistical analysis to extract simple demographic features by comparing user profiles [2] (e.g., ages, genders, and so on) can not find out personal context, i.e., what they are looking for in a certain situation. In other words, the personal recommendation for each user is supposed to be more specific.

In order to solve this problem, we mainly take into account two more conditions. Firstly, social affinity is regarded as a reasonable evidence to predict the personal context. For example, social relations (particularly, kin relations and friendships) can be assumed to identify each person's context more specifically. When he is looking for his father's birthday present, it is much more probable that he is looking for what his father wants than what he does. As aggregating the social networks, we can build a social network for making various social relations extractable. This social network can play a role of integrating multiple contexts which are inter-related between each other (e.g., parents and children).

Second condition is location, i.e., geographical position where you are. The personal context basically changes over time. In order to support better personalization, the service should be timely activated. For example, a user who is in a department store is expected to buy a certain product, rather than to go to restaurant.

More importantly, these two types of conditions can be merged for better personalized recommendation. Given two person who are (1) linked (highly related) on a social network and (2) located in (or moving to) a close place, we can recommend very reasonable information to them. Especially, in this research project, we have been focusing on the mobile users joining KTF (KT Freetel) services. The problem is that the social networks are hidden. Thereby, we want to discover the hidden social network from usage patterns of mobile devices.

10.6 Related Work and Discussion

Most similarly, there have been two works. In [17], they have proposed a way of measuring the closeness between two persons to build a social network. Mainly they are focusing on the calling patterns, when (and how frequent) people are calling. Also, in [6], their project "reality mining" has introduced experimental results for evaluating several hypothesis. These hypothesis has been compared to self-reports provided by the human users.

Personalization based on multi-agent systems has been introduced in MAPIS [26]. With regards to the business-oriented work, in [4], personalization process on e-commerce has been conducted by three modules; (1) marketing strategies, (2) promotion patterns model, and (3) personalized promotion products. Especially, location-based personalization services has been implemented, e.g., NAMA [21].

10.7 Concluding Remarks and Future Work

This work is a research project for delivering personalized content to mobile users. In this chapter, we have described our research project for building social network between mobile users. In order to do so, we have introduced our interactive approach to construct meaningful social networks between mobile users. Each context included in a social network has been combined with spatial context to better recommendation.

Future work, we are planning to put the calling patterns into the social network which has been built by expert's heuristics. It will make the social network more robust, and dynamically evolvable. Furthermore, evaluation method has been consider to verify whether the personalized service is reasonable or not.

Acknowledgements This work was supported by the Korean Science and Engineering Foundation (KOSEF) grant funded by the Korean government (MEST). (2008-0058292). This chapter has been significantly revised from the paper [14] published in Expert Systems with Applications, Vol. 36 (pp. 11950–11956) in 2009.

References

1. Tim Berners-Lee. The semantic web. *Scientific American*, 285(5):34–43, 2001
2. Philip Bonhard, Clare Harries, John McCarthy, and M. Angela Sasse. Accounting for taste: using profile similarity to improve recommender systems. In *CHI '06: Proceedings of the SIGCHI conference on Human Factors in computing systems*, pages 1057–1066, ACM, NY, 2006
3. Giacomo Cabri, Letizia Leonardi, Marco Mamei, and Franco Zambonelli. Location-dependent services for mobile users. *IEEE Transactions on Systems, Man, and Cybernetics – Part A: Systems and Humans*, 33(6):667–681, 2003
4. S. Wesley Changchien, Chin-Feng Lee, and Yu-Jung Hsu. On-line personalized sales promotion in electronic commerce. *Expert Systems with Applications*, 27(1):35–52, 2004
5. Rob Cross, Ronald E. Rice, and Andrew Parker. Information seeking in social context: Structural influences and receipt of information benefits. *IEEE Transactions on Systems, Man, and Cybernetics - Part C: Applications and Reviews*, 31(4):438–448, 2001
6. Nathan Eagle and Alex Pentland. Reality mining: sensing complex social systems. *Personal and Ubiquitous Computing*, 10(4):255–268, 2006
7. Jérôme Euzenat and Petko Valtchev. Similarity-based ontology alignment in OWL-Lite. In Ramon López de Mántaras and Lorenza Saitta, editors, *Proceedings of the 16th European Conference on Artificial Intelligence (ECAI'2004), Valencia, Spain, August 22-27, 2004*, pages 333–337. IOS Press, 2004
8. Jonathan L. Herlocker, Joseph A. Konstan, and John Riedl. Explaining collaborative filtering recommendations. In *CSCW '00: Proceedings of the 2000 ACM conference on Computer supported cooperative work*, pages 241–250, ACM, NY, 2000
9. Francisco Herrera and Luis Martínez. A model based on linguistic 2-tuples for dealing with multigranular hierarchical linguistic contexts in multi-expert decision-making. *IEEE Transactions on Systems, Man, and Cybernetics – Part B: Cybernetics*, 31(2):227–234, 2001
10. Tzung-Pei Hong and Shian-Shyong Tseng. A generalized version space learning algorithm for noisy and uncertain data. *IEEE Transactions on Knowledge and Data Engineering*, 9(2):336–340, 1997
11. R. H. Irving and D. W. Conrath. The social context of multiperson, multiattribute decisionmaking. *IEEE Transactions on Systems, Man and Cybernetics*, 18(3):348–357, 1988
12. Jason J. Jung. Ontological framework based on contextual mediation for collaborative information retrieval. *Information Retrieval*, 10(1):85–109, 2007
13. Jason J. Jung. Ontology-based context synchronization for ad-hoc social collaborations. *Knowledge-Based Systems*, 21(7):573–580, 2008
14. Jason J. Jung. Contextualized mobile recommendation service based on interactive social network discovered from mobile users. *Expert Systems with Applications*, 36:11950–11956, 2009
15. Jason J. Jung and Jérôme Euzenat. Towards semantic social networks. In Enrico Franconi, Michael Kifer, and Wolfgang May, editors, *Proceedings of the 4th European Semantic Web Conference (ESWC 2007), Innsbruck, Austria*, volume 4519 of *Lecture Notes in Computer Science*, pages 267–280. Springer, Berlin, 2007
16. Jason J. Jung, Hojin Lee, and Kwang Sun Choi. Contextualized recommendation based on reality mining from mobile subscribers. *Cybernetics and Systems*, 40(2):160–175, 2009

17. Przemyslaw Kazienko. Expansion of telecommunication social networks. In Yuhua Luo, editor, *Proceedings of the 4th International Conference on Cooperative Design, Visualization, and Engineering (CDVE 2007)*, volume 4674 of *Lecture Notes in Computer Science*, pages 404–412. Springer, Berlin, 2007
18. Jon M. Kleinberg. Small-world phenomena and the dynamics of information. In Thomas G. Dietterich, Suzanna Becker, and Zoubin Ghahramani, editors, *Advances in Neural Information Processing Systems 14 [Neural Information Processing Systems: Natural and Synthetic, NIPS 2001, December 3-8, 2001, Vancouver, British Columbia, Canada]*, pages 431–438. MIT, MA, 2001
19. Joseph A. Konstan, Bradley N. Miller, David Maltz, Jonathan L. Herlocker, Lee R. Gordon, and John Riedl. Grouplens: applying collaborative filtering to usenet news. *Communications of the ACM*, 40(3):77–87, 1997
20. Panu Korpipaa, Jani Mantyjarvi, Juha Kela, Heikki Keranen, and Esko-Juhani Malm. Managing context information in mobile devices. *IEEE Pervasive Computing*, 2(3):42–51, 2003
21. Ohbyung Kwon, Sungchul Choi, and Gyuro Park. NAMA: a context-aware multi-agent based web service approach to proactive need identification for personalized reminder systems. *Expert Systems with Applications*, 29(1):17–32, 2005
22. Farid MELGANI, Sebastiano B. SERPICO, and Gianni VERNAZZA. Fusion of multitemporal contextual information by neural networks for multisensor image classification. In *Proceedings of the 2001 IEEE International Geoscience and Remote Sensing Symposium (IGARSS '01)*, pages 2952–2954. IEEE Computer Society, 2001
23. Gerald Mollenhorst, Beate Völker, and Henk Flap. Social contexts and personal relationships: The effect of meeting opportunities on similarity for relationships of different strength. *Social Networks*, 30(1):60–68, 2008
24. Gautam Pant and Padmini Srinivasan. Link contexts in classifier-guided topical crawlers. *IEEE Transactions on Knowledge and Data Engineering*, 18(1):107–122, 2006
25. Michael J. Pazzani. A framework for collaborative, content-based and demographic filtering. *Artificial Intelligence Review*, 13(5-6):393–408, 1999
26. Christelle Petit-Rozé and Emmanuelle Grislin-Le Strugeon. MAPIS, a multi-agent system for information personalization. *Information & Software Technology*, 48(2):107–120, 2006
27. Odysseas Sekkas, Christos B. Anagnostopoulos, and Stathes Hadjiefthymiades. Context fusion through imprecise reasoning. In *Proceedings of the 2007 IEEE International Conference on Pervasive Services (ICPS)*, pages 88–91. IEEE Computer Society, 2007
28. Thomas Strang and Claudia LinnhoffPopien. A context modeling survey. In *Proceedings of the Workshop on Advanced Context Modelling, Reasoning and Management colocationed with UbiComp 2004*, 2004

Chapter 11
Online Identities and Social Networking

Muthucumaru Maheswaran, Bader Ali, Hatice Ozguven, and Julien Lord

11.1 Introduction

People identification on the Internet is one of the open problems that affect its day-to-day operations. For example, when we receive emails we often use the address field to ascertain the identity of the sender. This can be misleading because the "from address" can be easily spoofed (falsified) or a known sender could use an unfamiliar address. The address-based approach for people identification is prevalent in other applications besides email. One example is Wikipedia, where the IP address of the client's machine is used to track users making changes to the content on Wikipedia.

Despite its drawbacks, the address-based approach to identification is widely used because the Internet naturally supports it. Further, until recently most Internet applications were server-centric, where users access shopping, news, and search services from well-known providers. In these applications, users had to authenticate themselves to manage user related data at the servers. Only in limited cases, users had to identify other users to experience the services provided by the applications.

In recent years, the Internet has undergone significant changes [22] driven by trends such as crowd-sourced services, user-generated content, and social networking. One of the outcomes is the transformation of the Internet from a web that provides access to large volumes of data to a social web that interconnects people. In the *social web* [9] people use tools such as blogs, wikis, social networking sites [4], and messaging services to share information and collaborate with each other. One of the distinguishing features of the social web is its intervention at the social level, which makes people identification an important facet of the social web.

The social web provides a number of mechanisms to construct online identities using a hodgepodge of information with diverse origins and quality [22]. While identity information on the social web is predominantly self declared [4], other sources such as external inference, and community opinions also make significant

M. Maheswaran (✉)
School of Computer Science, McGill University, Montreal, QC, Canada H3A 2A7
e-mail: maheswar@cs.mcgill.ca

B. Furht (ed.), *Handbook of Social Network Technologies and Applications*,
DOI 10.1007/978-1-4419-7142-5_11, © Springer Science+Business Media, LLC 2010

contributions. The self declared information can be explicitly presented such as pseudonym, age, and interests in online profiles or implicitly stated via personal opinions in blogs. External inferences such as querying an Internet search engine using salient profile information of a user can yield results that indicate activities such as forum posts, blog posts, and open source contributions of the user. While such queries can yield valuable information to augment the identity of a user, considerable errors can occur in correlating the activities to the user. Another important source of identity information is the community opinion [11]. For instance, in e-commerce websites, opinions expressed by the community make important contributions to the identity of a seller.

There are three major issues associated with online identities on the social web: form, content, and accuracy. Usernames and passwords are the predominant form of user authentication on the web. One recently proposed alternative to usernames is OpenID [26] that uses uniform resource locators (URLs) to identify users. While usernames are simple, they localize the identities at a site level. In most cases, online identities have information voluntarily disclosed by the users. However, the type of information (e.g., type of user attributes) making up online identities can vary across different sites. Many factors impact the accuracy of the information associated with online identities. A study by Krasnova et al. [19] found that in online social networks (OSNs), users are mostly truthful but are selective in disclosing information. The study also found that users are increasingly uneasy about *organizational* threats that emerge from OSN operators than *social* threats that emerge from members of their social circle.

With the predominant role OSNs play in interconnecting people, it is interesting to examine the connection between online identities and social networking, which is the subject of this chapter. Due to the enormous popularity of OSNs, many networks have emerged with each catering for slightly different purposes. For instance, OSNs are created for business networking, meeting old classmates, and socializing with friends. The OSNs provide many opportunities for identifying the users. The simplest way to identity management is to use OSNs to manage online profiles, which is the most popular use of OSNs. Another way OSNs can contribute to identity management is by enabling new identification techniques that leverage the large volume of structural information held by these networks.

The central task in people identification is associating data with a person. For example, a college identifies its students by associating a student identity number with each enrolled person. The association of the data with the person should be securely verifiable for identification to be secure. The OSNs allow users to create online profiles through which users can project their identities in the social web. The online profiles are tailored by the users to present the most favorable identity for them on the social web [19]. The online profiles are bound to the person by the community and the integrity is maintained by the secure access provided by the OSN. Identifying users based on their connections in a social network is an emerging idea [5] that can have privacy concerns as well [3].

Section 11.2 examines basic issues in civil and digital identities, people identification problem, and requirements on digital identities. Section 11.3 describes
different approaches where social relations are used for people identification.
Section 11.4 presents a brief overview of a scheme for developing social digital
identities that capture the social relations a user has in the social web. By using the
social digital identity, a user can present and verify social connections outside OSN
where the relations are created and maintained. This section also discusses potential
applications of identities generated using social information. Section 11.5 describes
various threats faced by identities particularly in the context of the social web.

11.2 Background on Digital Identities

11.2.1 Civil vs. Digital Identities

Identity is a rather controversial topic, making it difficult to come up with an acceptable definition of the concept. For the purposes of this chapter, we define *identity* as
the distinctive description of the character, as well as a collection of claims about
the character, of a thing or an individual.

There is very little argument that identity is a useful concept when we deal
with things. For instance, cars have identities called *vehicle identification numbers*
(VINs) that are useful to relate information to a particular car. The motor vehicle
information databases use VINs to associate accident and recall repair information
to particular vehicles. To maintain the integrity of the vehicle information, most
jurisdictions have laws the prohibit tampering with the VIN tags on vehicles.

The identity of people is a much contentious topic with arguments for and against
the creation of unified civil identities for people. In [17], Gutwirth argues that the
"concept of identity offers little hope" when it relates to individuals. The major
concern raised by Gutwirth is that the *concept of identity* implies that individuals
are *static* beings who's characterization do not change. In reality individuals continuously undergo transformations through interactions, adventure, and exploration.
Given the concerns, one may ask about the necessity or benefits of individuals having identities.

One of the clear benefits of having a "civil identity" such as a birth certificate is
the access to basic services. It is inconceivable to implement basic political, social,
and human rights on a crowd of people without civil identities. Therefore, civil identities despite their many shortcomings [17] are an integral part of the management
structure of the society.

A similar case can be made for the necessity of online identities in the social
web as well. Without reliable online identities it is difficult or near impossible to
efficiently manage user related functions on the social web. In particular, Sybil [14]
identities (fake identities created by malicious users) lead to a lack of accountability
on the Internet. On a social web, where trust among participants is very important

for sustaining high level interaction, this is a problem. Example issues created by Sybil identities include:

- Email spamming from accounts created under pseudonyms.
- Content pollution attacks on peer-to-peer networks by uploading bogus or infected content.
- Distorting online reputation systems by creating false reputation reports.
- Collusion attacks in online gaming system.

Online identities can be developed in many different ways. One important aspect of any approach for online identity is the connection between online and offline identities of the individual [31]. The simplest way of creating reliable online identity that is still in widespread use on the Internet is to link an online identity to an offline credential such as a credit card. Unless an abundant supply of stolen credit card information is available to the malicious user, he is prevented by this approach from creating Sybil identities.

Another approach for creating online identities is to leverage social information. An online identity that is produced based on the social context created by the user's online activities is more representative of the user in the social web. Such an identity might actually feel more "real" to the user holding it [24]. For instance, an online gamer feels more connected to the gaming community and is well known there. While the importance and impacts of social aspects of online identity increases at a rapid pace, existing online identity creation systems do not fully support the social aspect. Further, even personal claims made by a user in a social network should be taken in the social context. Taking the claim in isolation and binding it with the user outside the context created by the social network can be misleading and often wrong. Further, field research has shown that online relationships and identities are intricately related and rooted in the "offline" life and identity of the individual, both personally and socially [6, 8], and there exists a mutual interaction and influence between online and offline relationships [31].

It is easy to see the potential benefits of an approach that takes into account the social aspects of online identities constructed for the same user in different social networks and integrates them into a holistic identity for the user. As more and more areas of daily life involves digital transactions, having a holistic identity with sufficient privacy controls becomes a necessity.

11.2.2 The People Identification Problem

For the purposes of this chapter, following Clarke [10], we define the people identification problem as "the problem of associating data with a person." In both physical and digital world settings, identification serves one important purpose. It allows rapid recall of relevant attributes of the person. For example, once Alice establishes that she is dealing with Bob (her friend) in a particular transaction she can immediately associate the trust and other parameters she knows about Bob with the person engaged in the current transaction. This reduces the uncertainty associated with a particular transaction.

Because identification is a fundamental human activity, many different approaches with correspondingly different levels of integrities have been developed. The primary means used for identification in these approaches include: appearance, names and codes, knowledge and tokens, physical or biological characteristics, and social behavior. In the physical world, appearance is defined using a collection of attributes (e.g., color of the hair, skin complexion, birthmarks). Although a single attribute such as hair color is meaningless as an identifier, large number of attributes taken together can be a weak but useful identifier of a person.

Names and codes are two of the most widely used identifiers of humans. Although names in general are not unique, given sufficient context such as father's or grandfather's name, it is possible to disambiguate conflicts. Because of the complexities of the disambiguation processes, to meet the efficiency requirements, names are often supplanted with codes in computer systems. The codes are selected by the issuing organizations (i.e., driving license number) and can encode certain attributes of the person. For example, a code could encode gender, age, and location information such that obvious misuses of the code can be detected at the point of authentication.

The user identification process implemented by most operating systems and restricted-access web portals use a knowledge-based approach, where the user should demonstrate the possession of secret knowledge such as passwords and personal identification numbers (PINs). The secret knowledge can be setup by the user (e.g., user selected passwords) provided by the organization (e.g., assigned PINs), and use deeply personal information supposedly unknown to outsiders (e.g., mother's maiden name). The limitations of this approach are becoming evident with the implosion of web-based service portals. One particularly acute and practical problem is the increasing number of passwords and PINs a user is expected to maintain as she increases the number of participating web portals. To address this problem, single sign-on technologies such as OpenID [26] and identity selector technologies such as InfoCards [7] have been proposed.

Token-based approaches for identification are widely used both on and off the Internet. A token is some form of documentary evidence that can be presented by the holder to establish her identity. Examples of token-based identities in the physical world include driver's license, passports, credit cards, and library cards. The token-based identifiers are often dependent on a seed or breeder document. For example, a passport is a token-based identifier that is most often based on a birth certificate. A token-based identifier can be considered as establishing the membership of the holder in a particular group. A passport, for instance, establishes that the holder is a member of the country issuing the passport. Similarly, a driver's license establishes that the holder is a member of the set of people authorized to drive a particular class of vehicles.

On the Internet, the token-based approach for identification is used in two ways. When digital tokens are used for identifying people, some way of binding the token to the person is necessary. This binding can be achieved using biometric techniques or secret knowledge such as passphrases. Tokens are also used by proxies to authenticate one another. This authentication is sometimes an indirect identification of a user. Examples of tokens used for identification on the Internet include Smartcard, security assertion markup language (SAML) assertions, and Public Key Infrastructure (PKI) certificates.

The integrity of an identification scheme that depends on physical and biological characteristics tends to depend on the intrusiveness of the approach. For example, methods that use appearance-based physical characteristics such as height, hair color, facial expressions, and weight tend to be unreliable. Whereas, methods such as fingerprints, DNA analysis, retina scans, and fingerprints tend to be more reliable than the ones based on less intrusive characteristics. It is also possible to impose physical characteristics on humans for precise identification (e.g., implanted chips). These methods invariably cause lot of privacy concerns.

Social behavior is another feasible approach for identifying people. In the physical world, social behavior such as style of speech, body language, and voice characteristics are used along with other approaches for identification. Like the appearance-based approaches, one social behavior based attribute can be a weak identifier of a person.

11.2.3 Requirements on Digital Identities

The importance of digital identification has prompted several studies [7, 10, 12] to investigate the requirements for digital identities. The requirements with regard to digital identities can be viewed in two different ways: (1) creating and assigning digital identities and (2) managing digital identities. The second group of requirements have received significant attention from the commercial and academic communities in the last few years. The primary motivator for the focus on identity management is the view that an Identity metasystem inspired by the architecture of the Internet is the best solution for the digital identity problem.

The seven laws of identity report [7] authored by Cameron from Microsoft is the most recent and important work that outlines the requirements that should be met by an *identity management system* for the Internet. For completeness, we repeat the *seven* laws of identity here with a commentary on the connections it has with the social approach described in this chapter.

- *User control and consent:* This law requires the system to obtain user consent while making important decisions on identity information flow. The law expects to improve user's trust on the identity management software by engaging the user in making important information flow decisions and alerting the user about the risks in making the different decisions.
- *Minimum disclosure for a constrained use:* This law is an extension of the well-known least privileges policy that is pervasively applied in secure computing systems. The main purpose of this law is to minimize the risk of unintended identity information leak due to software breaches. Assuming software breaches

cannot be ruled out, the law uses the need-to-know and need-to-retain policies to minimize the spread of sensitive information within the Internet.

- *Justifiable parties:* This law requires that identities should be released among parties that have mutually acceptable identity management policies. A typical digital identity could include valuable information about the subject. Consequently, the disclosure policies of the involved parties should be verified before releasing identity information.
- *Directed identity:* This law is based on the notion that identities can be classified as omni-directional and uni-directional. Omni-directional identities are held by well-known services on the Internet. This law stresses the care that should be exercised in assigning omni-directional identities.
- *Pluralism of operators and technology:* This law calls for an inter-operability based approach much like the Internet for identity management on the Internet. Because digital identities are an important element on the Internet and is likely to be created and used under diverse protocols, it is hard to expect an integrated architecture to provide a one-size-fits all solution.
- *Human integration:* This law emphasizes the human-machine links that are crucial in ensuring end-to-end security of computer-based transactions. Breakdown of the human-machine links can eventually reduce the effectiveness of overall security. Some of the issues plaguing the Internet such as phishing are a form of human-machine link breakdown.
- *Consistent experience across contexts:* In most cases, operator errors are directly related to their unfamiliarity of the computer system. This law suggests making a consistent element for a digital identity within the identity management infrastructure such that all applications run by a user can access her digital identity via this element.

Although the seven laws are meant for identity management infrastructures, some of the laws are applicable while creating and assigning digital identities. Next, we present the requirements put forward by Clarke in [10] for systems that create and assign digital identities. As noted in [10], the requirements given below are internally conflicting, which illustrates the complex nature of digital identities.

- *Universality of coverage:* A digital identity system should be capable of providing an identifier for each person. Taken with the seven laws this requirement need not be met by a single digital identity system. We should have a digital identity system within the identity metasystem that is able to provide an identity for each person.
- *Uniqueness:* This requirement means we should have a one-to-one binding between a person and the digital identity. That is a user cannot have more than one identity and no two users can have the same identity. The first part is often violated by legitimate identity assignment procedures for valid reasons (for example, workers with sensitive jobs such as undercover law enforcement can have multiple identities).
- *Permanence:* This requirement calls for an identity that does not change with time. Identities based on biometrics fit this requirement well. Obviously,

identities meeting this requirement would satisfy the uniqueness requirement as well. Appropriateness of such a permanent digital identity on the Internet is questionable given the possibility that identities can get maligned for false reasons.

- *Indispensability:* This requirement dictates that identifiers should be based on inherent characteristics of a person. The biometric identities meet the indispensability requirement.
- *Collectability:* This requirement says identities should be collectable by anyone. For a digital identity that works on the Internet, collectability requirement should be interpreted within the seven laws of identity. One interesting outcome of this is the interaction with direction. The directed identity law states that we should exercise caution in making identities omni-directional.
- *Storability:* Most digital identities should have no problem meeting this requirement which requires the identities to be storable with ease. One of the issues that can affect digital identities is the format changes. We need a clearly defined storage format so that archived identities can be processed.
- *Exclusivity:* This requirement means we should only have one approach for identification. On a large-scale system such as the Internet, exclusivity cannot be attained by any single approach. This non-exclusive nature is the underlying thrust for the Internet metasystem notion. However, it is possible to achieve exclusivity by requiring a digital identity that is part of the Identity metasystem to be sufficient.
- *Precision:* The digital identities created by the system for different people should be sufficiently varied so that one identity is less likely to be mistaken for another identity. With digital identities, operator error can be major source of errors.
- *Simplicity:* For digital identities the simplicity requirements can originate from users, programmers, and managers. For users and managers, the digital identifiers should be simple so that they could be deployed with minimal risk of unintentional information leaks. For programmers, simplicity is equally important.
- *Cost:* The cost of creating, storing, and maintaining digital identities should not be excessive. For a digital identity, major portion of the cost comes from processing and storage requirements.
- *Convenience:* One of the major concerns with respect to convenience is the amount off-line transactions needed to setup a digital identity.
- *Acceptability:* The digital identities should be socially acceptable. For example, biometric identities despite meeting majority of the above requirements can still face difficulties due to lack of social acceptability.

In [12], Dhamija and Dusseault provide an interesting set of pitfalls of identity management which they refer to as the *seven flaws*. We repeat the seven flaws and discuss each briefly.

- *Identity management is not a goal in itself.* Identity management is not an important concern to most users, while most are concerned about identity theft or other forms identity related attacks. Therefore, a new system for identity management cannot get users' interest solely based on being a *better* identity manager.

- *Users follow the path of least resistance.* Users want solutions that integrate well with existing systems so changes can be minimized. Also, legacy sites and systems should be supported by new proposals.
- *Cognitive scalability is as important as technical scalability.* Cognitive scalability is the problem often pointed out with usernames and passwords. Many proposals to ameliorate this problem also have cognitive scalability issues in subtly different ways. For instance, replacing usernames and passwords with URLs can introduce a problem where users need to scrutinize URLs and web destinations more carefully.
- *User consent could lead to maximum disclosure.* In most situations, user is considered the ultimate arbiter in security decisions such as installing software and providing access. If a user is stressed to make many decisions, the user is likely to over disclose information to reduce the effort.
- *We need mutual authentication and not just user authentication.* Most identity management systems require the server to have a valid certificate to establish a secure connection. However, establishing the trust of the server side is a much harder problem where users often play a role.
- *Relying parties want to control the customer experience.* Relying parties are the websites that consume the user identities. They would like to control the user experience in their sites according to their business strategies.
- *Trust must be earned and is hard for users to evaluate.* Trust is a dynamic parameter that can change with time. A user may not have sufficient information to place the proper level of trust on a remote site.

11.2.4 Classes of Digital Identities

We classify existing digital identities into three classes: integrated identity, federated identity, and user-centric identity. The integrated identity systems are obviously the simplest systems, where identities are provided by a single or tightly coupled system of identity providers. The federated identity is a generalization of the above system, where several independently operated identity providers come together to supply digital identities for the users.

In a federated identity management system, a user would create and store identity profile with one of the providers in the federation. When a user visits a service that is handled by another identity provider, an inter-identity provider protocol is responsible for exchanging identity information so that the user can log into the remote service. For example, a wireless user roaming into a remote network contacts her home identity provider through the foreign identity provider. The home and foreign identity providers cooperate the authenticate the user so that the user can obtain the wireless connectivity service at the roaming location. While federated architectures solve various identity related issues, they create their own. One of the primary issues is the way sensitive identity information is shared among the inter-operating identity providers. Because the identity providers are operated by large corporations or governments, users are anxious about information sharing among the different identity providers and the extent to which privacy concerns are taken into consideration in the sharing process. To address some of these concerns user-centric identity was proposed.

11.2.5 Taxonomy of Approaches to Identities

The taxonomy presented in Fig. 11.1 summarizes many issues discussed so far in this section regarding the producer, methodology of production, nature of identity, and usage of identity.

Simplest way to produce a digital identity is for the user to select an ad hoc label and attach it to her digital presence. One example of this approach is an email handle such as `user-selected-name@gmail.com`. Another way of producing a digital identity is for a responsible corporate entity to issue an identifier to a person. For instance, many universities issue emails to student and staff. These identifiers tend to have more trust associated with them. Yet another way of obtaining an identity is through the community. While this approach to identity generation is prevalent in actual communities, a counterpart in the Internet is absent.

An identity can be produced in digital form or non-digital form. Both forms be either secure or non-secure. For instance, a passport is a highly tamper resistant identity document whereas a birth certificate is a less tamper resistant identity document. Digital identities such as pseudonyms have less integrity associated with them while certificates issued by certification authorities carry higher level of integrity.

As discussed above, nature and usage are other important factors to consider in the creation of digital identities.

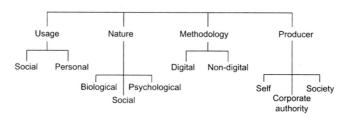

Fig. 11.1 Taxonomy of digital identity

11.3 Putting Social Relations to Work

11.3.1 Overview

While OSNs provide a platform for creating online profiles, posting data, and passing messages among friends, the major function of OSNs is to catalog social relations. In OSNs, social relations connect a user profile with other user profiles. In [4], Boyd and Ellison observe that most links made in OSNs have offline relations behind them. Although OSNs provide the opportunity to socialize online, very few relations are created from online meet ups. As a result, it is well accepted that links in OSNs indicate trusted relations [29, 32, 33] among individuals and many applications have been proposed to leverage these connections.

User profiles in OSNs have valuable personal information that can be used by an attacker to clone a user's profile in another OSN [2]. Similarly, information about the social connections among users is also valuable for marketers, phishers, spammers, credit rating agencies, and employers. This has created a new problem called *social graph privacy* [3]. Unlike the user's profile information which is solely guarded by the user, social graph is guarded by users and OSN operators.

Facebook which is one of the largest OSN operators has "public search listings" for visitors to preview information about members without joining the network [3]. The public listings show a person's photograph and up to eight of her friends. In [3], Bonneau et al. investigate how valuable information about the social graph can be reconstructed from the public listings shown by Facebook. By reconstructing the social graph (at least approximately) marketers, phishers, and spammers can approach a victim with personalized *bait* messages. For instance, knowing the social neighborhood, a phisher could craft a convincing bait message to send to a potential victim pretending to be a friend in distress who needs emergency financial assistance.

At present, most large OSNs (e.g., Facebook, MySpace, Orkut) are centrally controlled and operated. This means the social graphs created by the users and defining the connections among them are held exclusively by the operator of the OSNs. The OSN operators provide *application programming interfaces* (APIs) to export social graph and other information for processing in outside applications. The Open Social API from Google is an interface supported many OSN operators.

In this section, we discuss many different ways of putting social relations to work in many familiar security and trust management problems.

11.3.2 User Authentication Using Social Relations

User authentication is central to most applications on the web. Traditionally, user authentication has relied on usernames and passwords that use "something you know" factor for recognizing the rightful users. When additional security is needed, the "something you have" factor such as a secure token is added to the authentication requirements. With two factors, a user is successfully authenticated only if the user is able to show both factors. Another factor that is often used in addition or instead of one of the above is the "something you are" factor such as fingerprints, retinal scans, and voice recognition.

In [5], Brainard et al. suggested that a fourth factor "someone you know" could be used in addition or instead of the above factors for authenticating users. They have applied this technique for emergency authentication where the users have left behind a token or forgotten a password and is unable to meet the requirements for normal authentication.

The fourth factor or social authentication is based on the following process of a friend vouching for a user. First, the user asks a friend to vouch for him. Second, the friend recognizes the user and issues some proof of this recognition. Third, the user uses the proof as a temporary credential to log in to the service. In [5], vouching was done explicitly, with the user contacting a friend and literally asking for a vouching code. In [27], this idea is extended to the social web by using mobile computing to automate the process.

The vouching process can be performed in two different ways: one involves direct contacts with friends from a pre-authorized list and the other involves indirect contact via an OSN. In the social authentication approach presented in [27] a user obtains *vouching* tokens from friends, whenever she has a phone conversation or a Bluetooth sighting with them. The important feature of this approach is that the user's friends are contacted directly (by phone or Bluetooth), and this contact is used to prove the user's identity when logging in to a site or service. Some details of the social authentication method in [27] are given below.

The user starts by declaring a list of friends who will *vouch* for his identity based on offline relations. This list is stored on a central server. After a phone call with one of these friends the user will receive a token indicating that a communication took place. A token is only issued after a phone call that is longer than a minimum duration. This duration is determined by analyzing the distribution of the user's call durations. The idea is that it is unlikely that an intruder will be able to make a phone call long enough to receive a token, without alerting the other side that something is wrong.

Similarly if the user meets a friend in his declared list within the Bluetooth sensing distance, a token will be received confirming this sighting. Bluetooth sightings are trickier because the long range (about 10 m) doesn't mean that the users actually made contact. Thus the Bluetooth sightings are augmented in two ways. First, a rough estimate of the distance of the other user is made by measuring the time it takes to establish a Bluetooth connection. Second, the user is prompted to confirm the sighting of the other party. After both of these take place the vouching messages are exchanged.

The user proofs his identity to a social authentication server by showing a quorum of valid tokens collected during a given period of time. After validation of the presented tokens, the central server issues credentials that can be used by the user to access other services. These credentials are time limited and need to be used with a PIN number.

11.3.3 Connection Establishment Using Social Relations

The first step in securely communicating over the Internet is connection establishment. Normally, connection establishment involves authenticating the endpoints using a shared secret or trusted certificates. For arbitrary endpoints (or users), sharing a secret is not a possibility. Therefore, trusted certificates are used by the endpoints to verify each other before establishing the secure connection.

In [25], Ramachandran and Feamster proposed a system called the *Authenticatr* for establishing end-to-end trusted communication channels using social links on OSNs. Authenticatr implements an overlay API for OSNs that allows applications outside OSNs to securely discover and connect to peers. In a social network such as Facebook, users can define access control policies such as "share data X only with my friends." This facility is not available for applications running outside OSNs because the notion of friendship is valid only within OSNs. Authenticatr framework extends the notion of friendship to desktop applications by providing them the overlay API.

Authenticatr provides mailbox style APIs for sending and receiving messages. One example use of Authenticatr is a peer discovery application that uses social network based APIs to determine IP address, available ports, running services on remote machines managed by a friend of the user.

SocialVPN [16] by Figueiredo et al. provides a user-friendly architecture to create self-configuring virtual overlay networks. It provides all the necessary functions to interconnect hosts across private address realms, network address translators, and firewalls. A SocialVPN deployment can be managed through the high-level interface provided by OSNs. The SocialVPNs provide three distinct functions: (1) trusted certificate exchange facility, (2) peer address management for private address realms, and (3) user-friendly names.

In SocialVPN, the OSNs are used as trusted certificate exchanges through which endpoints can exchange public-key certificates that verify their end-point addresses. The security of the trusted certificate exchange depends on the security of the OSN. With private address realms, hosts on the Internet do not have bi-directional addressing capabilities. The SocialVPN provides private address management functions such that a host can access other hosts irrespective of their location.

11.3.4 Malware Propagation and Social Relations

While the above systems leverage the social relations in a beneficial manner, there are instances where social relations are exploited by malicious users or even governments to launch various forms of information security attacks [18, 23]. We discuss two forms of attacks where social relations are exploited to intrude hosts: social phishing and social malware.

In his popular book [21], Kevin Mitnick describes how "social engineering" is a vital step in breaking into computer networks. In the context of computer network intrusion, friends do not break into friends' machines. In this case, the intruder uses "pretexting" to engage potential victims in a friendly manner before launching the real attack. So the attacker is trying to become a friend of the victim and put himself in the comfort zone of the victim. This way the victim is more likely to reveal valuable information to the attacker, which he could use in launching a successful network attack.

Phishing is a well-known form of attack where the intruder sends a bait message to lure a victim to a bogus site that is setup like a bank, school, or an organization where the victim would normally reveal personal credentials. Using phishing, the attacker can gain at the least valuable identification information such as usernames and passwords. In certain cases, attackers can also gain other useful information such as social insurance, mailing addresses, and family names by setting up convincing attack scenarios. While phishing attacks is a major concern, the success rate of this class of attack is very low (about 4%) when the bait messages originate from strangers.

In social phishing [18], the bait messages are forged to have originated from a known person. Because the purported origin is familiar, a victim is likely to open the message and even act on the message such as clicking on a link contained in the message. For example, if an attacker is able to access emails in a school and figure out the student-teacher relationship, he can exploit it to send highly effective bait messages. The attacker can fake an email as originating from a teacher and having exam related information which is likely to get a response from the students. In the process, the attacker can gain valuable login information from the students. Social phishing attacks similar to this one has already taken place [18]. In [18], Jagatic et al. found that victims are likely to fall prey for a bait if the purported origin is a friend or from the same social context. They also found that females are more likely than males to fall prey for phishing attacks.

Another form of attack that exploits social relations and is becoming a concern is *social malware* [23]. In [23], Nagaraja and Anderson describe a social malware attack by Chinese intelligence agencies on the Tibetan movement headquarters. The authors posit that the following sequence of events could have led to the installation of the surveillance software in Tibetan computers.

1. Tibetan monks visiting discussion forums and revealing their identities and interests. Intelligence agencies profiling key monks and crafting bait emails for the selected targets.
2. Intelligence agents launching the bait emails and getting the victims to run the programs with malware or lure them to sites containing malware.
3. Successful attack leading to the installation of the surveillance software on the Tibetan computers. The surveillance software further propagating the malware by piggybacking them on normal communications within the community.
4. The surveillance software snooping on received files and other activities (e.g., key logging) in the infected computers and communicating actionable intelligence data back to servers at intelligence agencies.

In the above scenario, social relations are exploited in two steps. The Tibetan monks received bait emails purportedly originating from other monks or members of the Tibetan community. By leveraging the social connections, attackers can increase the attack's success rate. After intrusion, the attackers use legitimate communication among the members to further propagate their surveillance software within the Tibetan movement.

11.4   Social Digital Identity

11.4.1   Overview

In this section, we briefly describe a new social approach to identity generation that leverages the structural properties of the social networks. As mentioned earlier, edges in social networks represent trusted relations between people. A path formed by a sequence of such edges represents a trust chain in a social network which represents a set of relations among people who can transitively vouch for the person where the chain ends. The strength of the vouch depends on the source of the chain, length of the chain, and the integrity of each edge that is part of the chain. To increase the confidence on the identity of a person, multiple vouches can be requested from different source nodes in the social network. Ideally, the different vouches on the identity of a person should be independent so that one vouch can strengthen another vouch. We can obtain independent vouches in two different ways by tracing node disjoint paths or edge disjoint paths through the social graph. With node disjoint paths, a person cannot participate in two different vouches for the identity of a target. In edge disjoint vouches, a relation cannot be reused in two different vouches for the identity of a target.

11.4.2   Generating a Seed Digital Identity

The social identity generation schemes described below works on social graphs that can be directly obtained using the application programming interfaces provided by OSNs such as Facebook or Myspace. We can also obtain similar social graphs by examining the adjacency graphs generated by communication applications such as email.

Consider a portion of an example social graph as shown in Fig. 11.2. The nodes in the graph represent people and directed edges represent relations among the people. For instance, a directed edge from **a** to **b** indicates that node **a** has a trusted relation with node **b**. From an identity point-of-view we consider an edge from node **a** to node **b** as an *identity attestation* from node **a** to node **b** (i.e., node **a** is attesting the veracity of node **b**'s identity). Each node independently names the relations it has

Fig. 11.2 Example
social graph

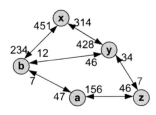

Fig. 11.3 Attaching the
landmark to the social graph

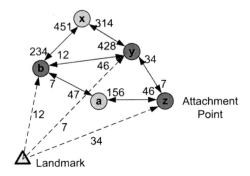

with other nodes (i.e., its outgoing edges). In Fig. 11.2, node **a** labels its relations
with nodes **b** and **z** using labels *47* and *156*, respectively. Each node uses unique
32-bit unsigned integers to labels its outgoing edges. In most cases, the friendship
between people is symmetric. That is, if node **x** has a trusted relation labeled α
with node **y**, node **y** has a trusted relation labeled β with node **x**. Because the nodes
choose the labels independently the value α need not be equal to β. The local scope
of the edge labels is very much similar to the local names proposed as part of simple
PKI [15].

The origin of social digital identity system is a landmark server that is placed
outside the social graph. As shown in Fig. 11.3, this landmark is attached to the
social graph by connecting it to strategically chosen attachment points on the social
graph. The edges that form the newly introduced connections from the landmark
into the social graph are labeled by the landmark.

The attachment points can be chosen using different strategies: random selection,
prestige-based selection, and optimized selection. The random selection is simple
where the attachment points are randomly selected from the set of nodes on the
social graph. The prestige of a node is given by its in-degree. In prestige-based selection, the nodes with higher prestige are given preference when attachment points
are selected. In optimized selection, the attachments points are placed such that several objectives are optimally satisfied. For instance, number of attachment points,
length of the identifier chains, and number of edge disjoint paths to the landmark
are some of the parameters to be considered in the attachment point selection process. In all of the above selection schemes, the landmark should ensure that the
attachment points are real (i.e., non Sybil nodes [32, 33]). This is essential to prevent bogus identity generation by malicious users.

Fig. 11.4 Example level
set computation process

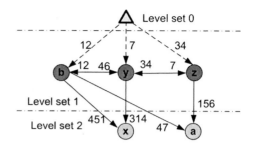

Once the attachment points are selected, the augmented social graph (social graph plus landmark) is divided into level sets. The purpose of dividing the nodes into level sets is to constrain the identity assignment process such that the privilege of providing an identifier is restricted. Suppose we are given a social graph where the edges do not have any weight (or equal weight), the level set computation can use a simple breadth-first search (BFS) algorithm. With the BFS, the landmark is the only node in level set 0. The level set 1 consists of attachment points. The level set i consists of those nodes that are directly connected to the nodes in level set $i-1$ and not in level sets 0 to $i-2$. The result of using a simple BFS for level set assignment on the sample social graph is shown in Fig. 11.4. When the edges have weights (i.e., heterogeneous edges), the level set assignment gets complicated. One situation that causes heterogeneity among the edges is the creation of new edges and deletion of old ones. The failure of an edge closer to the landmark can affect more paths than failure of edges further away from the landmark. Therefore, the level set assignment process should take the stability of the edge into consideration. If we assume that long-standing relations are likely to be more stable than newer relations, we can use the creation time of an edge in the level set assignment process.

11.4.3 Binding a Person to a SDI Token

The SDI token for a user is formed by the collection of SDI labels describing the edge-disjoint paths leading to the node from the landmark. This SDI token should be bound to the user such that only the user can issue it. The SDI token binding process has two phases: (1) computing the set of paths or validating previously computed set of paths and (2) creating certificates that associate the SDI labels with a particular user.

The first phase runs within the social identity provider as shown in Fig. 11.5. The SDI labels are computed using a maximal edge-disjoint path computation procedure. The primary purpose of the computations performed in the first phase is to ascertain the correctness of the SDI labels. In particular, we want to ensure that all the paths defined by the SDI label are active. Because a path from the landmark to a given node is made up of several edges, the path can fail if one or more edges along the path fail. To detect any failures, we propagate heartbeat messages through the social graph.

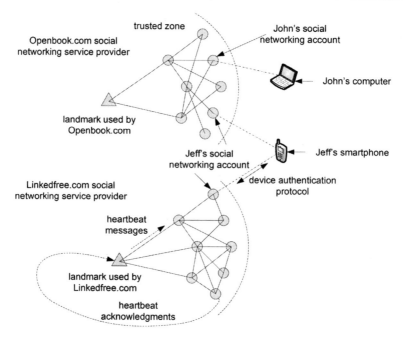

Fig. 11.5 User obtaining SDI tokens from social identity providers

The second phase of the SDI label binding is concerned with creating certificates that associate the SDI labels with a particular user. Consider the scenario depicted in Fig. 11.5 where we illustrate the SDI label assignment process for two users: Jeff and John. In this example, Jeff is a member of two OSNs (Openbook.com and Linkedfree.com) while John is a member of one OSN (Openbook.com). We assume that Jeff and John use a user-centric identity selection framework such as InfoCards [7]. The user-centric identity selectors run on user devices to initiate the transactions requiring identification. Suppose John is using his computer to login to a Blogging server, the identity selector running on John's machine interacts with the Blogging server to determine the minimum identification requirements. Once these requirements are determined, the identity selection framework presents John with a set of alternate credentials he can use to login to the Blogging server. Below we describe how John could adapt a user-centric identity selector to use SDI tokens for authenticating to the Blogging server.

John creates a public-private key pair for his device (computer) and registers it with his social identity provider service. Once the device is registered by John, the user-centric identity selector running on the device can request an SDI token from the social identity provider. The social identity provider can use a challenge-response protocol for authenticating the device originating the request for the SDI token. Before the SDI token is issued the social identity provider ensures that paths that are part of the SDI token are active using a heartbeat message based checking routine.

11.4.4 Example Deployment Scenario for SDI

In its basic form the SDI token of a person shows how that person is connected to other members of the community. The SDI token claims the interconnections the holder has within the community and a proof that verifies the specified claims. Using this facility, a person engaging in a transaction with Alice over the Internet could claim his identity as Ted (a friend of Bob). To proof his identity, Ted shows his SDI that Alice could verify using the SDI verification service.

Figure 11.6 shows the major components of a SDI infrastructure. The SDI provider is the central component of SDI infrastructure. An OSN service provider wanting to provide its users the social identity facility should connect with a SDI provider. An SDI provider can have more than one OSNs connected to it. Because current OSNs do not support inter-network linkages (i.e., a facebook.com user linking with linkedin.com user), the SDI provider treats the social graphs exported by the different social network providers as independent components.

The interactions that take place between a social networking provider and SDI provider are denoted by Step (1) in Fig. 11.6. One of the major pieces of information transferred from the social network provider to the SDI provider is the social graph that defines the interconnections among the people in the social network. This social graph is likely to be sub-graph of the actual graph maintained by the social network because a user may select only a subset of her friends for identification purposes. Further, new friendships are created and some old friendships may be deleted with time. We assume that the deletion rate of old friendships is very small.

Once the social graph or changes on an existing social graph are loaded into the SDI provider, it computes the SDI tokens for each user on the social graph.

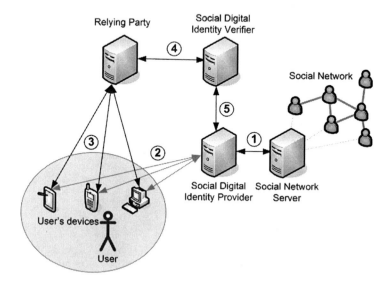

Fig. 11.6 An example deployment scenario for social digital identities

An SDI token has two parts: the label and certificate. The label is a declaration of the connectivity the holder of the SDI token has within the community. The certificate is proof of authenticity of the SDI token. As shown in Fig. 11.6 a user may interact with web-based services from a variety of devices such as PCs, smart phones, and tablet devices. We want SDI to provide device independent identification of people. For example, Alice could be using multiple devices (PCs and smart phones) to access Internet-based services. Alice may desire to be identified the same no matter what device she is using for accessing the services.

Step (2) in Fig. 11.6 shows the interactions between client devices and the SDI provider. We assume that the client devices have a user-centric identity management framework (e.g., InfoCards [7]) that is possibly extended to handle the SDI infrastructure on them. Suppose Alice wants to use her PC with the SDI infrastructure, she logs into the SDI provider either directly or through her social network provider (e.g., facebook.com) to configure her PC as one of her authorized identity keepers. Then the PC can interact with the SDI provider to download the SDI token containing the label and certificate components. Because the certificate associated with a SDI token has a time limited validity, it may be downloaded only on demand with each interaction requiring a confirmation from Alice.

The SDI token distributed to a device can include an end-point specific designation embedded in the token. This designation allows the SDI verifier service to know the exact submission process of the token. Further, identification events could be logged in the user-friendly manner at the social network provider and audited by Alice.

Step (3) in Fig. 11.6 shows the interactions between a relying party (i.e., an Internet-based service) that Alice is trying to access and the client device Alice is using for that purpose. These interactions are mostly determined by the protocols already formalized as part of a user-centric identity infrastructure such as InfoCards [7].

Once an SDI token is presented by a user device for identification purposes, the relying party should contact a SDI verification service to determine the authenticity of the token. These interactions are shown in Step (4) in Fig. 11.6. In addition, the relying party can use the label embedded in the SDI token to infer the connectivity of Alice within the community and determine whether any friends of interest for Alice are using or used the Internet-based service.

The SDI verification service should synchronize with the SDI provider so that it can validate the SDI token issued by the SDI provider. We can have multiple SDI verifiers to provide a high throughput verification service.

11.4.5 Example Applications of SDI

The SDI can be useful in many Internet-based applications. The primary advantage of SDI is that it provides a mechanism to identify people based on the friendships among people.

- *Password-less authentication:* The primary purpose of SDI is to provide a digital identity by harvesting the trusted friend-of-a-friend relations on social networks. Once registered by the user, a device such as a smartphone or computer could pull an valid SDI token from the social identity provider on behalf of the user. Using the SDI token, the user should be able to login to a web-based service that accepts SDI credentials.
- *Portable social networking:* One of the practical problems with existing OSNs is that they confine the social activities of the users to their sites. For example, consider Alice and Bob who are friends and are connected in an OSN. Suppose Alice and Bob visit a blogging site that is not hosted by their social network provider they may not be able to recognize each other. With SDI, Alice and Bob could use their SDI tokens to log into the blogging service. By examining the SDI tokens, the blogging service can determine that Alice and Bob are friends and alert them accordingly.
- *Peer to peer networks:* Peer-to-peer networks such as Kazza and Bittorrent are widely used for exchanging content on the Internet. They rely on the availability of massive number of replica servers from where content can be downloaded. One of the problems these systems face is the corrupt or bogus content that is introduced into the system by malicious users. While reputation management has been successfully used to minimize the impact of malicious users, corrupt and bogus content remains a problem. Further, peer-to-peer networking is an ideal platform for more than file sharing. It can be used for information sharing such as peer-to-peer news systems and peer-to-peer blogging services.
- *Email signing:* Spam is a major problem troubling both email providers and users. To combat the spam problem a variety of different tools have been developed. The inability to identify users accurately is one of the core issues that make email spam harder to solve. With SDI, we can require signed emails. Emails signed by SDI tokens can be easily identified because it quickly identifies the sender with respect to the receiver. This is analogous to memos exchanged in the physical world, where signatures are used to validate documents. Once a document is validated the trust or importance of the document relies on the relationship the sender has with the receiver. Unsigned memos are assumed to have zero or little value and can be subjected to traditional screening processes for viruses or spam.
- *Intelligent firewalls:* Firewalls are one of the important elements in the Internet defense system. Despite their widespread use, firewalls operate based on an antiquated trust model. In this model, trust is applied on traffic streams defined based on network protocol parameters such as end-point addresses, protocol types, and port numbers. Very recently, deep packet inspection engines have enabled firewall implementations that examine application specific parameters in their admission control processes. Application developers (e.g., peer-to-peer file sharing system developers) have routinely developed techniques to bypass the impediments imposed by the firewall devices. Many techniques including piggybacking the data onto other protocols in unintended ways have been used to traverse firewall enforced borders. Using SDI, we can develop intelligent firewall

designs that can enforce a person-to-person trust model instead of the protocol-centric trust model currently enforced.

- *Auto updates for information storage:* Locating information on old friends is one of the initial motivations for social networking. Although online storages such as websites and social networks are capable of holding valuable contact information such as email addresses, IM addresses, and phone numbers, they often have outdated information. This is particularly true for individual contact or profile information that is held by sites that rely on a single person for updates. By tagging pieces of information such as email addresses by SDIs automatic update of contact and profile information becomes feasible.
- *Validating user generated content:* User generated content is becoming an increasingly important part of data found on Internet. The people-centric identification provided by SDI is ideal for tagging user-generated content.

11.5   Information and Threats in Social Networks

11.5.1   Information on Social Networks

The information relating to a user on OSNs can be classified into three types: (1) information explicitly posted by the user, (2) information implicitly created by the user, (3) information created by others that relates to the user. The type of explicit information created on an OSN depends on the type of network. In many cases, it includes the following type of data: full name, contact address, phone, email, instant messaging contact identifier, hobbies, interests, work information. Specialized social networks can include fields more pertinent to their goals (e.g., current and previous employers for LinkedIn). Explicit information can also extend into vaguely defined fields such as favorite food, celebrities, and music.

Implicitly created information includes data not directly added by the user, but that still holds value in determining the activities of the user. For instance, pictures posted by the user in her album can contain EXIF data that contains information where the pictures were taken (longitude and latitude) and when they were taken. Therefore, the EXIF data extracted from the pictures posted by a user can help in inferring the places visited by the user in a vacation trip. Similarly, information stated about the user in message board on the social network such as "enjoy your trip to Cancun" implies that the user is going to visit Cancun.

The implicit information available on OSNs is vast. Following are some types of implicit information about a user: (a) names of friends and family, (b) pictures of friends and family, (c) information created by neighbors in the social graph, (d) information extracted from data objects, and (e) group relationships. A user's identity on the social network represents their individual mix of implicit and explicit information. It's important to note that while implicit information may seem inconsequential at first glance, it can prove quite revealing in certain cases. Several users have reported encountering problems (repercussions in their professional life mostly) due to information about them on social networks.

In [13], Donath argues that online identity includes the attitude and style of the person creating the profile. Separate profiles created by the same user could be linked by intangible properties like writing style, specific vocabulary usage, and communication tone. The subconscious nature of these aspects of communication means it is quite likely that separate accounts can show traces of the originating user [13].

The incorporation of personal photographs to the explicit information pool can be seen as an attempt to link an ambiguous online identity with its physical, real world equivalent. This leads to the assumption that communications which can be traced back to a personal photograph should be deemed "more secure," in the sense that the identity of the communicating party is more easily verifiable. There is one flaw to this argument: it only holds when the photograph is a reliable reference to the real world identity (i.e., human body [13]). If the friendship relation between two users was established purely based on online acquaintance, any personal photos linked to both users are no more reliable than any other piece of information. Additionally, should a false profile be created by a malicious user, publicly available pictures could be used to dupe users into creating fraudulent friendships links.

Profile cloning [2] is a well-known attack strategy where the victim's profile from one network is cloned onto another network and her friends are invited to link to it. For example, Alice has a public Facebook account, with pictures. Bob knows Alice and they are friends both online and offline. Bob also has an account on a separate social network (say MySpace). Eve, in an attempt to exploit Bob's friend-only information, creates a profile on MySpace using information taken from Alice's public Facebook profile. Eve, impersonating [20] as Alice sends a request to create a link between the fake Alice and Bob on MySpace. If Bob accepts the request, Eve can have access to Bob's friend-only information.

There are several simple ways to reduce the incidence of this type of fraud. If Alice has made it clear, through any channel, that she is not creating any further profiles, Bob would have reason to doubt the incoming MySpace request. Also, Alice could make her Facebook profile private, stopping Eve from getting the necessary information to create the fraudulent account (This counter measure can however be flawed if Alice and Eve are linked thereby giving Eve access to the private profile anyway). Lastly, Bob could verify the fraudulent MySpace request with Alice through a secondary channel which they both trust (in person, on the phone, or even on Facebook).

11.5.2 Information for Establishing Identity

Social networks present a natural "identity vouching" process. A new, unconnected user has no links in the network. Without any links, the new user has no traction inside the network. Links can only be created in a request-response setting.

Established users need to include the new user in their social connections so that he could take part in various network activities such as file exchange and communication.

One of the challenges that emerges in making links in OSNs is identifying the person requesting connection. The approach widely used for online identification is information recall such as asking for "Mother's maiden name" and "Which high school did you attend?" As personal information becomes widely available on OSNs, an attacker wanting to make fake relations can easily answer such questions. To prevent sensitive information from landing into inconspicuous hands, users need to keep their personal information private and to only create links with trusted users. However, closed and small communities tend not to thrive and it is generally encouraged to create large personal networks. In particular, OSN operators prefer that their users create large networks.

The above discussion implies that users should be vary of lone or weakly connected nodes seeking connections. This is somewhat misleading. A malicious user can develop variations of the impersonation attack, where he creates numerous profiles and links them together thereby creating a small community of users. If we assume a trust model based on community attachment, as suggested by Ba, each user in this community seems at least somewhat trustworthy to anyone outside the community [1]. This level of trust can be used by the attacker to lure real users to create links to the fraudulent profiles. After a legitimate user falls prey to such an attack, valuable private data could be compromised or the connections can be used to create further connections with real users.

In reality, a successful Sybil attack in a social network requires a tremendous amount of effort. This effort can be somewhat diminished if combined with simple identity theft (i.e., by having one or more of the nodes in the fraudulent community represent users that the attack target knows).

11.5.3 Identity vs. Privacy

Privacy in OSNs is a highly interesting topic not only within the academia but also within the public discourse. With the immense influence exerted by OSNs in the daily lives of their users, a previously unimagined amount of personal and social information about individuals are made accessible often to the whole world online and as expected this has added a whole new dimension to the issue of "online privacy."

Even some of the basic aspects of the problem, such as users' specific concerns about privacy, their level of satisfaction, and trends in information disclosure are rather inconclusive and blurry [19]. Several research reports show that people are highly concerned about their privacy and are becoming inclined towards reducing the amount of information they disclose in OSNs [19]. Simultaneously, other research shows that despite privacy concerns, actual information disclosure proceeds unabated in OSNs [28, 30]. A recent study has shown that the most prevalent privacy concern is organizational and governmental threats, specifically misuse of the information collected by social networks for commercial gain rather than individual threats like easy access to the information disclosed by fellow users, identity theft, or impersonation [19]. This is understandable considering that most privacy settings in social networks allow users to define layers of information, and in a way "layers of identity" that are accessible to different parties; friends can see more of the person's online identity, while an unknown visitor can see less of the person's online identity. However, users are not able to intervene a lot to the process of how their identities are managed at the organizational level and how it may be reused by the social network for different purposes, including commercial uses like advertising. Whether this affects users' identities by leading them to reduce the amount of information they provide or disclose to the or in the OSN is, as mentioned before, a matter of debate.

Another point that connects privacy concerns with identity within the framework of an OSN is the issue of whether the more readily available information related to one's identity makes the identity more robust and hence harder to forge, or does it make it more prone to attacks from individuals and organizations. The lack of research in this area prevents us from making further conclusions about this dilemma, but it is surely one of the interesting complexities caused by the intricate relation between privacy and identity, especially within an OSN context.

11.6 Summary

Online identities and social networking have an interesting connection between them. Despite many technical proposals over the last decade, implementing socially acceptable online identities remains an open problem. The social networking, on the other hand, has flourished on the Internet and is leading the transformation of the web into a *social* web. The online implementations of social networks provide the tools for users to create online profiles and link with other people. In many ways these online profiles, data associated with the online profiles, and the connections formed with the profiles can be considered as online identities of people. However, there is no framework or methodology for validating the information that is available on online social networks. As a result, the level of assurance that can be placed by the online identities developed on online social networks remain low.

References

1. Ba, S.: Establishing online trust through a community responsibility system. Decision Support Systems **31**(3), 323–336 (2001)
2. Bilge, L., Strufe, T., Balzarotti, D., Kirda, E.: All your contacts are belong to us: Automated identity theft attacks on social networks. In: 18th International Conference on World Wide Web, pp. 551–560 (2009)

3. Bonneau, J., Anderson, J., Anderson, R., Stajano, F.: Eight friends are enough: Social graph approximation via public listings. In: SNS '09: Second ACM EuroSys Workshop on Social Network Systems, pp. 13–18 (2009)
4. Boyd, D.M., Ellison, N.B.: Social network sites: Definition, history, and scholarship. Journal of Computer-Mediated Communication 13(1) (2007)
5. Brainard, J., Juels, A., Rivest, R.L., Szydlo, M., Yung, M.: Fourth-factor authentication: Somebody you know. In: CCS '06: 13th ACM conference on Computer and communications security, pp. 168–178 (2006)
6. Burkhalter, B.: Reading race online: Discovering racial identity in usenet discussions. In: M.A. Smith, P. Kollock (eds.) Communities in Cyberspace, pp. 60–75. Routledge, London (1999)
7. Cameron, K., Jones, M.B.: Design rationale behind the identity metasystem architecture. In: ISSE/SECURE 2007 Securing Electronic Business Processes, pp. 117–129 (2007)
8. Carter, D.: Living in virtual communities: An ethnography of human relationships in cyberspace. Information, Communication and Society 8(2), 148–167 (2005)
9. Chi, E.H.: The social web: Research and opportunities. IEEE Computer 41(9), 88–91 (2008)
10. Clarke, R.: Human identification in information systems: Management challenges and public policy issues. Information Technology and People 7(4), 6–34 (1994)
11. Craik, K.H.: Reputation: A Network Interpretation. Oxford University Press, NY (2009)
12. Dhamija, R., Dusseault, L.: The seven flaws of identity management: Usability and security challenges. IEEE Security and Privacy 6(2), 24–29 (2008)
13. Donath, J.: Identity and deception in the virtual community. In: M.A. Smith, P. Kollock (eds.) Communities in Cyberspace, pp. 27–58. Routledge, London (1999)
14. Douceur, J.R.: The sybil attack. In: First international Workshop on Peer-To-Peer Systems (2002)
15. Ellison, C.M.: The nature of a useable PKI. Computer Networks: The International Journal of Computer and Telecommunications Networking 31(9), 823–830 (1999)
16. Figueiredo, R., Boykin, P.O., Juste, P.S., Wolinsky, D.: Social VPNs: Integrating overlay and social networks for seamless P2P networking. In: IEEE WETICE/COPS 2008 (2008)
17. Gutwirth, S.: Beyond identity? Identity in the Information Society 1(1), 123–133 (2008)
18. Jagatic, T.N., Johnson, N.A., Jakobsson, M., Menczer, F.: Social phishing. Communications of the ACM 50(10), 94–100 (2007)
19. Krasnova, H., Gnther, O., Spiekermann, S., Koroleva, K.: Privacy concerns and identity in online social networks. Identity in the Information Society 2(1), 39–63 (2009)
20. Marshall, A.M., Tompsett, B.C.: Identity theft in an online world. Computer Law and Security Report 21(2), 128–137 (2005)
21. Mitnick, K.D., Simon, W.L., Wozniak, S.: The Art of Deception. Wiley, NY (2002)
22. Nabeth, T.: Social web and identity: A likely encounter. Identity in the Information Society 2(1), 1–5 (2009)
23. Nagaraja, S., Anderson, R.: The snooping dragon: Social-malware surveillance of the Tibetan movement. Tech. Rep. UCAM-CL-TR-746, University of Cambridge Computer Laboratory (2009)
24. O'Hara, K., Tuffield, M.M., Shadbolt, N.: Lifelogging: Privacy and empowerment with memories for life. Identity in the Information Society 1(1), 155–172 (2008)
25. Ramachandran, A.V., Feamster, N.: Authenticated out-of-band communication over social links. In: First Workshop on Online Social Networks, pp. 61–66 (2008)
26. Recordon, D., Fitzpatrick, B.: Openid authentication 1.1. http://openid.net/specs/openid-authentication-1_1.html (2006)
27. Soleymani, B., Maheswaran, M.: Social authentication protocol for mobile phones. In: 2009 International Conference on Computational Science and Engineering, pp. 436–441 (2009)
28. Stutzman, F.: An evaluation of identity-sharing behavior in social network communities. Journal of the International Digital Media and Arts Association 3(1) (2006)
29. Tran, N., Min, B., Li, J., Subramanian, L.: Sybil-resilient online content voting. In: 6th USENIX Symposium on Networked Systems Design and Implementation, pp. 15–28 (2009)

30. Tufekci, Z.: Can you see me now? Audience and disclosure regulation in online social network sites. Bulletin of Science Technology Society **28**(1), 20–36 (2008)
31. Xie, B.: The mutual shaping of online and offline social relationships. Information Research **13**(3) (2008)
32. Yu, H., Kaminsky, M., Gibbons, P.B., Flaxman, A.: Sybilguard: defending against sybil attacks via social networks. SIGCOMM Computer Communication Review **36**(4), 267–278 (2006)
33. Yu, H., Gibbons, P.B., Kaminsky, M., Xiao, F.: Sybillimit: A near-optimal social network defense against sybil attacks. In: IEEE Symposium on Security and Privacy, pp. 3–17 (2008)

Chapter 12
Detecting Communities in Social Networks

Tsuyoshi Murata

12.1 Introduction

Relations of real-world entities are often represented as networks, such as social networks connected with friendships or co-authorships. In many cases, real social networks contain denser parts and sparser parts. Denser subnetworks correspond to groups of people that are closely connected with each other. Such denser sub-networks are called "communities" in this chapter. (There are many definitions of communities which will be described later.) Detecting communities from given social networks are practically important for the following reasons:

1. Communities can be used for information recommendation because members of the communities often have similar tastes and preferences. Membership of detected communities will be the basis of collaborative filtering.
2. Communities will help us understand the structures of given social networks. Communities are regarded as components of given social networks, and they will clarify the functions and properties of the networks.
3. Communities will play important roles when we visualize large-scale social networks. Relations of the communities clarify the processes of information sharing and information diffusions, and they may give us some insights for the growth the networks in the future.

In general, detecting communities is not an easy task. There are many difinitions of communities and most of them are computationally expensive. For example, detecting communities by optimizing modularity is NP-hard.

This chapter explains the definitions of communities, criteria for evaluating detected communities, methods for community detection, and tools for community detection. The words "cluster" and "community" are often used interchangeably. In this chapter, we use the latter since the former can be used also for the group of unstructured entities (such as document clusters).

T. Murata (✉)
Tokyo Institute of Technology, W8-59 2-12-1 Ookayama, Meguro, Tokyo, 152-8552 Japan
e-mail: murata@cs.titech.ac.jp

B. Furht (ed.), *Handbook of Social Network Technologies and Applications*,
DOI 10.1007/978-1-4419-7142-5_12, © Springer Science+Business Media, LLC 2010

12.2 Definition of Community

The word "community" intuitively means a subnetwork whose edges connecting inside of it (intracommunity edges) are denser than the edges connecting outside of it (intercommunity edges). Definitions of community can be classified into the following three categories.

- Local definitions
- Global definitions
- Definitions based on vertex similarity.

12.2.1 Local definitions

The attention is focused on the vertices of the subnetwork under investigation and on its immediate neighborhood. Local definitions of community can be further divided into self-referring ones and comparative ones. The former considers the subnetwork alone, and the latter compares mutual connections of the vertices of the subnetwork with the connections with external neighbors.

The examples of self referring definitions are clique (a maximal subnetworks where each vertex is adjacent to all the others), n-clique (a maximal subnetwork such that the distance of each pair of vertices is not larger than n), and k-plex (a maximal subnetwork such that each vertex is adjacent to all the others except at most k of them).

The examples of comparative definitions are LS set (a subnetwork where each vertex has more neighbors inside than outside of the subnetwork), and weak community (the total degrees of the vertices inside the community exceeds the the number of edges lying between the community and the rest of the network).

12.2.2 Global definitions

Global definitions of community characterize a subnetwork with respect to the network as a whole. These definitions usually starts from a null model, in another words, a network which matches the original network in some of its topological features, but which does not display community structure. Then, the linking properties of subnetworks of the initial network are compared with those of the corresponding subnetworks in the null model. If there is a wide difference between them, the subnetworks are regarded as communities. The simplest way to design a null model is to introduce randomness in the distribution of edges among vertices. The most popular null model is that proposed by Newman and Girvan [14]. It consists of a randomized version of the original network, where edges are rewired at random,

Fig. 12.1 Dendrogram

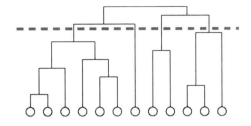

under the constraint that each vertex keeps its degree. This null model is the basic concept behind the definition of modularity, a function which evaluates the goodness of partitions of a network into communities.

12.2.3 Definitions Based on Vertex Similarity

Definitions of the last category is based on an assumption that communities are groups of vertices which are similar to each other. Some quantitative criterion is employed to evaluate the similarity between each pair of vertices. Similarity measures are at the basis of the method of hierarchical clustering. Hierarchical clustering is a way to find several layers of communities that are composed of vertices similar to each other. Repetitive merges of similar vertices based on some quantitative similarity measures will generate a structure shown in Fig. 12.1. This structure is called dendrogram, and highly similar vertices are connected in the lower part of the dendrogram. Subtrees obtained by cutting the dendrogram with horizontal line correspond to communities. Communities of different granurality will be obtained by changing the position of the horizontal line. In the case of Fig. 12.1, four communities are obtained.

12.3   Evaluating Communities

In general, there are many ways of partitioning given network into communities. It is necessary to establish which partition exihibit a real community structure. Therefore, we need a quality function for evaluating how good a partition is. The most popular quality function is the modularity of Newman and Girivan [12]. It can be written in several ways.

$$Q = \frac{1}{2m} \sum_{ij} \left(A_{ij} - \frac{k_i k_j}{2m} \right) \delta(C_i, C_j) \qquad (12.1)$$

where the sum runs over all pairs of vertices, A is the adjacency matrix, k_i is the degree of vertexi i and m is the total number of edges of the network. The element of A_{ij} of the adjacency matrix is 1 if vertices i and j are connected, otherwise it is 0. The δ-function yields 1 if vertices i and j are in the same community, 0 otherwise.

Modularity can be rewritten as follows.

$$Q = \sum_{s=1}^{n_m} \left[\frac{l_s}{m} - \left(\frac{d_s}{2m} \right)^2 \right] \qquad (12.2)$$

where n_m is the number of communities, l_s is the total number of edges joining vertices of community s, and d_s is the sum of the degrees of the vertices of s. In the above formula, the first term of each summand is the fraction of edges of the network inside the community, whereas the second term represents the expected fraction of edges that would be there if the network were a random network with the same degree for each vertex. Therefore, the comparison between real and expected edges is expressed by the corresponding summand of the above formula. Figure 12.2 illustrates the meaning of modularity.

The latter formula implicitly shows the definition of a community: a subnetwork is a community if the number of edges inside it is larger than the expected number in modularity's null model. If this is the case, the vertices of the subnetwork are more tightly connected than expected. Large positive values of Q are expected to indicate good partitions. The modularity of the whole network, taken as a single community, is zero. Modularity is always smaller than one, and it can be negative as well. Modularity has been employed as quality function in many algorithms. In addition, modularity optimization is a popular method for community detection.

However, there are some caveats on the use of modularity. Modularity values cannot be compared for different networks. Another thing we have to remember is that modularity optimization may fail to identify communities smaller than a scale which depends on the total size of the network and on the degree of interconnectedness of the communities, which is called resulution limit [7].

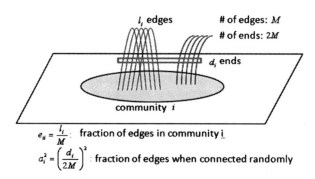

Fig. 12.2 Modularity

12.4 Methods for Community Detection

There are naive methods for dividing given networks into subnetworks, such as graph partitioning, hierarchical clustering, and k-means clustering. However, these methods needs to provide the numbers of clusters or their size in advance. It is desirable to devise methods that have abilities of extracting a complete information about the community structure of networks. The methods for detecting communities are roughly classified into the following categories: (1) divisive algorithms, (2) modularity optimization, (3) spectral algorithms, and (4) other algorithms.

12.4.1 Divisive Algorithms

A simple way to identify communities in a network is to detect the edges that connect vertices of different communities and remove them, so that the communities get disconnected from each other.

The most popular algorithm is that proposed by Girvan and Newman [8]. In this algorithm, edges are selected according to the values of measures of edge centrality, estimating the importance of edges according to some property on the network. The steps of the algorithm are as follows: (1) Computation of the centrality of all edges, (2) Removal of edge with largest centrality, (3) Recalculation of centralities on the running network, and (4) Iteration of the cycle from step (2).

Girvan and Newman focuses on the concept of edge betweenness. Edge betweenness is the number of shortest paths between all vertex pairs that run along the edge. It is intuitive that intercommunity edges have a large value of the edge betweenness, because many shortest paths connecting vertices of different communities will pass thorugh them. In the example of Fig. 12.3, two communities will be obtained by removing the central edge, whose edge betweenness is the largest (12).

12.4.2 Modularity Optimization

As mentioned above, modularity is a quality function for evaluating partitions. Therefore, the partition corresponding to its maximum value on a given network

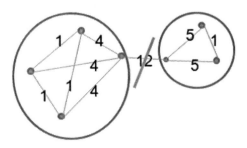

Fig. 12.3 Detecting communities based on edge betweenness

should be the best one. This is the main idea for modularity optimization. An exhaustive optimization of Q is impossible since there are huge number of ways to partiton a network. It has been proved that modularity optimization is an NP-hard problem. However, there are currently several algorithms that are able to find fairly good approximations of the modularity maximum in a reasonable time. One of the famous algorithms for modularity optimization is CNM algorithm proposed by Clauset et al. [4]. Another examles of the algorithms are greedy algorithms and simulated annealing.

12.4.3 Spectral Algorithms

Spectral algorithms are to cut given network into pieces so that the number of edges to be cut will be minimized. One of the basic algorithm is spectral graph bipartitioning. As a concrete procedure, Laplacian matrix L of given network is used. The Laplacian matrix L of a network is an $n \times n$ symmetric matrix, with one row and column for each vertex. Laplacian matrix is defined as $L = D - A$, where A is the adjacency matrix and D is the diagonal degree matrix with $D_{ii} = \sum_k A_{ik}$. All eigenvalues of L are real and non-negative, and L has a full set of n real and orthogonal eigenvectors. In order to minimize the above cut, vertices are partitioned based on the signs of the eigenvector that corresponds to the second smallest eigenvalue of L. In general, community detection based on repetative bipartitioning is relatively fast. Newman proposes a method for maximizing modularity based on the spectral algorithm [13].

12.4.4 Other Algorithms

There are many other algorithms for detecting communities, such as the methods focusing on random walk, and the ones searching for overlapping cliques. Danon compares the computational costs and their accuracies of major community detection methods [5].

12.5 Tools for Detecting Communities

Several tools have been developed for detecting communities. These are roughly classified into the following two categories: detecting communities from large-scale networks, and interactively analyzing communities from small networks.

12.5.1 Tools for Large-Scale Networks

Clauset et al. propose CNM algorithm [3] of community detection based on modularity optimization, and its implementation is available online. They claims that the algorithm is applicable for large-scale networks of a few million vertices. Wakita improves their algorithm and opens his implementation to public [17].

12.5.2 Tools for Interactive Analysis

There are many tools for interactively visualizing and analyzing small networks. (Detailed lists can be found in [16]).

- JUNG
  (http://jung.sourceforge.net/)
- Netminer
  (http://www.netminer.com/NetMiner/overview_01.jsp)
- Pajek
  (http://vlado.fmf.unilj.si/pub/networks/pajek/)
- igraph
  (http://igraph.sourceforge.net/)
- SONIVIS
  (http://www.sonivis.org/)
- Commetrix
  (http://www.commetrix.de/)
- Network Workbench
  (http://nwb.slis.indiana.edu/)
- visone
  (http://visone.info/)
- CFinder
  (http://www.cfinder.org/)

As an example, community detection of igraph is shown below. Igraph is a free software for network analysis, and it can be used as the libraries of C programing language, and as the combination with R, a programming language for statistical analysis. Figure 12.4 is the screenshot of the combination R+igraph. Details of R are available at http://cran.r-project.org/, and details of igraph are available at http://igraph.sourceforge.net/.

As a typical example in the field of social network analysis, Zachary's karate club network (Fig. 12.5) is used. This network shows the relations of certain Karate club members in a university. While Zachary was observing the relations of the members, a club administrator and a teacher were opposed to each other and the club was splitted into two factions. Figure 12.5 shows the vertices that belong to each faction. Reproducing the factions from given social network is often employed as a testbed of community detection methods. Karate club network represented in GML

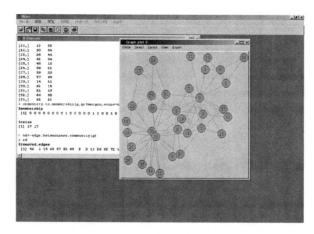

Fig. 12.4 Screenshot of R+igraph

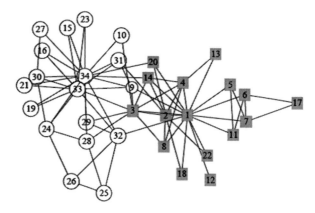

Fig. 12.5 Karate club network (cited from [14])

format can be downloaded from Mark Newman's Web site, for example [13]. Graph modelling language (GML) is one of the formats for representing networks. The following shows the processes of community detection of R+igraph. Explanation of each command are shown after #.

Figure 12.8 shows the result of community detection by fastgreedy, which maximize modularity in a greedy approach. The command read.graph loads network data, and the command tkplot perform visualization (Fig. 12.6). Initial positions of vertices are assigned randomly, and users can select major algorithms for visualization, such as Kamada–Kawai and Fruchterman–Reingold. Positions of vertices can be adjusted manually.

The command fastgreedy.community is for maximizing modularity greedily, and its results are stored in variable gr. The variable gr is composed of gr\$modularity (a list of modularity values in the process of maximization) and gr\$merge (vertex IDs

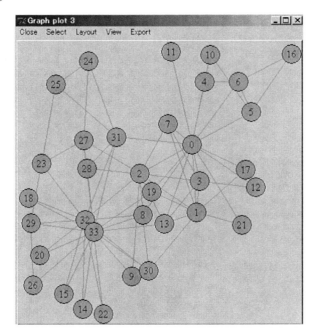

Fig. 12.6 Visualization of karate club network by igraph

that are merged at each step). The command communty.to.membership generates m$membership (membership of each vertex) and m$csize (size of each community). This example shows that the first eight vertices of lower numbers belong to community 0 and the sizes of the two communities are both 17. After storing the membershop m$membership to V(g)$color, the second tkplot command specifies a visualization algorithm and colors of vertices in order to perform visualization. Vertices of each community are colored as shown in Fig. 12.7.

As you can see from the figures, the only difference between the communities obtaind by fastgreedy and actual factions in Fig. 12.5 is the tenth vertex in Fig. 12.5 (the ninth vertex in Fig. 12.7). Please keep in mind that numbers starts from 1 in R, while from 0 in igraph.

Other methods for detecting communities are also available in igraph. Figure 12.9 shows community detection based on edge betweenness.

The command edge.betweenness.community detect communities by repetitively removing edges of high edge betweenness. The contents of the obtained variable ed is different from previous fastgreedy.community: ed$removed.edges (list of removed edges), ed$edge.betw eenness (list of edge betweenness), ed$merges (list of vertices that are merged in a dendrogram), and ed$bridges (list of bridging edges). Edge betweenness divides given network in an top-down manner, while ed$merges shows list of vertices in a reversed order (just like bottom-up manner). You can see that communities detected based on edge betweenness are differnet from the actual factions in Fig. 12.5.

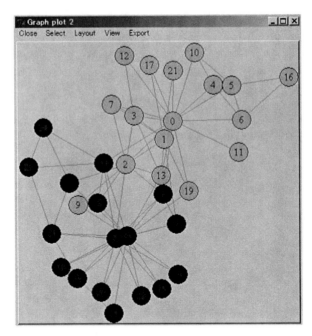

Fig. 12.7 Community detection by fastgreedy algorithm

```
> library("igraph")                          #load igraph library
> setwd("R")                                 #change directory
> dir()                                      #show files
[1] "karate.gml"
> g<-read.graph("karate.gml",format="gml")   #load network data
> tkplot(g)                                  #visualize network
[1] 1
> gr<-fastgreedy.community(g)                 #modularity optimization
> gr$modularity                              #list of modularity values
  [1] -0.04980276 -0.03763971 -0.01397107 -0.00147929  0.01775148  0.04906312
...
[31]   0.37598619  0.38067061  0.37179487  0.00000000
> gr$merge                                   #list of merged vertices
       [,1]  [,2]
  [1,]    5   16
...
[33,]    65   63
> m<-community.to.membership(g,gr$merges,steps=nrow(gr$merges)-1)
                                             #store membership and size
> m                                          #show the contents
$membership
  [1] 0 0 0 0 0 0 0 0 1 0 0 0 0 0 0 1 1 0 0 1 0 1 0 1 1 1 1 1 1 1 1 1 1 1
$csize
[1] 17 17
> V(g)$color<-m$membership                    #store membership
> V(g)$color
  [1] 0 0 0 0 0 0 0 0 1 0 0 0 0 0 0 1 1 0 0 1 0 1 0 1 1 1 1 1 1 1 1 1 1 1
> tkplot(g,layout=layout.kamada.kawai,vertex.color=V(g)$color)
                                             #visualize network
[1] 2
>
```

Fig. 12.8 Community detection by fastgreedy in R + igraph

```
> ed<-edge.betweenness.community(g)        #detect communities
> ed                                       #show result
$removed.edges                             #list of removed edges
 [1]  46   1  15  63  67  50  44   2   5  13  26  62  72  17   7   8   6  18  76  60  73  36  39  16
...
[73]  57  70  48  58  74  77
$edge.betweenness                          #list of edge betweenness
 [1]   71.392857  66.895177  77.317399  82.002906 123.232917 100.205556
...
[73]   1.500000   3.000000   1.000000   1.000000   2.000000   1.000000
$merges                                    #list of merged vertices
       [,1]  [,2]
 [1,]   32    33
...
[33,]   65    64
$bridges                                   #list of bridges
 [1]  78  77  75  74  71  70  68  67  66  65  63  61  58  55  53  50  49  47  45  43  41  39  37  35
[25]  33  31  29  27  25  24  18  14  11
> community.to.membership(g,ed$merges,steps=nrow(ed$merges)-1)
                                           #membership of two communities
$membership
 [1] 1 1 0 1 1 1 1 0 0 1 1 1 1 0 0 1 1 0 1 0 1 0 0 0 0 0 0 0 0 0 0 0 0 0
$csize
 [1] 19 15
> community.to.membership(g,ed$merges,steps=nrow(ed$merges)-2)
                                           #membership of three communities
$membership
 [1] 0 0 1 0 0 0 0 0 1 2 0 0 0 0 1 1 0 0 1 0 1 0 1 1 1 1 1 1 1 1 1 1 1 1
$csize
 [1] 15 18  1
> community.to.membership(g,ed$merges,steps=nrow(ed$merges)-3)
                                           #membership of four communities
$membership
 [1] 1 1 0 1 2 2 2 1 0 3 2 1 1 1 0 0 2 1 0 1 0 1 0 0 0 0 0 0 0 0 0 0 0 0
$csize
 [1] 18 10  5  1
>
```

Fig. 12.9 Community detection based on edge betweenness in R+igraph

The command edge.betweenness.community generates a dendrogram shown in Sect. 12.2.3. Communities of different granurality can be obtained from the dendrogram: if two communities of size 19 and 15 are divided further, communities of size 18, 1, 10, and 5 are obtained.

Many other methods for community detection are installed in R+igraph.

label.propagation.community   community detection by label propergation
leading.eigenvector.community   community detection by spectral partitioning
spinglass.community   community detection based on statistical mechanics
walktrap.community   community detection by random walk

12.6   Conclusion

This chapter explains the definitions of communities, criteria for evaluating detected communities, methods for community detection, and tools for community detection and visualization. More detailed survey can be found in [6]. And there are some online materials regarding community detection and visualization [16].

References

1. Barber, M. J., *Modularity and community detection in bipartite networks*, Physical Review E, 76(066102), 1–9, 2007
2. Chakrabarti, D., Kumar, R., Tomkins, A., *Evolutionary Clustering*, Proceedings of the 12th ACM SIGKDD International Conference on Knowledge Discovery and Data Mining (KDD06), pp. 554–560, 2006
3. Clauset, A., *Fast modularity community structure inference algorithm*, http://www.cs.unm.edu/~aaron/research/fastmodularity.htm
4. Clauset, A., Newman, M. E. J., Moore, C., *Finding community structure in very large networks*, Physical Review E, 70(066111), 1–6, 2004
5. Danon, L., Diaz-Guilera, A., Duch, J., Arenas, A., *Comparing community structure identification*, Journal of Statistical Mechanics, P09008, 1–10, 2005
6. Fortunato, S., *Community detection in graphs*, Physics Reports, 486, 75–174, 2010
7. Fortunato, S., Barthelemy, M., *Resolution limit in community detection*, Proceedings of the National Academy of Sciences (PNAS), 104(1), 36–41, 2007
8. Girvan, M., Newman, M. E. J., *Community structure in social and biological networks* Proceedings of the National Academy of Sciences (PNAS), 99(12), 7821–7826, 2002
9. Guimera, R., Sales-Pardo, M., Amaral, L. A. N., *Module identification in bipartite and directed networks*, Physical Review E, 76(036102), 1–8, 2007
10. Leskovec, J., Lang, K. J., Dasgupta, A., Mahoney, M. W., *community structure in large networks: Natural cluster sizes and the absence of large well-defined clusters*, arXiv:0810.1355, http://arxiv.org/abs/0810.1355, 2008
11. Lin, Y.-R., Chi, Y., Zhu, S., Sundaram, H., Tseng, B. L., *FacetNet: A Framework for Analyzing Communities and Their Evolutions in Dynamic Networks*, Proceedings of the 17th International World Wide Web Conference (WWW2008), pp. 685–694, 2008
12. Newman, M. E. J., *Modularity and community structure in networks*, Proceedings of the National Academy of Sciences (PNAS), 103(23), 8577–8582, 2006
13. Newman, M. E. J., *Network data*, http://www-personal.umich.edu/~mejn/netdata/
14. Newman, M.E.J., Girvan, M., *Finding and evaluating community structure in networks*, Physical Review E, 69(026113), 1–16, 2004
15. Palla, G., DerE'nyi, I., Farkas, I., Vicsek, T., *Uncovering the overlapping community structure of complex networks in nature and society*, Nature 435, 814–818, 2005
16. Vakali, A., Kompatsiaris, I., *Detecting, understanding and exploiting web communities*, http://www2009.org/tutorials.html, 2009
17. Wakita, K., *Ken Wakita – Community analysis software*, http://www.is.titech.ac.jp/~wakita/en/software/community-analysis-so-ftware/
18. Xu, J., Chen, H., *The topology of dark networks*, Communications of the ACM, 51(10), 58–65, 2008
19. Zhou, H., *Network landscape from a Brownian particlefs perspective*, Physical Review E 67(041908), 1–5, 2003

Chapter 13
Concept Discovery in Youtube.com Using Factorization Method

Janice Kwan-Wai Leung and Chun Hung Li

13.1 Introduction

In the Web 2.0 era, people can interact effectively in the Internet instead of just retrieve data. Social networks such as forums, blogs, video sharing sites are examples of applications. Social networks like Facebook [3], Bebo [1], Flickr [4] are blooming with user generated contents which can be in forms outside text such as images or videos.

Recent years online video sharing systems are burgeoning. In video sharing sites, users can upload and share videos with other users. YouTube [6] is one of the most successful and fast-growing systems. In YouTube, users can share their videos in various categories. Among these video categories, music is one of the most popular one and the number of music videos overly excess that of other categories [10, 22]. Users are not only allowed to upload videos but tag videos but leave comments on them as well. With more than 65,000 new videos being uploaded every day and 100 million video views daily, YouTube becomes a representative community among video sharing sites [7].

Due to the incredible growth of video sharing sites, video searching is no longer a easy task and more effort should be paid by users to search their desire videos from the entire video collection. To address this problem, grouping videos with similar contents together and indexing are necessary. As such, information about video content is needed for the objective mentioned above. However, it is an even challenging problem to find out accurate information about the uploaded videos. Currently, videos on YouTube are only coarsely grouped into some predefined high level categories (e.g., music, entertainment, sports, etc.) in which category of a video is just decided by a single user who put up the video. Under this policy of predefining categories, videos in a single category still span through a wide range of varieties. For example, in the music category, we may find music from various

J.K.-W. Leung (✉)
Department of Computer Science, Hong Kong Baptist University, Kowloon Tong,
Kowloon, Hong Kong
e-mail: janice@Comp.HKBU.Edu.HK

B. Furht (ed.), *Handbook of Social Network Technologies and Applications*,
DOI 10.1007/978-1-4419-7142-5_13, © Springer Science+Business Media, LLC 2010

countries or with different musical styles. Though some other video sharing sites, such as DailyMotion [2] and MySpace [5], have a lower level of category for music videos, the categorization just follow the basic music genre. However, people attentions to music are not limited to these simple genre. Furthermore, the predefined categories maybe too subjective to capture the real attracted issue of singers to the majority of users since they are only defined by a small group of people. Finally, the current categories on YouTube are fixed and it is hard to add/remove categories too often. As time goes by, some categories may become obsolete and some new topics may be missing from the categories.

These observations motivate us to explore a new way of video categorization for facilitating video search. In this work, we extend our previous proposed novel commentary-based clustering techniques by utilizing user comments for achieving this goal [18]. Unlike the traditional approaches of predefining some categories by human, our categorization is learnt from user comments. The advantage of our proposed approach is three-fold. First, our approach can capture public attentions more accurately and fairly than that of the predefined categories approach as we have taken the user opinions into consideration. In other words, the resulting categories are contributed by public users rather than a small group of people; Second, since user attentions can be changed from time to time, the categories of our method can be changed dynamically according to the recent comments by users; Finally, as users comments are in the form of natural language, users can describe their opinions in details with rich text. Therefore, by commentary-based clustering, we can obtain clusters which represent fine-grained level ideas of videos.

In the literature, various clustering techniques have been proposed for video categorization [17, 29]. However, this type of techniques did not take user opinion into consideration and thus the clustering results do not capture public interested issues.

Apart from predefined categories, YouTube also provides tagging to assist video searching service. Indexing videos with some words describing the videos should theoretically be helpful in the context of video understanding while users would not have any idea before viewing a video. Nevertheless, the tags are usually too loose and not structural which are hardly to give enough description of videos.

Some researchers have proposed to use the user tags on videos for clustering [16, 19]. Though user tags can somehow reflect user feelings on videos, tags are, in many cases, too brief to represent the complex ideas of users and thus the resulting clusters may only carry high-level concepts. Another stream of works which use commonly fetched objects of users for clustering [12] suffer similar shortcoming of neglecting object content. In [28], they proposed to adopt a multi-modal approach for video categorization. However, their work required lots of human efforts to first identified different categories from a large amount of videos.

We want to remark that although commentary-based clustering can theoretically obtain more fine-grained level clusters, it is much more technically challenging than that of tag-based clustering. The reason is that user comments are usually in the form of natural language and thus pre-processing is necessary for us to clean up the noisy data before using them for clustering.

The rest of the chapter is organized as follows. Section 13.2 discusses previous works in the context of social network mining. Section 13.3 explains our proposed approach for video categorization in video sharing sites. Section 13.4 briefly introduces our web crawler. Section 13.5 presents the details of pre-processing of the raw data grabbed by our crawler. Section 13.6 describes our video clustering algorithm. Section 13.7 presents and discusses our experimental results. Section 13.8 concludes the chapter.

13.2   Related Works

Since the late eighties, data mining has became a hot research field. Due to the advancing development of technologies, there is an increasing number of applications involving large amount of multimedia. For this reason, researches in the field of data mining are not limited to text mining but multimedia mining. Qsmar R. Zaine et al. [29] developed a multimedia data mining system prototype, MulitMediaMiner, for analyzing multimedia data. They proposed modules to classify and cluster images and videos based on the multimedia features, Internet domain of pares referencing the image of video, and HTML tags in the web pages. The multimedia features used include size of image or videos, width and height of frames, date on which the image or video was created, etc. Kotsiantis et al. [17] presented a work to discover relationships between multimedia objects based on the features of a multimedia document. In their work, features of videos such as color or grayscale histograms, pixel information, are used for mining the content of videos.

Motivated by the bloom of social networks, plenty of works have been done involving the study or analysis of online social networks. Different approaches are proposed to discover user interests and communities in social networks. Tag-based approach is one of the invented methods. In [19], Xin Li et al. developed a system to found common user interests, and clustered users and their saved URLs by different interest topics. They used the dataset from a URLs bookmarking and sharing site, del.icio.us. User interests discovery, and user and URLs clustering were done by using the tags users used to annotate the content of URLs. Another approach introduced to study user interests is user-centric which detects user interests based on the social connection among users. Schwartz et al. [23] discover people's interests and expertise by analyzing the social connections between people. A system, Vizster [15], was designed and developed to visualize online social networks. The job of clustering networks into communities was included in the system. For this task, Jeffrey and Danah identified group structures based on linkage. Except the use of sole tag-based or user-centric approaches, there are works done with a hybrid approach by combing the two methods. In [16], user interests in del.icio.us are modeled using the hybrid approach. Users are able to make friends with others to form social ties in the URLs sharing network. Julia Stoyanovich et al. examined user interests by utilizing both the social ties and tags users used to annotate content of URLs. Some researchers proposed the object-centric approach for social interests detection. In this approach, user interests are determined by the analysis of commonly fetched objects in social communities. Figuring out common interests is also a useful task in peer-to-peer networks since shareds interests facilitate the content locating of desire objects. Guo et al. [12] and Sripanidkulchai [25] presented in their works the algorithms of examining shared interests based on the common objects which users requested and fetched in peer-to-peer systems.

13.3 Public Attention Based Video Concept Discovery and Categorization for Video Searching

With the ceaseless growth of media content, it is increasingly a tense problem for video searching. It is usual that users hardly find their desire videos from the immense amount of videos. There are two main directions to ease the process of video searching, one is enhancing the text-based search engine whilst the other one is designing a better directory. In this chapter, we focus on the former approach.

Though many video sharing sites allowed tagging function for users to use tags to annotate videos during the upload process, it is very common for user to tag videos by some high level wordings. As such, tags are usually too brief for other users to locate the videos by using the text-based search engine. In our method, as user comments usually describe the videos in details, we can use them for video clustering to obtain fine-grained categories. By identifying the concept words for each categories, we can use them as latent tags for the corresponding categories in order to facilitate the video searching process.

In music domain, music videos in sharing systems are always categorized according to their types of musical sounds (e.g., pop, metal, country, etc.) under the music genre. However, except music styles, people may have many different attitudes and preferences (e.g., appearance of singers, event of performance, age of songs, etc) towards music in different regions. Therefore, to categorize music based on publicly interested issues, music genre is not a good categorical construct for video searching.

Our aim is to find a categorization where videos in each video group are representing a popular topic of interest and improve index with the in-depth concept of videos. In our algorithm, public attentions are modeled and video concepts are discovered by clustering videos into groups with the utilization of user-left comments.

Previously, computer scientists have tried many ways to find user interests. Tags are very popular to help in this context [19]. However, in a previous study of tagging in Youtube, it has been observed that many tags could not enhance the description of video as a result of system constraints [11].

Several disadvantages would be raised in this manner. Tags on a video are manually given by the one who uploads the video, thus the tags are just expressing a single user's feeling about the video. A study of content interactions in Youtube shows that tagging is unreliable as a result of self-promotion, anti-social behavior as well as other forms of content pollution [8]. Therefore, tags on a video would have a strong bias and are not fair enough to exactly describe what the video is actually about. On the contrary, comments can get rid of this problem as commentary authority is open to public and can be in large-scale. Since anyone can leave comments on videos, unlike tags, size of comment would be large enough to prevent being overwhelmed by malicious and meaningless rush comments. Furthermore, single-user given tags are definitely not representative of public feelings about the video. To address the sparsity and ambiguity of tagging, folksonomy search has been suggested [21] to improve existing tags in video. However, such systems still depends on a set of content category tag which is self found in youtube.com.

Moreover, videos are often tagged with a small number of words. As such, often fails to give enough description on the video. Though there is a previous work classifying videos from youtube.com by using the tags, the reported average number of tags per video is just 8–9 which is far fewer than the amount of comments per video [24]. Therefore, tags are insufficient to provide detailed information about videos. Another study of tagging across four major social media websites has shown that only 0.58% of tags in youtube.com belongs to the content category. Such percentage is the lowest among the four major social media websites of study [14]. In other words, only a very small amount of tag can identify the content category of the video in youtube.com. Since comments can be given by any users on any videos as feedbacks, they express different users thoughts about a video. Thus, contain more in-depth information about the videos. Also, by allowing every user to leave feedbacks, the number of comments on a video are usually much more than that of tags. Hence, utilizing comments instead of tags to find out the attracted issues can solve the above difficulties.

In a study of video search in youtube.com, it is found that search services are critical to social video websites but users often cannot contribute to the search service [13]. In our proposed work, such problem can be addressed by involving the user-left comments to enhance video searching.

Mentioned above, though tagging is popularly used as an assistant in video sharing sites, it is yet far from perfect for video searching. Our proposed work is aimed to supplement the tagging technique to achieve the goal of providing a better video searching service for users.

Beside tag-based, some researchers proposed the content-based approach to categorize videos [26]. Using video content as categorizing materials can group similar videos together according to their actual content. Nevertheless, video content itself only provide objective information about the videos but nothing about users' idea. Consequently, this approach fails to group videos according to public attentions. In contrast, user-left comments include users' view about the videos. Therefore, comments can, undoubtedly, be used to categorize videos based on public attentions.

Video features can also be used to achieve the goal of video clustering [17]. Video features, however, do not bare any subjective views by the public towards the videos. Also, using video features to cluster videos suffers the same shortcomings of content-based as well. Due to these reasons, comments, which contain both video content and users' views on videos, can provide more information for clustering videos.

13.4 Dataset Collection

YouTube is a video sharing platform on which users can upload their own videos for sharing purpose. Along with each video, a short description can be entered by the uploading user and tags as well. Apart from the video upload user, other registered users can also contribute to the video surrounding text by leaving comments on the video. In this chapter, we focused on the user comments of videos of Hong Kong singers in YouTube and did a comparison between comments and tags.

We first defined a set of 102 Hong Kong singer/group names. Given the set of singer/group names, we developed a crawler to firstly visit the YouTube web site and automatically search from the site the related videos based on video titles and video descriptions. From the resulting videos, the crawler saves the URL of each videos for further process. For the convenience of gathering user comments, the crawler transforms the fetched URLs to links which link to the pages of "all comments" mode of corresponding videos. With all the transformed video URLs, for each link, the crawler is able to scrape the video web page and grab the video title, all the user comments and the user names of who left comments on the video.

In the data set acquired by our crawler, 19,305 videos are grabbed with 102 singers and 7,271 users involved.

13.5 Data Pre-Processing

To ease the process of video searching by discovering the public attentions and categorizing videos, larger amount of data is required from video sharing sites. However, only with the large-scale collection of text-formatted raw data is not applicable for further processing. Large-sized dataset always need to undergo data pre-processing in the field of data mining. Here is no exception in our algorithm. After crawling YouTube, the mass data need to be pre-processed before performing video clustering.

Here are two steps of data pre-processing involved in our introduced algorithm,

1. Data Cleaning
2. Text Matrix Generation

13.5.1 Data Cleaning

As the comments left on YouTube videos are written in natural languages which consist lots of non-informative words, such as "thank," "you," etc, text processing with such materials must be caution. To avoid resulting a poor clustering, data cleaning is necessary for handling the noisy words.

In natural languages, there are many words that are not informative for clustering. These words would make the entire dataset very noisy. Applying a stoplist is one of the ways to clean up these words. Since some words are obviously not informative, it is easy to define a stoplist of noise. With a predefined stoplist, non-informative or distractive words can be strained from the dataset. After removing all the useless words by the stoplist, the dataset is then passed to the process of matrix generation.

13.5.2 Text Matrix Generation

Text-formatted data is not easy for further processing, it is more convenient to transform the data from text to matrix representation beforehand.

For example, the dataset can be represented by matrix A of size $n \times m$ where n is number of videos in the dataset and m equals to number of unique case-insensitive words in the dataset. In A, each row is a vector of video words and element $a_{i,j}$ is the frequency count of word j occurs in comments left on video i.

To transform the textual data into a more easy-computed text matrix, a dictionary is firstly built with the case-insensitive words in all the comments in the dataset. As comments are all in texts, linguistically, there exist many meaningless words in comments. These meaningless words, e.g., "is," "am," "the," "a," always occur in an extremely high frequency. Therefore, words occur in frequency exceeding a threshold should be discarded. On the other hand, words that seldom occur are probably not the important ones, so words with few occurrence should also be neglected. Therefore, we set an upper bound and a lower bound for word occurring frequency. All the words with frequency less than the lower bound or larger than the upper bound are filtered out. After filtering all the meaningless words, dictionary can then be built and matrix can be generated as well.

13.6 Video Processing via Clustering

In order to facilitate the video searching process, finding fine-grained video concepts and constructing a video category based on public attentions are crucial as there is no way to match a video with the desired ones without a deep understand of video content and people do searching with their interests in the usual practice.

As video comments left by users provide opinions about the video or singers in the video, some words in the comments are actually describing the fine-grained level concept of videos. Therefore we can find video concepts analyzing the video comments. With the concept words discovered from comments, video indexing can be improved by incorporating those concept words. Hence, facilitating video searching and make it be done in a more accurate manner.

With the reason that public attentions are reflected from the comments users left on videos, grouping similarly commented videos together is a possible way to provide a good video categorization. Since the objective of clustering is to distinguish substantial amount of data and group similar objects together, clustering is an adequate algorithm for constructing a video category that can guide user to his/her desire videos.

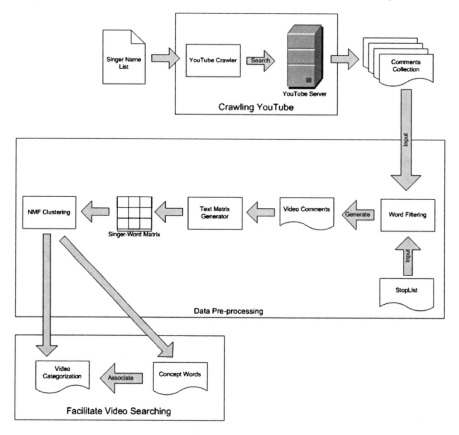

Fig. 13.1 Video concept discovery and video categorization of Hong Kong singer videos in YouTube

Figure 13.1 shows the procedures of finding video concepts, discovering public attentions to Hong Kong singers and categorizing Hong Kong singer videos from YouTube.

13.6.1 Video Clustering and Concept Discovery

For our purpose of building a good video category and learn the video concept for easier video searching, Non-negative matrix factorization (NMF) is the chosen clustering algorithm [27]. We propose to apply NMF for clustering based on three reasons. First of all, NMF is a bi-clustering method. With a bi-clustering algorithm, comment words and videos can be clustered simultaneously. Thus, the main characteristics of video groups can be drawn while grouping videos with similar user views together. Additionally, NMF does not provide an absolute assignment of videos to groups. Absolute assignment clustering algorithms are not suitable for singer video clustering. In practice, a video can belongs to multiple groups. For example, a classic music video can be performed by a singer who is passed away. The video is said to be in both "classic" group and "died singer" group. As NMF calculates possibility coefficients of each video to different groups, a single video can be assigned videos to multiple groups. Finally, NMF is effective for clustering. Since we need to cluster a large amount of data, effectiveness is one of the concerns. An effective low-dimensional linear factor model is desired.

Comments on a video often capture users feelings about the video or describe the video. Videos are clustered into the same group if they bear comments with similar contents. Similar videos, therefore, can be grouped together and with their characteristics be revealed as publicly attracted ones.

Let A be the $n \times m$ video-word matrix generated in the process of data pre-processing, where n and m are the number videos and number of words in dictionary respectively. As all the elements in A are the occurrence counts of words in documents, they are greater or equal to zero. This makes matrix A a non-negative matrix.

Since the importance of a term to a document can be reflected by it's number of appearance, the well-known keyword measure in Information Retrieval $tf - idf$ is adopted for extracting important words. Within the dataset, all the comments of a video is aggregated and considered as a document. Importance of term i in document j is $w_{i,j}$ which is computed by using $tf_{i,j}$ (term frequency of term i in document j) and idf_i (inverse document frequency of term i). Terms that are important to a document are expected to appear many times in the document. For this reason, the term frequency is used to measure the normalized frequency of a term in a document. Suppose there are t distinct terms in document j, $tf_{i,j}$ can be computed as,

$$tf_{i,j} = \frac{f_{i,j}}{\sqrt{\sum_{k=1}^{t} f_{k,j}^2}} \tag{13.1}$$

where $f_{i,j}$ is the number of times that term i appears in document j. As words appear in many documents are not useful for distinguishing documents, a measure idf is used to scale down the importance of these widely-used terms. The inverse document frequency of term i is defined as,

$$idf_i = log\frac{N}{n_i} \tag{13.2}$$

where N is the total number documents in the dataset, and n_i is number of documents that containing term i.

After computing the term frequency and inverse document frequency, the importance weight of a term i in document j is defined as the combination of $tf_{i,j}$ and idf_i,

$$w_{i,j} = tf_{i,j} \times idf_i \tag{13.3}$$

The greater the weighting, the more the importance is the term to the respecting document.

From matrix A, a non-negative matrix X can be produced by calculating the importance weights. Each element in X is defined as,

$$x_{j,i} = w_{i,j} = \frac{f_{i,j}}{\sqrt{\sum_{k=1}^{t} f_{k,j}^2}} \times log \frac{N}{n_i} \tag{13.4}$$

By fitting a k-factor model to matrix X, where k equals to number of groups to be obtained, X is decomposed into two non-negative matrices W and H, such that $X = WH + U$. After matrix decomposition, W is in size of $n \times k$ and H is in size of $k \times m$.

Our objective is to find W and H such that $X \approx WH$. By iteratively updating W and H, we can obtain W and H by minimizing the following function,

$$F(W, H) = ||X - WH||^2 \tag{13.5}$$

with respect to W and H and subject to constraints that $W, H \geq 0$.

Figure 13.2 shows the decomposition of video dataset matrix. From the resulting matrices, relationships between words, videos and clusters are revealed. Matrix W shows the relationships between videos and different clusters, whilst H clarifies the relationships between words and clusters. In W, value held in $w_{n,k}$ is the coefficient indicated how likely video n belongs to cluster k. To fit the purpose of our research, we have refined the method of group assigning in NMF. The original application of NMF algorithm assigns an object to a group in a maximum coefficient approach. However, in our method, video n is treated to be in group k if $w_{n,k}$ has the a value greater than a threshold β_k within vector n in W, where the value of threshold β_k is data dependent. The threshold should be chosen in a coefficient distribution depending manner. Videos can then be grouped into clusters based on their similarities. We define the set of clusters for video V_n that it belongs to as,

$$C_n = \{k \in K \mid \forall\, W_{n,k} > \beta_k\} \tag{13.6}$$

where K is set of all clusters.

Matrix H provides the information about the characteristics of the video groups. Concept words of a cluster can be found with H as $h_{k,m}$ is the coefficient of the term

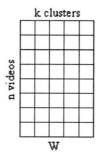
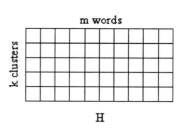

Fig. 13.2 NMF decomposition for video clustering

m belongs to cluster k. As the coefficient indicates how heavily a term associated with a cluster, the larger the coefficient, the more likely the term to be associated with the cluster. For each cluster, the top ten words, with respect to the term-cluster coefficient, are considered to be the concept words for the cluster, which the words states the properties of a group of videos and gives an in-depth description for the videos. Enhancing video index by incorporating the discovered concept words can consequently improve users video searching experience.

13.6.2   Factorized Component Entropy Measures for Vocabulary Construction

While matrix factorization methods and latent Dirichlet methods have often been successful applied to process news articles and technical papers, applications of such algorithms to short and terse statements in commentary pose significant difficulties. Misspellings and the very short length of the commentary are often the norms in comments in youtube.com. We propose the use of factorized component entropy as a measure to construct good vocabulary for analyzing noisy commentary.

Figure 13.3 shows size of the vocabulary as a function of the global minimum word frequency where we can see a sharp drop in the size of vocabulary when the global word frequency is increased.

The two matrices W and H generated from factorization have the effect of indicating the cluster membership. The cluster membership c_i of the ith concept is simply given by

$$c_i = \arg\max_j W_{ij},$$

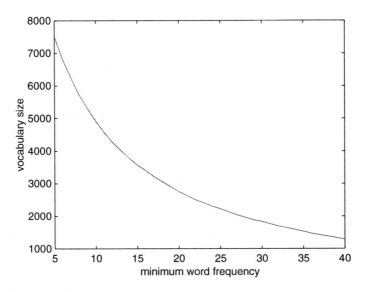

Fig. 13.3 Vocabulary size

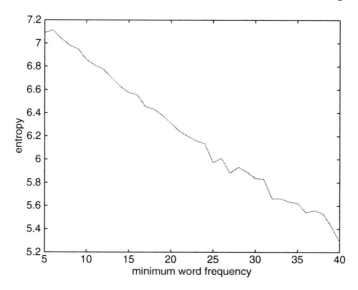

Fig. 13.4 Word-concept entropy

where j is the concept label. To evaluate how the words are distributed among the different concepts, we can compute the word-concept entropy of the jth concept using the following formula,

$$Ef_j = -\sum_i \left(H_{ij}/\sum_i H_{ij} \right) \log \left(H_{ij}/\sum_i H_{ij} \right). \qquad (13.7)$$

A small word-concept entropy implies that the words in the features have coefficients in H that is distributed across a smaller number of features and is thus more favorable. A large concept entropy implies that the words have coefficients evenly distributed across the different concepts and thus cannot be clearly differentiated.

Figure 13.4 shows the word-concept entropy as a function of the global word frequency. As the global word frequency increase, and the size of vocabulary decreases which leads to a reduction in word-concept entropy.

By taking the discrete derivative of the entropy, we can measure the change in entropy where the large drop in entropy represents the suitable size for vocabulary construction. Figure 13.5 shows the derivative of the word-concept entropy.

Similarly, we can also define the video-concept entropy which represents how well video commentary are grouped together using the following video-concept entropy formula,

$$Es_i = -\sum_j \left(W_{ij}/\sum_j W_{ij} \right) \log \left(W_{ij}/\sum_j W_{ij} \right), \qquad (13.8)$$

where Es_i is the video-concept entropy of the jth video commentary.

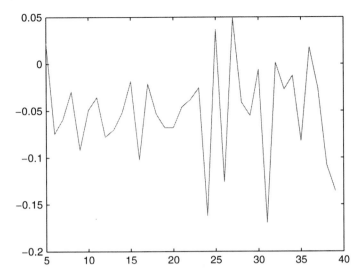

Fig. 13.5 Derivative of word-concept entropy

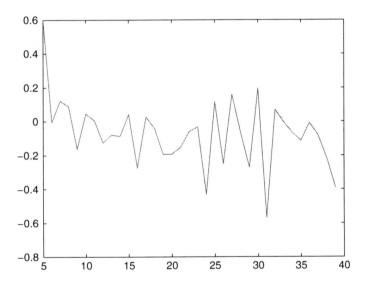

Fig. 13.6 Derivative of joint entropy

In the end, the joint entropy can be obtained by multiplying the video-concept entropy, word-concept entropy and the entropies similarly obtained by taking the transpose of W and H. The derivative of the joint entropy is shown in Fig. 13.6, where the noises are further suppressed.

13.7 Experimental Evaluation

A proof-of-concept experiment was done to with videos in Hong Kong regional music domain. An Intel(R) Core(TM)2 Quad 2.40GHz PC with 4GB RAM was used to conduct our experiment. Our web crawler was implemented in VC++ and the core algorithm was implemented in Matlab.

13.7.1 Empirical Setting

As the videos were grabbed by searching from the YouTube site with predefined list of singer names, there are possibilities that some videos are grabbed more than one time. For those videos preformed by more than one singer, as long as there are more than one singer names annotated in the video title, the video will be collected in times equals to the number of hits the predefined singer name hits the video title. To achieve a more accurate clustering result, duplicated videos are removed from the dataset.

In comments, users are used to mention the singer names when they are commenting on him/her. This will make the singer names dominate in every group of concept words. However, it is not conspicuous enough to reveal detailed concept of videos by singer names. Therefore, in our experiment, we add singer names to the stoplist as well.

Furthermore, some videos are less popular or just been uploaded for a short time that only have a few comments. These videos which have relatively few words are non-informative for video clustering. Videos with commentary words less than the threshold discovered in earlier section are removed.

The videos are clustered into k groups with the clustering algorithm discussed in Sect. 6. As number of cluster k is obviously an important parament that could influence the adequacy of video clustering, k should be chosen carefully. By averaging the entropies of all the clusters with different k which values in a specific range, we choose the k which resulting the smallest mean entropy. Because a small number of video groups would mix videos with various concepts together and a large number of video groups would break a conceptual-similar video group into many small pieces, so we set an appropriate range of 10–35 video groups for testing and picking a better k. From experiment, k is set to be 20.

Experiment was done twice with the above parameter setting, once with threshold β_i regarding cluster i to be mean coefficient of all videos,

$$\beta_i = meanCoef_i = \frac{\sum_{j=1}^{n} w_{j,i}}{n} \tag{13.9}$$

To compensate the poor performance caused by the extremely uneven distribution of coefficient, we chose the threshold to be mean coefficient plus standard deviation of all videos for the second experiment. β_i regarding cluster i is defined as,

$$\beta_i = meanSdCoef_i = \frac{\sum_{j=1}^{n} w_{j,i}}{n} + \sqrt{\frac{1}{n} \sum_{j=1}^{n} \left(w_{j,i} - \frac{\sum_{j=1}^{n} w_{j,i}}{n} \right)^2} \qquad (13.10)$$

where n is total number of videos being clustered.

13.7.2 Video Categories and Concepts

Since video clustering is a complete clustering analysis, publicly attracted music categories in Hong Kong can be found by clustering the videos. We deployed NMF as our clustering method. Applied the clustering algorithm to the video dataset in the way discussed in Sect. 6.1, with the experimentally chosen number of cluster of 20, videos were clustered into groups based on the words in their comments. The mean coefficient of videos to a cluster is set as the threshold. Videos with coefficient higher than the threshold of a cluster are said to be in that cluster. Under this strategy, videos can belong to several clusters as they may have multiple characteristics. Table 13.1 shows the discovered categories and concepts from our dataset.

Table 13.1 Latent video categories discovered in Hong Kong music video domain from YouTube

Group	Concept words
1	beautiful lyrics melody
2	female makeup dress
3	cute pretty handsome
4	sex photos scandal
5	funny hilarious laughing
6	rap raps hip
7	movie film story
8	cantonese mandarin language
9	commercial pepsi coke
10	piano piece ear grade
11	japanese japan korean
12	china olympic games
13	old classic memories
14	dance dancer moves
15	guitar band rock
16	award tvb gold
17	english chinese accent
18	sad legend died
19	together couple two
20	voice pretty talent

Unlike the generic music video categorization of some famous video sharing sites, such as DailyMotion divides music videos into eight classes (Pop, Rock, Rap, R&B, Jazz, Metal, Covers, and Electros), we categorized videos of local singers into twenty classes which are far more specific.

From our clustering result, we noticed that videos of singers are not only limited to general music videos, but also funny clips, award presentations, commercial advertisements as well as event promotion clips. Looking at the music videos alone, by clustering users' comments, we found that people's attitude towards Hong Kong music are not only target on the music styles. There are also other features of music which people are interested in, like languages, age of music, music instruments, type of singers, singer's voice, composition goodness, etc.

Furthermore, categorize singer videos with the proposed clustering algorithm, people can identify dance-oriented videos (Group 14), cross-culture produced music (Group 11) or even movie theme songs (Group 7) easily. Other than simply categorizing singer video clips, some up-to-date news in the local music circle, like scandals (Group 4), can also be found.

Tags are popularly investigated in the contest of topic detection. To compare the effect of concept finding by comment with tags, an experiment was conducted with the same setting but video meta data as the dataset. Video meta data are all the video surrounding tests including title, tags and description. Contrastingly, representative words of clusters extracted from video meta data cannot bring any idea of the video groups. Table 13.2 lists the top three representative words of each resulting video group derived from meta data. From the words listed in the table, nothing about the video concept of the groups can be told. With this table and Table 13.1, we can easily

Table 13.2 Cluster representative words extracted from video meta data

Group	Top three cluster representative words
1	sin story her
2	ltd invisible target
3	grain privilege shadow
4	characters editing exclusive
5	hkpca awards artist
6	andrew yun fung
7	family food sheh
8	actors chin stephen
9	quot buenos zero
10	south little repeat
11	finally earth day
12	bigboy2000 blogspot search
13	chi stephen derek
14	lollipop terry inch
15	label gold koon
16	takes goes bliss
17	xuite daily blog
18	bird carina kar
19	lap jennifer wealthy
20	mahjong tak spirit

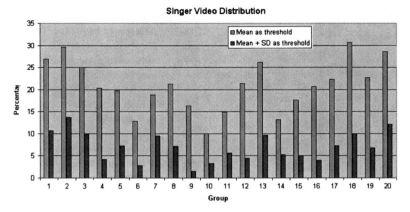

Fig. 13.7 Singer video distribution in YouTube

Table 13.3 Precision of objective clusters

		Precision	
Group	Concept words	Mean as threshold	Mean + SD as threshold
A	sex photos scandal	21.64%	81.58%
B	old classic memories	61.04%	78.16%
C	sad legend died	35.86%	60.34%
D	together couple two	64.44%	79.82%
Average		45.75%	74.96%

compare the effectiveness of comment and meta data for concept finding. The tables show that tags, titles or short descriptions are not sufficient for concept discovery of online videos.

Figure 13.7 illustrates the distribution of Hong Kong singer videos in YouTube according to the proposed algorithm using mean and mean + SD as thresholds. From the figure, we can see that the distribution of videos diverse over different threshold values. With the mean coefficient as the threshold, compared to the video groups resulted from the algorithm with mean + SD coefficient as threshold, larger groups of videos can be obtained. In the other words, algorithm associated with a smaller group assigning threshold would result heavier overlapped video groups.

The video clustering results are evaluated by human experts. To make the evaluation less controvertible, we only show the precisions of objective video groups in Table 13.3 where groups A, B, C, D are cluster 4, 13, 18, 19 respectively in our clustering. In the table, we noticed that assigning videos to groups with a smaller threshold may sometimes lower the precision. This will be caused in the groups which are very distinct to others. As a video group is too specific, the video-group coefficients to the group hold the extreme values. Also, closely related videos to the distinct group is always much fewer than videos which do not. Hence, videos are condense at the lower extreme side regarding the coefficients distribution. As a result, lowered the mean coefficient and caused the poor precision. On the other

Table 13.4 Clustering
and representative words
of videos by LDA

Group	Top three cluster representative words
1	able simply lots
2	old chinese lyrics
3	says nothing search
4	love her beautiful
5	isnt point pop
6	famous wanted body
7	sick sex stupid
8	crap language girls
9	cute pretty voice
10	movie story film
11	together funny type
12	voice pretty love
13	funny trying cute
14	shame fake admit
15	sad two during
16	love fantastic sad
17	voice talented rock
18	every may seriously
19	else word comment
20	top mind call

hand, we can see that the algorithm which assigns videos into groups with a larger threshold yields far better precisions. The average precision of the larger-threshold clustering groups in the table is 74.96% whilst that of the lower-threshold clustering is just 45.75%. The difference between the precisions resulted from clustering with the two different thresholds reflects the degree of extraordinary of the video group. The larger the difference, the more the special the group is. For example, in group 4, the two precisions differ from each other by a large percentage at about 60%, and from the concept words we can know that this group is about scandal of singers involving their sex photos. This is obviously an extremely distinct group.

Since Latent Dirichlet Allocation (LDA) is a popular clustering method for topic detection, we compared our proposed algorithm with LDA [9]. The top three representative words of video groups clustered by LDA are shown in Table 13.4. As shown in the table, the clustering results by LDA are not as good as our proposed algorithm in finding video concepts. It is experienced by many research experts that NMF outperforms LDA in clustering [20, 30].

13.7.3 User Comments vs. User Tags

As tags are believed to be an accurate description of an object and have been widely used for finding user interests and grouping objects, it is necessary to examine the virtues of user comments over tags before utilizing comments to capture public attentions and categorize videos to facilitate the video search in video sharing sites.

Table 13.5 Examples of concept words from user comments and user tags in four video clusters

Cluster I	Top 10 concept words in user comments	old classic memories drama childhood love 80s memory loved san
	Top 10 frequent user tags	chinese chan mv cheung wong love music mtv top anita
Cluster II	Top 10 concept words in user comments	sad legend two died missed heaven star superstar crying talented
	Top 10 frequent user tags	cheung chan leslie anita mui chinese mv danny hong wong
Cluster III	Top 10 concept words in user comments	guitar solo band rock cover drummer chords intro crap violin
	Top 10 frequent user tags	chinese beyond wong kong cheung ka kui hong nicholas paul
Cluster IV	Top 10 concept words in user comments	sex photos stupid fake victims private innocent scandal girls stop
	Top 10 frequent user tags	gillian chung sex photo edison chen gill cheung cecilia chan

One important observation from our experimental results is that user comments usually contains more in-depth information than that of user tags. Table 13.5 shows both the top ten concept words found from user comments and the top ten user tags of four clustered groups. From the concept words in the user comments, we can make a reasonable prediction that cluster I is about some music videos of some old songs. From the user tags, however, we can only find some singer names or some high-level descriptions (e.g., music, mv, mtv). Same as cluster II, from the concept words, this cluster is probably talking about some superstars who are already died. Nevertheless, the most frequent tags are only names of those dead superstars which do not reveal the low-level description of the group. Cluster III is the similar case as the above two clusters. Concept words from user comments state that this group is about the band sound and rock music but the tags only list out the name of a local popular band, "Beyond," and some of the band members. Tags of the other clusters suffer the similar problem as the above mentioned clusters. From the table, we can see that the user tags actually agree with our discovered concept words though the tags just exhibit the high-level sketch of the groups. In the other words, our algorithm gives an in-depth characterization of the videos with the concept words which the characterization cannot be exposed by the user tags, and in the mean time, the concept words achieve a strong agreement with the tags.

From this observation, we can conclude that if we want to obtain clustering results in a more fine-grained level, using commentary-based clustering technique is more suitable. For the purpose of facilitating video search, it is beyond doubt that result of fine-grained level clustering involving user points of attention is more desirable.

To give a more in-depth analysis of comments and tags, we have compared concept words against tags in different clusters. Table 13.6 records the portion of videos whose tags cover the concept words of different groups and there are two

Table 13.6 Percentage of videos with tags covering concept words across groups

		Covering concept words from group			
		A	B	C	D
Percentage of videos from group	A	34.04%	4.02%	0%	2.13%
	B	0%	15.79%	0%	0%
	C	0.84%	0.84%	7.58%	0.84%
	D	0%	10.17%	3.39%	5.26%

major observations from the table. First, we can see that there are at least 65% of videos whose tags cannot cover the concept words of the group they belongs to. This implies tag-based clustering cannot completely capture user opinions and video content. Second, we can see that the concept words of each group are mostly covered by tags of its own group. This once again verify the accuracy of our proposed method.

13.8 Conclusion and Future Work

In this chapter, we have proposed a novel commentary-based matrix factorization technique to cluster videos to facilitate searching and generate concept words to improve indexing. We propose the use of factorized component entropy as a measure to construct good vocabulary for analyzing sparse and noisy social media data. Experimental results showed that our commentary-based clustering yields better performance than that of tag-based approach which was proposed previously in the literature. On the other hand, we have successfully discovered some non-trivial categories among the videos of Hong Kong singers. Since our categorization is learnt from user feedbacks, it can provide an easy way for users to reach their desired videos via our list of categories.

In our future work, we plan to extend the commentary-based technique from video clustering to user and singer clustering. After we have obtained the three types of clusters, we can acquire the relationships among different videos, singers and users by analyzing the inter-cluster similarity. As such, social culture can be studied by combining and analyzing the discovered relationships. With the video-video, singer-singer, user-singer, and user-user relationships found by clustering, we can know the changes in music styles and singer styles over the ages, the trend of music, the ways people appreciate music, and even the special relationships of singers reflected by news, and more. Relationships observed by clustering are not only useful for social scientists to study social culture, but also beneficial for businesses, entertainment companies, fans clubs, social network systems and system users. With the help of examined user-user relationships, businesses can be profited from reducing advertising costs by advertise only to the potential customer groups. User-signer relationships define user-idol groups, entertainment companies can effectively promote to the target groups. Determining the user-singer relationships, in addition to profits for entertainment companies, fans groups can easily be managed.

Other than the advantages for some specific parties, general users are also benefited. Well-clustered groups of videos and singers equipped with a batch of concept words leads to a effort saving video searching for users. Also, social network systems are able to detect and refine incorrect tags with the concept words resulted from clustering. As a result, description of videos are more precise and thus improves the video searching function.

References

1. http://www.bebo.com
2. http://www.dailymotion.com
3. http://www.facebook.com
4. http://www.flickr.com
5. http://www.myspace.com
6. http://www.youtube.com
7. Usa today. youtube serves up 100 million videos a day online
8. F. Benevenuto, F. Duarte, T. Rodrigues, V. A. Almeida, J. M. Almeida, and K. W. Ross. Understanding video interactions in youtube. In *MM '08: Proceeding of the 16th ACM international conference on Multimedia*, pages 761–764, ACM, NY, 2008
9. D. M. Blei, A. Y. Ng, and M. I. Jordan. Latent dirichlet allocation. *J. Mach. Learn. Res.*, 3:993–1022, 2003
10. X. Cheng, C. Dale, and J. Liu. Understanding the characteristics of internet short video sharing: Youtube as a case study. *In CoRR abs*, Jul 2007
11. G. Geisler and S. Burns. Tagging video: conventions and strategies of the youtube community. In *JCDL '07: Proceedings of the 7th ACM/IEEE-CS joint conference on Digital libraries*, pages 480–480, ACM, NY, 2007
12. L. Guo, S. Jiang, L. Xiao, and X. Zhang. Fast and low-cost search schemes by exploiting localities in p2p networks. *J. Parallel Distrib. Comput.*, 65(6):729–742, 2005
13. M. J. Halvey and M. T. Keane. Exploring social dynamics in online media sharing. In *WWW '07: Proceedings of the 16th international conference on World Wide Web*, pages 1273–1274, ACM, NY, 2007
14. M. Heckner, T. Neubauer, and C. Wolff. Tree, funny, to read, google: what are tags supposed to achieve? a comparative analysis of user keywords for different digital resource types. In *SSM '08: Proceeding of the 2008 ACM workshop on Search in social media*, pages 3–10, ACM, NY, 2008
15. J. Heer and D. Boyd. Vizster: Visualizing online social networks. *IEEE Symposium on Information Visualization*, 2005
16. C. M. C. Y. Julia Stoyanovich, Sihem Amer-Yahia. Leveraging tagging to model user interests in del.icio.us. In *AAAI '08: Proceedings of the 2008 AAAI Social Information Spring Symposium*. AAAI, 2008
17. P. P. Kotsiantis S., Kanellopoulos D. Multimedia mining. In *WSEAS Trans. Syst.*, 3(10): 3263–3268, 2004
18. J. K.-W. Leung, C. H. Li, and T. K. Ip. Commentary-based video categorization and concept discovery. In Proceeding of the 2nd ACM Workshop on Social Web Search and Mining (Hong Kong, China, November 02 - 02, 2009), SWSM '09, pages 49–56, ACM, New York, NY, 2009
19. X. Li, L. Guo, and Y. E. Zhao. Tag-based social interest discovery. In *WWW '08: Proceeding of the 17th international conference on World Wide Web*, pages 675–684, ACM, NY, 2008
20. N. Oza, J. P. Castle, and J. Stutz. Classification of aeronautics system health and safety documents. *Trans. Sys. Man Cyber Part C*, 39(6):670–680, 2009

21. J. Z. Pan, S. Taylor, and E. Thomas. Reducing ambiguity in tagging systems with folksonomy search expansion. In *ESWC 2009 Heraklion: Proceedings of the 6th European Semantic Web Conference on The Semantic Web*, pages 669–683, Springer, Berlin, 2009
22. C. G. R. A. A. F. L. Rodrygo L. T. Santos, Bruno P. S. Rocha. Characterizing the youtube video-sharing community. 2007
23. M. F. Schwartz and D. C. M. Wood. Discovering shared interests using graph analysis. *Commun. ACM*, 36(8):78–89, 1993
24. A. S. Sharma and M. Elidrisi. Classification of multi-media content (video's on youtube) using tags and focal points. Unpublished manuscript
25. K. Sripanidkulchai, B. Maggs, and H. Zhang. Efficient content location using interest-based locality in peer-to-peer systems. In *INFOCOM 2003. Twenty-Second Annual Joint Conference of the IEEE Computer and Communications Societies. IEEE*, 3:2166–2176, 2003
26. S. Tsekeridou and I. Pitas. Content-based video parsing and indexing based on audio-visual interaction, 2001
27. W. Xu, X. Liu, and Y. Gong. Document clustering based on non-negative matrix factorization. In *SIGIR '03: Proceedings of the 26th annual international ACM SIGIR conference on Research and development in informaion retrieval*, pages 267–273, ACM, NY, 2003
28. L. Yang, J. Liu, X. Yang, and X.-S. Hua. Multi-modality web video categorization. In *MIR '07: Proceedings of the international workshop on Workshop on multimedia information retrieval*, pages 265–274, ACM, NY, 2007
29. O. R. Zaïane, J. Han, Z.-N. Li, S. H. Chee, and J. Y. Chiang. Multimediaminer: a system prototype for multimedia data mining. In *SIGMOD '98: Proceedings of the 1998 ACM SIGMOD international conference on Management of data*, pages 581–583, ACM, NY, 1998
30. L. Zunxiong, Z. Lihui, and Z. Heng. Appearance-based subspace projection techniques for face recognition. *Intelligent Interaction and Affective Computing, International Asia Symposium on*, pages 202–205, 2009

Chapter 14
Mining Regional Representative Photos from Consumer-Generated Geotagged Photos

Keiji Yanai and Qiu Bingyu

14.1 Introduction

The development of World Wide Web, and the popularization of digital photography, as well as the advent of public media-sharing websites such as Flickr and Picasa, have led to tremendous growth in large online multimedia resource. As a result, the problem of managing, browsing, querying and presenting such collections effectively and efficiently has become critical. However, these rich community-contributed collections are usually organized in an irregular way which makes it difficult to obtain relevant, accurate and complete results. For example, a search for the "noodle" images on the photo sharing site Flickr as well as many other similar sites returns results which contain many visually unrelated photos to the target category.

Community-contributed photo sharing sites collect metadata in addition to photos. While keywords and comments are common as metadata, recently some users attach "geotags" to their uploaded photos. A "geotag" means metadata which represents a location where the corresponding photo was taken, which is usually expressed by a set of a latitude and a longitude.

An accurate geotag can be obtained with a GPS device or a location-aware camera-phone. However, since it forces us to use relatively special devices, GPS-based geotags have not been common so far. Instead, map-based geotags have become common, after Flickr, which is the largest photo sharing site in the world, launched an online geotagging interface in 2006. Then, Flickr also became the largest "geotagged" photo database in the world. According to the Flickr official blog, the number of geotagged photo stored in Flickr exceeded 100,000,000 in February 2009, which corresponds to 3.3% of the total number of Flickr photos. These geotagged photos would be valuable not only for browsing and finding individual concepts, but also for helping us understand how specific objects or scenes are distributed and different over the world.

K. Yanai (✉)
Department of Computer Science, The University of Electro-Communications,
Chofugaoka 1–5–1, Chofu-shi, Tokyo 182–8585, Japan
e-mail: yanai@cs.uec.ac.jp

B. Furht (ed.), *Handbook of Social Network Technologies and Applications*,
DOI 10.1007/978-1-4419-7142-5_14, © Springer Science+Business Media, LLC 2010

Our objective is thus to facilitate a system which can automatically select relevant and representative photographs for the general object or scene categories corresponding to given keywords in the worldwide dimensions. In particular, we consider the geotagged photos on Flickr, identify the representative image groups, and generate an aggregate representation based on locations that allows navigation, exploration and understanding of the general concepts.

From a technical perspective, our approach for selecting the representative images is constituted of three main stages. First, we apply clustering techniques to partition the image set into similar groups, based on bag-of-visual-words feature vectors [1]. By evaluating the intra-cluster densities as well as the cluster member numbers, we discard most of the irrelevant images and obtain a reduced set of images which are visually similar each other. This stage could be regarded as the "Filtering Stage". Then, we geographically cluster the reduced set of images and select large geographic clusters as representative regions. Here we use the k-means clustering algorithm based on the photos' geographic latitude and longitude. Finally, for each representative region, we perform the Probabilistic Latent Semantic Analysis (PLSA) [2] to identify the distinct "topics," and do additional clustering on the entire topic vectors and select the "significant" cluster as the representative results for this geographic region. In addition, with the help of map service, a map-based UI is designed to support the browsing photos in context and understanding of the general object concepts.

The remaining part of this paper is organized as follows. Section 14.2 gives an overview of the related work. Section 14.3 describes our approach for region-based selection of the representative photos. Experimental results are reported and analyzed in Sect. 14.4. Finally, we present our conclusions and discuss the future work in Sect. 14.5.

14.2 Related Work

Until several years ago, researches on geotagged images focused on only location-based photo browsing for a personal geotagged photo collection [3, 4], since it is almost impossible to obtain a large number of geotagged images. The situation has been changed after Flickr launched an online geotagging interface in 2006. At the present, Flickr has become the largest geotagged photo database in the world. Geotagging with GPS devices is too expensive to spread, but Flickr online geotagging system allows users to indicate the place where photos are taken by clicking the online map. In addition, Flickr database is open to everyone via FlickrAPI which allows users' program to search Flickr photo databases for geotagged images.

Therefore, some works on geotagged image recognition with huge Flickr geotagged image database has been proposed recently. Cristani et al. [5] and Cao et al. [6] proposed methods on event recognition of geotagged images by integrating visual features and geographical information. In general, a geotag represents a pair of values on latitude and longitude. It is a just 2-dimensional vector. To convert a

2-d vector into more rich representation, [7] and [8] converted geotags into visual information from the sky using aerial images, and [9] transformed geotags to words using reverse geo-coding technique. On the other hand, [10] used GPS trace data which is a series of geotags instead of using just a pinpoint geotag in order to classify images into several pre-defined events. [11] used time and seasons for geotagged image recognition in addition to visual information and geo-location data. While event or scene recognition on geotagged images is common, "IM2GPS" project [12] proposed a unique idea of estimating a place from just one non-geotagged image with 6 million geotagged images gathered from Flickr.

As extension of location-based photo browsing, several recent researches have considered the problem of selecting representative or canonical photographs for online image collections. Jaffe et al. [13] select a summary set of photos from a large collection of geotagged photographs based on only tags and geotags. By analyzing the correlations between tags and geotags, a map-based visualization "Tag Map" is developed to help indicate the most important regions and the concepts represented in those regions. Our work similarly identifies the most important regions and select representative photos for these regions. A key difference is that in [13], the concepts are learn which could be mostly affected by users' photographic behavior. While in our work, we aim to select representative photographs for particular concepts by applying computer vision techniques. Simon et al. [14] have proposed a method to select canonical views for the landmarks by clustering images based on the visual similarity between two views. Like [14], Kennedy et al. [15] attempt to generate representative views for the world's landmarks based on the clustering and on the generated link structure. Unlike the works [14] and [15], we choose the general category objects or scenes as our target, but not the identical objects like landmarks which rely on 3D structure or viewpoint. Crandall et al. [16] extended the work by Kennedy et al. [15] to the worldwide dimension by using 35 million geotagged photos. In addition, Crandall et al. [16] introduced the meanshift clustering [17] to detect representative regions instead of k-means clustering, which allows users to give a scale of representative regions in a natural way instead of the number of regions.

The work by Raguram et al. [18] another similar work. They aim to select iconic images to summarize general visual categories, like "love," "beauty," "closeup" and "apple." Since general visual or abstract concepts usually have many semantic "themes," their canonical view selection is hence defined as select a small number of salient images for each semantic "theme." Our goal is different as we aim to select representative photos for geographic regions in the worldwide dimensions, and we concentrate on the general concrete concepts such as "noodle" and "waterfall" as well [19]. [20] also treated with generic concepts. However, we select canonical images on generic concepts regarding several regions in the worldwide dimension, while they treated with general concepts within only given regions.

14.3 Proposed Approach

In this section, we propose a novel method to select representative photographs for regions in the worldwide dimensions, which helps detect cultural differences over the world.

14.3.1 Overview

Our approach for selecting the representative images for representative local regions from geotagged images consists of three main stages as shown in Fig. 14.1: (1) removing irrelevant images to the given concept, (2) estimating representative geographic regions, and (3) selecting representative images for each region.

First, we apply clustering techniques to partition the image set into similar groups, based on bag-of-features (BoF) vectors [1]. By evaluating the intra-cluster densities as well as the cluster member numbers, we discard most of the irrelevant images and obtain a reduced set of images which are visually similar each other. This stage could be regarded as the "Filtering Stage." The method employed in this stage is based on the method proposed by Raguram et al. [18].

Then, we geographically cluster the reduced set of images and select large geographic clusters as representative regions. Here we use the k-means clustering algorithm based on the geographic latitude and longitude of photos to obtain representative regions in the world for the given concept.

Finally, for each representative region, we perform the Probabilistic Latent Semantic Analysis (PLSA) [2] to identify the distinct "topics," do additional clustering on the entire topic vectors, and select the "significant" cluster as the representative results for this geographic region. In addition, with the help of map service, a UI is designed to support the browsing photos in context and understanding of the general object concepts.

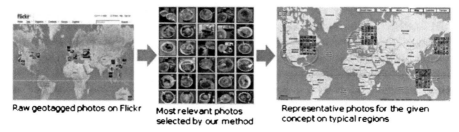

Raw geotagged photos on Flickr   Most relevant photos selected by our method   Representative photos for the given concept on typical regions

Fig. 14.1 After collecting geotagged photo related to the given concept by the tag-based search, we remove noise images, cluster regions and select regional representative images

14.3.2   Filtering Irrelevant Images

At most of the public photo sharing sites, the photos are organized by textual tags. Therefore, collecting photos using an input of query keywords normally returns many irrelevant or visually unrelated photos to the query concepts. Hence, in this stage we attempt to select most relevant photos to the concept from a large raw image set. As noted above, this stage can be regarded as "Filtering Stage" which based on clustering on bag-of-visual-words feature vectors and the intra-cluster similarity evaluation.

As follows, we describe bag-of-visual-words representation, visual clustering, and selecting the most relevant clusters by the evaluation of intra-cluster similarity in a detail way.

14.3.2.1   Image Representation

We adopt bag-of-visual-words model from [1] as the image representation. This model was first proposed for the text document analysis and recently applied in visual object recognition which has been found to be extremely powerful in tasks of representing the image features. The construction of bag-of-visual-words feature vectors for images involves several steps: (1) a set of points of interest are automatically detected in the image and local descriptors are computed over each point; (2) all the descriptors are quantized to form visual words; (3) for each image, we count the occurrences of each visual word to form a histogram of visual words which can be regarded as a bag-of-visual-words feature vector.

In our experiment, we first apply grid-based policy to detect the points of interest, and then compute the local descriptors by the Scale Invariant Feature Transform (SIFT) descriptor [21]. The SIFT descriptors are computed at 8 orientation directions over a 4×4 parts of spatial location, forming 128-dimensional vectors. Then we apply the k-means clustering algorithm over all extracted descriptors and computer the means to form visual words. Here we tried $k = 500$ and form a vocabulary of size 500. Finally, for each image, we assign all SIFT vectors to the nearest visual word and convert these vectors into one k-bin histogram which represents the bag-of-visual-words feature vector.

In our experiment, we still have used the color-based feature representation for the images as the comparison to the bag-of-visual-words representation. The performance of both methods is shown in the results part.

14.3.2.2   Visual Clustering

After building bag-of-visual-words representation for all raw images, we perform clustering using k-means algorithm over the bag-of-visual-words feature vectors to partition images into similar groups. In order to ensure a clear partition, we choose a high number of clusters k ($\approx$200 clusters for a dataset of about two thousand images). Since most irrelevant and visually unrelated photos tend to fall into the small clusters, we can discard such small clusters based on a minimum threshold (usually less than 10 cluster members in our experiment).

14.3.2.3 Selecting the Most Relevant Clusters

Since there may still exist some clusters with large noises (irrelevant images), in order to detect such irrelevant clusters and select the most relevant clusters, we employ the method of evaluating the intra-cluster similarity for the remaining clusters. The intra-cluster similarity is the average similarity between the images that belong to the cluster and the similarity between two images P_i and P_j can be calculated using the cosine metric between two image vectors V_i and V_j:

$$sim(P_i, P_j) = \frac{V_i \cdot V_j}{\sqrt{\mid V_i \mid \mid V_j \mid}} \tag{14.1}$$

The (1) indicates that, if the cosine angle between two image vectors equals to $0°$, the two images are very similar, whereas if the cosine angle between two image vectors equals to $90°$, the two images are very dissimilar.

Then given a cluster of n photos, $\mathbb{C} = \{P_1, \ldots, P_n\}$, we can define the intra-cluster similarity as:

$$SIM(\mathbb{C}) = \frac{\sum_{P_i, P_j \in \mathbb{C}, i \neq j} sim(P_i, P_j)}{{}_nC_2} \tag{14.2}$$

which denotes the average similarity between two photos within one cluster.

By computing the intra-cluster similarity value for each cluster and sorting all clusters in the descending order of the SIM values, we select several top ones as the most relevant clusters (We selected 40 clusters in our experiments).

14.3.3 Detecting Representative Regions

In this stage, given the remaining most relevant photos, we attempt to detect representative regions based on the photos' geographic locations. For simplicity, we perform k-means clustering algorithm, based on the photos' geographic latitude and longitude (with the help of geotags), using geographical distance as the distance metric. Then we select several largest geo-clusters to form the representative regions since they have more relevant photos and the number of photos taken in a region is an indication of the relative importance of that region for the particular concept. (In our experiment, for simplicity, we generally select about four or five representative regions for each concept.)

14.3.4 Generating Representative Photographs

At this point, we have obtained the most relevant or visually similar photos, and the corresponding representative regions. To generate a set of representative photos for these representative regions, we explore the Probabilistic Latent Semantic Analysis (PLSA) [2] model, which is recently applied to recognize object categories in an unsupervised manner.

As a generative model, PLSA was originally used to discover latent topics in the text documents represented by bag-of-words. In a similar consideration, since images can be regarded as "documents" and represented by bag-of-visual-words, hence PLSA can be applied to images for discovering the object categories in each image. In terms of images, suppose we have a set of images $D = (d_1, \ldots, d_n)$, each containing the visual words from the visual vocabulary $W = (w_1, \ldots, w_m)$. By introducing a mediator known as latent topics $Z = (z_1, \ldots, z_k)$, we can build a joint probability model over images and visual words, defined as:

$$P(w, d) = P(d) \sum_{z \in Z} P(w|z) P(z|d) \qquad (14.3)$$

where every image is modeled as a mixture of topics, $P(z|d)$, and $P(w|z)$ represents probability occurrence of visual words within a topic. We can learn the unobservable mixture parameters $P(z|d)$ and topic distributions $P(w|z)$ by the EM algorithm. Refer to [2] for a full explanation of the PLSA model.

As in our experiment, for each representative region, we apply the PLSA method to all the photos belonging to the region with a given number of topics, and get the probability distributions of all topics over each image, $P(Z|d)$, which can be regarded as topic vectors to represent an image. In the experiment, the number of topics was set to 20. After that, we aggregate photos according to the distributions of mixture topics by doing an additional step of clustering the topic vectors, $P(Z|d)$. In our experiments, we obtained the best results by applying k-means clustering with $k = 5$. Then the set of photos in the largest cluster are selected as representative photos of the given region, which is the final output of the proposed system.

14.4 Experimental Results

To test and verify if our approach works in practice, we conducted experiments with photos collected directed from Flickr. In order to ensure that the results would make a significant impact in practice, we concentrated on the most popular concepts including "noodle," "flower," "castle," "car," "waterfall," and "beach." The first four concepts are "object" concepts, while the rest are "scene" concepts. For each concept, we collected about 2000 most relevant geotagged photos distributed evenly in the world wide areas. As follows, we first provide numeric evaluation on our proposed method for extracting the most relevant photos. In the second part, we primarily demonstrate the representative set of photos selected for several representative regions.

14.4.1 Quantitative Evaluation

To evaluate our method for extracting the most relevant photos described in Sect. 14.3.1, we use the precision, which is defined as $N_R/(N_R + N_{IR})$, and the recall, which is defined as $N_{R_{sel}}/N_{R_{col}}$, where N_R, N_{IR}, $N_{R_{sel}}$, and $N_{R_{col}}$ are the number of relevant photos, the number of irrelevant photos, the number of relevant photos in selected photos, and the number of relevant photos in raw collected photos, respectively.

For comparison, we still have applied color-based method to this selection task. This method is based on the color-feature representation [22] for the images. First, we quantized the RGB color space into 64 (4 for each axis) bins, and made a color distribution histogram for each image. Based on the distance (histogram intersection) between images, we clustered all images into groups using k-means algorithm, and finally selected the largest clusters to form the most relevant image set. In addition, for more intuitively comparing, we kept the number of images selected by this method is almost equivalent to selecting by the proposed method.

In Table 14.1, we present the evaluation results which show the precision of raw photos directly collected from Flickr, the precision and recall of photos selected by color-based method and our proposed method. We obtain an average precision of 80% and an average recall of 74% by using our proposed method, which outperform the 59% and 54% by using color-based method. It also shows that our method can identify and select most of relevant photos effectively, though the raw dataset has many irrelevant ones. For a clear comparison on the precision, we also show the evaluation in Fig. 14.1.

Table 14.1 Evaluation results. This table describes the number of raw photos directly collected from Flickr (the numerical value in the parenthesis represents the precision), the number of photos selected by color-based method and our proposed method (two numerical values in the parenthesis represents the precision and the recall)

Concepts	Raw photos from Flickr	Selection by color-based method	Selection by proposed method
noodle	2,080 (42)	769 (60, 54)	752 (90, 80)
flower	2,225 (60)	703 (71, 37)	705 (85, 45)
castle	1,848 (35)	780 (52, 61)	761 (70, 81)
waterfall	1,901 (39)	689 (63, 59)	672 (78, 70)
beach	1,917 (38)	824 (51, 58)	813 (80, 90)
car	1,908 (43)	817 (56, 55)	800 (77, 75)
TOTAL/AVG.	11,879 (43)	4,582 (59, 54)	4,503 (80, 74)

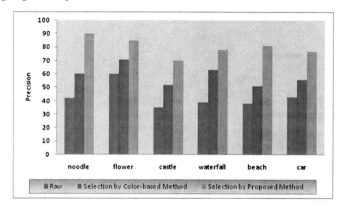

Fig. 14.2 Precision of raw photos directly collected from Flickr, photos selected by color-based method and our proposed method

14.4.2 Examples of Regional Representative Photos

In this subsection, we show the representative photos selected for several representative regions, while these regions were generated automatically based on geographic locations of the most relevant photos selected in the Sect. 14.4.1.

Figs. 14.3–14.7 show the results for the concept "noodle," each presents the most representative photos generated for the approximate regions: Japan, South East Asia, Europe as well as Mideast US, respectively. Without doubt, these results can help us understand about the "noodle" in these local areas. For example, Fig. 14.3 demonstrates many "ramen" photos in Japan, Fig. 14.4 demonstrates "spaghetti" photos in the European area, and Fig. 14.5 shows many noodles in the South East Asia area containing some Taiwanese style noodles and spicy Thai noodles, while others presents all kinds of peculiar "noodle" photos in other local areas.

We show the results for the concept "flower" in Figs. 14.8–14.12. The results demonstrate many species of flowers from five main approximate areas in the world: South East Asia, Europe, Central and South America, and South America. By combining the concept "flower" with geographic location, our system can not only help visualize varied and colorful appearance of the flowers, but also explore representative flowers for a concrete location, like Netherlands national flower "Tulip" (Fig. 14.9), North Carolina State flower "American Dogwood," Kansas State flower "Sunflower" (Fig. 14.11), and so on. With a larger set of "flower" photos, it is convinced that more representative regional flowers can be discovered.

While for the scene concept "waterfall," we extracted the representative photos for four large regions: Asia, Europe, North America, and South America. Figure 14.13 for the region of Asia and Fig. 14.14 for the region of South America. From the results, it is clear to find that waterfalls in South America seem to be more powerful, while waterfalls in the Asian area are somehow more beautiful. Such kinds of implications would be of importance in guiding travels around the world.

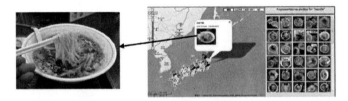

Fig. 14.3 Representative "noodle" photos for the region of Japan. Chinese-style noodle "ramen" is popular

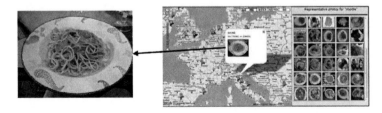

Fig. 14.4 Representative "noodle" photos for the region of Europe. Most of the photos are "Spaghetti"

Fig. 14.5 Representative "noodle" photos for the region of South East Asia

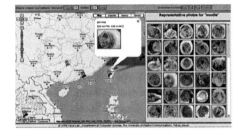

Fig. 14.6 Representative "noodle" photos for the region of Mideast US

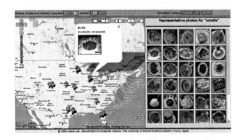

Fig. 14.7 Representative "noodle" photos generated for the region of Western US

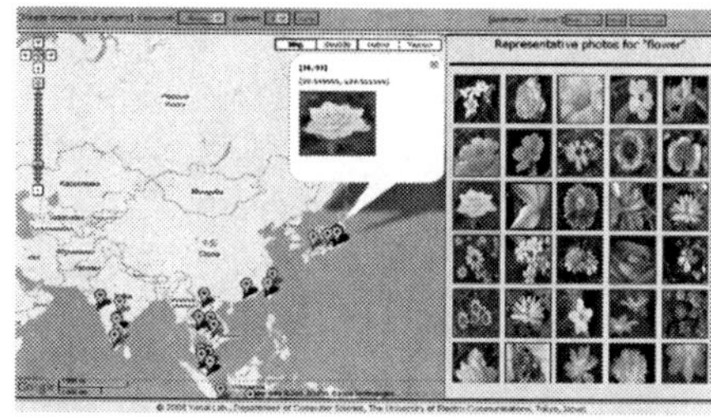

Fig. 14.8 Representative
"flower" photos for the region
of South East Asia

Fig. 14.9 Representative
"flower" photos for the region
of Europe

Fig. 14.10 Representative
"flower" photos generated for
the region of Oceania

Fig. 14.11 Representative
"flower" photos for the region
of Central and South America

Fig. 14.12 Representative
"flower" photos for the region
of South America

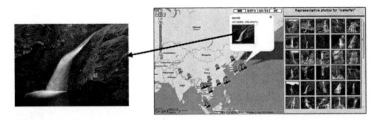

Fig. 14.13 Representative "waterfall" photos for the region of Asia. They are somewhat beautiful

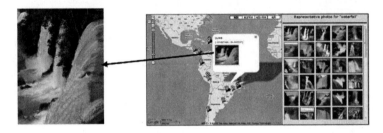

Fig. 14.14 Representative "waterfall" photos for the region of South America. They are more powerful

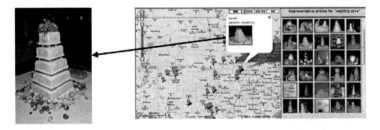

Fig. 14.15 "Wedding cake" in Mid US. Tall cakes are common. This is five-layered

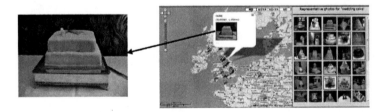

Fig. 14.16 "Wedding cake" in Europe. They are much shorter and simpler than US

Figs. 14.15 and 14.16 correspond to "wedding cake" in Europe and in Mid US, respectively. We can find many of the wedding cakes in Mid US are much taller than ones in Europe. To see more results for other concepts, please visit the following Web page: http://img.cs.uec.ac.jp/yanai/ASRP/

14.5 Conclusion and Future Work

In this paper, we proposed a novel method to select representative photographs for typical regions in the worldwide dimensions, which helps detect cultural differences over the world regarding given concepts.

For future work, we plan to propose a method to discover cultural differences for many concepts from a geotagged image database automatically, and think out some other strategies in detecting more representative regions with a more precise scope. In addition, we will conduct some evaluations on the representativeness of the photos selected for the corresponding region.

References

1. G. Csurka, C. Bray, C. Dance, and L. Fan. Visual categorization with bags of keypoints. In *Proc. of ECCV Workshop on Statistical Learning in Computer Vision*, pages 59–74, 2004
2. T. Hofmann. Unsupervised learning by probabilistic latent semantic analysis. *Machine Learning*, 43:177–196, 2001
3. K. Toyama, R. Logan, A. Roseway, and P. Anandan. Multiple instance learning for sparse positive bags. In *Proc. of ACM International Conference Multimedia*, pages 156–166, 2003
4. M. Naaman, Y.J. Song, A. Paepcke, and H. Garcia-Molina. Automatic organization for digital photographs with geographic coordinates. In *Proc. of ACM International Conference Multimedia*, pages 53–62, 2004
5. M. Cristani, A. Perina, U. Castellani, and V. Murino. Geo-located image analysis using latent representations. In *Proc. of IEEE Computer Vision and Pattern Recognition*, 2008
6. L. Cao, J. Luo, H. Kautz, and T. Huang. Annotating collections of geotagged photos using hierarchical event and scene models. In *Proc. of IEEE Computer Vision and Pattern Recognition*, 2008
7. J. Luo, J. Yu, D. Joshi, and W. Hao. Event recognition: Viewing the world with a third eye. In *Proc. of ACM International Conference Multimedia*, 2008
8. K. Yaegashi and K. Yanai. Can geotags help image recognition? In *Proc. of Pacific-Rim Symposium on Image and Video Technology*, 2009
9. D. Joshi and J. Luo. Inferring generic activities and events from image content and bags of geo-tags. In *Proc. of ACM International Conference on Image and Video Retrieval*, 2008
10. J. Yuan, J. Luo, H. Kautz, and Y. Wu. Mining GPS traces and visual words for event classification. In *Proc. of ACM SIGMM International Workshop on Multimedia Information Retrieval*, 2008
11. J. Yu and J. Luo. Leveraging probabilistic season and location context models for scene understanding. In *Proc. of ACM International Conference on Image and Video Retrieval*, pages 169–178, 2008
12. J. Hays and A. A. Efros. IM2GPS: Estimating geographic information from a single image. In *Proc. of IEEE Computer Vision and Pattern Recognition*, 2008
13. A. Jaffe, M. Naaman, T. Tassa, and M. Davis. Generating summaries and visualization for large collections of geo-referenced photographs. In *Proc. of ACM SIGMM International Workshop on Multimedia Information Retrieval*, 2006
14. I. Simon, N. Snavely, and S.M. Seitz. Scene summarization for online image collections. In *Proc. of IEEE International Conference on Computer Vision*, 2007
15. L. Kennedy and M. Naaman. Generating diverse and representative image search results for landmarks. In *Proc. of the International World Wide Web Conference*, pages 297–306, 2008
16. D. Crandall, L. Backstrom, D. Huttenlocher, and J. Kleinberg. Mapping the world's photos. In *Proc. of the International World Wide Web Conference*, 2009

17. D. Comaniciu and P. Meer. Mean shift: A robust approach toward feature space analysis. *IEEE Transactions on Pattern Analysis and Machine Intelligence*, 25(5):603–619, 2002
18. R. Raguram and S. Lazebnik. Computing iconic summaries of general visual concepts. In *Proc. of IEEE CVPR Workshop on Internet Vision*, 2008
19. B. Qiu and K. Yanai. Objects over the world. In *Proc. of Pacific-Rim Conference on Multimedia*, 2008
20. T. Quack, B. Leibe, and L.V. Gool. World-scale mining of objects and events from community photo collections. In *Proc. of ACM International Conference on Image and Video Retrieval*, pages 47–56, 2008
21. D.G. Lowe. Distinctive image features from scale-invariant keypoints. *International Journal of Computer Vision*, 60(2):91–110, 2004
22. M.J. Swain and D. H. Ballard. Color indexing. *International Journal of Computer Vision*, 7(1):11–32, 1991

Chapter 15
Collaborative Filtering Based on Choosing a Different Number of Neighbors for Each User

Antonio Hernando, Jesús Bobadilla, and Francisco Serradilla

15.1 Introduction

We present here a new technique for making predictions on recommender systems based on collaborative filtering. The underlying idea is based on selecting a different number of neighbors for each user, instead of, as it is usually made, selecting always a constant number k of neighbors. In this way, we have improved significantly the accuracy of the recommender systems.

Recommender Systems are programs able to make recommendations to users about a set of articles or services they might be interested in. Such programs have become very popular due to the fast increase of Web 2.0 [11, 12, 15] and the explosion of available information on the Internet. Although Recommender Systems cover a wide variety of possible applications [3, 4, 16, 19, 21], Movie recommendation websites are probably the best-known example for common users and therefore they have been subject to significant research [2, 14].

Recommender Systems are based on a filtering technique trying to reduce the amount of information available to the user. So far, collaborative filtering is the most commonly used and studied technology [1, 5, 9] and thus judgment on the quality of a recommender system depends significantly on its Collaborative Filtering procedures [9]. The different methods on which Collaborative Filtering is based are typically classified as follows:

- Memory-based methods [13, 18, 20] use similarity metrics and act directly on the matrix that contains the ratings of all users who have expressed their preferences on the collaborative service; these metrics mathematically express a distance between two users on behalf of their respective ratings.
- Model-based methods [1] use the matrix with the users' ratings to create a model on which the sets of similar users will be established. Among the most widely used models of this kind we have: Bayesian classifiers [6], neural networks [10] and fuzzy systems [22].

A. Hernando (✉)
Depto. de Sistemas Inteligentes Aplicados, Universidad Politécnica de Madrid, Spain
e-mail: ahernando@eui.upm.es

B. Furht (ed.), *Handbook of Social Network Technologies and Applications*,
DOI 10.1007/978-1-4419-7142-5_15, © Springer Science+Business Media, LLC 2010

317

Generally speaking, commercial Recommender Systems use memory-based methods [8], whilst model-based methods are usually associated with research Recommender Systems. Regardless of the approach used in the Collaborative Filtering stage, the technical purpose generally pursued is to minimize the prediction errors, by making the accuracy [7,8,17] of the Recommender Systems as high as possible. This accuracy is usually measured by the mean absolute error (MAE) [1,9].

In this paper, we will focus, among the Memory-based methods, those which rely on the user-based nearest neighborhood algorithm [1,5]: The K most similar users to one given (active) user are selected on behalf of the coincidence ratio between their votes as registered within the database. In this paper, a variant of this algorithm is presented. This is based on choosing, for each different user, not a constant, but a variable number of neighbors. As we will see, our algorithm improves significantly the accuracy as compared to the typical user-based nearest neighborhood algorithm with a constant number of neighbor users.

In Sects. 15.2 and 15.3, we formalize some concepts on recommender systems and the memory-based methods of collaborative filtering. In Sects. 15.4 and 15.5, we present new techniques based on the idea of choosing a variable number of neighbors for each user. In Sect. 15.6, we discuss how our algorithm improves significantly the K-nearest neighborhood algorithm. Finally, in Sect. 15.7, we set our conclusions.

15.2 Recommender Systems

We will consider a recommender system based on a database consisting of a set of m users, $U = \{1, \ldots, m\}$, and a set of n items, $I = \{1, \ldots, n\}$ (in the case of a movie recommender system, U would stand for the database users registered in the system and I would refer to the different movies in the database).

Users rate those items they know with a discrete range of possible values $\{min, \ldots, max\}$, associating higher values to their favorite items. Typically, this range of values is $\{1, \ldots, 5\}$ or $\{1, \ldots, 10\}$.

Given a user $x \in U$ and a item $i \in I$, the expression $v(x, i)$, will represent the value with which the user x has rated the item i. Obviously, users may have not rated every item in I. We will use the symbol $\bullet$ to represent that a user has not made any rating concerning an item i. In this way, the possible values in the expression $v(x, i)$ is the set $V = \{min, \ldots, max\} \cup \{\bullet\}$.

In order to offer reliable suggestions, recommender systems try to make accurate predictions about how a user x would rate an item, i, which has not been rated yet by the user x (that is to say, that $v(x, i) = \bullet$). Given a user $x \in U$ and an item $i \in I$, we will use the expression $v^*(x, i)$, to denote the system's estimation of the value with which the user x is expected to rate the item i.

Different methods have been used so far in order to achieve good estimations on the users' preferences. The quality of these techniques is typically checked in an empirical way, by measuring two features of the recommender system:

- The error made in the predictions
- The amount of predictions that the system can make.

Regarding error made in the estimation, different measures have been proposed. The most used one is probably the MAE [9] (see Definition 15.1) which conveys the mean of the absolute difference between the real values rated by the users, $v(x, i)$, and the estimated values $v^*(x, i)$. As may be seen in Definition 15.1, in the hypothetical case that the recommender system cannot provide any estimation, then we would consider that $MAE = 0$.

Definition 15.1 (MAE). Let $J = \{(x, i) | x \in U \ i \in I \ v(x, i) \neq \bullet \ v^*(x, i) \neq \bullet\}$

$$MAE = \begin{cases} \frac{1}{|J|} \sum_{(x,i) \in J} |v(x, i) - v^*(x, i)| & \text{if } J \neq \emptyset \\ 0 & \text{otherwise} \end{cases}$$

In order to quantify the amount of predictions that the recommender system can make, it is often used the coverage of a recommender system (see Definition 15.2), being defined as the percentage of predictions actually made by the system over the total amount of every possible prediction within the system. In the hypothetical case that all of the users had rated every item in the database, we would consider that the coverage is 1.

Definition 15.2 (Coverage). Let $A = \{(x, i) | x \in U, i \in I, v(x, i) = \bullet\}$
Let $B = \{(x, i) | x \in U, i \in I, v(x, i) = \bullet, v^*(x, i) \neq \bullet\}$

$$coverage = \begin{cases} \frac{|B|}{|A|} & \text{if } |A| \neq \emptyset \\ 1 & \text{otherwise} \end{cases}$$

15.3 Memory-Based Methods of Collaborative Filtering

In this section, we will focus on how recommender systems perform a prediction about the value with which the user $x \in U$ would rate the item $i \in I$, $v^*(x, i)$. These methods are based on the following idea: if we find a user $y \in U$ who has rated very similarly to $x \in U$, then, we can conclude that the user x's tastes are akin to those of the user y. Consequently, given an item $i \in I$ which the user x has not rated yet while the user y already has, we could infer that the user x would probably rate the item i with a similar value to the one given by the user y.

Thus, methods of this kind search, for each user, $x \in U$, a subset of k users, $y_1 \in U, ..., y_k \in U$ (called 'neighbors') who have rated very similarly to the user x. In order to predict the value with which the user x would rate an item $i \in I$, the recommender system examines first the values with which the neighbors $y_1, ..., y_k$ have rated the item i, and then, uses these values to make the prediction $v^*(x, i)$. Consequently, two main issues must be considered in order to make predictions:

- Evaluating how similar two users are in order to select, for each user x, a set of users, $y_1, ..., y_k$ (called 'neighbors') with similar tastes to the user x.
- Given a user x, and an item i, estimating the value with which the user x would rate the item i, $v^*(x, i)$, by considering the values with which the neighbors of x have rated this item i, $v(y_1, i),...,v(y_k, i)$.

As far as the first issue is concerned, there are several possible measures for quantifying how similar the ratings between two different users are [18]. The similarity measure between two users $x, y \in U$ is defined on those items who have been rated by both x and y. That is to say, we define the set $C(x, y)$, of the common items between $x, y \in U$ as follows:

Definition 15.3 (Common Items). Given $x, y \in U$, we define $C(x, y)$ as the following subset of I:

$$C(x, y) = \{i \in I \,|\, v(x, i) \neq \bullet, \, v(y, i) \neq \bullet\}$$

The Mean Square Difference, MSD, may be regarded as the simplest similarity measure:

$$MSD(x, y) = \frac{1}{|C(x, y)|} \sum_{i \in C(x,y)} (v(x, i) - v(y, i))^2$$

As may be seen, MSD is based on a known metric distance[1] and $MSD(x, y) \geq 0$. When $MSD(x, y) = 0$, then we have that x and y have assigned exactly the same values to those items which both users have rated. Besides, the lower $MSD(x, y)$ is, the more similar the users x and y are.

The cosine between two vectors, cos, or the correlation coefficient, $\rho(x, y)$, are the similarity measures most used:

- The cosine similarity:

$$\cos(x, y) = \frac{\sum_{i \in C(x,y)} v(x, i) v(y, i)}{\sqrt{\sum_{i \in C(x,y)} v(x, i)^2} \cdot \sqrt{\sum_{i \in C(x,y)} v(y, i)^2}}$$

- The correlation coefficient or Pearson similarity:

$$\rho(x, y) = \frac{\sum_{i \in C(x,y)} (v(x, i) - \bar{x})(v(y, i) - \bar{y})}{\sqrt{\sum_{i \in C(x,y)} (v(x, i) - \bar{x})^2} \cdot \sqrt{\sum_{i \in C(x,y)} (v(y, i) - \bar{y})^2}}$$

where $\bar{x} = \frac{1}{|C(x,y)|} \sum_{i \in C(x,y)} v(x, i)$ and $\bar{y} = \frac{1}{|C(x,y)|} \sum_{i \in C(x,y)} v(y, i)$

[1] Indeed, $\sqrt{MSD}$ fulfills the definition of distance given in metric spaces when $\forall x \in U \; \forall i \in I \; v(x, i) \neq \bullet$.

Unlike $MSD(x, y)$, the measures $\cos(x, y)$ and $\rho(x, y)$ do not fulfill the conditions related to distance in metric spaces.[2] Indeed, both measures lie within the range $[-1, 1]$ and, when the higher $\cos(x, y)$ or $\rho(x, y)$ are, the more similar the users x and y are.

Once a similarity measure has been chosen, the recommender system selects, for each user x, a subset of the k users most similar to it, $N(x) = \{y_1, ..., y_k\}$, and then, these are used to predict how the user x will rate an item i: $v^*(x, i)$.

As for this late issue, the simplest way to determine $v^*(x, i)$ consists of calculating the mean of the values rated by the k users $N(x) = \{y_1, ..., y_k\}$. That is to say:

$$v^*(x, i) = \frac{1}{|B(x, i)|} \sum_{y \in B(x, i)} v(y, i) \qquad (15.1)$$

where $B(x, i) = \{y \in N(x) | v(y, i) \neq \bullet\}$

The estimation $v^*(x, i)$ can be improved significantly by weighting more the values from the users who are more similar to x over those given by the users who are not so similar. If we consider a measure, sim, like ρ or $\cos$, we could perform this easily in the following way:

$$v^*(x, i) = \frac{\sum_{y \in N(x)\ v(y,i) \neq \bullet} sim(x, y) \cdot v(y, i)}{\sum_{y \in N(x)\ v(y,i) \neq \bullet} sim(x, y)} \qquad (15.2)$$

As may be seen, the Expression 15.2 works perfectly when using similarity measures like ρ or $\cos$, since they give the higher values to those users who are more similar to a given one. However, the Expression 15.2 does not work when dealing with a function like MSD, since it gives lower values to those items who are more similar (indeed, when two users, x, y have rated exactly with the same values, the value $MSD(x, y) = 0$). Consequently, when using MSD, the estimation is calculated using the Expression 15.1.

Once we have selected the similarity measure and the estimation expression, the recommender system based on collaborative filtering has been just designed. Both the evaluation of the recommender system in relation to MAE (see Definition 15.1) and the *coverage* (see Definition 15.2) depend strongly on the constant k, the number of neighbors for each user. Indeed, the optimal value associated to this constant depends on the recommender system and is often hard to find out.

15.4 Choosing Variable Number of Neighbors for Each User

As we have described in the previous section, typical recommender systems based on collaborative filtering select, for each user x, the set of the k most similar users (neighbors), and then use these neighbors to make predictions about how the user x will rate the different items.

---

[2] In metric spaces, the distance $d(x, y)$ must fulfill that $d(x, x) = 0$. However, as may be seen, $\rho(x, x) = \cos(x, x) = 1$.

In this section, we discuss a new technique to select the neighbors and calculate the estimations. This is based on choosing a variable number of neighbors (instead of choosing always k neighbors) for each user. This idea is inspired by the fact that, as it usually happens, a certain user x may have much more than k highly similar neighbors, while another one, y, may have much less than k. When this happens, in order to make predictions on x, we are in fact discarding a certain number of users which are highly similar to x, and in the same way, while making predictions on y, we would be including some users which are not similar enough to y, but are merely necessary to complete the fixed number of k neighbors.

In order to avoid this drawback, with our technique, a variable amount of neighbors is associated to each user in the following way. First we need to define a function, $d : U \times U \longrightarrow \mathbb{R}^+$, where $d(x, y)$ measures the inadequacy of user y's rates in order to predict the ratings of x. A user y will be considered as a neighbor of x when $d(x, y)$ lies under a constant value α (see Definition 15.6). This function d, like ρ and cos, is based on linear regression.

Next it must be dealt with obtaining this function d. We will consider that a user $y \in U$ is completely suitable to predict the ratings of user $x \in U$, if there is a value $b(x, y)$ such that for every item common to both users x and y, (that is to say, $\forall i \in C(x, y)$) the following holds:

$$v(x, i) = b(x, y) \cdot v(y, i) \tag{15.3}$$

In case the user $y \in U$ is not completely suitable to predict the user $x \in U$, there will be an error in the previous expression, and this expression will turn to be:

$$v(x, i) = b(x, y) \cdot v(y, i) + e(x, y, i) \tag{15.4}$$

Given $b(x, y)$, we evaluate the general error in the statement as follows:

$$\frac{1}{|C(x, y)|} \sum_{i \in C(x,y)} e(x, y, i)^2 \tag{15.5}$$

In order to define the unsuitability degree, d, of a user y to predict the user x, we will consider the value $b(x, y) \in \mathbb{R}$ such that the Expression 15.5 is minimum. As is commonplace in mathematics (using linear regression), this happens when $b(x, y)$ takes the value described in Definition 15.4.

Definition 15.4. We define $b : U \times U \longrightarrow \mathbb{R}$ as follows:

$$b(x, y) = \begin{cases} \dfrac{\sum_{i \in C(x,y)} v(x, i) \cdot v(y, i)}{\sum_{i \in C(x,y)} v(y, i)^2} & \text{if } C(x, y) \neq \emptyset \\ \infty & \text{otherwise} \end{cases}$$

Factor $b(x, y)$ is used in order to consider the case that two users employ different scales when rating items, even though they have similar tastes. That is to say, we will consider that users x and y have a similar taste when $\forall i \in C(x, y) v(x, i)$ tends to be very close to $b(x, y) \cdot y(i)$ (where $b(x, y)$ is a constant associated to both users x and y).

The function $d(x, y)$ is the minimum possible value in Expression 15.5 above.

$$d(x, y) = \min \frac{1}{|C(x, y)|} \sum_{i \in C(x,y)} e(x, y, i)^2 \tag{15.6}$$

It is not too hard to prove that this expression is completely equivalent to the one given in Definition 15.5. In this expression we have considered that d is infinite when there are no items common to both users x and y (that is to say, $C(x, y) = \emptyset$).

Definition 15.5. We define $d : U \times U \longrightarrow \mathbb{R}^+$ as follows:

$$d(x, y) = \begin{cases} \frac{1}{|C(x,y)|} \cdot \left(\sum_{i \in C(x,y)} v(x, i)^2 - \frac{(\sum_{i \in C(x,y)} v(x,i) \cdot v(y,i))^2}{\sum_{i \in C(x,y)} v(y,i)^2} \right) & \text{if } C(x, y) \neq \emptyset \\ \infty & \text{otherwise} \end{cases}$$

Besides, by Proposition 15.1, if we know the value $d(x, y)$, we could bound the value of the mean absolute error between the users x and the prediction made by user y, that is to say:

$$\frac{1}{|C(x, y)|} \sum_{i \in C(x,y)} |e(x, y, i)| = \frac{1}{|C(x, y)|} \sum_{i \in C(x,y)} |v(x, i) - b(x, y) \cdot v(y, i)|$$

Proposition 15.1. *Let $\gamma > 0$ be a positive real number. We have that if $d(x, y) \leq \gamma^2$, then:*

$$\frac{1}{|C(x, y)|} \sum_{i \in C(x,y)} |e(x, y, i)| \leq \gamma$$

Proof.

According to Expression 15.6, we have that:

$$d(x, y) = \frac{1}{|C(x, y)|} \sum_{i \in C(x,y)} e(x, y, i)^2$$

The following expression

$$\frac{1}{|C(x, y)|} \sum_{i \in C(x,y)} |e(x, y, i)|$$

reaches the maximum value for the users $x, y \in U$ fulfilling that:

$$d(x, y) = \frac{1}{|C(x, y)|} \sum_{i \in C(x,y)} e(x, y, i)^2 \leq \gamma^2$$

when

$$\forall i \in C(x, y) \ |e(x, y, i)| = \gamma$$

Consequently, we have that:

$$\frac{1}{|C(x, y)|} \sum_{i \in C(x,y)} |e(x, y, i)| \leq \frac{1}{|C(x, y)|} \sum_{i \in C(x,y)} \gamma = \gamma$$

□

The following proposition is immediately proven by taking into account the above one.

Proposition 15.2. *Let γ such that $0 \leq \gamma \leq 1$.*
Let $y \in N(x)$ such that $d(x, y) \leq \gamma^2 \cdot (max - min)^2$.
We have that:

$$\frac{1}{|C(x, y)|} \sum_{i \in C(x,y)} |e(x, y, i)| \leq \gamma \cdot (max - min)$$

Once we have defined the function d, we can state that a user y is a neighbor of x if the value of $d(x, y)$ keeps under constant α.

Definition 15.6 (Neighborhood). Given $x \in U$, we define $N(x)$ as the following set of users:

$$N(x) = \{y \in U \,|\, d(x, y) \leq \alpha\}$$

Although the parameter α may be defined arbitrarily and may depend on the specific recommender system in use, we suggest employing the following number (note that the possible values with which a user can rate an item are $\{min, \ldots, max\}$):

$$\alpha = \frac{(max - min)^2}{100}$$

When α takes this number, we can be sure, by Proposition 15.2, that for every neighbor, $y \in N(x)$, the mean absolute error between the users x and y is below the 10% of the difference $max - min$, that is to say:

$$\frac{1}{|C(x, y)|} \sum_{i \in C(x,y)} |e(x, y, i)| \leq 0.1 \cdot (max - min)$$

Once we have selected the neighbors of a user, $x \in U$, we can make an estimate on with which value the user x would rate an item i, by taking into consideration the neighbors of x.

Given an item $i \in I$ and a neighbor, $y \in N(x)$, who has rated the item i, we can estimate as $b(x, y) \cdot v(y, i)$ the value with which the user x would rate the item i. In the same way as in Expression 15.1, we take into account all the neighbors who have rated the item i to make the estimation $v^*(x, i)$ (see Definition 15.7).

In this way, we make an average of all the estimations arisen from the neighbors of x who have rated the item i. In case there are no neighbors which have rated the item i, we would say that $v^*(x,i) = \bullet$ (that is to say, we cannot estimate the value with which the user x would rate the item i).

Definition 15.7 (Estimation). We define the function $v^* : U \times U \longrightarrow \mathbb{R} \cup \{\bullet\}$ such that $\forall x \in U$ and $\forall i \in I$:

$$
v^*(x,i) =
\begin{cases}
\dfrac{1}{|B(x,i)|} \sum_{y \in B(x,i)} b(x,y) \cdot v(y,i) & \text{if } B(x,i) \neq \varnothing \\
\bullet & \text{otherwise}
\end{cases}
$$

where $B(x,i) = \{y \in N(x) | v(y,i) \neq \bullet\}$

15.4.1   Example

Next, we will consider an example in order to illustrate what we have stated above.

Let us consider four users $x, y, z, t \in U$ and the items $i_1, i_2, i_3, i_4, i_5 \in I$. Let us consider that $V = \{1, 2, 3, 4, 5\}$. Just consider the following ratings made by the users:

$$
\begin{array}{lllll}
v(x, i_1) = 1 & v(x, i_2) = \bullet & v(x, i_3) = 2 & v(x, i_4) = 3 & v(x, i_5) = 5 \\
v(y, i_1) = \bullet & v(y, i_2) = 2 & v(y, i_3) = 3 & v(y, i_4) = 3 & v(y, i_5) = 5 \\
v(z, i_1) = 5 & v(z, i_2) = \bullet & v(z, i_3) = \bullet & v(z, i_4) = 3 & v(z, i_5) = 1 \\
v(t, i_1) = 2 & v(t, i_2) = 4 & v(t, i_3) = 4 & v(t, i_4) = 5 & v(t, i_5) = \bullet
\end{array}
$$

We calculate the value α:

$$
\alpha = \frac{(5-1)^2}{100} = 0.16
$$

In order to make a recommendation to user x, we need to calculate the neighbors of this user x. Consequently, we calculate previously the following:

$$
\begin{aligned}
C(x, y) &= \{i_3, i_4, i_5\} \quad |C(x, y)| = 3 \\
b(x, y) &= \frac{2 \cdot 3 + 3 \cdot 3 + 5 \cdot 5}{3^2 + 3^2 + 5^2} = 0.93 \quad d(x, y) \\
&= \frac{1}{3}\left(2^2 + 3^2 + 5^2 - \frac{(2 \cdot 3 + 3 \cdot 3 + 5 \cdot 5)^2}{3^2 + 3^2 + 5^2}\right) = 0.26 > \alpha
\end{aligned}
$$

$$
\begin{aligned}
C(x, z) &= \{i_1, i_4, i_5\} \quad |C(x, z)| = 3 \\
b(x, z) &= \frac{1 \cdot 5 + 3 \cdot 3 + 5 \cdot 1}{5^2 + 3^2 + 1^2} = 0.66 \quad d(x, z) \\
&= \frac{1}{3}\left(1^2 + 3^2 + 5^2 - \frac{(2 \cdot 3 + 3 \cdot 3 + 5 \cdot 1)^2}{5^2 + 3^2 + 1^2}\right) = 3.07 > \alpha
\end{aligned}
$$

$$C(x,t) = \{i_1, i_3, i_4\} \quad |C(x,t)| = 3$$

$$b(x,t) = \frac{1{\cdot}2 + 2{\cdot}4 + 3{\cdot}5}{2^2 + 4^2 + 5^2} = 0.55 \quad d(x,t)$$

$$= \frac{1}{3}\left(1^2 + 2^2 + 3^2 - \frac{(1{\cdot}2 + 2{\cdot}4 + 3{\cdot}5)^2}{2^2 + 4^2 + 5^2}\right) = 0.04 \le \alpha$$

As a result, there is only one neighbor of x, namely, t. That is to say,

$$N(x) = \{t\}$$

Now, we can estimate how user x would rate the item i_2 in the following way:

$$v^*(x, i_2) = \frac{1}{1}(b(x,t) \cdot v(t, i_2)) = 0.55 \cdot 4 = 2.2$$

15.5 The Coverage Improvement

As will be seen in Sect. 15.6, when evaluating the technique described in the previous section, we can see that (when α is low), the MAE level is extraordinarily good, but the coverage is very low. That is to say, the recommender system makes real good but few predictions.

In this section, we deal with a way to get a better coverage, while preserving to the greater possible extent the quality of the system's predictions.

First of all, we will study why the recommender system makes so few predictions. The main reason lies in the fact that since we only select as neighbors those users who are very suitable so as to predict the rating of a user x, the resulting set of neighbors is usually very small, and consequently it often happens that $B(x,i) = \emptyset$ for many $x \in U$ and $i \in I$.

In order to correct this, we propose to get a bigger set of the neighbors $N(x)$ of a user x, taking into account also some users, y, which, although might not be considered as very suitable to predict the ratings of x, were indeed useful for making predictions on some items which cannot be predicted by the set of neighbors $N(x)$ alone. This new enlarged set of neighbors of a user x will be called $N^*(x)$.

For each user, $x \in U$, and each item, $i \in I$, we will consider the neighbor $w(x,i)$, who is the user most suitable to predict the ratings of x among the users who have rated the item i (see Definition 15.8).

Definition 15.8. We define a function $w : U \times I \longrightarrow U$ fulfilling that

$$w(x,i) = y \Leftrightarrow d(x,y) = \min_{\substack{z \in U \\ v(z,i) \neq \bullet}} d(x,z)$$

For each user, $x \in U$, we include as neighbors every user $w(x, i)$ where $i \in I$ (see Definition 15.9). Consequently, in this new set of neighbors, not only we include very suitable neighbors to predict the ratings of x, but also those which let us get a closer prediction on how the user x would rate the items.

Definition 15.9 (New Neighborhood). Given $x \in U$, we define $N^*(x)$ as the following set of users:

$$N^*(x) = N(x) \cup \{w(x, i) | i \in I\}$$

where $N(x) = \{y \in U | d(x, y) \leq \alpha\}$

According to this definition, the coverage of the recommender system would be the highest possible, since we are considering for each user $x \in U$ and each item $i \in I$, the best neighbor of x who has rated the item i. Indeed, an item $i \in I$ cannot be predicted on behalf of the user x if and only if this item i has not been rated by any users.

Once we have defined the neighbors of each user, we will focus on how to make estimations. Unlike Definition 15.6, the new definition of neighbors of $x \in U$ in Definition 15.9 involves the possibility of including users who are not very suitable so as to predict the ratings of x. In order to have good levels of MAE, we need to weight (unlike the estimation proposed in Definition 15.7) the inadequacy levels of each neighbor of x, in such way that those users more suitable to predict the ratings of x will have more importance. Although this is the underlying idea already implied in Expression 15.2 in Sect. 15.3, we cannot use this expression since, unlike the similarity measures like ρ or cos, the lesser $d(x, y)$ is, the higher will be the adequacy level of user y in order to predict the ratings of x.

In order to weight the unsuitability degrees of each neighbor, we need to design a function f_α (see Definition 15.10):

Definition 15.10. Let $\alpha > 0$
We define the function $f_\alpha : \mathbb{R}^+ \longrightarrow [0, 1]$ as follows:

$$f_\alpha(x) = \frac{\alpha^4}{x^4 + \alpha^4}$$

This function fulfills the following properties:

Proposition 15.3. *Let $\alpha > 0$. The previous function f_α has the following properties:*

i) $f_\alpha(0) = 1 \; f_\alpha(\alpha) = 1/2$
ii) *If $0 \leq x_1 < x_2$, then $0 < f_\alpha(x_2) < f_\alpha(x_1) \leq 1$*
iii) *If $x \leq 0.5 \cdot \alpha$, then $f_\alpha(\alpha) > 0.9$*
iv) *If $x \geq 2 \cdot \alpha$, then $f_\alpha(\alpha) < 0.1$*

The function f_α is suitable to weigh the neighbors of x when making estimations. As may be seen in Definition 15.11, we weigh, by means of f_α, the inadequacy degree of the neighbors of x.

Definition 15.11 (New Estimation). Let $x \in U$.

We define the function $v^* : U \times U \longrightarrow \mathbb{R} \cup \{\bullet\}$ such that $\forall x \in U$ and $\forall i \in I$, the following holds:

$$v^*(x,i) = \begin{cases} \dfrac{\sum_{y \in N^*(x)\ v(y,i) \neq \bullet} f_\alpha(d(x,y)) \cdot b(x,y) \cdot v(y,i)}{\sum_{y \in N^*(x)\ v(y,i) \neq \bullet} f_\alpha(d(x,y))} & \text{if } \exists y \in N^*(x)\ v(y,i) \neq \bullet \\ \bullet & \text{otherwise} \end{cases}$$

According to the properties of f_α, we give much more importance to those neighbors $y \in N(x)$ with $d(x,y) \leq \alpha$, than to those fulfilling $d(y,x) \geq \alpha$. Consequently, when there are neighbors $y \in U$ who have rated an item $i \in I$ (that is to say, $v(y,i) \neq \bullet$) and with unsuitability degree lower than α (that is to say, $d(x,y) \leq \alpha$), the estimation calculated in Definition 15.11 is very close to that which ensues from Definition 15.7 in the previous section. Besides, as we have said above, we are considering the highest possible value of coverage.

15.6 Evaluation of Our Techniques

In this section, we will analyze the value of coverage and MAE of our techniques in relation to the k-neighborhoods based on the metrics, MSD, ρ ('correlation') and cos. We have used the "MovieLens" database [23], which has been a reference for many years in research carried out in the area of Collaborative Filtering. The database contains 943 users, 1,682 items and 100,000 ratings, with a minimum of 20 items rated per user. The items represent motion pictures and the rating values range from 1 to 5.

In relation to the techniques presented here, we calculate the constant α as we suggested in a previous section:

$$\alpha = \frac{(5-1)^2}{100} = 0.16$$

In relation to the techniques presented in Sects. 15.4 and 15.5, we have obtained the values of MAE and coverage described in Table 15.1. As may be seen, although the MAE of this second technique is not so good in as the first technique, the coverage level has been increased significantly.

Figure 15.1 illustrates the MAE and coverage values of the algorithm of the k nearest neighbors for different values of k (15, 30, 60, 90, 120, 150, 180, 210 and 240), covering from 1.6 to 25% of the total number of users.

Table 15.1 Evaluation of the techniques presented in the paper

Technique	MAE	Coverage
Technique 1 (Sect. 15.4)	0.099	35.99%
Technique 2 (Sect. 15.5)	0.504	100%

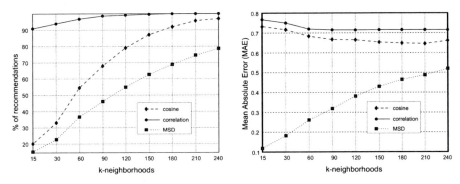

Fig. 15.1 MAE and Coverage for the k nearest neighbors algorithm based on the metrics MSD, ρ and cos

Although *MSD* provides the best results in relation to MAE, the coverage level keeps very low (until the value of k is high). Instead, the similarity measure ρ ("correlation") keeps good levels of coverage and MAE (this is an example which helps understand why correlation is often used instead of *MSD*).

As may be seen, the values the algorithm k-nearest neighbors provides for any of the three similarity measures and for any value in the constant k are consistently worse than those obtained by the technique presented in Sect. 15.5. Besides, our technique presents the advantage that it does not need to find the value for any parameter, unlike the classic algorithm, whose results depend significantly on the parameter k (and consequently, it is always necessary to find out the optimal value for this parameter beforehand).

15.7 Conclusions

In this paper, we have presented a new technique for making predictions on recommender systems based on collaborative filtering. The underlying idea is based on selecting a variable number of neighbors for each user on behalf of the number of high similar users (neighbors) in the database (instead of, as it is usually made, selecting always a constant number k of neighbors). Thanks to this new technique, we can get a significant improvement of both the value MAE and the coverage.

References

1. G. Adomavicius and A. Tuzhilin, Toward the Next Generation of Recommender Systems: a survey of the state-of-the-art and possible extensions, IEEE Transactions on Knowledge and Data Enginnering, Vol. 17, No 6, 2005, pp. 734–749
2. N. Antonopoulus and J. Salter, Cinema screen recommender agent: combining collaborative and content-based filtering, IEEE Intelligent Systems, 2006, pp. 35–41

3. R. Baraglia and F. Silvestri, An Online Recommender System for Large Web Sites, Proceedings of the IEEE/WIC/ACM International Conference on Web Intelligence, 2004, pp. 199–205
4. J. Bobadilla, F. Serradilla and A. Hernando, Collaborative Filtering adapted to Recommender Systems of e-learning, Knowledge Based Systems, Vol. 22, 2009, pp. 261–265
5. J.S Breese, D. Heckerman and C. Kadie, Empirical Analysis of Predictive Algorithms for Collaborative Filtering, Proceedings of the 14th Conference on Uncertainty in Artificial Intelligence, pp. 43–52, 1998
6. S.B. Cho, J.H. Hong and M.H. Park, Location-Based Recommendation System Using Bayesian Users Preference Model in Mobile Devices, Lecture Notes on Computer Science, 4611, pp. 1130–1139, 2007
7. I. Fuyuki, T.K. Quan and H. Shinichi, Improving Accuracy of Recommender Systems by Clustering Items Based on Stability of User Similarity, Proceedings of the IEEE International Conference on Intelligent Agents, Web Technologies and Internet Commerce, pp. 61–61, 2006
8. G.M. Giaglis and G. Lekakos, Improving the Prediction Accuracy of Recommendation Algorithms: Approaches Anchored on Human Factors, Interacting with Computers, Vol. 18, No. 3, 2006, pp. 410–431
9. J.L. Herlocker, J.A. Konstan, J.T. Riedl and L.G. Terveen, Evaluating collaborative filtering recommender systems, ACM Transactions on Information Systems, Vol. 22, No. 1, 2004, pp. 5–53
10. H. Ingoo, J.O. Kyong and H.R. Tae, The collaborative filtering recommendation based on SOM cluster-indexing CBR, Expert Systems with Applications, Vol. 25, 2003, 413–423
11. T. Janner and C. Schroth, Web 2.0 and SOA: Converging Concepts Enabling the Internet of Services, IT Pro, 2007, pp. 36–41
12. M. Knights, Web 2.0, IET Communications Engineer, Vol. 5, No. 1, 2007, pp. 30–35
13. F. Kong, X. Sun and S. Ye, A Comparison of Several Algorithms for Collaborative Filtering in Startup Stage, Proceedings of the IEEE networking, sensing and control, 2005, pp. 25–28
14. J.A. Konstan, B.N. Miller and J. Riedl, PocketLens: toward a personal recommender system, ACM Transactions on Information Systems, Vol. 22, No. 3, 2004, pp. 437–476
15. K.J. Lin, Building Web 2.0, Computer, Vol. 40, No. 5, 2007, pp. 101–102
16. F. Loll and N. Pinkwart, Using Collaborative Filtering Algorithms as eLearning Tools, 42nd Hawaii International Conference on System Sciences HICSS '09, 2009, pp. 1–10
17. Y. Manolopoulus, A. Nanopoulus, A.N. Papadopoulus and P. Symeonidis, Collaborative recommender systems: combining effectiveness and efficiency, Expert Systems with Applications, Vol. 34, No. 4, 2008, pp. 2995–3013
18. J.L. Sanchez, F. Serradilla, E. Martinez and J. Bobadilla, Choice of Metrics used in Collaborative Filtering and their Impact on Recommender Systems, Proceedings of the IEEE International Conference on Digital Ecosystems and Technologies (DEST'08), 2008, pp. 432–436
19. S. Staab, H. Werthner, F. Ricci, A. Zipf, U. Gretzel, D.R. Fesenmaier, C. Paris and C. Knoblock, Intelligent Systems for Tourism, Intelligent Systems, Vol. 17, No. 6, 2002, pp. 53–64
20. P. Symeonidis, A. Nanopoulos and Y. Manolopoulos, Providing Justifications in Recommender Systems, IEEE Transactions on Systems, Man and Cybernetics, Part A, Vol. 38, No. 6, 2008, pp. 1262–1272
21. K. Wei, J. Huang and S. Fu, A survey of e-commerce recommender systems, Proceedings of the International Conference on Service Systems and Service Management, 2007, pp. 1–5
22. R.R. Yager, Fuzzy Logic Methods in Recommender Systems, Fuzzy Sets and Systems, Vol. 136, No.2, 2003, pp. 133–149
23. http://www.movielens.org

Chapter 16
Discovering Communities from Social Networks: Methodologies and Applications

Bo Yang, Dayou Liu, and Jiming Liu

16.1 Introduction

Network communities refer to groups of network nodes, within which the links connecting nodes are dense but between which they are sparse. A network community mining problem (NCMP for short) can be stated as the problem of finding all such communities from a given network. A large variety of problems can be translated into NCMPs, ranging from graph partition applications, such as VLSI layout [1,2], large-scale scientific computing [3,4], load balance for distributed computing [5,6], and image segmentation [7], to complex network analysis, such as social network analysis [8–10], biological network analysis[11–13], and Web pages clustering [14–16].

Network communities in different application contexts may imply different meanings and serve different purposes. For example, they may be sets of electronic units closely placed on a VLSI circuit board, collections of processes that frequently communicate with each other, segments of an image, circles of a society within which people share common interests and keep frequent contacts, classes of Web pages related to common topics, or groups of proteins exhibiting similar functions. Discovering such hidden patterns from networks will enable us to better understand the structural and/or functional characteristics of networks and to more effectively utilize them.

The remainder of this chapter is organized as follows: Section 16.2 introduces some of the existing methods for solving NCMPs. Section 16.3 presents several interesting applications of NCMPs as related to social network analysis. Finally, Section 16.4 concludes the chapter.

B. Yang (✉)
School of Computer Science and Technology, Jilin University, China
e-mail: ybo@jlu.edu.cn

B. Furht (ed.), *Handbook of Social Network Technologies and Applications*,
DOI 10.1007/978-1-4419-7142-5_16, © Springer Science+Business Media, LLC 2010

16.2 Methodologies of Network Community Mining

In view of the basic strategies adopted, most of the existing community mining
algorithms can be classified into two main categories: *optimization based algorithms*
and *heuristic based algorithms* (Fig. 16.1). The former solves an NCMP by transforming it into an optimization problem and trying to find an optimal solution with
respect to a pre-defined objective function, such as various cut criteria adopted by
spectral methods [2,7,17–20], the evaluation function introduced by the Kernighan–
Lin algorithm [21], the network modularity employed in several algorithms [13,22–
25] and others [26]. On the contrary, heuristic algorithms do not explicitly state
optimization objectives, and they solve an NCMP based on certain intuitive assumptions or heuristic rules. For example, the heuristic rule used in the maximum
flow community (MFC) algorithm [15] is based on the assumption that "flows"
through inter-community links should be larger than those of intra-community
links. Similarly, the heuristic rule employed by the GN algorithm [8] is that the
the "edge betweenness" of inter-community links should be larger than that of
intra-community links. Others such as the Wu-Huberman algorithm [27], the HITS
algorithm [14], the CPM [28], and the FEC [29] have adopted different assumptions.

16.2.1 Optimization Based Algorithms

Spectral methods and local search based methods are two representatives of optimization based algorithms for solving NCMPs.

Spectral methods optimize certain pre-defined *cut* criteria by using the quadratic
optimization technique. In graph theory, the *cut* of a bipartition of a network is
defined as the number of inter-group links. An optimal bipartition of a network
is the one with the minimum cut. Yet, in most cases, the minimum cut criterion

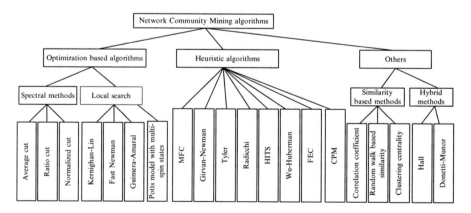

Fig. 16.1 The classification chart for some of the existing community mining algorithms [31]

will lead to bias partitions. In order to avoid this problem, other criteria, such as *average cut* [17, 18], *ratio cut* [20], *normalized cut* [7], and their variants, have been proposed to compute the density, instead of the number, of inter-group links. Unfortunately, the problems of finding different optimal cuts have been proven to be NP-complete [7, 30]. Based on matrix theory, the spectral methods try to find an approximately optimal cut by transforming the problem into a constraint quadratic optimization problem represented as $min(X^T MX)/(X^T X)$, where X denotes the indicator vector of a bipartition, and M is a symmetric positive semi-definite matrix. In the case of minimizing the average cut, M corresponds to the Laplacian matrix of a given graph. In the case of minimizing the ratio cut, normalized cut, or others, M corresponds to a variant of the Laplacian matrix. Thus, an approximately optimal solution of the constraint quadratic optimization problem can be obtained by means of calculating the second smallest eigenvector of M.

Generally speaking, computing all eigenvectors of a matrix will take $O(n^3)$ time, where n is the number of nodes. While in a sparse matrix, the second smallest eigenvector can be calculated with the time complexity of $O(m/(\lambda_2 - \lambda_3))$ by applying the Lanczos method. Here, m denotes the number of links in a network, and λ_2 and λ_3 denote the second and third smallest eigenvalues of M, respectively. These two eigenvalues dominate the performance of spectral methods. They will run very slowly when the gap between and is small.

In fact, the spectral methods are bipartition methods that try to split a graph into two, with a balanced size and the minimum cut. Therefore, for a network that contains multiple communities, one can find all of the communities with a hierarchical structure in a recursive way until a pre-defined stopping criterion is satisfied.

The Kernighan–Lin algorithm [21], the fast Newman algorithm [22], and the Guimera–Amaral algorithm [13] are three popular local search based optimization methods for solving NCMPs. They adopt quite a similar idea in finding a neighbor of the current solution in the problem space during each iteration, but adopt different optimization objectives and different strategies for regulating the local search process.

The Kernighan–Lin algorithm [21] (or KL for short) aims to minimize an evaluation function defined as the difference of the numbers of intra-community links and inter-community links. Starting from an initial partition of a network, in each iteration, KL moves or swaps nodes between communities in order to decrease the evaluation function. This iterative process stops when the evaluation function remains unchanged. KL runs moderately fast with the time complexity of $O(n^2)$. During the local search process, KL only accepts better neighbor solutions and rejects all worse ones, and thus it often finds a local, rather than a global, optimal solution. The principal restriction of KL is that it needs to have some prior knowledge, such as the number, as well as the average size of, communities in order to generate an initial partition. KL is also sensitive to initial partitions; that is, a bad one could result in a slow convergence and hence a poor solution.

Newman has presented a faster algorithm (or FN for short) for detecting community structures with the time complexity of $O(mn)$ [22]. In essence, FN is also a local search based optimization method. Starting from an initial state in which each community only contains a single node, FN repeatedly joins communities together in pairs by choosing the best merge, until only one community is left. In this bottom-up way, the *dendrogram* of community structure is constructed. In order to choose the best merge in each iteration, a new metric, *modularity*, is proposed to quantitatively measure how well-formed a community structure is. The modularity of a given network in terms of a Q-function is defined as follows:

$$Q = \sum_i e_{ii} - a_i^2 \tag{16.1}$$

where e_{ij} denotes the fraction of all weighted links in networks that connect the nodes in community i to the those in community j, and $a_i = \sum_j e_{ij}$. It is expected that better partitions of a given network will be those with larger Q-values.

The algorithm proposed by Guimera and Amaral [13] (or GA for short) also tries to find a partition of a network with the maximum modularity. However, different from FN, GA adopts simulated annealing (SA) to regulate the local search process in order to obtain a better solution. Similar to KL, starting from an initial partition of a network, GA generates, evaluates, accepts or rejects a new neighbor partition from the current one in each iteration. To generate a new neighbor partition, GA moves or swaps nodes between groups, divides a group or merges two groups. Then GA evaluates the new partition by calculating its modularity and decides whether or not to accept it by using the *metropolis* criterion given in (16.2) based on the current system temperature.

$$p = \begin{cases} 1, & C_{t+1} \le C_t \\ e^{-(C_{t+1}-C_t)/T}, & C_{t+1} > C_t \end{cases} \tag{16.2}$$

where $C_t = -Q_t$, p is the probability of accepting the solution obtained at time $t + 1$, and T is the system temperature at time $t + 1$.

As argued by authors, GA has a good performance, due to the capability of SA, in finding a globally optimal solution. While the efficiency of GA is dominated by the convergent speed of SA, which is usually slow and very sensitive to its parameters, such as the initial layout and the strategies of finding a neighbor solution, and the cooling system temperature. GA outputs a partition of a network without a hierarchical structure, and does not require prior knowledge, such as the number of communities.

It should be noticed that it is not always safe for us to use the modularity as the optimization objective. For example, the actual partitions of some social networks correspond to locally maximum modularity values rather than global optima, as shown in Fig. 16.2 [31]. Also, as reported by Guimera and his colleagues [32], some random networks without well defined community structures may have quite high modularity values due to fluctuations. Additionally, as Fortunato and Barthelemy argued [33], modularity optimization methods tend to discover coarse rather than fine ones. In those cases, the optimization based methods that maximize modularity values may not be able to find the real community structures hidden in networks.

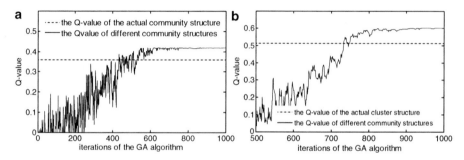

Fig. 16.2 The local search process of the GA algorithm [31]. In (**a**), GA is applied to the karate network. The detected optimal community structure consists of four communities, and the corresponding Q-value is 0.42, which is greater than 0.37, the Q-value of the actual 2-community partition of this network. In (**b**), GA is applied to the football association network. The detected optimal community structure contains 10 communities with a Q-value of 0.60. Again, this global optimum is larger than 0.51, the locally optimal Q-value of the real 12-community structure of this network

In the literature, there are also other optimization based algorithms for addressing NCMPs. For example, Reichardt and Bornholdt considered a network as a multiple-state Potts model, in which each node is a spin with q values [34]. They suggested that the best network partition corresponds to the most stable state of the Potts model, that is, the state with the minimum energy, in which the spins with the same values constitute one community. They found such a distribution of spin values by minimizing a pre-defined energy function using a Monte Carlo optimization method combined with the simulated annealing algorithm.

16.2.2 Heuristic Methods

The maximum flow community (MFC) algorithm [15], the Girvan–Newman algorithm (GN) [8] and its improvements [35, 36], the Hyperlink Induced Topic Search algorithm (HITS) [14], the Wu–Huberman algorithm (WH) [27] and the Clique percolation method (CPM) [28] are typical heuristic based algorithms for solving NCMPs.

The MFC algorithm was proposed by Flake et al. based on the Max Flow-Min Cut theorem in graph theory [15]. The basic assumption behind is that the maximum flow through a given network is decided only by the capacity of network "bottlenecks," which is the capacity of the Min-Cut sets, and the sparse inter-community links can be regarded as the "bottlenecks" in the flow within the network. Therefore, the inter-community links can be discovered by calculating the Min-Cut sets. By iteratively removing "bottleneck" links, involved communities will be gradually separated from each other. Based on MFC, Flake and his colleagues proposed a method for discovering Web communities and verified an interesting hypothesis through their experiments, that is, self-organized and hyperlink-based Web community are highly topic-related [37]. So far, the best time for calculating the Min-Cut sets of a graph is $O(mnlog(n^2/m))$ [38,39], which decides the time of each bipartition happened in MFC. But in practice, MFC runs fast because the Min-Cut computation is restricted within a fairly small area around some pre-selected Web pages rather than the global Web.

Similarly, the GN algorithm detects all communities by recursively breaking inter-community links [8]. But, different from MFC, the heuristic rule introduced in GN is that the inter-community links are those with the maximum "edge betweenness," which is defined as the number of geodesic paths running through a given link. The GN algorithm is a hierarchical method and can produce a dendrogram of community structure in a top-down fashion. Its time complexity is $O(m^2n)$, which makes it not suitable for large-scale networks. In order to speed up the basic GN algorithm, several improvements have been proposed.

Tyler et al. introduced a statistical technique into the basic GN algorithm [36]. Instead of computing the exact edge betweenness of all links, they used the Monte Carlo method to estimate an approximate edge betweenness value for a selected link set. Inevitably, an improvement in speed is gained at the price of a reduction in accuracy.

Because calculating edge betweenness is time-consuming, Radicchi et al. defined a new metric, called *link clustering coefficient*, to replace it [35]. The assumption behind their method is that inter-community links are unlikely to belong to a short loop, such as triangles and squares; otherwise, links in the same loop would likely be across communities, and thus such links would inevitably increase the density of inter-community links. Using this heuristic rule, they define the link clustering coefficient as the number of triangles or squares in which a link is involved. In each iterative step, links with the minimum link clustering coefficient will be cut off. The average time complexity for computing the link clustering coefficient of all links is $O(m^3/n^2)$, lower than that for computing edge betweenness, which is $O(mn)$. Thus, their method is on average faster than GN with the time complexity of $O(m^4/n^2)$.

Similar to MFC, HITS presented by Kleinberg [14] aims to discover hyperlink-based Web communities. The basic assumption behind HITS is that there exist authorities and hubs on the Web, and authorities are often pointed to by hubs that preferentially point to authorities. Based on the mutually reinforcing relationship between authorities and hubs, they developed an iterative method for inferring such authority-hub communities from the Web by computing the principal eigenvectors of two special matrices in terms of the adjacency matrix of the Web. A search engine based on HITS can return the most topic-related pages to users.

In the WH algorithm proposed by Wu and Huberman [27], a network is modeled as an electrical circuit by allocating one unit resistor on each link. Then, it selects two nodes from two distinct communities as the positive and negative poles, respectively. The assumption of the WH algorithm is that the resistance within communities will be much less than that between communities because the intra-community links are much denser than inter-community links, and thus the voltage difference of distinct communities should be more significant. Based on this heuristic, the WH algorithm can separate the group with a high voltage and the group with a low voltage from a network, by finding two maximum gaps in the node sequence sorted by their respective voltage values. Then, it determines the final division by considering the co-occurrence of nodes in such separated groups. As authors argued, their method is very fast with a linear time in terms of the size of a network. However, the WH algorithm depends heavily on its prior knowledge, which is hard to obtain beforehand. For instance, it needs to identify two "poles" belonging to different communities. Also, it needs the approximate size of each community in order to find multiple communities.

Palla and his colleagues presented CPM to discover an overlapping community structure [28]. They assumed that a network community is made of "adjacent" k cliques, which share at least $k - 1$ nodes with each other. Each clique uniquely belongs to one community, but cliques within different communities may share nodes. Using the above heuristic information, CPM is able to find the overlaps of communities. For a given K, CPM first locates all k cliques ($k \leq K$) from a given network, and then build a clique-clique overlap matrix to find out communities in terms of different k. But in practice, for an unknown network, it is not easy to decide what value of k will result in a more reasonable community structure.

16.2.3   Other Methods

Besides the above-discussed two main categories, there exist some other algorithms for solving NCMPs. For example, we can cluster a network through a bottom-up approach by repetitively joining pairs of current groups based on their similarities, such as correlation coefficients [40] and random walk similarities [41], which are defined in terms of their linkage relation. Also, we can first transform an NCMP into a clustering problem in a vector space by allocating a k-dimensional coordinate to each node, and then cluster such spatial points using any typical spatial clustering algorithm, such as k-mean. Back in 1970, Hall had proposed an efficient way for transforming a network into a group of one-dimensional points by using a weighted quadratic equation in order that the nodes with dense links will be put close together, and those with sparse links will be put far away from each other [42]. Recently, Donetti and Munoz proposed a method for solving NCMPs based on quite a similar idea [43]. Their method maps a network into a k-dimensional vector space using the k smallest eigenvectors of the Laplacian matrix before clustering spatial points.

16.3   Applications of Community Mining Algorithms

In this section, we will present some applications of community mining, with respect to various tasks in social network analysis.

16.3.1 Network Reduction

Network reduction is an important step in analyzing social networks. In this section, we will illustrate how to reduce a complex network into a dendrogram, by means of community mining. The example discussed here is taken from the work as reported in [44], in which the network was constructed from the bibliography of the book entitled "graph products: structure and recognition [45]". The bibliography contains 360 papers written by 314 authors. Its corresponding network is a bipartite graph, in which each node denotes either one author or one paper, and link (i, j) represents author i publishing a paper j, as shown in Fig. 16.3.

Figure 16.4 provides the community structure as detected using a community mining algorithm, called ICS [44], in which 147 communities are uncovered from the bibliography network. As one would have expected, each community contains some papers and their corresponding coauthors.

Most of the detected communities are self-connected components. The component A is the biggest one containing 13 communities, 158 papers, and 86 authors. Figure 16.5 shows the network indicating the collaborations among these 86 coauthors, in which link (i, j) with weight w denotes authors i and j have coauthored w papers. Then, ICS is again applied to the coauthor network and totally 14 communities are uncovered, as shown in Fig. 16.6a, in which different gray degrees indicate different communities.

Moreover, the clustered coauthor network can be reduced into a much smaller one by condensing each community as one node, as shown in Fig. 16.6b. Finally,

Fig. 16.3 The bibliography network for the book entitled "graph products: structure and recognition" [44]

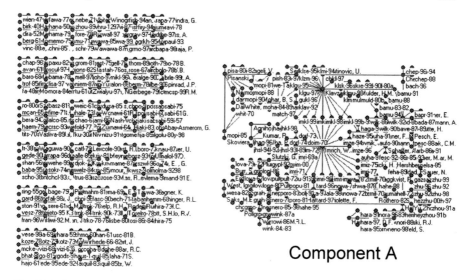

Fig. 16.4 The community structure of the bibliography network as detected using ICS [44]

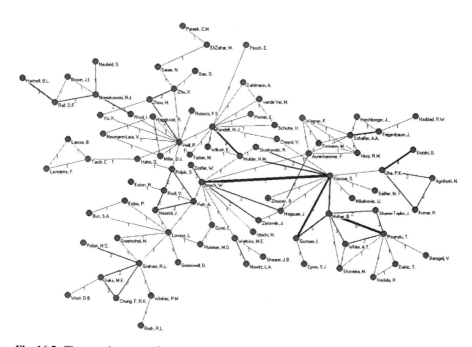

Fig. 16.5 The coauthor network corresponding to the biggest component [44]

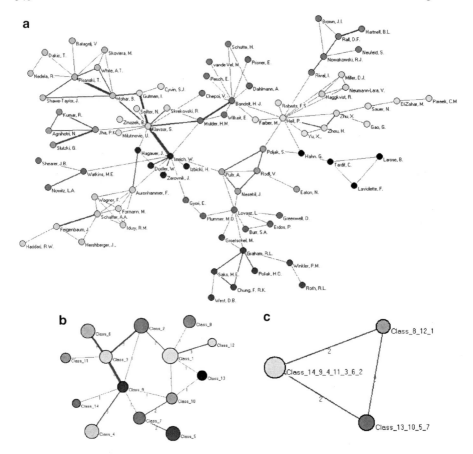

Fig. 16.6 The reduction of a coauthor network [44]. (**a**) The community structure of the network. (**b**) The condensed network. (**c**) The top-level condensed network

the top-level condensed network corresponding to a 3-community structure is constructed by using ICS from the condensed network, as shown in Fig. 16.6c. In this way, a dendrogram corresponding to the original coauthor network can be built, as shown in Fig. 16.7.

16.3.2 Discovering Scientific Collaboration Groups from Social Networks

In this section, we will show how community mining techniques can be applied to the analysis of scientific collaborations among researchers using an example given in [46]. Flink is a social network that describes the scientific collaborations among 681 semantic Web researchers (http://flink.semanticweb.org/). The

48 Neumann-Lara, V. (12)
41 Miller, D.J.   (12)
27 Haggkvist, R.   (12)
51 Pareek, C.M.   (1)
14 El-Zahar, M.   (1)
65 Sauer, N.   (1)
19 Gao, G.   (1)
84 Zhu, X.   (1)
83 Zhou, H.   (1)
82 Yu, X.,   (1)
16 Farber, M.   (1)
62 Roberts, F.S.   (1)
30 Hell, P.   (1)
49 Nowakowski, R.J. (8)
61 Rival, I.   (8)
5   Brown, J.I.   (8)
60 Rall, D.F.   (8)
29 Hartnell, B.L.   (8)
78 West, D.B.   (5)
64 Saks, M.E.   (5)
8   Chung, F. R.K.   (5)
56 Pollak, H.O.   (5)
20 Graham, R.L.   (5)
22 Groetschel, M.   (5)
63 Roth, R.L.   (5)
81 Winkler, P.M.   (5)
6   Burr, S.A.   (7)
21 Greenwell, D.   (7)
15 Erdos, P.   (7)
40 Lovasz, L.   (7)
54 Plummer, M.D.   (7)
24 Gyori, E.   (7)
58 Pultr, A.   (10)
45 Nesetril, J.   (10)
55 Poljak, S.   (10)
13 Eaton, N.   (10)
59 Redl, V.   (10)
38 Larose, B.   (13)
39 Laviolette, F.   (13)
74 Tardif, C.   (13)
28 Hahn, G.   (13)
76 Wagner, F.   (4)
32 Idury, R.M.   (4)
2   Aurenhammer, F.   (4)
18 Formann, M.   (4)
66 Schaffer, A.A.   (4)
25 Haddad, R.W.   (4)
17 Feigenbaum, J.   (4)
31 Hershberger, J., (4)
37 Kumar, R.   (11)
1   Agnihotri, N.   (11)
71 Slutzki, G.   (11)
35 Jha, P.K.   (11)
72 Skoviera, M.   (6)
43 Mohar, B.   (6)
79 White, A.T.   (6)
69 Shawe-Taylor, J. (6)
53 Pisanski, T.   (6)
4   Batagelj, V.   (6)
46 Nedela, R.   (6)
11 Dakic, T.   (6)
50 Nowitz, L.A.   (14)
70 Shearer, J.B.   (14)
77 Watkins, M.E.   (14)
9   Cyvin, S.J.   (3)
23 Gutman, I.   (3)
42 Milutinovic, U.   (3)
36 Klavzar, S.   (3)
68 Seifter, N.   (3)
85 Zmazek, B.   (3)
73 Skrekovski, R.   (3)
7   Chepoi, V.   (2)
80 Wilkeit, E.   (2)
44 Mulder, H.M.   (2)
57 Prisner, E.   (2)
75 vande Vel, M.   (2)
52 Pesch, E.   (2)
3   Bandelt, H.-J.   (2)
67 Schutte, H.   (2)
10 Dahlmann, A.   (2)
34 Izbicki, H.   (9)
26 Hagauer, J.   (9)
86 Zerovnik, J.   (9)
12 Dorfler, W.   (9)
33 Imrich, W.   (9)

Collaboration In Bibliography
of Book Graph Products

Fig. 16.7 The dendrogram of the coauthor network as shown in Fig. 16.5

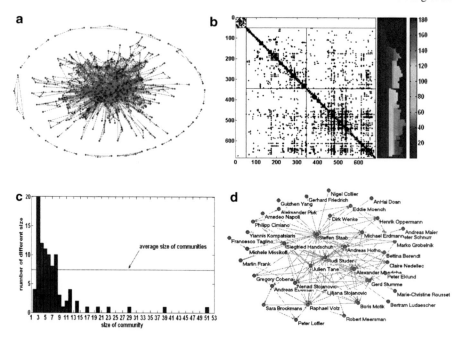

Fig. 16.8 Mining a scientific collaboration network [46]. (**a**) The network of Flink. (**b**) The matrix with a hierarchical structure. (**c**) The statistics of detected communities. (**d**) An illustrated community

network was constructed based on semantic Web technologies and all related semantic information was automatically extracted from "Web-accessible information sources", such as "Web pages, FOAF profiles, email lists, and publication archives". Directed links between nodes, as shown in Fig. 16.8a, denote "know relationships," indicating scientific activities happening between researchers. The weights on the links measure the degrees of collaboration. From the perspective of social network analysis, one may be especially interested in such questions as: (1) among all researchers, which ones would more likely to collaborate with each other? (2) what are the main reasons that bind them together? Such questions can be answered by means of applying the above-mentioned community mining techniques.

Figure 16.8a shows the network structure of Flink, while Fig. 16.8b presents the output of the NCMA community algorithm proposed in [46], where each dot denotes a non-zero entry in the adjacency matrix and the gray bar at the righthand side encodes the hierarchical community structure in which different shades denote different hierarchical levels. Three biggest groups in the first level can be detected, which, respectively, contain 51, 294, and 336 members, as separated by the solid lines in the matrix. The first group is almost separated from the entire network, and its 49 members constitute the outside cycle of Fig. 16.8a. In total, 93 communities are detected and the average size of a community is 7.32, as shown in Fig. 16.8c.

The self-organized communities would provide the answer to the first question. By referring to them, one can know the specific collaboration activities among these researchers. Approximately, we can observe a power-law phenomenon; most communities have a small size, while a small number of communities contain quite a large number of members.

After manually checking the profiles of members within different communities, an interesting fact has been confirmed. That is, most of communities are organized according to the locations or the research interests of their respective members. As an example, we can look into details of the largest community in which Steffen Staab is in the center, as shown in Fig. 16.8d. In this community, 22 of 39 come from Germany, 21 come from the same city, Karlsruhe, and 12 out of such 21 come from the same university, the University of Karlsruhe, where Steffen Staab works. Moreover, the community is research topic related; most of its members are interested in the topic related to ontology learning. These results might offer the clue to answer the second question, i.e., researchers in adjacent locations and with common interests prefer to intensively collaborate with each other.

16.3.3   Mining Communities from Distributed and Dynamic Networks

Most of the existing methods for addressing NCMPs are centralized, in the sense that they require complete information about networks to be processed. Moreover, they assume the structures of networks will not dynamically change. However, in the real world, many applications involve distributed and dynamically-evolving networks, in which resources and controls are not only decentralized but also updated frequently. In such a case, we need find a way to solve a more challenging NCMP [47]; that is to adaptively mine hidden communities from distributed and dynamic networks. One promising solution is based on an Autonomy-Oriented Computing (AOC) approach, in which a group of self-organizing agents are utilized. The agents will rely only on their locally acquired information about networks. In what follows, we will highlight its main ideas through an example from [47].

Intelligent Portable Digital Assistants (or iPDAs for short) that people carry around can form a distributed network, in which their users communicate with each other through calls or messages. One useful function of iPDAs would be to find and recommend new friends with common interests, or potential partners in research or business, to the users. The way to implement it will be through the following steps: (1) based on an iPDA user's communication traces, selecting individuals who have frequently contacted or been contacted with the user during a certain period of time; (2) taking the selected individuals as the input to an AOC-based [48, 49] algorithm [47], which will in turn automatically compute other members within the same community of this user in a decentralized way, by exchanging a limited number of messages with related iPDAs; (3) ranking and recommending new persons, who might not be included the current acquaintance book, the user. In such a way, people can periodically receive recommendations about friends or partners from their iPDAs.

16.4 Conclusions

In this chapter, we have introduced the network community mining problems (NCMPs), and discussed various approaches to tackling them. Generally speaking, methods for effectively and efficiently solving NCMPs can be of fundamental importance from the viewpoints of both theoretical research and practical applications. In view of their respective rationales and formulations, most of the existing methods can be classified into two categories: optimization based methods and heuristic methods.

Community mining approaches have been widely used in different areas, ranging from Web search, recommender systems, bio-informatics, to social network analysis. In this chapter, we have presented three interesting applications: network reduction, discovering scientific collaboration and distributed recommender system.

Acknowledgements This work was funded by the National Natural Science Foundation of China under Grant Nos. 60773099, 60873149 and 60973088, the National High-Tech Research and Development Plan of China under Grant Nos. 2006AA10Z245 and 2006AA10A309, the Open Project Program of the National Laboratory of Pattern Recognition (NLPR), and the basic scientific research fund of Chinese Ministry of Education under Grant No. 200903177.

References

1. B. Krishnamurthy, An improved min-cut algorithm for partitioning VLSI networks, IEEE Trans. Comp., Vol. 33, No. 5, 1984, pp. 438–446
2. L. Hagen, and A.B. Kahng, New spectral methods for ratio cut partition and clustering, IEEE Trans. Computer-Aided Design, Vol. 11, No. 9, 1992, pp. 1074–1085
3. M.T. Heath, E.G.Y. Ng, and B.W. Peyton, Parallel algorithm for sparse linear systems, SIAM Rev., Vol. 33, 1991, pp. 420–460
4. Pothen, H. Simon, and K.P. Liou, Partitioning sparse matrices with eigenvalues of graphs, SIAM J. Matrix Anal. Appl., Vol. 11, No. 3, 1990, pp. 430–452
5. H. Simon, Partitioning of unstructured problems for parallel processing, Comput. Syst. Eng., Vol. 2, No. 3, 1991, pp. 135–148
6. B. Hendrickson, and R. Leland, An improved spectral graph partitioning algorithm for mapping parallel computations, SIAM J. Comp. Sci., Vol. 16, No. 2, 1995, pp. 452–469
7. J. Shi, and J. Malik, Normalized cuts and image segmentation, IEEE Trans. Pattern Anal. Mach. Intell., Vol. 22, 2000, pp. 888–904
8. M. Girvan and M.E.J. Newman, Community structure in social and biological networks, Proc. Natl. Acad. Sci., Vol. 9, 2002, pp. 7821–7826
9. M.E.J. Newman and M. Girvan, Finding and evaluating community structure in networks, Phys. Rev. E, Vol. 69, 2004, 026113-026115
10. G. Palla, A.L. Barabasi, T. Vicsek, Quantifying social group evolution, Nature, Vol. 446, No. 7136, 2007, pp. 664–667

11. V. Spirin, L.A. Mirny, Protein complexes and functional modules in molecular networks, Proc. Natl. Acad. Sci., Vol. 100, No. 21, 2003, p. 12123
12. D.M. Wilkinson, B.A. Huberman, A method for finding communities of related genes, Proc. Natl. Acad. Sci., Vol. 101, 2004, pp. 5241–5248
13. R. Guimera, and L.A.N. Amaral, Functional cartography of complex metabolic networks, Nature, Vol. 433, 2005, pp. 895–900
14. J.M. Kleinberg, Authoritative sources in a hyperlinked environment, J. ACM, Vol. 46, No. 5, 1999, pp. 604–632
15. G.W. Flake, S. Lawrence, C.L. Giles, F.M. Coetzee, Self-organization and identification of Web communities, IEEE Comp., Vol. 35, No. 3, 2002, pp. 66–71
16. H. Ino, M. Kudo, A. Nakamura, Partitioning of Web graphs by community topology, Proc. of the 14th International Conference on World Wide Web (WWW'05), 2005, pp. 661–669
17. M. Fiedler, Algebraic connectivity of graphs, Czechoslovakian Math. J., Vol. 23, 1973, pp. 298–305
18. M. Fiedler, A Property of eigenvectors of nonnegative symmetric matrices and its application to graph theory, Czechoslovakian Math. J., Vol. 25, 1975, pp. 619–637
19. A. Pothen, H. Simon, and K.P. Liou, Partitioning sparse matrices with eigenvectors of graphs, SIAM J. Matrix Anal. Appl., Vol. 11, 1990, pp. 430–452
20. Y.C. Wei and C.K. Cheng, Ration cut partitioning for hierarchical designs, IEEE Trans. Computer-Aided Design, Vol. 10, No. 7, 1991, pp. 911–921
21. B.W. Kernighan, and S. Lin, An efficient heuristic procedure for partitioning graphs, Bell System Technical, Vol. 49, 1970, pp. 291–307
22. M.E.J. Newman, Fast algorithm for detecting community structure in networks, Phys. Rev. E, Vol. 69, 2004, pp. 066133
23. Z. Wang, and J. Zhang, In search of the biological significance of modular structures in protein networks, PLOS Comp. Bio., Vol. 3, No. 6, 2007, p. e107
24. J.M. Pujol, J. Bejar, and J. Delgado, Clustering algorithm for determining community structure in large networks, Phys. Rev. E, Vol. 74, 2006, p. 016107
25. M.E.J. Newman, Modularity and community structure in networks, Proc. Natl. Acad. Sci., Vol. 103, No. 23, 2006, pp. 8577–8582
26. J. Reichardt and S. Bornholdt, Detecting fuzzy community structures in complex networks with a potts model, Phys. Rev. Let., Vol. 93, No. 19, 2004, p. 218701
27. F. Wu and B.A. Huberman, Finding communities in linear time: a physics approach, Euro. Phys. J. B, Vol. 38, 2004, pp. 331–338
28. G. Palla, I. Derenyi, I. Farkas, and T. Vicsek, Uncovering the overlapping community structures of complex networks in nature and society, Nature, Vol. 435, No. 7043, 2005, pp. 814–818
29. B. Yang, W.K. Cheung, and J. Liu, Community mining from signed social networks, IEEE Trans. Knowledge and Data Eng., Vol. 19, No. 10, 2007, pp. 1333–1348
30. M.R. Garey, and D.S. Johnson, Computers and Intractability: A Guide to the Theory of NP-Completeness, W. H. Freeman, CA, 1979
31. B. Yang, D. Liu, J. Liu, D. Jin, and H. Ma, Complex network clustering algorithms, J. Software, Vol. 20, No. 1, 2008, pp. 54–66
32. R. Guimera, M. Sales and L.A.N. Amaral, Modularity from fluctuations in random graphs and complex networks, Phys. Rev. E, Vol. 70, 2004, 025101
33. S. Fortunato, M. Barthelemy, Resolution limit in community detection, Proc. of the National Academy of Science, Vol. 104, No. 1, 2007, pp. 36–41
34. J. Reichardt and S. Bornholdt, Detecting fuzzy community structures in complex networks with a potts model, Phys. Rev. Let., Vol. 93, No. 19, 2004, p. 218701
35. F. Radicchi, C. Castellano, F. Cecconi, V. Loreto, and D. Parisi, Defining and Identifying communities in networks, Proc. Natl. Acad. Sci., Vol. 101, No. 9, 2004, pp. 2658–2663
36. J.R. Tyler, D.M. Wilkinson, and B.A. Huberman, Email as spectroscopy: automated discovery of community structure within organizations, Proc. of the 1st International Conference on Communities and Technologies, 2003

37. W.Y. Chen, D. Zhang, E.Y. Chang, Combinational collaborative filtering for personalized community recommendation, Proc. of the 14th ACM SIGKDD International Conference on Knowledge Discovery and Data Ming (KDD'08), 2008

38. A.V. Goldberg and R.E. Tarjan, A new approach to the maximum flow problem, J. ACM, Vol. 35, No. 4, 1988, pp. 921–940

39. A.V. Goldberg, Recent developments in maximum flow algorithms, Proc. of the 6th Scandinavian Workshop on Algorithm Theory, 1998

40. S. Wasserman and K. Faust, Social network analysis, Cambridge University Press, Cambridge, 1994

41. P. Pons, and M. Latapy, Computing communities in large networks using random walks, J. Graph Algorithms Appl., Vol. 10, No. 2, 2006, pp. 191–218

42. K.M. Hall, An r-dimensional quadratic placement algorithm, Management Science, Vol. 17, No. 3, 1970, pp. 219–229

43. L. Donetti and M.A. Munoz, Detecting network communities: a new systematic and efficient algorithm, J. Stat. Mech, Vol. 10, 2004, p. P10012

44. B. Yang, and J. Liu, Discovering global network communities based on local centralities, ACM Trans. on the Web, Vol. 2, No. 1, 2008, Article 9, pp. 1–32

45. W. Imrich and S. Klavzar, Product graphs: structure and recognition, Wiley, New York, 2000

46. B. Yang, and J. Liu, An efficient probabilistic approach to network community mining, Proc. of Joint Rough Set Symposium (JRS'07), 2007, pp. 267–275

47. B. Yang, J. Liu, D. Liu, An autonomy-oriented computing approach to community mining in distributed and dynamic networks, Autonomous Agent Multi-Agent System, Vol. 20, No. 2, 2010, pp. 123–157

48. J. Liu, X. Jin, K.C. Tsui. Autonomy oriented computing. Springer, Berlin, 2004

49. J. Liu, X. Jin, K.C. Tsui. Autonomy oriented computing (AOC): formulating computational systems with autonomous components, IEEE Trans. Systems Man Cybernetics, Part A: Systems and Humans, Vol. 35, No. 6, 2005, pp. 879–902

Part III
Social Network Infrastructures and Communities

Chapter 17
Decentralized Online Social Networks

Anwitaman Datta, Sonja Buchegger, Le-Hung Vu, Thorsten Strufe,
and Krzysztof Rzadca

17.1 Introduction

Adapted from the original definition in [9], we define an online social network
(OSN) as an online platform that (1) provides services for a user to build a public profile and to *explicitly* declare the connection between his or her profile with
those of the other users; (2) enables a user to share information and content with
the chosen users or public; and (3) supports the development and usage of social
applications with which the user can interact and collaborate with both friends and
strangers.

Current online social networks are extended in two main directions towards the
capabilities of the provided services and the decentralization of the supporting infrastructures, as depicted in Fig. 17.1.

Along the first dimension, the features and services provided by online social networks have been extended significantly. Early social networking sites, from a simple
online tool to manage personal and professional contacts, such as in SixDegrees
and Friendster, to an effective tool for sharing several kind of information and contents with a viral spread. Popular OSNs such as Facebook offer users even more
services and applications, as third-parties are allowed to develop and plug their
applications into the site. The OSN has come closer to being a full-fledged development platform for social applications. If a Web browser becomes an operating
system for the next-generation computing devices as predicted by various technological experts, it is very likely that online social network service would be the user
interface of that operating system, i.e., it provides users a portal to manage their
Web-wide personal and social information sources.

Another trend of extending current online social network services is towards
the decentralization of the backend infrastructure. Centralized social networking services are prone to some problems, some of which have even led to the
demise of many early-generation OSN sites such as SixDegrees and Friendster [9].

A. Datta (✉)
School of Computer Engineering, NTU Singapore, Nanyang Avenue, Singapore 639798
e-mail: anwitaman@ntu.edu.sg

B. Furht (ed.), *Handbook of Social Network Technologies and Applications*,   349
DOI 10.1007/978-1-4419-7142-5_17, © Springer Science+Business Media, LLC 2010

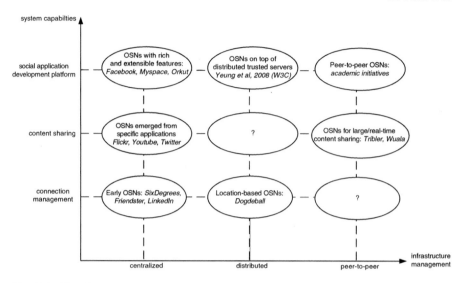

Fig. 17.1 Classification and development trend of online social network services

The problems include both technical and social issues that emerge as a consequence of a centralized management of the services. On the technical side, the centralized management of a social network with rapid growth in user popularity has led to various performance scalability issues, most notably the frequent down-time of the micro-blogging service Twitter and similar slowness and unresponsiveness of Facebook to many users.[1] Along with the increasing popularity of the service comes the increasing cost of management and maintaining the infrastructures to ensure a smooth continuation and reasonable performance of the provided services. On the social side, the unlimited sharing capability of information has also led the social collisions in the sense that the fast growth of the networking sites, without proper privacy preserving schemes, leads to a collapse in social contexts, for instance, users had to face their bosses and acquaintances alongside their close friends and so information is shared to many unwanted contacts. The ruptures of trust between the users and the site providers were also among the key problems leading to the collapse of such early social networking services.

A decentralized online social network is an online social network implemented on a distributed information management platform, such as a network of trusted servers or a peer-to-peer systems. In contrast to centralized OSNs where the vendor bears all the cost in providing the services, a distributed or peer-to-peer OSN offers a cost-effective alternative. In fact, a P2P approach helps lower the cost of the provider drastically, e.g., the case of Skype [29]. Other benefits of a DOSN include better control of user privacy and the enhancement of innovative development [7, 42]. By decentralizing OSNs, the concept of a service provider is changed,

---

[1] http://www.watchmouse.com/en/SPI/2008/performance_social_networking_sites.php

as there is no single provider but a set of peers that take on a share of the tasks needed to run the system. This has several consequences: in terms of privacy (no central data collection, reduced economic incentive for advertisement) and operation, nor any central entity that decides or changes the terms of service whimsically. Moving from a centralized web service to a decentralized system also means that different modes of operations become possible: using one's own storage or cloud storage, delay-tolerant social networks, and local treatment of local content, to name some of them.

DOSNs combine *social* and *decentralized* elements. The path to a system with these properties vary: a DOSN can be achieved by adding one of these two properties to an existing system and thus transforming it, as by taking centralized OSNs and decentralizing them or by adding a social component to current decentralized applications that do not have a social component yet. It can also be achieved by adding both properties at the same time: decentralizing and adding a social component to current centralized applications. We discuss the first of these transformations, i.e., going from a generic OSN to a DOSN in Sect. 17.4 and decentralizing application specific OSNs in Sect. 17.5, and adding social functionalities to distributed systems in Sect. 17.6 on social distributed systems.

17.1.1 Scope of the Chapter

In this chapter, we provide an overview of current (mostly, ongoing) approaches to realize DOSNs. We summarize what each of these projects plan to achieve and what their current status is, as well as what key innovations have been achieved in these mostly nascent initiatives. We discuss several design choices and challenges first in general and then in the context of particular projects.

In addition to entire self-contained DOSN systems, there is a range of individual functionalities that can be combined and integrated in a DOSN. Generic mechanisms for distributed systems, such as cryptography for privacy, key management, storage distribution, numbers and location of replicas, incentives for cooperation and resource-sharing, topology, p2p substrate and administration tasks, trust needed for the program, etc. may be developed either within the context of DOSNs from the start or be adapted from other contexts. We touch upon several of these generic mechanisms in the following sections when needed, but an exhaustive treatment of these enabling techniques is out of the scope of this chapter.

17.2 Challenges for DOSN

In this section, we list some challenges for decentralized social networks. While many of them are technical in nature, some are trade-offs that depend on preference, such as whether privacy should be prioritized or search. Such trade-offs are closely connected to technical questions and are thus included.

Decentralizing the existing functionality of online social networks requires finding ways for distributed storage of data, updates propagation and versioning, a topology and protocol that enables search and addressing, i.e., a mechanism to find friends in the topology, robustness against churn, openness for third-party applications, and means for content revocation (by encryption and/or time), dealing with heterogeneity of user resources, demands, online behavior, etc. We discuss these challenges in more detail below.

Storage. Where should content be stored? Should they be stored exclusively at nodes run by friends, or be encrypted and stored at random nodes, or should the nodes be chosen using some other heuristics such as in a DHT or based on uptime history? As in file-sharing, there will be several answers to this question. The requirement for redundancy to provide availability of data depends to a large extent on the duration and distribution of time peers are online. These activity patterns are also influenced by the geographic distribution of the peers and shifted by time zones. The distribution of interested and authorized peers and the desired probability of availability are to be traded off with storage requirements, especially if the system should allow for storing of media files and not only links to websites where such media files can be found.

Updates. How can we deal with updates, e.g., status updates of friends? In peer collaboration systems, updates, e.g., of a workplace, are sent to a small group of peers via a decentralized synchronization mechanism. In P2P social networks, with distributed storage and replication – and a potential need for scalability, the requirements change. P2P publish/subscribe mechanisms are a possibility, but their security in terms of access control will have to be developed further. Unlike a traditional peer-to-peer environment, where many peers are involved, each of the sub-networks will be much smaller (though larger than typical collaborative groups), making it relatively simpler to realize quorum systems and deal with updates.

Topology. Should nodes be connected according to their social connection? This would cluster friends in the overlay network, which would facilitate updates. As a downside, given the possibility of a relatively small set of friends, this would limit the availability and robustness of data access. How can we build a decentralized, p2p topology suitable for social networks? In pure file-sharing networks, the topology does not depend on whether the peers know each other and nodes exchange content with any other nodes in the network. At the other end of the spectrum, existing examples of decentralized social networks (in the widest sense) are mostly platforms for collaboration or media sharing and they tend to consist of collaborative groups that are relatively closed circles, e.g., using a "ring of trust" or darknets. In contrast, online social networking services have overlapping circles.

Search, Addressing. Related to the topic of updates above, how can users find their friends from the real social network in the P2P virtualization thereof, and conversely, how can they discover new friends by virtue of common interests. Over multiple sessions, peers may change their physical address. In a typical file sharing network, this is not an issue. One just needs to find some peer with the content it is looking for.

However friends and trust links of a social network are essential, and so it is crucial to both be able to find back friends even if they have changed their physical address, and also authenticate the identity. Traditionally, peer identity is tied with an IP address [36] which clearly is not sufficient. However, handling peer identity in a self-contained manner in a P2P system is also feasible [2] (also partially in Skype [39]). It may also be difficult to maintain a complete ring like in traditional structured overlays as an index structure, if the network is based on only social links. Recent advances in realizing distributed indexing with a ringless overlay [20] potentially holds the key to this issue. These mechanisms composed together potentially can help maintain social network links under churn. Another search issue is – how can users find out about information available concerning their interests? In social networks, tagging or folksonomies is the basic mechanism to annotate content. Recently, there have also been advances made in enabling decentralized tagging [25], which paves another step towards realizing social networks on top of a P2P infrastructure. Note that there is a trade-off between privacy protection and search capabilities.

Openness to New Applications. One of the most alluring features of current online social networks is that they are open to third-party applications, which enables a constant change of what a social networking service provides to the users. There is a core functionality for maintaining social ties, such as profile information, connection to friends, status updates, internal messaging, posting on each other's sites, events notification. In addition, third-party applications provide more and unpredictable ways of contacting users, finding out about other users' interests, forming groups and group identities, etc. This openness to extensions potentially provides great benefits for the users. The price for these benefits is the risk that comes with opening the service to untrusted third parties, extending the privacy problem from the single service provider to all application providers. In a decentralized environment, if some users choose to enable a third-party application, their choice should not affect other users or even users connected directly to them. How to draw this boundary is an open and challenging question.

Security. Keeping control over their data with the user implies the need for security support, so the classical requirements for security (confidentiality, access control, integrity, authentication, non-repudiation) apply, albeit modified for the context of decentralized social networks. The main questions for user control are in the domain of access control, e.g., how can we ensure that only authorized friends can access content. For distributed storage with other peers that the user not necessarily wants to access data, the content has to be encrypted, as done for example for file backup [1] or anonymous peer-to-peer file-sharing [15, 16]. To manage access to encrypted data, key distribution and maintenance have to be handled such that the social network group can access data but be flexible enough to handle churn in terms of going offline and coming back, additions and removal to the user's social network. Group membership research has dealt with questions of key management and renewal and how to give access to new members of a group by issuing new keys in rounds [41]. Likewise darknets [19] also share a key within the group. Such existing mechanisms are however grossly inadequate to meet the finer granularity of access control needs for social network features.

Even in the most simple scenario, where all members are allowed full access, if one wishes to realize control on membership itself, then sharing a secret key is not enough. Any member who already has the shared key can pass it on to new members. Therefore, keys and identities need to be combined for access control, but without access to a file system, mechanisms like access control lists are not feasible. In many online networks (for example Yahoo! Groups[2]), a smaller subset of members own and moderate the membership of a group. Thus even a minor variation of the basic groups like darknets, to realize a group where all members still have equal access to content, but only a subset of members control the membership itself, is non-trivial in a decentralized setting.

There is on top of that the need for a finer granularity of access control, determining who can read, write or modify and delete each shared object, and how to enforce such access control in a decentralized setting, while still guaranteeing non-repudiation as well as preventing impersonation and replay. Achieving such finer granularity of access control in a decentralized manner is, we believe one of the hardest security challenges, and the biggest hurdle in realizing a P2P infrastructure for social networking applications.

Other security issues like prevention of DDoS and Sybil attacks, enforcing co-operation and preventing free-riding or content pollution, and establishing trust are also of course long-standing issues in the community, but since they have been in the spotlight for years now, we do not highlight these here. That of course does not mean that these are trivial, or even practically solved. However, in the social network context, some of these issues may actually get simpler to deal with [46].

For peer identities, one can take advantage of opportunistic networks and peer authentication by in-person contact, when friends meet in real life and exchange keys over their phones. For bootstrapping authentication, a central authority (trusted third party) seems hard to avoid.

Robustness. Against misbehavior: In a centralized system, one can turn to the provider in case of user misbehavior, there is usually a process defined for dealing with such complaints. In a decentralized system, there is no authority that can ban users for misbehavior or remove content. Robustness against free-riding: Without the monetary incentive offered by advertising, other incentives have to come in to make users shoulder the responsibilities for keeping up the infrastructure, providing storage and ensuring availability by staying online. Robustness and Trust: Once access to content is granted, it is difficult to revoke that right. When a user allows a friend to see a message, the friend can store the message and keep access to it even after a change of key. Trust has to be at least equal to assigned access rights, due to this difficulty.

Limited Peers. To take advantage of the decentralized nature of social networks, a mapping of physical social network to virtual and vice versa enables extensions to offering access via web browsers by phone applications and direct exchange of data

---

[2] http://groups.yahoo.com/

in physical proximity. A major impedance to widespread adoption of a decentralized system for OSNs will be users' reluctance to install yet another software. Consequently, it will be essential to allow for two classes of users, a core network of users who run the decentralized infrastructure software as well as a web service front-end, and the other, who are essentially clients accessing this service. This of course throws open Pandora's box with lots of questions, including technological feasibility as well as game theoretic issues like incentives and fairness in such a two tier system. Another immediate benefit however of allowing such two-tier system is that users can then participate in the social network with resource constrained (e.g., mobile) devices, which they may use as an auxiliary, even when they contribute resources to the core of the system with their primary device.

Locality. Using direct exchange between devices, real-life social networks can be used to support the decentralized social networking application. In addition to such opportunistic networks between users, a distributed architecture also enables us to take advantage of geographic proximity and its correlation with local interests. For example, most access routers for home Internet access now come with USB slots where storage can be added or they already have unused storage on the device itself. These routers are typically always on and thus would provide some stability for availability of data of local interest. This local interest can arise from the locality of events but also from the locality of typical real-life social networks of friends and neighbors. How to best harness this locality remains to be seen.

17.2.1 Differences to Other Decentralized or P2P Applications

While there are properties common to peer-to-peer approaches that we can take advantage of for decentralized social networks, in this section we focus on what makes the requirements for social networks different from other peer-to-peer services in order to point out where new solutions are needed.

Peer-to-peer storage has been done successfully for file-sharing. These results can, however not be directly applied to social networks: In P2P file-sharing, any copy of a music, video, media file, potentially present in high numbers, will do. These copies are usually not updated, although new versions or different content get added to the system. In social networks, information, such as the current status of a person, is updated often and it makes a difference which version gets downloaded, the value of outdated information is much less than that of timely information that enables users to react to content changes.

In most file-sharing systems, files are not encrypted. When they are [15, 16], mostly for reasons of plausible deniability, the keys to the files can be obtained. For peer-to-peer social networks privacy is even more important as it concerns personal information, so storing content unencrypted at other peers whom the user does not want to access personal information is not an option. Files should only be readable by peers that are specifically allowed to access them.

This access control has been also required for peer-to-peer collaborative work support (CSCW), albeit for smaller groups than the typical user base of online social networks. Work colleagues are added or removed from a working group at a lower rate than expected churn for social networks. For DOSN we need a way of dealing with dynamic relations, that is churn both in terms of online/offline behavior and of adding/removing friends and corresponding access rights.

This dynamic behavior coupled with a different distribution of interest add requirements to availability. In file-sharing, a file is potentially of interest to a large population of users, a Zipf-law distribution of file popularity and thus download availability has been observed. For social networks, this distribution is expected to be different and often limited to a number of friends that is not directly correlated with the network size. The information about a person is of interest to their social network, not typically the general public, there are different economies of scale and scope at play.

Who is interested and authorized to access in social networks also differs from peer-to-peer backup/storage systems, where there is typically one owner of data, so granting access rights and key management is much simplified. Peer-to-peer storage for file backup has been addressed by numerous systems such as Farsite [1] for individuals but these do not address the issues arising from social networks, nor utilize the opportunities of ingrained mutual trust.

For social networks, we need a large-scale peer-to-peer network with fine-grained access control for reading and writing, with changing files (versions), small number of interested peers compared to overall population, and enable a list of features including file-sharing, chat, news-feeds, public and private asynchronous messaging, search, notifications. This means that there are components we can take from other peer-to-peer services, but need to modify and extend them as described above.

17.3   The Case for Decentralizing OSNs

Keeping user data centralized or even just distributed but connected allows the service providers of online social networks, third-party application providers and, in cases where there is no deliberate protection, indeed anyone to crawl the network and find out about content or at least about connectivity and access patterns. The information gathered can then be used for data mining, direct advertising, censorship, or other purposes. Moreover, a centralized depository or fully connected network is more susceptible to virus or malware spreading than mostly local social networks that can be partitioned.

An immediate advantage of a DOSN is rather straightforward: it is not centralized, not owned by a single entity. The central storage of user information and ownership by a company, along with commercial exploitation of this information e.g., for ad revenue, raises privacy concerns that could be better addressed by a decentralized approach, with encryption and appropriate key management.

Of course at this juncture it is legitimate to ask, why use a decentralized infrastructure for supporting social networks, when the good old client-server architecture works fine. One can give the traditional arguments that P2P scales well, since a growing user base naturally brings in more infrastructural resources. This definitely can be a good incentive for people with good ideas but little money to support and expand overnight if their popularity increases. Also, if popularity declines over time, there is less exposure. However, given the success of numerous upstart companies, which have managed to scale well to not just millions but even hundreds of millions of users, the traditional scalability argument alone does not justify the hassles of a decentralized infrastructure.

Privacy has become a major concern. Particularly privacy and protection from massive data-mining and "big-brotherly" treatment of the users by the social networking service providers. This is expected eventually to lead to a significant population of users, who while they would like to enjoy the benefits and fun of social networks, may also want to restrict access to their personal data not only from fellow users who happen to be strangers, but also from any provider or indeed the general public. This disaffected population is expected to be the early adopters of decentralized social networks with encryption.

Besides privacy and other related security concerns, a decentralized approach also enables content creators to execute greater control over their content, as well as avoid censorship either by the website owner, or censorship of the hosting website by a third party.

While some sites follow up with corrective measures because of users' outcry, e.g., [6], and one may also argue about legislative solutions to protect users' privacy, there is no guarantee that in the future the users' data will not be misused. The objective decentralized privacy-preserving OSNs is thus to aim for a system which makes it technologically harder (ideally, impossible) to violate the users' privacy and large scale data mining, even while the users continue to enjoy the advantages of social networking.

Given the reality of privacy breaches by centralized online social network providers, as exemplified by Facebook's beacon application [35] among others [23], there is a motivation for giving the control over data back to the users and not have one entity access to all personal data of the participants in the social network. With a peer-to-peer approach, decentralization is a given, and combined with appropriate encryption users can determine whom they allow access to their data.

Essentially, a decentralized approach seems promising to be the right technology to achieve both privacy and freedom of speech. For this reason, user-provided content and participatory media creation suit themselves better to a peer-to-peer rather than a client-server model. Another incentive for users to embrace such a model is to evade any constraints put by the service provider in the present or future (e.g., for the amount of storage space, or subscription fees, or service shut down).

Realizing an application layer Internet on top of diverse networking infrastructure, including the Internet, but also mobile – cellular as well as ad-hoc, and supporting Web 2.0 applications on top of such an application layer Internet, can also help making them ubiquitous.

By supporting the direct exchange of information between devices, be it between users that meet or between adjacent nodes of a city mesh network, a peer-to-peer infrastructure can take advantage of real social networks and geographic proximity. In contrast to a centralized web server, local connectivity already facilitates social networking without Internet access.

While access control by encryption for user data privacy would be possible in a centralized system, it does not go as far as a peer-to-peer approach in ensuring user control. First, whoever would be willing to provide the centralized service and infrastructure would also be able to cease to provide the service or change its terms. Second, due to the lack of data mining and advertising possibilities, there would be fewer incentives and means to provide a good service and all the servers necessary for a centralized solution. Third, a centralized service requires more trust by the users than a distributed system that limits the risk of privacy breaches by not providing a central repository of user data, so that only a small fraction of protected data may be exposed at any time, should the encryption be broken.

In addition to addressing the privacy aspects in general, there is an opportunity to support a non-commercialized self-organized service. Web-based centralized online social networks today bring together the social sphere of family and friends with the commercial sphere. This combination enables targeted advertising thanks to profile information and data mining and thus based on a person's revealed preferences and extends it to a more precise targeting by taking into account social information. We envision a peer-to-peer social network that separates these spheres and enables users to maintain their social network without commercial prompting by advertisement.

User control of data, as provided by a peer-to-peer and secured social network, has consequences beyond privacy and freedom from advertisement. One such consequence is that users can also exercise control over the content they create in terms of intellectual property. User control in this sense means control over who can access their content and what they are allowed to do with that content, e.g., access control can be combined by licensing models of the user's choice (e.g., creative commons licenses) allowing for flexible content rights, as opposed to the current practice of copyright for the online social network providers. Likewise, users also can enjoy freedom of speech, without fearing censorship or other obstacles (like a subscription fee), which a central service provider can impose at its whim.

Another aspect of control is how the social network can be accessed. Moving down the layers from application to network to physical access, there is another instance of peer-to-peer paradigm suitability that has been overlooked: decentralized access via various means (such as direct exchange, as in opportunistic networks) for ubiquitous social networks as opposed to those limited to the web.

Centralized web-based social networks do not match the inherent peer-to-peer nature of both social networks themselves and of participatory media creation. User-provided content and participatory media creation suit themselves better to a community-driven peer-to-peer rather than a client-server model. By mapping a peer-to-peer application to a peer-to-peer infrastructure, direct connections can be exploited such that locality can be taken into account. Peers can carry information for each other in a delay-tolerant fashion and use local access points for local information. We thus have a matching of the distributed nature of human social networks with a distributed service, and we can also match the service to a local environment and make it a ubiquitous service. By supporting the direct exchange of information between devices, be it between users that meet or between adjacent nodes of a city mesh network, a peer-to-peer infrastructure can take advantage of real social networks and geographic proximity. In contrast to a centralized web server, local connectivity already facilitates social networking without Internet access.

17.4 General Purpose DOSNs

To give the readers a better overview of existing approaches towards the decentralization of online social network services, we propose a reference architecture of a general-purpose DOSN platform is given in Fig. 17.2. The reference architecture consists of six layers and provides an architectural abstraction of variety of current related approaches to decentralized social networking in the research literature. The lower layer of this architecture is the physical communication network, which can be the Internet or a (mobile) ad hoc network (in case we consider a mobile online social network). The distributed or P2P overlay management provides core functionalities to manage resources in the supporting infrastructure of the system, which can be a distributed network of trusted servers or a P2P overlay. Specifically, this layer provides higher layers the capabilities of looking up resources, routing messages, and retrieving information reliably and effectively among nodes in the overlay.

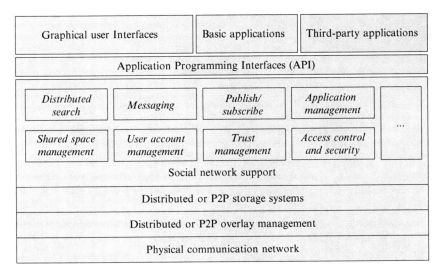

Fig. 17.2 The general architecture of a distributed online social network

On top of this overlay is the decentralized data management layer, which implements functionalities of a distributed or peer-to-peer information system to query, insert, and update various persistent objects to the systems.

The social networking layer implements all basic functionalities and features that are provided by contemporary centralized social networking services. Among these functionalities the most important ones are given in Fig. 17.2, namely the capability to search the system (Distributed search) for relevant information, the management of users and shared space (User account and share space management), the management of security and access control issues (Trust management, Access control and security), the coordination and management of social applications developed by third parties (Application management).

It is expected that the social networking layer exposes and implements an application programming interface (API) to support the development of new applications by freelance developers and other third-parties, as well as to enable the customization of the social network service to suit various preferences of the user. To enable better interoperability with available social network services, e.g., better portability of applications across OSN providers, this API should conform to existing API standards, e.g., OpenSocial.[3]

The top layer of the architecture includes the user interface to the system and various applications built on top of the development platform provided by the DOSN. The DOSN user is expected to provide the user the necessary transparency to use the DOSN as any other centralized OSN. Applications can be either implemented by the DOSN provider or developed by third-parties, and can be installed or removed from the system according to user's preferences.

17.4.1 Proposed DOSN Approaches

This section introduces and explains several existing approaches to implement general-purpose decentralized online social networks. They range from academic proposals without any implementation to first systems that exist as demonstrators or are even in the course of public testing, as of the time of this writing.

Safebook Safebook [13], an approach to provide a decentralized general purpose OSN, follows the main objective of protecting its users' privacy.

It considers adverse or erroneous behavior of a centralized service provider, possible adversaries which are misusing the functions of the social networking service, as well as external adversaries that could eavesdrop or modify data on the networking layer.

The main goals of offering the full set of services that centralized general purpose SNS usually implement, and of assuring the three security objectives of privacy, integrity, and availability, it is based on two simple assumptions: that decentralization and cooperation between friends will facilitate the implementation of a secure,

---

[3] www.opensocial.org

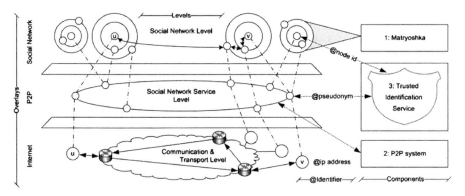

Fig. 17.3 Main design components of safebook

and privacy preserving OSN. Considering the centralized storage to be a potential risk, safebook chooses a distributed implementation architecture. The social links between friends, family members, and acquaintances, which are represented as the core intrinsic knowledge of an OSN, are leveraged for multiple purposes. Requests from a user and for a user's profile are anonymized hop-by-hop on recursive routing paths traversing links of the OSN. Additionally, since friends are assumed to cooperate, they are leveraged to increase the availability of profiles.

Safebook consists of three major different components, the TIS, matryoshkas, and a peer-to-peer location substrate (see Fig. 17.3).

All users have to acquire certificates from a *Trusted Identity Service (TIS)* upon joining the OSN, which they are able to do by invitation, only. The TIS is a stateless, offline service. It does not store any information, but simply implements a cryptographic function to issue keys, identifiers, and certificates based on the identity of the requesting user. It currently is run at the institutions participating in the Safebook development (Institut Eurécom and TU Darmstadt), but may be further distributed to other trusted third parties. The TIS represents a powerful entity in safebook, yet, it does not cause any threats, since it is only involved in the identification and certification of users, but does neither store nor retrieves or accesses any data of the users.

Safebook discerns between identified participation in the OSN, and anonymous participation to provide services to other users. In order to protect the identified participation, safebook introduces *matryoshkas*, which are specialized overlays encompassing each user. All contacts of a user represent the innermost shell of a user's matryoshka. Each user selected for a matryoshka in turn selects one of his contacts to be part of the next matryoshka shell, unless a predefined number of shells is reached. Current evaluation indicates that three to four shells represent a good trade-off between the resilience towards statistical identification attacks against the core, vs. the efficiency and performance of the system. The matryoshkas are used to anonymize requests, to hide the existence of the user in the center, and to increase the availability of the user's profile, by replicating it among the devices the matryoshka consists of.

For the purpose of locating other users' matryoshkas, safebook implements a peer-to-peer substrate. Considering response times of requests to be a main requirement, the developers have adapted Kademlia [33], an existing peer-to-peer system known to achieve fast lookup. Safebook implements the original routing structure and distance metric as Kademlia, simply switching for iterative to recursive routing and stochastically including access through contacts to protect the identity of the requesting user. The identifier used for the peer-to-peer substrate additionally is derived from the certificates, and hence determined by the TIS, which prevents denial of service attacks on the peer-to-peer overlay.

Safebook initially has been analyzed in formal models and large scale simulations. A first functional prototype to date is tested by the developers, which predict a first version for the public to be available by the end of 2010.

FOAF Yeung et al. [30] presents another practical approach to decentralize management of current social networks. The framework enables users to export their FOAF[4] profiles, store them on dedicated trusted servers. Users query and manage these profiles through open Web-based protocols such as WebDAV[5] or SPARQL/Update.[6] A clear advantage of this approach is its compatibility to current social networking platforms and its entirely Web-based nature. The use of a set of trusted servers for storing user's data, however, raises some other security issues that necessitates further considerations. We believe this approach has a high potential of being adopted, as it is supported by the W3C consortiums.

Another related work is Social VPNs [18]. Users may query different social networks to discover friends to build a Virtual Private Network (VPN) with them. The prototype integrates with Facebook, use the IP2IP virtual networks and IPsec security infrastructure to build a VPN platform for a number of interactive applications such as instant messaging, file sharing, etc.

NEPOMUK[7] is an on-going EU project with close relation to DOSN. The goal of NEPOMUK is to develop a middleware for sharing users' desktops with friends for online collaborations and sharing of knowledge by exploiting Semantic Web technologies.

LifeSocial Considering the immense increase of users that online social networks have experienced in the recent past, and which are expected for the future, too, LifeSocial [24] primarily aims at keeping social networking services scalable by distributing the load to their users' resources.

The main functional components of OSNs are data storage and interaction. Both are classic domains of peer-to-peer systems, and have very successfully been implemented as file sharing[8] and instant messaging (jabber), or telephony

---

[4] http://www.foaf-project.org/

[5] http://www.webdav.org/

[6] http://jena.hpl.hp.com/~afs/SPARQL-Update.html

[7] http://www.nepomuk.org

[8] Gnutella [12], Kazaa [27], and Bittorrent [14] are only some of the more prominent examples.

(skype) applications. With current social network providers being central entities, who have to provide the entire resources for storing the data uploaded to the OSN and for making it accessible, they are soon to become a bottle neck when the number of users increases further. LifeSocial hence proposes to distribute the service provision in a peer-to-peer fashion in order to mitigate the resource problem and to balance the service load to the resources at the users' devices.

LifeSocial is designed with the main premise to leverage on existing and proven components and to create a modular plugin-architecture to assure extensibility. It consequently is assembled using FreePastry,[9] a structured peer-to-peer overlay for data storage, and PAST[10] to achieve reliable replication of the data. LifeSocial implements its own access control scheme on top of these components. Some plug-ins are mandatory to implement a general purpose OSN: The whole system demands plugins for profile management, friend management, group management and photo albums as a minimum set. Additional plugins, such as a whiteboard and a chat system have been proposed.

The different components of LifeSocial, and the overall system, have been evaluated in simulation studies. It additionally is one of the few systems of which a prototype exists at the time of this writing (see Fig. 17.4). The prototype consists of all mandatory plugins, as well as basic white-board and chat functions. It has been presented in different conferences and exhibitions and the system currently is tested between the group of its developers.

PeerSoN   PeerSoN[11] [7, 10] aims at keeping the features of OSNs but overcoming two limitations: privacy issues and the requirement of Internet connectivity for all transactions. To address the privacy problem, it uses encryption and access control coupled with a peer-to-peer approach to replace the centralized authority of classical OSNs. These two measures prevent privacy violation attempts by users, providers, or advertisers. Extending the decentralized approach, PeerSoN also enables direct exchange of data between devices to allow for opportunistic, delay-tolerant networking. This includes making use of ubiquitous storage to enable local services.

The main properties of PeerSoN are encryption, decentralization, and direct data exchange. In a nutshell, encryption provides privacy for the users, and decentralization based on the use of a P2P infrastructure provides independence from OSN providers. Decentralization makes it easier to integrate direct data exchange between users' devices into the system. Direct exchange allows users to use the system without constant Internet connectivity, leveraging real-life social networking and locality.

The current PeerSoN implementation replicates the following features of OSNs. In the category of social links, users (peers) can become friends and thus establish a social link between each other. Digital personal spaces are provided in that users can maintain their own profile and a wall, a space for items posted by themselves

---

[9] http://www.freepastry.org/

[10] http://www.freepastry.org/PAST/default.htm

[11] http://www.peerson.net

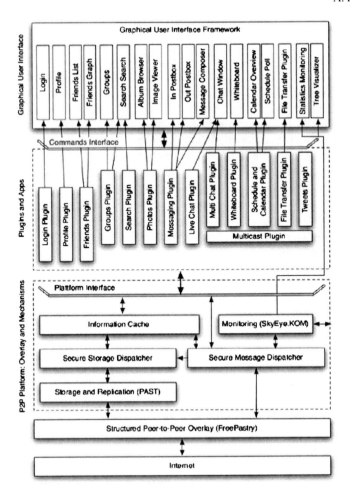

Fig. 17.4 LifeSocial plugin architecture

or their friends. Communications between users are directly peer-to-peer when both are online, and the implementation supports asynchronous messaging when this is not the case.

PeerSoN uses a DHT as a lookup system and then lets peers connect directly; all data is encrypted and keys for accessing an object are encrypted for the exclusive use of authorized users and stored in a separate file associated with a particular object, such as a user's profile. The prototype implementation has been tested on PlanetLab and uses OpenDHT for the lookup service. Using OpenDHT facilitated the PeerSoN deployment on PlanetLab but will be replaced for the next iteration of the implementation.

Likir Likir [4] is a Kademlia-based DHT that is aimed to protect the overlay against attacks common to these systems, by embedding a strong identity notion at

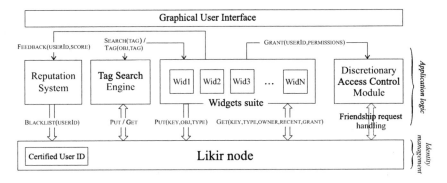

Fig. 17.5 Likir architecture

overlay level. This increases the reliability of the overlay and offers many identity-based services that well suit social applications [5]. Likir targets at the main goals of avoiding a centralized storage of personal information, offering reliability, and integrating the identities of users deep into the system.

The main motivation of Likir is to avoid a central data repository, for both the reason to avoid a single point of failure and aggregation of user data. The rationale is to use a reliable, identity-based DHT layer, to provide the main services. The applications built on top of this substrate consequently are relieved from identity management, as it is already provided by the underlying DHT (see Fig. 17.5). Likir is designed to achieve full confidentiality of data as well as anonymity of the users. It additionally provides access control in a granularity to applications: "authorized disclosure" ensures that malicious applications installed at some individual's device is unable to access data disclosed to other applications.

Likir builds its core properties on introducing cryptography in a plain DHT-based approach. All nodes are furnished with an identifier in the form of an OpenId by a certification service. Subsequent communication events consequently are encrypted and authenticated by both communicating parties. A supplemental access control scheme is integrated that requires all service providing nodes to check grants that are appended to each request before returning any data.

In addition to an analytical study on the bandwidth and computational overhead consumed by Likir, the authors have run large scale emulations on PlanetLab. A prototype of the Likir middleware has been published and is available for download, including a simple chat application for the purpose of demonstrations.

17.5   Specialized Application Centric DOSNs

Besides decentralized counterparts of general purpose online social networking applications as described above, there are also initiatives to realize decentralized counterparts of niche applications such as video sharing, social bookmarks and libraries, and micro-blogging to name a few.

17.5.1 Social-Based P2P File Sharing

Among works in this category, the most well-developed initiative is Tribler [37], which is basically a P2P content sharing system that leverages the existing social relationships and taste similarities among its users for fast discovery and recommendation of digital contents.

Initiated from the EU project P2P-Next[12] whose goal is to provide end-to-end professional streaming content based on P2P technologies and low-cost commodity hardware devices, i.e., user computers, Tribler has been extensively developed and provides a rich set of functionalities for its users, e.g., discovery and recommendation of friends with similar preferences, as well as providing fast and low overhead delivering video-on-demand such as television programs. The system, implemented as an social-based extension of the BitTorrent engine, is freely available[13] and has been evaluated at small and medium scales. The most recently public trial of Tribler, reported in [31] in mid July 2008, which lasted in 9 days, consists a global deployment of nearly 5,000 unique peers for live streaming a free video. The system has shown to yield a relative good performance, e.g., the pre-buffering time before playing back the video is from 3 to 10 times shorter than that of the two existing deployed P2P live stream systems reported in [45, 48].

To facilitate the social group formation between users, Tribler uses a de-anonymized approach to manage the peer identities. During the registration phase, each participating user is given by email a secure, unique, permanent identifier (*PermID*). PermIDs are obtained via a public key generation scheme with challenge-response mechanism to prevent spoofing. Existing contacts of a user (a peer with a PermID) can also be imported from other social networks such as MSN and GMail. For boostrapping the networks, any newly joined peer can contact one in a list of pre-known superpeers, from which to obtain a list of other peers already available in the systems. The boostrapping of the networks is done via an epidemic protocol [44].

A peer in Tribler uses many types of caches to store locally any contextual information relevant to its interests and tasted. These so-called Megacaches (each less than 10 MB) of a peer may store various information related to its friend lists, the altruism levels, the preferences of its friends, and meta-data of the files and contents posted in the network. With existing BitTorrent networks, the number of files injected per day is sufficiently small such that the caches of file meta-data can be fully replicated among all peers. Thus there is no need to perform network-wide searching for interested content, but only the browsing of the local meta-data cache.

Peers in Tribler are clustered into many groups, each of which contains those peers with similar preferences and interests, or taste buddies group. The interest commonality between two peers are given by the similarity in their preferences of in the same or related content. Fore example, each peer's preference can

---

[12] http://www.p2p-next.org

[13] http://tribler.org/

be defined as its zapping behavior profile, which is the percentage of length the online television program actually watched by the peer, compared to the length of the complete program on air. The formation of such taste buddies group is done via the epidemic protocol BuddyCast [44]. The BuddyCast protocol requires a peer to periodical connect to either an existing friend (the exploitation phase) or a randomly peer (the exploration) and exchange a BuddyCast message with the selected peer. The BuddyCast message usually consists of the number of taste buddies with top-10 preference lists, e.g., the type of TV programs the peer is interested in, a number of random peers, and the top-50 preference of the sending peer. The exploration-to-exploitation ratio can be adapated to limit the randomness of the exploration. To ensure that a BuddyCast message has a high probability to be replied, the random peer in an exploration phase is selected based on its freshness to increase the chance it is still online, i.e., newly joined peers are more likely to be selected.

The exchange of a BuddyCast message enables the two contacting peers to discovery whether they have similar preferences. Overtime the social network of peers would also be clustered into different groups of users with related interests. Thus the BuddyCast protocol in fact implements a decentralized collaborative filtering technique to recommend programs and potential friends of interests to a user. This will also facilitate the content delivery to end-users, since the downloading of contents relies on the collaboration among users in such social groups.

The download of contents from the system is according to a collaborative downloading protocol 2Fast [21], in which a peer asking its friends to help it in downloading. The assumption is that peers would behave altruistically in favor of their friends, thus a peer will be willing to help uploading the content which it is not interested int. Peers that are not in a social group would follow an uncooperative downloading scheme, which is the default Tit-for-Tat strategy in BitTorrent.

The 2Fast protocol has been deployed for testing in a real environment and gives promising results for small-scale experiments. With around 1,900 peers, 6% seeds to download a 1.2 GB file, the download time decreased by a factor from 2 to almost 6 for different types of connections from the downloading peers. Larger scale experiments have not been carried out with more realistic workloads from existing BitTorrent networks or available video streaming systems, however to evaluate the overall system performance more thoroughly.

Recently, a light weight message exchange protocol using a reputation metric, BarterCast [34], has also been proposed to prevent the free-riding problem in the system. Consider the social networks of peers as a graph and define the capacity of an edge from a peer u to a peer v as the total number of bytes (of data content) u has uploaded to v in the past. The subject reputation $R_i(j)$ of a peer j, as evaluated by a peer j is proportional to the difference in the max-flow of bytes from i to j with the max-flow of bytes in the opposite direction. Therefore, this $R_i(j)$ represents the service that j has provided to other peers in the system from the viewpoint of i. A peer is classified by another peer as a sharer, neutral, or free-rider peer depending on whether its subjective reputation falls below a certain threshold. Given the reputation, a peer may rank or ban another peer from downloading certain pieces of content from it, and thus free-riding incentives are reduced or eliminated.

17.5.2 Shared Bookmarks and Collaborative Search

Diki[14] is a social bookmarking service that allows users to encrypt and share their bookmarks with trusted friends via the Extensible Messaging and Presence Protocol (XMPP), a real-time Web-based communication protocol for Internet services.[15] User privacy is preserved via three design principles: to enable data exchange only between trusted friends, not storing any data centrally, and any stored data is encrypted.

User data is encrypted using the PGP private key encryption scheme, stored locally, and exchanged to trusted friends using the XMPP protocol. A user may establish his own XMPP server or use existing ones to communicate with the others.

Since the XMPP servers only handle the exchange of encrypted data between users, without knowing the content of the exchanges, the system ensures that the information, e.g., URLs a user shares with his or her friends is kept secret. In short, Diki provides a decentralized, privacy-preserving version of the highly popular social bookmarking service Delicious.[16]

Using such an XMPP protocol, it is completely possible to implement the decentralized, privacy-preserving, and secured versions of other existing social applications such as Twitter.

Shared bookmarks and other meta-information can in turn be used for implicit or explicit collaborative online search. Some recent initiatives such as Gossple[17] and COBS[18] pursue such an approach of leveraging peer-to-peer/hybrid infrastructure based social networks and interest communities to facilitate collaborative search.

17.5.3 Micro-Blogging

FETHR[42] is a light-weight protocol enabling users to use any existing microblogging service to communicate with other users on top of HTTP with near real-time guarantee. Users who follow the FETHR protocol can subscribe to each other's updates (tweaks) and receive these tweaks in real-time. Published entries are signed digitally by the publisher and linked together in a chain in reverse chronological order. Each entry in the list contains the hash of the previous entry for detecting any tampering in the content of the tweak. A FETHR publisher also includes the hashes of prior tweaks from his o her friends, thus integrating the timelines of many

---

[14] http://www.pace-project.org/

[15] http://xmpp.org

[16] http://delicious.com/

[17] www.gossple.fr/

[18] http://code.google.com/p/socialcobs/

participants into a directed acyclic graph of tweaks spanning the whole network. This provides a provable order of events happening, as well as enabling the reconstruction of conversation threads.

According to the FETHR protocol, the publishers (the micro-blogger) push the entire (assumedly small) contents of the messages (tweaks) to the subscribers. This is different from Twitter: in Twitter the followers are simply notified of the new tweaks, whose contents are still stored on the servers.

The current implemented prototype, BirdFeeder,[19] can be considered as a distributed alternative to the existing so-called microblogging platform Twitter.[20] It aims to target the weaknesses of Twitter, whose centralized architecture is shown to be the main cause to its performance bottleneck and single point of failure.

FETHR is designed as an entirely new protocol to be applied on existing microblogging services, thus its success much dependent on the widely adoption of the service provider communities. Also, the implemented prototype is still in early phase, and there is little study and analysis on the security and effciency of FETHR.

17.6 Social Distributed Systems

Besides the initiatives to emulate specifically online social networks, as described in the previous section, there is also a growing trend to develop *social distributed systems* (SocDS) which provide equivalent functionalities to non-social (and sometimes, also centralized) systems. Such initiatives try to leverage and translate the social trust into properties leading to system reliability. This trend of coupling real life social networks with distributed systems is gaining traction in recent times. For example, distributed hash tables realized using exclusively social links can provide robustness against Sybil attack. Likewise, P2P storage systems relying on social trust to do data backup provide resilience against free-riding address limitations of computational trust models and stand-alone algorithmic solutions. Such social distributed systems can be used for carrying out any task the non-social counterparts are typically used for, but additionally, and naturally, SocDS are ideal to be used as substrates and building blocks for distributed/decentralized online social networks.

Essentially, one can argue that with the use of SocDS, we have a two way symbiotic design. Distributed/peer-to-peer infrastructure for OSNs provide desirable properties and addressing the shortcomings and constraints of traditional OSNs which use centralized resources provided by OSN service providers. On the other hand leveraging on social networks to design robust distributed systems provide new systems design opportunities which are beyond the scope of traditional algorithmic

---

[19] http://brdfdr.com/

[20] http://twitter.com/

solutions. Such distributed systems can be used for different applications, but are of-course naturally suitable to form the underlying substrates for decentralized online social networks.

We next discuss social distributed systems design for some basic building blocks such as indexing and routing using distributed hash tables (DHTs) and p2p storage & back-up systems. For each of these building blocks, there are non-social counterparts which have been studied in traditional systems research, which we will point out whenever necessary. The benefits (as well as possible drawbacks) of the "social" counterparts will also be briefly explained.

17.6.1 Social DHT: SocialCircle

Structured overlays, e.g., Distributed Hash Tables (DHTs) provide essential indexing and resource discovering in distributed information systems. Typically, structured overlays are based on enhanced rings, meshes, hypercubes, etc., leveraging on the topological properties of such geometric structures. The ring topology is arguably the simplest and most popular structure used in various overlays. In a ring based overlay network like Chord [40] nodes are assigned to distinct points over a circular key-space, and the ring invariant is said to hold if each node correctly knows the currently online node which succeeds it (and the one which precedes it) in the ring. The ring is both a blessing and a curse.

On the one hand, an intact ring is sufficient to guarantee correct routing. Hence, historically, all existing structured overlays over circular key space have considered it necessary de facto. Previous attempts have used social network links to bolster DHTs, e.g., Sprout [32], preferring social links whenever possible, but nevertheless requiring links to random/unknown nodes also. Such an approach still relies on using the untrusted links most of the time, but was arguably as good as it could get under the older paradigm of DHT designs, where a completely connected underlying graph and ring invariance were considered necessary.

In the recent years several radical DHT designs have been proposed, for example VRR [11] proposed for ad-hoc environments and Fuzzynet [20] designed specifically to avoid ring maintenance. Neither of these two rely on sanctity of a ring or fully connected underlying graph. SocialCircle [47] adapts and hybridizes ideas from these two DHTs. In the description of SocialCircle below we also point out which of the features are derived from which of VRR or Fuzzynet respectively.

Virtual ring routing (VRR) is a DHT style overlay layer approach used to define the underlying network's routing mechanism. It is implemented directly on top of the link layer and provides both traditional point-to-point network routing and DHT routing to the node responsible for a hashed key, without either flooding the network or using location dependent addresses. While traditional DHTs take for granted point-to-point communication between any pair of participating nodes, VRR extends the idea, using only link layer connectivity. Essentially this means that the VRR scheme relaxes the traditional DHT assumption of a completely

Fig. 17.6 Sybil attack
resistant *SocialCircle* DHT
exploiting social connections.
This example of DHT over
Tom & Jerry's social graph is
adapted from the virtual ring
figure in [11] for routing in
ad-hoc networks

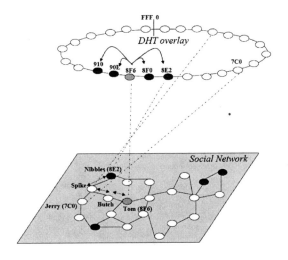

connected underlying graph. Each node in VRR has an unique address and location independent fixed identifier, organized in a virtual ring, emulating Chord style network. Each node keeps a list of $r/2$ closest clockwise and counter-clockwise neighbors for the node on the virtual ring. Such a set of neighbors is called the node's virtual neighbor set (*vset*).

Typically, members in a node's *vset* won't be directly accessible to it through the link layer. Thus each node also maintains a second set called the physical neighbor set (*pset*), comprising nodes physically reachable to it through the link layer. In SocialCircle, this idea in exploited by replacing VRR's *pset* with the set of friends a node has - its social set *sset*.

Thus, instead of exploiting the physical layer connectivity as VRR does, Social-Circle builds the overlay over the *social plane* exploiting people's social connections. In Fig. 17.6 the lower plane shows the social graph, while the upper plane shows the SocialCircle DHT. Adaption of VRR to exploit social links rather than physical neighbors provides a good abstraction, enabling SocialCircle to realize a Sybil attack [17] resistant DHT, where end-to-end routing can be achieved following a web or trust of friends-of-friends.

Finally, each peer maintains a routing table, which comprises of routes to its *vset* neighbors using its *sset*. These routes can be established and maintained using different strategies typically inspired by mobile ad-hoc routing protocols. Like in VRR, nodes in SocialCircle also keep track of the routes that pass through them. The advantage of using the DHT abstraction to do the routing over social graph is same as the use of DHTs instead of using flooding based search in a typical peer-to-peer system. The DHT abstraction ensures efficiency and certainty of routing to the appropriate target.

Thus, in the example from Fig. 17.6, *Tom* with logical identifier $8F6$ on the SocialCircle has $8F0$, $8E2$, $90E$ and 910 in its *vset*. *Spike* has *Jerry*, *Nibbles* and *Butch* in its *sset* since they are his direct social connections.

Tom needs to maintain routes to all its *vset* nodes, and thus, for $8E2$, he will have a route through his *sset* entry *Butch*, who will route through his *sset* entry *Spike*.

So when *Tom* needs to route a message to $7C0$, then it will try to forward the message closest to the target on the SocialCircle, which happens to be $8E2$. While the message is being routed to $8E2$ following the *sset* nodes at each peer, *Spike* will observe that the ultimate destination is $7C0$, for which it may already have a route passing through it, and will thus forward the message to *Jerry*, instead of sending it to the intermediate destination *Nibbles*. *Jerry* processes the routing request, and forwards it to the final destination *Quacker*, who happens to have the identifier $7C0$ on SocialCircle.

VRR works in an opportunistic manner where the route is forwarded along the virtual ring, but discovers shortcuts, so that the search is still efficient. SocialCircle preserves the same benefits by routing over the social links. Each hop on the social link involves IP level routing, which may need several hops, just like any logical overlay hop of traditional DHTs.

While the routing in SocialCircle follows the ideas from VRR, it use Fuzzynet's data-management ideas [20] for storing and retrieving key-value pairs in SocialCircle. The details of SocialCircle's data-management are not relevant here.

Given the exclusive use of social links to realize a DHT, SocialCircle is naturally resilient against Sybil attacks and also provides a means to more effectively use trust mechanisms to deal with free-riding and other anti-social/non-cooperative behaviors. It is also a natural primitive to be used in DOSNs, and specifically has been used to realize a directory service facilitating search for friends which is a common functionality required in online social networks.

Robustness against churn, scalability of the SocialCircle overlay with respect to the number of peers, and performance under partial knowledge of social networks (i.e., when an individual is yet to add all its friends) are unaddressed issues which will need further investigation to determine SocialCircle's usability in large-scale real life deployments.

17.6.2 Storage/Back-up

A p2p storage (or back-up) system uses the storage space of its participants to increase the availability or the survivability of the data. Coupled with mechanisms for content sharing and privacy, a distributed storage system is a building block for a DOSN. For instance, it can ensure that, when a user is off-line, her profile is available through the replicas. At the same time, real-world relations between people can be used as a basis for replication agreements. As in any other p2p system, one of the key issues in a p2p storage system is to provide incentives for peers to act fairly: not to consume disproportional amount of other peers' bandwidth or storage and to provide stored data on a request. Basing replication agreements on real friendships can mitigate the need for more explicit incentives: in general, a friend is less likely to free-ride on our resources than a stranger (or, even if a friend free-rides, we are more likely to forgive her and the system).

Many distributed storage systems have the option of sharing stored objects among a group of users. OceanStore [26] is one of the first distributed storage infrastructures, focusing on storing objects. As all the objects are encrypted, read sharing (i.e., many agents accessing an object) is accomplished through sharing of the encryption key. OceanStore also permits multiple agents to modify the same object through Access Control Lists (ACL), which are OceanStore object themselves (a write on an object is authenticated by a trusted server against an ACL associated with the object).

Wuala[21] is an on-line storage system that combines distributed and centralized elements. Data is stored both on users' machines and on Wuala's servers; the algorithm associating data with particular machines is most probably centralized. Wuala can act as a crude DOSN as it enables its users to share files in a group of "friends"; however other OSN features, such as profile information, are missing.

BlockParty [28] and FriendStore [43] are p2p backup system in which data is stored only on designated peers corresponding to real-world "friendships" between users. In fact, the "friendship" relation acts as a proxy for a simple reputation system: it verifies user identities and provides off-system discouragement for free-riding. Moreover, [28] argues that friendship-based system will have less permanent node departure; and thus the data survivability will depend on (rare) hardware failures rather than permanent departures frequent in usual p2p systems. Friendship-based systems can be thus more forgiving to transient errors [43] instead of assuming a permanent departure and, consequently, large-scale data transmissions, longer delays can be used.

The main disadvantage of friendship-based p2p backup systems is that, in general, systems that constrain choice of replicating nodes have lower survivability (see e.g., [22] for analysis with locality constraints). In a friendship-based system, achieved data survivability strongly depends on survivability of machines of friends – and friendships are fostered rather based on the person's character, and not her computer's up-time, which is the important factor for the system's reliability.

Approaches mixing traditional algorithmic solutions, for example, uptime history based choice of peers in a storage system with real life social trust to build a robust system are still in their nascence, and with great potentials and research opportunities.

17.7 Delay-Tolerant DOSN

Once the functionality is distributed, social networks are no longer dependent on Internet connectivity for every transaction – in contrast to current web-based services. We therefore have the opportunity to take into account locality, both in terms of connectivity by direct exchange between devices, and in terms of content, such as

---

[21] http://www.wuala.com

local community interests and events. This way, social networking applications can benefit from local storage, connectivity, and delay-tolerant data transfer via social encounters. The local communities, in turn, can benefit from the social networking applications enabled by such a system, e.g., by finding neighbors with similar interests.

Current online social networking services require the user to be connected to the Internet for every interaction, not only for real-time information but also for older information such as data posted by the user or her friends in the past. Since online social networks are part of the so-called Web 2.0, they run on dedicated web servers.

All information in the online social network is thus stored on logically central servers, even though they may be replicated or cached in different geographic regions using content distribution services. Due to such centralization, there is no distinction between information of global or exclusively local relevance.

We propose to implement online social network functionality in a distributed, delay-tolerant way. Intermittent Internet connectivity can be used to connect with the wider user community, while users can exchange data among each other in direct physical proximity during offline times. The need for constant Internet connectivity, which can be costly, is thus eliminated. When information is of local relevance only, it need not be transferred to a central server that is potentially far away. These needless long-distance transfers can be replaced by local storage. In addition, it becomes easier to take locality into account logically when keeping local information also local physically.

While portable user devices, such as phones, laptops, an personal digital assistants (PDAs) can be used to exchange data directly, also fixed devices can contribute resources. Schioeberg [38] proposed to use storage on home routers, such as ADSL modems with WLAN capabilities to support peer-to-peer social networks. Many home routers now have unused storage or can at least be extended by USB sticks or external hard drives. Fixed devices that typically are switched on irrespective of user activity not only contribute resources but also increase availability and robustness of a system for delay-tolerant social networks.

Such delay-tolerant, local social networks allow us to build on other proposals and new opportunities. For example, Antoniadis et al. [3] proposed to use local wireless networks to enhance communities such as neighborhoods in towns. Collectively, users would build wireless neighborhood networks by pooling their resources to support the creation and operation of the underlying communication network. They envision user participation and cooperation at several layers, physic, access, network, and application layers. They argue that *the design of communities suitable for this environment will encourage users to participate, enable trustworthy network creation, and provide a social layer, which can be exploited in order to design cross-layer incentive mechanisms that will further encourage users to share their resources and cooperate at lower layers.* The goal is to bridge the gap between online and offline communities.

The way we envision delay-tolerant social networks can be a vehicle to such fostering of communities. Beyond the features of current social networks that allow users to keep in touch and up-to-date with the friends they already have and, increasingly, the new ones they found thanks to the service itself, delay-tolerant social networks would allow users to benefit from locality. They could find others who live nearby and have similar interests, find or start events in the neighborhood, organize or collaborate for creative of political collective action, found local marketplaces of ideas, goods, or services, edit local information repositories or wikis, to name just a few possibilities.

Local social networks could also be established to never connect to a wider collection of networks but form islands of social networks, effectively making censorship or data mining prohibitively difficult.

The possibilities of use of delay-tolerant social networks are of course not limited to the examples given above, once the technology is available, users may come up with novel and original applications, as has been the case with online social networks or indeed the advent of the Internet and the World-Wide Web itself. Delay-tolerant social networks can thus be seen as enablers for applications or uses not yet foreseen.

Taking a wider perspective, we contend that there is a feedback loop between society and technology, and there are interesting dynamics in both directions, raising questions such as the following. How can we develop and use technology to enhance people's lives and society as a whole and how can we take societal phenomena and changes into account to improve technology? Delay-tolerant social networks can serve as an example to allow us to explore these questions directly. First, by experimenting how local user communities can benefit from social networks that do not require Internet connectivity. Second, by analysing how user behavior, such as mobility and use of ubiquitous computing resources, can support distributed social networks.

17.8 Conclusion

Most of the early commercial initiatives for DOSN do not have a large user base due to the dominance of their existing centralized social application counterparts that offer equivalent functionalities. The major obstacles to the wide adoption of these decentralized social applications are their immaturity in features and the acceptance of existing users. Data portability issues also hinder the popularity of the new systems, even if these new ones offer much more security and privacy-preserving features. Another reason is the network effect problem: users of an existing social networking service do not want to switch to another one without their friends doing so, since maintaining these connections is important for them. Therein a chick-and-egg problem emerges: a newly developed decentralized social system is less appealing to new users due to its lack of benefits, while the system itself relies on a certain critical mass of participants before it can offer its users any significant values. While this is true also for centralized OSNs, the problem is excacerbated when involving a change away from web-based services. Additionally, various performance issues, mostly related to the availability, latency, and throughput in data access due to data encryption and replication, of these decentralized social applications have still yet to be investigated carefully to compare with their existing centralized approaches.

Despite the above challenges, we believe that development and research on DOSNs still are very important and have significant impact. Due to scalability issues, major social networking providers may want to switch to use a decentralized infrastructure for their services. Furthermore, such decentralized alternatives are also less costly compared to centralized architectures. In this chapter, we made a case for using a decentralized infrastructure for social networks to address problems other than purely technical ones stemming from a centralized service-provider owned approach, such as privacy and access limitations. We listed a variety of research challenges and opportunities that result from decentralization, e.g., security issues to enable user control of data, storage, topology, search, and update management. Research into the area of DOSN has become very active, and we discussed several recent approaches in this paper, in terms of general-purpose DOSN, DOSNs with a focus on a specialized application, and the emerging trend of social applications. Once decentralized, the functionality of OSNs can be expanded by allowing for direct data exchange between devices, enabling ad-hoc social communities, data locality, and delay-tolerant social networks.

Acknowledgments Anwitaman Datta and Krzysztof Rzadca's work was funded by ACRF Tier-1 Grant Number RG 29/09 and A*Star SERC Grant Number 072 134 0055. Le-Hung Vu is partially supported by the FP7 EU Large-scale Integrating Project OKKAM: Enabling a Web of Entities, contract number ICT-215032.

References

1. A. Adya, W. Bolosky, M. Castro, R. Chaiken, G. Cermak, J. Douceur, J. Howell, J. Lorch, M. Theimer, and R. Wattenhofer. In *Proceedings of the 5th Usenix Symposium on Operating Systems Design and Implementation (OSDI)*, Farsite: Federated, available, and reliable storage for an incompletely trusted environment, 2002.
2. Karl Aberer, Anwitaman Datta, and Manfred Hauswirth. Efficient, self-contained handling of identity in peer-to-peer systems. *IEEE Transactions on Knowledge and Data Engineering*, 16(7):858–869, 2004.
3. P. Antoniadis, B. Le Grand, L. Satsiou, A.and Tassiulas, R.L. Aguiar, J.P. Barraca, and S. Sargento. Community building over neighborhood wireless mesh networks. *IEEE Technology and Society Magazine*, 27:48–56, 2008.
4. Luca Maria Aiello, Marco Milanesio, Giancarlo Ruffo, and Rossano Schifanella. Tempering Kademlia with a robust identity based system. In *P2P '08: Proceedings of the 2008 Eighth International Conference on Peer-to-Peer Computing*, pages 30–39, 2008.
5. Luca Maria Aiello and Giancarlo Ruffo. Secure and Flexible Framework for Decentralized Social Network Services. In *SESOC 2010: IEEE International Workshop on SECurity and SOCial Networking*, 2010.
6. Maria Aspan. Quitting Facebook Gets Easier, Feb. 2008. http://www.nytimes.com/2008/02/13/technology/13face.html.
7. Sonja Buchegger and Anwitaman Datta. A case for P2P infrastructure for social networks – opportunities and challenges. In *Proceedings of WONS 2009, The Sixth International Confer-*

ence on Wireless On-demand Network Systems and Services, Snowbird, Utah, USA, February 2–4, 2009.

8. Sonja Buchegger and Anwitaman Datta. A case for P2P infrastructure for social networks – opportunities and challenges. In *WONS 2009, 6th International Conference on Wireless On-demand Network Systems and Services, Snowbird, Utah, USA*, February 2009.

9. Danah Boyd and Nicole B. Ellison. Social network sites: Definition, history, and scholarship. *Journal of Computer-Mediated Communication*, 13(1–2), November 2007.

10. Sonja Buchegger, Doris Schiöberg, Le Hung Vu, and Anwitaman Datta. PeerSoN: P2P social networking - early experiences and insights. In *Proceedings of the Second ACM Workshop on Social Network Systems Social Network Systems 2009, co-located with Eurosys 2009*, Nürnberg, Germany, March 31, 2009.

11. M. Caesar, M. Castro, E.B. Nightingale, G. O'Shea, and A. Rowstron. Virtual ring routing: network routing inspired by dhts. In *SIGCOMM, Proceedings*, 2006.

12. clip2. The gnutella protocol specification v0.4. `http://rfc-gnutella.sourceforge.net/`, letzter Abruf: 19.04.2007, 2002.

13. Leucio-Antonio Cutillo, Refik Molva, and Thorsten Strufe. Safebook: a Privacy Preserving Online Social Network Leveraging on Real-Life Trust. *IEEE Communications Magazine*, 47(12):94–101, December 2009.

14. Bram Cohen. Incentives build robustness in bitorrent. In *Proceedings of the 1st Workshop on Economics of Peer-to-Peer Systems*, 2003.

15. Ian Clarke, Oskar Sandberg, Brandon Wiley, and Theodore W. Hong. Freenet: A distributed anonymous information storage and retrieval system. In *Proceedings of Designing Privacy Enhancing Technologies: Workshop on Design Issues in Anonymity and Unobservability*, pages 46–66, July 2000.

16. Roger Dingledine, Michael J. Freedman, and David Molnar. The free haven project: Distributed anonymous storage service. In H. Federrath, editor, *Proceedings of Designing Privacy Enhancing Technologies: Workshop on Design Issues in Anonymity and Unobservability*. Springer-Verlag, LNCS 2009, July 2000.

17. J.R. Douceur. The sybil attack. In *Peer-To-Peer Systems: First International Workshop, IPTPS, Revised Papers*. Springer, 2002.

18. Renato J. Figueiredo, Oscar P. Boykin, Pierre St. Juste, and David Wolinsky. Social VPNs: Integrating overlay and social networks for seamless P2P networking. In *17th IEEE International Workshop on Enabling Technologies: Infrastructures for Collaborative Enterprises*, June 2008.

19. Justin Frankel. Waste P2P Darknet, 2003. http://waste.sourceforge.net/.

20. Sarunas Girdzijauskas, Wojciech Galuba, Vasilios Darlagiannis, Anwitaman Datta, and Karl Aberer. Fuzzynet: Zero-maintenance Ringless Overlay. Technical report, 2008.

21. P. Garbacki, A. Iosup, D.H.J. Epema, and M. van Steen. 2fast: Collaborative downloads in p2p networks (best paper award). In *6-th IEEE International Conference on Peer-to-Peer Computing*, pages 23–30. IEEE Computer Society, sep 2006.

22. F. Giroire, J. Monteiro, and S. Pérennes. P2p storage systems: How much locality can they tolerate? Technical Report 7006, INRIA, 2009.

23. Jennifer Golbeck. Quechup: Another Social Network Enemy!, Sept. 2007. Oreillynet.com.

24. Kalman Graffi, Sergey Podrajanski, Patrick Mukherjee, Aleksandra Kovacevic, and Ralf Steinmetz. A distributed platform for multimedia communities. In *IEEE International Symposium on Multimedia (ISM'08)*, page 6, Berkley, USA, Dec 2008. IEEE, IEEE Computer Society Press.

25. Olaf Gorlitz, Sergej Sizov, and Steffen Staab. Pints: Peer-to-peer infrastructure for tagging systems. *IPTPS*, 2008.

26. J. Kubiatowicz, D. Bindel, Y. Chen, S. Czerwinski, P. Eaton, D. Geels, R. Gummadi, S. Rhea, H. Weatherspoon, C. Wells, et al. Oceanstore: An architecture for global-scale persistent storage. *ACM SIGARCH Computer Architecture News*, 28(5):190–201, 2000.

27. Eng Keong Lua, Jon Crowcroft, Marcelo Pias, Ravi Sharma, and Steven Lim. A survey and comparison of peer-to-peer overlay network schemes. *IEEE Communications Surveys & Tutorials*, 7(2):72–93, 2005.

28. J. Li and F. Dabek. F2F: Reliable storage in open networks. In *IPTPS, Proceedings*, 2006.
29. Nicolas Liebau, Konstantin Pussep, Kalman Graffi, Sebastian Kaune, Eric Jahn, André Beyer, and Ralf Steinmetz. The impact of the p2p paradigm. In *Proceedings of Americas Conference on Information Systems 2007*, Aug 2007.
30. Ching man Au Yeung, Ilaria Liccardi, Kanghao Lu, Oshani Seneviratne, and Tim Berners-Lee. Decentralization: The future of online social networking. In *W3C Workshop on the Future of Social Networking Position Papers*, 2009.
31. J.J.D. Mol, A. Bakker, J. Pouwelse, D.H.J. Epema, and H.J. Sips. The design and deployment of a bittorrent live video streaming solution. In *ISM 2009*. IEEE Computer Society, December 2009.
32. S. Marti, P. Ganesan, and H. Garcia-Molina. Dht routing using social links. In *The 3rd International Workshop on Peer-to-Peer Systems*. Springer, 2004.
33. Petar Maymounkov and David Mazieres. Kademlia: A Peer-to-Peer Information System Based on the XOR Metric. In *LNCS: International Workshop on P2P-Systems*, volume 2429, pages 53–65, 2002.
34. M. Meulpolder, J.A. Pouwelse, D.H.J. Epema, and H.J. Sips. Bartercast: A practical approach to prevent lazy freeriding in p2p networks. In State University of New York Yuanyuan Yang, editor, *Proceedings of the 23rd IEEE International Parallel and Distributed Processing Symposium*, pages 1–8, Los Alamitos, USA, May 2009. IEEE Computer Society.
35. Juan Carlos Perez. Facebook's Beacon More Intrusive Than Previously Thought, Nov 2007. http://www.pcworld.com/article/id,140182-c,onlineprivacy/article.html.
36. J.A. Pouwelse, P. Garbacki, J. Wang, A. Bakker, J. Yang, A. Iosup, D.H.J. Epema, M. Reinders, M. van Steen, and H.J. Sips. Tribler: A social-based peer-to-peer system. *Concurrency and Computation: Practice and Experience*, 20:127–138, 2008.
37. J.A. Pouwelse, P. Garbacki, J. Wang, A. Bakker, J. Yang, A. Iosup, D.H.J. Epema, M. Reinders, M. van Steen, and H.J. Sips. Tribler: A social-based peer-to-peer system. *Concurrency and Computation: Practice and Experience*, 20:127–138, 2008.
38. Doris Schiöberg. A peer-to-peer infrastructure for social networks. Diplom thesis, TU Berlin, Berlin, Germany, December 17, 2008.
39. Skype.com. Skype P2P telephony explained, 2004. http://www.skype.com/intl/en/download/explained.html.
40. I. Stoica, R. Morris, D. Liben-Nowell, DR Karger, MF Kaashoek, F. Dabek, and H. Balakrishnan. Chord: a scalable peer-to-peer lookup protocol for internet applications. *Networking, IEEE/ACM Transactions on*, 11(1):17–32, 2003.
41. M. Steiner, G. Tsudik, and M. Waidner. Key agreement in dynamic peer groups. *IEEE Transactions on Parallel and Distributed Systems*, 11(8):769–780, 2000.
42. Daniel R. Sandler and Dan S. Wallach. Birds of a fethr: Open, decentralized micropublishing. In *8th International Workshop on Peer-to-Peer Systems (IPTPS '09) April 21, 2009*, Boston, MA, 2009.
43. D.N. Tran, F. Chiang, and J. Li. Friendstore: cooperative online backup using trusted nodes. In *SocialNets '08: Proceedings of the 1st Workshop on Social Network Systems*, pages 37–42. ACM, 2008.
44. J. Wang, J.A.Pouwelse, J.E. Fokker, A.P. de Vries, and M.J.T. Reinders. Personalization on a peer-to-peer television system. *Multimedia Tools and Applications*, 36:89–113, 2008.
45. Susu Xie, Gabriel Y. Keung, and Bo Li. A measurement of a large-scale peer-to-peer live video streaming system. *Parallel Processing Workshops, International Conference on*, p. 57, 2007.
46. Haifeng Yu, Michael Kaminsky, Phillip B. Gibbons, and Abraham Flaxman. Sybilguard: defending against sybil attacks via social networks. In *SIGCOMM*, 2006.
47. Lukasz Zaczek and Anwitaman Datta. Mapping social networks into p2p directory service. In *SocInfo, International Conference on Social Informatics*, 2009.
48. Xinyan Zhang, Jiangchuan Liu, Bo Li, and Tak shing Peter Yum. Coolstreaming/donet: A data-driven overlay network for peer-to-peer live media streaming. In *in IEEE Infocom*, 2005.

Chapter 18
Multi-Relational Characterization of Dynamic Social Network Communities

Yu-Ru Lin, Hari Sundaram, and Aisling Kelliher

18.1 Introduction

The emergence of the mediated social web – a distributed network of participants creating rich media content and engaging in interactive conversations through
Internet-based communication technologies – has contributed to the evolution of
powerful social, economic and cultural change. Online social network sites and
blogs, such as Facebook, Twitter, Flickr and LiveJournal, thrive due to their fundamental sense of "community". The growth of online communities offers both
opportunities and challenges for researchers and practitioners. Participation in online communities has been observed to influence people's behavior in diverse ways
ranging from financial decision-making to political choices, suggesting the rich potential for diverse applications. However, although studies on the social web have
been extensive, discovering communities from online social media remains challenging, due to the interdisciplinary nature of this subject. In this article, we present
our recent work on characterization of communities in online social media using
computational approaches grounded on the observations from social science.

Motivation: human community as meaning-making eco-system. A key idea from
situated cognition is that knowledge is fundamentally situated within the activity
from which it is developed [1]. Brown, Collins and Duguid [1] offers an analysis
of how we make meaning with the lexical and grammatical resources of language –
people can interpret indexical expressions (containing such words as *I*, *you*, *here*,
now, *that*, etc.) only when they can find what the indexed words might refer to. The
concept of *indexicality* suggests [1] that "knowledge, which comes coded by and
connected to the activity and environment in which it is developed, is spread across
its component parts, some of which are in the mind and some in the world much as
the final picture on a jigsaw is spread across its component pieces." In other words,
knowledge does not solely reside in the mind of an individual, but is distributed

H. Sundaram (✉)
School of Arts, Media and Engineering, Arizona State University, Tempe, AZ, USA
e-mail: Hari.Sundaram@asu.edu

B. Furht (ed.), *Handbook of Social Network Technologies and Applications*,
DOI 10.1007/978-1-4419-7142-5_18, © Springer Science+Business Media, LLC 2010

and shared among co-participants in authentic situations. The meaning-making eco-social systems, denoted by Lemke [2], shape and create meaning not by individual components (people, media, objects, etc.), but by their co-participation in an activity situation.

Being influenced by this theory, we believe that semantics is an *emergent artifact of human activity that evolves over time*. Human activity is mostly social, and the social networks of human are conceivable loci for the construction of meaning. Hence, it is crucial to identify real human networks as *communities of people interacting with each other through meaningful social activities, and producing stable associations between concepts and artifacts in a coherent manner*.

Motivating applications. The discovery of human communities is not only philosophically interesting, but also has practical implications. As new concepts emerge and evolve around real human networks, community discovery can result in new knowledge and provoke advancements in information search and decision-making. Example applications include:

- Context-sensitive information search and recommendation: The discovered community around an information seeker can provide context (including objects, activities, time) that help identify most relevant information. For example, when a user is looking at a particular photo, the community structure may be used to identify peers or objects likely co-occurring with the photo.
- Content organization, tracking and monitoring: The rapid growth of content on social media sites creates several challenges. First, the content in a photo stream (either for a user or a community) is typically organized using a temporal order, making the exploration and browsing of content cumbersome. Second, sites including Flickr provide frequency based aggregate statistics including popular tags, top contributors. These aggregates do not reveal the rich temporal dynamics of community sharing and interaction. Community structure may be used to reflect the social sharing practice and facilitate the organization, tracking and monitoring of user-generated social media content.
- Behavioral prediction: Studies have shown that individual behaviors usually result from mechanisms depending on their social networks, e.g. social ebeddedness [3] and influence [4]. Community structure that accounts for inherent dependencies between individuals embedded in a social network can help understand and predict the behavioral dynamics of individuals.

Data characteristics and challenges. Large volumes of social media data are being generated from various social media platforms including blogs, FaceBook, Twitter, Digg, Flickr. The key characteristics of online social media data include:

- Voluminous: Recent technological advances allow hundreds of millions of users to create social and personal content instantly. The amount of data and the rate of data production can be enormous.
- Dynamic: Users' online actions are constantly archived with timestamps. These online activity records enable a fine-grained observation on the dynamics of human interactions and interests.

- Context-rich: Most social media platforms allow a wide array of actions for managing and sharing media objects – e.g. uploading photos, submitting and commenting on news stories, bookmarking and tagging, posting documents, creating web-links, as well as actions with respect to other users (e.g. sharing media and links with a friend), or on media objects produced by other users. The complex social interactions among users result in multi-relational network data.

The large-scale, fine-grained, rich online interaction records pose new challenges on community discovery:

- Lack of well-defined attributes: Traditional studies of human communities are often based on fixed demographic characteristics [5, 6]. Within online social networks, individuals may shift fluidly and flexibly among communities depending on their online social actions (e.g. who they recently interact with, what they recently share with each other, etc.) [7].
- Limitation in network centric analysis: Classical social network analyses mostly focus on static interpersonal relationships (e.g. self-reported friendships), with a primary interests on the graph topological properties These studies range from well-established social network analysis [6] to recent successful graph mining algorithms such as HITS [8], PageRank [9] and spectral analysis [10]. These methods are limited in discovering important aspects of online communities since the interpersonal relationships may evolve with their online interactions and may involve rich media contexts (e.g. tags, photos, time, and space).
- Scalability requirement: The Internet scale social network data requires a scalable analysis framework to support community discovery based on information latent in the multi-relational social network data [11].

Problem overview. We are interested in characterizing human communities that emerge from online interpersonal social activities. Given the challenges discussed above, we have focused on the following research problems:

- *How to identify meaningful interpersonal relationship from online social actions?* In social network literature, community discovery usually refers to detecting cohesive subgroups of individuals within networked data collected based on well-defined social relationship such as self-reported friendship [6]. Characterization of communities in online social networks deviates from traditional social network analysis because the social meaning of the networks is not definite.
- *How to identify sustained evolving communities from dynamic networks?* Online communities are temporal phenomena emerge from sustained human actions and interests, and the actions and interests may evolve over time. Traditional analysis of social networks focuses on the properties of a static graph (aggregation or snapshot of network), which overlooks the temporal characteristics of communities. Discovering communities based sustained activities and at the same time characterizing their temporal evolution is challenging.
- *How to identify communities with rich interaction context?* Online social media websites (e.g. Flickr, Facebook) enable rich interaction between media and users, as well as complex social interactions among users – two users may share similar

tags or read the same feeds. Discovery communities from such complex social interactions pose technical challenges that involve dealing with networked data consisting of multiple co-evolving dimensions, e.g. users, tags, feeds, comments, etc. Existing high dimensional data mining techniques are usually computational intensive and not suitable for dealing with large scale social networked data.

Our approach. Our work concerns approach to the three problems (see Fig. 18.1 for illustrating summarization):

- *Mutual awareness*: We propose mutual awareness (Fig. 18.1a), a bi-directional relationship indicating how well a pair of bloggers is aware of each other, as fundamental property of a community. We provide computational definition to quantify mutual awareness and use it as a feature for community discovery. Then, we capture the amount of mutual awareness expanding on the entire network using a random walk based distance measure, commute time, which estimates the probability that two bloggers are aware of each other on the network (Fig. 18.1b). We propose an efficient iterative mutual awareness expansion algorithm to extract communities, which partitions the network by maximizing the commute time distance between two sets of bloggers. The experimental results for community extraction in terms of standard evaluation metrics are promising.

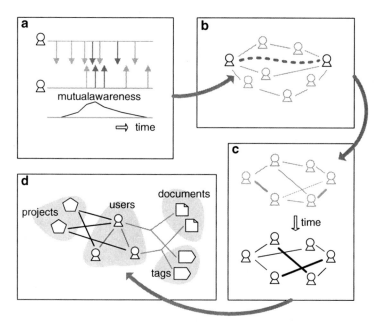

Fig. 18.1 Our work concerns multiple aspects on community analysis: (**a**) Mutual awareness – a bi-directional relationship indicating how well a pair of bloggers is aware of each other, as fundamental property of a community. (**b**) Mutual awareness expansion – a random walk based distance measure which estimates the probability that two bloggers are aware of each other on the network. (**c**) FacetNet – for analyzing communities and their evolutions in a unified process. (**d**) MetaFac – the first graph-based multi-tensor factorization framework for analyzing the dynamics of heterogeneous social networks

- *FacetNet*: We introduce the FacetNet framework to analyze communities and their evolutions in a unified process. In our framework (Fig. 18.1c), the community structure at a given timestep is determined both by the observed networked data and by the prior distribution given by historic community structures. Algorithmically, we propose the first probabilistic generative model for analyzing communities and their evolution. The experimental results suggest that our technique is scalable and is able to extract meaningful communities based on social media context. (e.g., dramatic change in a short time is unlikely).

- *MetaFac*: We propose MetaFac, the first graph-based tensor factorization framework for analyzing the dynamics of heterogeneous social networks (Fig. 18.1d). In this framework, we introduce metagraph, a novel relational hypergraph representation for modeling multi-relational and multi-dimensional social data. Then we propose an efficient multi-relational factorization algorithm for latent community extraction on a given metagraph. Extensive experiments on large-scale real-world social media data and from the enterprise data suggest that our technique is able to extract meaningful communities that are adaptive to social media context.

Organization. The rest of this article is organized as follows. Section 18.2 presents community discovery based on mutual awareness. Section 18.3 presents method for extracting sustained evolving communities. Section 18.4 presents method for extracting communities with rich interaction context. Section 18.5 concludes with future directions.

18.2   Actions, Networking and Community Formation

In this section we study the online blog network and propose computational approach for discovering communities in the blogosphere. Blogs (or weblogs) have become popular self-publishing social media on the Web. Although they are a type of websites, the analysis of blog communities is different from traditional Web analysis literature. The differences lie in the different semantics and structures of the hyperlinks in the context of blogosphere. A blog is typically used as a tool for communication. Driven by an event (such as a real-world news), bloggers publish entries that refer to each other. Thus links among blog entries are considered to be *interactions* between two bloggers and have significant temporal locality. On the Web, it is common that a new page refers to a relevant page that exists for a long time, such as an authoritative page [8, 9]. A "community of web pages" due to the links of *relevance* is thus different from a "community of bloggers" formed due to the links of interactions. The analysis of blog network also deviates from traditional social network analysis [6] because the *social meaning* of the blog network is not as well-defined as in traditional social networks (e.g. links represent friendship). Hence, community discovery in the blogosphere requires a new analytical framework grounded in the unique characteristics of the blog media.

18.2.1 Mutual Awareness and Community Discovery

The notion of *virtual community*, or online community, has been discussed extensively in prior research. Rheingold [12] defined virtual communities to be "social
aggregations that emerge from the Net when enough people carry on those public
discussions long enough, with sufficient human feeling, to form webs of personal relationship in cyberspace." Jones [13] considered four characteristics as the necessary
conditions for the formation of a virtual community: interactivity, communicators,
virtual common-public-place where the computer-mediated communication takes
place, and sustained membership. These conditions echo Garfinkel's observation
on the necessity of mutually observable actions [14]. The same idea that interactivity forms a social reality has also been discussed by Dourish [15]. According to
Dourish, interaction involves presence (some way of making the actors present in
the locale) and awareness (some way of being aware of the other's presence). In
what Dourish called an *action community*, members share the common sense un-
derstandings through the reciprocal actions. The common aspect of the prior work
is the emphasis on the significance of action and interaction in online communities.
However, little work has studied the counter perspective – how to discover
communities due to actions.

We introduce *mutual awareness* that is fundamental to blog community formation. By mutual awareness of action we mean that individual blogger actions must
lead to bloggers becoming aware of each other's presence. The idea is in the light of
Locale theory [15] that discusses how social organization of activity is supported in
different spaces. While the domains of activity must provide means for the community members to act, the space must also accord members' presence and facilitate
mutual awareness.

Note that mutual awareness may be related to, but is different from, *link reciprocity*, which refers to the tendency of vertex pairs to form mutual connections
between each other [16]. It is also related to *tie strength* discussed in the social network literature [17] – "the strength of a tie is a (probably linear) combination of the
amount of time, the emotional intensity, the intimacy (mutual confiding), and the
reciprocal services which characterize the tie." However, quantifying tie strength
based on these elements remains challenging. In fact, mutual awareness can be considered as a mechanism for tie strength situated in particular communication media.

18.2.2 Extracting Communities Based on Mutual Awareness Structure

We propose a computational approach for community discovery in the blogosphere.
Grounded on the actions of individual bloggers, we propose to discover community
based on the idea of mutual awareness. We propose a computational definition for
determining mutual awareness in the blog network. Then, using mutual awareness
as features, we propose methods for extracting blog communities.

18.2.2.1   Computable Definition for Mutual Awareness

Let us examine the actions of individual bloggers – how bloggers read and communicate ideas with other bloggers. The bloggers can act in the blogosphere, in several ways: surf/read, create entries (containing entry-to-entry links, entry to blog/web, or no link), comment or change blogroll. Some actions (e.g. surf/read) may be hidden, while others may be observable.

How a specific blogger action leads to mutual awareness may depend on (a) if the action is mutually observed, and (b) the importance of the action for the blogger who performs the action. Note that some blogger actions are not observable by other bloggers. For example, let us consider two hypothetical bloggers, Mary and John. Let us assume that Mary creates an entry with a hyperlink that points to John's blog. In this case John would be unaware of Mary's entry. On the other hand, if Mary leaves a comment on John's entry, then John is immediately aware of her presence. If Mary mostly leaves comments on other bloggers, and the importance of a comment for Mary is low – while many bloggers are aware of Mary, she may not feel that she in engaged in dialogue with them. The assessment of mutual awareness is the first step toward the discovery of blog communities.

We thus characterize mutual awareness as follows (see Fig. 18.2 for an illustration): mutual awareness between two bloggers is affected by the type of action, the number of actions for each type, and when the action occurred. It depends on sustained actions – it increases if there are follow-up actions that lead to mutual awareness and decreases if actions are not sustained over time.

We represent the set of bloggers in the blogspace as a weighted directed graph $G = (V, E)$, where each node $v \in V$ represents a blogger, each edge between any pair of nodes u and v represents an action performed by u with respect to v. The weight on each edge $f(u, v)$ indicates the mutual awareness between two bloggers u and v. The corresponding matrix $\mathbf{M}$ with each entry $\mathbf{M}_{uv} = f(u, v)$ is called mutual awareness matrix and is defined as follows.

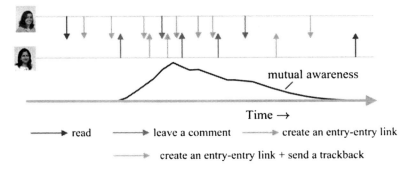

Fig. 18.2 Mutual awareness between two bloggers is affected by the type of actions, the number of such actions, and when such actions occur. The arrow direction indicates the source and the destination blogger on whom the action is performed. A mutual awareness curve is plotted to show the action impacts

Definition 18.1. (*Mutual awareness matrix*):

$$\mathbf{M} = \sum_k \alpha_k \min(\hat{\mathbf{X}}_k, \hat{\mathbf{X}}_k^T) \qquad (18.1)$$

where the index k is used to denote a specific action (e.g. leaving a comment, or creating an entry-to-entry link) and α_k represent the importance of the actions and is usually empirically determined. $\mathbf{X}_k$ is aggregated action matrix for the action type k. Since mutual awareness due to earlier actions will gradually diminish, the temporal effect can be modeled as a decaying exponential function:

$$\mathbf{X}_k = \sum_{t=t_0}^{T} \mathbf{X}_{k;t} e^{-\lambda_k (T-t)} \qquad (18.2)$$

where λ_k is the decaying factor for the action type k. Different types of actions may decay at different rate. $\mathbf{X}_{k;t}$ denotes all-pair type-k actions occurring at time t, and $\mathbf{X}_k$ aggregates these actions from time t_0 to time T.

Mutual awareness is a bi-directional relationship indicating how well a pair of bloggers is aware of each other. This semantics results in a symmetric mutual awareness matrix. The reciprocity condition (the minimum value) in (18.1) makes the possibility of both bloggers being aware of each other to be high.

Empirical Evaluation. We have studied the effectiveness of mutual awareness (MA) matrix on real-world blog datasets [18]. We use the subgroup extraction procedure described in [18] to extract subgroups, and evaluate the quality of these subgroups in terms of different metrics. Compared with the baseline adjacency matrices (with entries indicating the total number of entry-to-entry links), the subgroups extracted using mutual awareness matrices are usually of higher quality. The quality evaluation is based on several metrics, including conductance, interesting coefficient, etc. (see the definitions of the metrics in [18]). Figure 18.3a shows the performance comparison of results from the WWE 2006 Workshop Blog Dataset [18]. An example subgroup is shown in Fig. 18.3b – the group is observed to have cohesive topic about mystery novels based on the top keywords from their blog contents.

18.2.2.2 Mutual Awareness Expansion

We extend the idea of mutual awareness to community extraction. Mutual awareness quantifies the relationship between two bloggers. To extract a set of bloggers having high mutual awareness, we hypothesize how mutual awareness expands in a blog network:

- Transitivity: One could become aware of a member without direct interaction since he or she can observe his or her direct peers interacting with other people.

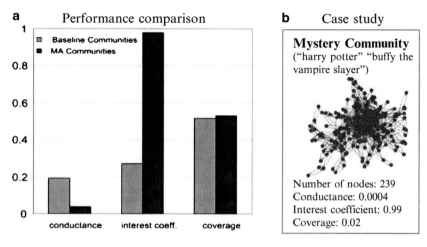

Fig. 18.3 (a) Performance comparison between the Baseline communities and the MA communities in terms of metrics conductance, interest coefficient, and coverage. (b) An example subgroup cohesive topic about mystery novels, extracted using MA matrix

Thus awareness is transitive. (The transitivity property in social network has been first examined in Travers and Milgram's well-known small world experiment [19], which motivates our proposed algorithm [20].)

- Reciprocity: Such transitive awareness must be reciprocal. If expansion of awareness is only one directional, one might not feel belonging to the community
- Frequency: The amount of observed interaction must be sufficient for members to feel connected to each other

We characterize such *mutual awareness expansion* process by a random walk model. The probability that two bloggers are aware of each other on the entire network is quantified using the random walk expected length between two nodes corresponding to the bloggers. We refer to this expected length as *symmetric social distance*. It is computed as follows: Given a direct graph $G = (V, E)$ and the mutual awareness matrix $\mathbf{W}$ associated with G, the random walk on G is defined to be the Markov chain with state space V and the transition matrix $\mathbf{P} = \mathbf{D}^{-1}\mathbf{W}$, where $\mathbf{D}$ is a diagonal matrix with element $d_{ii} = \sum_j w_{ij}$. A random walker at a node i on G will follow the transition probability $p_{ij} = P_{ij}$ to visit the next node j. Note that by construction $w_{ii} = \sum_j w_{ij}$ (i.e. $p_{ii} = 1/2$) for $i \neq j$.

Let $\tau_{u \to v}$ denote the one-way social distance from node u to v, i.e. the expected number of steps to reach node v from node u. We define $\tau_{u \to v}$ to have the *transitive awareness* property:

Definition 18.2. (*Transitive awareness property*):

$$
\tau_{u \to v} = \begin{cases} 1 + \sum_{(u,x) \in E} p_{ux} \tau_{x \to v} & \text{if } u \neq v \\ 0 & \text{if } u = v \end{cases} \tag{18.3}
$$

Fig. 18.4 Transitive
awareness property – the
social distance from node u
to v is defined by the expected
number of steps before node v
is visited, starting from node

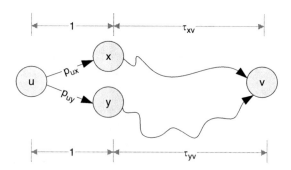

where p_{ux} is the transition probability from u to x. The equation can be illustrated
in Fig. 18.4: To reach v from u, the random walker takes one step to get to the next
node x with transition probability p_{ux}, and then calculates the rest expected distance
to v. The symmetric social distance is defined by $\tau_{u \leftrightarrow v} = \tau_{u \rightarrow v} + \tau_{v \rightarrow u}$.

Solution 18.1. Based on property in (18.3), the solution for $\tau_{u \leftrightarrow v}$, denoted by $\tau_{u \leftrightarrow v}$,
can be derived by using Green's function [21]:

$$\tau_{u \leftrightarrow v} = vol \sum_{i=2}^{k} \frac{1}{\lambda_i}(\phi_i(u) - \phi_i(v))^2 \qquad (18.4)$$

where $vol = \sum_{u,v \in V} w_{uv}$, φ_i's and λ_i's$(0 = \lambda_1 < \lambda_2 \leq \ldots \leq \lambda_n)$ are the eigenvectors and corresponding eigenvalues of the Laplacian matrix $\mathbf{L} = \mathbf{D} - \mathbf{W}$. The solution
is computed by truncating after the k-th smallest eigen-pair for $k < n$. Intuitively,
$\tau_{u \leftrightarrow v}$ is the random walk expected path length from u to v and back to u, which takes
into account the indirect interactions between u and v derived by their interactions
with other nodes over the entire network.

Community Extraction. We use the symmetric social distance as a criterion to
extract a community. Given a set of bloggers V, a subset S from V can be seen
as a community if the symmetric social distance among members of S is short compared to those with non-members. Therefore, we iteratively split the set V into two
sets S and $V \backslash S$ by maximizing the symmetric social distance as follows:

$$S = \text{argmax}_{S \subset V} \omega(S, V) \sum_{u \in S, v \in V \backslash S} \tau_{u \leftrightarrow v} \qquad (18.5)$$

Where $\omega(S, V)$ is a weighted function used to obtained desirable properties (e.g.
balance partition) of the set of communities. Details of the algorithm can be found
in [20].

Empirical Evaluation. We compare our community extraction method with
well-known baseline clustering algorithms, including the kernel k-means [22],

normalized cut [10] and iterative conductance cutting [23]. The results indicate that our method outperforms all baseline methods in terms of low conductance, high coverage, and low entropy [20].

18.2.3   Application: Query-Sensitive Community Extraction

We apply the community extraction algorithm to the extraction of *query-sensitive communities*, i.e. blog communities that have a strong content related theme with respect to a given query. We summarize the idea as follows (see [20] for more details):

- Step 1: Given a query topic Q, extract query-sensitive graph G_Q to represent interactions relevant to the topic.
- Step 2: Given G_Q, extract communities as described in Sect. 18.2.2.

In the first step, we construct a weighted action matrix with respect to a query Q. Q contains query keywords that represent the given topics, e.g. "Katrina", "london bomb", etc. The weight of an interaction is determined by the relevance score of the blog content involved in the interaction. Because the query keywords in Q are relatively short, in order to further incorporate relevant blogs in G_Q, we compute the "query relevancy" by employing a web-based similarity function [20, 24].

Figure 18.5 shows an example from our experiment. In this case, we extract communities with respect to the query keyword is "katrina", which is about a natural disaster caused by the hurricane Katrina in August 2005. In order to understand

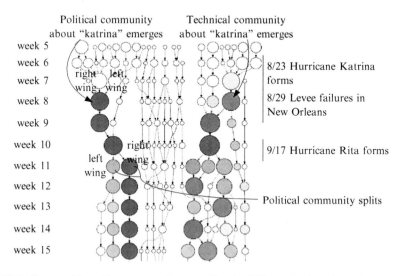

Fig. 18.5 Communities with respect to the query "katrina." The node size reflects the number of community members and the reddish shade of node is proportional to the query relevancy for the keyword "katrina"

the "meaningfulness" of the extracted communities, we employ a heuristic method [20] to examine the relationship between the topic and the communities over time: We connect those communities extracted from different time snapshots based on an interaction similarity measure.[1] In Fig. 18.5, each node represents a detected community where the communities detected during the same week are aligned horizontally and the communities at different time snapshots are connected by arrows. The grayscale of an arrow is proportional to the interaction similarity between the two communities. The node size reflects the number of community members and the reddish shade of node is proportional to the query relevancy for the keyword "katrina". More saturated node represents more relevant community.

The interactions among the extracted communities are quite interesting. Two dominated communities, one with a focus on politics (shown on the left) and the other with a focus on technology (shown on the right), emerged and evolved due to the Katrina event. When the event Katrina occurred at week 7, we found community merged from left-wing to right-wing members, due to debates about the government response as well as cooperation of fund-raising. Later at week 11, the community split into stable communities that correspond to their political preferences. The results suggest that for queries such as "Katrina", community extraction help identifies people with different viewpoints based on their sustained interactions.

Summary. A key idea in this work was that observable actions lead to the emergence of human communities, and awareness expansion was critical to community formation. We provide computational definition to quantify mutual awareness and use it as a feature to extract subgroups in the blogosphere. The effectiveness of mutual awareness features is verified on real-world blog datasets.

We showed how to detect blog communities based on mutual awareness expansion, given a specific query. We proposed a symmetric social distance measure that captures the expansion process and use it to detect communities. The community evolution with respect to a query reveals interesting community dynamics.

There are some open issues in this work. (1) The communities are independently extracted at consecutive timesteps and then the evolutions are characterizes to explain the difference between these communities over time. Such a two-stage approach may result in community structures with high temporal variation, and undesirable evolutionary characteristics may have to be introduced in order to explain such high variation in the community structures. A more appropriate approach is to analyze communities and their evolutions in a unified framework. (2) In order to extract communities with strong content related themes, we construct networks with query-dependent edge weights with respect to given concepts. However, the theme of a community may not be known in advance, and it may emerge and evolve over time, depending on the content and context associated with the interactions. This will require a new approach for extracting communities from rich interaction contexts. We shall discuss these directions in next two sections.

---

[1] A more systematical solution will be presented in next section.

18.3   Analyzing Communities and Evolutions in Dynamic Network

In this section, we present the FacetNet framework that analyzes communities and their evolutions in a unified process. Traditional analysis of social networks treats the network as a static graph, where the static graph is either derived from aggregation of data over all time or taken as a snapshot of data at a particular time. These studies range from well-established social network analysis [6] to recent successful applications such as HITS [8] and PageRank [9]. However, this research omits one important feature of communities in networked data – the temporal evolution of communities.

18.3.1   Sustained Membership, Evolution and Community Discovery

If evolution is a nature characteristic of human communities, how are they different from a chance meeting of casual individuals? Jones [13] argued that a virtual community is not a chance meeting of casual individuals but should involve long term, meaningful conversations among humans, and this condition suggests that there should be a minimal level of sustained membership. Lemke described *community ecology* as follows: "they have a relevant history, a trajectory of development in which each stage sets up conditions without which the next stage could not occur," "the course of their development depends in part on information laid down (or actively available) in their environments from prior (or contemporary) systems of their own kind."

Recently, there has been a growing body of analytical work on communities and their temporal evolution in dynamic networks (e.g. [20,25,26]). However, a common weakness in these studies, is that communities and their evolutions are studied separately – usually community structures are independently extracted at consecutive timesteps and then in retrospect, evolutionary characteristics are introduced to explain the difference between these community structures over time. Such a two-stage approach has two issues: (a) At each timestep, communities are extracted without considering sustained membership (temporal smoothness of clustering). (b) It may result in community structures with high temporal variation, and undesirable evolutionary characteristics may have to be introduced in order to explain such high variation in the community structures.

Sustained membership is the key to discovery time-evolving communities. We introduce the FacetNet framework to extract sustained and evolving communities from dynamic social networks.

18.3.2 Extracting Sustained Evolving Communities

We present the formulation of our model, and describe how to extract communities
and their evolutions from the solution of our model.

18.3.2.1 Problem Formulation

We assume that edges in the networked data are associated with discrete timesteps.
We use a snapshot graph $G_t = (V_t, E_t)$ to model the interactions at time t, where
in G_t, each node $v_i \in V_t$ represents an individual, each edge $e_{ij} \in E_t$ represents
the presence of interactions between v_i and v_j, and $w_{t;ij} = (W_t)_{ij}$ denotes the edge
weight of e_{ij}. Note the edge weight can represent mutual awareness, or more generally, the frequency of interactions between nodes i and j observed at time t.
Assuming G_t has n nodes, $W_t \in \Re_+^{n \times n}$ (nonnegative matrix of size $n \times n$) is the
corresponding weight matrix for G_t. Over time, the interaction history is captured
by a sequence of snapshot graphs $G_1, \ldots, G_t, \ldots$ indexed by time.

   The basic principles (as illustrated in Fig. 18.6) behind our models are the community structure at time t is determined by (1) the data observed at time t (i.e. W,
which is short for W_t), and (2) the community structure at time $t - 1$. We propose
to use the community structure at time $t - 1$ (already extracted) to regularize the
community structure at current time t (to be extracted). To incorporate such a regulation, we introduce a cost function to measure the quality of community structure
at time t, where the cost consists of two parts – a *snapshot cost* and a *temporal cost*:

$$cost = \alpha \cdot \mathcal{CS} + (1 - \alpha) \cdot \mathcal{CT} \tag{18.6}$$

This cost function is first proposed by Chakrabarti et al. [27, 28] in the context of
evolutionary clustering. In this cost function, the snapshot cost $\mathcal{CS}$ measures how
well a community structure fits W, the observed interactions at time t. The temporal
cost $\mathcal{CT}$ measures how consistent the community structure is with respect to historic
community structure (at time $t - 1$). The parameter a is set by the user to control the
level of emphasis on each part of the total cost.

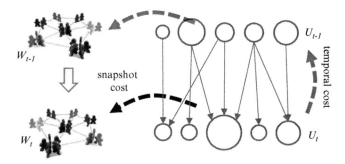

Fig. 18.6 The community structure at time t (denoted as U_t) is determined by (**a**) the data observed
at time t (denoted as W_t), and (**b**) the community structure at time $t - 1$ (denoted as U_{t-1})

A community structure at time t should fit W well, where W is the observed interaction matrix at time t. This requirement is reflected in the snapshot cost $\mathcal{CS}$ in the cost function (18.6). We adopt a stochastic block model first proposed in [29]. Assume that there exist m communities at time t, and that the interaction w_{ij} is a combined effect due to all the m communities. That is, we approximate w_{ij} using a mixture model $w_{ij} = \sum_{k=1}^{m} p_k \cdot p_{k \to i} \cdot p_{k \to j}$, where p_k is the prior probability that the interaction w_{ij} is due to the k-th community, $p_{k \to i}$ and $p_{k \to j}$ are the probabilities that an interaction in community k involves node v_i and v_j, respectively. Written in a matrix form, we have $W \approx X \Lambda X^T$, where $X \in \mathfrak{R}_+^{n \times m}$ is a non-negative matrix with $x_{ik} = p_{k \to i}$ and $\sum_i x_{ik} = 1$. In addition, Λ is an $m \times m$ non-negative diagonal matrix with $\lambda_k = p_k$, where λ_k is short for λ_{kk}. Matrices X and Λ (or equivalently, their product $X\Lambda$) fully characterize the community structure in the mixture model. Based on this model, we define the snapshot cost $\mathcal{CS}$ as the error introduced by such an approximation, i.e.,

$$CS = D(W \| X \Lambda X^T) \qquad (18.7)$$

where $D(A \| B) = \sum_{i,j} \left(a_{ij} \log \frac{a_{ij}}{b_{ij}} - a_{ij} + b_{ij} \right)$ is the KL-divergence between A and B. The snapshot cost is high when the approximate community structure $X \Lambda X^T$ fails to fit the observed data W well.

In the cost function (18.6), the temporal cost $\mathcal{CT}$ is used to regularize the community structure. We propose to achieve this regularization by defining $\mathcal{CT}$ as the difference between the community structure at time t and that at time $t-1$. Recall that the community structure is captured by $X\Lambda$. Therefore, with $Y = X_{t-1}\Lambda_{t-1}$, the temporal cost is defined as:

$$CT = D(Y \| X\Lambda) \qquad (18.8)$$

where $D(\cdot \| \cdot)$ is the KL-divergence as defined before. The temporal cost $\mathcal{CT}$ is high when there is a dramatic change of community structure from time $t - 1$ to t.

Putting the snapshot cost $\mathcal{CS}$ and the temporal cost $\mathcal{CT}$ together, we have an optimization problem as to find the best community structure at time t, expressed by X and Λ, that minimizes the following total cost:

$$cost = \alpha \cdot D(W \| X \Lambda X^T) + (1 - \alpha) \cdot D(Y \| X\Lambda) \qquad (18.9)$$

subject to $X \in \mathfrak{R}_+^{n \times m}$, $\sum_i x_{ik} = 1$, and Λ being a $m \times m$ non-negative diagonal matrix. Solving this optimization problem is the core of our FacetNet framework.

Solution 18.2. We provide an iterative EM algorithm to find the optimal solutions for (18.9) as follows:

$$x_{ik} \leftarrow x_{ik} \cdot 2\alpha \sum_j \frac{w_{ij} \cdot \lambda_k \cdot x_{jk}}{(X \Lambda X^T)_{ij}} + (1 - \alpha) \cdot y_{ik}$$

then normalized such that $\sum_i x_{ik} = 1 \forall k$

$$\lambda_k \leftarrow \lambda_k \cdot \alpha \sum_{ij} \frac{w_{ij} \cdot x_{ik} \cdot x_{jk}}{(X \Lambda X^T)_{ij}} + (1 - \alpha) \cdot \sum_i y_{ik}$$

then normalized such that $\sum_k \lambda_k = 1$ \hfill (18.10)

Details about the proposed model and the convergence of the solution can be found in [30]. Different from the matrix factorization formulation presented here, in [30], the problem is reformulated in terms of maximum a posteriori (MAP) estimation and we show a close connection between the optimization framework for solving the evolutionary clustering problem and our proposed generative probabilistic model.

18.3.2.2 Extracting Communities and Evolutions

Community Membership. Assume we have computed the result at time $t - 1$, i.e., (X_{t-1}, Λ_{t-1}), and the result at time t, i.e., (X_t, Λ_t). We define a diagonal matrix D_t, whose diagonal elements $d_{t;ii} = \sum_{ij}(X_t \Lambda_t)_{ij}$. Then the i-th row of $D_t^{-1} X_t \Lambda_t$ indicates the "soft" community memberships of v_i at time t.

Community Evolution. To derive the community evolutions, we align the two bipartite graphs, that at time $t - 1$ and that at time t, side by side by merging the corresponding network nodes v_i's (as illustrated in Fig. 18.7). A natural definition of community evolution (from community $c_{i;t-1}$ at time $t - 1$ to community $c_{j;t}$ at time t) is the probability of starting from $c_{i;t-1}$, walking through the merged bipartite graphs, and reaching $c_{j;t}$. A simple derivation shows that $P(c_{i;t-1}, c_{j;t}) = \left(\Lambda_{t-1} X_{t-1}^T D_t^{-1} X_t \Lambda_t\right)_{ij}$ and $P(c_{j;t}|c_{i;t-1}) = \left(X_{t-1}^T D_t^{-1} X_t \Lambda_t\right)_{ij}$. Each node and each edge contribute to the evolution from $c_{i;t-1}$ to $c_{j;t}$. That is, all individuals and all interactions are related to all the community evolutions, with different levels. This is more reasonable compared to traditional methods where the analysis of community evolution assumes all members having identical importance in a community.

Fig. 18.7 The evolution of communities from time $t - 1$ to t, is obtained by merging the bipartite graphs through corresponding nodes v_i's – as the probability of starting from $c_{i;t-1}$ (community nodes at $t - 1$), walking through the merged bipartite graphs, and reaching $c_{j;t}$ (community nodes at t)

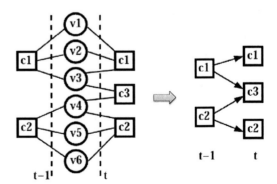

18.3.3   Application: Time-Dependent Ranking in Communities

We apply the FacetNet algorithm on the DBLP co-authorship dataset (see [30] for more details). In Fig. 18.8a we list the extracted top authors in two of the extracted communities, Data Mining (DM) and Database (DB), where the rank is determined by the value x_{ik}, i.e., $p_{k \to i}$. Recall that $p_{k \to i}$ indicates to what level the k-th community involves the i-th node, where the value is derived based on both the current and the historic community structures. So from our framework, we can directly infer who the important members in each community are. Note that the importance of a node in a community is determined by its contribution to the community structure.

We can also track the role each individual plays in a community by looking the value of $p_{k \to i}$ over time. In Fig. 18.8b, c We demonstrate one top author (Philip S. Yu) in the DM community whose community membership remains stable over all the timesteps and another top author (Laks V. S. Lakshmanan) whose community membership varies very much over the 5 timesteps. In the figure, each compass indicates a pair $(p_{k_1 \to i}, p_{k_2 \to i})$ where k_1 and k_2 correspond to the DB and the DM communities, respectively. So in a compass, a vertical arrow (which has a large projection on the y-axis) indicates a large value of the community membership in the DM community and a horizontal arrow (which has a large projection on the

a   Top members in two communities

Data Mining	**Philip S. Yu**, Jiawei Han, Jian Pei, Wei Wang, Haixun Wang, Beng Chin Ooi, Kian-Lee Tan, Charu C. Aggarwal, Jiong Yang, Hongjun Lu, Mong-Li Lee, Jeffrey Xu Yu, Tok Wang Ling, Anthony K. H. Tung, Dimitris Papadias, Wynne Hsu, Bing Liu, Ke Wang, Yufei Tao, Xifeng Yan, Wei Fan, **Laks V. S. Lakshmanan**, Sourav S. Bhowmick, Guozhu Dong, Jianyong Wang
Database	Divesh Srivastava, Nick Koudas, Divyakant Agrawal, Hans-Peter Kriegel, Surajit Chaudhuri, Amr El Abbadi, H. V. Jagadish, Rajeev Rastogi, Minos N. Garofalakis, S. Muthukrishnan, Jennifer Widom, Rakesh Agrawal, Elke A. Rundensteiner, Jeffrey F. Naughton, Rajeev Motwani, Flip Korn, Michael J. Franklin, Johannes Gehrke, Hector Garcia-Molina, Vivek R. Narasayya, Raghu Ramakrishnan, **Laks V. S. Lakshmanan**, Walid G. Aref, Christos Faloutsos, Sihem Amer-Yahia

b   Philip S. Yu

1997–1998   1999–2000   2001–2002   2003–2004   2005–2006

c   Laks V. S. Lakshmanan

1997–1998   1999–2000   2001–2002   2003–2004   2005–2006

Fig. 18.8 (**a**) Top members in the Data Mining (DM) and Database (DB) communities, sorted by $p_{k \to i}$. (**b, c**) The evolution of community memberships for two top authors. In the compasses, an *arrow* close to the vertical axis indicates a large value of the community membership in the DM community and to the horizontal axis indicates a large value of the community membership in the DB community. Hence, the first author consistently played an important role mainly in the DM community, whereas the second author had a varying role in both communities

x-axis) indicates a large value of the community membership in the DB community. We can see that the first author consistently played an important role mainly in the DM community, whereas the second author had a varying role in both the two communities.

Compared to prior link analysis algorithms, such as HITS and PageRank, our FacetNet has two advantages: (a) Localized measures: Unlike most of the ranking algorithms that give global measures, In FacetNet, we obtain individual importance (in terms of his/her participation in each community) and community membership simultaneously. The importance measures are localized (per community) and can be aggregated as global measures on the entire network. (b) Temporal variation: The importance of a node, and the context in which the node is deemed important, may vary over time. A simple function for discounting the historic data is not sufficient to capture different types of variation. FacetNet allows understanding how the nodes' global and local importance change over time.

Summary. The analysis of communities and their evolutions in dynamic temporal networks is a challenging research problem with broad applications. In this work, we proposed a framework, FacetNet, that combines the task of community extraction and the task of evolution extraction in a unified process. To the best of our knowledge, our framework is the first probabilistic generative model that simultaneously analyzes communities and their evolutions. The results obtained from our model allow us to assign soft community memberships to individual nodes, to analyze the strength of ties among various communities, to study how the affiliations of an individual to different communities change over time, as well as to reveal how communities evolve over time. The experimental results on time-dependent ranking in the DBLP communities demonstrate utility of our FacetNet framework. It reveals the community membership evolution for an individual or the evolutions of the communities, and to discover many interesting insights in dynamic networks that are not directly obtainable from existing methods.

We are currently extending this framework in two directions. First, our current model only considered the link information. In many applications, the content information (e.g., the contents of blog entries and the abstracts of papers) is also very important. We are investigating how to incorporate content information into our framework. Second, so far we only use our model to explain the observed data. To extend our model to predict future behaviors of individuals in a dynamic social network is also an important research topic. We shall investigate some of these directions in next section.

18.4 Community Analysis on Multi-Relational Social Data

This work aims at discovering community structure in rich media social networks, through analysis of the time-varying multi-relational data. As an example scenario, let us consider the use of social media in enterprises, which have increasingly

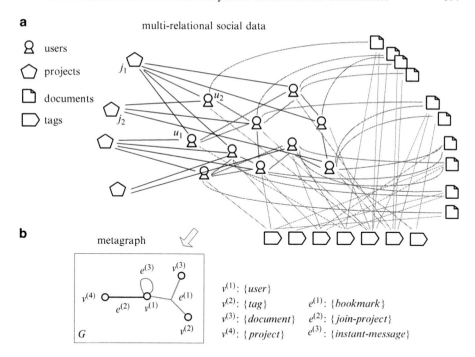

Fig. 18.9 (**a**) Users and related objects in an enterprise. (**b**) A metagraph that represents the enterprise social context

embraced social media software to promote collaboration. Such social media, including wikis, blogs, bookmark sharing, instant messaging, emails, calendar sharing, and so on, foster dynamic collaboration patterns that deviates from the formal organizational structure (e.g. cooperate departments, geographical places, etc.). People who are close in the formal organizational structure (e.g. formal collaboration network) might be far apart in the communication network (e.g. the network of instant messaging). On the other hand, users' document access patterns might be related to their corporate roles as well as personal interests. Figure 18.9a shows an example of such multi-relational social data. The complex and dynamic interplay of various social relations and interactions in an enterprise reflects the day-to-day collaboration practice – how people assemble themselves for a task or activity, how ideas are shared or propagated, through which communication means, who are considered to be expert at some tasks, or what pieces of information are relevant to a particular task, and so on.

In this section, we introduce the first graph-based tensor factorization algorithm to analyze the dynamics of heterogeneous social networks, which can flexibly discover communities along different dimensions (membership, content, etc.), and can help predict users' potential interests.

18.4.1 Embeddedness, Artifacts and Community Discovery

Studies have shown that individual behaviors usually result from mechanisms depending on their social networks. Social embeddedness [3] indicates the choices of individuals depend on how they are integrated in dense clusters or multiplex relations of social networks. For example, social embeddedness in cohesive structures can lead people to make similar political contributions [31]. A similar idea has been grounded in situated cognition. According to Dewey, an individual's actions will always be interrelated to all others within certain social medium that forms the individual membership in a community. Once membership is established, the individual begins to share the same supply of knowledge that the group possesses. Accordingly, this shared experience forms an emotional tendency to motivate individual behavior in such a way that it creates purposeful activity evoking certain meaningful outcomes [32].

This work has suggested the behavioral dynamics of individuals occur under complex, social conditions that simultaneously give rise to the community structure (i.e. the "dense cluster" or "community membership"). While the conditions may be ambiguous, situated cognition theorists have suggested that "artifacts holding historic and negotiated significance within a particular context." Based on the idea, we presume the community structure latent in multiplex relations based on shared artifacts affects and is affected by individual choices. That is, community structure that accounts for inherent dependencies between individuals embedded in a multi-relational network can help understand and predict the behavioral dynamics of individuals.

18.4.2 Extracting Communities from Rich-Context Social Networks

We focus on the multi-relational network observed from the social media. We define the problem as discovering latent community structure from the context of user actions represented by multi-relational social networks. The problem has three parts: (1) how to represent multi-relational social data, (2) how to reveal the latent communities consistently across multiple relations, and (3) how to track the communities over time.

18.4.2.1 Problem Formulation

We formally represent multi-relational social data through *tensor algebra* and *metagraph representation*.

Tensor Algebra. A tensor is a mathematical representation of a multi-way array. The order of a tensor is the number of modes (or ways). A first-order tensor is a vector, a second-order tensor is a matrix, and a higher-order tensor has three or more modes. We use $\mathbf{x}$ to denote a vector, $\mathbf{X}$ denote a matrix, and $\mathcal{X}$ a tensor. Each entry (i, j, k) in a tensor, for example, could represent the number of times the user i submitted an entry on topic j with keyword k.

Metagraph Representation. We introduce *metagraph*, a relational hypergraph for representing multi-relational and multi-dimensional social data. We use a metagraph to configure the relational context specific to the system features – this is the key to make our community analysis adaptable to various social media contexts, e.g. an enterprise or a social media website like Digg. We shall an enterprise example to illustrate three concepts: *facet, relation*, and *relational hypergraph*.

As shown in Fig. 18.9a, assume we observe a set of users in an enterprise. These users might collaborate under different working projects, e.g. the user u_1 and u_2 work for the project j_1, and user u_2 belong to two projects j_1 and j_2 at the same time. Collaboration can occur implicitly across different social media such as instant messenger or email, e.g. user u_3 frequently IM with u_1 and u_2. We denote a set of objects or entities of the same type as a *facet*, e.g. a user facet is a set of users, a project facet is a set of projects. We denote the interactions among facets as a *relation*; a relation can involve two (i.e. binary relation) or more facets, e.g. the "join-project" relation involves two facets (user, project), and the "bookmark" relation involves three facets (user, document, tag). A facet can be implicit, depending on whether the facet entities interact with other facets, e.g. the set of bookmark object might be omitted due to no interaction with other facets. Formally, we denote the q-th facet as $v^{(q)}$ and the set of all facets as V. A set of instantiations of an M-way relation e on facets $v^{(1)}, v^{(2)}, \ldots, v^{(M)}$ is a subset of the Cartesian product $v^{(1)} \times \ldots \times v^{(M)}$. We denote a particular relation by $e^{(r)}$ where r is the relation index. The observations of an M-way relation $e^{(r)}$ are represented as an M-way data tensor $\mathcal{X}^{(r)}$.

Now we introduce a *multi-relational hypergraph* (denoted as *metagraph*) to describe the combination of relations and facets in a social media context (Fig. 18.9b). A hypergraph is a graph where edges, called *hyperedges*, connect to any number of vertices. The idea is to use an M-way hyperedge to represent the interactions of M facets: each facet as a vertex and each relation as a hyperedge on a hypergraph. A metagraph defines a particular structure of interactions among facets, not among facet elements. Formally, for a set of facets $V = \{v^{(q)}\}$ and a set of relations $E = \{e^{(r)}\}$, we construct a metagraph $G = (V, E)$. To reduce notational complexity, V and E also represent the set of all vertex and edge indices, respectively. A hyperedge/relation $e^{(r)}$ is said to be incident to a facet/vertex $v^{(q)}$ if $v^{(q)} \in e^{(r)}$, which is represented by $v^{(q)} \sim e^{(r)}$ or $e^{(r)} \sim v^{(q)}$. E.g., in Fig. 18.9b, the vertex $v^{(1)}$ represents the user facet, the hyperedge $e^{(1)} = \{v^{(1)}, v^{(2)}, v^{(3)}\}$ represents the "bookmark" relation.

Based on the discussed in Sect. 18.4.1, we assume the interaction between any two entities (users or media objects) i and j in a community k, written as x_{ij}, can be viewed as a function of the relationships between community k with entity i, and k with j. If we consider the function to be stochastic, i.e. let $p_{k \to i}$ indicate how likely an interaction in the k-th community involves the i-th entity and p_k is the probability of an interaction in the k-th community, we can express x_{ij} by $x_{ij} \approx \sum_k p_{k \to i} \cdot p_{k \to j} \cdot p_k$ (as discussed in Sect. 18.3.2). Likewise a 3-way interaction among entity i_1, i_2 and i_3 is $x_{i_1 i_2 i_3} \approx \sum_k p_k \bullet p_{k \to i_1} \bullet p_{k \to i_2} \bullet p_{k \to i_3}$. A set of such interactions among entities in facet $v^{(1)}$, $v^{(2)}$ and $v^{(3)}$ can be written by:

$$\mathcal{X} \approx \sum_{k=1}^{K} p_k \mathbf{u}_k^{(1)\circ} \mathbf{u}_k^{(2)\circ} \mathbf{u}_k^{(3)} = [\mathbf{z}] \prod_{m=1}^{3} \times_m \mathbf{U}^{(m)} \qquad (18.11)$$

where $\mathcal{X} \in \mathfrak{R}_{+}^{I_1 \times I_2 \times I_3}$, is the data tensor representing the observed three-way interactions among facet $v^{(1)}$, $v^{(2)}$ and $v^{(3)}$. $p_{k \to i_q}$ is written as an (i_q, k)-element of $\mathbf{U}^{(q)}$ for $q = 1, 2, 3$. $\mathbf{U}^{(q)}$ is an $I_q \times K$ matrix, where I_q is the size of $v^{(q)}$. The probabilities of communities are elements of $\mathbf{z}$, i.e. $p_k = \mathbf{z}_k$. We use $[\mathbf{z}]$ to denote a superdiagonal tensor, where the operation $[\cdot]$ transforms a vector $\mathbf{z}$ to a superdiagonal tensor by setting tensor element $z_{k...k} = \mathbf{z}_k$ and other elements as 0. The decomposition defined in (18.11) is similar to the CP/PARAFAC tensor decomposition [33, 34] except that the *core tensor* $[\mathbf{z}]$ and the *factor matrices* $\{\mathbf{U}^{(q)}\}$ are constrained to contain nonnegative probability values. Under the nonnegative constraints, the 3-way tensor factorization is equivalent to the three-way aspect model in a three-dimensional co-occurrence data [35].

The nonnegative tensor decomposition can be viewed as community discovery in a single relation. The interactions in social media networks are more complex – usually involving multiple two- or multi-way relations. By using metagraphs, we represent a diverse set of relational context in the same form and define community discovery problem on a metagraph, with the following two technical issues: (a) how to extract community structure as coherent interaction latent spaces from observed social data defined on a metagraph, and (b) how to extract community structure as coherent interaction latent spaces from time evolving data given a metagraph. The problems are formally stated as follows.

Definition 18.3. (*Metagraph Factorization or MF*): given a metagraph $G = (V, E)$ and a set of observed data tensors $\{\mathcal{X}^{(r)}\}_{r \in E}$ defined on G, find a nonnegative core tensor $[\mathbf{z}]$ and factors $\{\mathbf{U}^{(q)}\}_{q \in V}$ for corresponding facets $V = \{v^{(q)}\}$. (Since E also represents the set of all edge indices, the notations $r \in E$ and $e^{(r)} \in E$ are exchangeable. Likewise, $q \in V$ and $v^{(q)} \in V$ are exchangeable).

Definition 18.4. (*Metagraph Factorization for Time evolving data, or MFT*): given a metagraph $G = (V, E)$ and a sequential set of observed data tensors $\left\{ \mathcal{X}_t^{(r)} \right\}_{r \in E}$ defined on G for time $t = 1, 2, \ldots$, find nonnegative core tensor $[\mathbf{z}_t]$ and factors $\left\{ \mathbf{U}_t^{(q)} \right\}_{q \in V}$ for corresponding facets $V = \{v^{(q)}\}$.

We will present our method in two steps: (1) present a solution to MF (next section); (2) extend the solution to solve MFT (Sect 18.4.2.3).

18.4.2.2 Metagraph Factorization

The MF problem can be stated in terms of optimization. Let us first consider a simple metagraph case. Assume we are given a metagraph $G = (V, E)$ with three vertices $V = \{v^{(1)}, v^{(2)}, v^{(3)}\}$ and two 2-way hyperedges $E = \{e^{(a)}, e^{(b)}\}$ that describe the interactions among these three facets, as shown in Fig. 18.10. The observed data corresponding to the hyperedges are two second-order data tensors (i.e. matrices) $\{\mathcal{X}^{(a)}, \mathcal{X}^{(b)}\}$ with facets $\{v^{(1)}, v^{(2)}\}$ and $\{v^{(2)}, v^{(3)}\}$ respectively. The facet $v^{(2)}$ is shared by both tensors.

The goal is to extract community structure from data tensors, through finding a nonnegative core tensor [**z**] and factors $\{\mathbf{U}^{(1)}, \mathbf{U}^{(2)}, \mathbf{U}^{(3)}\}$ corresponding to the three facets. The core tensor and factors need to consistently explain the data, i.e. we can approximately express the data by $\mathcal{X}^{(a)} \approx [\mathbf{z}] \times_1 \mathbf{U}^{(1)} \times_2 \mathbf{U}^{(2)}$ and $\mathcal{X}^{(b)} \approx [\mathbf{z}] \times_2 \mathbf{U}^{(2)} \times_3 \mathbf{U}^{(3)}$, as illustrated in Fig. 18.10. The core tensor [**z**] and facet $\mathbf{U}^{(2)}$ are shared by the two approximations, and the length of **z** is determined by the number of latent spaces (communities) to be extracted. Since both the left- and the right-hand side of the approximation are probability distributions, it is natural to use the KL-divergence (denoted as $D(\cdot||\cdot)$) as a measure of approximation cost.

We can generalize Fig. 18.10 to any metagraph G, as: given a metagraph $G = (V, E)$, the objective is to factorize all data tensors such that all tensors can be approximated by a common nonnegative core tensor [**z**] and a shared set of nonnegative factors $\{\mathbf{U}^{(q)}\}$, i.e. to minimize the following cost function:

$$J\,(G) = \min_{\mathbf{z}, \{\mathbf{U}^{(q)}\}} \sum_{r \in E} D(\mathcal{X}^{(r)} || [\mathbf{z}] \prod_{m:v^{(m)} \sim e^{(r)}} \times_m \mathbf{U}^{(m)})$$

$$\text{s.t. } \mathbf{z} \in \mathfrak{R}_+^{1 \times K}, \mathbf{U}^{(q)} \in \mathfrak{R}_+^{I_q \times K} \forall q, \sum_i \mathbf{U}_{ik}^{(q)} = 1 \forall q \forall k \qquad (18.12)$$

where K is the number of communities, and $D(\cdot||\cdot)$ is the KL-divergence as described above. The constraint that each column of $\{\mathbf{U}^{(q)}\}$ must sum to one is added

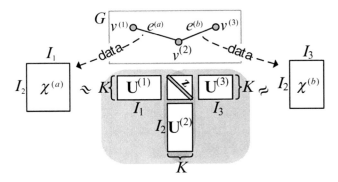

Fig. 18.10 An example of the metagraph factorization (MF). Given observed data tensors $\{\mathcal{X}^{(a)}, \mathcal{X}^{(b)}\}$ and a metagraph G that describes the interaction among facets $\{v^{(1)}, v^{(2)}, v^{(3)}\}$, find consistent community structure expressed by core tensor [z] and facet factors $\{\mathbf{U}^{(1)}, \mathbf{U}^{(2)}, \mathbf{U}^{(3)}\}$

due to the modeling assumption that the probability of an occurrence of a relation on an entity is independent of other entities in a community. This equation can be easily extended to incorporate weights on relations.

Solution 18.3. By employing the concavity of the log function (in the KL-divergence), we derive a local minima solution to (18.12). The solution can be found by the following updating algorithm:

$$\mathbf{z}_k \leftarrow \sum_{r \in E} \sum_{i_1 \cdots i_{M_r}} \mathcal{X}^{(r)}_{i_1 \cdots i_{M_r}} \mu^{(r)}_{i_1 \cdots i_{M_r} k}$$

$$U^{(q)}_{i_q k} \leftarrow \sum_{l:e^{(l)} \sim v^{(q)}} \sum_{i_1 \cdots i_{q-1} i_{q+1} \cdots i_{M_l}} \mathcal{X}^{(l)}_{i_1 \cdots i_{M_l}} \mu^{(l)}_{i_1 \cdots i_{M_l} k}$$

$$\text{where } \mu^{(r)}_{i_1 \cdots i_{M_r} k} \leftarrow \frac{\mathbf{z}_k \prod_{m:v^{(m)} \sim e^{(r)}} \times_m \mathbf{U}^{(m)}_{i_m k}}{([\mathbf{z}] \prod_{m:v^{(m)} \sim e^{(r)}} \times_m \mathbf{U}^{(m)})_{i_1 \cdots i_{M_r}}} \tag{18.13}$$

where $\mathbf{z}$ is a length K vector, $L = |E|$ denotes the total number of hyperedges on G.

After updates, each column of $\mathbf{U}^{(q)}$ and the vector $\mathbf{z}$ are normalized to sum to one. Because of this normalization step, we have omitted the scaling constant for updating $\mathbf{z}$ and $\mathbf{U}^{(q)}$. This iterative update algorithm is a generalization of the algorithm proposed by Lee et al. [36] for solving the single nonnegative matrix factorization problem. In metagraph factorization, the update for core tensor [$\mathbf{z}$] depends on all hyperedges on the metagraph, and the update for each facet factor $\mathbf{U}^{(q)}$ depends on the hyperedges incident to the facet. The details of this algorithm can be found in [37].

18.4.2.3 Time Evolving Extension

In the MFT problem, the relational data is constantly changing as evolving tensor sequences. We propose an online version of MF to handle dynamic data. Since historic information is contained in the community model extracted based on previously observed data, the new community structure to be extracted should be consistent with previous community model and new observations, which is similar to evolutionary clustering discussed in Sect. 18.3. To achieve this, we extend the objective in (18.12) as follows.

A community model for a particular time t is defined uniquely by the factors $\left\{\mathbf{U}_t^{(q)}\right\}$ and core tensor [$\mathbf{z}_t$]. (To avoid notation clutter, we omit the time indices for t.) For each time t, the objective is to factorize the observed data into the nonnegative factors $\{\mathbf{U}^{(q)}\}$ and core tensor [$\mathbf{z}$] which are close to the prior community model, [$\mathbf{z}_{t-1}$] and $\left\{\mathbf{U}_{t-1}{}^{(q)}\right\}$. We introduce a cost l_{prior} to indicate how the new community structure deviates from the previous structure in terms of the KL-divergence. The new objective is defined as follows:

$$J_2(G) = \min_{\mathbf{z},\{\mathbf{U}^{(q)}\}} (1-\alpha) \sum_{r \in E} D\left(\mathcal{X}^{(r)} \| [\mathbf{z}] \prod_{m:v^{(m)} \sim e^{(r)}} \times_m \mathbf{U}^{(m)}\right) + \alpha l_{prior}$$

$$\text{with } l_{prior} = D(\mathbf{z}_{t-1}\|\mathbf{z}) + \sum_q D\left(\mathbf{U}_{t-1}^{(q)}\|\mathbf{U}^{(q)}\right)$$

$$\text{s.t. } \mathbf{z} \in \mathfrak{R}_+^{1 \times K}, \mathbf{U}^{(q)} \in \mathfrak{R}_+^{I_q \times K} \forall q, \sum_i \mathbf{U}_{ik}^{(q)} = 1 \forall q \forall k \qquad (18.14)$$

where α is a real positive number between 0 and 1 to specify how much the prior community model contributes to the new community structure. l_{prior} is a regularizer used to find similar pair of core tensors and pairs of facet factors for consecutive time. The new community structure will be a solution incrementally updated based on a prior community model.

Solution 18.4. Based on a derivation similar to the discussion in Sect. 18.4.2.2, we provide a solution to (18.14) as follows:

$$z_k \leftarrow (1-\alpha) \sum_{r \in E} \sum_{i_1 \cdots i_{M_r}} \mathcal{X}^{(r)}_{i_1 \cdots i_{M_r}} \mu^{(r)}_{i_1 \cdots i_{M_r} k} + \alpha z_{k;t-1}$$

$$U_{i_q k}^{(q)} \leftarrow (1-\alpha) \sum_{l:e^{(l)} \sim v^{(q)}} \sum_{i_1 \cdots i_{q-1} i_{q+1} \cdots i_{M_l}} \mathcal{X}^{(l)}_{i_1 \cdots i_{M_l}} \mu^{(l)}_{i_1 \cdots i_{M_l} k} + \alpha U_{i_q k;t-1}^{(q)} \quad (18.15)$$

where $\mathbf{z}$ is a length K vector, $\mu^{(l)}_{i_1 \cdots i_{M_l} k}$ is defined as in (18.13). After updates, each column of $\mathbf{U}^{(q)}$ and the vector $\mathbf{z}$ are normalized to sum to one. Because of this normalization step, we have dropped the scaling constant for updating $\mathbf{z}$ and $\mathbf{U}^{(q)}$. It can be shown that the parameters in the previous model ($\mathbf{z}_{t-1}$ and $\left\{\mathbf{U}_{t-1}^{(q)}\right\}$) act as Dirichlet prior distribution to inform the solution search [38], thus the solution is consistent with previous community structure.

18.4.3 Application: Context-Sensitive Prediction in Enterprise

We design a prediction task to illustrate how our community tracking algorithm can be utilized to predict users' future interests based on the multi-relational social data. Specifically, given data D_t at time t, we extract communities to predict users' future use of tags, and compare the prediction with the ground truth in data D_{t+1}. We collected collaboration relationships from the employee profiles and social media (e.g. bookmarks, wiki, etc.) in an enterprise. We then construct multiple relations from the different data sources.

In our experiment, the time interval is 1 month. The overall prediction performance is obtained by taking average prediction performance over 10-month data. We compare our method with two baseline methods: (1) *recurring interests* – predicting future tags (at $t + 1$) as the tags mostly frequently used by the user at t. (2) *collective interests* (pLSA) – predicting future tags by using a well-known collective filtering method (probabilistic latent semantic analysis [39] or pLSA) on the user-tag matrix.

We generate predictions base on the community structure extracted by our method, denoted by MF and MFT. The MF algorithm outputs community structure from relational data of each time slot t_-1. The MFT algorithm uses the same data as MF, with an aid of prior community model extracted for time t-2 as an informative prior. Hence MFT gives results incrementally. From an extracted community model we obtain the probability of a community k, i.e. $p(k)$, and the probability of a user u and a tag q, given community k, i.e. $p(u|k)$ and $p(q|k)$. Then a prediction is made based on the condition probability $p(q|u) \propto p(u, q) \approx \Sigma_{k'} p(k) p(u|k') p(q|k')$. The detailed experiment setting can be found in [37]. Our method can also be applied to a *cold-start* setting by incorporating a folding-in technique (e.g. [35]) to overcome the situation where $p(q|k)$ may not be directly available from the model parameters (e.g. q is a new tag which has not been used before t).

Figure 18.11 shows the relevant improvement compared with the first baseline method, i.e. the recurring interests. The results indicate the prediction given by our community tracking algorithms outperform the baseline methods by 36–250% on the average, which suggest that our method can better capture the cohesive structures of the contexts around users' interests.

Summary. We proposed the MetaFac framework to extract community structures from various social contexts and interactions. There were three key ideas: (1) metagraph, a relational hypergraph for representing multi-relational social data; (2) MF algorithm, an efficient non-negative multi-tensor factorization method for

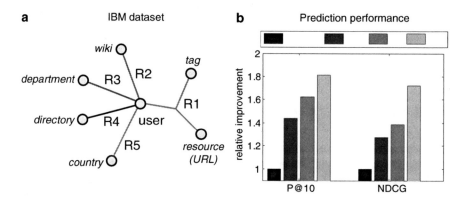

Fig. 18.11 (**a**) IBM dataset: R1, ..., R5 are different relations among the seven facets, e.g. bookmark (R1), join-wiki (R2), etc. The sizes of these relational data from R1∼R5 are: 3K × 12K × 61K, 3K × 1K, 3K × 2K, 3K × 90 and 3K × 42. (**b**) Prediction performance: Our framework improves the prediction of users' future tag use

community extraction on a given metagraph; (3) MFT, an on-line factorization method to handle time-varying relations. To illustrate the utility of our method, we design a tag prediction task in an enterprise context. We generated the predictions based on the extracted community models and compare results with baselines. Our method outperformed baselines up to an order of magnitude. We show significant improvement of our method due to (a) incorporating a historic model and (b) leveraging diverse relations through a metagraph.

There are some open issues in this work. For example, there are different aspects of community evolution, including change in the community size, change in the number of communities and change in the community content or features (what the community is about). To study the evolution within communities, our method has assumed the number of communities does not change across time (i.e. we do not consider the second aspect). Learning and comprehending several evolution aspects in a unified process is a challenging issue.

Nevertheless, our work can lead to several interesting directions. (1) As our algorithm does not tie to a specific data schema, it can be easily extended to deal with schema changes. (2) By combining various social relations of data, it can be used to identify effective social relations based on model selection approaches. As a potential extension of this framework, we are interested in utilizing the relational hypergraph to study the correlation between networks and the behavioral dynamics of individuals.

18.5   Conclusions and Future Directions

In this article, we have discussed our current work on community analysis in dynamic, multi-relational social networks. Our work includes several key ideas: (1) We introduce mutual awareness, a fundamental property of communities in online social media, which is computationally defined based on observable individual actions within the social media context. The effectiveness of mutual awareness features is empirically verified on large-scale real-world blog datasets. We propose an efficient iterative mutual awareness expansion algorithm for community extraction using a random walk based distance measure that quantifying the amount of mutual awareness expanding on the entire network. The community evolution with respect to a query reveals interesting community dynamics. (2) We propose FacetNet framework, the first probabilistic generative model that simultaneously analyzes communities and their evolutions. The results obtained from our method allow us to assign soft community memberships to individual nodes, to analyze the strength of ties among various communities, to study how the affiliations of an individual to different communities change over time, as well as to reveal how communities evolve over time. Extensive experimental studies demonstrated that by using our FacetNet framework, we are able to discover many interesting insights in dynamic networks that are not directly obtainable from existing methods, such as the evolution of individuals' contribution to different communities.

(3) We propose MetaFac, the first graph-based tensor factorization framework for analyzing the dynamics of heterogeneous social networks. We introduce metagraph for modeling multi-relational and multi-dimensional social data. Then we propose an efficient non-negative multi-tensor factorization method for community extraction on a given metagraph. In addition, we provide an on-line extension of this method to handle time-varying multi-relations. Extensive experiments on enterprise and large-scale social media data suggest that our technique is scalable and can help predict users' future interests based on the cohesive structure of contexts extracted by our method.

Our current work has led to several interesting research directions. In social media like Facebook, users often experience overload of online social connections, shared interests and information, as well as the interplay of people and subject matter. For people who are interested in certain topics, it is difficult to understand how the topics (or media items) are, and have been, shared and discussed by different people. This leads to important technical questions on how to disentangle and display the complex dynamic relationships between people and subjects over time. Our methods can be used to support interactive visualization that allows users to explore and query multiple aspects of community activities, such as relevant topics, representative users and artifacts (e.g. tweets, photos) of the communities, as well as their relationships and evolutions.

Our work can also contribute to research in social science. For example, anthropologists are interested in material cultural transition based on artifacts and their association with time and space. Our work on community analysis has identified several relevant structural elements from large scale observable interpersonal activities in social media, including community awareness (mutual and transitive awareness), community composition (degree of individuals' participation in communities), community inter-structure (the relationship among communities and how it changes over time), community context (e.g. time and location associated with community activities) and community artifacts (e.g. tags and photos generated by communities). We have used these structural elements to discover interesting cultural patterns among communities, e.g. the interaction of right-wing and left-wing communities in blog data. We plan to extend the current approach to discover the structural changes of a community as well as the context where the changes occur, to support the search and detection of emergent or transitional cultural patterns. Ethnographic investigation is needed in order to reveal finer-grained patterns of human interactions as well as qualitative understanding of the extracted structures. Extracting the evolution of inter-structure among different communities will help understand the condition and impact of social media as a new communicative practice.

Acknowledgement This material is based upon work supported in part by NEC Labs America, an IBM Ph.D. Fellowship and a Kauffman Entrepreneur Scholarship. We are pleased to acknowledge Yun Chi, Shenghuo Zhu, Belle Tseng, Jun Tatemura and Koji Hino, from NEC Labs America, for providing the invaluable advices on community discovery and the NEC Blog dataset. We are indebted to Jimeng Sun, Paul Castro and Ravi Konuru, from IBM T.J. Watson Research Center, for providing advices on tensor analysis and the IBM enterprise data.

References

1. J. Brown, A. Collins, et al. (1989). *Situated Cognition and the Culture of Learning*. Educational Researcher **18**(1): 32.
2. J. Lemke (1997). *Cognition, Context, and Learning: A social Semiotic Perspective*. In: Situated Cognition: Social, Semiotic, and Psychological Perspectives. Erlbaum, Mahwah, NJ, pp 37–56.
3. M. Granovetter (1985). *Economic Action and Social Structure: A Theory of Embeddedness*. American Journal of Sociology **91**(3): 481–510.
4. N. Friedkin and E. Johnsen (1999). *Social Influence Networks and Opinion Change*. Advances in Group Processes **16**: 1–29.
5. L. Backstrom, D. Huttenlocher, et al. (2006). *Group Formation in Large Social Networks: Membership, Growth, and Evolution*. SIGKDD, 44–54, 2006.
6. S. Wasserman and K. Faust (1994). Social Network Analysis: Methods and Applications. Cambridge University Press, Cambridge.
7. L. Backstrom, R. Kumar, et al. (2008). *Preferential Behavior in Online Groups*. Proceedings of the International Conference on Web Search and Web Data Mining, 117–128.
8. J. M. Kleinberg (1999). *Authoritative Sources in a Hyperlinked Environment*. Journal of the ACM **46**(5): 604–632.
9. S. Brin and L. Page (1998). *The Anatomy of a Large-Scale Hypertextual Web Search Engine*. Computer Networks and ISDN Systems **30**(1–7): 107–117.
10. J. Shi and J. Malik (2000). *Normalized Cuts and Image Segmentation*. IEEE Transactions on Pattern Analysis and Machine Intelligence **22**(8): 888–905.
11. T. Kolda and J. Sun (2008). *Scalable Tensor Decompositions for Multi-aspect Data Mining*. ICDM, 2008.
12. H. Rheingold (1899). Virtual Community: Homesteading on the Electronic Frontier. MIT Press, London.
13. Q. Jones (1997). *Virtual-Communities, Virtual Settlements & Cyber-Archaeology: A Teoretical Outline*. Journal of Computer Mediated Communication **3**(3): 35–49.
14. H. Garfinkel (1984). Studies in Ethnomethodology. Polity Press, Cambridge.
15. P. Dourish (2001). Where the Action Is: The Foundations of Embodied Interaction. MIT Press, Cambridge.
16. D. Garlaschelli and M. Loffredo (2004). *Patterns of Link Reciprocity in Directed Networks*. Physical Review Letters **93**(26): 268701.
17. M. Granovetter (1973). *The Strength of Weak Ties*. American Journal of Sociology **78**(6): 1360.
18. Y.-R. Lin, H. Sundaram, et al. (2006). *Discovery of Blog Communities Based on Mutual Awareness*. The 3rd Annual Workshop on the Weblogging Ecosystems: Aggregation, Analysis and Dynamics.
19. J. Travers and S. Milgram (1969). *An Experimental Study of the Small World Problem*. Sociometry **32**(4): 425–443.
20. Y.-R. Lin, H. Sundaram, et al. (2007). *Blog Community Discovery and Evolution Based on Mutual Awareness Expansion*. IEEE/WIC/ACM International Conference on Web Intelligence, 2007.
21. F. Chung and S. Yau (2000). *Discrete Green's Functions*. Journal of Combinatorial Theory (A) **91**(1–2): 191–214.
22. I. Dhillon, Y. Guan, et al. (2005). *A Unified View of Kernel k-Means, Spectral Clustering and Graph Partitioning*. Technical Report. University of Texas, Austin.
23. R. Kannan, S. Vempala, et al. (2004). *On Clusterings: Good, Bad and Spectral*. Journal of the ACM **51**(3): 497–515.
24. M. Sahami and T. Heilman (2006). *A web-based kernel function for measuring the similarity of short text snippets*. Proceedings of the 15th International Conference on World Wide Web, 377–386, 2006.
25. S. Asur, S. Parthasarathy, et al. (2007). *An Event-based Framework for Characterizing the Evolutionary Behavior of Interaction Graphs*. Proceedings of the 13th ACM SIGKDD International Conference on Knowledge Discovery and Data Mining.

26. G. Palla, A. Barabasi, et al. (2007). *Quantifying Social Group Evolution*. Nature **446**: 664–667.
27. D. Chakrabarti, R. Kumar, et al. (2006). *Evolutionary Clustering*. SIGKDD, 554–560.
28. Y. Chi, X. Song, et al. (2007). *Evolutionary Spectral Clustering by Incorporating Temporal Smoothness*. SIGKDD.
29. K. Yu, S. Yu, et al. (2005). *Soft Clustering on Graphs*. NIPS'05.
30. Y.-R. Lin, Y. Chi, et al. (2009). *Analyzing Communities and Their Evolutions in Dynamics Networks*. Transactions on Knowledge Discovery from Data (TKDD) **3**(2): 1–31.
31. J. Moody and D. White (2003). *Structural Cohesion and Embeddedness: A Hierarchical Concept of Social Groups*. American Sociological Review **68**: 103–127.
32. A. Agostino (1999). *The Relevance of Media as Artifact: Technology Situated in Context*. Educational Technology & Society **2**(4): 46–52.
33. J. Carroll and J. Chang (1970). *Analysis of Individual Differences in Multidimensional Scaling Via an N-way Generalization of "Eckart-Young" Decomposition*. Psychometrika **35**(3): 283–319.
34. R. Harshman (1970). *Foundations of the PARAFAC Procedure: Models and Conditions for an "Explanatory" Multi-Modal Factor Analysis*. UCLA Working Papers in Phonetics **16**(1): 84.
35. A. Popescul, L. H. Ungar, et al. (2001). *Probabilistic Models for Unified Collaborative and Content-Based Recommendation in Sparse-Data Environments*. UAI 2001, 437–444.
36. D. Lee and H. Seung (2001). *Algorithms for Non-Negative Matrix Factorization*. NIPS, 556–562, 2001.
37. Y.-R. Lin, J. Sun, et al. (2009). *MetaFac: Community Discovery via Relational Hypergraph Factorization*. SIGKDD, 2009.
38. Y.-R. Lin, Y. Chi, et al. (2008). *FaceNet: A Framework for Analyzing Communities and Their Evolutions in Dynamics Networks*. Proceedings of the 17th International World Wide Web Conference, 2008.
39. T. Hofmann (1999). *Probabilistic Latent Semantic Indexing*. SIGIR, 1999.

Chapter 19
Accessibility Testing of Social Websites

Cecilia Sik Lányi

19.1 Introduction

There is no doubt that social websites have become one of the greatest inventions of the twenty-first century. Maintaining social connections, getting new and new friends, online entertainment: these are the very things we expect a good portal to provide. The concept of the social websites is that upon registration users share a desired amount of personal data with other users and after that they build a so called friend network using their acquaintances as building elements. The more acquaintances are present the more information is accessible during a certain period of time.

Although the goals of these sites are somewhat common, the audience is not always the same. Among these social systems we can distinguish between two main categories, regarding their user sets. One of these are the ISN (International Social Networking) systems, which usually cover closed, invitation based communities, linked by common factors of interests (school, workplace, etc.). The other group is called ESN (External Social Networking) which characterises the well known social websites like Facebook, iWiW. Although most of the ESN sites are also invitation based, receiving an invitation doesn't require special privileges, only a contact on the certain site. It is also interesting that ESN sites may hold ISN sites protected by passwords or invitation by their creators. But the very question arises: are these social sites usable by anyone?

Most software engineering companies do not develop products for special users, because they do not see potentiality in this limited market. It is a fact, that 10% of the population worldwide is handicapped [1].

Due to the growing age of workforce and high accident rates in some countries, the number of handicapped people will increase [2]. In the USA 14% of the population is estimated to suffer from a disability. When we look at people, aged 65 and over, this figure becomes 50%. Disabilities are strongly linked with age. Our

C.S. Lányi (✉)
Virtual Environment and Imaging Technologies Laboratory, Department of Electrical Engineering, University of Pannonia, Veszprem, Hungary
e-mail: lanyi@almos.uni-pannon.hu

B. Furht (ed.), *Handbook of Social Network Technologies and Applications*,
DOI 10.1007/978-1-4419-7142-5_19, © Springer Science+Business Media, LLC 2010

societies are facing a growing number of people aged 75 and more, who are likely to have impairments or disabilities. In Europe this group will total up to 14.4% of the population in 2040, compared with 7.5% in 2003: it will almost double [3]. By 2020, 25% of the EU's population will be over 65. Spending on pensions, health and long-term care is expected to increase by 4–8% of the GDP in forthcoming decades, with total expenditures tripling by 2050. However, older Europeans are also important consumers with a combined wealth of over €3,000 billion [4].

We know very well, the elderly people have several health problems. The number of the elderly people grows dramatically. A paradigm shift is needed: producers should put these consumers from margin to the mainstream, because the main users will no longer be children and young, or middle aged healthy adults. The now mainstream consumers use the Internet and obviously are members of social sites. They surely would like to continue using these services in their "silver years" in order to maintain their social connections easier. Will they really be able to do so? To do so we have to examine, are those websites barrier free?

Average web-designers do not take into consideration the specific needs of handicapped users, although there are several guidelines available to help software developers to produce accessible software product with minimal effort. In recent times, lots of efforts are being made to build accessibility and usability standards of international quality, especially for Web content. These guidelines usually warrant minimal requirements from the part of the users [5]. For example the current amount of keyboard support in most common web sites is far from being sufficient [6].

When we talk of Social Websites, the first thing, that comes into our mind is, that these are web sites or in other words web pages for building and reflecting social networks or social relations among people, e.g., who share interests and/or activities or just would like to build a community based on the same interest. If we sum up the number of the registered users of several social networks [7] we will get about 1,173,000,210 registered users of these sites. Yes, maybe some people are member of not only one social side but several sites, still we can say that nowadays 1/5 of the earth's population is a member of a social website. It is a huge number. If we consider, that more than 10% of the members have special needs, it is more than 117,300,000 people. It is a nonsense, not to take into consideration the needs of these people, not to ensure equal opportunity for them in the fields of information communication technology.

Numerous validator programmes are available as free service, to test accessibility, for example W3C Quality Assurance Tools [8], WebXACT [9], Opera [10]. Naturally, each one has advantages and disadvantages. The W3C Quality Assurance Tools are almost universal for validating Web Standards, languages and CSS stylesheets. Moreover they have Specific Tools – for Specific Needs, for example: RDF Validator [11] checks and visualizes RDF documents. XML Schema Validator [12] is a form for checking a schema, which is accessible via the Web. Almost all of these tools are web-based, they are available both as downloadable sources, and as free services on the w3.org site.

Unfortunately none of these services is universal, none of them is able to test accessibility and usability aspects of the following user groups at the same time: standard users (mainstream users), blind people, visually impaired people, deaf people, hearing impaired people, people with mobility and movement problems, people with cognitive problems and elderly people.

Therefore, we have developed a checklist and validator software: XValid [13] for testing home pages from the viewpoint of universal design, based on the guidelines of WCAG 2.0.

The XValid validator [13, 14] is a human controlled testing tool for specific needs, in light of accessibility and usability. Usability in the Web design has to cope with important elements like: Perceptibility, Understandability, Operability, Memorability, Efficiency, Technical robustness. Accessibility and usability have technical aspects as well as human interaction aspects [15]. The XValid validator software examines these elements too. As far as we know, there is no other existing validator responding to WCAG 2.0 yet.

With the use of XValid based on the WCAG 2.0 Guidelines, the most well known social websites: Facebook, iWiW, MySpace, YouTube were tested. The tests were followed by a statistical analysis based on the test results. Based on these statistics, the most frequently occurring errors were determined. In this chapter you can find results of this analysis.

19.2 Social Websites and Their User Interfaces

A social network service focuses on building and reflecting social networks or social relationships between people, e.g., who share interests and/or activities [7]. In this section you will read about the functionality and user interfaces of the tested social websites. (Facebook, iWiW, MySpace, YouTube).

Facebook is a social networking website, that is operated and privately owned by Facebook, Inc [16]. It is a social utility, that connects people, to keep in touch with friends, upload photos, share links and videos. Users can add friends and send them messages, and update their personal profiles to notify friends about themselves. Additionally, users can join networks organized by living places, workplaces, schools, or regions. More than 350 million people around the world are using Facebook, to share their lives online [17].

Facebook features a series of creative and funny applications glueing young people in front of the computer displays for hours. There are a huge number of flash games to try. Those games are created to generate some kind of competition between the users based on their shared statistics.

19.2.1 Facebook Lite

This is Facebook's simplified menu system. The new interface is more simple and cleaner. The biggest difference between "classic" and "lite" is the absence of the navigation and information panels on the left side. The input field itself is also replaced by buttons like write, post photo, post video. Based on the changes above, the certain input methods are only displayed and accessible in case, they are really needed. Furthermore, the Friends menu has been replaced by the Events menu. All of the subpages are now more transparent, offering quicker access of the necessary information.

iWiW *(abbreviation for International Who is Who) i*s a Hungarian social networking web service, started on April 14, 2002 as *WiW* (*Who Is Who*). By the end of 2008 the number of the users registered on iWiW reached four million (the number of the Hungarian population is ten million) [18].

Nowadays a decrease in numbers takes place because there are a lot of users who abandon "the path of enlightment" by relocating their virtual headquarters to Facebook. It can also cause problems, that the data, published on such a site can be reached by anybody, even those you would not like to share information with.

The features of iWiW are: multilingual options (15 languages), grouping of contacts, user advertisement system, image storage, enhanced profile and contact display map, personal data visibility settings, user contact listing, city based grouping, system messages, e-mail notifications, message board, message subsystem, forum. All these features contribute to the popularity of iWiW.

MySpace was awarded the most popular social networking site in the United States in June 2006. MySpace is also winning market shares from other social networks. In June 2006, it captured 80% of social networking traffic [19]. MySpace set up a Developer Platform (MDP) which allows developers to share their ideas and write their own MySpace applications. The MDP is based on the Open Social API. The first public beta of the MySpace applications was released on March 5, 2008, with around 1,000 applications [20]. MySpace allows users to customize their user profile pages. Users also have the option to add music to their profile pages via MySpace Music.

YouTube is a video sharing website on which users can upload and share videos: Uploading, tagging and sharing videos worldwide! Before the launch of YouTube in 2005, there were few easy methods available for ordinary computer users who wanted to post videos online. With its simple interface, YouTube made it possible for anyone with an Internet connection to post a video that a worldwide audience could watch within a few minutes [21]. One of the key features of YouTube is the ability of users to view its videos on web pages outside the site. Each YouTube video is accompanied by a piece of HTML, which can be used to embed it on a page outside the YouTube website. This functionality is often used to embed YouTube videos in social networking pages and blogs [22]. YouTube uses Adobe Flash to render content.

Lets take a quick look to the structure and possibilities of these sites. The first point of view according to which we proceed with our investigation is the look and feel. Almost all of these sites, following the latest trends, use prism based layouts on their main pages. The larger, more important prisms contain the main elements displaying the latest events and interactions of our contacts. The borders themselves contain ads or usability enhancement features.

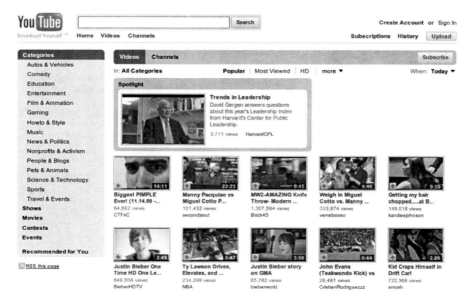

Fig. 19.1 YouTube category view

Most of the popular sites avoid the use of bright colours in order to achieve a clear look and feel. However we should not mix up transparency and a clean or lithe layout. Although iWiW may look crowded at first sight but on Facebook a novice user will require more time to find even the basic functions (which procedure becomes much harder if the user doesn't speak English). All the inspected sites offer the accessibility of their functions in a certain TAB order. Let's have a look at for example Myspace. If you try to sign up, it seems to be easy, but actually it is not (Figs. 19.1 and 19.2).

Another example: try to log in using only the TAB button, we can not be sure, which menu is active (Fig. 19.3).

Without a mouse, logging into the site is close to impossible. To log in, the user needs to push the TAB button at least 35–40 times. However the menus are well ordered, and grouped, the font size is too small for users with low vision, and the color schema is not correct too. As we can see the submenus are logically ordered and can be accessed easily (Fig. 19.4).

Without special hardware devices, which emulate mouse, it is hard to access any menu or submenu on the site. The site structure is well organised, users can do anything what they want with one or two clicks, of course if we suppose that they are using a mouse or equivalent device. Users with low vision can not change the appearance of the site, there are no accessibility settings such as changing font size or contrast.

On Facebook, you need to push the TAB button:

- 56 times at least to make a new comment,
- 80 times to change the language of the page,

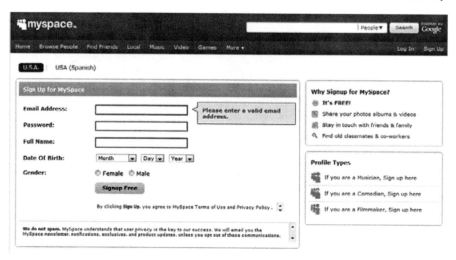

Fig. 19.2 Myspcace, trying to sing up

Fig. 19.3 Myspcace "Where am I"?

- about 45 times to harvest the money from your businesses at Bangkok in MafiaWars ® application,
- To reach the chat function? Forget it, it is impossible with using keyboard only!

Needless to say, all of the layout feature ads are displayed in hope of a great income. In the choice of the displayed ads the age of the targeted users is reflected heavily. Our belief is, that great success may be achieved if social website owner

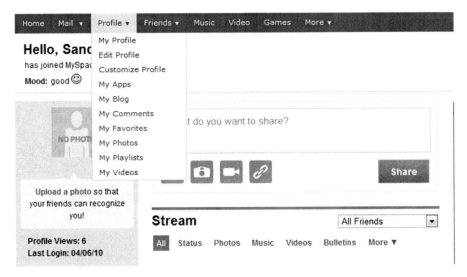

Fig. 19.4 Menu structure of Myspcace

companies successfully integrate accessible applications into their traditional marketing procedure. With web designers taking the elderly and handicapped people into consideration can even an ultimate breakthrough be achieved.

19.3   WEB Accessibility Analysis

The Web Content Accessibility Guidelines 1.0, were created in 1999 by the W3C, aiming to explain to web designers how to make the web content accessible for people with disabilities [23]. The document includes fourteen guidelines, or general principles of accessible web design. Each guideline includes a statement and an explanation. The Web Content Accessibility Guidelines 2.0 was published on December 2008. We conducted our tests before this date, when WCAG 2.0 was under construction and it had four principles and 12 guidelines [24].

19.3.1   The Main Principles and Structure of WCAG 2.0

19.3.1.1   Structure of WCAG 2.0

- Principles – Top four principles
- Guidelines – 12 guidelines provide the basic goals.
- Success criteria – For each guideline, testable success criteria are provided.
- Levels of conformance – Three levels of conformance are defined: A (lowest), AA, and AAA (highest).

- Sufficient and advisory techniques – An informative list of typical mistakes and good-practice techniques is provided. Techniques fall into two categories: those that are sufficient for meeting the success criteria, and those that are advisory.
- Common Failures – it describe authoring practices known to cause Web content not to conform to WCAG 2.0

19.3.1.2   Guideline 1. Perceivable

Information and user interface components must be presentable to users in ways they can perceive.

This means that users must be able to perceive the information being presented (it can't be invisible to all of their senses).

1.1. Text Alternatives: Provide text alternatives for any non-text content so that it can be changed into other forms people need, such as large print, braille, speech, symbols or simpler language.
1.2. Time-based Media: Provide alternatives for time-based media.
1.3. Adaptable: Create content that can be presented in different ways (for example simpler layout) without losing information or structure.
1.4. Distinguishable: Make it easier for users to see and hear content including separating foreground from background.

19.3.1.3   Guideline 2. Operable

User interface components and navigation must be operable.

This means that users must be able to operate the interface (the interface cannot require interaction that a user cannot perform).

2.1. Keyboard Accessible: Make all functionality available from a keyboard
2.2. Enough Time: Provide users enough time to read and use content.
2.3. Seizures: Do not design content in a way that is known to cause seizures.
2.4. Navigable: Provide ways to help users navigate, find content and determine where they are.

19.3.1.4   Guideline 3. Understandable

Information and the operation of user interface must be understandable.

This means that users must be able to understand the information as well as the operation of the user interface (the content or operation cannot be beyond their understanding).

3.1. Readable: Make text content readable and understandable.
3.2. Predictable: Make Web pages appear and operate in predictable ways.
3.3. Input Assistance: Help users avoid and correct mistakes.

19.3.1.5 Guideline 4. Robust

Content must be robust enough that it can be interpreted reliably by a wide variety of user agents, including assistive technologies.

This means that users must be able to access the content as technologies advance (as technologies and user agents evolve, the content should remain accessible).

4.1. Compatible: Maximize compatibility with current and future user agents, including assistive technologies.

19.3.2 The XValid Software

XValid was developed with.Net framework 2.0. The code license of validation core is free, so anyone can build, modify or distribute it. It's a traditional desktop application, but because the validation core is a standalone library an online version is possible. XValid's main advantage is WCAG 2.0 conformity and the free availability. The application is divided into two parts: the validation core and the graphical user interface. Validation core is a standalone library, and it's capable to work without the GUI, so a later online version, or a non-Windows version is possible (although, the P/Invoked FreeImage may be a problem in this case). The application can analyze local files from the computer's file system, or a specific URL. In the first case the user clicks on the "Browse" button, and in the well-known Windows-way, selects a file. In the second case the user enters the exact URL into the textbox. After that the "Check" button can be pressed and some seconds later the report is appearing in the large white area. This report can be saved with the "Save Report" button. Figure 19.5 shows the validation process.

The following guidelines are checked at this stage [13]:

1.1.1. Alternative texts, Image maps (client- and server-side), Short descriptions, Long descriptions
1.3.1. Alternative texts
2.4.3. Titles

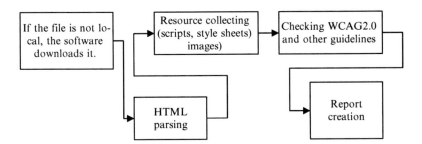

Fig. 19.5 The validation process

2.4.4. Alternative texts
3.1.1. Text direction and language
3.2.5. User requestable functions
4.1.1. Tag closings, Unique ids
4.1.2. Captions, Labels

The validation core tries to analyze every image for improper sizing, every script for unsafe functions (windows.open(), window.alert(), browser-specific codes. . .) and every style sheet for improper styles (although not capable to cover every problem).

The software uses the following third party libraries:

– FreeImage.NET 3 – this is a free wrapper for the excellent FreeImage (which is used under the "FreeImage Public License – Version 1.0"), a free open source graphics library.
– Self-modified version of MIL HTML Parser.

The process (and application usage) is very simple from the user's point of view. After starting the application, the following form is displayed (see Figs. 19.6–19.8).

The most known social websites have been tested with XValid: Facebook, iWiW, MySpace, YouTube. The statistical analysis of our test is shown in Tables 19.1–19.5.

The most serious problems based on our tests are that the WEB designers:

- do not take care of giving alternative short texts for all non text elements,
- do not give a long description although it may be necessary (Table 19.1),
- do not use <label> element to associate text label with form control (Table 19.2),

Fig. 19.6 Testing the Facebook page with XValid (XValid found altogether 98 errors and remarks)

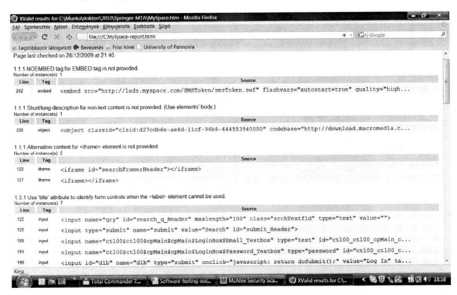

Fig. 19.7   Testing the MySpace page with XValid (XValid found altogether 55 errors and remarks)

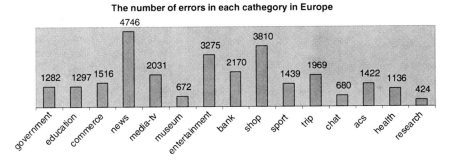

Fig. 19.8   Number of errors in each category occurring on WEB pages in Europe

- do not provide the availability of all functions are available form the keyboard (Table 19.3),
- the <html> elements doesn't have "dir" attributes (Table 19.4),
- do not use the html tags correctly causing severe errors if assistive technologies try to parse the content (Table 19.6).

Table 19.2 shows the analyses of testing Guideline 1.3. The typical error was forgetting the use of <label> element.

We did not found any errors in respect of the Guideline 1.2 and 1.4. We did not found errors in respect of the Guideline 2.2–2.4.

We did not found any errors in respect of the Guideline 3.2 and 3.3.

Table 19.1 Checkpoint errors of guideline 1.1 of principle 1: perceivable

Guideline 1.1 Text alternatives: Provide text alternatives for any non-text content so that it can be changed into other forms people need, such as large print, braille, speech, symbols or simpler language	Social Website	Number of errors	Summa
If a short description can not serve the same purpose and present the same information as the non-text content a long description is necessary	Facebook iWiW MySpace YouTube	1 10 – 24	35
Short text alternative for non-text content is not provided	Facebook iWiW MySpace YouTube	4 15 – 30	49
Short text alternative for non-text content is too long	Facebook iWiW MySpace YouTube	– – – 7	7
NOEMBED tag for EMBED tag is not provided	Facebook iWiW MySpace YouTube	– – 1 –	1
Short/long description for non-text content is not provided. (Use elements' body.)	Facebook iWiW MySpace YouTube	– – 1 –	1
Alternative content for <iframe> element is not provided	Facebook iWiW MySpace YouTube	– 1 2 –	3

The importance of the findings of the tests are justified not only by the special needs users (handicapped people), but by anybody's needs. If we take into consideration that for mainstream users it is much more convenient to use a well designed site than a non-barrier free design, we can say, it is not only a humanitarian standpoint, but potential market and financial question too. If a site is not easy to use, the users will fall away from this site.

For a disabled user, when using a web application, it is very important to achieve nearly the same performance as a non-handicapped, mainstream user. If this is not guaranteed, disabled users may not be able to handle a web application and are thus potentially not able to work in certain areas [5].

We have found altogether 98 errors at Facebook, 110 errors at iWiW, 50 errors at MySpace and 601 errors at YouTube.

Table 19.2 Checkpoint errors of guideline 1.3 of principle 1: perceivable

Guideline 1.3 Adaptable: Create content that can be presented in different ways (for example simpler layout) without losing information structure	Social Website	Number of errors	Summa
Use "title" attribute to identify form controls when the <label> element cannot be used	Facebook	17	37
	iWiW	8	
	MySpace	7	
	YouTube	5	
Use <label> element to associate text label with form control	Facebook	18	112
	iWiW	8	
	MySpace	7	
	YouTube	79	
Advisory information provided with "title" attribute is too short	Facebook	—	52
	iWiW	—	
	MySpace	—	
	YouTube	52	

Table 19.3 Checkpoint errors of guideline 2.1 of principle 2: operable

Guideline 2.1 Keyboard accessible: Make all functionality available from a keyboard	Social website	Number of errors	Summa
Some elements uses pointing device based event handlers. These functions aren't accessible without a pointing device	Facebook	18	206
	iWiW	5	
	MySpace	25	
	YouTube	158	

Table 19.4 Checkpoint errors of guideline 3.1 of principle 3: understandable

Guideline 3.1 Readable: Make text content readable and understandable	Social website	Number of errors	Summa
The <html> element doesn't have "dir" attribute, which specifies the base direction of directionally neutral text. (The default direction is left–right.)	Facebook	1	4
	iWiW	1	
	MySpace	1	
	YouTube	1	
The <html> element doesn't have "lang" attribute, which specifies the base language of text content	Facebook	—	1
	iWiW	1	
	MySpace	—	
	YouTube	—	
The <html> element although has "xml:lang" attribute but doesn't have "lang" attribute	Facebook	—	1
	iWiW	—	
	MySpace	1	
	YouTube	—	

Table 19.5 Checkpoint errors of guideline 4.1 of principle 4: robust

Guideline 4.1 Compatible: Maximize compatibility with current and future user agents, including assistive technologies	Social website	Number of errors	Summa
This tag is not closed correctly. Assistive technologies may can't parse the content accurately	Facebook	–	99
	iWiW	5	
	MySpace	–	
	YouTube	94	
The "id" attribute isn't unique	Facebook	3	13
	iWiW	2	
	MySpace	–	
	YouTube	8	
The "language" attribute is deprecated and not conforms to the current HTML/XHTML specifications. Use "type" instead	Facebook		30
	iWiW	28	
	MySpace	2	
	YouTube	–	
The "type" attribute is missing	Facebook	–	13
	iWiW	7	
	MySpace	–	
	YouTube	6	
The script file has an unusual extension	Facebook	–	1
	iWiW	1	
	MySpace	–	
	YouTube	–	
Use "title" attribute to identify form controls when the <label> element cannot be used	Facebook	17	37
	iWiW	8	
	MySpace	7	
	YouTube	5	
Use <label> element to associate text label with form control	Facebook	18	105
	iWiW	8	
	MySpace	–	
	YouTube	79	
Advisory information provided with "title" attribute is too short	Facebook	–	52
	iWiW	–	
	MySpace	–	
	YouTube	52	
Using <legend> element allows authors to assign a caption to a <fieldset> and improves accessibility	Facebook	–	1
	iWiW	1	
	MySpace	–	
	YouTube	–	

Table 19.6 The number of the tested WEB sites by countries (country/number of tested sites)

Continent	Country	Number of tested site
Europe	Austria	16
	France	37
	Germany	51
	Greece	14
	Hungary	50
	Italy	13
	Lithuania	24
	Norway	13
	Poland	48
	Slovakia	31
	Switzerland	18
	UK	25
Summa in Europe		340
Outside of Europe	Arabic language countries	17
	Israel	26
	Japan	21
	Peru	25
	USA	39
	Taiwan	40
Summa outside of Europe		168

19.4   Compare the Results with Other Website's Accessibility

In our earlier researches [13, 14] we tested 18 countries' sites in 15 categories (Table 19.6): journals-, Web Shops-, Government-, commercial-, healthcare-, TV channels'-, time table-, bank-, assistive technology-, free time-, museums'-, chat-, sport news- sites, e-learning and education sites, approximately 500 sites, with XValid. We made a statistical analysis based on our test not only for Europe but outside Europe, in all 15 mentioned categories. The results are shown by Figs. 19.5 and 19.6.

It is true, not a representative sample of the websites was taken, still the number of the tested websites (>500) is enough to find the most serious problems.

The highest numbers of the errors are in the category of news papers, shop and entertainment and TV channels in Europe (Fig. 19.8). Outside Europe the highest number of the category is news, trip and bank (Fig. 19.9).

As it is shown by Tables 19.1–19.5, we found altogether 98 errors at Facebook, 110 errors at iWiW, 50 errors at MySpace and 601 errors at YouTube. Comparing the analysis of social websites to earlier inspected websites in 15 categories in 18 countries (Figs. 19.8–19.9), we can claim that the investigated social sites are very good because we found less than 100 errors at Facebook and MySpyce websites. These websites are almost barrier free. The other two investigated websites iWiW and YouTobe have more errors.

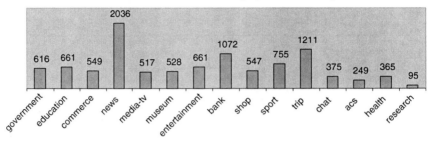

Fig. 19.9 Number of errors in each category occurring on WEB pages outside of Europe

19.5 Conclusions

We developed a new validator software called XValid for specific needs in light of design for all. We used this validator to test well known social websites: Facebook, iWiW (Hungarian site), MySpace, YouTube. We made a statistical analysis based on our test results and compared these results to other sites' accessibility. We determined the most frequently occurring errors based on these statistics. People with disabilities could reach the internet barrier free if WEB designers gave attention to these typical errors. We know we tested only a few social websites, still, by this article, we would like to call the attention of web designers to a very important issue. It is our firm belief, that **websites should be barrier free**.

Avoiding the typical errors, would not require extra investment, neither would it take much more time. The extra effort put into an accessible web-page will surely be returned.

For web designers, we strongly recommend to test the home page with several validators and to test by special needs users too, in order to ensure its accessibility and usability – for the satisfaction of their users [25].

Whether a social website is barrier free or not, is important, because it is not only the youngest generation, who visits one or more social websites, but middle aged or elder people too. Moreover, today's middle aged generations, will be the elderly people in 10 or 20 years. Surely they will require social websites, because they got used to their provided features. Regarding the growing numbers of the elderly people, developing accessible social websites is a huge market. Therefore it is important to pay attention to the barrier free feature of social websites.

Acknowledgements The authors would like to return thanks for the help of Mr. Sándor Forrai, who developed the XValid software as an MSc thesis work at the University of Pannonia.

References

1. Sik Lányi C. "Multimedia Software Interface Design for Special Needs Users", Encyclopedia of information science and technology, 2nd Edition, IGI Global, 2008
2. WHO: "Situation Analysis for Health at Work and Development of the Global Working Life" from: http://www.who.int/occupational_health/publications/globstrategy/en/index4.html
3. EU Commission: "2010: A Europe Accessible for All", Report from the Group of Experts set up by the European Commission, from: http://europa.eu.int/comm/employment_social/index/final_report_ega_en.pdf
4. EC Europa: "Ageing Well in the Information Society" from: (http://ec.europa.eu/information_society/newsroom/cf/itemdetail.cfm?item_id=3457
5. R. Jani, M. Schrepp. "Are the Web Accessibility Guidelines Applicable and Sufficient for Web Applications?" 8th European conference for the advancement of assistive technology in Europe: Assistive technology from virtuality to reality (AAATE 2005), IOS Press, 2005, pp. 499–503
6. M. Schreep, R. Jani. "Efficient Keyboard Support in Web-Pages", 8th European conference for the advancement of assistive technology in Europe: Assistive technology from virtuality to reality (AAATE 2005), IOS Press, 2005, pp. 504–508
7. Wikipedia, "List of Social Networking Websites" from: http://en.wikipedia.org/wiki/List_of_social_networking_websites
8. W3C Quality Assurance Tools from: http://www.w3.org/QA/Tools/
9. WebXACT from: http://webxact.watchfire.com/
10. Opera from: http://www.opera.com/
11. RDF Validator from: http://www.w3.org/RDF/Validator/
12. XML Schema Validator from: http://www.w3.org/2001/03/webdata/xsv
13. C. Sik Lányi, S. Forrai, N. Czank, Á. Hajgató. "On Developing Validator Software XValid for Testing Home Pages of Universal Design", 12th international human computer interaction conference: universal access in HCI (HCII 2007), LNCS 4554, Springer, 2007, pp. 284–293
14. C. Sik Lányi, S. Forrai, N. Czank, Á. Hajgató. "Are the WEB Sites Barrier-Free, if they are not, How Many of the Sites are Barrier-free?" 9th European conference for the advancement of assistive technology in Europe: challenges for Assistive Technology, (AAATE 2007), IOS Press, 2007, pp. 627–932
15. K. Miesenberger, F. Pühretmair. "Help.gv.at – Accessible e-Government in Austria," 8th European conference for the advancement of assistive technology in Europe: Assistive technology from virtuality to reality (AAATE 2005), IOS Press, 2005, pp. 489–493
16. VentureBeat from: http://venturebeat.com/2008/12/18/2008-growth-puts-facebook-in-better-position-to-make-money/
17. M. Zuckerberg, Blog Facebook: "An Open Letter from Facebook Founder Mark Zuckerberg" 2009, from: http://blog.facebook.com/blog.php?post=190423927130
18. iWiW, "iWiW User Count Passed 4 Million", from: http://www.penzcentrum.hu/cikk/1015273/1/atlepte_a_4_milliot_az_iwiw_felhasznalok_szama
19. Mashable, the Social Media Guide, "MySpace, America's Number One", from: http://mashable.com/2006/07/11/myspace-americas-number-one/
20. Wikipedia, MySpace, from: http://en.wikipedia.org/wiki/MySpace
21. Wikipedia, YouTube, from: http://en.wikipedia.org/wiki/YouTube
22. YouTube, Help, from: http://www.google.com/support/youtube/bin/answer.py?answer=57788
23. WCAG 1.0, from: http://www.w3.org/TR/1999/WAI-WEBContent-19990505
24. WCAG 2.0, from: http://www.w3.org/TR/WCAG20/
25. C. Sik Lányi, "Testing the Accessiblity of WEB Sites", In Press in Special Issue Web for All, International Journal of Knowledge and Web Intelligence, Inderscience Publishers, Volume 2, Number 1, January 2011

Chapter 20
Understanding and Predicting Human Behavior for Social Communities

Jose Simoes and Thomas Magedanz

20.1 Introduction

Over the last years, with the rapid advance in technology, it is becoming increasingly feasible for people to take advantage of the devices and services in the surrounding environment to remain "connected" and continuously enjoy the activity they are engaged in, be it sports, entertainment, or work. Such a ubiquitous computing environment will allow everyone permanent access to the Internet anytime, anywhere and anyhow [1]. Nevertheless, despite the evolution of services, social aspects remain in the roots of every human behavior and activities. Great examples of such phenomena are online social networks, which engage users in a way never seen before in the online world. At the same time, being aware and communicating context is a key part of human interaction and is a particularly powerful concept when applied to a community of users where services can be made more personalized and useful. Altogether, harvesting context to reason and learn about user behavior will further enhance the future multimedia vision where services can be composed and customized according to user context. Moreover, it will help us to understand users in a better way.

However, despite all the technological revolutions, for the end user (Humans) it is the perceived Quality of Experience (QoE) that counts, where QoE is a consequence of a user's internal state (e.g., predispositions, expectations, needs, motivation, mood), the characteristics of the designed system (e.g., usability, functionality, relevance) and the context (or the environment) within which the interaction occurs (e.g., social setting, meaningfulness of the activity) [2].

Dealing with the previously enumerated challenges and trying to achieve the aforementioned goal, we propose an architectural framework and a methodology, which together will pave the way to understand and predict human behavior in

J. Simoes (✉)
Fraunhofer Institute FOKUS, Berlin, Germany
e-mail: jose.simoes@fokus.fraunhofer.de

B. Furht (ed.), *Handbook of Social Network Technologies and Applications*,
DOI 10.1007/978-1-4419-7142-5_20, © Springer Science+Business Media, LLC 2010

future social-aware multimedia systems. Furthermore, our work overviews some application scenarios, which could benefit from such innovation, namely advertising, augmented reality and self-awareness systems.

20.2   User Data Management, Inference and Distribution

Current service creation trends in telecommunications and web worlds are showing the convergence towards a Future Internet of user-centric services. In fact, some works [3] already provide user-oriented creation/execution environments, but these are usually tied to specific scopes and still lack on the capability to adapt to the heterogeneity of devices, technologies and the specificity of each individual user. Based on these limitations, the research in [4] identifies flexibility and personalization as the foundation for users' satisfaction, where the demand for different types of awareness needs to be present across the entire value of chain of a service.

Despite most initiatives require or propose some sorts of user profile management systems; these are usually proprietary and include limited information about user preferences and contexts. Therefore, in order to apply user information across a range of services and devices, there is a need for standardization of user related data and the architecture that enables their interoperability. These efforts have been seen at both fixed and mobile worlds and are usually taken under the European Telecommunications Standards Institute (ETSI), the Third Generation Partnership Project (3GPP), Open Mobile Alliance (OMA), among others. Considering data requirements from a wide range of facilities and from different standardization organizations, the concept of Common Profile Storage (CPS) is defined by 3GPP in [5] as a framework for streamlining service-independent user data and storing it under a single logical structure in order to avoid duplications and data inconsistency. Being a logically centralized data storage, it can be mapped to physically distributed configurations and should allow data to be accessed in a standard format. Indeed, several approaches have been proposed to guarantee a certain interoperability degree and can be grouped into three main classes: the syntactic, semantic and modeling approaches. The work in [6] proposes a combination of them to enable interoperability of user profile data management for a Future Internet.

Independently from the technology, all systems should allow user related data to be queried, subscribed or syndicated and ideally through web service interfaces. However, standardization, interoperability, flexibility and management are not the only challenges. To improve the degree of services personalization it is important to generate new information from the existing one. In this sense, social networks, user modeling and reality mining techniques can be empowered to study patterns and predict future behaviors. Consequently, all the adjacent data necessary to perform such operations must be managed within the scope of a user/human profile. Nevertheless, due to the sensitiveness of the information we are referring to, it is important to efficiently control the way this information is stored, accessed and distributed, preserving users privacy, security and trust.

With the aim of inferring users needs, desires or intentions, several research initiatives from different fields (e.g., eHealth, Marketing, Telecoms) are starting to become a reality. Despite the different methodologies and approaches, the user requirements and the technologies involved to address the problems are usually the same. They commonly involve social network analysis, context-awareness and data mining. The basic motivation is the demand to exploit knowledge from various amounts of data collected, pertaining to social behavior of users in online environments. A prime example of this are the research efforts dedicated towards the Enron email dataset [7]. Together, these techniques proved to be useful for analysis of social network data, especially for large datasets that cannot be handled by traditional methods.

Real world situations usually have to be derived from a complex set of features. Thus, context or behavior aware systems have to capture a set of features from heterogeneous and distributed sources and process them to derive the overall situation. Therefore, recent approaches are intended to be comprehensive, i.e., comprise all components and processing steps necessary to capture a complex situation, starting with the access and management of sensing devices, up to the recognition of a complex situation based on multiple reasoning steps and schemes. To handle complex situations, the concept of decomposition is applied to the situation into a hierarchy of sub-situations. These sub-situations can be handled autonomously with respect to sensing and reasoning. In this way, the handling of complex situations can be simplified by decomposition [8]. Another similar perspective is called layered reasoning, where the first stage involves feature extraction and grouping (i.e., resulting in low-level context), the second event, state and activity recognition (i.e., originating mid-level context), while the last stage is dedicated to prediction and inference of new knowledge [9]. In what concerns social networks, research usually focuses on quantifying or qualifying the relationship between peers, where algorithms such as centrality and prestige can be used to calculate the proximity, influence or importance of a node in a network [10], while clustering and classification can be applied to similarity computation, respectively [11, 12]. In addition, when user related data is associated with time and space dimensions, by empowering data mining techniques it is possible to find hidden patterns that can be used in any of the previously identified stages of reasoning.

In this sense, combining all of pre-enunciated concepts with ontologies and semantic technologies, we present a generic framework for managing user related data, which, together with a specific methodology will pave the way to understanding and predicting future human behavior within social communities.

20.3   Enabling New Human Experiences

After over viewing how the challenges related with the user data management and new knowledge inference are dealt, it is important to understand what are the technologies behind it, how to link them and what can they achieve when combined in synergy. Altogether, dealing with different aspects, they are capable of covering both the emotional and rational aspects inherent to human behavior.

20.3.1 The Technologies

20.3.1.1 Social Networks

Humans in all cultures at all times form complex social networks; the term social network here means ongoing relations among people that matter to those engaged in the group, either for specific reasons or for more general expressions of mutual solidarity. Likewise, social networks among individuals who may not be related can be validated and maintained by agreement on objectives, social values, or even by choice of entertainment. They involve reciprocal responsibilities and roles that may be altruistic or self-interest based. Usually, network members tend to trust and rely on each other, and to provide information that other members might find useful and reliable. Social networks are trusted because of shared experiences and the perception of shared values and shared needs [13]. This phenomenon has recently created and converted existing online communities into complex online social networks. Although the behavior of individuals in online networks can be slightly different from the same individuals interacting in a more traditional social network (reality), it gives us invaluable insights on the people we are communicating with, which groups are we engaged, which are our preferences, etc.

20.3.1.2 Reality Mining

To overcome the discrepancy between online and "offline" networks, reality mining techniques can be empowered to approximate both worlds, proving awareness about people actual behavior. It typically analyzes sensor data (from mobiles, video cameras, satellites, etc) to extract subtle patterns that help to predict and understand future human behavior. These predictive patterns begin with biological "honest signals," human behaviors that evolved from ancient primate signaling mechanisms, and which are major factors in human decision making [14]. In fact, these systems enable us to have the "big picture" of specific social contexts by aggregating and averaging the collected data (e.g., identify and prevent epidemics). Moreover, it allows data/events correlation and consequently future occurrences extrapolation.

20.3.1.3 Context-Awareness

In today's services, the sought to deal with linking changes in the environment with computer systems is becoming increasingly important, allowing computers to both sense and react based on their environment. Additionally, devices may have information about the circumstances under which they are able to operate and based on rules, or an intelligent stimulus, react accordingly [15]. By assessing and analyzing visions and predictions on computing, devices, infrastructures and human interaction, it becomes apparent that:

a. context is available, meaningful, and carries rich information in such environments,
b. that users' expectations and user experience is directly related to context,
c. acquiring, representing, providing, and using context becomes a crucial enabling technology for the vision of disappearing computers in everyday environments.

20.3.2 Architectural Framework and Methodology

In order to enable human behavior understanding and prediction, there are several independent but complementary steps that can be grouped into three different categories: Data Management, New Knowledge Generation and Service Exposure and Control. Figure 20.1 depicts these relationships as well as the sequence of activities involved.

20.3.2.1 Data Management

This activity usually starts with data acquisition. This process involves gathering information from different information systems. In our experiments we included user preferences, social networks, devices, policies, profiling algorithms, external

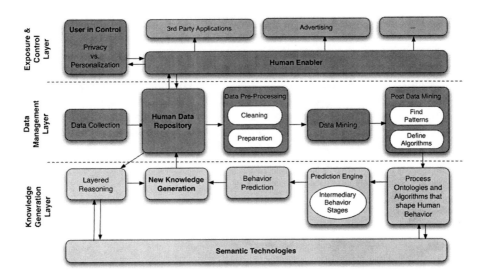

Fig. 20.1 Human Behavior Understanding and Prediction process

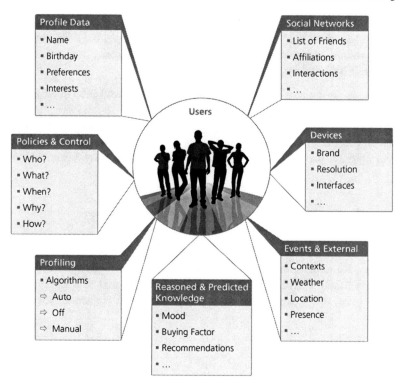

Fig. 20.2 Example of information to be stored in the Human Data Repository

contexts, as well as reasoned and predicted knowledge. Figure 20.2 exemplifies the type of information that can be stored in the Human Data Repository, a set of properties build within a generic structure that allow services of the future to use user related information, while respecting their privacy, needs and concerns [16].

Due to real systems limitations, data is usually not captured without errors, therefore it is necessary to pre-process it in advance (before mining), otherwise it would not be possible to correlate information correctly. Once this is done, data is mined by using two different approaches: the first, uses know statistical algorithms to help pattern recognition and consequent algorithmic modeling, the second uses the opposite approach, where specific algorithms are designed to identify patterns in the data (this requires previous modeling). Combining both, allows us to address the specifics of our applications, and at the same time, automatically detect new relevant correlations that might occur after a few iterations.

20.3.2.2 Knowledge Generation

New information inference is based on user related data, which we call context and can be separated into three different categories: real-time, historical data and

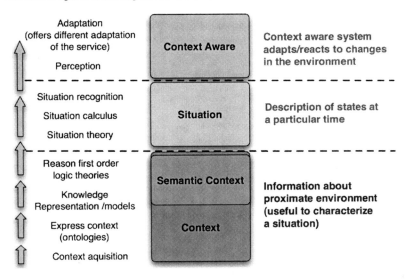

Fig. 20.3   Context layering model

reasoned context. Nevertheless, only real-time information is considered as context in the real meaning of this term. As illustrated in Fig. 20.3, there are several layers of abstraction in a context-aware system and any context-aware middleware or architecture must therefore be capable of building representations and models of these abstractions. However, these high-level abstractions can only be made from lower level context, which requires some form of context management function (performed by a Context Broker). In our case, this is performed at the Human Data Repository.

The main context management features are context acquisition, context aggregation & fusion, context dissemination, discovery and lookup. In order to manipulate context information, it must be represented in some form that is compatible with the models that will be used in the reasoning and situation recognition processes. These models could be object oriented, ontological, rule based, logic based, based on semantic graphs or fuzzy logic sets. Expressing context using just one representation is almost impossible since the range is from the most specific, for example a temperature reading, to the most abstract, the state of happiness. Furthermore, the representation must lend itself to the reasoning and inference techniques to be used, such as classification, filtering, aggregation, feature extraction, taxonomies, data mining, clustering, pattern recognition and prediction. Reasoning mechanisms allow high-level context to be deduced or situations to be recognized and often, the output of one process can be used as an input to another. Moreover, reasoning is also used to check the consistency of context and context models.

Transposing this ideology to the methodology presented in Fig. 20.1, once the data is prepared, it is run through a set of algorithms and ontologies (which also make use of existing semantics systems) that were designed to predict intermediary states (e.g., mood, stress, receptivity, engagement, etc.), used to infer human behavior. Afterwards, the information is passed to the prediction engine, which, depending on its configuration, reasons new possible behaviors. It is very important to stress that the prediction does not necessarily anticipates the user wishes or desires, but a possible future that could be interesting for the user.

20.3.2.3 Service Exposure and Control

The third layer is divided into two main capabilities. The first is user-centric and relates to the ability of the user to stay in control of the whole scenario, enabling it to specify when, what, why, who, where and how the data is or can be accessed. This opens the doors for opportunistic communications, as user context is disclosed according to contextual privacy policies and settings, enabling systems and devices to sense how, where and why information and content are being accessed and respond accordingly. Furthermore, through the Human Enabler, users are able to influence the way their behavior is predicted, by controlling how there are being profiled (automatic, off, manually personalized). In an extreme situation, they can build their own profiling algorithms. In fact, people will wish to manage their identities in different ways, sometimes opting for full disclosure, at other times disclosing it only in an anonymous way to preserve their privacy. This is essential for establishing and managing trust and for safeguarding privacy, as well as for designing and implementing business security models and policies. The second set of features is associated with the capacity of exposing this information (both raw data and inferred one) to third party service providers (such as advertising agencies), through well-defined web service interfaces. Once again, always considering the users privacy restrictions. Besides exposing user related information, the human enabler allows data to be subscribed, syndicated or updated on request.

20.3.3 Innovations

The analysis of the first results indicated the following key findings:

- It is possible to infer user behavior based on user preferences, social networks and context-aware systems, with the help of reality/data mining techniques.
- Proximity and Similarity are great weight indicators for inferring influence and can be computed or calculated analytically.
- Both online and offline social networks have influence over a person's behavior.
- User perceived QoE is improved as the methodology delivers personalization, contextualization, interactivity, adaptation and privacy.
- Users are willing to participate in their own profiling experience and the results are positive.

Applying these techniques into different fields of computer social sciences may have significant applicability in different parts of the value chain. Here are some examples:

- Infer and suggest missing information in users profile according to his/her peers contextual information.
- Understand how a specific user can be influenced by another user or community and vice versa.
- Understand how similar two users are, even if they do not have friends in common.
- Infer strengths of relationships by analyzing interactions within multimedia content available on social networks.
- Improve visualization of social relationships according to a set of know or inferred parameters.
- Improve users perceived Quality of Experience by focusing on aspects such as personalization, contextualization, interactivity, adaptation and privacy.
- Enable users to participate in their own profiling experience.
- Leverage user behavior predictions to be accessible to third party providers while concerning user privacy, preferences, desires and intentions.
- Improve recommendation systems with predictions that correspond to what users want, need or desire. In other words, it is a personalized and automated electronic word of mouth that reasons contextualized information for a specific user or set of users.

20.4 The Social Enabler

Giving particular emphasis on social communities and with the purpose of enabling next generation social services, our work defines some goals, requirements and challenges:

- Sophisticated user social context and data exposure layer, where information can be requested or subscribed.
- Enhanced security, privacy and trust mechanisms, where entities requesting user related context data are duly authenticated and authorized.
- Standardized interfaces to get information from different social communities.
- Provide a common framework that allows real-time social network metrics analysis and new knowledge inference: similarity, distance, influence.

To accomplish these objectives and to be compliant with the social requisites and innovations specified in Sects. 20.2 and 20.3, respectively, we propose an entity called Social Enabler (SE), which is responsible for providing social context information that can then be securely requested or subscribed according to user self-defined policies. Being inserted within the previously introduced framework, the SE can use the data mining and reasoning platforms to transform raw social data, acquired

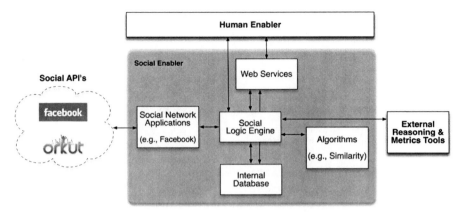

Fig. 20.4 Distribution of the social enabler modules and associated entities

from the online social networks applications, into enriched information about the social network and their peers. Figure 20.4 shows the entities and sub-components involved.

To allow flexibility, the SE is decomposed into four distinct but complementary modules. The Social Network Application is responsible for using the external API's to request data about the users and their network. Furthermore, it represents the (visual) interface towards the end user. The Social Logic Engine contains the intelligence of the enabler. It accepts requests, processes queries, manages data internally (store, delete, access) and invokes metrics, as well as algorithm calculations. The Internal Database represents the physical storage of the social attributes as well as the results from special operations executed by the logic engine. Moreover, it maps information from different social communities into a single logical entity, the user, whose data is fully accessible at the Human Enabler (HE). This data is periodically refreshed due to a keep-alive mechanism implemented on the logic engine, which informs the HE about its data structure.

Based on such info, the HE updates its registries by invoking the respective web services. Alternatively, the HE might be informed on every social context update. As all information has a validity, whenever it expires and there is an entity requesting it (directly or through the HE), it is automatically fetched from the SE. To allow future extensions, we created a separate module where a set of Algorithms can be implemented without affecting the internal structure of the enabler. These usually use raw social data stored inside the databases and request complex combinations of data before proceeding to the final calculation. In our tests, we developed formulas for similarity, influence and distance. Lastly, External Reasoning & Metrics Tools are used to improve the type of leveraged information about user's social networks. They typically provide information regarding network metrics such as: centralities, clustering, diameter, among others, which might be helpful indicators for understanding the behavior and social position of each individual within a social network.

20.4.1   The Algorithms

Assuming the initial goal of enabling, understanding and predicting social-aware behaviors, the system must focus on people in the first place. For this reason, to quantify the relationship between two users we use the concept of Distance, while to qualify it, we defined Similarity. The third, Influence, represents a mix of both. The first indicates how many people exist in the path between two individuals, plus one (first level contacts have distance one). The second reflects how many aspects, preferences or features two people have in common and it is standardized in a percentage between zero and one (being 100% a perfect match). Together, the complementary attributes will play a key role in the reasoning and prediction modules, which will use these metrics to infer new knowledge (inside the HE).

20.4.1.1   Distance

Although this concept is easy to understand, due to the restrictions imposed inside social networks, we need to recur to iterative processes requesting friends of friends and social groups, users are associated with. Despite its extreme computational effort, the Distance (D) between user A and B is expressed by (20.1), where $f(x)$ represents the set of friends of "x" and $g(x) = f(y_1) \cup f(y_2) \ldots \cup f(y_n)$, being $y_1, y_2 \ldots y_n$ all elements in the set of "x". Moreover we assume $A \backslash B$ means the set that contains all elements of A that are not in B.

$$D_{A.B} = \begin{cases} 0, & B \in \emptyset \; or \; Set_n = Set_{n+1} \\ 1, & B \in Set_1 = f(A) \\ 2, & B \in Set_2 = g(Set_1) \backslash Set_1 \\ n, & B \in Set_2 = g(Set_{n-1}) \backslash Set_{n-1} \end{cases} , \qquad (20.1)$$

20.4.1.2   Similarity

Currently, this method is based on a weighted keyword matching between both profiles. To avoid disassociation between data, each property (attribute) on the user's profile is compared to its equivalent. Being "p" the total number of matched keywords within a property, "L" the total number of profile attributes, "a" an attribute and "w" the weight of each attribute, the Similarity (S) between user Alice and Bob is given by (20.2), where "T" represents the total number of keywords from a specific profile attribute.

$$S = \sum_{a=0}^{L} \frac{2 \times w_a \times p}{T_a \, (alice) + T_a \, (bob)} \quad where \quad \sum_{0}^{L} w_a = 1 \qquad (20.2)$$

By using weights it is possible to give more importance to specific user properties, making the algorithm more flexible. The "2" in the equation is used to average the amount of attributes between both users. Obviously, fields like name and gender are not considered, as they are not relevant to this comparison. Interests, affiliations, groups and other personal preferences are given priority (using the weights). Furthermore, depending on the definition of similarity, the weights might be considered differently. In our interpretation, a particular emphasis is given towards the number of friends, groups, albums, photos, attended events and pages (being fan of) users have in common. Although this method is not optimal, in the future, it can be significantly improved when combined or extended with semantic and ontology technologies.

20.4.1.3 Influence

Deals with the assessment of the directed proximity (influence) between two people. The algorithm uses the amount of interactions from one user to the other. Within social networks, this can be measured by the number of comments or posts made on a user albums, photos, links or the personal user profile itself (called 'Wall' on Facebook). The Influence ($I_{A,B}$) value is given by (20.3), where "L" represents the total number of interaction types, "a" the specific interaction type (so far we used wall posts and comments, photo comments and link comments and the associated 'Like' events). "$M(n_a)$" is the maximum amount of specific interactions a user received and "n_a" the number of specific interactions that the user being compared (B) did. As previously defined, "W_a" represents the weight value of a specific interaction type.

$$I = \sum_{a=0}^{L} \frac{w_a \times n_a}{M(n_a)} \quad where \quad \sum_{0}^{L} w_a = 1 \tag{20.3}$$

It is important to notice that influence is directional, that is, the value of influence of user A towards user B, may not be the same as user B towards user A. Furthermore, as this is a very simplistic reasoning, the obtained value between 0 and 1 (being 1 the highest influential level), merely represents an approximation.

20.4.1.4 Adjustments

Due to the simplicity of the presented equations, and to approximate the calculation results of both similarity and influence with what would be expectable, we propose a transformation of the final results to follow the normal distribution. In this sense, (20.4) shows how this can be done.

$$f(x) = \frac{1}{\sigma\sqrt{2\pi}} \exp\left(-\frac{(x-\mu)^2}{2\sigma^2}\right) \tag{20.4}$$

Where "x" is the previously computed value, "μ" the mean of the entire set of calculations and "σ" the standard deviation. This will allow a better approximation as in real life, within a group of friends, usually, only a few are very similar and capable of highly influencing the other peers. By analogy, the ones that do not share common interests or interact often, are likely to be different and not capable of influencing. In between will stay the majority of the friends/peers.

To better understand this concept, Fig. 20.5 illustrates an example of a similarity result for a user with 250 friends. The top graphics show the distribution of similarity values for each friend (Index) and the frequency of each similarity interval. The down part shows (in terms of density) the difference between the actual calculated values (left and blue) and what would be expected in a normal distribution (right and red).

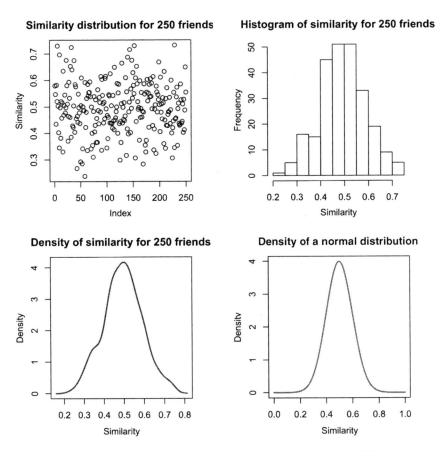

Fig. 20.5 Frequency and density representation of similarity for a network of 250 peers

20.4.2 Technological Considerations

Within this environment, when not contemplating the users and our system, we have an outside world that comprises both third party entities and the social networks. Although it is interesting for social networks to expose their capabilities to external service providers, their regulations usually restrict them to run under a closed and supervised environment. Therefore, the same appealing opportunities that social networks leverage, are excluding external multimedia services from using them. In this sense, most of the times, the user itself must fill its own personal data in order to be legal to store this information. Other restrictions also refer to a limited period of time under which the information may be stored (outside the SN) within the application. Furthermore, most of the information can only be requested when the user is using the application. This limitation creates the need for the applications to be both useful and catchy, making the user return and stay online time enough to collect all the necessary data, respectively. Otherwise, the social enabler cannot address real-time scenarios with updated user information.

From a conceptual point of view, the social enabler can be run by different entities, namely telecommunication providers, media and marketing agencies, the public sector, etc. In fact, Vodafone recently launched the Vodafone 360 service, which integrates some of the presented concepts. Nevertheless, it is important to remember that due to the sensitivity of the data being collected and analyzed, the entity responsible for controlling the SE must have a strong trust relationship with the customers/users (to allow opt-in/out and privacy control). Another alternative, which is very often adopted within commercial products, is to offer rewards in exchange for the collected data. Either way, trust is a necessary requirement as information is not only internally used but also exposed on request or subscription by third party providers.

20.5 Applications

When applying the previously introduced framework to real-world scenarios, its applications are countless. Nevertheless, in this article we will be focusing on social communities. The first one presents a new way of interacting in a new immersive social experience, while the second shows how it can be used to visualize social self-awareness. The last one introduces a simple use case that illustrates how it can be used to improve existing business models and consequently generate revenue when applied to an advertising scenario. From the applications described, although the information leveraged by them is available and can be reasoned by the proposed framework, it was not yet tested in the presented scenarios.

20.5.1   The Augmented Social Experience

Merging a set of different social networks and different context providers into a single interface is not new, yet challenging and in vogue. What if there was a way for users to simply point their mobiles at people and automatically know more about them? By combining the proposed solution with facial and object recognition techniques, it is possible to emerge in a new way of interacting with people. Figure 20.6 provides some examples of what could be possible to achieve. In scenario (a), the user wants to know more about the publicly available information regarding the Facebook profile of the person currently being tracked, while (b) on the other hand provides basic profile information that the person in the picture decided to share at that precise moment within that context, improved with the system inferred information. Case (c) presents a summary of keywords that better define a someone's profile within the Digg community (this could give a quick overview of someone's interests). In this sense, we can see that the services presented can be provided directly by the Human Data Repository (exposed by the Human Enabler) but at the same time, can be a combination of previously reasoned information with specific application data itself.

As mentioned earlier, all the information disclosed by the user is dynamically managed by himself and can be updated in real-time. Depending on the time of the day or event the user is attending, he can decide which information can be retrieved by the system. Such application will also help to promote collaboration and enrichment of existing content, as it can provide the interface to interact with it and consequently the user himself. If the user does not have permission to edit the content, he can still tag it by associating an event to it. Such ubiquitous augmented reality scenarios will become possible and we will embrace a new era

Fig. 20.6 Example of a Human Social application: (**a**) Facebook option, (**b**) Personal Profile option, (**c**) Digg option

of context-aware social communications. Furthermore, depending on the type of ontologies deployed on the system, the amount of inferred information can vary. While Fig. 20.6 introduces a couple of examples, by combining different contextual information, the possibilities are unlimited.

20.5.2 Future Self-Awareness

A creative integration of emerging digital technologies and the appropriate methods of futures studies enables the creation of an adaptive and context-sensitive personal future simulation system. Such a system can be used to produce comprehensible and informative future simulations by utilizing the unprecedented amount of continuously cumulating personal digital data. These future simulations should be generated using the standards and principles that have been negotiated and approved by the users of the system.

The emerging future simulation consists of interconnected interactive micro future scenarios that depict an individual's future, focusing on her daily activities, decisions and choices. Educational simulations provide additional context-sensitive information, alternative future paths and recommendations based on an individual's personal circumstances and environment. The creation of comprehensible micro future scenarios is based on an effective analysis and processing of the personal data deriving from the versatile networked digital environments and personal digital applications like social networking sites, micro blogging services, community platforms, information management systems, email programs and web browsers.

The creation of a functional digital future simulation system would enable new ways to approach the future from personal and social perspectives. Through an adaptive future simulation system – implemented as an active part of an individual's life – the "future discourse" could have comprehensible everyday applications and concrete consequences at the level of everyday choices and decisions. The future simulation would become a platform for the emergent personal and social intellectual processes. Informative and interactive micro scenarios could connect and contextualize an individual's mundane existence to wider social, cultural, political, economical and ecological realities. Simultaneously, the system would enhance an individual's ability to recognize the variety of alternative paths and worlds possible for them in the future. Substantially, the creation of an appropriate number of personal future simulations would allow the observation and analysis of wider patterns of potential future development. The futures of communities, societies and even humanity could be studied and extrapolated through the accumulating personal future simulations.

20.5.3 Advertising

Despite not being exactly a business model, advertising is for sure one of the most successful revenue models in today's industries. In fact, due to its preponderance, it is one of the services that most evolved in the last years. Today, most products or services are very well described and in the digital words, this information is usually presented in a standardized way in any metadata format. Consequently, if there is a technical way of matching it with users profile information, interests and affiliations, it is possible to improve the targeting accuracy and user satisfaction. Nevertheless, alone this information is not very useful. A user may like sports but does not mean he is interested in being advertised about it. Therefore, the main change must occur in the way advertising is perceived by the end user. What if we could shape it into a recommendation enhanced with the word of mouth effect?

Indeed, online social networks provide most of the required data to make this vision a reality. Like explained earlier, within social networks there are a couple of algorithms that might be preponderant in reasoning new knowledge. Within this context, similarity between users (by matching profiles, affiliations, friends in common, shared media, etc) can be used as a predictive factor of interest. It is likely that people with similar profiles like the same things. Another good parameter is proximity. With it, it is possible to understand how close two individuals (or group of people) are. Usually, people that are directly connected within social networks have something in common. Applying data mining technologies might help to identify what is or are the common denominators between people and explore this link on future reasoning processes. Lastly, if advertisers can measure the influence users have on each other, they can differentiate and prioritize offers accordingly. Inside social networks this is usually possible to infer based on the amount of interactivity between peers (e.g., number of comments on a wall, photos or groups and participation in similar events) and the number of shared multimedia objects (e.g., photos, videos, links). Furthermore, as the Human Data Repository includes information other than user profile and its social activities, advertisers can explore the amount of context data associated with it. Advertisements (ads) are no longer limited to static demographic information. Instead, it is possible to dynamically target users according to external context information such as weather, location, traffic, influence among his peers, or other reasoned data. In addition, this information can be delivered in a personalized and adapted way (if the multimedia content is available in such format), has it is possible to know at each moment what type of devices the user has enabled.

In what concerns the way the ads are displayed or consumed, it should also be possible to use the social exposure layer to present the recommendation results, benefiting from the viral effect social media offers us. What would happen if a user publishes to his contact list, in a non-intrusive way (e.g., social networks), that he just bought a particular product? In a first instance advantages might only be seen for the advertisers, but what if he got a discount for that? What if he could add a recommendation to it (can be in the form of an event)? After all, Electronic Word of Mouth (eWOM) is one of the most important decision factors in today's society (e.g., when choosing an Hotel online). Moreover, if this recommendation comes from a known peer, the influence factor is much higher.

Ideally, recommendations should occur only when user predicted needs, intents or desires match a specific advertising offer (I am hungry vs. I offer food). As an example, we have profiled that a specific user usually drinks coffee after lunch, when the weather is sunny. From past behaviors, if this set of situations occur, it is likely that the user will have the same idea. Therefore, if in the system there is an advertisement to be targeted only within a specific location (where the user is currently) and when the user fits a specific profile group, it should be triggered/delivered accordingly. If this ad is made in a form of special discount, it is likely to be well received by the end user. In the future, if all privacy issues associated with advertising can be efficiently tacked, advertising might even co-exist as a service itself.

20.6 Conclusions and Future Work

Merging digital and physical worlds will create unprecedented ubiquitous user interfaces enabling a set of seamless rewarding user experiences. In our work, by extending regular user profile data (user preferences) to accommodate social, context, device and policy related information, we open the path to a new era of services where these can become user behavior aware, paving the way to understand user needs, desires and intents. Moreover, by applying a set of methodologies to it, it became possible to reason new knowledge about people actual behaviors. Exposing these data to third party providers in an application friendly way will enable unique ubiquitous and pervasive scenarios. Together with other security aspects (authentication, privacy and trust) this work will have considerable social and economical impact in the services of the future. In a way, it will improve users perceived Quality of Experience by changing the way they see, use, consume and interact with content and services in any futuristic scenario. In the future, we would like to explore further the possibility to integrate our work with the Internet of things, extending the Human Enabler concept to any other object, focusing on how they can be described, characterized, consumed and correlated with people.

References

1. N. Baker, M. Zafar, B. Moltchanov, and M. Knappmeyer, "Context-Aware Systems and Implications for Future Internet." Future Internet Conference and Technical Workshops, Prague, Czech Republic, May 2009.
2. G. Antoniou and F. Harmelen, "A Semantic Web Primer", 2nd Edition. The MIT Press, Cambridge, ISBN 0262012421, 2008.
3. C. Baladrón, et al., "User-Centric Future Internet and Telecommunication Services", Towards the Future Internet, IOS Press, 2009.

4. M. Hassenzahl and N. Tractinsky, "User Experience – A Research Agenda", Behaviour & Information Technology, Vol. 25(2), 2006, pp. 91–97.
5. 3GPP TR.32.808: 3rd Generation Partnership Project: Technical Specification Group Services and System Aspects; Telecommunication management; Study of Common Profile Storage (CPS) Framework for User Data for Network Services and Management (Release 8).
6. G. Bartolomeo and T. Kovacikova, "User Profile Management in Next Generation Networks", Proceedings of the 5th Advanced International Conference on Telecommunications, Venice, May 2009.
7. R. Bekkerman, A. McCallum, and G. Huang, "Automatic Categorization of Email into Folders: Benchmark Experiments on Enron and SRI Corpora", CIIR Technical Report IR-418, 2004.
8. T. Spring, et al., "A Comprehensive Approach for Situation-Awareness Based on Sensing and Reasoning about Context", Ubiquitous Intelligence and Computing, LNCS, Vol. 5061, 2009, pp. 143–157.
9. M. Knappmeyer, N. Baker, S. Liaquat, R. Tönjes, "A Context Provisioning Framework to Support Pervasive and Ubiquitous Applications", EuroSSC 2009, LNCS 5741, 2009, pp. 93–106.
10. U. Khan and A. Khan, "Social Networks Identification and Analysis Using Call Detail Records", 2nd international Conference on interaction Sciences: information Technology, Culture and Human, ACM, Vol. 403, 2009, pp. 192–196.
11. D. Crandall, D. Cosley, D. Huttenlocher, J. Kleinberg, and S. Suri, "Feedback Effects Between Similarity and Social Influence in Online Communities", Preceedings of the 14th ACM SIGKDD international Conference on Knowledge Discovery and Data Mining, Las Vegas, USA, 2008, pp. 160–168.
12. J. Mori, T. Tsujishita, Y. Matsuo, and M. Ishizuka, "Extracting Relations in Social Networks from the Web Using Similarity Between Collective Contexts", The Semantic Web – ISWC 2006, Springer LNCS, Vol. 4273, 2006, pp. 487–500.
13. E. Clemons, S. Bernett, and A. Appadurai, "The Future of Advertising and the Value of Social Network Websites: Some Preliminary Examinations," Proceedings of the 9th International Conference on Electronic Commerce, ACM Press, Minnesota, 2007.
14. A. Pentland, "Honest Signals: How They Shape Our World," The MIT Press, Cambridge, ISBN-13:978–0262162562, 2008.
15. B. Schilit, N. Adams, and R. Want, "Context-Aware Computing Applications," IEEE Workshop on Mobile Computing Systems and Applications (WMCSA'94), Santa Cruz, CA, US, 1994, pp. 89–101.
16. J. Simoes, P. Weik, and T. Magedanz, "The Human side of the Future Internet", Towards the Future Internet, IOS Press, 2010, pp. 183–192, doi:10.3233/978-1-60750-539-6-183.

Chapter 21
Associating Human-Centered Concepts with Social Networks Using Fuzzy Sets

Ronald R. Yager

21.1 Introduction

The rapidly growing global interconnectivity, brought about to a large extent by the Internet, has dramatically increased the importance and diversity of social networks. Modern social networks cut across a spectrum from benign recreational focused websites such as Facebook to occupationally oriented websites such as LinkedIn to criminally focused groups such as drug cartels to devastation and terror focused groups such as Al-Qaeda. Many organizations are interested in analyzing and extracting information related to these social networks. Among these are governmental police and security agencies as well marketing and sales organizations. To aid these organizations there is a need for technologies to model social networks and intelligently extract information from these models. While established technologies exist for the modeling of relational networks [1–7] few technologies exist to extract information from these, compatible with human perception and understanding. Data bases is an example of a technology in which we have tools for representing our information as well as tools for querying and extracting the information contained. Our goal is in some sense analogous. We want to use the relational network model to represent information, in this case about relationships and interconnections, and then be able to query the social network using intelligent human-centered concepts. To extend our capabilities to interact with social relational networks we need to associate with these network human concepts and ideas. Since human beings predominantly use linguistic terms in which to reason and understand we need to build bridges between human conceptualization and the formal mathematical representation of the social network. Consider for example a concept such as "leader". An analyst may be able to express, in linguistic terms, using a network relevant vocabulary, properties of a leader. Our task is to translate this linguistic description into a mathematical formalism that allows us to determine how true it is that a particular

R.R. Yager (✉)
Machine Intelligence Institute, Iona College, New Rochelle, NY, 1080, USA
e-mail: yager@panix.com

B. Furht (ed.), *Handbook of Social Network Technologies and Applications*,
DOI 10.1007/978-1-4419-7142-5_21, © Springer Science+Business Media, LLC 2010

Fig. 21.1 Paradigm for Intelligent Social Network Analysis (PISNA)

node is a leader. In this work we look at the use of fuzzy set methodologies [8–10] to provide a bridge between the human analyst and the formal model of the network.

Our rational for focusing on this fuzzy technology is based on the confluence of two important factors. One of these is that fuzzy set theory and particularly Zadeh's paradigm of computing with words [11, 12] was especially developed for the task of representing human linguistic concepts in terms of fuzzy subsets. In addition fuzzy logic has a large repertoire of operations that allows for the combination of these sets in ways that mimic the logic of human reasoning and deduction. The second important factor is that the standard formal model used to represent a social network is a set–based mathematical structure called a relationship. Using this structure the members of the network constitute a set of elements, the connections in a network are represented as pairs of elements and the network is viewed as the set of all these pairs. The key observation here is that the standard form of network representatives is in terms of **set theory**. The fact that the underlying representation of the social network is in set theoretic terms makes it to well suited to a marriage with the fuzzy set approach.

An introduction to some basic ideas of graph (relational network) theory is first provided. We then discuss some concepts the fuzzy set paradigm of computing with words. The natural connection between graph theory and granular computing, particularly fuzzy set theory, is pointed out. This connection is grounded in the fact that these are both set based technologies. Our objective here is to take a step toward the development of intelligent social network analysis using fuzzy set methods. In particular one can start by expressing in a human focused manner concepts associated with social networks then formalize these concepts using fuzzy sets and then evaluate these concepts with respect to social networks which have been represented using set based relational network theory. We capture this approach in what we call the paradigm for intelligent social network analysis, PISNA. Using this paradigm we provide definitions of a number of concepts related to social networks. In Fig. 21.1 we show the **Paradigm for Intelligent Social Network Analysis (PISNA)**.

21.2 An Introduction to Relational Network Theory

In this section we introduce some of the basic ideas from mathematical graph theory. Our purpose here is to focus on the view of a graph as a mathematical relationship. The view will be useful when we bring fuzzy set theory in to model human concepts. Since we are drawing heavily from the ideas of classic mathematics here we shall

Fig. 21.2 Typical undirected
graph

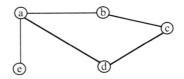

most often use the mathematicians preferred term of graph however for our ultimate purposes a more intuitive designation would be a relational network. However for the most part we use the term graph and social/relational network synonymously.

Two major classes of graphs are undirected and directed. Since for the most part we shall concentrate on undirected graphs we shall use the unmodified term graph to mean undirected and specifically use the modifier directed when we refer to directed graph.

A typical graph is shown in Fig. 21.2. It consists of a set of vertices (nodes) with some of them connected with undirected lines. We denote this graph as $G = <V, E>$ here $V = \{a, b, c, d, e\}$ is the set of vertices and $E = \{ab, ad, ae, bc, cd\}$ is the collection of undirected lines called edges. The number of vertices in V is called the *order* of G. The number of edges in E is called the *size* of G. We shall find it convenient to let U indicate the collection of all distinct unordered pairs Using this we see that $E \subseteq \mathcal{U}$. We shall also find it useful to designate $\mathcal{U}_x$ for any $x \in V$ as the subset of $\mathcal{U}$ consisting of the terms involving x.

If xy is an edge of G we say that x and y are *adjacent*. The word incident can be used synonymously with adjacent. We say that a graph G is *complete* if there is an edge between all vertices.

For our purposes we will find it useful to associate with G a relationship R: $V \times V \to \{0, 1\}$ such that $R(x, y) = R(y, x) = 1$ if xy is an edge of G and $R(x, y) = R(y, x) = 0$ if xy is not an edge of G. In an undirected graph R is a symmetric relation, $R(x, y) = R(y, x)$. For some purposes it will be useful to assume that R is reflexive, $R(x, x) = 1$.

An important operation in graphs is moving between vertices, graph transversal. Here we define some important ideas in this regard. If x and y are two distinct vertices and an x–y *path* in G is a sequence of distinct vertices beginning with x and ending with y so that there is an edge between any two adjacent vertices in the sequence. Consider the sequence of distant nodes $a_1 a_2 a_3 \ldots a_q$ this can be said to provide a path for a_1 to a_q if $\underset{i=1\,\text{to}\,q-1}{\text{Min}} [R(a_i, a_{i+1}] = 1$. We note in an undirected graph if $a_1\, a_2\, a_3 \ldots a_q$ is a path from a_1 to a_q then its reverse $a_q\, a_{q-1} \ldots a_2 a_1$ is a path from a_q to a_1.

Two vertices x and y are said to connected if there is an x–y path. A graph G is said to be connected if every two vertices in G are connected. A cycle is an x–y path in which $x = y$ and contains at least three edges. It must contain at least three distant vertices.

Assume $G = < V, E >$ is a graph in which $x \in V$ and $e \in E$. By $G - e$ we mean the subgraph $< V, E - e >$, it contains all edges except e and has the same vertices as G. By G-x we mean the subgraph $< V - x, E - \mathcal{U}x >$. It contains all the vertices of G except x and all the edges of G except those that are incident on x.

A number of measures have been associated a graph. Among the most useful of these is the degree of a vertex, denoted deg(v). It is the number of edges incident to the vertex. For example in the graph of Fig. 21.1 we have deg(a) = 3.

Another important idea is the length of a path, defined as the number of edges the path contains. The distance between two vertices is the length of the shortest path between them. We refer to a shortest path as a geodesic and denote the shortest path between x and y as Geo(x, y). If we use Len(p) to indicate the length of a path then the *distance*(x, y) = Len(Geo(x, y)). If no path exists between two vertices we say that the distance is infinite.

We shall find a graph's description in terms of its relationship R to be extremely useful in many applications. This will be particularly the case when we try to associate human cognitive concepts with a graph.

A useful mathematical operation associated with relationships is composition. Assume R_1 and R_2 are relationships over the same vertex set V. The composition of R_1 and R_2 denoted $R_1 \blacklozenge R_2$ is also a relationship on V defined so that

$$R_1 \blacklozenge R_2(x, z) = \text{Max}_{y \in V}[\text{Min}(R_1(x, y), R_2(y, z)]$$

It can be shown that the composition operator is associative and hence

$$R_1 \blacklozenge R_2 \blacklozenge R_3 = (R_1 \blacklozenge R_2) \blacklozenge R_2 = R_1 \blacklozenge (R_2 \blacklozenge R_3)$$

A special case of composition is $R \blacklozenge R$, the composition of a graph with itself, we shall denote this R^2. More generally we shall denote the composition of R with its self k times as R^k,

$$R^k = R \blacklozenge R \blacklozenge \ldots \blacklozenge R$$

We observe that since R(x, x) = 1 then

$$R^2(x, z) = \text{Max}_y[(R(x, y) \wedge R(y, z)] \geq R(x, x) \wedge R(x, z) \geq R(x, z)$$

More generally it can be shown that $R^k(x, y) \leq R^{k+1}(x, y)$ and $R^k(x, x) = 1$. From this we see $R^k \subseteq R^{k+1}$ for all $k \geq 1$.

It is most important to observe that if $R^k(x, y) = 1$ then there exists a path of at least length k from x to y. Thus distance(x, y) can be seen as the smallest k for which $R^k(x, y) = 1$. Thus we see composition operation provides a useful tool for working with paths.

In the preceding we have introduced some of the basic ideas of mathematical graph theory as we now turn to some applications in the following we shall find it more intuitively appealing to refer to graphs as relational or social networks.

21.3   Computing with Words

As we have indicated our goal here is to extend our capabilities of analyzing re-lational networks by associating with these networks various concepts with which humans understand the world. As already noted human beings predominantly use linguistic terms in which to communicate, comprehend and reason. Machines on the other hand require much more formal symbols in which to "comprehend and reason." One of the most useful approaches to providing a bridge between man and machine comprehension is Zadeh's fuzzy set based paradigm of computing with worlds [11, 12] and the more general idea of granular computing [13]. These technologies allow for a high level of man–machine cooperation by providing a framework in which concepts and knowledge can be modeled in a manner amenable to both man and machine. Here we are interested in using this framework for mu-tual understanding in the domain of social network analysis. As previously noted the potential here is particularly promising given that computers understanding of these networks is in terms of a mathematical relationship, which is a type of set object.

In the following we shall introduce some ideas from these fuzzy set based ap-proach to computing with words.

Let U be some attribute that takes its value in a space Y. An example of this is a person's age. For humans this takes its value in the set $Y = \{1 \text{ to } 100\}$. A linguistic value is some word that can be used to describe the value of U. In the case of age some examples of linguistic values are "old", "young" and "about 30". A linguis-tic value can be seen as a granule, it is a collection of values from X. In providing information about U in addition to using precise values people also use linguistic values as well as other granular objects such as ranges. By a communal vocabu-lary associated with an attribute we mean a collection of linguistic values that are used to discuss the attribute and are commonly understood. It is part of the social environment.

Fuzzy sets have provided a useful tool for formalizing the idea of vocabulary in a way that allows for the type of formal computation needed by machines. Here if W is a linguistic value about the attribute U then we can express it as a fuzzy subset W over the domain Y of U. In particular for any element $y \in Y$ its membership grade in W, $W(y) \in [0, 1]$, indicates the compatible of the value y with the linguistic concept W.

With the aid of fuzzy sets we are able to bridge the gap between man and machine by allowing the man to define the common vocabulary that they will in terms of fuzzy sets. Thus here man can communicate his ideas using words and the machine can understand these words as fuzzy sets. The fuzzy sets are in a form that the machine can manipulate. This is what Zadeh [11, 12] has referred to as machine precisiation. We are making the world understandable to the machine.

In studying social networks there are a number of attributes about which it will be useful to have vocabularies. One such attribute is strength of connection between vertices. This is an attribute whose domain is the unit interval, $I = [0.1]$. Terms like strong, weak, none would be linguistic values that would be part of a vocabulary associated with this attribute. In this case we would define the word "strong" as a fuzzy subset S of [0, 1] such that for any $y \in [0, 1]$ the value $S(y)$ would indicate the degree to which y satisfies the communal definition of the concept strong.

Another attribute for which it would be useful to have a communal vocabulary is the number of links in a path, link-length. Here we can express this in terms of fuzzy subsets defined over the domain $Y = \{0, \ldots, N\}$.

Linguistic values in addition to being associated with attributes corresponding to physical objects can be associated with variables corresponding to universal type concepts. One such example we shall find useful is proportion. Here U is an attribute that takes its value in the set $I = [0.1]$ where $r \in [0, 1]$ is a proportion. Examples of linguistic values that would be part of a vocabulary associated with this attribute are "many", "most", "about half" and "few". As noted by Zadeh [14] these terms provide a generalization of the quantifiers "all" and "none" often used in logic. We can refer to this as linguistic quantifiers.

In the following we shall use the linguistic modeling capability of fuzzy sets to provide more realistic formulation of some concepts available in social networks analysis as well as some new some concepts. Since our goal is to focus on the procedures and operations involved in providing this type of capability we shall not dwell upon the construction of the vocabulary but assume that all necessary linguistic terms are available as appropriate fuzzy sets. In addition with an understanding of the mechanism provided we are certain that future researchers can provide alternative formulations of the concepts then those provided here.

21.4 On the Concept of Node Importance

A useful concept introduced in the social network literature involves the idea of importance of a vertex in a network. This is related to the centrality of a node [3]. The basic measure of centrality, sometimes called local centrality, is the number of vertices adjacent to a node. Thus $C(x_i) = \sum_{\substack{j=1 \\ j \neq i}}^{n} R(x_i, x_j)$. Here we are measuring the centrality of a vertex by the number of other vertices to which it directly connected. A somewhat more general definition is to measure the number of nodes it is connected to by at most k steps. In this we get

$$C^k(x_i) = \sum_{\substack{j=1 \\ j \neq i}}^{n} R^k(x_i, x_j)$$

Since $R^k(x_i, x_j) \geq R^p(x_i, x_j)$ for $k > p$ then we see that $C^k(x_i) \geq C^p(x_i)$ for $k > p$.

A softening of this concept can be had if we consider the "number of *close* connections". In order to do this we take advantage of the OWA aggregation operator [15] and the ability of fuzzy subsets to express linguistic terms. Here we assume the linguistic term *close* is in our communal vocabulary. In particular we have a definition of the concept *close* as a fuzzy subset Q on the space $N = \{1, 2, \ldots, n, n + 1\}$. Here for each $j \in N$ we have $Q(j) \in [0, 1]$ as the degree to which being connected at most by j links is considered as close. We note that such a definition for close must satisfy the following properties: 1. $Q(j) \geq Q(k)$ if $j < k$ 2. $Q(1) = 1$ and 3. $Q(n + 1) = 0$.

Using this definition obtain a set of n weights to be used as the parameters for the OWA aggregation operator, $w_k = Q(k) - Q(k + 1)$. We note that the w_k satisfy the following two conditions $w_k \geq 0$ and $\sum_{k=1}^{n} w_k = 1$

Using these weights we calculate the number of *close* connections that x_i has as

$$C^{Close}(x_i) = \sum_{k=1}^{n} w_k C^k(x_i)$$

A special case of *close* is where $Q(j) = 1$ for $j \leq q$ and $Q(j) = 0$ for $j > q$. This corresponds to a definition of *close* as "at most q links." Using this definition we obtain that $w_k = 1$ for $k = q$ and $w_k = 0$ for $k \neq q$. In this case we get $C^{Close}(x_i) = C^q(x_i)$.

Another special case is where $Q(j) = 1$ for $j \leq q_1$, $Q(j) = \alpha$ for $q_1 < j \leq q_2$ and $Q(j) = 0$ for $j > q_2$. In this case we get: $w_k = \alpha$ for $k = q_1$, $w_k = 1 - \alpha$ for $k = q_2$ and $w_k = 0$ for all other k. Using this we get $C^{Close}(x_i) = \alpha g^{q_1}(x_1) + (1-\alpha)C^{q_2}(x_1)$.

Another notable definition of *Close* is the following quasi-linear type. Here we define *Close* as follows

$$Q(j)\frac{q - j}{q - 1} \text{ for } j < q \text{ and } Q(j) = 0 \text{ for } j \geq q.$$

In this case $w_k = 0$ for $k \geq q$ and $w_k = Q(k) - Q(k - 1) = \frac{1}{q-1}$ for $k < q$. Using this definition we get $C^{Close}(x_i) = \frac{1}{q-1} \sum_{k=1}^{q-1} C^k(x_i)$.

Recalling that that $C^k(x_i)$ is the number of nodes connected to x_i by at most k steps let us define $T^k(x_i) = C^k(x_i) - C^{k-1}(x_i)$. Here $T^k(x_i)$ is the number of nodes whose **shortest path** to x_i is **equal** to k steps. We note here that $C^0(x_i) = 0$. From this we see that $C^k(xi) = \sum_{j=1}^{k} T^j(x_i)$. Using this with the quasi-linear definition of *Close* we get

$$C^{Close}(xi) = \sum_{k=1}^{q-1} \frac{q - k}{q - 1} T^k(x_i)$$

Here then $C^{Close}(x_i)$ is a weighted sum of the number of nodes that have shortest path to x_i of length k. We further observe that the weights are a linearly decreasing function of k.

Fig. 21.3 Close in proportional terms

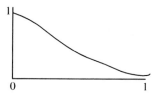

An alternative and perhaps more universal expression for $C^{Close}(x_i)$ can be obtained if we define a path as *Close* in terms of the proportion of internal vertices it contains rather than the absolute number of links. In order to accomplish this introduce term $Close_p$ standing for close in proportional terms, which we define using a membership function f: $[0, 1] \rightarrow [0, 1]$. We illustrate this in Fig. 21.3. Here with $p \in [0, 1]$ indicating a proportion of the vertices term f(p) indicates the degree to which two vertices being connected through at most p proportion of the other vertices in network are considered as being close. Here we observe that $f(p_1) \geq f(p_2)$ if $p_1 < p_2$, $f(0) = 1$ and $f(1) = 1$.

We can use this to generate a value for number of close connections to x_i. Here again

$$C^{Close}(x_i) = \sum_{k=1}^{n-1} w_k C^k(x_i)$$

But in this case we have $w_k = f(\frac{k-1}{n-2})$.

Once having had calculated the number of close connections to x_1, $C^{Close}(x_i)$, we can answer a question such as "as does x_i have at least five close connections ?". More generally using the ability of fuzzy subsets to represent linguistic numeric concepts we can answer questions as to whether x_i has *many* or *few* close connectors. In particular if L is a linguistic quantity such as *many, few* or *about twenty* we can define it as a fuzzy subset L of the real line R. Here for any number $y \in R$, L(y) indicates the degree to which y satisfies the concept L. Using this we can express the answer to the question how true is it that x_i has L close connections by obtaining $L(C^{Close}(x_i))$, the membership grade of $C^{Close}(x_i)$ in L. We note that if we define $\mathcal{L}$ as a proportional fuzzy subset L_p on [0, 1] then we obtain the answer to the question as $L_p(\frac{C^{Close}(x_i)}{n})$.

21.5 Generalizing the Concept of a Cluster

The concept of a cluster of nodes and the related idea of clique are important ideas in social networks. Again let $G = <V, E>$ be an undirected graph representing a social network. Assume R is the associated relationship. A subset $S \subseteq V$ is called a cluster of order k if

(a) For all $x, y \in S$ we have $Geo(x, y) \leq k$
(b) For all $z \notin S$ we have $Geo(x, z) > k$ for some $x \in S$.

In terms of R we see that for all x, y ∈ S we must have $R^k(x, y) = 1$ and for $z \notin S$ then $R^k(x, z) = 0$ for at least one x ∈ S.

Here we suggest a softer definition of the idea of clique, more in the spirit of human perception of the concept of a clique. With the aid of fuzzy sets we are able to precisiate this concept to provide a machine understandable interpretation of the definition.

Following is our proposed definition of the concept of a clique. A subset S is a clique if most of elements in S are closely connected, none of the elements are too far from each other and no element not in the clique is better connected to the members of the clique then any element in the clique. We can see that the concept of clique requires the satisfaction of three criteria. Let us look at these criteria and then see how to evaluate their satisfaction

C_1: Most of the elements in S are closely connected
C_2: None of the elements in S are too far from any of the others
C_3: No element not in the clique is better connected to the members of the clique then any element in the clique

Our procedure for the determining whether a subset S is a clique will be the following. For the subset S we shall find for each of the criteria C_j the value $C_j(S) \in [0, 1]$ indicating the degree to which the subset S satisfies the criteria C_j. Once having these values we obtain degree to which S is a clique, $Clique(S) = Min_j[C_j(S)]$.

Our focus now becomes on the how do evaluate each of these criteria. We must provide a machine understanding of each of these criteria. We start with the first criteria. Here we must use two linguistic concepts from our communal vocabulary, *Closely Connected* and *Most*. Closely connected can be defined using a function $Q : \{Positive\ Integers\} \rightarrow [0, 1]$ such that $Q(k)$ is the degree to which a shortest path between two nodes of at most k edges is considered as close. A prototypical example of such a function is

$$Q(k) = 1 \text{ for } k \leq a, Q(k) = \frac{b-k}{b-a} \text{ for } a \leq k < b \text{ and } Q(k) = 0 \text{ for } k \geq b$$

Here a shortest distance of *a* or less is considered as close. A shortest distance of equal or greater then b is not close. Distances between these extremes partially satisfy the concept close (Fig. 21.4).

Now for any two nodes x and y we can calculate the degree to which they are close as

$$Close(x, y) = \underset{k=1\,to\,b}{Max} [Q(k) \wedge R^k(x, y)]$$

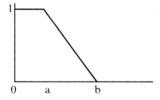

Fig. 21.4 Prototypical definition of close

Fig. 21.5 Concept *Most* as a
fuzzy set

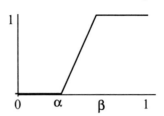

We note that if the shortest distance between x and y is q then $R^k(x, y) = 0$ for
$k < q$ and $R^k(x, y) = 1$ for $k \geq q$ and since $Q(k)$ is monotonically decreasing then
$Close(x, y) = Q(q)$.

The next concept we need is *Most*. Formally most can be expressed as a fuzzy
subset $M : [0, 1] \rightarrow [0, 1]$ where for any $p \in [0, 1]$ the value $M(p)$ indicates
the degree to which the proportion p satisfies the concept of *Most* We see the
fuzzy subset set M should have the following properties: $M(0) = 0$, $M(1) = 1$ and
$M(p_2) \geq M(p_1)$ if $p_2 > p_1$. A basic form for the fuzzy subset M corresponding to
the concept *Most* is shown in Fig. 21.5.

A special case of this is where $\alpha = 0.5$ and $\beta = 0.75$. Using this we get

$M(p) = 0$ for $p \leq 0.5$

$M(P) = \frac{0.75-p}{0.25} = 3 - 4p$ for $0.5 < p \leq 0.75$

$M(P) = 1$ for $p > 0.75$

Using these linguistic concepts we can now describe a procedure to obtain $C_1(S)$.
Assume $S = \{x_1, \ldots, x_{nS}\}$ is some subset of nodes where n_S indicates the number
of elements in S. For each pair x_i and x_j in S we can calculate $Close(x_i, x_j) = Q(q_{ij})$
where q_{ij} is the shortest distance between x_i and x_j. For each x_i we can calculate the
degree to which it is close to *Most* of the other elements in S as $W(x_i) = M(p_i)$
where

$$p_i = \frac{\sum_{\substack{j=1 \\ j \neq i}}^{n_S} Close(x_i, x_j)}{n_s - 1}$$

Using this we can calculate $C_1(S) = \underset{x_i \in S}{Min}[W(x_i)]$.

We now consider the second criteria, "none of the elements in S are far from
any other element in S." We first need the concept *Far*. To obtain this we start with
a fuzzy subset from the non-negative real numbers, $F:\mathbf{R} \rightarrow [0, 1]$ so that $F(k)$ is
the degree to which a shortest distance of k links is *Far*. We see that F should be
a monotonically increasing function prototypically illustrated in Fig. 21.6. A crisp
definition of *Far* can be had if we make $c = d$.

We now obtain from this the concept not far. We denote this as a fuzzy set $\bar{F}$ and
express it as the negation of F thus $\bar{F}(k) = 1 - F(k)$. Using this we can obtain the
degree to which any two nodes are not far

$$Not.Far(x, y) = \underset{k=1 \text{ to } n}{Max} [R^k(x, y) \wedge \bar{F}(k)].$$

Fig. 21.6 Fuzzy set *Far*

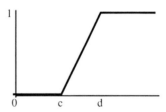

Let U_s indicate the collection of distinct unordered pairs of elements in S. Once having obtained for every pair $u \in U_s$ a measure of the degree to which they are not far as calculated above we then can obtain $C_2(s) = \mathrm{Min}[\mathrm{Not.Far}(u)]$. Thus here $_{u \in U_s}$
we simply need to find the furthest pair of vertices in S and calculate the degree to which they are not far.

The third condition requires that no element not in S be better connected to the elements in S then any of the elements in S. We shall suggest a method for precisiation of this condition. We note that the method is not unique other ways can surely be envisioned for capturing this condition, our goal here is more to be illustrative then definitive.

Our definition will be based on the requirement that all the elements in S should be closer to *most* of the other elements in S than any element not in S. Thus if $y \notin S$ we can calculate degree to which it is close to *most* of the elements in S as

$$W(y/S) = \mathrm{Most}\, \frac{\sum\limits_{j=1}^{n_S} \mathrm{Close}(y, x_j)}{n_S}$$

In addition for any $x_i \in S$ we can calculate as we have already have shown

$$W(x_i/S) = \mathrm{Most}\, \frac{\sum\limits_{\substack{j=1 \\ j \neq i}}^{n_S} \mathrm{Close}(x_i, x_j)}{n_S - 1}$$

We now order the $w(y/S)$ and $w(x_i/S)$ for $x_i \in S$ and $y \notin S$ in descending order. If one of the y is ahead of any of the x_i on this list then $C_3(S) = 0$ otherwise $C_3(s) = 1$.

21.6 Congested Nodes

The concept of path in an undirected graph $G = <X, R>$ is clearly defined. A sequence of nodes $\rho = x_1 x_2 \ldots x_q$ is a path between x_1 and x_q if $\mathrm{Min}_{i=1\,\mathrm{to}\,q}[R(x_i, x_{i+1}] = 1$. Here we want to consider an idea of congestion and try to formulate an idea of an un-congested path. Our interest here is motivated by the observation that in some applications the number of arcs incident upon a node can interfere with the performance of the node in a path.

Consider a social networking system such as LinkedIn. This is a system in which people, generally for the purpose of business, try to make connection with another person using connections through other people. Here for example assume **A** wants to contact **B** who is a person he doesn't know. **A** however sees that **M**, a person he knows, has a connection with **B**. **A** therefore has a path to **B** thru **M**. In this LinkedIn social network **A** would contact **M** and ask him to make an introduction to **B**. However, if **M** has a lot of connections, incident nodes, he may be very congested and not be very efficient in making the connection. If **A** has an alternative connection to **B** through **D** a node with not many incident nodes he may prefer to go through **D**. Even if the path through **D** requires him also to go through an additional node **E** he may prefer this to the path thru **M** if **E** also has not many incident nodes. Typically binary social networks don't have the capability to make these kinds of distinctions. Here we begin to look into the inclusion of these types of considerations by introducing the idea of "un-congested" path and the related idea of path duration.

We first introduce a predicate "congested node" which we can express as a fuzzy set C over the set X of nodes in the network. Here for each node $x_i \in X$ the value $C(x_i) \in [0, 1]$ indicates the degree to which x_i is a congested node. This membership grade is the truth of the statement x_i is a congested node. We must now define what we mean by a congested node. We shall start here with a simple definition, although one that is cointensive with our idea of congestion. We shall say that a node is a congested node if it has *many* incident nodes. It has a high density. In order to take advantage of this definition we must make machine understandable the term *many*. The approach we shall use is to express *many* as a fuzzy subset. Let $N = \{0, 1, 2, \ldots, n\}$ where n is the number of nodes in the network. We now define *many* as a fuzzy subset MANY over the space N such that for any $y \in N$ the value $MANY(y) \in [0, 1]$ indicates the degree to which the quantity y satisfies the concept *many*. We can see that MANY must be a monotonically increasing function of y, this if $y_2 > y_1$ the $MANY(y_2) \geq MANY(y_1)$. A prototypical example of the concept of many is shown in Fig. 21.7.

Using as our definition of a congested node as one with *many* incident nodes and our precisiation of the concept *many* by the fuzzy subset MANY we can obtain the degree to which a node x_i is congested node

Fig. 21.7 Many incident nodes

$$C(x_i) = \text{MANY} \left(\sum_{\substack{j=1 \\ j \neq i}}^{n} R(x_i, x_j) \right)$$

It is the degree to which the number of incident nodes on x_i satisfies MANY.

Using the concept of a congested node we can consider the formulation of the meaning of the idea of an un-congested path in a social network $< X, R >$. Here we shall use a very basic understanding of the concept un-congested path as a sequence of nodes that is a path in which all intermediary nodes are un-congested. Let us now see to what degree the sequence $\rho = x_1 x_2 \ldots x_q$ provides an un-congested path from x_1 to x_q.

For any node x_i in the sequence ρ we can obtain the degree to which it is un-congested node as $\overline{C}(x_i) = 1 - C(x_i)$ where $C(x_i)$ is the degree to which it is a congested node.

We can now calculate the degree to which "all the intermediary nodes are not congested as $\underset{i=2 \text{ to } q-1}{\text{Min}} [\overline{C}(x_i)]$. In addition we can calculate the degree to it is true that the sequence ρ is a path from x_1 to x_q as $\text{Path}(\rho) = \underset{i=2 \text{ to } q-1}{\text{Min}} [R(x_i, x_{i+1})]$.

Using these we can now express the concept uncongested path as a predicate UNCONG that we can associate we any sequence of nodes $\rho = x_1 x_2 \ldots x_q$ and evaluated as

$$\text{UNCONG}(\rho) = \text{Path}(\rho) \wedge \underset{i=2 \text{ to } q-1}{\text{Min}} [\overline{C}(x_i)].$$

Here then for the sequence $\rho = x_1 x_2 \ldots x_q$ we have that $\text{UNCONG}(\rho)$ is

$$R(x_1, x_2) \wedge \overline{C}(x_2) \wedge R(x_2, x_3) \wedge \overline{C}(x_3) \wedge \ldots \ldots \wedge R(x_{q-2}, x_{q-1})$$
$$\wedge \overline{C}(x_{q-1}) \wedge R(x_{q-1}, x_q))$$

It is intuitively interesting that we rewrite this as

$$\text{UNCONG}(\rho) = R(x_1, x_2) \wedge \underset{i=2 \text{ to } q-1}{\text{Min}} [\overline{C}(x_i) \wedge R(x_i, x_{i+1})]$$

Here the term $D(x_i) = \overline{C}(x_i) \wedge R(x_i, x_{i+1})$ can be viewed the degree to which the node x_i can effectively perform its leg of path.

Actually for this case where $R(x_i, x_j) \in [0, 1]$ we will get that either $\text{UNCONG}(\rho) = 0$ if the sequence is not a path or $\text{UNCONG}(\rho) = \underset{i=2 \text{ to } q-1}{\text{Min}} [\overline{C}(x_i)]$.

While the approach just suggested is a basic approach the framework that it provides is rich enough to allow for the inclusion of more sophisticated considerations with respect to the idea of congestion and more generally ease of attainment of connection. We shall now investigate some of the available extensions.

We first begin with the definition of the concept of congested node which we described in terms of how many incident arcs a node has. We suggested that the degree of congestion of node x_i is equal to the truth-value of the predicate **the node x_i has many incident nodes**, $C(x_i) = \text{MANY}(\sum_{\substack{j=1 \\ j \neq i}}^{n} R(x_i, x_j)))$ where MANY is defined as a fuzzy subset of the space $N = \{0, 1, \ldots, n\}$, it is fuzzy subset over the set of integers. We first note that we can define *Many* in terms of a proportion rather then an absolute value. That is we can define *Many* as $MANY_P: [0, 1] \rightarrow [0, 1]$, here for any proportion y of nodes in the network $MANY_P(y)$ indicates the degree to what y satisfies the concept *many*. In this case

$$C(x_i) = MANY_p \left(\frac{\sum\limits_{j \neq i, j=1}^{N} R(x_i, x_j)}{N} \right)$$

This allows for a more universal definition of Many.

More generally we can define a predicate *congested node* using a Takagi-Sugeno type fuzzy systems model [16]. Let V be a variable denoting the number of incident arcs on a node. Let C indicate the degree to which it is true that a node is a congested node. Let A_i, $i = 1$ to r, be a collection of linguistic terms describing the number of arcs incident on a node. Here then the A_i will be terms like few, many, about 10, etc. Using these terms we can formulate a fuzzy systems model definition of the concept congested node using r rules of the form

If V is A_i then C is α_i.

Here $\alpha_i \in [0, 1]$ is the degree to which it is true the node is considered as congested. In order to calculate the degree of congestion of an arbitrary node x_j we first calculate the number of incident arcs it has, $q_j = \sum\limits_{\substack{k=1 \\ k \neq j}}^{n} R(x_j, x_k)$. Using this we obtain

$$C(x_j) = \frac{\sum\limits_{i=1}^{r} A_i(q_j)\alpha_i}{\sum\limits_{i=1}^{r} A_i(q_j)}$$

Even more generally we can use additional features of the node external to its network parameters to calculate degree to which it is a congested node. These features will of course dependent on the type of object the node is representing. Let U be some additional feature associated with nodes. Let B_i, $i = 1$ to be some predicate describing values of the feature U. In addition assume for any node x_j we can obtain $B_i(x_j) \in [wsg1]sg$ he degree to which feature value B_i is satisfied by node x_j. A typical example of a feature value is a fuzzy subset, however other descriptions are possible.

Using these ideas we can now formulate our definition of the degree of congestion of a node using a collection of r rules of the form

If V is A_i and U is B_i then C is α_i.

With q_j as calculated above being the number of arcs incident on x_j we can obtain

$$C(x_j) = \frac{\sum_{i=1}^{r} A_i(q_j)B_i(x_j)\alpha_i}{\sum_{i=1}^{r} A_i(q_j)B_i(x_j)}$$

The main point is that we can use in addition to information of the network structure sophisticated knowledge about a node to determine whether it will smoothing perform its task or introduce congestion into a path. In social networks such as Linked In knowledge of the personality and objectives of individual, node, will be useful.

Let us now look at another aspect of our framework for calculating the degree to which a path constitutes an uncongested path. Our definition was that *all* the nodes on the path must be uncongested. A softer definition of this concept can be obtained if we use in our definition that *most* of the nodes on the path are uncongested, that is we replace all with most. More generally use can use any quantifier such as *all*, *almost all* or *some* to specify what we mean by an uncongested path. We further recall that these types of linguistic quantifiers can be expressed as a fuzzy subset $Q : [0, 1] \rightarrow [0, 1]$ so that for any proportion $p \in [0, 1]$ the value $Q(p)$ indicates the degree to which the proportion p satisfies the concept of the quantifier [14]. Furthermore these types of quantifiers display the properties that $Q(0) = 0, Q(1) = 1$ and $Q(p_1) \geq Q(p_2)$ if $p_1 > p_2$.

In [17] Yager showed how one could use the OWA operator to evaluate the truth of the predicates such as

Q of the nodes on the path are uncongested

In particular assume we have a path with m intermediary nodes. Let $\bar{C}(x_i) = 1 - C(x_i)$ be the degree to which the ith intermediate node on the path is uncongested. Using these values and the fuzzy set Q we are able to determine UNCONG(ρ), the degree to which path ρ satisfies our definition of being an uncongested path. We describe the procedure as follows. We first calculate a set of m weights associated with the quantifier Q as $w_j = Q(\frac{j}{m}) - Q(\frac{j-1}{m})$ for $j = 1$ to m. These are a set of weights lying in the unit interval and summing to one. Next we let b_j be the jth largest of $\bar{C}(x_j)$. Using these we then calculate UNCONG(ρ) $= \sum_{j=1}^{m} w_j b_j$.

We point out that in the special case where $w_n = 1$ and $w_j = 0$ for $j \neq n$ we get

$$\text{UNCONG } (\rho) = b_m$$

where b_m is the smallest of the $\bar{C}(x_i)$, that is UNCONG(ρ) $= \text{Min}_i[\bar{C}(x_i)]$ which was our original formulation.

21.7 Duration

In describing paths in networks a useful concept is the number of links or length of the path. Here we shall provide a generalization of this idea by introducing the concept of duration which will allow us to consider the impact of congestion on the length of a sequence of nodes. Consider the sequence of nodes $\rho = x_1 x_2 \ldots x_q$. We shall define the duration of ρ as

$$\text{Dura}(\rho) = \sum_{j=1}^{q-1} \frac{1}{R(x_j, x_{j+1})} + \sum_{j=2}^{q-1} \left(\frac{1}{\overline{C}(x_j)} - 1 \right)$$

Let us first consider this for the standard case where we don't consider congestion, which is obtained by letting $\overline{C}(x_i) = 1$. In this case

$$\text{Dura}(\rho) = \sum_{j=1}^{q-1} \frac{1}{R(x_j, x_{j+1})}$$

If ρ is a true path then $R(x_j, x_j + 1) = 1$ for all j we get to $\text{Dura}(\rho) = q - 1$, the number of links in the path. If any of $R(x_j, x_{j+1}) = 0$, then the sequence ρ is not a path. In this case $\text{Dura}(\rho) = \infty$ since $\frac{1}{0} = \infty$. Thus a sequence that is not a path has $\text{Dura}(\rho) = \infty$

Now let us look at situations where we can have some congestion. First consider the term $\frac{1}{\overline{C}(x_i)} - 1 = \frac{C(x_i)}{1-C(x_i)}$, we see it is the ratio of the degree of congestion divided by the degree of non-congestion. If the congestion is zero then $\frac{C(x_i)}{1-C(x_i)} = 0$ on the other if $C(x) = 1$ then this becomes infinite. Most generally in the case where ρ is a true path then $\text{Dura}(\rho) = \#$ of links $+ \sum_{j=2}^{q-1} \frac{C(x_j)}{1-C(x_j)}$. Here we can refer to $\frac{C(x_i)}{1-C(x_i)}$ as the delay associated with node x_i.

21.8 Directed Graphs

Another class of graphs are those shown in Fig. 21.8. These are called directed graphs or digraphs. A digraph consists of a number of vertices or nodes with directed lines between. These lines are referred to as directed edges or arcs. We can denote this directed graph as $D = \ <V, A>$ where V is the set of nodes and A the collection of arcs. The arc denoted (a, b) is used to indicate a directed edge from a to b.

We can associate with D a reflexive relationship R on V. Thus R: $V \times V \rightarrow \{0, 1\}$. In this relationship $R(x, y) = 1$ if there is a directed edge from x to y. In point of fact an undirected graph can be seen as a special case of a directed graph in which R is symmetric, $R(x, y) = R(y, x)$. Thus at the formal level we can view both undirected and directed graphs as the same type of objects, both are relationships

$R : V \times V \to \{0, 1\}$ the only difference between them is that an undirected graph is symmetric. As a result of this unification many of the concepts we have introduced for (undirected) graphs are valid for digraphs.

The operation of composition, $R \blacklozenge R = R^2$ is the same for these digraphs,

$$R^2(x, z) = Max_y[R(x, y) \wedge R(y,z)]$$

The concept of path naturally extends. If x and y are two distinct vertices an x–y path is a sequence of distinct vertices beginning with x and ending with y so that there is a directed edge between any two adjacent vertices. More formally if x and y are two distinct vertices an x–y path is a sequencing of distinct vertices beginning with x and ending with y so that $R(a, b) = 1$ for any two adjacent vertices in the sequence. Formally we say that the sequencing $a_1 \ a_2 \ a_3 \ldots a_q$ is a path from a_1 to a_q if $R(a_1, a_2) \wedge R_2(a_2, a_3) \wedge \ldots \wedge R(a_{q-1}, a_q) = 1$. This is thus degree to which this is a path.

The concept of degree of a node can be generalized to the case of digraph, however here we need two concepts in-degree, Deg_i and out-degree, Deg_o. In particular $Deg_i(x) = \sum\limits_{y \in V - \{x\}} R(x.y)$ it is the number of edges coming into x. The out-degree is $deg_o(x) = \sum\limits_{y \in V - \{x\}} R(x.y)$.

21.9 Authority Figures

A prototypical directed graph is hierarchical structure or rooted tree shown in Fig. 21.9. Here we are interested in providing a generalization of the node #1 for any directed relational network by introducing a node type concept called an **authority figure.** Our object is to define some procedure via some network features so that for any node x_j in a directed graph we can determine the degree of truth of the statement x_j is an authority-figure. We shall formulate this as a fuzzy subset AFig over the set of nodes, X. Thus for any node x_j its membership grade $AFig(x_j)$ will be the degree to which it is an authority figure.

Our procedure will be to define what properties constitute our concept of authority figure and provide a mechanism that allows us to calculate whether a node satisfies these conditions in terms of using the network structure. Here we shall consider a network $< X, R >$ in which $R : X \times X \to [0, 1]$ such $R(x, y) = 1$

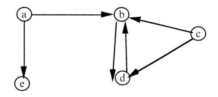

Fig. 21.8 Typical directed graph

if there is an edge from x to y and R(x, y)=0 if no edge exists. The fact that it is a direct network means that R(x, y) and R(y, x) are not necessarily equal. We assume R is a reflexive relationship, R(x, x) = 1.

We now consider our generalization of the concept of an authority figure. We first see that the basic feature of node x_1 in Fig. 21.9 is that all nodes have a path *from* x_1 while no nodes have a path *to* x_1. We shall now provide a generalization in this idea.

What must be kept in mind is that our generalization will be subjective in that it is our perception of the concept of an authority figure. Thus while we feel that our definition basically captures the idea of authority figure other people may have somewhat different variations of our formulation. However what is of importance here is that the procedure that will be described to implement our definition is general enough to be used to implement other specific formulations of this concept.

We shall define authority figure type node as one that satisfies the following conditions

C_1: The node has a path to all other nodes in the network
C_2: For most nodes the path from the authority node to it is short
C_3: Few nodes have a path *to* the authority node

Here then we need to satisfy three criteria. We now suggest how to determine the satisfaction of each of these criteria using the network structure $< X, R >$. We shall assume the cardinality of the network is $|X| = n$. We recall that for any network $R^k(x_i, x_j) = 1$ if there exists a path from x_i to x_j with at most k edges. If no such path exists it is zero. Using this we can easily formulate the first criteria. For any node x_i we can define

$$C_1(x_i) = Min_j(R^{n-1}(x_i, x_j))$$

The second condition requires us to use fuzzy sets to introduce two concepts "most" and "short". We first define the concept *most* using a fuzzy subset Q on the unit interval, $Q : [0, 1] \rightarrow [0, 1]$, where for any proportion p the value Q(p) indicates the degree to it satisfies the concept *most*. Such a fuzzy subset should satisfy the conditions: $Q_1(0) = 0$, $Q_1(1) = 1$ and if $p_2 > p_2$ then $Q(p_2) \geq Q(p_1)$. A prototypical example of this using a piecewise linear definition for *most* such as

$Q(p) = 0$ if $p \leq a$
$Q(p) = \frac{p-a}{b-a}$ if $a < p \leq b$
$Q(p) = 1$ if $p > b$

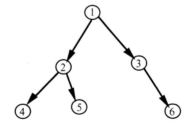

Fig. 21.9 Typical
hierarchical network

Alternatively we can use a power type function such as $Q(p) = p^r$ with $r > 2$.

The concept of short path can also be expressed as a fuzzy subset S defined on the set of positive integers. Here S must be such that $S(1) = 1$ and $S(l_1) \geq S(l_2)$ if $l_1 < l_2$. Again a prototypical definition of this concept can be had using a piece-wise linear fuzzy subset as shown in Fig. 21.10.

Our interest now is to determine $C_2(x_i)$, the degree to which the node x_i has a short path to most nodes. First we determine for any x_j the truth of the proposition that there is a short path from x_i to x_j. Here we shall let the $SP_i(x_j)$ denote this value and express it as

$$SP_i(x_j) = \underset{k=1 \text{ to } n-1}{\text{Max}} [S(k) \wedge R^k(x_i, x_j)].$$

Since $S(k)$ is decreasing with respect to k we see $SP_i(x_j)$ will be equal to $S(k)$ for the first k for which there is a path from x_i to x_j. If we denote this k_j then $SP_i(x_j) = S(k_j)$.

Using the preceding we can obtain for each $x_j \neq x_i$ the value $SP_i(x_j)$ the degree to which there is a short path for x_i to x_j.

We now use a version of the OWA aggregation operator [18] to determine, $C_2(x_1)$ the degree to which x_i has a short path to most of the other nodes. We proceed as follows. We first order the $SP_i(x_j)$ and let d_k be the value of the kth largest of the $SP_i(x_j)$. Using this and the fuzzy subset Q representing our concept of most we calculate

$$C_2(x_i) = \underset{k=1 \text{ to } n-1}{\text{Max}} \left[Q(\frac{k}{n-1}) \wedge d_k \right]$$

An alternative way of obtaining $C_2(x_i)$ is to use the regular OWA operator. Here we first obtain $w_k = Q(\frac{k}{n-1}) - Q(\frac{k}{n-1})$ for $k = 1$ to $n - 1$ and then we obtain

$$C_2(x_i) = \sum_{k=1}^{n-1} w_k d_k$$

We now consider the third requirement, *few* nodes have a path to the authority, x_i. Here we can define *few* in similar way to how we defined *most*. Let it be a fuzzy set $F : [0, 1] \rightarrow [0, 1]$ such for any proportion p, $F(p)$ indicates its satisfaction to the concept *few*. Here F must be such that: $F(0) = 1$, $F(1) = 0$ and if $p_1 < p_2$ then $F(p_1) \geq F(p_2)$.

Since $R^r(x_j, x_i) = 1$ if there is a path of length of at most r links from x_j to x_j then $R^{n-1}(x_j, x_i) = 1$ if there is any path from x_j to x_i. If there is no path $R^{n-1}(x_j,$

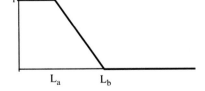

Fig. 21.10 Fuzzy subset corresponding to concept short path

$x_i) = 0$. For each x_j we let $h_j = 1 - R^{n-1}(x_j, x_i)$. We then order the h_j and let g_k be the kth smallest of h_j. Using this we obtain

$$C_3(x_i) = \max_{k=1 \text{ to } n} \left[g_k \wedge F\left(\frac{k-1}{n-1}\right) \right]$$

Let us look at this. Assume that k_i is the number of nodes for which $R(x_j, x_i) = 1$. In this case $h_j = 0$ for k_i values and $h_j = 1$ for $(n-1) - k_i = n - (k_i + 1)$ values. In this case $g_k = 1$ for $k \geq k_1 + 1$ and hence $C_3(x_i) = F(\frac{k_i}{n-1})$]. It is degree to which $\frac{k_i}{n-1}$ satisfies the concept few.

We are now in a position to determine the truth of the statement that x_i is an authority figure. We first calculate the value of $C_1(x_i)$, $C_2(x_i)$ and $C_3(x_i)$ and then

$$AFig(x_i) = \min [C_1(x_i), C_2(x_2), C_3(x_3)]$$

21.10 Conclusion

We provided an introduction to the basic ideas of graph (relational network) theory. We discussed some concepts from the fuzzy set paradigm of computing with words. The natural connection between these two technologies was pointed out. Our main objective here was to introduce a paradigm to help in development of intelligent social network theory using granular computing. Using this paradigm one starts by expressing, in a human focused manner, concepts associated with social networks. We then formalize these concepts using fuzzy sets. Having this set based formulation we can evaluate these concepts with respect to a given social network which have been represented using set based relational network theory. This approach forms the basis of what we call the paradigm for intelligent social network analysis, PISNA. Using this paradigm we provided definitions of a number of concepts related to social networks.

References

1. Carrington, P. J., Scott, J. and Wasserman, S., Models and Methods in Social Network Analysis, Cambridge University Press: New York, 2007.
2. Wasserman, S. and Faust, K., Social Network Analysis: Methods and Applications, Cambridge University Press: New York, 1994.
3. Scott, J., Social Network Analysis, SAGE: Los Angeles, 2000.
4. Chartrand, G., Introductory Graph Theory, Dover Publications: Mineola, NY, 1977.
5. Bollobas, B., Modern Graph Theory, Springer: New York, 2000.
6. Berge, C., The Theory of Graphs, Dover Publications: Mineola, NY, 2001.
7. Newman, M., Barabási, A. L. and Watts, D. J., The Structure and Dynamics of Networks, Princeton University Press: Princeton, NJ, 2006.
8. Zadeh, L. A., "Fuzzy sets," Information and Control 8, 338–353, 1965.

9. Yager, R. R. and Filev, D. P., Essentials of Fuzzy Modeling and Control, Wiley: New York, 1994.

10. Nguyen, H. T. and Walker, E. A., A First Course in Fuzzy Logic, Chapman and Hall: Boca Raton, FL, 2005.

11. Zadeh, L. A., "Fuzzy logic = computing with words," IEEE Transactions on Fuzzy Systems 4, 103–111, 1996.

12. Zadeh, L. A., "Generalized theory of uncertainty (GTU) – principal concepts and ideas," Computational Statistics and Data Analysis 51, 15–46, 2006.

13. Bargiela, A. and Pedrycz, W., Granular Computing: An Introduction, Kluwer Academic: Amsterdam, 2003.

14. Zadeh, L. A., "A computational approach to fuzzy quantifiers in natural languages," Computing and Mathematics with Applications 9, 149–184, 1983.

15. Yager, R. R., "On ordered weighted averaging aggregation operators in multi-criteria decision making," IEEE Transactions on Systems, Man and Cybernetics 18, 183–190, 1988.

16. Pedrycz, W. and Gomide, F., Fuzzy Systems Engineering: Toward Human-Centric Computing, Wiley: New York, 2007.

17. Yager, R. R., "Quantifier guided aggregation using OWA operators," International Journal of Intelligent Systems 11, 49–73, 1996.

18. Yager, R. R., "Applications and extensions of OWA aggregations," International Journal of Man-Machine Studies 37, 103–132, 1992.

Part IV
Privacy in Online Social Networks

Chapter 22
Managing Trust in Online Social Networks

Touhid Bhuiyan, Audun Josang, and Yue Xu

22.1 Introduction

In recent years, there is a dramatic growth in number and popularity of online social networks. There are many networks available with more than 100 million registered users such as Facebook, MySpace, QZone, Windows Live Spaces etc. People may connect, discover and share by using these online social networks. The exponential growth of online communities in the area of social networks attracts the attention of the researchers about the importance of managing trust in online environment. Users of the online social networks may share their experiences and opinions within the networks about an item which may be a product or service. The user faces the problem of evaluating trust in a service or service provider before making a choice. Recommendations may be received through a chain of friends network, so the problem for the user is to be able to evaluate various types of trust opinions and recommendations. This opinion or recommendation has a great influence to choose to use or enjoy the item by the other user of the community. Collaborative filtering system is the most popular method in recommender system. The task in collaborative filtering is to predict the utility of items to a particular user based on a database of user rates from a sample or population of other users. Because of the different taste of different people, they rate differently according to their subjective taste. If two people rate a set of items similarly, they share similar tastes. In the recommender system, this information is used to recommend items that one participant likes, to other persons in the same cluster. But the collaborative filtering system performs poor when there is insufficient previous common rating available between users; commonly known as cost start problem. To overcome the cold start problem and with the dramatic growth of online social networks, trust based approach to recommendation has emerged. This approach assumes a trust network among users and makes recommendations based on the ratings of the users that are directly or indirectly trusted by the target user. In such a system; trust is used

T. Bhuiyan (✉)
School of Information Technology, Queensland University of Technology, Australia
e-mail: t.bhuiyan@qut.edu.au

B. Furht (ed.), *Handbook of Social Network Technologies and Applications*,
DOI 10.1007/978-1-4419-7142-5_22, © Springer Science+Business Media, LLC 2010

for neighborhood formation. Trust could be used as supplementary or replacement method of widely used collaborative filtering system. Services offered and provided through the Web including online social network have varying quality, and it is often difficult to assess the quality of a service before accessing and using it. Trust and reputation systems can be used in order to assist users in predicting and selecting the best quality services. We have described briefly the current status of the online social networks and trust related issues in online environment. In the following sections of this chapter; we also describe how Bayesian reputation systems can be combined with trust modeling based on subjective logic to provide an integrated method for assessing the quality of online services. This will not only assist the user's decision making, but will also provide an incentive for service providers to maintain high quality, and can be used as a sanctioning mechanism to discourage deceptive and low quality services.

Online trust and reputation systems are emerging as important decision support tools for selecting online services and for assessing the risk of accessing them. It has been previously proposed and studied Bayesian reputation systems [1–4] and trust models based on subjective logic [5–8]. Binomial Bayesian reputation systems normally take ratings expressed in a discrete binary form as either positive (e.g. *good*) or negative (e.g. *bad*). Multinomial Bayesian reputation systems allow the possibility of providing ratings with discrete graded levels such as e.g. *mediocre – bad – average – good – excellent* [4]. It is also possible to use continuous ratings in both binomial and multinomial reputation systems [9]. Multinomial models have the advantage that scores can distinguish between the case of polarized ratings (e.g. a combination of strictly good and bad ratings) and the case of only average ratings.

Trust models based on subjective logic are directly compatible with Bayesian reputation systems because a bi-jective mapping exists between their respective trust and reputation representations. This provides a powerful basis for combining trust and reputation systems for assessing the quality of online services. A general characteristic of reputation systems is that they provide global reputation scores, meaning that all the members in a community will see the same reputation score for a particular agent. On the other hand, trust systems can in general be used to derive local and subjective measures of trust, meaning that different agents can derive different trust in the same entity. Another characteristic of trust systems is that they can analyze multiple hops of trust transitivity Reputation systems on the other hand normally compute scores based on direct input from members in the community which is not based on transitivity. Still there are systems that have characteristics of being both a reputation system and a trust system. The matrix below shows examples of the possible combinations of local and global scores, and trust transitivity or not. In this work we describe a framework for combining these forms of trust and reputation systems. Because Bayesian reputation systems are directly compatible with trust systems based on subjective logic, they can be seamlessly integrated. This provides a powerful and flexible basis for online trust and reputation management.

22.2 Online Social Networks

Professor J. A. Barnes has introduced the term "Social Network" in 1967 to describe the associations of people drawn together by family, work, hobby etc.; for emotional, instrumental, appraisal and information support [10]. These networks may operate in many levels from family level to a level of nations and can play important roles in communications among people, organizations and even nations; as well as the way how problems are solved and how organizations may run in better way. In its simplest form, a social network is a map of the relevant ties between the individuals, organizations, nations etc. being studied. With the evolution of digital age, Internet provides a greater scope of implementing social networks online. Online social networks have broader and easier coverage of members worldwide to share information and resources.

The first online social networks were called UseNet Newsgroups (www.usenet.com) designed and built by Duke University graduate students Tom Truscott and Jim Ellis in 1979. Since then the online social networks have a continuous growth in size and numbers. In February 2010; online social network giant Facebook cross the massive 370 million registered monthly active user. The Table 22.1 below shows a brief timeline of the history of online social networking [11].

A January 2009 compete.com study ranked Facebook as the most used social network by worldwide monthly active users, followed by MySpace [12]. Table 22.2 shows the top 10 most popular online social networks in terms of user's visit. As on February 2010, Facebook also secured the first position in terms of number of registered users (Table 22.4).

Based on number of registered user and monthly visit; Facebook is the largest and most popular online social network at this moment (www.insidefacebook.com). It had 350 million Monthly Active Users (MAU) at the beginning of January 2010. But it has been growing too fast around the world since then. Now, at the beginning of February 2010, the number increases to 373 million MAU across the world. As on 10 February 2010, roughly 23 million more people are using Facebook compared to 30 days ago, many in countries with big populations around the world. This is an interesting shift from much of Facebook's international growth to date. Once Facebook began offering the service in multiple languages (it's available in more than 70 of them as of today), it started blowing up in many countries like Canada, Iceland, Norway, South Africa, Chile, etc. The United States is at the top with more than five million new users; it also continues to be the single largest country on Facebook, with 108 million MAU. That's 35% of the total US population. Table 22.3 shows a growth comparison MAU of top ten countries between January and February 2010.

Going down the list, we first see some regulars: Indonesia, Turkey, the U.K. and France. These all have been growing for months. Mexico is on its way to become the largest Spanish-speaking country on Facebook; with a gain of slightly less than a million new users; it is close to the largest, Spain, Argentina and Colombia.

Table 22.1 Brief Timeline of online social networking

1971	Ray Tomlinson invents email
1973	First group chat program
1975	First mailing list, called *MsgGroup*
	First computer conferencing system
1978	First Multi-User Dungeon (MUD) for multi-user gaming
1979	*USENET* newsgroups created
1984	Birth of the *Fido* network of Bulletin Board Systems (BBSes)
1985	Whole Earth Letronic Link (WELL) community begins
1988	Internet Relay Chat (IRC) invented
1991	Tim Berners-Lee posts "World-Wide Web: Executive Summary" to *USENET* Group. "Gopher", the first simple menu-driven client to Internet resources launches
1992	Berners-Lee creates his "What's New?" page, arguably the first blog
1993	Howard Rheingold publishes *The Virtual Community*
	Mosaic Web browser is released
1994	"Christ is coming" is the first spam on *USENET*
1995	Ward Cunningham launches the first wiki
	AltaVista, the first full Web search engine, launches
1996	ICQ: first peer-to-peer instant messaging appears
	January: 100,000 Web servers
1997	April: 1,000,000 Web servers
	Slashdot, the first blog to enable reader comments, goes online
	Jorn Barger coins the term "Weblog"
1998	Open Directory Project (DMOZ), later acquired by *Netscape*
1999	Peter Merholz coins the term "blog" as a contraction of "Weblog"
	LiveJournal and *Blogger* launch
	Kuro5hin, a blog where users vote for what goes to the front page, launches
2000	*HotOrNot.com* created with zero capital
2001	*Wikipedia*, an open collaborative wiki encyclopedia, goes live
	Movable type (leading blog software) initial beta release
2002	10,000,000th Web server goes live
	10,000,000th post on *Blogger*
	Friendster launches
2003	Venture capital investment in social network space exceeds $50 million
	LiveJournal and *Friendster* pass one million accounts
	Skype released
	LinkedIn, social network focused on business professionals, secures
	Series A financing of $4.7 million led by Sequoia Capital
2004	*Skype* hits ten million downloads
	Social Networking *Metalist* (SocialSoftware.BlogsInc.com) lists more than 200 different social networking systems
2005	*Skype* hits 100 million downloads
2006	*Google* acquires *YouTube*, video social network, for a stock transaction worth $1.65 billion

(continued)

Table 22.1 (continued)

2007	IBM launches enterprise social networking suite
	LinkedIn surpasses 10,000,000 members
	Germany social networking site *OpenBC/Xing* successful IPO
	Wikipedia exceeds 1,700,000 English articles
2008	The fastest growing sites were Twitter (664%), Tagged (421%), and Ning (303%)
	MySpace had 58.4 million unique visitors in December, Facebook had 55.2 million
	Facebook passed MySpace in time per person: 2 h, 7 min–1 h, 40 min
2009	*Facebook* hits 350 million registered users

Table 22.2 Top ten mostly visited social networks in Jan'09– based on MAU

Rank	Site	Monthly visit
1	facebook.com	1,191,373,339
2	myspace.com	810,153,536
3	twitter.com	54,218,731
4	flixster.com	53,389,974
5	linkedin.com	42,744,438
6	tagged.com	39,630,927
7	classmates.com	35,219,210
8	myyearbook.com	33,121,821
9	livejournal.com	25,221,354
10	imeem.com	22,993,608

Table 22.3 Country wise monthly growth of Facebook users- as on Feb 2010

Country	1/1/2010	1/2/2010	Change	Change (%)
U.S.	102,681,240	108,062,900	5,381,660	5
Indonesia	15,301,280	17,301,760	2,000,480	13
Turkey	16,961,140	18,556,840	1,595,700	9
U.K.	23,076,700	24,342,820	1,266,120	5
France	14,301,020	15,498,220	1,197,200	8
Mexico	6,671,560	7,624,120	952,560	14
Germany	5,796,940	6,674,740	877,800	15
India	5,658,080	6,342,800	684,720	12
Philippines	8,806,300	9,317,180	510,880	6
Brazil	2,373,520	2,869,920	496,400	21

22.3 Trust in Online Environment

Trust has become important topic of research in many fields including sociology, psychology, philosophy, economics, business, law and IT. It is not a new topic to discuss. In fact, it has been the topic of hundreds books and scholarly articles over a long period of time. Trust is a complex word with multiple dimensions. A vast literature on trust has grown in several area of research but it is relatively confusing and sometimes contradictory, because the term is being used with a variety of meaning [13]. Also a lack of coherence exists among researchers in the definition of

Table 22.4 Top ten largest social networks in Feb'10 – based on registered users

No.	Network name	Web link	Reg user
1	Facebook	www.facebook.com	350,000,000
2	QZone (Chinese)	http://qzone.qq.com	200,000,000
3	MySpace	www.myspace.com	130,000,000
4	Windows Live Spaces	http://home.spaces.live.com	120,000,000
5	Habbo	www.habbo.com.au	117,000,000
6	Orkut	www.orkut.com	100,000,000
7	Friendster	www.friendster.com	90,000,000
8	Hi5	www.hi5.com	80,000,000
9	Flixster	www.flixster.com	63,000,000
10	Netlog	www.netlog.com	59,000,000

trust. Though dozens of proposed definitions are available in the literature, a complete formal unambiguous definition of trust is rare. In many occasions, trust is used as a word or concept with no real definition. Hussain and Chang [14] present an overview of the definitions of the terms of trust and reputation from the existing literature. They have shown that none of these definitions is fully capable to satisfy all of the context dependence, time dependence and the dynamic nature of trust. Trust is such a concept that crosses disciplines and also domains. The focus of definition differs on the basis of the goal and the scope of the projects. Two generalized definitions of trust defined by Jøsang et al. [15] which they called reliability trust (the term "evaluation trust" is more widely used by the other researchers, therefore we use this term) and decision trust respectively will be used for this work. Evaluation trust can be interpreted as the reliability of something or somebody. It can be defined as the subjective probability by which an individual, A, expects that another individual, B, performs a given action on which its welfare depends. On the other hand, the decision trust captures broader concept of trust. It can be defined as the extent to which one party is willing to depend on something or somebody in a given situation with a feeling of relative security, even though negative consequences are possible.

22.4 Related Work

The issue of trust has been gaining an increasing amount of attention in a number of research communities including online service provision. There are many different views of how to measure and use trust. Some researchers use trust and reputation as same meaning while others are not. Though the meaning of trust is different to different people, a brief review on these models is a good starting point to research in the area of Trust. As trust is a social phenomenon, the model of trust for the artificial world like Internet should be based on how trust works between people in society [16]. The rich literature growing around trust systems for Syber Space gives a strong indication that this is an important technology. Unfortunately, the systems being proposed are usually designed from scratch, and only in very few cases are authors building on proposals by other authors. The period we are in can therefore be seen as a period of pioneers. Consolidation around a set of sound and well recognized principles is needed in order to get the most benefit out of trust systems.

Stephen Marsh [17] is one of the pioneers to introduce a computational model for trust in the computing literature. For his PhD thesis, Marsh investigates the notions of trust in various contexts and develops a formal description of its use with distributed, intelligent agents. But the model is complex, mostly theoretical and difficult to implement. Abdul-Rahman et al. [16] proposed a model for supporting trust in virtual communities, based on direct experiences and reputation. However, there are certain aspects of their model that are ad-hoc which limits the applicability of the model in broader scope. Schillo et al [18] proposed a trust model for scenarios where interaction result is Boolean, either good or bad, between two agents trust relationship. Though, they did not consider the degrees of satisfaction. Two one-on-one trust acquisition mechanisms are proposed by Esfandiari et al. [19] in their trust model. The first is based on observation. They proposed the use of Bayesian networks and to perform the trust acquisition by Bayesian learning. In the model proposed by Yu and Singh [20], the information stored by an agent about direct interactions is a set of values that reflect the quality of these interactions. Only the most recent experiences with each concrete partner are considered for the calculations. This model failed to combine direct information with witness information. When direct information is available, it is considered the only source to determine the trust of the target agent. Only when the direct information is not available, the model appeals to witness information.

Mui et al. [21] proposed a computational model based on sociological and biological understanding. The model can be used to calculate agent's trust and reputation scores. They also identified some weaknesses of the trust and reputation study which is the lack of differentiation of trust and reputation and the mechanism for inference between them is not explicit. Trust and reputation are taken to be the same across multiple contexts or are treated as uniform across time and the existing computational models for trust and reputation are often not grounded on understood social characteristics of these quantities. They did not examine effects of deception in this model. Pujol et al. [22] proposed a method for calculating the reputation of a given member in a society or in a social network by making use of PageRank algorithm. Dimitrakos [23] presented and analysed a service-oriented trust management framework based on the integration of role-based modelling and risk assessment in order to support trust management solutions. They provided evidence of emerging methods, formalisms and conceptual frameworks which, if appropriately integrated, can bridge the gap between systems modelling, trust and risk management in e-commerce.

Selcuk et al. [24] proposed a reputation-based trust management protocol for P2P networks where users rate the reliability of the parties they deal with and share this information with their peers. Sabater et al. [25] have proposed a modular trust and reputation system oriented to complex small/mid-size e-commerce environments which they called ReGreT, where social relations among individuals play an important role. O'Donovan et al [26] distinguished between two types of profiles in the context of a given recommendation session or rating prediction. The consumer profile and the producer profile. They described "trust" as the reliability of a partner profile to deliver accurate recommendations in the past. They described two models of trust which they called profile-level trust and item-level trust.

Guha et al [27] proposed a method based on PageRank algorithm for propagating both trust and distrust. They identified four different methods for propagating the net beliefs values, namely direct propagation, co-citation, transpose and coupling. The Advogato maximum flow trust metric has been proposed by Levien [28] in order to discover which users are trusted by members of an online community and which are not. Trust is computed through one centralized community server and considered relative to a seed of users enjoying supreme trust. Local group trust metrics compute sets of agents trusted by those being part of the trust seed. Advogato, only assigns Boolean values indicating presence or absence of trust. It is a global trust algorithm which uses the same trusted nodes to make trust calculation for all users. It makes the algorithm suitable for P2P networks. As the trust inference algorithm has released under a free software license, it became the basis of many research paper. Appleseed trust metric was proposed by Ziegler [29]. AppelSeed is closely based on PageRank algorithm. It allows rankings of agents with respect to trust accorded. One of the major weaknesses is that a person who has made many high trust ratings will have lower value than if only one or two people had been rated. Another weakness of this model is; it requires exponentially higher computation with increasing number of user which makes it non-scalable.

Shmatikov et al. [30] proposed a reputation-based trust management model which allows mutually distrusting agents to develop a basis for interaction in the absence of central authority. The model is proposed in the context of peer-to-peer applications, online games or military situations. Teacy [31] proposed a probabilistic framework for assessing trust based on direct observations of a trustees behavior and indirect observations made by a third party. They claimed that their proposed mechanism can cope with the possibility of unreliable third party information in some context. Xiong [32] also proposed a decentralized reputation based trust supporting framework called PeerTrust for P2P environment. The have focused on models and techniques for resilient reputation management against feed back aggregation, feedback oscillation and loss of feedback privacy. Jøsang et al [6] proposed a model for trust derivation with Subjective Logic. They argued that Subjective logic represents a practical belief calculus which can be used for calculative analysis trust networks. TNASL requires trust relationships to be expressed as beliefs, and trust networks to be expressed as DSPGs in the form of canonical expressions. They have described how trust can be derived with the belief calculus of subjective logic. Xue and Fan [33] proposed a trust model for the Semantic Web which allows agents to decide which among different sources of information to trust and thus act rationally on the semantic web. Tian et al [34] proposed trust model for P2P networks in which the trust value of a given peer was computed using its local trust information and recommendation from other nodes. In a recent work [35] proposes a new algorithm called TrustWalker to combine trust-based and item-based recommendation. Though the proposed method is limited to centralised system only.

22.5 Trust Models Based on Subjective Logic

Subjective logic [36–38] is a type of probabilistic logic that explicitly takes uncertainty and belief ownership into account. Arguments in subjective logic are subjective opinions about states in a state space. A binomial opinion applies to a single proposition, and can be represented as a Beta distribution. A multinomial opinion applies to a collection of propositions, and can be represented as a Dirichlet distribution.

Subjective logic defines a trust metric called *opinion* denoted by $\omega_X^A = (\vec{b}, u, \vec{a})$, which expresses the relying party A's belief over a state space X. Here $\vec{b}$ represents belief masses over the states of X, and u represent uncertainty mass where $\vec{b}, u \in [0, 1]$ and $\sum \vec{b} + u = 1$. The vector $\vec{a} \in [0, 1]$ represents the base rates over X, and is used for computing the probability expectation value of a state x as $E(x) = \vec{b}(x) + \vec{a}(x)u$, meaning that $\vec{a}$ determines how uncertainty contributes to $E(x)$. Binomial opinions are expressed as $\omega_x^A = (b, d, u, a)$ where d denotes disbelief in x. When the statement x for example says "*David is honest and reliable*", then the opinion can be interpreted as reliability trust in David. As an example, let us assume that Alice needs to get her car serviced, and that she asks Bob to recommend a good car mechanic. When Bob recommends David, Alice would like to get a second opinion, so she asks Claire for her opinion about David. This situation is illustrated in Fig. 22.1 below where the indexes on arrows indicate the order in which they are formed.

When trust and referrals are expressed as subjective opinions, each transitive trust path Alice $\rightarrow$ Bob $\rightarrow$ David, and Alice $\rightarrow$ Claire $\rightarrow$ David can be computed with the *transitivity operator*, where the idea is that the referrals from Bob and Claire are discounted as a function Alice's trust in Bob and Claire respectively. Finally the two

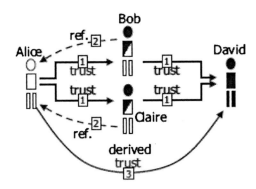

Fig. 22.1 Deriving trust
from parallel transitive chains

paths can be combined using the cumulative or averaging fusion operator. These operators form part of *Subjective Logic* [37, 38], and semantic constraints must be satisfied in order for the transitive trust derivation to be meaningful [39]. Opinions can be uniquely mapped to beta PDFs, and in this sense the fusion operator is equivalent to Bayesian updating. This model is thus both belief-based and Bayesian.

A trust relationship between A and B is denoted as [A:B]. The transitivity of two arcs is denoted as ":" and the fusion of two parallel paths is denoted as "$\diamond$". The trust network of Fig. 22.1 can then be expressed as:

$$[A, D] = ([A, B] : [B, D]) \diamond ([A, C] : [C, D]) \qquad (22.1)$$

The corresponding transitivity operator for opinions denoted as "$\otimes$" and the corresponding fusion operator as "$\oplus$". The mathematical expression for combining the opinions about the trust relationships of Fig. 22.1 is then:

$$\omega_D^A = \left(\omega_B^A \otimes \omega_D^B \right) \oplus \left(\omega_C^A \otimes \omega_D^C \right) \qquad (22.2)$$

Arbitrarily complex trust networks can be analysed with TNA-SL which consists of a network exploration method combined with trust analysis based on subjective logic. The method is based on simplifying complex trust networks into a directed series parallel graph (DSPG) before applying subjective logic calculus.

22.6 Trust Network Analysis

Trust networks consist of transitive trust relationships between people, organisations and software agents connected through a medium for communication and interaction. By formalising trust relationships, e.g. as reputation scores or as subjective trust measures, trust between parties within a domain can be derived by analysing the trust paths linking the parties together. A method for trust network analysis using subjective logic (TNA-SL) has been described by Jøsang et al [6, 7, 15]. TNA-SL takes directed trust edges between pairs as input, and can be used to derive a level of trust between arbitrary parties that are interconnected through the network. Even in case of no explicit trust paths between two parties exist; subjective logic allows a level of trust to be derived through the default vacuous opinions. TNA-SL therefore has a general applicability and is suitable for many types of trust networks. A potential limitation with the TNA-SL is that complex trust networks must be simplified to *series-parallel* networks in order for TNA-SL to produce consistent results. The simplification consisted of gradually removing the least certain trust paths until the whole network can be represented in a series-parallel form. As this process removes information it is intuitively sub-optimal.

22.6.1 Operators for Deriving Trust

Subjective logic is a belief calculus specifically developed for modeling trust relationships. In subjective logic, beliefs are represented on binary state spaces, where each of the two possible states can consist of sub-states. Belief functions on binary state spaces are called *subjective opinions* and are formally expressed in the form of an ordered tuple $\omega_x^A = (b, d, u, a)$, where b, d, and u represent belief, disbelief and uncertainty respectively where b, d, $u \in [0, 1]$ and $b + d + u = 1$. The base rate parameter $a \in [0, 1]$ represents the base rate probability in the absence of evidence, and is used for computing an opinion's probability expectation value $E\left(\omega_x^A\right) = b + au$, meaning that a determines how uncertainty shall contribute to $E\left(\omega_x^A\right)$. A subjective opinion is interpreted as an agent A's belief in the truth of statement x. Ownership of an opinion is represented as a superscript so that for example A's opinion about x is denoted as ω_x^A. Subjective logic has a sound mathematical basis and is compatible with binary logic and traditional Bayesian analysis. Subjective logic defines a rich set of operators for combining subjective opinions in various ways [40]. Some operators represent generalizations of binary logic and probability calculus, whereas others are unique to belief calculus because they depend on belief ownership.

Transitivity is used to compute trust along a chain of trust edges. Assume two agents A and B where A has referral trust in B, denoted by ω_B^A, for the purpose of judging the functional or referral trustworthiness of C. In addition B has functional or referral trust in C, denoted by ω_C^B. Agent A can then derive her trust in C by discounting B's trust in C with A's trust in B, denoted by $\omega_C^{A:B}$. By using the symbol "$\otimes$" to designate this operator, we define

$$\omega_C^{A:B} = \omega_B^A \otimes \omega_C^B \begin{cases} b_C^{A:B} = b_B^A b_C^B \\ d_C^{A:B} = b_B^A d_C^B \\ u_C^{A:B} = d_B^A + u_B^A + b_B^A u_C^B \\ a_C^{A:B} = a_C^B. \end{cases} \tag{22.3}$$

The effect of discounting in a transitive chain is that uncertainty increases, not disbelief. Cumulative *Fusion* is equivalent to Bayesian updating in statistics. The cumulative fusion of two possibly conflicting opinions is an opinion that reflects both opinions in a fair and equal way. Let ω_C^A and ω_C^B be A's and B's trust in C respectively. The opinion $\omega_C^{A \diamond B}$ is then called the fused trust between ω_C^A and ω_C^B, denoting an imaginary agent $[A, B]$'s trust in C, as if she represented both A and B. By using the symbol "$\oplus$" to designate this operator, we define

$$\omega_C^{A \diamond B} = \omega_B^A \oplus \omega_C^B \begin{cases} b_C^{A \diamond B} = \left(b_C^A u_C^B + b_C^B u_C^A\right)/\left(u_C^A + u_C^B - u_C^A u_C^B\right) \\ d_C^{A \diamond B} = \left(d_C^A u_C^B + d_C^B u_C^A\right)/\left(u_C^A + u_C^B - u_C^A u_C^B\right) \\ u_C^{A \diamond B} = \left(u_C^A u_C^B\right)/\left(u_C^A + u_C^B - u_C^A u_C^B\right) \\ a_C^{A \diamond B} = a_C^A. \end{cases} \tag{22.4}$$

where it is assumed that $a_C^A = a_C^B$. Limits can be computed [40] for $u_C^A = u_C^B = 0$. The effect of the cumulative fusion operator is to amplify belief and disbelief and reduce uncertainty.

22.6.2 Trust Path Dependency and Network Simplification

Transitive trust networks can involve many principals, and in the examples below, capital letters A, B, C and D will be used to denote principals We will use basic constructs of directed graphs to represent transitive trust networks, and add some notation elements which allow us to express trust networks in a structured way. A single trust relationship can be expressed as a directed edge between two nodes that represent the trust source and the trust target of that edge. For example the edge [A, B] means that A trusts B. The symbol ":" is used to denote the transitive connection of two consecutive trust edges to form a transitive trust path. The trust relationships between four principals A, B, C and D connected serially can be expressed as:

$$([A, D]) = ([A, B] : [B, C] : [C, D]) \tag{22.5}$$

Let us now turn to the combination of parallel trust paths, as illustrated in Fig. 22.1. We will use the symbol "$\diamond$" to denote the graph connector for this purpose. The "$\diamond$" symbol visually resembles a simple graph of two parallel paths between a pair of agents, so that it is natural to use it for this purpose. In short notation, A's combination of the two parallel trust paths from her to D in Fig. 22.1 is then expressed as:

$$([A, D]) = (([A, B] : [B, D]) \diamond ([A, C] : [C, D])) \tag{22.6}$$

It can be noted that Fig. 22.3 contains two parallel paths. Trust networks can have dependent paths. This is illustrated on the left-hand side of Fig. 22.2.

The expression for the graph on the left-hand side of Fig. 22.2 would be:

$$([A, D]) = (([A, B] : [B, D]) \diamond ([A, C] : [C, D]) \diamond ([A, B] : [B, C] : [C, D])) \tag{22.7}$$

A problem with (22.7) is that the arcs [A, B] and [C, D] appear twice, and the expression is therefore not canonical. Trust network analysis with subjective logic may produce inconsistent results when applied directly to non-canonical expressions.

Fig. 22.2 Network simplification by removing weakest path

It is therefore desirable to express graphs in a form where an arc only appears once. A canonical expression can be defined as an expression of a trust graph in structured notation where every edge only appears once.

A method for canonicalization based on network simplification was described in [7]. Simplification consists of removing the weakest, i.e. the least certain paths, until the network becomes a directed series-parallel network which can be expressed on a canonical form. Assuming that the path $([A, B]:[B, C]:[C, D])$ is the weakest path in the graph on the left-hand side of Fig. 22.2, network simplification of the dependent graph would be to remove the edge $[B, C]$ from the graph, as illustrated on the right-hand side of Fig. 22.2. Since the simplified graph is equal to that of left side of Fig. 22.2, the formal expression is the same as (22.6).

22.7 Trust Transitivity Analysis

Assume two agents A and B where A trusts B, and B believes that proposition x is true. Then by transitivity, agent A will also believe that proposition x is true. This assumes that B recommends x to A. In our approach, trust and belief are formally expressed as opinions. The transitive linking of these two opinions consists of discounting B's opinion about x by A's opinion about B, in order to derive A's opinion about x. This principle is illustrated in Fig. 22.3 below. The solid arrows represent initial direct trust, and the dotted arrow represents derived indirect trust.

Trust transitivity, as trust itself, is a human mental phenomenon, so there is no such thing as objective transitivity, and trust transitivity therefore lends itself to different interpretations. We have identified two main difficulties. The first is related to the effect of A disbelieving that B will give a good advice. What does this exactly mean? We will give two different interpretations and definitions. The second difficulty relates to the effect of base rate trust in a transitive path. We will briefly examine this, and provide the definition of a base rate sensitive discounting operator as an alternative to the two previous which are base rate insensitive.

22.7.1 Uncertainty Favoring Trust Transitivity

A's disbelief in the recommending agent B means that A thinks that B ignores the truth value of x. As a result A also ignores the truth value of x.

Fig. 22.3 Principle of trust transitivity

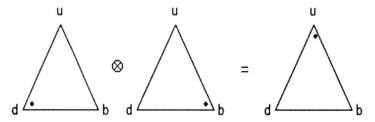

Fig. 22.4 Example of applying the discounting operator for independent opinions

Definition 22.1 (Uncertainty Favoring Discounting). Let A and B be two agents where A's opinion about B's recommendations is expressed as $\omega_B^A = \{b_B^A,\ d_B^A,\ u_B^A,\ a_B^A\}$, and let x be a proposition where B's opinion about x is recommended to A with the opinion $\omega_x^B = \{b_x^B,\ d_x^B,\ u_x^B,\ a_x^B\}$ Let $\omega_x^{A:B} = \{b_x^{A:B},\ d_x^{A:B},\ u_x^{A:B},\ a_x^{A:B}\}$ be the opinion such that:

$$
\begin{cases}
b_x^{A:B} = b_B^A b_x^B \\
d_x^{A:B} = d_B^A d_x^B \\
u_x^{A:B} = d_B^A + u_B^A + b_B^A u_x^B \\
a_x^{A:B} = a_x^B
\end{cases}
$$

then $\omega_x^{A:B}$ is called the uncertainty favoring discounted opinion of A. By using the symbol $\otimes$ to designate this operation, we get $\omega_x^{A:B} = \omega_B^A \otimes \omega_x^B$.

It is easy to prove that this operator is associative but not commutative. This means that the combination of opinions can start in either end of the path, and that the order in which opinions are combined is significant. In a path with more than one recommending entity, opinion independence must be assumed, which for example translates into not allowing the same entity to appear more than once in a transitive path. Figure 22.4 illustrates an example of applying the discounting operator for independent opinions, where $\omega_B^A = \{0.1,\ 0.8,\ 0.1\}$ discounts $\omega_x^B = \{0.8,\ 0.1,\ 0.1\}$ to produce $\omega_x^{A:B} = \{0.08,\ 0.01,\ 0.91\}$.

22.7.2 Opposite Belief Favoring

A's disbelief in the recommending agent B means that A thinks that B consistently recommends the opposite of his real opinion about the truth value of x. As a result, A not only disbelieves in x to the degree that B recommends belief, but she also believes in x to the degree that B recommends disbelief in x, because the combination of two disbeliefs results in belief in this case.

Definition 22.2 (Opposite Belief Favoring Discounting). Let A and B be two agents where A's opinion about B's recommendations is expressed as $\omega_B^A = \{b_B^A, d_B^A, u_B^A, a_B^A\}$, and let x be a proposition where B's opinion about x is recommended to A as the opinion $\omega_x^B = \{b_x^B, d_x^B, u_x^B, a_x^B\}$. Let $\omega_x^{A:B} = \{b_x^{A:B}, d_x^{A:B}, u_x^{A:B}, a_x^{A:B}\}$ be the opinion such that:

$$\begin{cases} b_x^{A:B} = b_B^A b_x^B + d_B^A d_x^B \\ d_x^{A:B} = b_B^A d_x^B + b_B^A d_x^B \\ u_x^{A:B} = u_B^A + (b_B^A + d_B^A)u_x^B \\ a_x^{A:B} = a_x^B \end{cases}$$

then $\omega_x^{A:B}$ is called the opposite belief favoring discounted recommendation from B to A. By using the symbol $\otimes$ to designate this operation, we get $\omega_x^{A:B} = \omega_B^A \otimes \omega_x^B$.

This operator models the principle that *"your enemy's enemy is your friend"*. That might be the case in some situations, and the operator should only be applied when the situation makes it plausible. It is doubtful whether it is meaningful to model more than two arcs in a transitive path with this principle. In other words, it is doubtful whether the enemy of your enemy's enemy necessarily is your enemy too.

22.7.3 Base Rate Sensitive Transitivity

In the transitivity operators defined in Sects. 27.3.1 and 27.3.2 above, a_B^A had no influence on the discounting of the recommended (b_x^B, d_x^B, u_x^B) parameters. This can seem counterintuitive in many cases such as in the example described next.

Imagine a stranger coming to a town which is know for its citizens being honest. The stranger is looking for a car mechanic, and asks the first person he meets to direct him to a good car mechanic. The stranger receives the reply that there are two car mechanics in town, David and Eric, where David is cheap but does not always do quality work, and Eric might be a bit more expensive, but he always does a perfect job. Translated into the formalism of subjective logic, the stranger has no other info about the person he asks than the base rate that the citizens in the town are honest. The stranger is thus ignorant, but the expectation value of a good advice is still very high. Without taking a_B^A into account, the result of the definitions above would be that the stranger is completely ignorant about which of the mechanics is the best. An intuitive approach would then be to let the expectation value of the stranger's trust in the recommender be the discounting factor for the recommended (b_x^B, d_x^B) parameters.

Definition 22.3 (Base Rate Sensitive Discounting). The base rate sensitive discounting of a belief $\omega_x^B = \{b_x^B, d_x^B, u_x^B, a_x^B\}$ by a belief $\omega_B^A = \{b_B^A, d_B^A, u_B^A, a_B^A\}$ produces the transitive belief $\omega_x^{A:B} = \{b_x^{A:B}, d_x^{A:B}, u_x^{A:B}, a_x^{A:B}\}$ where

$$\begin{cases} b_x^{A:B} = E\left(\omega_B^A\right) b_x^B \\ d_x^{A:B} = E\left(\omega_B^A\right) d_x^B \\ u_x^{A:B} = 1 - E\left(\omega_B^A\right) \left(b_x^B + d_x^B\right) \\ a_x^{A:B} = a_x^B \end{cases}$$

where the probability expectation value $E\left(\omega_B^A\right) = b_B^A + a_B^A u_B^A$.

However this operator must be applied with care. Assume again the town of honest citizens, and let the stranger A have the opinion $\omega_B^A = (0, 0, 15, 0.99)$ about the first person B she meets, i.e. the opinion has no basis in evidence other than a very high base rate defined by $a_B^A = 0.99$. If the person B now recommends to A the opinion $\omega_x^B = (1, 0, 0, a)$, then, according to the base rate sensitive discounting operator of Definition 22.3, A will have the belief $\omega_x^{A:B} = (0.99, 0, 0.01, a)$ in x. In other words, the highly certain belief $\omega_x^{A:B}$ is derived on the basis of the highly uncertain belief ω_B^A, which can seem counterintuitive. This potential problem could be amplified as the trust path gets longer. A safety principle could therefore be to only apply the base rate sensitive discounting to the last transitive link.

There might be other principles that better reflect human intuition for trust transitivity, but we will leave this question to future research. It would be fair to say that the base rate insensitive discounting operator of Definition 22.2 is safe and conservative, and that the base rate sensitive discounting operator of Definition 22.3 can be more intuitive in some situations, but must be applied with care.

22.7.4 Mass Hysteria

One of the strengths of this work is in its analytical capabilities. As an example, consider how mass hysteria can be caused by people not being aware of dependence between opinions. Let's take for example; person A recommend an opinion about a particular statement x to a group of other persons. Without being aware of the fact that the opinion came from the same origin, these persons can recommend their opinions to each other as illustrated in Fig. 22.5.

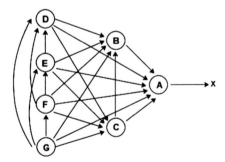

Fig. 22.5 The effects of unknown dependence

The arrows represent trust so that for example $B \rightarrow A$ can be interpreted as saying that B trusts A to recommend an opinion about statement x. The actual recommendation goes, of course, in the opposite direction to the arrows in Fig. 22.5. It can be seen that A recommends an opinion about $x - 6$ other agents, and that G receives six recommendations in all. If G assumes the recommended opinions to be independent and takes the consensus between them, his opinion can become abnormally strong and in fact even stronger than A's opinion.

As a numerical example, let A's opinion ω_x^A about x as well as the agents' opinions about each other $\left(\omega_A^B, \omega_A^C, \omega_B^C, \omega_A^D, \omega_B^D, \omega_C^D, \omega_A^E, \omega_B^E, \omega_C^E, \omega_D^E, \omega_A^F,\right.$ $\omega_B^F, \omega_C^F, \omega_D^F, \omega_E^F, \omega_A^G, \omega_B^G, \omega_C^G, \omega_D^G, \omega_E^G, \omega_F^G\left.\right)$ all have the same value given by $(0.7, 0.1, 0.2, a)$.

In this example, we will apply the consensus operator for *independent* beliefs to illustrate the effect of unknown dependence. We also apply the uncertainty favoring discounting operator which does not take base rates into account. Taking all the possible recommendations of Fig. 22.5 into account creates a relatively complex trust graph, and a rather long notation. In order to reduce the size of the notation, the transitivity symbol ":" will simply be omitted, and the cumulative fusion symbol $\diamond$ will simply be written as ",". Analyzing the whole graph of dependent paths, as if they were independent, will then produce:

$$\omega_x \begin{pmatrix} \text{GA, GBA, GCA, GCBA, GDA, GDBA, GDCA, GDCBA, GEA, GEBA, GECA,} \\ \text{GECBA, GEDA, GEDBA, GEDCA, GEDCBA, GFA, GFBA, GFCA, GFCBA,} \\ \text{GFDA, GFDBA, GFDCA, GFDCBA, GFEA, GFEBA, GFECA, GFECBA,} \\ \text{GFEDA, GFEDBA, GFEDCA, GFEDCBA} \end{pmatrix} = (0.76, 0.11, 0.13, a)$$

For comparison, if G only took the recommendation from A into account (as he should), his derived opinion would be $\omega_x^{G:A} = \{0.49, 0.07, 0.44, a\}$. In real situations it is possible for recommended opinions to return to their originator through feedback loops, resulting in even more exaggerated beliefs. When this process continues, an environment of self amplifying opinions, and thereby mass hysteria, is created.

22.8 The Dirichlet Reputation System

Reputation systems collect ratings about users or service providers from members in a community. The reputation centre is then able to compute and publish reputation scores about those users and services. Figure 22.6 illustrates a reputation centre where the dotted arrow indicates ratings and the solid arrows indicate reputation scores about the users.

Multinomial Bayesian systems are based on computing reputation scores by statistical updating of Dirichlet Probability Density Functions (PDF), which therefore

Fig. 22.6 Simple reputation
system

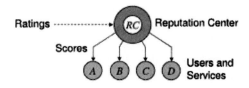

are called Dirichlet reputation systems [4, 9]. A posteriori (i.e. the updated) reputation score is computed by combining a priori (i.e. previous) reputation score with new ratings.

In Dirichlet reputation systems agents are allowed to rate others agents or services with any level from a set of predefined rating levels, and the reputation scores are not static but will gradually change with time as a function of the received ratings. Initially, each agent's reputation is defined by the base rate reputation which is the same for all agents. After ratings about a particular agent have been received, that agent's reputation will change accordingly.

Let there be $k\psi$ different discrete rating levels. This translates into having a state space of cardinality $k\psi$ for the Dirichlet distribution. Let the rating level be indexed by i. The aggregate ratings for a particular agent are stored as a cumulative vector, expressed

$$\text{as: } \vec{R} = (\vec{R}(L_i)|i = 1 \dots k).\psi\psi \tag{22.8}$$

This vector can be computed recursively and can take factors such as longevity and community base rate into account (22.8). The most direct form of representing a reputation score is simply the aggregate rating vector $\vec{R}_y\psi$ which represents all relevant previous ratings. The aggregate rating of a particular level $i\psi$ for agent $y\psi$ is denoted by $\vec{R}_y(L_i)\psi$.

For visualisation of reputation scores, the most natural is to define the reputation score as a function of the probability expectation values of each rating level. Before any ratings about a particular agent y have been received, its reputation is defined by the common base rate $\vec{a}$. As ratings about a particular agent are collected, the aggregate ratings can be computed recursively (8, 9) and the derived reputation scores will change accordingly. Let $\vec{R}$ represent a target agent's aggregate ratings. Then the vector $\vec{S}$ defined by:

$$\vec{S}_y : \left(\vec{S}_y(L_i) = \frac{\vec{R}_y(L_i) + C\vec{a}(L_i)}{C + \sum_{j=1}^{k} \vec{R}_y(L_j)}; |i = 1 \dots k \right). \tag{22.9}$$

is the corresponding multinomial probability reputation score. The parameter C represents the non-informative prior weight where $C = 2$ is the value of choice, but larger value for the constant C can be chosen if a reduced influence of new evidence over the base rate is required.

The reputation score $\vec{S}$ can be interpreted like a multinomial probability measure as an indication of how a particular agent is expected to behave in future transactions. It can easily be verified that

$$\sum_{i=1}^{k} \vec{S}(L_i) = 1\psi. \tag{22.10}$$

While informative, the multinomial probability representation can require considerable space on a computer screen because multiple values must be visualised. A more compact form can be to express the reputation score as a single value in some predefined interval. This can be done by assigning a point value v to each rating level L_i, and computing the normalised weighted point estimate score σ.

Assume e.g. k different rating levels with point values $v(L_i)$ evenly distributed in the range [0, 1] according to $v(L_i) = \frac{i-1}{k-1}$. The point estimate reputation score of a reputation $\vec{R}$ is then:

$$\sigma = \sum_{i=1}^{k} v(L_i)\vec{S}(L_i). \tag{22.11}$$

A point estimate in the range [0, 1] can be mapped to any range, such as 1–5 stars, a percentage or a probability.

Bootstrapping a reputation system to a stable and conservative state is important. In the framework described above, the base rate distribution $\vec{a}$ will define initial default reputation for all agents. The base rate can for example be evenly distributed over all rating levels, or biased towards either negative or positive rating levels. This must be defined when setting up the reputation system in a specific market or community.

As an example we consider five discrete rating levels, and the following sequence of ratings:

Periods 1–10: L1 Mediocre
Periods 11–20: L2 Bad
Periods 21–30: L3 Average
Periods 31–40: L4 Good
Periods 41–50: L5 Excellent

The longevity factor is $\lambda = 0.9$, and the base rate is dynamic (22.8, 22.9). The evolution of the scores of each level as well as the point estimate are illustrated in Fig. 22.7.

In Fig. 22.7 the multinomial reputation scores change abruptly between each sequence of ten periods. The point estimate first drops as the score for L1 increases during the first ten periods. After that the point estimate increases relatively smoothly during the subsequent 40 periods. Assuming a dynamic base rate and an indefinite series of L5 (Excellent) ratings, the point estimate will eventually converge to 1.

Fig. 22.7 Scores and point
estimate during a sequence
of varying ratings

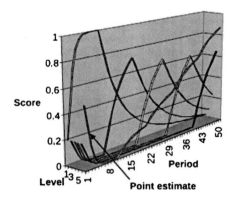

22.9 Combining Trust and Reputation

A bijective mapping can be defined between multinomial reputation scores and
opinions, which makes it possible to interpret these two mathematical representations as equivalent. The mapping can symbolically be expressed as:

$$\omega \leftrightarrow \vec{R} \tag{22.12}$$

This equivalence which is presented with proof in (3) is expressed as:

Theorem 22.1. Equivalence Between Opinions and Reputations. *Let* $\omega =$
$(\vec{b}, u, \vec{a})$ *be an opinion, and* $\vec{R}$ *be a reputation, both over the same state space*
X *so that the base rate* $\vec{a}$ *also applies to the reputation. Then the following equiva-*
lence holds (22.3):

For $u \neq 0$:

$$
\begin{cases}
\vec{b}(x_i) = \dfrac{\vec{R}(x_i)}{C + \sum_{i=1}^{k} \vec{R}(x_i)} \\[3mm]
u = \dfrac{C}{C + \sum_{i=1}^{k} \vec{R}(x_i)}
\end{cases}
\Longleftrightarrow
\begin{cases}
\vec{R}(x_i) = \dfrac{C\vec{b}(x_i)}{u} \\[3mm]
u + \sum_{i=1}^{k} \vec{b}(x_i) = 1
\end{cases}
\tag{22.13}
$$

For $u = 0$:

$$
\begin{cases}
\vec{b}(x_i) = \eta(x_i) \\[2mm]
u = 0
\end{cases}
\Longleftrightarrow
\begin{cases}
\vec{R}(x_i) = \eta(x_i) \sum_{i=1}^{k} \vec{R}(x_i) = \eta(x_i)\infty \\[3mm]
\sum_{i=1}^{k} m(x_i) = 1
\end{cases}
\tag{22.14}
$$

The case $u = 0$ reflects an infinite amount of aggregate ratings, in which case the
parameter η determines the relative proportion of infinite ratings among the rating

levels. In case $u = 0$ and $\eta(x_i) = 1$ for a particular rating level x_i, then $\vec{R}(x_i) = \infty$ and all the other rating parameters are finite. In case $\eta(x_i) - 1/k$ for all $i = 1 \dots k$, then all the rating parameters are equally infinite. As already indicated, the non-informative prior weight is normally set to $C = 2$.

Multinomial aggregate ratings can be used to derive binomial trust in the form of an opinion. This is done by first converting the multinomial ratings to binomial ratings according to (22.15) below, and then to apply Theorem 22.1.

Let the multinomial reputation model have k rating levels $x_i; i = 1, \dots k$, where $\vec{R}(x_i)$ represents the ratings on each level x_i, and let σ represent the point estimate reputation score from (22.11). Let the binomial reputation model have positive and negative ratings r and s respectively. The derived converted binomial rating parameters (r, s) are given by:

$$\begin{cases} r = \sigma \sum_{i=1}^{k} \vec{R}_y(x_i) \\ s = \sum_{i=1}^{k} \vec{R}_y(x_i) - r \end{cases} \tag{22.15}$$

With the equivalence of Theorem 22.1 it is possible to analyse trust networks based on both trust relationships and reputation scores. Figure 22.8 illustrates a scenario where agent A needs to derive a measure of trust in agent F.

Agent B has reputation score $\vec{R}_B^{RC}$ (arrow 1), and agent A has trust ω_{RC}^A in the Reputation Centre (arrow 2), so that A can derive a measure of trust in B (arrow 3). Agent B's trust in F (arrow 4) can be recommended to A so that A can derive a measure of trust in F (arrow 5). Mathematically this can be expressed as:

$$\omega_F^A = \omega_{RC}^A \otimes \vec{R}_B^{RC} \otimes \omega_F^B \tag{22.16}$$

The compatibility between Bayesian reputation systems and subjective logic makes this a very flexible framework for analysing trust in a network consisting of both reputation scores and private trust values.

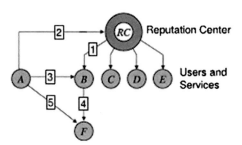

Fig. 22.8 Combining trust and reputation

22.10 Trust Derivation Based on Trust Comparisons

It is possible that different agents have different trust in the same entity, which intuitively could affect the mutual trust between the two agents. Figure 22.9 illustrates a scenario where A's trust $\omega_B^A\psi$ (arrow 1) conflicts with B's reputation score $\vec{R}_B^{RC}$ (arrow 2). As a result $A\psi$ will derive a reduced trust value in the Reputation Centre (arrow 3). Assume that $A\psi$ needs to derive a trust value in E, then the reduced trust value must be taken into account when using RC's reputation score for computing trust in E. The operator for deriving trust based on trust conflict produces a binomial opinion over the binary state space $\{x, \bar{x}\}$, where $x\psi$ is a proposition that can be interpreted as x: "RC provides reliable reputation scores", and $\bar{x}$ is its complement. Binomial opinions have the special notation $\omega_x = (b, d, u, a)$ where $d\psi$ represents disbelief in proposition x.

What represents difference in trust values depends on the semantics of the state space. Assume that the state space consists of five rating levels, then Fig. 22.10a represents a case of polarised ratings, whereas Fig. 22.10b represents a case of average ratings. Interestingly they have the same point estimate of 0.5 when computed with (22.11).

We will define an operator which derives trust based on point estimates as defined by (22.11). Two agents having similar point estimates about the same agent or proposition should induce mutual trust, and dissimilar point estimates should induce mutual distrust.

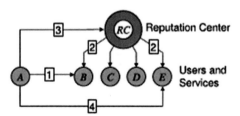

Fig. 22.9 Deriving trust
from conflicting trust

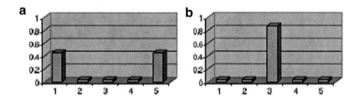

Fig. 22.10 Comparison of polarized and average reputation scores. (**a**) Reputation score from polarized ratings (**b**) Reputation score from avg ratings

Definition 22.4 (Trust Derivation Based on Trust Comparison). Let ω_B^A and ω_B^{RC} be two opinions on the same state space $B\psi$ with a set rating levels. A's trust in $RC\psi$ based on the similarity between their opinions is defined as:

$$\omega_{RC}^A = \omega_B^A \downarrow \omega_B^{RC} \text{ where } \begin{cases} d_{RC}^A = \left| \sigma\left(\vec{R}_B^A\right) - \sigma\left(\vec{R}_B^{RC}\right) \right| \\ u_{RC}^A = Max\left[u_B^A, u_B^{RC}\right] \\ b_{RC}^A = 1 - b_{RC}^A - u_{RC}^A \end{cases}$$

The interpretation of this operator is that disbelief in $RC\psi$ is proportional to the greatest difference in point estimates between the two opinions. Also, the uncertainty is equal to the greatest uncertainty of the two opinions.

With the trust comparison trust derivation operator, $A\psi$ is able to derive trust in $RC\psi$ (arrow 3). With the above described trust and reputation measures, $A\psi$ is able to derive trust in $E\psi$ expressed as:

$$\omega_E^A = \omega_{RC}^A \otimes \omega_E^{RC} \tag{22.17}$$

This provides a method for making trust derivation more robust against unreliable or deceptive reputation scores and trust recommendations.

By considering the scenario of Fig. 22.9, assume that $RC\psi$ has received five mediocre and five excellent ratings about $B\psi$ as in Fig. 22.10a, and that $A\psi$ has had ten average private experiences with B, as in Fig. 22.10b. Then $\sigma\left(\vec{R}_B^{RC}\right) = \sigma\left(\vec{R}_B^A\right) = 0.5$, so that $d_{RC}^A = 0$. According to (22.15) we get $u_B^{RC} = u_B^A = 1/6$, so that $u_{RC}^A = 1/6$, and according to (22.13) we get $b_{RC}^A = 5/6$. With $a_{RC}^A = 0.9$ the derived binomial opinion is $\omega_{RC}^A = (5/6, 0, 1/6, 0.9)$, which indicates a relatively strong, but somewhat uncertain trust.

Assume further the aggregate ratings $\vec{R}_E^{RC} = (0, 4, 2, 2, 0)$, i.e. reflecting 0 mediocre, 4 bad, 2 average, 2 good and 0 excellent ratings about E. The base rate vector is set to $\vec{a} = (0.1, 0.2, 0, 2, 0.4, 0.1)$ and the non-informative prior weight $C = 2$. Using (22.9), the multinomial reputation score is. The point values for each level from mediocre to excellent are: 0.00, 0.25, 0.50, 0.75 and 1.00. Using (22.11) the point estimate reputation is $\sigma = 0.46$.

Using (22.15) and the fact that $\sum_{i=1}^{k} \vec{R}_E^{RC}(x_i) = 8$, the reputation parameters can be converted to the binomial $(r, s) = (3.68, 4.32)$. Using (22.13) RC's trust in $E\psi$ in the form of a binomial opinion can be computed as $\omega_E^{RC} = (0.368, 0.432, 0.200, 0.500)$ where the base rate trust has been set to $a_E^{RC} = 0.5$.

The transitivity operator can now be used to derive A's trust in E. The base rate sensitive operator from (22.11) will be used, which for this example is expressed as:

$$\begin{cases} b_E^{A:RC} = (b_{RC}^A + a_{RC}^A u_{RC}^A) b_E^{RC} \\ d_E^{A:RC} = (b_{RC}^A + a_{RC}^A u_{RC}^A) d_E^{RC} \\ u_E^{A:RC} = 1 - b_E^{A:RC} - d_E^{A:RC} \\ a_E^{A:RC} = a_E^{RC} \end{cases} \tag{22.18}$$

A's trust in $E \psi$ can then be computed as the opinion $\omega_E^A = (0.362, 0.425, 0.213, 0.500)$, which in terms of probability expectation value is $\mathrm{E}\left(\omega_E^A\right) = 0.4686$. This rather weak trust was to be expected from the relatively negative ratings about E.

22.11 Conclusion

The current online community is suffering the lack of trust or confidence on the opinion expressed in the web-based social network where the degree of trust among the members is absent. The members are facing the quality problem in terms of poor quality and even deceptive opinions or recommendations. In this research work, we have surveyed the current scholars work in the area of trust management in online social networks. We also discuss the method of trust propagation in a trust networks. The proposed method will help to analyze trust network for effective management of trust in current online social networks. Trust and reputation management represents an important approach for stabilizing and moderating online markets and communities. Integration of different systems would be problematic with incompatible trust and reputation systems. Trust propagation does not manifest itself as a physical phenomenon in nature, but only exists on the mental and cognitive level. It is therefore difficult to assess whether computational models for trust propagation are adequate and reflect the way people reason about trust. A number of principles have been described to model the propagation of trust. We have discussed the shortcomings of computational trust based on subjective logic by the risk of over counting of trust evidence when opinions are not independent and have described a set of computational trust principles that reflect intuitive trust propagation constructs. Different situations require different trust models. With appropriate computational trust models, the principles of trust propagation can be ported to online communities of people, organizations and software agents, with the purpose of enhancing the quality of those communities. The specific computational trust operators must therefore be selected as a function of the situation to be modeled. We have also described how it is possible to elegantly integrate Bayesian reputation systems and trust analysis based on subjective logic. This provides a flexible and powerful framework for online trust and reputation management including online social networks.

References

1. A. Jøsang and R. Ismail, The Beta Reputation System. In Proceedings of the 15th Bled Electronic Commerce Conference, 2002.
2. A. Jøsang, S. Hird, and E. Faccer, Simulating the Effect of Reputation Systems on e-Markets. In P. Nixon and S. Terzis (Eds), Proceedings of the First International Conference on Trust Management (iTrust), Crete, Greece, 2003.
3. A. Withby, A. Jøsang, and J. Indulska, Filtering Out Unfair Ratings in Bayesian Reputation Systems. The ICFAIN Journal of Management Research, 4(2), 2005, 48–64.

4. A. Jøsang and J. Haller, Dirichlet Reputation Systems. In The Proceedings of the International Conference on Availability, Reliability and Security (ARES 2007), Vienna, Austria, 2007.
5. A. Jøsang and S. Pope, Semantic Constraints for Trust Tansitivity. In S. Hartmann and M. Stumptner (Eds), Proceedings of the Asia-Pacific Conference of Conceptual Modelling (APCCM) (Volume 43 of Conferences in Research and Practice in Information Technology), Newcastle, Australia, 2005.
6. A. Jøsang, R. Hayward, and S. Pope, Trust Network Analysis with Subjective Logic. In Proceedings of the 29th Australasian Computer Science Conference (ACSC2006), CRPIT, Vol 48, Hobart, Australia, 2006.
7. A. Jøsang, E. Gray, and M. Kinateder, Simplification and Analysis of Transitive Trust Networks. Web Intelligence and Agent Systems, 4(2), 2006, 139–161.
8. A. Jøsang and T. Bhuiyan, Optimal Trust Network Analysis with Subjective Logic, The Second International Conference on Emerging Security Information, Systems and Technologies, Cap Esterel, France, 2008.
9. A. Jøsang, X. Luo, and X. Chen, Continuous Ratings in Discrete Bayesian Reputation Systems. In The Proceedings of the Joint iTrust and PST Conferences on Privacy, Trust Management and Security, Trondheim, Norway, 2008.
10. J. A. Barnes, Politics in a Changing Society: A Political History of the Fort Jameson Ngoni, Manchester University Press, UK, 1967.
11. D. Teten, and S. Allen, The Virtual Handshake: Opening Doors and Closing Deals Online. AMACOM/American Management Association, 2005.
12. A. Kazeniac, Social Networks: Facebook Takes Over Top Spot, Twitter Climbs. Compete.com. http://blog.compete.com/2009/02/09/facebook-myspace-twitter-social-network/. Retrieved 10-02-2010, 2009.
13. D. H. McKnight and N. L. Chervany, What Trust Means in e-Commerce Customer Relationships: An Interdisciplinary Conceptual Typology. International Journal of Electronic Commerce, 6(2), 2002, 35–59.
14. F. K. Hussain and E. Chang, An Overview of the Interpretations of Trust and Reputation. The Third Advanced International Conference on Telecommunications, Mauritius, 2007.
15. A. Jøsang, R. Ismail, and C. Boyd, A Survey of Trust and Reputation Systems for Online Service Provision. Decision Support Systems, 43(2), 2007, 618–644.
16. X. Abdul-Rahman and S. Hailes, Supporting Trust in Virtual Communities. Proceedings of the Hawaii International Conference on System Sciences, USA, 2000.
17. S. Marsh, Formalising Trust as a Computational Concept. PhD thesis, University of Stirling, 1994.
18. M. Schillo, P. Funk, and M. Rovatsos, Using Trust for Detecting Deceitful Agents in Artificial Societies. Applied Artificial Intelligence, 14(8), 2000, 825–848.
19. B. Esfandiari and S. Chandrasekharan, On How Agents Make Friends: Mechanisms for Trust Acquisition. The Proceedings of the Fifth International Conference on Autonomous Agents Workshop on Deception, Fraud and Trust in Agent Societies, 2001.
20. B. Yu and M. P. Singh, Distributed Reputation Management for Electronic Commerce. Computational Intelligence, 18(4), 2002, 535–549.
21. L. Mui, M. Mohtashemi, and A. Halberstadt, A Computational Model of Trust and Reputation. In Proceedings of the 35th Hawaii International Conference on System Science, 2002.
22. J. M. Pujol, R. Sanguesa, J. Delgado, Extracting Reputation in Multi-Agent System by Means of Social Network Topology. The Proceedings of the First International Joint Conference on Autonomous Agents and Multi-Agent Systems, Italy, 2002, 467–474.
23. T. Dimitrakos, A Service-Oriented Trust Management Framework. International Workshop on Deception, Fraud, and Trust in Agent Societies, 2003, 53–72.
24. A. Selcuk, E. Uzun, and M. R. Pariente, A Reputation-Based Trust Management System for P2P Networks. IEEE International Symposium on Cluster Computing and the Grid, 2004.
25. J. Sabater and C. Sierra, Review on Computational Trust and Reputation Models. Artificial Intelligence Review, 24, 2005, 33–60.
26. J. O'Donovan and B. Smyth, Trust in Recommender Systems. IUI'05, USA, 2005.

27. R. V. Guha, R. Kumar, P. Raghavan, and A. Tomkins, Propagation of Trust and Distrust. The Proceedings of the 13th International World Wide Web Conference, USA, 2004, 403–412.
28. R. Levien, Attack-resistant Trust Metrics. Ph.D. thesis, University of California at Berkeley, USA, 2004.
29. C. N. Ziegler, Towards Decentralized Recommender Systems. PhD Thesis, University of Freiburg, Germany, 2005.
30. V. Shmatikov and C. Talcott, Reputation-Based Trust Management. Journal of Computer Security 13(1), 2005, 167–190.
31. W. T. L. Teacy, An Investigation into Trust & Reputation for Agent-Based Virtual Organisations. University of Southampton, UK, 2005.
32. L. Xiong, Resilient Reputation and Trust Management: Models and Techniques. PhD thesis, Georgia Institute of Technology, USA, 2005.
33. W. Xue and Z. Fan, A New Trust Model based on Social Characteristic and Reputation Mechanism for the Semantic Web. In the Proceedings of the Workshop on Knowledge Discovery and Data Mining, 2008.
34. C. Q. Tian, S. H. Zou, W. D. Wang, and S. D. Cheng, Trust Model Based on Reputation for Peer-to-Peer Networks. Journal on Communication, 29(4), 2008, 63–70.
35. M. Jamali and M. Ester, TrustWalker: A Random Walk Model for Combining Trust-based and Item-based Recommendation. KDD'09, 2009.
36. A. Jøsang, Artificial reasoning with subjective logic. In Proceedings of the 2nd Australian Workshop on Commonsense Reasoning, Perth, Australia, 1997.
37. A. Jøsang, A Logic for Uncertain Probabilities. International Journal of Uncertainty, Fuzziness and Knowledge-Based Systems, 9(3), 2001, 279–311.
38. A. Jøsang, Probabilistic Logic Under Uncertainty. In The Proceedings of Computing: The Australian Theory Symposium (CATS2007), CRPIT, Vol 65, Ballarat, Australia, 2007.
39. A. Jøsang and S. Pope, Semantic Constraints for Trust Tansitivity. The Proceedings of the Asia-Pacific Conference of Conceptual Modelling, Vol 43, Australia, 2005.
40. A. Jøsang, Subjective Logic, 2009. Draft Book available at http://persons.unik.no/josang/papers/subjective_logic.pdf

Chapter 23
Security and Privacy in Online Social Networks

Leucio Antonio Cutillo, Mark Manulis, and Thorsten Strufe

23.1 Introduction

Social Network Services (SNS) are currently drastically revolutionizing the way people interact, thus becoming *de facto* a predominant service on the web, today.[1] The impact of this paradigm change on socioeconomic and technical aspects of collaboration and interaction is comparable to that caused by the deployment of World Wide Web in the 1990s.

Catering for a broad range of users of all ages, and a vast difference in social, educational, and national background, SNS allow even users with limited technical skills to publish ***Personally Identifiable Information*** (PII) and to communicate with an extreme ease, sharing interests and activities.

An ***Online Social Network*** (OSN) offering, usually centralized, online accessible SNS contain digital representations of a subset of the relations that their users, both registered persons and institutions, entertain in the physical world. Spanning all participants through their relationships, they model the social network as a graph. Every OSN user can typically create his or her own *OSN profile* and use the available *OSN applications* to easily share information with other, possibly selected, users for either professional, or personal purposes. OSN with a more professional and business-oriented background are typically used as a facility geared towards career management or business contacts; such networks typically provide SNS with a more serious image. In contrast, OSN with a more private and leisure-oriented background are typically used for sharing and exchanging more personal information,

This work has partially been funded by IT R&D program of MKE/KEIT under grant number 10035587, DFG FOR 733 ("QuaP2P"), and the EU SOCIALNETS project, grant no 217141.

[1]According to reports, facebook.com. recently surpassed the previously most popular website google.com by both page visits and served bandwidth: http://www.hitwise.com/us/datacenter/main/dashboard-10133.html http://www.mercurynews.com/business/ci_14698296?nclick_check=1.

T. Strufe (✉)
TU Darmstadt & CASED, Darmstadt, Germany
e-mail: strufe@cs.tu-darmstadt.de

B. Furht (ed.), *Handbook of Social Network Technologies and Applications*,   497
DOI 10.1007/978-1-4419-7142-5_23, © Springer Science+Business Media, LLC 2010

like, e.g., contact data, photographs, and videos; OSN provided by such networks have usually a more youthful interface. The core OSN application is the creation and maintenance of *contact lists*. Through informing users automatically on profile changes of their contacts, the SNS thus helps users to stay up to date with news of their contacts and very often the popularity of users is measured in the size of their contact lists.

These properties of the SNS have led to the definition of boyd and Ellison [6], according to which *Social Network Sites* or *Online Social Network Services* are:

> " ... web-based services that allow individuals to (1) construct a public or semi-public profile within a bounded system, (2) articulate a list of other users with whom they share a connection, and (3) view and traverse their list of connections and those made by others within the system".

This definition, however, leaves aside some additional services that become apparent when observing the use of SNS. In particular, the communication of members through direct, sometimes instant message exchange, the annotation of profiles (e.g., via comments and recommendations), or the creation of links pointing to other profiles (picture tagging). The publication and browsing of images has grown to become a core function of these services [13]. Additionally, SNS typically provide support for a variety of third-party applications featuring advanced interactions between members ranging from simple "poking" of another member or the support for interest groups for a common topic to "likeness" testing with other members and the exchange of virtual gifts.

Maintenance and access to the OSN and their services are offered by commercial **Social Network Providers** (SNP), like Facebook Inc.,[2] LinkedIn Corp.,[3] Google Inc.,[4] XING AG,[5] and the likes. In general, a large amount of PII provided by the users is stored at the databases being under control of these providers, especially in the case of OSN targeting non-professional purposes. This data is either visible to the public, or, if the user is aware of privacy issues and able to use the settings of the respective SNS, to a somewhat selected group of other users. As profiles are attributed to presumably known persons from the real world, they are implicitly valued with the same trust as the assumed owner of the profile. Furthermore, any actions and interactions coupled to a profile are again attributed to the assumed owner of this profile, as well.

A SNP can, together with its SNS, also offer an application programming interface (API), allowing interested users to program a **Social Network Application** (SNA), thus extending and enhancing the functional range of the service.

Unfortunately, the popularity and broad acceptance of social networking services as platforms for interaction and social activities attracts not only faithful users, who are trying to add value to the community, but parties with rather adverse interests,

---

[2] www.facebook.com

[3] www.linkedin.com

[4] www.orkut.com

[5] www.xing.com

be they commercial or plain malicious, as well. Analyzing the OSN with respect to their security properties and the privacy of their users exposes some obvious threats. Different studies have shown that the participants clearly represent the weak link for security in OSN and that they are vulnerable to several types of social engineering attacks.[6] This partially is caused by a lack of awareness to the consequences of simple and presumably private actions, like accepting contact requests, tagging pictures, as well as acts of communication like commenting on profiles or leaving wall posts. However, the usability of privacy control mechanisms offered by the SNS and more importantly inherent trust assumptions on other users and their profiles, which are actually a desired social characteristic, certainly add to the problem.

The analysis of the privacy problems in current OSN demonstrates that even if all participants were aware and competent in the use of SNS, and even if a concise set of privacy measures were deployed, the OSN would still be exposed to potential privacy violations by either the omniscient service provider or an external attacker taking control of the OSN: the complete PII, directly or indirectly supplied by all participants, is collected and stored permanently at the databases of the providing company, which potentially becomes a *big brother* capable of exploiting this data in many ways that can violate the privacy of individual users or user groups.

The importance of this privacy exposure is underlined by the market capitalization of these providers, which ranges from 580 million US$ (acquisition of myspace through the news corp. in 2005) to 15 billion US$ (Facebook Inc, according to the investment of Microsoft in 2007) [1]. Even considering the commercial bodies that act as SNP to be trusted, hackers may be able to compromise their systems to gain access, unsatisfied employees may abuse their access to the data, or even imprudent publication of seemingly anonymized data may lead to the disclosure of PII, as it has happened in the past.[7] In consequence, we consider the protection of PII in OSN as an emerging topic, which is currently not addressed by the providers in the appropriate way.

23.1.1   Social Network Providers and Their Customers

Social network providers offer social networking services to the users and may further provide additional interfaces and services to other customers. These customers may come from different domains and pursue various goals.

In particular, *sponsors* belong to customers who advertise their services to the users through the OSN platform. Their advertisements may be of different kinds: plain commercial sponsors buy banner space or other marketing services from the SNP to advertise their products; SNS frequently contain "market pages" at which

---

[6] Several of these attacks have been shown to be successful in the past. A short selection of examples can be found in [5, 9] as well as at http://www.sophos.com/pressoffice/news/articles/2007/08/facebook.html and http://www.blackhat.com/html/bh-usa-08/bh-usa-08-archive.html.

[7] http://www.nytimes.com/2006/08/09/technology/09aol.html.

users can publish classified ads, job offers, and the likes, for which they may be billed. Also sponsors may create commercial interest groups or profiles inside the OSN.

Another type of OSN customers are ***third party service providers***, who extend the content and functionality of SNS with their own applications. These applications such as quizzes and games are typically executed on the servers under control of these third parties connected to the SNS via appropriate APIs. Often these applications have extensive access to the personal data of OSN users.

Finally, all sorts of ***data analysts*** may act as customers of SNP. These customers typically have data mining interests and may also get access to the personal information of users and their activities within the OSN. The analysis carried out by data analysts may serve different purposes, including scientific research (such as statistics, social behavior, or network-relevant aspects) and non-scientific data mining, typically for commercial purpose such as marketing.

Figure 23.1 illustrates the diversity of OSN customers and reflects their relationship to the SNS functionality and possible access to the personal information of the OSN users.

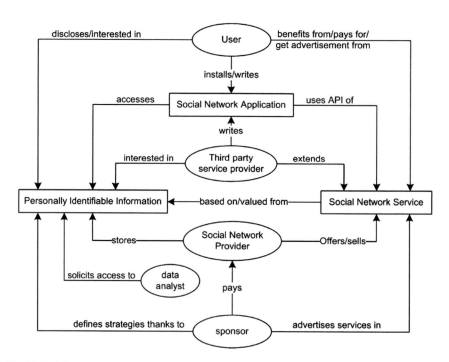

Fig. 23.1 OSN customers and their relationships to PII and SNS

23.1.2 Functional Overview of Online Social Networks

Even though each OSN is usually tailored to some specific use, the functional range of these platforms is essentially quite similar. Generally speaking, OSN functionality can be classified into three main types: The **networking functions** serve the actual purpose of OSN to foster social relationships amongst users within the virtual platform. In particular, they provide functionality for building and maintaining the social network graph. The **data functions** are responsible for the management of user-provided content and communications amongst the users. Their variety contributes to the enhancement of users' interaction and makes the platform more attractive. Finally, the **access control functions** aim to implement the user-defined privacy measures and to restrict unauthorized access to the user-provided data and information. In Fig. 23.2 we illustrate the functionality provided by a typical OSN platform and provide more details thereafter.

Networking functions. OSN users can typically build their profiles and establish relationships with each other. The set of networking functions includes all functions that update the vertices and the edges of the social network graph. In particular, the OSN user invokes the *profile creation* function upon his or her registration on the OSN platform. This function adds a new vertex representing that user to the social network graph. Thereafter, with *profile lookup* the user can find other users, who are also represented via vertices. Through the call to the *relationship link establishment* function the user can set up a new relationship with some other user. This function typically sends notification to that user, who in turn can accept or ignore the request. If the user accepts the request then users are added to the contact lists of each other and a new edge representing their relationship is added to the social network graph. The OSN users can also encounter profiles for possible relationships thanks to the *contact list browsing* function, which is realized through the traversal along the edges of the graph. Additional networking functions can be used to remove vertices and edges from the graph, for example upon the deletion of the user's profile.

Data functions. OSN users can typically advertise themselves via their own profiles and communicate with each other using various applications like blogs, forums, polls, chats, e-mails, and online galleries. Here we point out the *profile update*

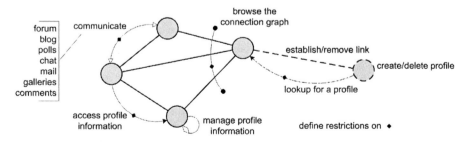

Fig. 23.2 Main functionality of a typical OSN platform

function, which allows the OSN users to maintain details on their own profiles and provide fresh information to other users, who may call the *profile retrieval* function, and hence visit the profile. Communication amongst users via blogs and forums is typically implemented through the *post* function, which inserts a block of information as an element into the main thread (sometimes called the "wall"). This block of information is not limited to plain text and can also contain videos, pictures, or hyperlinks. An OSN user willing to setup multimedia galleries typically calls the *upload* function, which transfers digital data from user's device to the OSN database. In case of content depicting other users, the *tag* function can create a link pointing to their profile. OSN users can typically evaluate content published by other users through the *like* or *dislike* functions. These functions can also be considered as a feedback to the publisher given by other users. In consequence, the user may either be encouraged, or discouraged to provide similar uploads and posts. Using the *comment* function OSN users can articulate their point of view in a more explicit way. OSN users can also exchange personal messages. Here, in particular, the *write to* function simulates the asynchronous offline communication (e.g., e-mail), whereas the *chat to* function allows for the synchronous real-time communication. An OSN user can send messages to individuals and also to subgroups of users from his or her contact list. The latter subgroup can be defined via the *regroup* function. Additionally, users may *create* interest groups, *advertise* own interest groups to other users, and *join* interest groups created by other users. The user who creates an interest group obtains administrator rights for this group by default; however, these rights can be changed thereafter, and distributed to other group members.

Access control functions. OSN users are usually allowed to define their own privacy settings through the some control functions. In particular, an OSN user may have control over the

- Visibility of the online presence within the OSN
- Visibility of contacts from the user's contact lists
- Visibility and access to his or her own profile information
- Access to his or her own uploaded content and posted communications

All these functions usually take as an input the information to be protected and the list of profiles having the rights to access it. The eligible profiles can be clustered into generic groups such as "friends", "friends of friends", "everybody", or user-defined groups, such as "family", "colleagues" and the like.

For example, the profile lookup function takes as an input a target's profile identifier, such as the name of the profile owner, and returns a list of possible candidates. An OSN user can apply output restrictions on this function to partially hide the own presence in the OSN. However, the protected profile would remain reachable due to the profile browsing functionality of the OSN. Nevertheless, sensitive relationships can be hidden from unauthorized users by imposing restrictions on the output of the contact list browsing function. Thus, combined with the restrictions on profile lookup, this constraint can completely hide some profile in the OSN, since this profile will become unreachable from other users outside of the profile's contact list. Note that new contacts could be still added to the profile owner's contact list on the initiative of the latter. Another example is the control on the output of the profile retrieval function, which allow the profile owner to control the disclosure of the profile to other users. This allows some OSN user to hide parts of the private profile information from selected partners. Finally, the data related to online or offline indicators, one-to-one or one-to-many communications, such as posts, walls, comments, positive or negative marks, tags and the like can be protected by the means of restrictions on the huge set of the communication functions.

23.1.3 Modelling Data Contained in Online Social Networks

The core information stored in OSN, the self generated and maintained data of the users and their profiles, can be classified into the following five types (cmp. Fig. 23.3):

1. Personal contact details, describing the user's identity
2. Connectivity, representing the connections in the social network graph
3. Interests of the user
4. Information on the curriculum vitae of the user
5. Communication, including all interactions with other OSN users of the SNS

These types encompass the amount of personally identifiable information, which is provided directly by the OSN user. Additional information about the OSN user is often generated and made accessible within the OSN by other users.

Personal contact details describe *'who the user is'*, providing not only some basic information such as user's name, picture, gender, birthday and birthplace, and marital status, but also some additional meta information with regard to the membership in the OSN, as well as the contact information aside of the OSN platform, such as (e)mail addresses, phone numbers, instant messaging identifiers, and personal web sites. Furthermore, it describes the personal profile of the user and may report about sexual, personal, political or religious interests and preferences. Users frequently can include a quick summary about themselves, describing their professional expertise, views and opinions, skills they "have to offer", as well as a short text on what they are looking for.

Connectivity describes *'whom the user knows'*, providing the user's contact list, possibly with annotated information about the type of the relationship (cf. family, colleagues, best friend, sports partner). Especially OSN platforms that with more private and leisure-oriented focus frequently ask the user to provide information on the relationship status, and in consequence the name and profile of their significant other. Users may further ask for recommendations by others. These recommendations may contain very detailed information about the user, and shed light on the relationship between the both.

Interests describe *'what the user likes and is interested in'*. These may contain user's personal interests, hobbies, and preferences: In particular, information about

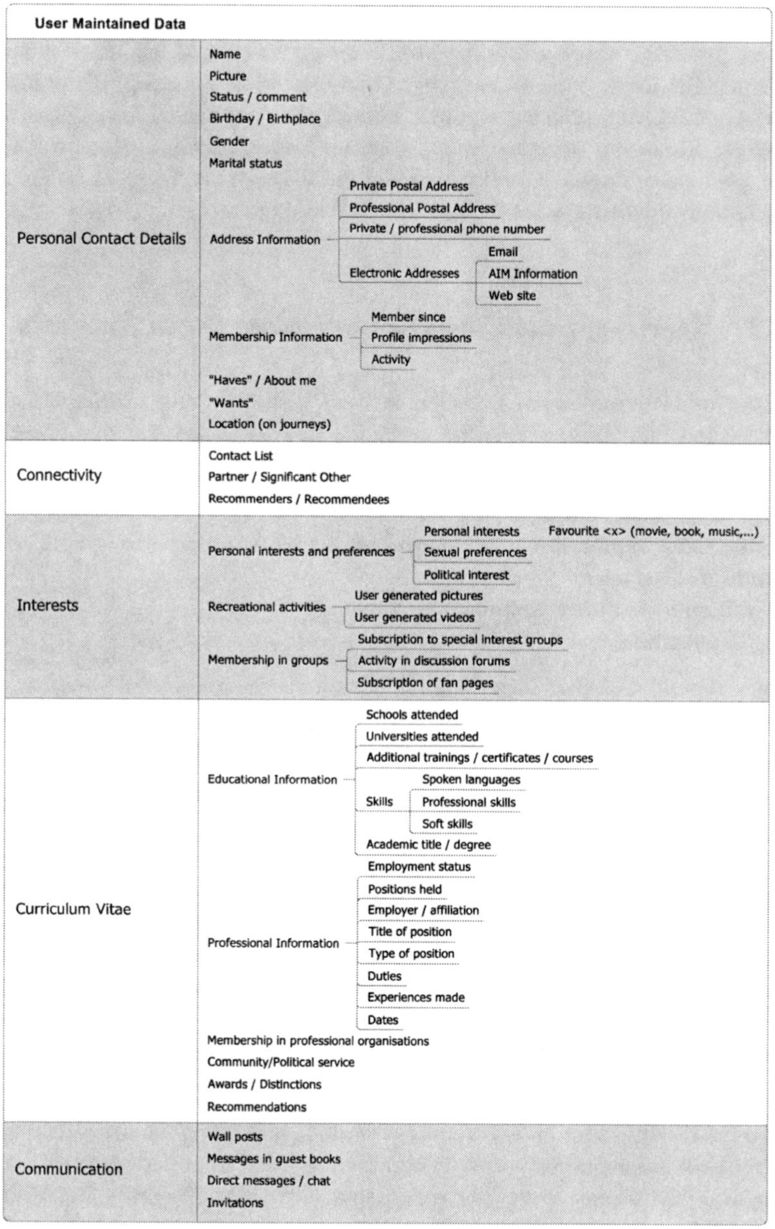

User Maintained Data

Personal Contact Details	Name
	Picture
	Status / comment
	Birthday / Birthplace
	Gender
	Marital status
	Address Information: Private Postal Address; Professional Postal Address; Private / professional phone number; Electronic Addresses (Email, AIM Information, Web site)
	Membership Information: Member since; Profile impressions; Activity
	"Haves" / About me
	"Wants"
	Location (on journeys)

Connectivity	Contact List
	Partner / Significant Other
	Recommenders / Recommendees

Interests	Personal interests and preferences: Personal interests (Favourite <x> (movie, book, music,...)); Sexual preferences; Political interest
	Recreational activities: User generated pictures; User generated videos
	Membership in groups: Subscription to special interest groups; Activity in discussion forums; Subscription of fan pages

Curriculum Vitae	Educational Information: Schools attended; Universities attended; Additional trainings / certificates / courses; Skills (Spoken languages, Professional skills, Soft skills); Academic title / degree
	Professional Information: Employment status; Positions held; Employer / affiliation; Title of position; Type of position; Duties; Experiences made; Dates
	Membership in professional organisations
	Community/Political service
	Awards / Distinctions
	Recommendations

Communication	Wall posts
	Messages in guest books
	Direct messages / chat
	Invitations

Fig. 23.3 Types of data commonly stored in OSN profiles

favorite movies or music style, their sexual, religious, and political views, recreational activities of the user (such as personal pictures and videos showing situations from their personal lives), and their subscription to fan-pages as well as membership in special interest groups inside the OSN (which usually can be resolved to reading their posts containing their opinions on different topics).

Information on the curriculum vitae of the user describes the *professional career* and *educational background*, including attended schools, colleges, and universities, advanced studies, academic titles and professional certificates, as well as professional and soft skills. This information may be very detailed and include the description of job positions the users currently hold or have previously had, usually including information on the duration and type of the position (e.g. full-time, part-time, freelance, self-employed), the duties and responsibilities fulfilled in the job, and experiences being collected.

In addition to this description of the career progression, some OSN platforms ask the users to provide information on their membership in professional organizations (past and present), their community and political services (memberships and positions in clubs, associations, political parties, and professional societies), awards and distinctions, as well as recommendations and references.

Communication describes *'which messages the user has exchanged and with whom'*. OSN platforms generally offer exchange of personal offline messages, asynchronous communication via posts on walls and guest books entries, which the profile owner may hide or disclose to other users, and synchronous communication such as chats. These are examples of direct communications initiated by the user. However, there are also some less direct communications provided by other functionalities of the OSN platforms, such as the utilization of SNS applications (e.g. "poking", "likeness tests", quizzes), as well as public or targeted invitations to organized events.

Indirect information disclosure about OSN users may occur through posted opinions and comments, or any type of annotations to profiles of other users. Even though the owners of the annotated profiles may be able to remove undesired annotations, they need to notice the annotations in the first place. Since many users do not explicitly search for annotations made by other users about their profiles, this indirectly disclosed information may remain publicly accessible over a longer period of time. Similarly, information about users may be disclosed via third party statements about the user made in forums of the interest groups, or as annotations or comments at the profiles of other users.

Any form of user-generated digital content may also cause third party information disclosure. For example, some OSN networks try to prevent users from posting photographs showing people on their profiles if the owner of the profile is not pictured there.[8] However, this does not prevent users from posting photographs picturing them together with others. Additionally, many OSN platforms offer "tagging"

---

[8] http://www.odnoklassniki.ru.

of pictured users, whose profiles will usually be directly linked to that picture. These tags may contain further comments added by the user who uploads the picture.

23.1.4 A Model for Social Network Services

Social Network Services (SNS) are structured along the following three layers with different responsibilities (see also Fig. 23.4):

- A *Social Network* (SN) level, building the digital representation of members and their relationships
- A *Application Service* (AS) level, constituting the application infrastructure managed by the SNS provider
- A *Communication and Transport* (CT) level representing the communication and transport services as provided by the network

The SN layer provides each member with a set of functions corresponding to social interactions in the real life. These functions can be divided in two classes. The first class deals with *Communication Management* and includes the real-time communication, such as chat and phone calls, as well as the offline communication, such as wall posts, mails and tweets. The second class deals with *Relations Management*, including friendship requests, friends lookups, profile access and reputation administration. To implement these functions, the SN layer relies on the AS layer. This layer includes either the whole infrastructure managed by the SNS provider and the web, storage, and communication services to create the SN service. The AS layer can implement data storage and its retrieval, indexing of the content, management of access permissions to data, and node join or leave, in a centralized or distributed fashion. In any case, redundancy and delegation are common strategies to enhance availability: both for organizational reasons or if a server faces failures or other inabilities to provide the service, it may delegate requests to secondary or fallback servers. The AS layer in turn relies on the transport and (inter)networking protocols and infrastructures, such as the classical Internet or the GPRS connectivity. This network infrastructure is thus implemented by the lowest CT layer and can be managed by one or more network providers.

23.2 Security Objectives: Privacy, Integrity, and Availability

Security objectives are requirements that have to be satisfied in order to protect the system from potential threats and attacks.

In this chapter we provide an overview of important security objectives for on-line social networks. First of all we notice that classical requirements (cf. [3]) of *confidentiality*, *integrity*, and *availability*, have a special touch when considered in the scope of OSNs. While integrity and availability have only subtle differences

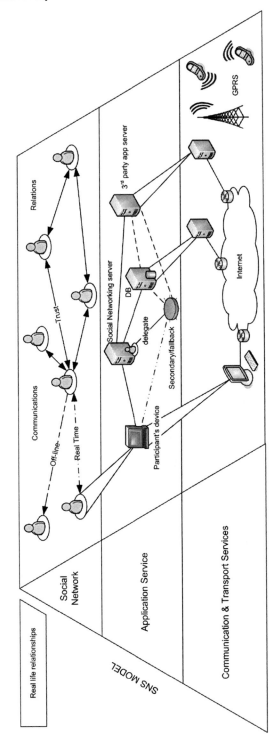

Fig. 23.4 Three architectural layers of social networking services

compared to other communication systems, in that they mostly address the content provided by the users, the requirement of confidentiality (usually associated with encryption) is no longer sufficient and should be extended to the more comprehensive security objective – *privacy*.

While potential breach of user privacy and integrity of user-provided contents may lead to economic damages for the users, cause embarrassing situations, and also tarnish their reputation (even in the real world), the missing availability of contents or services may also decrease the attractiveness of the actual OSN platform and harm its provider. It is extremely difficult to cope with all these goals simultaneously. Especially privacy of OSN users is challenging since the amount of personal information is huge and this information may be available not only from a particular OSN platform but also from the web.

In the following, we describe privacy, integrity and availability objectives for online social networks, while also mentioning potential threats with regard to not only the profile owner, but also other users and the system itself.

23.2.1 Privacy

Privacy is a relatively new concept, born and evolving together with the capability of new technologies to share information. Conceived as 'the right to be left alone'[15] during the period of newspapers and photographs growth, privacy now refers to the ability of an individual to control and selectively disclose information about him.

The importance of privacy is so relevant to have been reported in the Universal Declaration of Human Rights (art.12):

> *"No one shall be subjected to arbitrary interference with his privacy, family, home or correspondence, nor to attacks upon his honor and reputation. Everyone has the right to the protection of the law against such interference or attacks."*

In the internet age, where huge amount of sensitive data can be easily gathered, stored, replicated and correlated, the protection of privacy is even more seen as the main objective for the services provided by an OSN platform [2, 8].

Generally speaking, the protection of information which users publish at their profiles, presumably accessible by their contacts only, takes place with the *usage control* [12]: the control of the degree at which sensitive data is disclosed to selected other parties (i.e. access control) together with the control of its later usage, even after the information has been accessed. Access to the contents of a user profile may only be granted by the user directly, and this access control has to be as fine-grained as the profile itself. For example, if the profile contains several information blocks then access to each block has to be managed separately.

In addition, the protection of communication calls for inference techniques aiming at deriving any type of information with regard to: (1) *anonymity*, meaning that users should access resources or services without disclosing their own identities;

(2) *unobservability*, i.e. the requirement that no third party should gather any information about the communicating parties and the content of their communication; (3) *unlinkability*, which requires that obtaining two messages, no third party should be able to determine whether both messages were sent by the same sender, or to the same receiver; (4) *untraceability*, which demands that no third party can build a history of actions performed by arbitrary users within the system; in other words, it demands both anonymity and unlinkability.

In summary, the objective of privacy is to hide any information about any user at any time, even to the extent of hiding their participation and activities within the OSN in the first place. Moreover, privacy has to be met by default, i.e. all information on all users and their actions has to be hidden from any other party internal or external to the system, unless explicitly disclosed by the users themselves.

23.2.2 Integrity

The objective of integrity in online social networks is to prevent any unauthorized modification or tampering of user-generated content and profile information, as listed on Fig. 23.3. This encompasses the protection of real identity of users within the OSN platforms. In this sense, the meaning of integrity in such networks is somewhat extended in comparison to the conventional detection of modification attempts on data. Moreover, problems with integrity of user profiles and their contents may have devastating impact on the objectives put forth with respect to the privacy of OSN users. Since the creation of profiles in traditional OSNs is easy, it is a matter of facts, that protection of real identities is insufficient in today's platforms. In particular, none of the current major OSN providers is able (and perhaps even not interested in) to ensure that a profile is associated to the corresponding individual from the real world.

As users inherently trust the OSN providers, the aforementioned vulnerabilities can be thwarted through the appropriate authentication procedures to assure the existence of real people behind registered OSN profiles. Identity checks do not necessarily have to be performed by a centralized service, however, all identification services have to be trusted by all participants.

23.2.3 Availability

The objective of availability for online social networks aims at assuring the operability of the social network services in the face of attacks and faults. The insufficient guarantees for availability may prevent users from accessing the service and make of the OSN platform less attractive. Especially, for OSNs with professional focus, e.g. OSNs that aid their users to foster business relations or find new job positions, it is mandatory to keep users' data continuously available. Therefore, we consider availability of user-generated data and profiles as a basic requirement that should be provided by the platforms, even though for leisure-oriented OSN platforms the availability of certain content may appear not of prime importance at first sight.

The main concern of availability are **denial-of-service** attacks. In the context of social network services they may aim at either seizuring a victim's profile (or selected parts of it) or disrupting the possibility to communicate with the user. Furthermore, also integrity threats like data pollution and cloning may impair the availability of network services by affecting the quality of the service perceived by the users.

Remark 23.1. Also distributed services, which are implemented in a decentralized way, possibly via peer-to-peer systems, or which follow other types of service delegation, may be vulnerable to a series of attacks against availability as well. These attacks include *black holes*, aiming at collecting and discarding a huge amount of messages; *selective forwarding*, where some traffic is forwarded to the destination, but the majority is discarded; and *misrouting*, which aims to increase the latency of the system or to collect statistics on the network behavior. In any case, attacks on distributed social networks are more effective in case of *collusion* amongst malicious users or in the presence of Sybil nodes controlled by the attacker, which is not the case for the centralized OSNs.

Finally, we notice that while privacy has to address broader spectrum of threats and deal with different types of attackers, including the OSN and application providers, as well as external parties, both integrity and availability primarily address the latter, since OSN users have an inherent interest that these objectives are met.

23.3 Attack Spectrum and Countermeasures

The diversity of available OSN platforms opens doors for a variety of attacks on privacy of the users, integrity of their profiles, and the availability of the user-provided contents. In this section we will highlight main attack types against OSN platforms and discuss their impact on the aimed security objectives. Table 23.1 will serve as a background for our discussion. It illustrates different types of attacks and shows their relevance for the mentioned security objectives of privacy, integrity, and availability. We will discuss not only the purpose and impact of each attack but also explain the techniques needed to mount it, while referring to some real-world examples, where possible. We note, however, that technical realization behind an attack may strongly depend on the functionality and in particular on the use of different protection mechanisms within the OSN platform. Therefore, not every attack technique will have the same impact when used against different OSN platforms. Moreover, since OSN providers typically have full control over the network resources, no meaningful protection appears possible if the attacks are mounted by the provider itself.

Table 23.1   Attacks vs. security objectives in online social networks

Attacks	Security objectives		
	Privacy	Integrity	Availability
Plain impersonation	x	x	
Profile cloning	x	x	
Profile hijacking	x	x	
Profile porting	x	x	
Id theft	x	x	x
Profiling	x		
Secondary data collection	x		
Fake requests	x		
Crawling and harvesting	x		
Image retrieval and analysis	x		
Communication tracking	x		
Fake profiles and sybil attacks		x	
Group metamorphosis		x	
Ballot stuffing and defamation		x	
Censorship		x	x
Collusion attacks	x	x	x

23.3.1   Plain Impersonation

With *plain impersonation* attack the adversary aims to create fake profiles for real-world users as depicted on Fig. 23.5. In this sense a real-world user will be impersonated within the OSN platform. The success of this attack strongly depends on the authentication mechanisms deployed in the registration process. Since many OSNs tend to authenticate email addresses by requesting confirmations for the registration emails, this attack can be easily performed if an email address is created in advance. The consequence of plain impersonation is that the adversary can participate in the OSN applications on behalf of the impersonated user with all damaging consequences for the user. A currently very prominent secondary effect of all kinds of impersonation (Sects. 23.3.1–23.3.5) is the misuse of the trust that users inherently have in messages from their accepted contacts, and especially the "419" scam[9]: impersonating attackers engage in a dialog with contacts of the impersonated individual, and, by producing a credible story, ("My wallet was stolen in London and now I can't pay my flight home") successfully defraud the victim. This attack can

---

[9] http://www.419scam.org/.

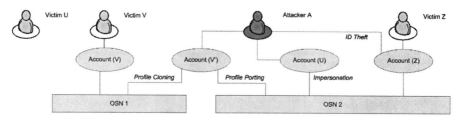

Fig. 23.5 Impersonation attacks: victim U doesn't have any OSN account, victim V has an account on OSN1 and victim Z on OSN2. The attacker V generates U's account on OSN1, a copy of V's account on OSN1 and OSN2, and logs on OSN2 with the credentials of Z

be thwarted only through the deployment of stronger authentication techniques. In particular, it is desirable to require some form of real-world identification from the user prior to switching on her account.

23.3.2 Profile Cloning

By *profile cloning* we understand a special type of impersonation attack that occurs within the same OSN platform [5], as depicted on Fig. 23.5. The goal of the adversary here is to create a profile for some user that is already in possession of some valid profile in the same network. From the technical point of view this attack can be realized through the registration of the new profile using the same (or similar) content as the existing one. This is feasible in most OSN platforms since each profile is associated with some unique administrative id and an email address used during the registration. Furthermore, many users hide their email address so that OSN users would not be able to distinguish between the original profiles and their clones registered with other email addresses. As a consequence the adversary can create confusion through impersonation of other registered users and possibly gain access to the private information communicated to that users. Moreover, with tools like iCloner [5] profile cloning can be automated. Such tools are able to collect public data of OSNs members, match them, create cloned profiles and then send friendship requests on their behalf. A possible solution for OSN providers to prevent profile cloning is to deploy mechanisms that are able to detect similarities between different profiles, in particular with regard to the personal information that is visible to the OSN users. Since cloned profiles typically have later registration date than the original ones, it should be feasible for the OSN provider to distinguish them and remove from the network.

23.3.3 Profile Hijacking

The goal of the adversary mounting a *profile hijacking* attack is to obtain control over some existing profile within an OSN platform. Many OSN platforms protect user access to their own profiles via passwords. Hence, from the technical point of view profile hijacking is successful if the adversary can obtain passwords of other users. This can be done by many means. First, it is a well-known fact that the majority of users choose weak passwords that can be recovered via an automated dictionary attack [7]. However, OSN providers typically deploy protection against such attacks by restricting the number of login attempts or by using techniques that require human interaction such as CAPTCHAs [14]. Nevertheless, there exist effective tools, e.g. as the one included in iCloner [5], that are able to analyze and bypass CAPTCHAs. Alternatively, the adversary may try to obtain passwords via social-engineering attacks such as phishing [11], or obtaining passwords for other online services, relying on the fact that most people use the same passwords across the majority of their accounts at different sites. The OSN functionality can be misused to distribute messages aiming to lure users to fake login websites.[10] Finally, we shouldn't forget that OSN providers themselves have full control over the registered profiles. Therefore, if some profile appears attractive for the OSN provider to be hijacked the password access to the profile can be changed accordingly.

23.3.4 Profile Porting

By *profile porting* we understand another type of impersonation where some profile that exists within one OSN platform is cloned into another OSN platform [5, 9], as depicted on Fig. 23.5. From the technical point of view this attack can be realized via registration of a profile using some new email address. Profile porting is appealing since not every user has her own profile on every available OSN platform. On the other hand, there might be some users that participate in both OSN platforms and thus will not be able to distinguish amongst ported profiles. The significance of profile porting (e.g. in comparison to profile cloning) is that users may be completely unaware that their profiles have been ported. The impact of profile porting is that the adversary can impersonate users in different OSN platforms. Thwarting profile porting is not that easy. In particular, profile similarity detection tools can still be used but only if they can work across multiple OSN platforms. Since every OSN platform is administrated by a different provider, the deployment of such tools would require cooperation amongst the providers. This is difficult to achieve, since OSN providers are cautious about granting any form of access to their profile database to competitors.

23.3.5 ID Theft

Under *ID theft* we consider the impersonation of OSN users in the real-world [5], as depicted on Fig. 23.5. An adversary mounting the ID theft attack should be able

---

[10] http://fraudwar.blogspot.com/2009/05/facebook-hack-reveals-trend-in.html.

to convince anyone about the ownership of some particular OSN profile. In this way the adversary can possibly misuse the reputation or expertise of the real profile owner for own benefit, while leaving the owner unaware of the attack. One way for a successful ID theft attack is to take control over the target profile. This requires the same effort as for the profile hijacking attack. However, this effort seems necessary only if the adversary has to actively use the profile for the ID theft attack, e.g. communicate via the OSN platform. Often it would simply suffice to claim the ownership of a profile and perform the actual communication via other channels. In this case thwarting ID theft attacks by technical means seems impossible. The only solution is to rely on other means of real-world identification such as national identity cards, driver's licenses, etc.

23.3.6 Profiling

In addition to the maintenance of own profiles modern OSNs provide users with various applications to express themselves via forums, guest books, discussions, polls, multimedia data, etc. These activities are observable by other users within the OSN platform. By *profiling* we understand an attack against any target OSN user aiming to collect information about OSN activities or further attributes of that user, e.g [4], see also Fig. 23.6. This attack can be typically performed by OSN users, possibly in an automated way, since the collectable information is usually publicly accessible by all OSN users. The risk of profiling attacks performed by OSN users can be diminished via fine-grained access control and anonymizing techniques. For example, users should be able to allow access to the personal parts of their profile

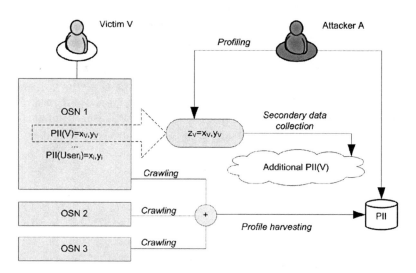

Fig. 23.6 Main PII related threats in current OSNs

on the individual basis and not only based on roles (e.g. friends) as realized in many current OSN platforms. However, the recent studies, e.g. [10], show that even if the personal information is hidden, it can still be inferred from public information and social activities of the user. An alternative solution could be to let users decide whether their activities (e.g. discussion comments) should be kept unlinkable to their profiles. Although these measures may help to reduce the risk of profiling performed by other OSN users, thwarting profiling performed by OSN providers[11] appears to be much more difficult.

23.3.7 Secondary Data Collection

By *secondary data collection* we understand an attack that aims to collect information about the owner of some OSN profile via secondary sources apart of the OSN platform, as depicted on Fig. 23.6. A typical example of secondary data collection is to use some Internet search engine to find information that can be linked to the profile owner. More effective is to use some Internet service[12] that aggregates all information it can find about some particular person. Through such an attack the adversary may obtain much more information about some user than available in the profile and misuse it against the user both in the virtual environment of the OSN platform and in the real life. Another example are recent de-anonymization attacks [16] that misused the group memberships of social network users for their unique identification. Furthermore, the existence of OSNs with public and private profiles simplifies the secondary data collection as many users tend to have accounts on different platforms [18]. There is no meaningful protection against secondary data collection attacks since the data is typically aggregated from different locations. Therefore, it appears in responsibility of the user to limit information kept in the profile in order to avoid its linkability with secondary sources.

23.3.8 Fake Requests

One of the main objectives of OSN platforms is to establish social contacts. This proceeds via connection requests that can be either accepted or rejected by the users. An adversary with own OSN profile that sends *fake requests* to other users aims less on the social contact with these users but is more interested to expand its own network. The dissemination of fake requests can be automated. Since many OSN users tend to accept fake requests,[13] the adversary can simplify access to their

---

[11] http://www.pcworld.com/article/191716/myspace_user_data_for_sale.html.

[12] http://www.123people.com/.

[13] http://www.columbiamissourian.com/stories/2005/09/01/a-new-kind-of-fame/.

profiles and activities and possibly obtain additional information, whose visibility is subject to the available direct or nth-grade connections. These connections can then be misused for the automated collection and aggregation of information. The actual dissemination of fake requests cannot be prevented since establishment of new connections is an important goal of OSN applications. Therefore, it is desirable that users behave more responsibly upon accepting new connection requests. Unfortunately, current studies, e.g. [5] show that users tend to accept fake requests.

23.3.9 Crawling and Harvesting

The goal of *crawling* is to collect and aggregate publicly available information across multiple OSN profiles and applications in an automated way [4, 5]; see also Fig. 23.6. Unlike profiling this attack does not target any particular user and unlike secondary data collection it is executed within the OSN environment. The expansion of own network connections by the adversary using fake requests can be seen as a preliminary step for crawling. The adversary is simply interested in collecting as much public information within the OSN platform as possible. This information can then be misused for different purposes, for example for selling data to marketing agencies, etc. Also it would allow for the offline analysis of social relationships and user activities, thus paving the way for targeted attacks on OSN users. Although some OSN platforms try to protect from crawling through the deployment of CAPTCHAs, the latter can be passed over with the appropriate solving tools [5]. Another attack by which the adversary simultaneously crawls across different OSN platforms is called *harvesting*. Typically harvesting results in larger datasets with larger amount on private information about the OSN users.

23.3.10 Image Retrieval and Analysis

Upload of images or other digital content and its discussion stimulates social interactions of OSN users. However, free accessibility to images and videos bear potential risks to the privacy of users. By *image retrieval and analysis* we understand an automated attack aiming to collect multimedia data (incl. images, videos, etc.) available with the OSN platform. This attack is typically followed by the subsequent analysis via automated pattern recognition tools (see e.g. [17] for a survey on face recognition) to find links to the OSN profiles of displayed users. Information distilled in this way can reveal more private information about users than they are willing to give. In particular, it may reveal information about friends or colleagues that are not necessarily part of the user's social network, or information about visited locations (location-tracking) shown on the photographs. The analysis of digital content can be further strengthened by considering secondary sources such as search over the Internet. Digital content retrieval attacks can be possibly thwarted through a more restrictive access control policies for the digital content.

23.3.11 Communication Tracking

OSN users communicate with each other using diverse OSN applications. By *communication tracking* we understand a profiling attack aiming to reveal information about communications of the same user. In this way the attacker may collect more information about the user than available in the profile. This attack can be mounted in an automated way by searching for comments left by the target user in various OSN applications.

23.3.12 Fake Profiles and Sybil Attacks

In many OSN platforms users can easily create several profiles under possibly different identities and contents. Since many OSN platforms lack of proper authentication such creation of *fake profiles* becomes easy [5]. On the technical side, the user has only to create a new email for the registration of a fake account. Fake profiles pave the way for *Sybil attacks* that may serve different purposes.[14,15] For example, owners of fake profiles can establish new connections without disclosing their real identities. In this way they may obtain more information about some person than by using some real account. Sybil account may also be created on behalf of the whole groups.[16] Furthermore, Sybil accounts can be misused against the functionality of the OSN platforms. This includes distribution of spam messages[17] or other illicit content such as malware[18] and phishing links,[19,20] illegal advertisement, bias of deployed reputation systems, etc. Creation of fake profiles can be seen as a special form of impersonation attacks. One solution for OSN providers to recognize fake profiles is to use IP traceback. Indeed, if logins to several profiles come from the same IP address then it is likely that some of these profiles are fake. However, an attacker may try to avoid IP traceback by using different proxies. Therefore, stronger identification and authentication mechanisms for admission of new users would offer a better protection.

---

[14] http://www.nature.com/news/2009/090423/full/news.2009.398.html.

[15] http://www.sophos.com/pressoffice/news/articles/2009/12/facebook.html.

[16] http://gadgetwise.blogs.nytimes.com/2010/03/18/fake-facebook-fan-pages/.

[17] http://www.pcworld.com/businesscenter/article/191847/facebook_users_targeted_in_massive_spam_run.html.

[18] http://content.usatoday.com/communities/technologylive/post/2009/12/koobface-compels-facebook-victims-to-help-spread-worm-/1.

[19] http://scitech.blogs.cnn.com/2010/03/19/facebook-responds-to-massive-phishing-scheme/.

[20] http://www.pcworld.com/businesscenter/article/174607/twitter_warns_of_new_phishing_attack.html.

23.3.13 Group Metamorphosis

A popular application provided by OSN platforms is the establishment of shared interest groups. These groups are usually administrated by OSN users and provide a platform for more focused discussions, specialized contact establishment, and dissemination of information, which may be interesting for a targeted audience. By *group metamorphosis* we understand an attack where group administrators change the group subject to persuade own interests, e.g. political.[21] Other OSN users who joined the group earlier may remain unaware of this change, which in turn may have negative impact on their reputation. A possible solution for OSN providers to thwart group metamorphosis attacks is to restrict control of administrators over the interest groups, in particular to prevent them from modifying any information that may have impact on the group as a whole.

23.3.14 Ballot Stuffing and Defamation

OSN platforms serve primarily the contact establishment and interaction amongst users. Hence, attacks biasing public perception and recognition of a target OSN user by others are undesirable. By *ballot stuffing* we understand an attack by which the attacker wishes to increase public interest to some target OSN user. This attack may increase the amount of personal messages or connection requests received by the target user resulting in a DoS attack on the physical resources of the OSN user. The attack may place the victim into the focus of public, possibly embarrassing discussions. On the other hand, ballot stuffing may increase popularity of the profile belonging to the attacker. This can be achieved through recommendations submitted by the attacker using fake profiles. In contrast, *defamation attacks* aim at decreasing public interest of a target user, in particular by tarnishing the reputation of the latter.[22] In particular, defamation may lead to blacklisting of the user in contact lists of other users and keep the user away from participation in communication applications such as shared interest groups and discussion forums. It may further have negative impact on the user's life in the real world.[23] Another form of defamation is the anti-advertising against companies[24] aiming to damage the reputation of the latter on the market.

---

[21] One incident has been reported for facebook, where a multitude of groups have been fostered under general topics and concertedly renamed to support Silvio Berlusconi, in 2009 http://www.repubblica.it/2009/12/sezioni/politica/giustizia-21/gruppi-facebook/gruppi-facebook.html.

[22] http://timesofindia.indiatimes.com/sports/off-the-field/Rachel-Uchitel-threatenslawsuit-over-Facebook-defamation/articleshow/5708237.cms.

[23] http://mybroadband.co.za/news/Internet/6580.html.

[24] http://blogs.bnet.com/businesstips/?p=6786.

Both ballot stuffing and defamation attacks have to be performed at a large scale in order to have a significant impact. An attacker may create fake profiles and use automated tools to disseminate information needed to increase or decrease interest to a specific OSN user. Another technique is to use the poll application provided by many OSN platforms and let users vote on information related to the victim.

23.3.15 Censorship

OSN providers typically have control over the whole data available within the network. As such they can deliberately manipulate the user-provided information and contents. In some cases this ability is necessary to prevent dissemination of illicit content. On the other hand, *censorship* when applied without substantial reasons may have negative impact on the OSN users. For example, in OSN platforms focusing on business contacts users often advertise their expertise. In this scenario censorship may be misused to favor some users over their competitors. Censorship may have many facets. It can be performed by active modification of user-provided contents, which might remain unnoticed by the user. Higher impact can be achieved through the target manipulation of search engines within the network. Since censorship can be performed by the OSN provider[25] without involving any other parties, there is little one can do to prevent this threat. Censorship may be applied not only by OSN providers but also by administrators of shared interest groups. They can deliberately modify or drop messages of group members. Although restricting group administrators from modification of other user contents appears to be an effective protection measure, it is unlikely to be used in practice, since this ability contradicts to the responsibility of group administrators for the content disseminated within the group.

23.3.16 Collusion Attacks

The "impact of a crowd" can be exhibited in OSNs through a *collusion* of users. In this attack several users join their malicious activities in order to damage other OSN users or mount attacks against applications of the OSN platform. In particular, colluding users may start defamation or ballot stuffing campaigns, increase each over reputations, bias the outcome of public polls or influence public discussions. Since colluding users have valid OSN profiles these attacks do not require creation of fake profiles. Furthermore, these attacks are more difficult to recognize than similar attacks mounted via fake profiles. The reason is that IP traceback would not help even if colluding users do not deploy any additional proxies.

---

[25] http://www.civic.moveon.org/pdf/myspace/.

23.4 Summary and Conclusion

This chapter deals with security in Online Social Networks (OSN). It introduces Online Social Networks as the digital representations of relationships, which their users entertain in the physical world. Social network providers (SNP), commonly commercial entities that offer Social Networking Services (SNS), the access to the OSN, and their users, are identified as the main actors in online social networking. Sponsors, application providers, and data analysts are third parties in this context and they represent further actors.

Analysing the typical users of OSN it becomes apparent that the seeming ease of use attracts especially individuals with limited knowledge about computers, the Internet, and computer security. The users provide and maintain a wealth of data to the OSN at the same time. Privacy concerns remain unaddressed, and the uploaded data largely consists of personally identifiable information (PII), and even private messages between the users.

In order to allow for the analysis of threats, this chapter attempts to formally divide typical SNS into a layered model of the Social Networking Layer, including the digital representation of their users' relationships, the Application Service Layer, comprising of the service infrastructure offering the social networking services, and the Communication and Transport Layer, which represents the underlying computer networks.

Comparing security objectives for online social networks to common security goals in computer science, which generally identified to be confidentiality, integrity, and availability, some similarities, and, more importantly, some differences become apparent.

Especially establishing confidential channels between senders and receivers is not sufficient for social networking services. The confidentiality objective hence has to be extended to provide *privacy* of the users. Considering the wealth of PII stored in OSN, and the extension through third party annotations, the accessibility of data more strictly has to be restricted in order to protect the identity and privacy of users. Threats to their users' privacy are abundant in OSN. The access to the data of users through the provided interfaces eases the automated gathering of data in order to profile single users, or to mine their data in multiple sources, thus allowing for secondary data collection. Even the harvesting of a large number of profiles becomes easily possible, thus collecting PII of not only particular, but even of large numbers of users. Different types of identity threats are direct consequences, with impersonation, profile cloning, and even the porting of profiles being feasible and quite simple to accomplish.

The integrity, being threatened by creation of faked profiles, or even defamation and ballot stuffing, as well as availability, mainly threatened by denial-of-service and censorship, generally are quite similar to their traditional definitions in computer science.

Considering these objectives, a plethora of attacks on SNS security are conceivable, and many of these not only have been shown in scientific work, but reported to have been conducted in the wild, too. The attacks are classified into nine distinct groups and described in detail. Academic, and, where reported, real world examples are given and explained to further describe them and illustrate their impact.

Online social networks currently are among the best accepted and most highly utilized networked applications on the Internet. Their immense user base, which by 2010 has exceeded 500 million distinct users, permits predicting that they will stay being one of the killer apps during the coming years. However, both their users and their providers have not learned to properly master their properties, and the vast number and severity of threats, as well as the plethora of reported attacks, underlines the importance of introducing and enforcing security measures, which are better than the rudimentary approaches that are implemented today.

References

1. Modelling the Real Market Value of Social Networks. http://www.techcrunch.com/2008/06/23/modeling-the-real-market-value- of-social-networks/, 2008.
2. danah m. boyd . Facebook's privacy trainwreck. *Convergence: The International Journal of Research into New Media Technologies*, 14(1):13–20, 2008.
3. A. Avizienis, J.-C. Laprie, B. Randell, and C. Landwehr. Basic concepts and taxonomy of dependable and secure computing. *IEEE Transactions on Dependable and Secure Computing*, 1(1):11–33, 2004.
4. M. Balduzzi, C. Platzer, T. Holz, E. Kirda, D. Balzarotti, and C. Kruegel. Abusing Social Networks for Automated User Profiling. Research Report RR-10-233, EURECOM, 2010. http://www.iseclab.org/papers/socialabuse-TR.pdf.
5. L. Bilge, T. Strufe, D. Balzarotti, and E. Kirda. All Your Contacts Are Belong to Us: Automated Identity Theft Attacks on Social Networks. In *18th Intl. World Wide Web Conference*, 2009.
6. d. m. boyd and N. B. Ellison. Social network sites: definition, history, and scholarship. *Journal of Computer-Mediated Communication*, 13(1), 2007.
7. D. Florencio and C. Herley. A Large-Scale Study of Web Password Habits. In *16th International Conference on World Wide Web (WWW 2007)*, pages 657–666. ACM, 2007.
8. R. Gross and A. Acquisti. Information Revelation and Privacy in Online Social Networks. In *ACM Workshop on Privacy in the Electronic Society*, pages 71–80, 2005.
9. T. N. Jagatic, N. A. Johnson, M. Jakobsson, and F. Menczer. Social phishing. *Communications of the ACM*, 94–100, 2007.
10. A. Mislove, B. Viswanath, K. P. Gummadi, and P. Druschel. You Are Who You Know: Inferring User Profiles in Online Social Networks. In *ACM International Conference on Web Search and Data Mining (WSDM 2010)*, pages 251–260. ACM, 2010.
11. T. J. Nathaniel, N. Johnson, and M. Jakobsson. Social phishing. *Communications of the ACM. Retrieved March*, 7, 2006.
12. J. Park and R. Sandhu. Towards Usage Control Models: Beyond Traditional Access Control. In *SACMAT '02: Proceedings of the Seventh ACM Symposium on Access Control Models and Technologies*, pages 57–64. ACM, New York, NY, USA, 2002.
13. F. Schneider, A. Feldmann, B. Krishnamurthy, and W. Willinger. Understanding Online Social Network Usage from a Network Perspective. In *ACM SIGCOMM conference on Internet measurement*, 2009.

14. L. von Ahn, M. Blum, N. J. Hopper, and J. Langford. CAPTCHA: Using Hard AI Problems for Security. In *EUROCRYPT 2003*. *LNCS*, vol 2656, pages 294–311. Springer, Heidelberg, 2003.
15. S. D. Warren and L. D. Brandeis. The right to privacy. *Harward Law Review*, 4(5):193–220, December 1890.
16. G. Wondracek, T. Holz, E. Kirda, and C. Kruegel. A Practical Attack to De-Anonymize Social Network Users. In *IEEE Symposium on Security and Privacy*. IEEE CS, 2010. http://www.iseclab.org/papers/sonda.pdf.
17. W. Zhao, R. Chellappa, P. J. Phillips, and A. Rosenfeld. Face recognition: a literature survey. *ACM Computing Surveys*, 35(4):399–458, 2003.
18. E. Zheleva and L. Getoor. To Join or Not to Join: The Illusion of Privacy in Social Networks with Mixed Public and Private User Profiles. In *WWW 2009*, pages 531–540. ACM, 2009.

Chapter 24
Investigation of Key-Player Problem in Terrorist Networks Using Bayes Conditional Probability

D.M. Akbar Hussain

24.1 Introduction

The communication disruption in social networks occurs when it is fragmented by the removal of a set of nodes, which means the said set of nodes are the key actors in the network. The key player problem (KPP) has two contexts; in the first case KPP-1 we have to find a set of k-nodes which may be called as kp-set of order k and if we remove this kp-set it will severely damage communication among the remaining nodes. Whereas in the second case KPP-2 we also find kp-set of order k which is maximally connected to all other nodes [1]. In the first context KPP-1, fragmentation occurs or distance between nodes becomes very large so in realistic terms practically disconnected. In the second context KPP-2, how many and who can reach as many nodes as possible directly or alternatively through shorter path ways. It has been pointed out that the centrality measures alone from graph theory for example betweenness, degree and closeness are not enough to solve the key player problem [1, 2]. Consider for example the kite network as shown in Fig. 24.1 from David Krackhardt, it can be seen that if we remove node 1 which has the highest degree centrality the communication setup remains intact for the remaining nodes as seen in Fig. 24.2. On the other hand if we remove node 8 which has the highest betweenness centrality measure, although the network is fragmented in two components but still the major portion of the network remains intact as seen in Fig. 24.3. Selecting a set of nodes to solve KPP-1 or KPP-2 problem is not the same as the selection of equal number of individual nodes to get an optimal KPP solution [3]. The reason is that some time their is redundancy with respect to node's position and its removal does not necessarily change the fragmentation as the nodes are essentially connected via other nodes. Borgatti presented an optimal measure to solve KKP-1 problem by selecting a kp-set in such a way that it maximize fragmentation and distance. The fragmentation measure suggested by him counts the number

D.M.A. Hussain (✉)
Automation and Control, Department of Electronic Systems, Aalborg University, Niels Bohrs
Vej 8, 6700 Esbjerg, Denmark
e-mail: akh@es.aau.dk

B. Furht (ed.), *Handbook of Social Network Technologies and Applications*,
DOI 10.1007/978-1-4419-7142-5_24, © Springer Science+Business Media, LLC 2010

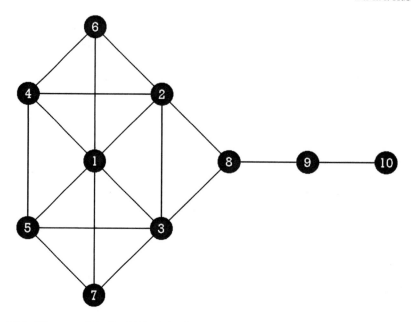

Fig. 24.1 Kite network by David Krackhardt

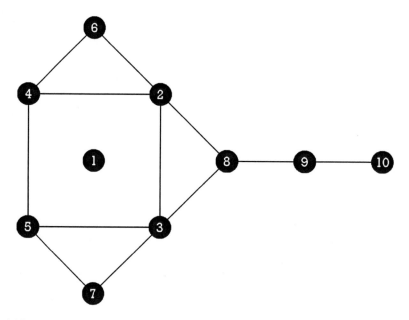

Fig. 24.2 Node with highest degree is removed

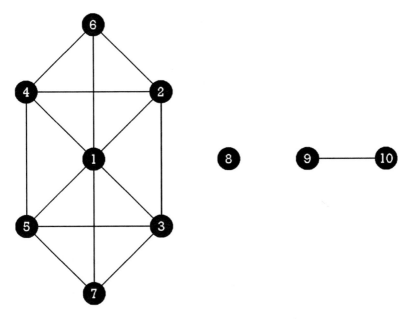

Fig. 24.3 Node with highest betweenness is removed

of pairs of nodes that are disconnected from each other for example a given matrix A in which $A_{ij} = 1$ if i can reach j otherwise $A_{ij} = 0$, fragmentation measure F is defined as:

$$F = 1 - \frac{2 \sum_i \sum_{j<i} A_{ij}}{n(n-1)} \qquad (24.1)$$

In the fragmented components nodes are mutually reachable so F can be rewritten based on their sizes S_k as:

$$F = 1 - \frac{\sum_k S_k(S_k - 1)}{n(n-1)} \qquad (24.2)$$

The above expression still does not include the shape and structure of the components, the solution is to measure sum of the reciprocals of distances, therefore re-writing (24.1) as;

$$D^F = 1 - \frac{2 \sum_{i>j} \frac{1}{d_{ij}}}{n(n-1)} \qquad (24.3)$$

the above equation is similar in respect as expression for F and in a similar way could achieve its maximum value 1 if all the nodes are disconnected.

In this paper we present a simulated study to investigate key player problem using Bayes probability theorem discussed later in Sect. 24.4, surprisingly, results are very similar to what Borgatti achieved through its distance fragmentation measure (we shall refer it as fragmentation index in the remaining text description) [1]. In our results presentation we have compared the two methods by removing each node individually and computing the distance fragmentation index, therefore, from these methods we can see both the probability of the individual node and the value of the fragmentation index. Our paper is organized in the following way; it provides a brief survey of SNA in Sect. 24.2, centrality measures and their mathematics used in the social network analysis is discussed in Sect. 24.3. This is necessary as we are using these measures in our proposed computational method. Bayes theory is briefly discussed in Sect. 24.4 in context of our implementation, Sect. 24.5 provides the proposed model, analysis and results, finally conclusion in Sect. 24.6.

24.2 SNA Survey

Social Network Analysis is a mathematical method for 'connecting the dots'. SNA allows us to map and measure complex, and sometimes covert, human groups and organizations [4]. Given any network where the nodes/agents are individuals, groups, organizations etc., a number of network measures such as centrality or cut-points are used to locate critical/important nodes/agents. Social network analysis is a multi-model multi-link problem so the challenges posed by such multi-dimensional task are enormous. The standard representation of a typical social network model is through a graph data structure. This type of model can be considered as an intellective simulation model, such types of models explain one particular aspect of the model abstracting other factors present in the model. The dynamics of larger social networks is so complex some time it becomes difficult to understand the various levels of interactions and dependencies just by mere representation through a graph. However, to overcome this limitation many analytical methods provide relationship dependencies, role of different nodes and their importance in the social networks. Insight visualization of any network typically focuses on the characteristics of the network structure. SNA measures indicate various roles of the nodes in a network, for example leaders, gatekeepers, role models etc. A node is central if it is strategically located on the communication route joining pairs of other nodes [5, 6]. Being central it can influence other nodes in the network, in other words potentially it can control the flow of information. The potential of control makes the centrality conceptual model for these nodes. The idea of centrality is not new it was first applied to human communication by Baveles in 1948 [5, 7]. In this study relationship between structural centrality and influence in group processes were hypothesized. Following Baveles it was concluded that centrality is related to group efficiency in problem-solving, perception of leadership and the personal satisfaction of participants [8–10]. In the fifties and sixties more research was conducted on these measures and it was concluded that centrality is relevant to the way groups get organized to solve problems. The following references provide a very deep and pioneering work on these measures [11–20]. The centrality concept is not exclusive to deal with group problem tasks, it has been used in other discipline as well [21, 22].

A number of centrality measures have been proposed over the past years. Most of the centrality measures are based on one of two quite different conceptual ideas and can be divided into two large classes [23]. The measures in the first class are based on the idea that the centrality of an individual in a network is related to how it is near to others. Second class of measures is based on the idea that central nodes stand between others on the path of communication [24–26]. A node being on the path of other nodes communication highway has the potential to control what passes through it. The simplest and most straightforward way to quantify the individual centrality is therefore the degree of the individual, i.e., the number of its immediate neighbors. In a graph if every node is reachable from any node in the graph it is called a connected graph also each path in the graph is associated with a distance equal to the number of edges in the path and the shortest path to reach a given pair of nodes is geodesic distance. Nieminen has provided a very systematic elaboration of the concept of degree [27]. Scott has extended the concept based on degree beyond immediate (first) neighbors by selecting the number of nodes an individual can reach at a distance two or three [28]. Similarly, Freeman produced a global measure based on the concept of closeness in terms of the distances among the various nodes [25]. The simplest notion of closeness is obtained by the sum of the geodesic distances from an individual to all the other nodes in the graph [29]. These traditional social network measures and the information processing network measures can help in revealing importance and vulnerabilities of the nodes/agents in the network. Since the start of this century many terrorism events have occurred around the globe. These events have provided a new impetus for the analysis, investigation, studying the behavior and tracking terrorist networks (individuals).

Apart from centrality measures social scientist have also developed highly efficient techniques like data mining and decision making tree methods to process large amount of data. Data Mining technique extract particular kind of information from this huge data. Typically, once a particular information is located the data mining application alerts either system or the human operator which determines whether the application has provided the requested information. Data mining also allows to record the search process, so that patterns of objects and information can be visualized as graph. This visualization is quite useful for large amount of data information. In the beginning data mining methodology has been developed largely for businesses applications to help with marketing it also has applications in medical profession. However, more recently it has been used in law enforcement and intelligence operations [30]. The development and implementation of these systems require a cooperative effort on the part of those who develop and those who operate them. The importance of such systems is that they must provide complete information based on the input and typically sound alarm when targeted information is located however, the final action or judgment is still made by the user. On the other hand decision tree methodology can be used to make decisions. The core idea behind decision tree technique is to correctly locate and identify the choice options which are explicitly evaluated in terms of the importance of their outcome. The probability of that outcome is used in creating a sequence of decision map from start to end. The most positive aspect of this method is that decision is made explicit so that others can use the decision tree if faced with the similar questions. Similar to data mining techniques for application in law enforcement and intelligent operations decision trees can also be used to guide decisions. Both of these tools; data mining and decision tree have applications in the analysis of social networks.

Application of the above mentioned tools/concepts on the complex socio-technical systems like SNA is very demanding to squeeze out the required information. Most of the above mentioned measures and tools work best when the data is complete; i.e., when the information is inclusive about the interactions among the nodes. However, the difficulty is that large scale distributed, covert and terrorist networks typically have considerable missing data. Normally, a sampled snapshot data is available, some of the links may be intentionally hidden (hence missing data may not be randomly distributed). Also data is collected from multiple sources and at different time scales and granularity. In addition inclusive and correct information may be prohibitive because of secrecy. Obviously, there could be other difficulties but even these provide little guidance for what to expect when analyzing these complex socio-technical systems with the existing tools. Therefore, new concepts are really required in this area for better understanding/investigation of these nodes one such example is the fragmentation concept from Borgatti [1]. Our method could also be regarded as a new way to locate important key actors in a terrorist network analysis context, which combines the standard centrality measures into Bayes conditional probability method.

Typically, one has to identify the following characteristics in the context of SNA:

(a) Key players in the network
(b) Potential threat from the network
(c) Important individual, event, place or group
(d) Dependency of individual nodes
(e) Leader-Follower identification
(f) Bonding between nodes
(g) Vulnerabilities identification
(h) Efficiency of overall network

Kathleen Carley has also provided the following key characteristics for classification and distinctiveness of nodes [31].

(a) An individual or group that if given new information can propagate it rapidly
(b) An individual or group that has relatively more power and can be a possible source of trouble, potential dissidents, or potential innovators
(c) An individual or group where movement to a competing group or organization would ensure that the competing unit would learn all the core or critical information in the original group or organization (inevitable disclosure)
(d) An individual, group, or resource that provides redundancy in the network

24.3 SNA Measures

Social networks provides mapping and the social network analysis measure relationships and movement between people, groups, events, organizations or other information/knowledge processing entities. People, organization and groups are represented as nodes in the network while the links show relationships or movement between the nodes. SNA provides both visual and mathematical analysis of human relationships. This methodology could also be used by the management to perform Organizational Network Analysis [4]. There are many ways to determine important members of a network. The most straightforward technique is to compute member's **degree**; the number of direct connections to other members of the network apart from **degree** more well known measures are **betweenness** and the **closeness**. A node with relatively few direct connections could still be important if it lies between two or more large groups. On the other hand a member could also be important if it has direct and indirect links in such a way that it is placed closest to all other members of the group, in other words the node has to go through fewer intermediaries to reach other members than anyone else. It is important to note that terrorist cells have complex, dynamical and decentralized structures and these standard measures alone may not be enough to reveal information about important actors in the network. SNA has been used with other measures to highlight important nodes in terrorist cells [32–34], other applications like Googles PageRank systems is using the concept of network theory and centrality, in medical field network analysis has been used to track the spread of HIV, more recently a very interesting research has been carried out for the understanding of relationships from Enron's email records [35].

24.3.1 Degree

To comprehend networks and their participants, we evaluate the location of participants in the network. Degree provides the relative importance and the location of a particular node in the network. Typically, centrality means degree, with respect to communication a node with relatively high degree looks important. In a social network a node that is directly connected with many other nodes actually see itself and be seen by others in the network as indispensable. This means a node with low degree is isolated from direct involvement and see itself and by others not to be a stakeholder. A general measure of centrality $D_c(p_i)$ based on degree for a node p_i is given by [25];

$$D_c(p_i) = \sum_{j=1}^{n} d(p_j, p_i) \quad (for\ all\ j \neq i) \tag{24.4}$$

where

$$d(p_j, p_i) = \begin{cases} 1 & \text{if } p_j, p_i \text{ directly connected} \\ 0 & \text{otherwise} \end{cases}$$

A node can be connected with maximum of $(n - 1)$ number of nodes in a n size network. Therefore, the maximum degree value is $(n - 1)$, so to have a relationship which is proportion of other nodes that are directly connected to p_i can be written as follows.

$$D'_c(p_i) = \frac{\sum_{j=1}^n d(p_j, p_i)}{(n - 1)} \tag{24.5}$$

24.3.2 Betweenness

Betweenness (also called load) measures to what extent a node can play the role of intermediary in the interaction between the other nodes. The most popular and simple betweenness measure based on geodesic path is proposed by Freeman and Anthonisse [24,26]. In many real scenarios however, communication does not travel exclusively through geodesic paths. For such situations two more betweenness measures are developed first based on all possible paths between couple of nodes [36] and second based on random paths [37]. Consider a graph $G = (V, E)$ with vertices V and edges E, a path from a source vertex to a target vertex is an alternating sequence of edges. The length of this path is the total number of edges from source to target and shortest path of these alternating routes is called the *geodesic*. Therefore, nodes located on many shortest paths (geodesics) between other nodes will have higher betweenness compared with others. For a graph $G = (V, E)$ with n vertices, the betweenness $B_c(k)$ for a vertex k is:

$$B_c(k) = \sum_{i \neq j, i \neq k} \frac{\sigma_{ij}(k)}{\sigma_{ij}} \tag{24.6}$$

where σ_{ij} is the number of shortest paths from i to j, and $\sigma_{ij}(k)$ is the number of shortest geodesic paths from i to j that pass through vertex k. It can be normalized by dividing through the number of pairs of vertices not including k, which is $(n - 1)(n - 2)$. Calculation of betweenness is quite complicated for networks when several geodesics connect a pair of nodes, which is the case in most real world networks. Also, $B_c(k)$ is dependent on the size of the network on which it is being calculated. Freeman [25] has provided relative centrality of any node in the network by the following relationship.

$$B'_c(k) = \frac{B_c(k)}{(n^2 - 3n + 2)/2} \tag{24.7}$$

The idea is that maximum value of $B_c(k)$ is achieved by the central point of the star that is given by;

$$\frac{(n^2 - 3n + 2)}{2} \tag{24.8}$$

Therefore, the relative betweenness centrality is determined by the ratio given in (24.7) and is re-written as (24.9).

$$B'_c(k) = \frac{2B_c(k)}{(n^2 - 3n + 2)} \tag{24.9}$$

24.3.3 Closeness

A more sophisticated centrality measure closeness based on geodesic distance can be defined, which is the mean geodesic (i.e., shortest path) distance between a node and all other nodes reachable from it. Closeness can be regarded as a measure of how long it will take information to spread from a given node to other nodes in the network. From retrospect closeness can provide the information about nodes independence. We are utilizing the closeness centrality in our implementation, so it is necessary to provide brief detail about closeness to complete the discussion on standard centrality measures typically used in SNA. The simplest mathematics for closeness centrality is provided by [29], which is determined by summing the geodesics from a node of interest to all other nodes in the network and taking its inverse. Closeness grows as the distance between node i and other nodes for example $(j....n)$ increases. The Closeness C_c for a node i is given by;

$$C_c(i) = \frac{1}{\sum_{j=1}^{n} d(p_j, \, p_i)} \tag{24.10}$$

where d is the geodesic distance between respective nodes, for all those nodes which are not connected the geodesic distance is infinity. The above expression is dependent on the size (number of nodes) of the network and it is appropriate to have an expression which is independent of this limitation. Beauchamp [38] suggested that relative Closeness (point centrality) for a node i is given by;

$$C'_c(i) = \frac{(n - 1)}{\sum_{j=1}^{n} d(p_j, \, p_i)} \tag{24.11}$$

24.4 Bayes Probability Theorem

Bayes' Theorem is a simple mathematical formula used for calculating conditional probabilities. Bayes' Theorem originally stated by Thomas Bayes and it has been used in a wide variety of contexts, ranging from marine biology to the development of "Bayesian" Spam blockers for email systems. Through the use of Bayes' Theorem precise measures can be obtained by showing how the probability that a theory is correct is affected by new evidence [39, 40]. In a Bayesian framework the conditional and marginal probabilities for stochastic events for example A and B are computed through this relationship:

$$P(A|B) = \frac{P(B|A)P(A)}{P(B)} \tag{24.12}$$

$$P(A|B) \propto P(B|A) \, P(A) \tag{24.13}$$

where $P(A)$ is the prior probability or marginal probability of A, $P(A|B)$ is the conditional probability given B also called posterior probability. $P(B|A)$ is conditional probability given A, $P(B)$ is prior probability and considered as normalizing constant. $P(B|A)$ is in-fact equal to $L(A|B)$ which is the likelihood of A given fixed B, however, at times likelihood L can be multiplied by a factor so that it is proportional to, but not equal probability P. It should be noted that probability of an event A conditional on another event B is generally different from the probability of B conditional on event A, however, there is a unique relationship between the two which is provided by Bayes theorem. We can formulate the above relationship as:

$$posterior = \frac{likelihood \times prior}{normalizing \ constant} \tag{24.14}$$

We can re-write (24.12) as the ratio $P(B|A)/P(B)$ which is typically called as standardized likelihood or normalized likelihood so it can be written as:

$$posterior = normalized \ likelihood \times prior \tag{24.15}$$

Bayes conditional probability from above expression can be expanded as;

$$P(A|B) = \frac{P(B|A) \, P(A)}{P(B|A) \, P(A) + P(B|A') \, P(A')} \tag{24.16}$$

$P(A)$ is the probability regardless of any other information; $P(A')$ is the complimentary event of A; $P(B|A)$ is the conditional probability; $P(B|A')$ is the probability of B given A'.

Bayesian approach have been used in dynamic SNA issues, statistical analysis and network measurement [40–43], our approach here is different, we are interested in evaluating the theory or hypothesis (24.12) for A based on B which is the new information (evidence) that can verify the hypothesis and $P(A)$ is our best estimate of the probability (known as the prior probability of A, prior to considering the new information). In other words we are interested to compute the probability that A is correct (true) with the assumption that the new information (evidence) is correct. The detailed implementation is discussed in the following Sect. 24.5.

24.5 Analysis & Results

We explain our model of computation by considering a network of 20 nodes as shown in Fig. 24.4, such a network is intentionally considered with some nodes having very large value of degree and vice versa, similar is the case for betweenness. We need four terms of the Bayes probability expression given by (24.16). $P(A)$ is the prior probability which is computed from the values of closeness and betweenness, the second term $P(A')$ which is complimentary mentioned earlier can be computed as $(1 - P(A))$. Now the conditional probability $P(B|A)$ is taken as the betweenness over the entire network, similarly, $P(B|A')$ is taken as the degree over the entire network, all these values are given in Table 24.1. In order to see graphically which node has higher value of degree or betweenness, we have also shown the network through the nodes individual size comparison for degree and betweenness in Figs. 24.5 and 24.6 respectively.

There could be many situations of interest for the analysis of this network, let us consider two cases for this network; node 1 and 11 and assume that these are key player nodes and we eliminate them from the network as shown in Figs. 24.7 and 24.8 respectively.

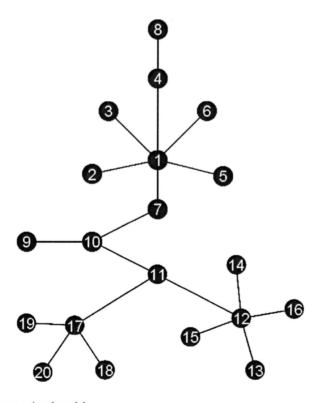

Fig. 24.4 Computational model

Table 24.1 Term values

Node numbers	$P(A)$	$(1 - P(A))$	$P(B|A)$	$P(B|A')$
1	0.409555	0.590445	0.497076	0.315789
2	0.123377	0.876623	0.000000	0.052632
3	0.123377	0.876623	0.000000	0.052632
4	0.158830	0.841170	0.064327	0.105263
5	0.123377	0.876623	0.000000	0.052632
6	0.123377	0.876623	0.000000	0.052632
7	0.404391	0.595609	0.450292	0.105263
8	0.102151	0.897849	0.000000	0.052632
9	0.141791	0.858209	0.000000	0.052632
10	0.459959	0.540041	0.532164	0.157895
11	0.495047	0.504953	0.602339	0.157895
12	0.342303	0.657697	0.362573	0.263158
13	0.123377	0.876623	0.000000	0.052632
14	0.123377	0.876623	0.000000	0.052632
15	0.123377	0.876623	0.000000	0.052632
16	0.123377	0.876623	0.000000	0.052632
17	0.296089	0.703911	0.280702	0.210526
18	0.120253	0.879747	0.000000	0.052632
19	0.120253	0.879747	0.000000	0.052632
20	0.120253	0.879747	0.000000	0.052632

Fig. 24.5 Degree comparison

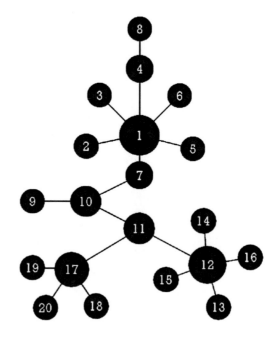

Fig. 24.6 Betweenness comparison

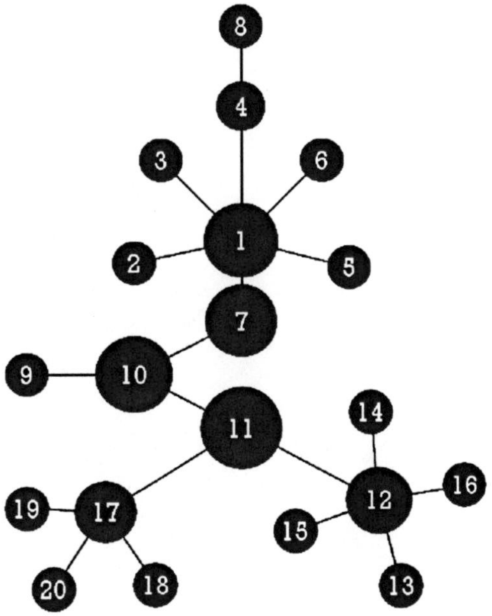

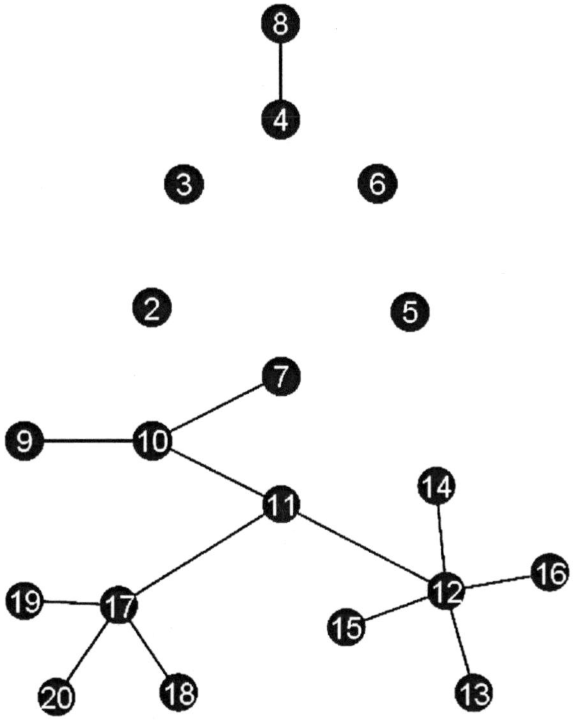

Fig. 24.7 Network structure with node 1 eliminated

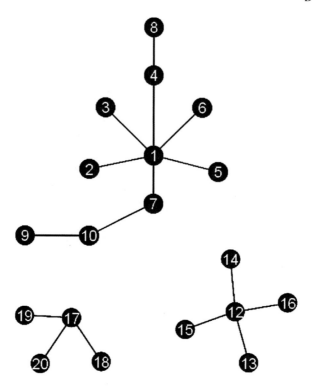

Fig. 24.8 Network structure with node 11 eliminated

Now if we analyze the structure of the network we can see that there are mainly three groups, one around node 1, second around node 12 and third around node 17, when node 1 is eliminated essentially first group is severely damaged but the other two groups are intact, the fragmentation index value is approximately 0.6 and our computed probability is approximately 50%, which is reasonable as it has effected nearly that percentage of the network. However, when we look at the case of node 11, it is quite evident that it has effected all three groups and the network is fragmented into three separate mini components, the fragmentation index is approximately 0.6 and the computed probability is much higher 80% indicating how important node 11 is in the network. The reason of higher probability value is because of our computational model, which is biased towards betweenness/closeness and as the betweenness for this particular node is quite high which caused induction and raising the probability value. Figure 24.9 has shown the probability values for all the nodes and it can be seen that nodes 1, 7, 10 and 11 are the key players in this network having over 50% probability.

The second network we have selected for our results is the kite network from David Krackhardt as shown in Fig. 24.1. In this network node 1 has the largest value in terms of degree and node 8 has the highest value of betweenness. As it is said earlier that it is also a unique network that even if we remove node 8 having largest betweenness the major portion of the network still remains intact and removal of

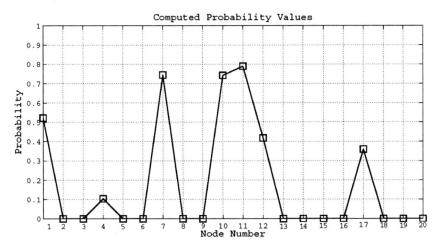

Fig. 24.9 Bayes conditional probability (random network)

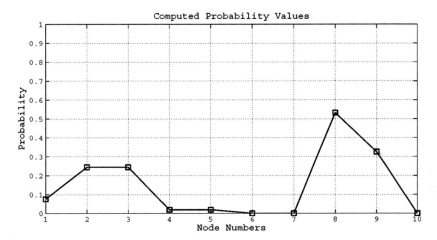

Fig. 24.10 Bayes conditional probability (Kite network)

node 1 cause no significance change and communication is still possible between most nodes but may be with a little extra overhead as the path ways are increased (structures are shown already in Figs. 24.2 and 24.3). The fragmentation index of node 1 if it is eliminated is very very low close to zero indicating that it not the key player and similarly probability computed is also low, less than 10%. The fragmentation index is little higher for the case of node 8 (approximately 0.2) and the computed probability is increased to about 50% , which in contrast to fragmentation index value is quite large the reason is again the same that the computed probability is biased towards betweenness/closeness which is the new evidence for correcting our earlier assumption in the Bayes conditional probability theorem. The conditional probability for each node of this network is shown in Fig. 24.10 for comparison, it

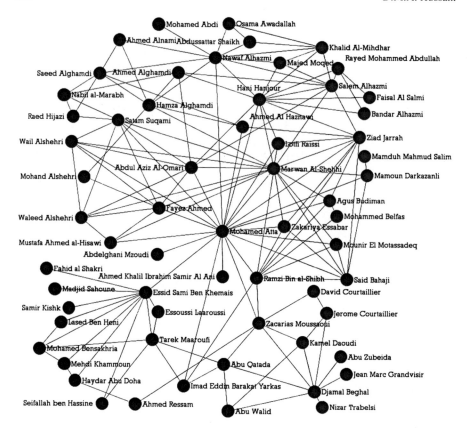

Fig. 24.11 9–11 Hijackers network (Valdis E. Krebs)

shows that node 2, 3 and 9 are the possible candidates for key player position apart from 9. It should be noted that the system has out rightly rejected node 1 to be a key player even though it has the largest value of degree centrality. The last network for the analysis is the 9–11 hijackers network [4] of 62 nodes as shown in Fig. 24.11 much has been said about this network our purpose of considering it here is to bench mark our results as most information about this network is complete. The corresponding node labels are given in Table 24.2 for convenience as we are more familiar with the names of these hijacker in contrast to their position/number in the network.

Table 24.3 shows the computed Bayes terms for the whole network. For this network we can consider many situations to see the important nodes, we all know that how important Mohamed Atta (node 33) was, so we will consider three situations node 20 (Essid Sami Ben Khemais), node 33 (Mohamed Atta) and node 39 (Marwan Al-Shehhi). Node 33 has both high degree and high betweenness measure, in contrast to this node 20 has high degree and reasonable betweenness on the other hand node 39 has low betweenness and very high degree measure. To visualize the effect

Table 24.2 Hijackers name
and node numbers

Node numbers	Names
1	Abu Zubeida
2	Jean-Marc Grandvisir
3	Nizar Trabelsi
4	Abu Walid
5	Djamal Beghal
6	Ahmed Ressam
7	Kamal Daudi
8	Jerome Courtaillier
9	Haydar Abu Doha
10	Mehdi Khammoun
11	Abu Qatata
12	Zacarias Moussaoui
13	David Courtaillier
14	Essoussi Laaroussi
15	Mohamed Bensakhria
16	Tarek Maaroudfi
17	Lased Ben Heni
18	Imad Eddin Barakat Yarkas
19	Seifallah ben Hassine
20	Essid Sami Ben Khemais
21	Fahid al Shakri
22	Mohammed Belfas
23	Adelghani Mzoudi
24	Ramzi Bin al-Shibh
25	Madjid Sahoune
26	Agus Budiman
27	Mounir El Motassadeq
28	Ahmed Khalil Ibrahim Samir
29	Samir Kishk
30	Mustafa Ahmed al-Hisawi
31	Zakariya Essabar
32	Mamduh Mahmud Salim
33	Mohamed Atta
34	Mamoun Darkazanli
35	Said Bahaji
36	Fayez Ahmed
37	Ziad Jarrah
38	Wail Alshehri
39	Marwan Al- Shehhi
40	Waleed Alshehri
41	Abdul Aziz Al Omari
42	Lotfi Raissi
43	Bandar Alhazmi
44	Satam Suqami
45	Ahmed Al Haznawi

(continued)

Table 24.2 (continued)

Node numbers	Names
46	Hani Hanjour
47	Rayed Mohammed Abdullah
48	Mohand Alshehri
49	Salem Alhazmi
50	Ahmed Alghamdi
51	Faisal Al Salmi
52	Majed Moqed
53	Nabil al-Marabh
54	Hamza Alghamdi
55	Raed Hijazi
56	Nawaf Alhazmi
57	Saeed Alghamdi
58	Khalid Al-Mihdhar
59	Ahmed Alnami
60	Osama Awadallah
61	Aduussattar Shaikh
62	Mohamed Abdi

Table 24.3 Term values

Node numbers	$P(A)$	$(1 - P(A))$	$P(B\|A)$	$P(B\|A')$
1	0.125000	0.875000	0.000000	0.016393
2	0.125000	0.875000	0.000000	0.016393
3	0.125000	0.875000	0.000000	0.016393
4	0.132581	0.867419	0.001093	0.049180
5	0.219540	0.780460	0.107559	0.131148
6	0.165877	0.834123	0.007286	0.032787
7	0.162084	0.837916	0.008106	0.065574
8	0.158851	0.841149	0.001639	0.065574
9	0.164033	0.835967	0.007013	0.049180
10	0.154314	0.845686	0.000546	0.049180
11	0.190337	0.809663	0.037978	0.081967
12	0.331109	0.668891	0.226503	0.131148
13	0.153266	0.846734	0.000000	0.032787
14	0.158031	0.841969	0.000000	0.032787
15	0.161826	0.838174	0.004281	0.065574
16	0.187560	0.812440	0.032423	0.098361
17	0.152500	0.847500	0.000000	0.032787
18	0.221774	0.778226	0.034153	0.065574
19	0.158031	0.841969	0.000000	0.032787
20	0.342359	0.657641	0.252095	0.180328
21	0.151741	0.848259	0.000000	0.016393

(continued)

Table 24.3 (continued)

Node numbers	$P(A)$	$(1 - P(A))$	$P(B\|A)$	$P(B\|A')$
22	0.163978	0.836022	0.000000	0.032787
23	0.185976	0.814024	0.000000	0.016393
24	0.246314	0.753686	0.053780	0.163934
25	0.151741	0.848259	0.000000	0.016393
26	0.201023	0.798977	0.011020	0.081967
27	0.195513	0.804487	0.000000	0.065574
28	0.185976	0.814024	0.000000	0.016393
29	0.151741	0.848259	0.000000	0.016393
30	0.196970	0.803030	0.002914	0.065574
31	0.196774	0.803226	0.000000	0.065574
32	0.140553	0.859447	0.000000	0.016393
33	0.582919	0.417081	0.579299	0.360656
34	0.201508	0.798492	0.016940	0.065574
35	0.200599	0.799401	0.002505	0.114754
36	0.217631	0.782369	0.025865	0.131148
37	0.223314	0.776686	0.020055	0.163934
38	0.203444	0.796556	0.002914	0.098361
39	0.276376	0.723624	0.087104	0.295082
40	0.167992	0.832008	0.000820	0.098361
41	0.224958	0.775042	0.023342	0.147541
42	0.209481	0.790519	0.012295	0.081967
43	0.156410	0.843590	0.000000	0.032787
44	0.230922	0.769078	0.049681	0.131148
45	0.207088	0.792912	0.015483	0.065574
46	0.286164	0.713836	0.123798	0.213115
47	0.158441	0.841559	0.000820	0.065574
48	0.156706	0.843294	0.000592	0.032787
49	0.190775	0.809225	0.014080	0.131148
50	0.173888	0.826112	0.006995	0.081967
51	0.156410	0.843590	0.000000	0.032787
52	0.164865	0.835135	0.000000	0.065574
53	0.163696	0.836304	0.002923	0.065574
54	0.192955	0.807045	0.024964	0.114754
55	0.157676	0.842324	0.000920	0.049180
56	0.298492	0.701508	0.154954	0.180328
57	0.172905	0.827095	0.012477	0.098361
58	0.170219	0.829781	0.007104	0.098361
59	0.162234	0.837766	0.000000	0.049180
60	0.155612	0.844388	0.000000	0.049180
61	0.155612	0.844388	0.000000	0.049180
62	0.154040	0.845960	0.000000	0.016393

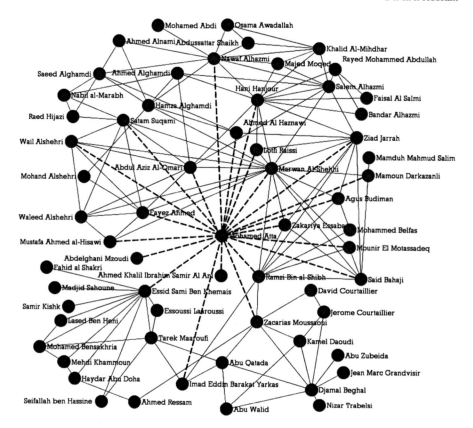

Fig. 24.12 Mohamed Atta eliminated

Figs. 24.12–24.14 shows the structures of the networks once these nodes are eliminated from the network, the removal is manifested through dotted lines on these figures rather than wiping off these connections because removal of one node out of 62 nodes visually does not make a significant impact. It is quite evident from the figures that node 33 and node 20 are the key actor nodes having a probability of 70 and 42% respectively. Whereas the probability value for node 39 is quite low about 10% which is quite right because this node does not have a central role in the network compared with other nodes. Also, there is redundancy because many nodes after its removal are still reachable from via other nodes in the network. The fragmentation indices are approximately 0.36, 0.31 and 0.25 for nodes 33, 20 and 39 respectively. Figure 24.15 shows the computed probability values for the whole network to see potentially possible key players in the network, which is quite in agreement with earlier results for this network.

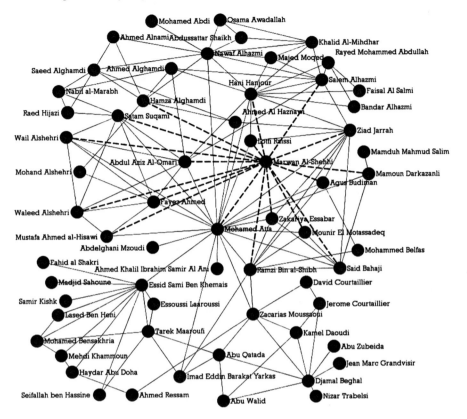

Fig. 24.13 Marwan eliminated

24.6 Conclusion

SNA has been performed by researchers in various contexts for example in Covert/Terrorist organizations to study the behavior of individual nodes. Although, typically SNA has mainly dealt with small quite bonded networks, the relationship between the nodes which are normally people is often very simple for example "friendship". However, there has been consensus among researcher that SNA can be applied to terrorist/covert networks [31,44] although they posses different structures compared with typical hierarchical organizations, they are more like cellular and distributed. The idea of applying typical SNA measures is that we can establish relationship between nodes of these networks and try to identify/isolate the important actors in the network by locating their position through centrality measures.

The study presented here is based on the similar assumption, we have considered that data is perfect that is there is no missing links etc when the sample is made. The results are provided with three different scenarios, two of these networks are well known and the information about them is easily accessible through literature.

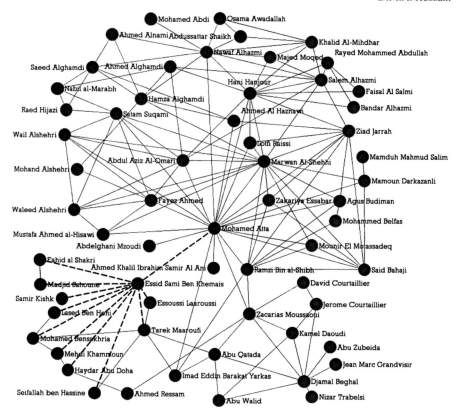

Fig. 24.14 Essid Sami Ben Khemais eliminated

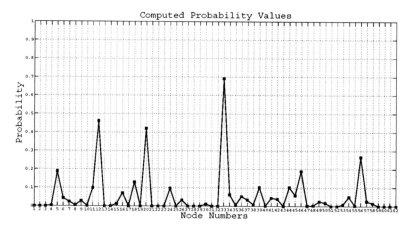

Fig. 24.15 Bayes conditional probability

The first network was intentionally created with some nodes having sort of low degree, betweenness and closeness and some having the inverse of these values. It has been shown through simulations that standard centrality measures can be combined and adopted to be used in Bayes conditional probability theorem. The results obtained through their utilization achieved a robust computational mechanism which can evaluate the likelihood probability of a node to be a key actor or otherwise in the network. The results as mentioned earlier are biased towards nodes having betweenness/closeness, which is a reasonable assumption due to two reasons one is that the most important centrality measure in SNA is betweenness and the second is the new evidence we consider is based on betweenness. Finally, the results are compared with the fragmentation index provided by Borgatti and it shows that the obtained results are consistent with his idea of distance fragmentation measure.

References

1. Borgatti S. P:. Identifying sets of key players in a network. Computational, Mathematical and Organizational Theory 12(1), pages 21–34, 2006.
2. Borgatti S. P:. The key player problem. In R. Breiger, K. Carley, and P. Pattison, (eds.), Dynamic social network modeling and analysis, workshop summary and papers. National Academy of Sciences Press, pages 241–252, 2003.
3. Borgatti S. P. and M. G. Everett:. The centrality of groups and classes. Journal of Mathematical Sociology 23(3), pages 181–201, 1999.
4. Valdis Krebs:. Connecting the dots, tracking two identified terrorists, 2002.
5. Bavelas A:. A mathematical model for group structures. Human Organization 7, pages 16–30, 1948.
6. Shaw M. E:. Group structure and the behaviour of individuals in small groups. Journal of Psychology 38, pages 139–149, 1954.
7. Bavelas A:. Communication patterns in task oriented groups. Journal of the Acoustical Society of America 22, pages 271–282, 1950.
8. Leavitt Harold J:. Some effects of communication patterns on group performance. Journal of Abnormal and Social Psychology 46, pages 38–50, 1951.
9. Smith Sidney L:. Communication pattern and the adaptability of task-oriented groups: an experimental study. Cambridge, MA, Group networks laboratory, research laboratory of electronics, Massachusetts Institute of Technology, 1950.
10. Bavelas A. and D. Barrett:. An expermental approach to organizational communication. Personnel 27, pages 366–371, 1951.
11. Glanzer M. and R. Glaser:. Techniques for the study of team structure and behaviour. Part II: Empirical studies of the effects of structure. Technical report, Pittsburgh, American Institute, 1957.
12. Glanzer M. and R. Glaser:. Techniques for the study of group structure and behaviour. Part II: Empirical studies of the effects of structure in small groups. Psychological Bulletin 58, pages 1–27, 1961.
13. Cohen A. M:. Communication networks in research and training. Personnel Administration 27, pages 18–24, 1964.
14. Shaw M. E:. Communication networks. In L. Berkowitz (ed.), Advances in experimental social psychology, vol. vi, pages 111–147, New York, Academic Press, 1964.
15. Stephenson K. A. and M. Zelen:. Rethinking centrality: methods and examples. Social Networks 11, pages 1–37, 1989.

16. Flament C:. Applications of graph theory to group structure. Englewood Cliffs, NJ, Prentice Hall, 1963.
17. Burgess R. L:. Communication networks and behavioural consequences. Human Relations 22, pages 137–159, 1968.
18. Snadowski A:. Communication network research: an examination of controversies. Human Relations 25, pages 283–306, 1972.
19. Rogers D. L:. Socio-metric analysis of inter-organizational relations: application of theory and measurement. Rural Socioeonv 39, pages 487–503, 1974.
20. Rogers D. L:. Communication networks in organizations. Communication in organizations, pages 108–148, New York, Free Press, 1976.
21. Cohn B. S. and M. Marriott:. Networks and centres of integration in indian civilization. Journal of Social Research I, pages 1–9, 1958.
22. Pitts F. R:. A graph theoretic approach to historical geography. The Professional Geographer 17, pages 15–20, 1965.
23. Latora V. and M. Marchiori:. A measure of centrality based on network efficiency, arxiv.org preprint cond-mat/0402050, 2004.
24. Freeman Linton C:. A set of measures of centrality based on betweenness. Sociometry 40, pages 35–41, 1971.
25. Freeman Linton C:. Centrality in social networks: conceptual clarification. Social Networks 1, page 215–239, 1979.
26. Anthonisse J. M:. The rush in a graph, University of Amsterdam Mathematical Centre, Amsterdam, 1971.
27. Nieminen J:. On centrality in a graph. Scandinavian Journal of Psychology 15, pages 322–336, 1974.
28. Scott J:. Social networks analysis, 2nd edition, London, Sage Publications, 2003.
29. Sabidussi G:. The centrality index of a graph. Psychometrika 31, pages 581–603, 1966.
30. Shaw M. J., C. Subramaniam, G. W. Tan and M. E. Welge:. Knowledge management and data mining for marketing. Decision Support Systems 31(1), pages 127–137, 2001.
31. Carley K. M., J.-S. Lee and D. Krackhardt:. Destabilizing networks, Dept. of Social and Decision Sciences, Carnegie Mellon University, Pittsburgh, PA 15143, November 2001.
32. Akbar Hussain D. M:. Destabilization of terrorist networks through argument driven hypothesis model. Journal of Software 2(6), pages 22–29, 2007.
33. Akbar Hussain D. M. and D. Ortiz-Arroy:. Locating key actors in social networks using bayes posterior probability framework, lecture notes in computer science. In Intelligence and Security Informatics, vol. 5376/2008.
34. Ortiz-Arroy D. and D. M. Akbar Hussain:. An information theory approach to identify sets of key players. In Intelligence and Security Informatics, vol. 5376/2008.
35. Adibi J. and J. Shetty:. Discovering important nodes through graph entropy the case of enron email database. In Linkkdd 2005: Proceedings of the 3rd international workshop on link discovery, pages 74–81, ACM, New York, 2005.
36. Freeman L. C., S. P. Borgatti and D. R. White:. Centrality in valued graphs, a measure of betweenness based on network flow. Social Networks 13, pages 141–154, 1991.
37. Newman M. E. J:. A measure of betweenness centrality based on random walks, cond-mat/0309045, 2003.
38. Beauchamp M. A:. An improved index of centrality. Behavioral Science 10, pages 161–163, 1965.
39. Oliver C. Ibe:. Fundamentals of applied probability and random processes, Elsevier Academics Press, ISBN 0-12-088508-5, 2005.
40. Montgomery D. C. and G. C. Runger:. Applied statistics abd probability for engineers, 4th edition, ISBN 978-0-471-74589-1, Wiley, 2006.
41. Koskinen J. H. and T. A. B. Snijders:. Bayesian inference for dynamic social network data. Journal of Statistical Planning and Inference 137, pages 3930–3938, 2007.

42. Siddarth K., H. Daning and C. Hsinchum:. Dynamic social network analysis of a dark network: identifying significant facilitators. In Proceedings of IEEE international conference on intelligence and security informatics, ISI 2007, New Brunswick, NJ, USA, May 23–24, 2007.
43. C. J. Rhodes and E. M. J. Keefe:. Social network topology: a bayesian approach. Journal of the Operational Research Society 58, pages 1605–1611, 2007.
44. Sparrow M.:. The application of netwrok analysis to criminal intelligence: an assessment of the prospects. Social Networks 13, pages 251–274, 1991.

Chapter 25
Optimizing Targeting of Intrusion Detection Systems in Social Networks

Rami Puzis, Meytal Tubi, and Yuval Elovici

25.1 Introduction

Internet users communicate with each other in various ways: by Emails, instant messaging, social networking, accessing Web sites, etc. In the course of communicating, users may unintentionally copy files contaminated with computer viruses and worms [1, 2] to their computers and spread them to other users [3]. (Hereafter we will use the term "threats", rather than computer viruses and computer worms). The Internet is the chief source of these threats [4].

The main means of combating these threats are intrusion detection systems (IDS) [5] that filter Internet traffic according to predefined attack signatures or source address blacklists. Both approaches are commonly implemented in software and hardware security solutions. Signatures of existing threats are obtained by careful study in antivirus laboratories. Detection of new threats must be performed rapidly in an automatic manner, in order to reduce the widow of opportunity that the new threats can exploit for propagation. To automate the process of detecting new threats, IDSs produce blacklists and signatures of potential attacks/threats using honey-pots [6] that are used to trap the threats or anomaly detection techniques [7] that are used to monitor the behavior of vulnerable systems and alert when a system is suspected to be compromised by a threat.

Weaver et al. [1] state that an effective IDS should be widely distributed across the network. In this study we assume that such an IDS is available. We also assume that this system is capable of detecting new threats, generating signatures, and cleaning Internet traffic. Examples of systems that detect malicious activity, based on the coordinated efforts of many detection units, can be found in [8].

Since it is not realistic to inspect the traffic generated by all Internet users, incoming and outgoing traffic can be inspected by IDSs deployed on a range of Internet service providers (ISPs). In [9] for example, it is proposed that only the traffic of

R. Puzis (✉)
Department of Information Systems Engineering and Deutsche Telekom Laboratories,
Ben-Gurion University of the Negev, Beersheba, Israel
e-mail: faramir.p@gmail.com

B. Furht (ed.), *Handbook of Social Network Technologies and Applications*,
DOI 10.1007/978-1-4419-7142-5_25, © Springer Science+Business Media, LLC 2010

users who have recently obtained an IP address should be inspected and cleaned. Theoretic models of epidemic propagation suggest immunizing the most significant users in order to slow down the threat propagation in the entire network [10].

In this paper we study a framework aimed at reducing the spread of threats between users belonging to a social network [11]. The framework comprises four parts. In the first part, we build a social network by analyzing the communication between users. In the second part, we identify a group of users that have the highest influence on the communication between users who belong to the social network. In the third part, we analyze the threat propagation in the social network assuming that IDS is monitoring the traffic of the central group of users. Various deployments are examined to determine the optimal deployment size and method. In the fourth part we demonstrate how ISPs can deploy the IDS to inspect and clean the traffic of users found in the third part.

The rest of the paper is structured as follows. In Sect. 25.2 we present the work related to this study. In Sect. 25.3 we present the new framework. In Sect. 25.4 we present the framework evaluation. In sect. 25.5 we conclude the paper with a summary and suggestions for future work.

25.2 Background

25.2.1 Epidemic Propagation in Social Networks

The propagation of Email viruses is very similar to the propagation of their biological counterparts. Common models of epidemic propagation categorize the population into three states: susceptible (S) individuals do not have the disease in question but can catch it if exposed to someone who does; infective (I) individuals have the disease and can pass it on; and removed (R) individuals have been disabled by the disease and cannot be infected or infect others.

Different epidemic propagation models define different transitions between the states. The SIR model assumes that any susceptible individual has a probability β of catching the disease in a unit of time from any infective entity. Infected entities are removed with a probability γ in a unit of time [12]. If we consider SIS as the basis for the model, we have a model of endemic disease in which carriers that are cured become susceptible. Since carriers can be infected many times, it is possible that the disease will persist indefinitely, circulating around the population and will never die out [13]. In this paper we use a SI model of epidemic propagation in which all individuals in the initially susceptible population eventually become infected. This model was used to simulate propagation of threats transferred through Email networks [14].

General epidemic models assume that the population is fully mixed. As a result the fractions s, i, and r of entities in the states S, I, and R can be expressed analytically by differential equations. In reality, diseases can only spread between entities that have actual contact. The nature of the contacts influences the disease propagation [13].

Email threats can propagate by sending themselves to randomly generated Email addresses. To increase the amount of successful infections, some threats (such as ILoveYou, Kletz, etc.) exploit address-books or Emails kept on the hosting computer. A threat can also search for stored Emails in order to retrieve addresses of potential victims. Sent and received Emails form a social network when two users are connected if an Email was sent from one to another or vice versa. This network can be extracted from logs of Email servers. Researchers usually study epidemic propagation in networks using stochastic simulations. In this study we employ stochastic simulations and "what if" scenario analysis based on the real Email logs of a community of 11,000-users.

Most epidemic models define $\lambda = \beta/\gamma$ to be the effective spreading rate of the infection. The epidemic threshold is a value λc such that for any $\lambda > \lambda c$ the infection is constantly spreading in the population until it reaches an equilibrium state. If $\lambda < \lambda c$, the infection dies out exponentially fast.

Recent work has highlighted the effect of a network's degree distribution on the behavior of epidemic spread. Particular attention was paid in these studies to scale-free networks, in which the probability that a vertex has degree k decays as $k^{-\alpha}$ for some constant α [15, 16]. The epidemic threshold is equal to zero in scale free networks meaning that any infection can spread in such a network regardless of its effective spreading rate [17, 18]. In order to slow down the epidemic propagation in networks various immunization strategies were proposed [10, 19, 20]. Infections spreading over scale-free networks are known to be highly resilient to random immunization strategies. However, it was shown that targeted immunization (of highly connected vertices, for example) can be very effective.

The degree distribution of networks based on sent and received Emails is continuous but does not follow a power law [3]. Tyler et al. [21] found that 80% of vertices in such networks must be protected in order to prevent epidemics, even if targeted vaccination is used.

25.2.2   Centrality Indexes

In order to analyze and understand the roles played by vertices in complex networks, many network-analytic studies in the last years have relied on the evaluation of centrality. These measures are used to rank the prominence of individual vertices according to their position in the network [22, 23]. Below we describe the primary types of centrality indexes of individual vertices and of groups of vertices.

25.2.2.1   Degree Centrality

Node degree [24] is the number of directed connections of that node. As a case in point, vertex 4 in Fig. 25.1 has the maximal number of connections as shown

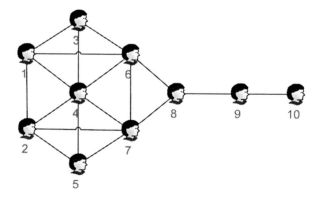

Fig. 25.1 Example of a small network

Table 25.1 The most central vertices in Fig. 25.1

Vertex	Degree	Closeness	Betweenness
#4	**6**	1/15	0.263
#6 or #7	5	**1/14**	0.357
#8	3	1/15	**0.470**

Table 25.2 The most central pairs in Fig. 25.1

Group of vertices	Group degree	Group closeness	Group betweenness
#4 and #9	**8(10)**	**1/8**	0.573
#6 and #7	6(8)	1/11	**0.660**

in Table 25.1. Targeted immunization strategies that prefer nodes with high Degree Centrality (DC) have been proposed in order to control epidemic propagation in a variety of networks [19, 20].

25.2.2.2 Group Degree Centrality

Group Degree Centrality (GDC) is defined as the number of non-group nodes adjacent to group members [25]. In this study we treat the degree of a group C as the size of its local neighborhood. The local neighborhood includes all vertices that are located not more than one hop away from a group member. Group degree is presented in Table 25.2 as two numbers: the number inside brackets is the size of the local neighborhood; the number outside the brackets is the number of non-group nodes adjacent to a group member. For example, in Fig. 25.1 the local neighborhood of the group {6, 7} includes eight nodes, while the local neighborhood of the group {4, 9} is the whole graph as shown in Table 25.2. Deployment of packet filters based on GDC was proposed in [26] in order to counter spoofed DDoS attacks and to contain Internet worms. The GD of a given group can be computed in time proportional to the total number of links emanating from the group members.

25.2.2.3 Closeness Centrality

Closeness Centrality (CC) [24] of a vertex is the sum of geodesic distances to all other vertices in the graph. In fact, this produces an inverse measure of closeness where small numbers indicate that the vertex is close to everyone all other vertices. In order to maintain consistency with other centralities, we compute closeness by taking the reciprocal summation of distances. For example, in Fig. 25.1, nodes 6 and 7 have the highest closeness in the network as shown in Table 25.1. Following is a sample calculation of closeness (6) where the distances of 6 from the nodes $\{1,2,\ldots,10\}$ are aggregated (left to right):

$$Closeness(6) = 1/(1 + 2 + 1 + 1 + 2 + 0 + 1 + 1 + 2 + 3) = 1/14.$$

A vertex with high CC will possess a low average time until it witnesses a new network flow [27]. Consider the following gossip example. Some nodes "tell" some secrets to all their neighbors. The neighbors in turn continue spreading the secrets to their neighbors and so on. The average time until a vertex in the network will "hear" the secrets decreases with the closeness of the vertex. IDS targeting strategies based on a higher degree of closeness are expected to improve the response time of the system.

25.2.2.4 Group Closeness Centrality

Group Closeness Centrality (GCC) of a group C has several alternative definitions [25]. In this study, we interpret GCC as a reciprocal sum of geodesic distances from all communicating nodes in the graph to the closest group member:

$$Closeness(C) = \frac{1}{\sum_{v \in V} \min_{m \in C}[dist(v, m)]}$$

The most central groups are groups with the highest GCC. All vertices in Fig. 25.1 are adjacent to either 4 or 9. Therefore, $\{4, 9\}$ is the group of two nodes with maximal closeness as shown in Table 25.2. After computing distances between each pair of nodes (using Dijkstra or Bellman–Ford algorithms [28]) GCC of a given group can be computed in $O(kn)$ time where k is the size of the group and n is the size of the network.

25.2.2.5 Betweenness Centrality

Another important centrality measure is the Shortest Path Betweenness Centrality. Betweenness Centrality (BC) measures the extent to which a vertex has control over information flowing between other vertices [25, 29]. The BC of a vertex is defined as the total fraction of shortest paths between all pairs of vertices in a network in which the vertex takes part. High BC scores indicate that the ratio of the shortest paths on which a vertex lies is high [30]. The shortest path between two vertices can be determined by an algorithm, such as Dijkstra's algorithm or Breadth-First Search (BFS). These algorithms devise paths in which the distance between two end vertices is minimal [30, 31].

For a given graph G = (V, E), let $\sigma_{s,t}$ be the number of shortest paths between s and t and let $\sigma_{s,t}(\upsilon)$ be the number of shortest paths between s and t that traverse υ. The BC of vertex υ is:

$$BC(\upsilon) = \sum_{s,t \in V | s \neq \upsilon \neq t} \left(\frac{\sigma_{s,t}(\upsilon)}{\sigma_{s,t}} \right)$$

25.2.2.6 Group Betweenness Centrality

The Betweenness Centrality of individual vertices can be naturally extended to groups of vertices. Let $C \subseteq V$ be a group of vertices. Group Betweenness Centrality (GBC) of C stands for the total fraction of shortest paths between all pairs of vertices that pass through at least one member of the group C [25]. Let $\ddot{\sigma}_{s,t}(C)$ be the number of shortest paths between s and t that traverse at least one member of the group C. GBC(C) is defined as follows:

$$GBC(C) = \sum_{s,t \in V | s \neq t} \left(\frac{\ddot{\sigma}_{s,t}(C)}{\sigma_{s,t}} \right)$$

A fast algorithm for computation of GBC was recently developed [32]. Using this algorithm and standard methods of combinatorial optimizations (such as simulated annealing, genetic algorithms, etc.) a central group of vertices can be found. In order to find the group of users that should be monitored, we use a greedy algorithm for GBC maximization. This algorithm incrementally constructs a group by adding vertices with the highest contribution to the GBC of the current group.

25.2.2.7 Random Walk Betweenness Centrality

Random Walk Betweenness-Centrality (RWBC), proposed by Newman [33], accounts for paths that are not necessarily short. In RWBC, shorter paths tend to considered more than longer ones. RWBC assumes that routes may contain cycles, which is not the case in most communication networks. However RWBC matches some rumor-spreading models. It is best suited for estimating the potential control a node may have over the communication flows in gossip networks where messages randomly wander through the network until they reach their intended target. To the best of our knowledge no group variant of RWBC has been suggested in the literature.

25.3   Experimental Setup

In this section we describe the experiment we designed in order to investigate
deployment strategies of a system for detecting and eliminating threats while
analyzing only part of the Email traffic. The study is composed of three parts. In
the first part, we derive several social networks by analyzing Email logs of a closed
community. In the second part, we pinpoint the optimal places to intercept the Email
traffic based on the network's topology. We locate groups of users with the most
influence on the network communication using several different centrality measures.
In the third part, we analyze the threat propagation in the social network for various
deployments. In this part we use a network simulation tool developed for this purpose (see Fig. 25.2) and derive several metrics of protection performance, such as,
the size of the infected population, the time when the threat is detected for the first
time, etc. The independent variables in this study are summarized in Table 25.3.

25.3.1   Extracting the Social Network

In the first part of our study, the social network is extracted from logs of Email
servers. Email Logs contain the addresses of senders and recipients of all outgoing

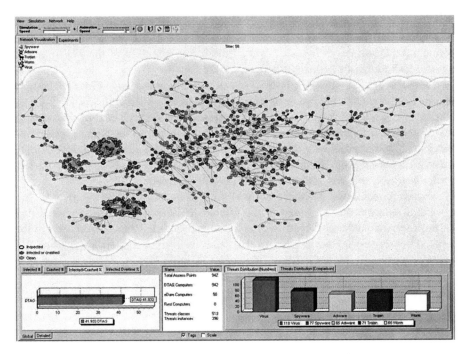

Fig. 25.2   A screenshot of the simulation tool. In the main frame, the social network is visualized.
At the *bottom* statistical information is presented

Table 25.3 Independent variables

Variable	Values
Network	Four networks extracted from Email logs.
IDS targeting strategy	DC, GDC, CC, GCC, BC, GBC, RWBC
IDS target group size	1,...,20
IDS false negative rate	0.1
Propagation rate	0.001
Simulation length	300 time units

Table 25.4 Statistical properties of the derived networks

	Snapshot 1	Snapshot 2	Snapshot 3	Snapshot 4
Number of vertices	1,035	1,104	970	1,130
Mean degree	2.08	2.39	2.54	2.20
Total number of edges	1,079	1,323	1,232	1,247

and incoming Emails. We create the social network based on Email addresses appearing in these logs. Each vertex in the graph represents a user (Email address) and each edge represents a social connection between the users (an Email sent from one user to another or vice versa).

The social network was constructed from 1 week's log of Email traffic at Ben-Gurion University. Every Email sent from one university member to another was recorded. Every record in the log contained five fields. The first field specified the exact date and time when the Email message was sent. Email addresses of senders and receivers were hashed to preserve the user's privacy. The log also contained the volume in bytes of every Email. The last field of the log indicated whether the addressee successfully received the Email.

There are several ways to construct social networks from logs. First, we assume that threats propagate via Email by sending themselves as attachments. In this case records of Emails of a volume lower than a certain threshold can be removed. Emails that did not reach their destination were also not interesting for threat propagation analysis. Since aggressive worms can propagate very fast even through the Email network, assuming that the users are active enough during the propagation period, we took subsets of users active in certain periods of time.

Next we constructed the social network formed by the relevant log records. Every Email address that appeared in the filtered log was mapped to a vertex. Two vertices were connected if there was at least one recorded Email from one to the other. The derived networks used in this study were unweighted and undirected. Other properties of the networks are described in Table 25.4.

25.3.2 Pinpointing Central Users

In the second part of our study the suggested users for intercepting threats in the social networks were found. To pinpoint central groups of users, we analyzed the graphs derived in the previous subsection. We located the group of users to be targeted by the IDS using the centrality measures described in Sect. 25.2.2. We numerically compared the effectiveness of targeting strategies based on the centrality of individual vertices to methods based on group centrality. For the former strategies we chose several vertices having the highest centrality. For the latter strategies we chose a set of vertices that were the most central as a group (i.e., having the highest group centrality).

It can be proven by straightforward reduction from the vertex cover problem [34] that finding a group of vertices of a given size with maximal Group Degree, Group Betweenness, or Group Closeness is NP-hard. Every set of vertices that has one of the above optima also has a member vertex attached to every edge in a graph and vice versa. In light of this fact we utilized algorithms that would be sufficiently fast for this study.

In this study we used a greedy optimization of group centralities. First we considered all users as potential targets of the IDS. Then, in order to construct a target group of k members we performed k iterations, each time choosing the next vertex having maximal absolute contribution to the centrality of the partial group as described by the following expression:

$$\text{maxarg}_{v \in V} \left[C(M \cup \{v\}) - C(M) \right]$$

where C represents a group centrality and M is the partial group.

In this study we chose to target the communications of one to twenty users in each one of the above Email networks. In total, the seven targeting strategies that correspond to seven centrality measures described in Sect. 25.2.3 resulted in 560 groups of users. In the next section we describe the simulation process for evaluating the role of these groups in detecting and slowing down propagation of Email threats.

25.3.3 Simulation

In the third part of the study, we analyzed the threat propagation in the presence of IDSs. In order to simulate threat propagation, we stochastically simulated epidemic propagation in social networks and the operation of IDSs targeted to groups of users as identified by the various targeting strategies.

In our simulation we used the SI model of epidemic disease propagation. Accordingly, a computer could be in one of the following states: a) Susceptible – a computer can become infected with a threat or b) Infective – a computer is infected with a threat and can infect others. In the beginning of each simulation one percent of random computers were in an infective state while other computers were susceptible.

Threats can be transferred unintentionally from one user to another as scripts or infected attachments accompanying regular communication of the users. For example, a Word document file infected with VBScript virus can be sent as a legitimate attachment. We assumed that each infected computer had a constant probability of infecting each one of its neighbors in each time unit. In current study this probability was set to 0.01%.

The simulated IDS was defined as being capable of detecting new threats and removing known threats. Once a threat was detected, a unique signature was generated that identified this class of threats. Then, threat instances of this class that were captured by the IDS were removed from the Email traffic. We assumed that the IDS could detect a threat and generate a signature on the first encounter. This was a reasonable assumption since Email delivery is hardly a real-time process and there are small delays that result from processing a portion of Email traffic. We also assumed that 10% of threats would evade IDS filtering mechanisms using techniques such as polymorphism. Email accounts targeted by IDS were chosen according to the ordered lists that were generated using the greedy centrality maximization described in the previous subsection. Only the Email traffic of the targeted accounts was inspected and cleaned. Note that only incoming and outgoing traffic could be inspected and filtered since IDSs do not have the capability for cleaning a user's computer once it is infected.

25.4 Experiment Results

In this section we discuss the results of simulating threat propagation through the Email networks under investigation. Every execution of the simulation was repeated 10 times and lasted 300 time units allowing the threats to propagate to all Email accounts in the network. The output of the simulation included: the average contamination level of the network; the time it took to detect a new threat; the half-life of the epidemic; and the actual effectiveness of the IDS. A complete list of the measurements taken during the simulation can be found in Table 25.5.

25.4.1 Threat Prevalence

The following figures describe the threat propagation in the Email networks from several perspectives. The focus is on the differences between IDS targeting strategies. In Fig. 25.3 we can see that when IDS has no effect on the propagation the infected population growth looks as if it were similar to a sigmoid. There is a first stage of exponential growth that becomes a linear growth when larger portions of the network are infected and the propagation slows down as it reaches the most distant regions of the network. The first stage of exponential growth is very short in our graphs since the epidemic begins with 1% of initially infected computers. This (quite large) portion of initially infected computers serves two goals. First, it makes our assumptions on threat detection more realistic since many suggested threat detection mechanisms expect a reasonable prevalence of the threat in the network.

Table 25.5 Dependent variables

Variable	Description
Threat prevalence	The number of Email accounts infected by a threat divided by the total number of Email accounts
Epidemic half-life	The number of time units that the simulation was executed before 50% of the Email accounts were infected
Detection time	The number of time units the simulation was executed before the threat was first spotted by IDS
Fraction of intercepted threats	The number of threats that were filtered out by IDS divided by the total number of threats sent via email
IDS effectiveness	The number of infected computers without IDS filtering out threats minus the number of infected computers with IDS divided by the number of infected computers without IDS. Let $|I_k|$ be the number of computers infected when IDS is targeting k Email accounts $$\text{IDS effectiveness} = \frac{|I_0| - |I_k|}{|I_0|}$$

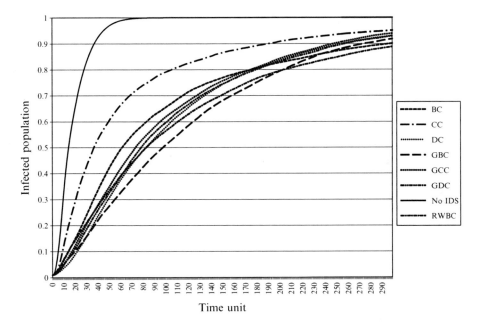

Fig. 25.3 The fraction of infected computers over time as IDS filters the Emails of 15 accounts chosen using various targeting strategies

Second, reasonable initial prevalence of the threat in the network reduces variability in the threat propagation during later stages and makes the simulation results less noisy.

In Fig. 25.3 we can see how the threat propagation changes when IDS targets approximately 1.5% of the Email accounts. Figure 25.4 presents the average threat prevalence as a function of the number of Email accounts targeted by the IDS (left)

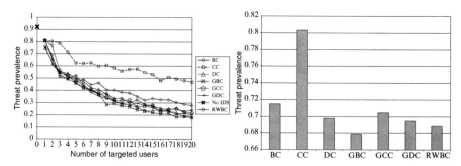

Fig. 25.4 The average fraction of infected computers: *left* – as the function of the target group size and *right* – average over all target group sizes

and the summary of threat prevalence (right) for various targeting strategies. We can clearly see from the plots that when IDS targets Email accounts with the highest individual closeness, the threat prevalence is the highest. The reason for such poor performance is that nodes with the highest closeness are positioned close to each other in what is presumed to be the center of the network. We can also see that strategies based on group centrality perform better than strategies based on centrality of individual nodes with GBC resulting in the lowest threat prevalence on average. Among strategies based on the centrality of individual nodes, the RWBC has the best performance. Unfortunately, to the best of our knowledge no group variant of random walk betweenness has been suggested so far in the literature.

25.4.2 Epidemic Half-Life

It is not apparent from Fig. 25.3 but the decay in the number of computers not affected by the propagating threat is very close to exponential. Figure 25.5 presents the log-plot of the fraction of the healthy population as a function of time. A straight line in this plot represents an exponentially decaying function. This allows us to regard the half-life time of the healthy population as a characteristic of the threat propagation.

Half-life time is the time it takes for a population to decrease by half. When the population of healthy computers decays exponentially, the half-life time is constant during the whole threat propagation process. We will refer to this measure as epidemic half-life. Figure 25.6 presents the epidemic half-life as a function of the number of targeted Email accounts (left) and the summary of epidemic half-life (right) for various targeting strategies. As in Fig. 25.4, we see that the GBC targeting strategy has the best performance (the slowest propagation); RWBC is the second best; and the strategy based on closeness of individual nodes has the poorest performance. In contrast to the threat prevalence, epidemic half-life dependence on the number of targeted Email accounts is roughly linear.

Fig. 25.5 Exponentially
decaying fraction of healthy
population over time without
IDS protection

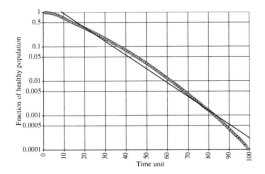

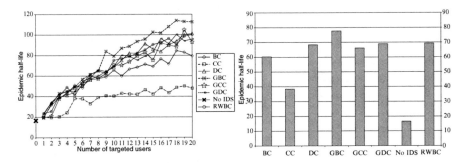

Fig. 25.6 Epidemic half-life for various IDS targeting strategies: *left* – as a function of the target group size and *right* – average over all target group sizes

25.4.3   Detection Time

In this subsection we analyze the simulation results from the point of view of the average threat detection time. Surprisingly, targeting strategies based on closeness (CC and GCC) perform poorly also from this perspective. We would expect that the nodes that are the closest to all other nodes in the network would be attacked very early during the threat propagation. However, as can be seen from Fig. 25.7, the nodes with the highest degree are attacked first.

25.4.4   Intercepted Threats

Next we discuss the ability of the IDS to intercept threats propagating through the Email network. As the graph on left side of Fig. 25.8 depicts, half of the attacks can be prevented by inspecting communications of twelve to fifteen Email accounts. However, these Email accounts should be chosen using targeting strategies based on DC, GBC, GCC, or GDC. In contrast to previous metrics, targeting nodes with the highest degree produces the best results. It is surprising that targeting strate-

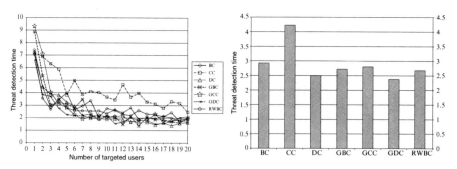

Fig. 25.7 Detection time for various IDS targeting strategies: *left* – as a function of the target group size and *right* – average over all target group sizes

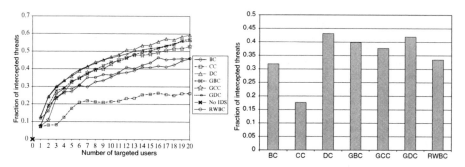

Fig. 25.8 Fraction of intercepted threats as a function of the target group size (*left*) and average over all target group sizes (*right*) for various IDS targeting strategies

gies based on BC and RWBC perform poorly in terms of threat interception. BC was originally suggested as an estimate of the control that a node may have over data flows in communication networks with shortest path routing. RWBC relaxes the shortest-path constraint and is applicable to gossip processes where data flows randomly through the network. Nevertheless, both strategies fail to select Email accounts through which most threats are "passing". We can see in Fig. 25.8 (right side) that the strategy based on the group variant of betweenness (GBC) performs well in contrast to betweenness of individual nodes (BC). However, both strategies based on DC and GDC outperform it.

The reason for such behavior lies in the simulation model employed in this study. We assumed that each infected computer has a constant probability of infecting each one of its neighbors in each time unit. Email accounts selected using DC and GDC have the maximal number of neighbors and are, therefore, being attacked rapidly throughout the simulation. Hence, there is a large number of threats intercepted while inspecting all communications of these Email accounts.

The number of threats intercepted by IDS can be regarded as the operating cost of network protection. Figure 25.9 presents the fraction of healthy population (benefit)

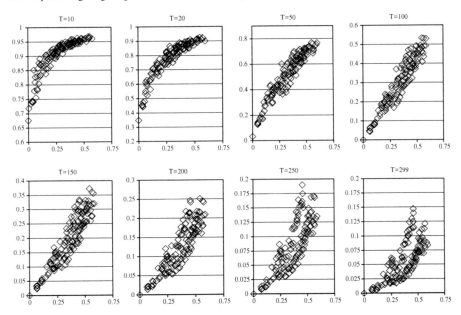

Fig. 25.9 Fraction of infected population (y-axis) as the function of the fraction of intercepted threats (x-axis) during various stages of the epidemic

vs. the fraction of intercepted threats (cost). We can see from this figure that during the initial stages of the simulation, a small increase in the fraction of intercepted threats results in a drastic increase in the fraction of healthy population. However, during later stages of the threat propagation, a drastic increase in the fraction of intercepted threats is required to maintain the healthy population. We can conclude that the fraction of intercepted threats alone does not reflect the effectiveness of the IDS targeting strategy.

25.4.5   IDS Effectiveness

In this subsection we use the definition of protection effectiveness suggested in [35]. Effectiveness of any protection (in our case assumed to be IDS) can be defined as the relative decrease in the damage caused to the system. Let $|I_k|$ be the number of computers infected when IDS is targeting k Email accounts. The IDS effectiveness can be defined as the number of infected computers when no IDS filters out threats,

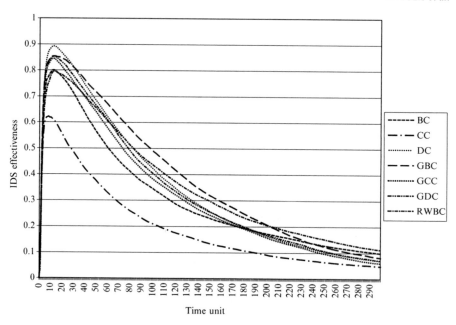

Fig. 25.10 IDS effectiveness over time when IDS targets 15 Email accounts using various strategies

minus the number of infected computers when IDS is active, divided by the number of infected computers without IDS:

$$\text{IDS effectiveness} = \frac{|I_0| - |I_k|}{|I_0|}$$

Figure 25.10 presents the IDS effectiveness over time. We can see that the IDS is mostly effective during time units 10–20 when the threat propagation rate (without IDS) is maximal (see Fig. 25.3). Puzis et al. show in [35] that the peak effectiveness of protection, such as IDS, does not depend on the epidemic model employed during the simulation. Therefore, peak IDS effectiveness can be regarded as characteristic of the IDS derived from its filtering capabilities and targeted Email accounts but not from the threat propagation properties. In Fig. 25.11 (right) we can see where a phase transition in peak IDS effectiveness occurs when three Email accounts are being targeted. Similar behavior can be seen also in plots of the detection time (Fig. 25.7, left). This behavior is less apparent but also noticeable in the plots of threat prevalence (Fig. 25.4, left).

Average IDS effectiveness (Fig. 25.11, left) is presented here as a reference. It cannot be regarded as the property of the IDS and its targeting mechanism since, for example, it highly depends on the duration of the simulation. The IDS simulated in this study is not perfect. Therefore, the whole network is eventually infected.

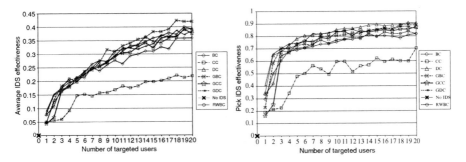

Fig. 25.11 Average (*left*) and peak (*right*) IDS effectiveness as a function of the target group size

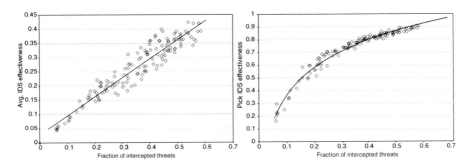

Fig. 25.12 Average (*left*) and peak (*right*) IDS effectiveness vs. fraction of intercepted threats

Continuing the simulation beyond the point where most of the network is infected will diminish the effect that slowing down the threat propagation may have on the average IDS effectiveness. In contrast, peak IDS effectiveness does not depend on the simulation duration as long as the initial stage of the threat propagation is over.

Figure 25.12 presents the effectiveness of IDS as the function of the fraction of intercepted threats. The dependence of average IDS effectiveness on the fraction of intercepted threats is linear while dependence of the peak IDS effectiveness is logarithmic. From the cost-benefit point of view, this means that the effectiveness of IDS over time is proportional to investments in IDS capabilities. However, small investments in IDS capabilities have a larger marginal effect on the IDS effectiveness during the most critical stages of threat propagation.

Finally, Fig. 25.13 presents the IDS effectiveness and fraction of intercepted threats. Targeting strategy based on BC results in the highest peak IDS effectiveness and the highest number of intercepted threats. Targeting strategy based on GBC results in the highest average IDS effectiveness.

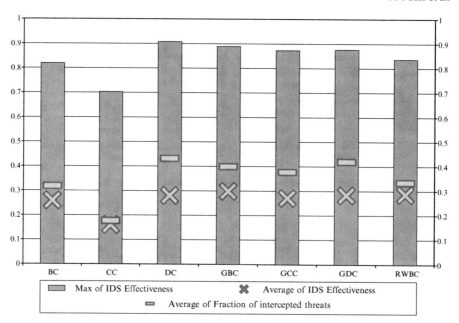

Fig. 25.13 IDS effectiveness and fraction of intercepted threats for various targeting strategies

25.5 Summary and Conclusions

In this paper we have shown that cleaning the traffic of central users in the social network can slow down or even prevent the propagation of threats and that intercepting the traffic of these users leads to faster detection time of new threats. We presented a study in which various strategies were investigated for selecting users whose traffic should be intercepted. To evaluate the user targeting strategies, we utilized stochastic simulation of epidemic propagation and derived several different metrics that describe the propagation and the effect that protection (such as IDS) may have on this propagation. For example, in the investigated Email networks, the decay in the number of computers unaffected by the propagating threat is very close to exponential. This allowed us to regard epidemic half-life as a characteristic of the threat propagation speed.

We showed that using IDS to inspect communications of selected Email accounts decreases the fraction of infected computers in the network and increases the half-life time of the healthy population. As the number of targeted Email accounts increases, the effectiveness of the IDS increases and the time required to detect the threat drops. The results showed that, in general, IDS targeting strategies based on group centrality perform better than strategies based on the centrality of individual nodes. GBC results in the lowest threat prevalence on average and the highest epidemic half-life. GDC results in the lowest threat detection times while DC results in the highest number of intercepted threats and the highest IDS effectiveness during the most critical stages of threat propagation.

References

1. N. Weaver, V. Paxson, S. Staniford, R. Cunningham, "A taxonomy of computer worms", In The First ACM Workshop on Rapid Malcode (WORM), 2003.
2. S. Staniford, V. Paxson, N. Weaver, "How to own the internet in your spare time", Proceedings of the 11th USENIX security symposium, 2002.
3. J. Balthrop, S. Forrest, M. E. J. Newman, M. M. Williamson, "Technological networks and the spread of computer viruses", Science 304, 527, 2004.
4. Symantec Internet Security Threat Report, Jan–June 2004.
5. X. Zhang, C. Li, W. Zheng, "Intrusion prevention system design", Proceedings – The fourth international conference on computer and information technology, 386–390, 2004.
6. Y. Tang, S. Chen, "Defending against internet worms. A signature based approach", IEEE INFOCOM, 2005.
7. A. Gupta, R. Sekar, "An approach for detecting self-propagating email using anomaly detection", In Proceedings of the international symposium on recent advances in intrusion detection, Sep 2003.
8. V. Yegneswaran, P. Barford, S. Jha, "Global intrusion detection in the DOMINO overlay system", In Proceedings of NDSS, San Diego, CA, 2004.
9. P. Blackburn, "Quarantining DHCP clients to reduce worm infection risk", http://www.giac.org/certified_professionals/practicals/gsec/3472.php
10. R. Pastor-Satorras, A. Vespignani, "Epidemics and immunization in scale-free networks", http://arxiv.org/abs/cond-mat/0205260, 2002.
11. M. Tubi, R. Puzis, Y. Elovici, "Deployment of DNIDS in social networks", IEEE ISI, 2007.
12. R. Huerta, L. S. Tsimring, "Contact tracing and epidemics control in social networks", Physical Review E, 66, 056115, 2002.
13. M. E. J. Newman, "The structure and function of complex networks", SIAM Review, 45(2), 167–256, 2003.
14. C. C. Zou, D. Towsley, W. Gong, "Email virus propagation modeling and analysis", Technical Report TR-CSE-03–04, University of Massachussets, Amherst, 2004.
15. A. L. Barabasi, R. Albert, H. Jeong, "Scale-free characteristics of random networks: the topology of the world-wide web", Physica A 281, 69–77, 2000.
16. A. L. Barabasi, R. Albert, "Emergence of scaling in random networks", Science 286, 509, 1999.
17. M. E. J. Newman, "The spread of epidemic disease on networks", Physical Review. E, 66, 016128, 2002.
18. R. Pastor-Satorras, A. Vespignani, "Epidemic spreading in scale-free networks", Physical Review Letters, 86(14), 3200–3203, 2001.
19. D. H. Zanette, M. Kuperman, "Effects of immunization in small-world epidemics". Physica A, 309, 445–452, 2002.
20. R. Pastor-Satorras, A. Vespignani, "Immunization of complex networks", Physical Review E, 65, 036104, 2002.
21. J. R. Tyler, D. M. Wilkinson, B. A. Huberman, "Email as spectroscopy: automated discovery of community structure within organizations. Communities and technologies", M. Huysman, E. Wenger, V. Wulf (Eds), pp. 81–95, 2003.
22. J. Scott, "Social network analysis: a handbook", Sage Publications, London, 2000.
23. S. P. Borgatti, M. G. Everett, "A graph-theoretic perspective on centrality", Social Networks, 28(4), 466–484, 2006.
24. L. C. Freeman, "Centrality in social networks conceptual clarification", Social Networks, 1, 215–239, 1979.
25. M. G. Everett, S. P. Borgatti, "The centrality of groups and classes", Mathematical Sociology, 23(3), 181–201, 1999.
26. K. Park, "Scalable protection against ddos and worm attacks. DARPA ATO FTN project AFRL contract F30602–01–2–0530", Purdue University, West LaFayette, 2004.
27. S.P. Borgatti, "Centrality and AIDS", Connections, 18(1), 112–114, 1995.

28. F. Harary, R. Z. Norman, D. Cartwright, "Structural models. An introduction to the theory of directed graphs", John Wiley and Sons, New York, 1965.
29. L.C. Freeman, "A set of measuring centrality based on betweenness", Sociometry 40, 35–41, 1977.
30. M. E. J. Newman, "Scientific collaboration networks. II. Shortest paths, weighted networks, and centrality", Physical Review E, 64, 016132, 2001.
31. U. Brandes, "A faster algorithm for betweenness centrality", Journal of Mathematical Sociology, 25(2), 163–177, 2001.
32. R. Puzis, Y. Elovici, S. Dolev. "Fast algorithm for successive computation of group betweenness centrality", Physical Review E, 76(5), 056709, 2007.
33. M. E. J. Newman, "A measure of betweenness centrality based on random walks", http://arXiv.org/abs/cond-mat/0309045, 2003.
34. R. G. Downey, M. R. Fellows, "Parametrized computational feasibility", Feasible Mathematics, 2, 219–244, 1995.
35. R. Puzis, M. D. Klippel, Y. Elovici, S. Dolev, "Optimization of NIDS placement for protection of intercommunicating critical infrastructures", Springer LNCS, EuroISI, 2008.

Chapter 26
Security Requirements for Social Networks in Web 2.0

Eduardo B. Fernandez, Carolina Marin, and Maria M. Larrondo Petrie

26.1 Introduction

A social network is a structure of individuals or organizations, which are connected by one or more types of interdependency, such as friendship, affinity, common interests or knowledge. Social networks have existed for a long time in a looser way than now. For example, in all of my research career I have communicated with other researchers working on similar areas. This exchange may include working on a project together, writing a paper, or just exchanging information or ideas. These networks were unstructured, people would come and go, and there was no control of who was in and what they could say. We all knew each other and the exchange was typically only technical. The Internet facilitated these exchanges enormously, regular mail was too slow to write papers in collaboration, for example. The early Internet, now referred to as Web 1.0, significantly lowered the cost of accessing or publishing content to a global audience, as well as keeping in contact with friends and collaborators. Anyone with a web site could publish papers, post product information, or display whatever they wanted. Anyone with an Internet connection could follow links to access content. The content of websites was generally controlled by the individual, company or organization that created it. Software tools were developed for contributing content and standards were developed for information and data exchange. E-mail and instant messaging tools made possible keeping in touch with existing contacts, and forum and chat-room spaces made possible to discover and temporarily interact with new people or groups. In that stage the Internet was mostly a repository of shared information with limited interaction [1].

Web 2.0 introduced some important changes, it allows anyone with a web connection to write as well as read. Anyone can have now its own web site and keep in contact with friends and collaborators in a simple and inexpensive way. Search engines, content-tagging by users, and user-generated content have made it much

E.B. Fernandez (✉)
Department of Electrical and Computer Engineering and Computer Science, Florida Atlantic University, Boca Raton, FL 33431, USA
e-mail: ed@cse.fau.edu

B. Furht (ed.), *Handbook of Social Network Technologies and Applications*,
DOI 10.1007/978-1-4419-7142-5_26, © Springer Science+Business Media, LLC 2010

easier to interact. Content from different sites can be combined and used for any purpose. However, in order to take advantage of these good things one now needs to join a structured social network. Many varieties of social networks have appeared, some just for keeping in contact with friends, but others for specialized uses. The idea is having a participatory group where everybody shares information and ideas with others in a shared space. Social network sites are structured as personal networks, with the individual at the center of their own community. People and their online interactions are captured as published content on the web in a way that allows content and people-as-content to be traversed through social, rather than thematic links. New categories of communication such as broadcast, narrowcast, and private messaging have been created. Virtually everything is read/write with space for added metadata and comments.

Software development in this environment presents new challenges because of its richness and the need for security. The large amount of information about individuals creates a significant privacy problem. Patterns are a way to simplify software development which we have been using in our work. A pattern is an encapsulated solution to a software problem in a given context and a good catalog of patterns can improve the quality of software. Patterns are fundamental when dealing with complex systems, security patterns can help apply security in complex systems [2].

There is a variety of security threats to social networks and several serious incidents have already occurred. The state of security in social networks is rather primitive; they contain mostly information about individuals but there is little protection against privacy violations [3]. Their platforms are also easy to penetrate by external attackers. We try to define here what security requirements should be imposed on these organizations to protect their users.

As indicated, we will express requirements in the form of a collection of patterns. Their most important value is to provide design guidelines for system designers that can implicitly add security as well as needed functional aspects. We start with an abstract version of the pattern, really an analysis pattern. This version can be used in the requirements and analysis stages of the lifecycle. They can also be used to evaluate existing systems. Systems usually need to comply with regulations, e.g. HIPAA for medical systems. Regulations can be described by a set of patterns and looking for the existence of those patterns in the system can convince us that the system complies with the regulations.

Section 26.2 of this chapter considers the security threats to social networks, as well as describing some incidents. Section 26.3 presents two patterns about social networks in the context of Web 2.0 technologies: the Participation-Collaboration Pattern describes the functionality of the collaboration between users in applications and the Collaborative Tagging Pattern is useful to share content using keywords to tag contents. Section 26.4 discusses some possible improvements. We end with some conclusions and ideas for future work.

26.2 Context, Threats, and Incidents

Social networks are complex systems that were not designed with security as a basic objective. Recently, there has been pressure from their users to make them more secure but as all security experts know, security is not an add-on, it must be considered from the beginning. This implies that new platforms and applications are needed. The original platforms and applications are easy to attack as shown by several incidents, some of which are described below.

Usability of the security mechanisms is another fundamental design flaw. It doesn't matter if the system has good security controls if they are too complex for the average users. Most privacy settings are confusing, cumbersome, and change frequently, so users lose track of their privacy restrictions. For example, Facebook's Privacy Policy has almost 6,000 words; its policies include 50 settings with over 170 options [4].

Many companies are encouraging their employees to use social networks as a way to reach potential clients or provide better service. That use may expose them to risks of illegal access to their corporate data or to their reputation [5]. Often these companies don't have any policies about the use of social networks by their employees.

The users themselves are a source of many security problems; many of them don't know or don't care about privacy. In surveys, e.g. the one mentioned in [24], many respondents were willing to let anyone see their full names, addresses, gender, and had few aspects that they wanted to hide (typically, religion or sexual preferences). In fact, some even bragged they did not have any secrets. A user in a survey said "I have nothing to hide", and we have heard this before from others. What these people don't realize is that information can be misinterpreted, propagated erroneously, and misused, e.g. for identity theft. This user even exposes his DNA record. Somebody could see in it a potential for some disease and he might not get a job, lose his girlfriend, or be denied insurance. The list of his purchases may identify him as liking books that some people might consider perverted or evil, with possible bad consequences. This position has started to reverse as many people are realizing that showing all this information is creating problems for them to get jobs.

In this moment the main source of privacy threats comes from the platform providers. Social networks are usually commercial enterprises that are trying to make money. They don't charge their users and provide nice functions to entice them to join. However, the providers sell this information or the access to the users to external parties to generate profits. They encourage users to provide as much information as possible and to share it with as many people as possible. Sometimes they use deceptive policies that confuse users and make them provide more information, not to protect their information, and even to share it with external entities [4]. Their privacy models allow internal applications to bypass the users' privacy settings and can collect all their information [3]. Facebook even allows third-party applications, which have not been checked for security, to run in its platform.

Important sources of threats in any commercial system are insiders, the people who work at the companies that provide platforms or applications for the social networks.

Threats also come from members trying to access information with poor privacy controls. Also, from external attackers who may take advantage of the platform weaknesses. Social engineering attacks, frequent in the Internet, become much faster and more effective using social networks, the attacker can reach much more people at one time. Spam can propagate farther and faster.

Not only privacy and security are at risk in poorly controlled social networks, reputation is another aspect that can suffer. People can post things about others, which can affect their lives. A company using the network can get a bad reputation if some users express the disapproval of their products or services.

Other threats include the standard Internet threats: Malware: viruses, worms, Trojan horses, spyware, identity theft, phishing, account hijacking [6].

Availability attacks can be very annoying to people used to keep track of their friends in real time. If you let others know always your location you are inviting burglars to your house. Web sites hosting social networks may keep your information indefinitely.

The effect of the platform and associated software is naturally very important, An example is ELGG, an open source platform [7]. Elgg runs on a combination of the Apache web server, MySQL database system and the PHP interpreted scripting language. These are open source products but they are not particularly secure. The use of mashups can bring data leakage. Mobile access to social networks and their applications will bring new problems [8]. Many social networks are using cloud-based platforms that may not have proper defenses.

Several incidents have shown the fragility of the current networks:

- A recent breach in Facebook allowed users to see private information from other users.
- Last December an attacker got into the master directory of Twitter's addresses and tampered with its DNS to redirect users to the site of the "Iranian Cyber Army" [9].

26.3 Two Patterns

As mentioned earlier, we can define security requirements for social networks by building functional patterns that include appropriate security patterns to restrict the users' actions needed to protect their privacy. We show two of these here but a more complete set is in preparation.

26.3.1 Participation-Collaboration

26.3.1.1 Intent

Describe the functionality of the collaboration between users participating in social networks, together with access and rights restrictions.

26.3.1.2 Example

A small company wants to create a manual covering the use of one of its products. The traditional approach is to gather a small set of experts to write it, hopefully reducing the potential for costly errors. However, manuals face a market of readers with different skill levels, and the company's writers may not always get everything right. Customers often know what they need better than the company does, but the flow of information has traditionally gone from the publisher to the customer, rather than the other way around. It is hard then to produce good-quality manuals [10].

26.3.1.3 Context

This pattern can be useful when a group of people has a common interest in sharing and communicating information about a specific subject. They all have access to the facilities of an environment such as the one provided by Web 2.0.

26.3.1.4 Problem

There are tasks where we need the collaboration of a large variety of people, who can provide unique points of view or expertise. How do we share information among people in different places and with different areas of expertise so they can work together?

The solution for this problem is affected by the following **forces**:

- There are issues that can be solved better when many people collaborate, we should provide a convenient way for them to interact.
- Consistent participation may provide a platform for some users to be recognized as experts. We want to know who are the users who have a high level of expertise in some area.
- A person needs to be designated to accept or reject the changes in the content made by the users; otherwise the collaboration may be overwhelmed by some users or become corrupted with spurious content.
- We should control who can propose new content to avoid spammers and similar input providers.

26.3.1.5 Solution

An open process may provide better results than having only a few people provide their knowledge and we want to let as many people as possible to participate under controlled conditions. Each collaboration should be received before acceptance. Only registered users should be able to add content.

Figure 26.1 presents the class diagram for this pattern. The **User** is authenticated by an **Authentication** system (pattern) [11]. The User has specific **Rights** with respect to the **Content**. The **Reviewer** approves the content provided by the user.

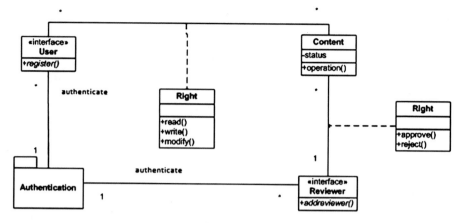

Fig. 26.1 Class Diagram for Participation and Collaboration pattern

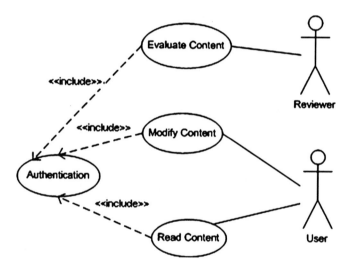

Fig. 26.2 Use Case Diagram for Participation and Collaboration pattern

26.3.1.6 Dynamics

The class diagram supports the use cases shown in Fig. 26.2.

The sequence diagram of Fig. 26.3 shows the use case modify content: First the user logs in the platform, then she can make changes but those changes are not published until the reviewer approves them.

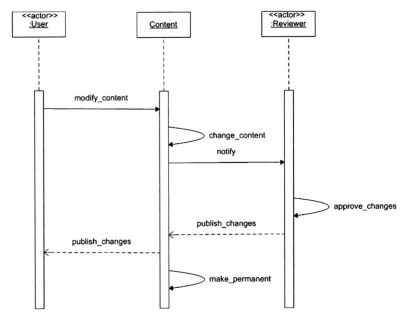

Fig. 26.3 Sequence Diagram for the use case Modify Content

26.3.1.7   Implementation

- Using the facilities of Web 2.0, implement a collaborative platform through which users or application actors can contribute knowledge, code, facts, and other material relevant to a discussion. The material can be made available, possibly in more than one format or language, and participants can then modify or append to that core content.
- The collaborative platform allows the user to modify an article, upload images, videos and audio. To do that, the user must have an account to be identified to the reviewer; it is important to use an appropriate authentication system.

26.3.1.8   Known Uses

- Platforms of collaboration such as Wikipedia, a free web encyclopedia [25].
- Facebook Wiki, a technical reference for developers interested in the Facebook Platform.
- Facebook Platform is a standards-based Web service with methods for accessing and contributing data [12].

26.3.1.9   Related Patterns

- The Authenticator pattern [11], is used to authenticate the users of the system.
- The Role-Based Access Control (RBAC) pattern [13] is used to define the rights of the users with respect to the contents.

26.3.1.10   Consequences

This pattern has the following advantages:

- Allows users in any place to modify content; they can share text, videos, images and can discuss any topic trying to collaborate and give different ideas.
- Experts demonstrate their knowledge or talent about certain topic and they can be recognized in their field of expertise.
- We can keep out spammers and other undesirable users.

Possible disadvantages include:

- Sometimes the reviewers don't know about a specific topic and they can eliminate important or useful content. They can also be biased. This means the reviewer should be carefully selected.

26.3.2   Collaborative Tagging

26.3.2.1   Intent

The Collaborative Tagging pattern makes content more meaningful and useful by using keywords to tag bookmarks, photographs, and other content.

26.3.2.2   Example

Consider a person tagging a photograph of broccoli. One person might label it "cruciform," "vegetable," or "nutritious," while another might tag it "gross," "bitter," or worse. We need some way to attach information to this item as a guide to possibly interest users about this vegetable [10].

26.3.2.3   Context

People in the internet need to search different kinds of content such as pictures, text, content, audio files, bookmarks, news, items, websites, products, blog posts, comments, and other items available online. They may want an item for a variety of reasons.

26.3.2.4   Problem

Often, we need to use a search system to find resources on the Internet. The resources must match our needs, and to find relevant information, we need to enter search terms. The search system compares those terms with a metadata index that shows which resources might be relevant to our search. The primary problem with such a system is that the metadata index is often built by a small group of people who determine the relevancy of those resources for specific terms [10]. The smaller the group that does this, the greater the chance that the group will apply inaccurate tags to some resources or omit certain relationships between the search terms and the resources' semantic relevancy. How do we let users guide the search for people with related interests?

The solution is affected by the following **forces**:

- The number of ways to classify an item is undefined and the choices can be as different as the users and all of these are valid in some sense.
- A specific item can belong to an unlimited number of categories. We want to have a variety of ways to find items.

26.3.2.5   Solution

Let the users add tags to items to indicate categorizations of interest to the members of the group.

Figure 26.4 shows the class diagram for this pattern. The **User** belongs to a **Domain** and applies **Tags** from this domain to **Resources**. A User is any human, application, process, or other entity that is capable of interacting with a resource. A domain is the total set of objects and actions that the language provides. Resource denotes any digital asset that can have an identifier. Examples of resources include online content, audio files, digital photos, bookmarks, news items, websites, products, blog posts, comments, and other items available online.

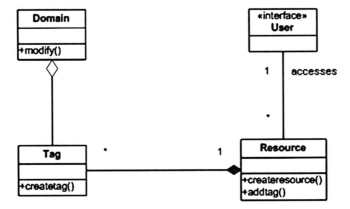

Fig. 26.4 Class Diagram for the Collaborative Tagging Pattern

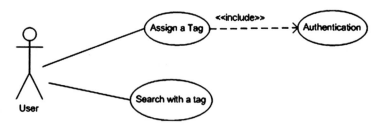

Fig. 26.5 Use Case Diagram for the Collaborative Tagging Pattern

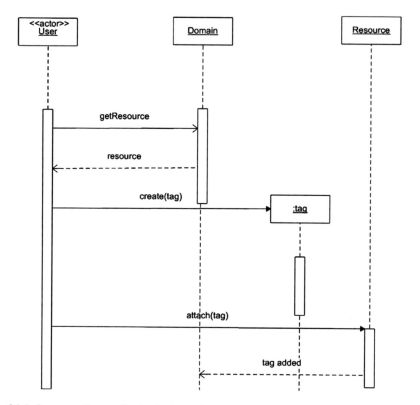

Fig. 26.6 Sequence diagram for the Assign a Tag use case

Figure 26.5 shows the use cases related to this pattern. Figure 26.6 shows a sequence diagram for the use case Tag a resource: First the user selects a resource, he then makes a semantic classification of the resource by adding a tag. The user has freedom to assign any word to a resource. After the user tags a resource, the domain changes its content and people can start to use the tag for searches.

26.3.2.6 Known Uses

- **Flickr** has implemented the capability to let individuals provide tags for digital photographs [14].
- **Technorati** lets individuals use tags for blog articles. It also it has published a microformat for tags in blog entries and indexes blogs using those tags (and category data) [15].
- **Slashdot's** beta tagging system lets any member place specific tags on any post [16].

26.3.2.7 Consequences

This pattern has the following advantages:

- Users can classify their collections of items in any way that they find useful.
- When users try to find an item, the results have more variety and meanings.
- Tags provide a way to measure aspects such as directionality and centrality.

Possible liabilities are:

- When users can freely choose tags, the resulting metadata can include the same tags used with different meanings and multiple tags for the same concept, which may lead to inappropriate connections between items and inefficient searches for information about a subject.
- There is no explicit information about the meaning of each tag.
- The personalized variety of terms can present challenges when searching and browsing.

26.4 Improvements

The excitement brought upon by the possibilities of Web 2.0 produced a flurry of applications, frameworks, and all kinds of social networks. Security was not a concern for them and many of these networks are unstructured, collect too much information, and once you join one of them it is very hard to leave. Reacting to the complaints of their users the social network providers have added mostly boundary defenses. For example, firewalls and IDS are mentioned in [6]. The state of security for social networks is rather primitive; they contain large amounts of information about individuals but there is little protection against privacy violations [3]. The increasing use of controllers and sensors will make the security situation even worse. Twitter has about 70,000 applications developed by external developers, none of which has been certified for security. Attempts to unify standards for social networks have not worked very well: OpenSocial defines a common API for social applications across multiple websites [17]. With standard JavaScript and HTML, developers can create apps that access a social network's friends and update feeds. As reported by TechCrunch on November 5, 2007, OpenSocial was also quickly cracked. The total time to crack the OpenSocial-based iLike on Ning was just 20 mins. according to TechCrunch, with the attacker being able to add and remove songs on a user's playlist, and to look into information on their friends.

To improve this situation, [23] proposes an architecture to enforce privacy automatically, including a framework and service model of privacy as a service. Safebook is a decentralized architecture which tries to protect privacy against the provider's misuses [18]. Usability is an area that can be improved significantly. For example, well known security models such as RBAC or multilevel can be applied by users if they have an appropriate interface [19].

While these are efforts in the right direction, we think we should start by defining precisely the security requirements of this environment and we are describing them as a collection of patterns. Their most important value is to provide design guidelines for system developers that implicitly add security as well as needed functional aspects. We usually start with an abstract version of the pattern, really an analysis pattern. This version can be used in the requirements and analysis stages of the lifecycle. For example, the Participation and Collaboration pattern solution in Fig. 26.1 shows the functional aspects of users collaborating in a social network, and it also shows that we need authentication in specific parts of the model. It additionally shows that users need specific rights to access content and that the Reviewer has the right to accept or reject new content. Using this pattern a developer who doesn't know much about social networks or security can build a system that has the required functions for this type of system and incorporates security at the right places. Patterns can be used to evaluate existing systems. Systems usually need to comply with regulations, e.g. HIPAA for medical systems. Regulations can be described by a set of patterns and looking for the existence of those patterns in the system can convince us that the system complies with the regulations.

26.5   Conclusions

We presented a perspective of security issues in social networks and proposed a way to define their security requirements using patterns. We presented two basic patterns for social network interaction: the Participation-Collaboration Pattern describes the functionality of the collaboration between users in applications, while the Collaborative Tagging Pattern is useful to share content using keywords to tag bookmarks, photographs and other contents. These patterns will be valuable for web designers defining the architecture of new systems.

We need to define patterns for other aspects that require improvement or more precise definition and study some other aspects of social network security. These include:

The Secure Mashup pattern. A mashup is a web application that combines data or functionality from several other applications or services to produce a new service [10]. We are producing also a variant for wireless mashups [8].

Social Network Usability patterns. We need a clear conceptual model of user interaction to provide a logical and simple model for a user to set her privacy preferences. We are starting some work on this direction [19].

Social Networks in a Cloud Environment. This work implies analyzing the threats to social networks when their platforms are based on clouds.

Support for social networks using web services. Web services have a set of well developed security standards [20]. Current social networks have not exploited this technology to provide security [21].

Secure software development methodology. The supporting software structure and any applications that run on it must be developed in a secure way. We have developed a general methodology to build secure systems that will be adapted to this environment [22].

References

1. A.C. Weaver and B.B. Morrison, "Social networking", Computer IEEE, Feb 2008, 97–100.
2. E.B. Fernandez, "Security patterns", Proceedings of the Eigth International Symposium on System and Information Security – SSI'2006, Keynote talk, Sao Jose dos Campos, Brazil, Nov 08–10, 2006.
3. E.M. Maximilien, T. Grandison, T. Sun, D. Richardson, S. Guo, and K. Liu, "Privacy-as-a-Service: Models, algorithms, and results on the Facebook platform", Proceedings of Web 2.0 Security and Privacy, 2009.
4. N. Bilton, "Price of Facebook privacy? Start clicking", The New York Times, May 13, 2010.
5. M. Brandel, "Baited and duped on Facebook", Computerworld, Oct 19, 2009, 28–35.
6. R. Westervelt, "Facebook attacks prompt investments in social networking security", Search-Security.com, Jan 11, 2010.
7. "Elgg–Open Source Social Networking Platform", http://www.elgg.org/
8. E.M. Maximilien, "Mobile mashups: Thoughts, directions, and challenges", Proceedings of the 2nd IEEE Internaional Conference on Semantic Computing, 2008.
9. J. Wortham and N. Bilton, "Big web attack on Twitter is third assault this year", The New York Times, Dec 19, 2009.
10. D. Hinchcliffe, N. Nickull, and J. Governor, "Web 2.0 Architectures", O'Reilly Media, 2009.
11. F.L. Brown, J. DeVietri, G. Diaz, and E.B. Fernandez, "The Authenticator pattern", Proceedings of Pattern Language of Programs (PloP'99), 2009.
12. Facebook Wiki, 2009, November 5, Wiki, http://wiki.developers.facebook.com/index.php/Main_Page
13. E.B. Fernandez and R. Pan, "A pattern language for security models", Proceedings of PLoP, 2001.
14. Flickr X, 2009, http://en.wikipedia.org/wiki/Flickr

15. Technorati, 2009, http://en.wikipedia.org/wiki/Technorati
16. Slashdot, http://en.wikipedia.org/wiki/Slashdot
17. Wikipedia, "OpenSocial", http://en.wikipedia.org/wiki/OpenSocial
18. L.A. Cutillo, R. Molva, and T. Strufe, "Safebook: A privacy-preserving online social network leveraging on real-life trust", IEEE Communications, Dec 2009, 94–101.
19. E.B. Fernandez and J. Munoz-Arteaga, "Extending a secure software methodology with usability aspects", position paper for the 3rd Workshop on Software Patterns and Quality (SPAQu'09), in conjunction with OOPSLA, 2009.
20. E.B. Fernandez, K. Hashizume, I. Buckley, M.M. Larrondo-Petrie, and M. VanHilst, "Web services security: standards and products", Chapter 8 in "Web services security development and architecture: theoretical and practical issues", Carlos A. Gutierrez, Eduardo F. Medina, and M. Piattini (Eds.), IGI Global Group, 2010, 152–177.
21. A. Ennai and S. Bose, "MobileSOA: A service oriented Web 2.0 framework for context-aware, lightweight and flexible mobile applications", Proceedings of EDOC, 2008.
22. E.B. Fernandez, M.M. Larrondo-Petrie, T. Sorgente, and M. VanHilst, "A methodology to develop secure systems using patterns", Chapter 5 in "Integrating security and software engineering: Advances and future vision", H. Mouratidis and P. Giorgini (Eds.), IDEA Press, 2006, 107–126.
23. M. Gotta, "Reference architecture for social network sites, in perceptions on collaboration and social software", 2008, http://mikeg.typepad.com/perceptions/2008/07/reference-archi.html
24. B. Stone, "Too much information? Hah! Sharing all online is the point", The New York Times, Apr 23, 2010.
25. Wikipedia, 2009, http://en.wikipedia.org/wiki/Wikipedia_(terminology)

Part V
Visualisation and Applications of Social Networks

Chapter 27
Visualization of Social Networks

Ing-Xiang Chen and Cheng-Zen Yang

27.1 Introduction

Social networks can structure the complex relationships between different groups of individuals or organizations, and thus they are helpful to analyze the social activities and relationships of actors, particularly over a large number of nodes (actors) [1, 2]. The concept of a small world and the six degree of separation[1] are the most well-known examples about social networks [3]. To represent a social network, a simple, straight way is to use a graph representation with individuals or actors as nodes, and relationships or interactions as edges. When a social network is constructed, the nodes and edges within the social network can be appropriately analyzed to discover the important actors and relationships. PageRank [4] and Hyperlink-Induced Topic Search (HITS) [5] are two famous representatives developed in late 1990s that still deeply affect the ranking schemes of Web sites until today.

As the rapid and explosive development of the Internet in the two decades, many social behaviors have been transformed from the human daily activities to the Internet. Various social relationships are thus created, connected, and migrated from our real lives to the Internet environment from different social groups. With the ubiquitous characteristic of the Internet, today many online social environments are also provided to connect people. For example, many social communities and relationships are quickly constructed and connected via instant personal messengers, blogs, Twitter, Facebook, and a great variety of online social services. On account of such vigorous growth of online social activities, social relationships between groups of individuals or organizations hence become more complex than before.

To aid the analysis on social networks, many studies have been investigated to present social networks with graph representations in social science [1, 6]. Since early 1930s, Moreno started to use different hand-drawn images to analyze the social relationships between different groups [6]. For example, he combined the

---

[1]http://en.wikipedia.org/wiki/Six_degrees_of_separation

I.-X. Chen (✉)
Telcordia Applied Research Centre - Taiwan, Telcordia Technologies, Piscataway, NJ 08854
e-mail: seanchen@research.telcordia.com

B. Furht (ed.), *Handbook of Social Network Technologies and Applications*,
DOI 10.1007/978-1-4419-7142-5_27, © Springer Science+Business Media, LLC 2010

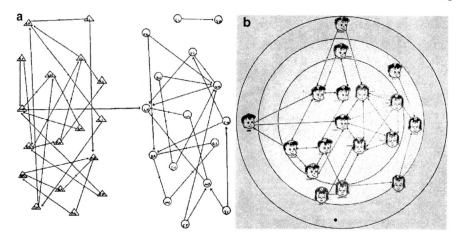

Fig. 27.1 Visualization of social network using hand-drawn images [6]. (**a**) Friendship choices among fourth grade children. (**b**) The sociogram of a first grade class

presentations of both the locations and the shapes to express additional information about the structural properties of social networks. In Fig. 27.1a, boys are shown as triangles and girls as circles. From the aspect of the locations with illustrating boys on the left and girls on the right, the friendship choices by genders are very clear that only one boy chose a girl and no girl chose any boy as a friend. In 1952, Grant further applied a more intuitive manner with icons to present the social relationships in a group of first grade children. Figure 27.1b displays the social relationships in a clearer way with visual icons and thus helps identify the genders and relationships easily.

Visualization is a powerful technique to facilitate exploring social relationships within social networks. With the advances of computer graphic technologies, visualizations of social networks have been evolved from hand drawn images in 1930s to the era of Web interfaces in 1990s [1]. Meanwhile, various visualization techniques and metaphors were proposed to improve the analysis of social networks and enhance the human computer interactions. For example, in 1950s, computational methods, such as factor analysis and multidimensional scaling (MDS), were proposed to lay out nodes in social networks [1]. Factor analysis was developed to reduce the number of nodes by mapping similar nodes into "factors". MDS was further utilized to lay out nodes in a 2D or 3D way that distances between pairs of nodes on the display correspond to distances between individuals in the data. With evolution of computer technologies and visualization techniques, machine-drawn images and screen-oriented graphics were developed to visualize social networks with more abundant visual components and interactions. Although many visualization techniques have been focused on the discussions, such as displaying fine graph layouts, coloring, and presenting clear node-edge relations, visualizing complex relations is still challenging to social network visualization.

In the recent decade, visualization technologies have been widely applied to social networks to facilitate accessibility and interoperability through the platform of Web browsers. Currently, many studies have attempted to visualize complex and multilayer node-edge relationships with innovative metaphors and techniques [39]. However, visualizing social networks with a large number of nodes and complex relationships on the Internet is still a challenging issue. Particularly in the era of Web 2.0, many forms of online sociality, including e-mail, instant personal messengers, blogs, and online social services, produced composite social networks and greatly involved our social lives. Visualizing social networks thus plays an important role of accessing social networks and connecting people in a more effective and efficient way.

Today, many visualization applications have been also employed in different online social networks to help people manipulate their social relationships and access the abundant resources on the Internet. The purpose of this chapter is to introduce and analyze social network visualization techniques and their applications. In the rest of this chapter, we will first introduce the background of social network analysis, visualization methods, and various novel visualization applications for social networks. In particular, more emphases are on describing the state-of-the-art visualizations of online social networks in different forms of sociality and discussing visualization from different views of social relationships. Finally, the last section concludes this chapter, and discusses the challenges and the future development of visualizing online social networks.

27.2 Social Network Analysis

Social networks are built when actors belonging to different social groups are connected to each other. In late 1800s and early 1900s, sociologists have been looking for social relationships, groups, positions, and organizations in human activities [1]. In early 1930s, Moreno brought in the concept of *sociograms* to represent social networks and started to explore the social relations in a formal study. Until today, social network analysis is still a hot issue that attracts many concerns, particularly for analyzing the online social networks. In this section, some important metrics for network analysis are described to give a brief overview of social network analysis.

27.2.1 Graph Theory

Many fundamental concepts and metrics in social network analysis are derived from graph theory, because graph theory formally represents social networks with structural properties. In the following descriptions of terms, some fundamental definitions related to graph theory and social network analysis are depicted mainly referring to [7].

- Node degree:

In graph theory, the degree of a node in a graph is the number of edges incident to the node. If there are loops in the graph, the degree of a node will be counted twice.

Therefore, the maximum number of unique edges in a graph can be obtained when the loops are excluded. There are at most $N^*(N-1)/2$ edges for an undirected graph and at most $N^*(N-1)$ edges for a directed graph, where N is the number of nodes.

- Node density:

The density of an undirected graph can be defined as $(2^*E)/N^*(N-1)$, where E is the number of edges. On the other hand, the density of a directed graph can be defined as $E/N^*(N-1)$.

- Path length:

The path length is the number of edges in the sequence that a walk follows. In a path, all nodes and edges appear only once in the sequence. Therefore, the path length can be defined as the distances between pairs of nodes in a network graph, and average path length is the average of these distances between all pairs of nodes.

- Component size:

When the component size is concerned, a connected graph needs to be discovered first since the component size is counted by the number of connected nodes in a graph. A graph is connected if all pairs of nodes are reachable, and for each pair of two nodes, one of them is reachable from the other. On the other hand, if a graph is not connected, the graph can be partitioned into several connected subgraphs where each component size can be calculated by the number of connected nodes in each subgraph.

27.2.2 Centrality

One of the key applications in social networks is to identify the most important or central nodes in the network. The measure of centrality is thus used to give a rough indication of the social power of a node based on how well they connect the network. HITS and PageRank are two most famous representatives using centrality for ranking. HITS analyzes the important nodes based on calculating Authorities (in-degrees) and Hubs (out-degrees) [5], and PageRank calculates node values based on out-degrees [4]. In social network analysis, "Degree", "Betweenness", and "Closeness" centrality are three most popularly adopted methods to measure the centrality of a social network. In the descriptions below, we depict the distinction between the three popular individual centrality measures: degree centrality, betweenness centrality, and closeness centrality.

- Degree centrality:

Degree centrality is defined as the number of edges incident upon a node, and thus it is usually the first way to calculate the nodes that are most potential to determine other nodes. For calculating degree centrality, the nodes that have direct connections to a large number of nodes are considered. If the edges in a graph are directed, the in-degree centrality is differentiated from the out-degree centrality.

- Betweenness centrality:

In addition to degree centrality, betweeness centrality is another key metrics for computing the extent to which a node lies between other nodes in the network. If a node is the only node that links two groups of nodes in the network, this node shall be seen as an important node for keeping the social network together. Therefore, betweenness centrality is to measure the connectivity of the neighbors of a node and to give a higher value for nodes which bridge clusters. Besides, this measure reflects the number of nodes which a node is connecting indirectly through the direct links [8].

- Closeness centrality:

The measure of closeness centrality is to take into account how distant a node is to the other nodes in the network. Hence, closeness centrality is to measure the order of magnitude that a node is near all other nodes in a social network by calculating the mean shortest path for a node to all other nodes in the graph. As mentioned in [2], nodes that are ranked high with closeness centrality can be seen as the nodes that are more likely to act as information distributors in the social network.

27.2.3 Clustering

Many social networks contain subsets of nodes that are highly connected within the subset and have relatively few connections to nodes outside the subset [2]. The nodes in such subsets are likely to share some attributes and form their own communities. Since the detection of these community structures is not trivial, how to efficiently and effectively discover such community structures is important. Therefore, the main measure described below is to help explore the grouping effects by clustering coefficient.

- Clustering coefficient:

A clustering coefficient is to measure the degrees of nodes to decide which nodes in a graph tend to be clustered together. Thus, the clustering coefficient measure is to quantify how close its neighbors are to being a complete graph. As the nodes grouped in the real-world social network tend to have relatively high density of ties, the clustering coefficient is also utilized for small world analysis [9].

From the descriptions above, we quickly overview some important metrics used for social network analysis. In the following, we will focus on introducing visualization techniques and their applications for online social networks. For more details and metrics about social network analysis, readers can refer to [7, 8].

27.3 Visualization

Visualization plays a crucial role of linking the human vision and computer, helping identify patterns, and extracting insights from large amounts of information [10–13, 40]. To help people understand different information structures, various visual representations and metaphors have been proposed for decades. Although many information visualization techniques have been developed, no single visualization method can fit all kinds of information structures. For visualizing social networks, some visual representations are considered appropriate to present network structures, such as node-edge diagrams and matrix representations. These visual representations have also been popularly employed in visualizing social networks. In the following, different visual representations are analyzed with their graph layouts for displaying social networks.

27.3.1 Node-Edge Diagrams

A node-edge diagram is an intuitive way to visualize social networks. With the node-edge visualization, many network analysis tasks, such as component size calculation, centrality analysis, and pattern sketching, can be better presented in a more straightforward manner. Many node-edge layouts have been presented to place the nodes in the graph for users to clearly recognize the structure of the social network. However, different layouts have their own pros and cons to display the network graph depending on the size, complexity, and structure of the social network. For example, some layouts are suitable to display social networks in a moderate size, but they are not suitable for showing larger networks. Three kinds of layouts, namely, random layout, force-directed layout, and tree layout, are described to explain the node-edge diagrams.

27.3.1.1 Random Layout

A random layout is to put the nodes at random geometric locations in the graph, and thus it may not yield very clear visualization results, particularly when the number of nodes immensely increases, e.g. more than thousands of nodes. However, since a random layout algorithm can efficiently draw the social network graph in linear time, $O(N)$, sometimes it can be usable to visualize very large network graphs. Therefore, random graphs have been proposed as a possible model to take into account the structural characteristics of instances that appear in many practical applications [14]. Figure 27.2a shows a random geographic layout.

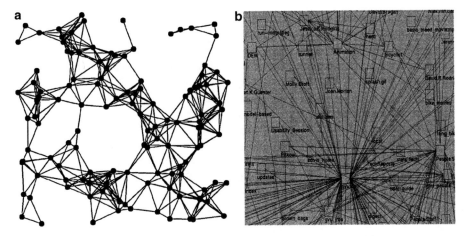

Fig. 27.2 Node-link graph layouts for social networks. (**a**) A random geographic layout [14]. (**b**) A force-based graph layout [15]

27.3.1.2 Force-Directed Layout

A force-directed layout is also known as a spring layout, which simulates the graph as a virtual physical system. In a force-directed layout, the edges act as spring and the nodes act as repelling objects, just like the Hooke's law and the Coulomb's law. Hence, there exists gravitational attraction or magnetic repulsion between each node in the graph. Generally, an initial random layout will be yielded first, and then the force-directed algorithms will run iteratively to adjust the positions of nodes until all graph nodes and attractive forces between the adjacent nodes run to convergence. Figure 27.2b displays a force-based graph layout for forming better layouts of the space [15].

Since a force-directed layout may take hundreds of iterations to obtain a stable layout, the running time is at least $O(N \log N)$ or $O(E)$, where N is the number of nodes and E is the number of edges. Compared with a random layout, the running cost of a force-directed layout is much higher than that of a random layout, especially when the number of nodes is large. It is therefore not suitable for graphs larger than hundreds of nodes.

27.3.1.3 Tree Layout

A basic tree layout is to choose a node as the root of tree, and the nodes connected to the root become children of the root node. Nodes that are at more levels away from the root become the grand-children of the root and so on. A tree layout can display a more structural layout than graph layouts by considering more contextual information. Because of the hierarchical nature of a tree layout, trees are more straightforward to grasp human eye than general graphs. Drawing a tree layout thus takes more constraints than drawing a general graph since tree structures are a special case of graphs. Meanwhile, more contextual information of a graph can be extracted to present a hierarchical layout and facilitate network analysis.

For a better visual presentation of domain specific information, more suitable variants of the tree layout were proposed, such as hyperbolic tree layout [16] and a radial tree layout [17]. These tree visualizations utilize the idea of focus + context to better the visualization effects with animation techniques and help users to obtain both global and local views of a social network in a 2D display. Figure 27.3a shows the visualization of a hyperbolic tree view [16], and Fig. 27.3b shows a radial tree layout [2]. In addition, an advanced visualization technique, called H3, further maps the hyperbolic tree into a 3D space with a fisheye effect to better utilize the visualization space. Figure 27.3c displays the H3 visualization [18].

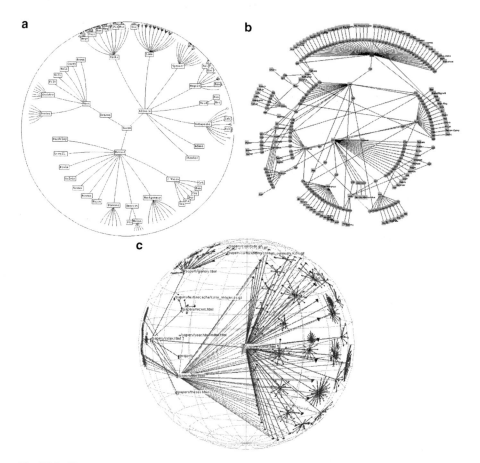

Fig. 27.3 Three kinds of tree layouts for social network visualization. (**a**) A hyperbolic tree view [16] (**b**) A radial tree layout [2]. (**c**) An H3 view [18]

27.3.2 *Matrix Representations*

Since a social network graph consists of nodes connected with edges, it can be transformed into a simple Boolean matrix whose rows and columns represent the vertices of the graph. Moreover, the Boolean values in the matrix can be further replaced with valued attributes associated with the edges to provide more informative network visualizations [19]. Since a matrix presentation can help minimize the occlusion problems caused by the node-edge diagram, the matrix-based representation of graphs offers an alternative to the traditional node-edge diagrams. With a matrix-based representation, clusters and associations among the nodes can also be better discovered when the number of nodes increases. Particularly, when the relationships are complex, a matrix-based representation can effectively outperform a node-edge diagram in readability since the high connectivity of a node-edge representation will easily diffuse the focus [19].

In 2006, an enhanced matrix-based representation, called MatrixExplorer, was developed to visualize social networks with a Dual-Representation. In [20], MatrixExplorer can provide users with two synchronized representations of the same network: matrix and node-edge. When a social network is composed of highly interlaced edges, the matrix-based view can help users quickly recognize the associations between nodes. Figure 27.4 illustrates a matrix-base view of MatrixExplorer with an initial order on the left and a traveling salesman problem (TSP) order on the right [20]. In Fig. 27.4, a reordered matrix can evidently help users find more clusters. A matrix-based visualization may not entirely replace a conventional node-edge diagram, yet it could complement the shortcomings of a node-edge diagram to better the social network visualization.

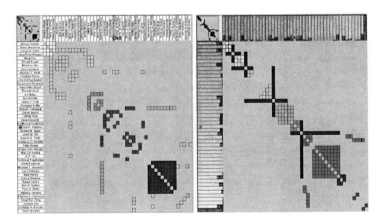

Fig. 27.4 MatrixExplorer: initial order (*left*) and TSP order (*right*) [20]

27.4   Visualizing Online Social Networks

As the fast development of the Internet, many online social network services are created to connect social relationships among people. Versatile visualization skills are employed to facilitate analyzing online social networks, and more in-depth studies have been investigated to improve the presentation of online social networks. When the attributes of sociality are concerned, online social networks can be classified into different social communities. In addition, from the daily social activities of various online social communities, social networks may evolve into different patterns of social structure. Therefore, visualizations of online social networks were developed according to the attributes of network sociality to present their network structure.

In this section, many state-of-the-arts visualization applications are surveyed to present the versatile social network visualizations on the Web. In the following, we first depict and analyze the visualization of online social networks according to their attributes of sociality, including Web communities, email groups, digital libraries, and Web 2.0 services. Then, the features of these up-to-date online social network visualizations are depicted and discussed with the illustrations of their visualization interfaces or screen shots. In the end of this section, we summarize online social network visualizations based on different views of social relationships, e.g. user-centric social relationships, content-centric social relationships, and hybrid social relationships.

27.4.1   Web Communities

After the six degrees of separation concept and Web services were becoming popular in late 1990s, different social network services were created on the Web to help people maintain their social relationships. The SixDegrees.com website was an early representative created on the basis of the Web interaction model during 1997 and 2001. Since the start of SixDegrees.com, various social network websites and Web-based dating services have been established to provide people more convenient ways to build up their social relationships and communities. In addition, many social network websites are developed with interactive visualization interfaces to facilitate people connecting their communities and maintaining social relationships.

In 2003, Club Nexus was established based on the friendship network data of Stanford students and allowed them to explicitly list their friends by their profiles [21]. For example, students registered on Club Nexus were provided with the profiles of their year in school, major, residence, gender, personalities, hobbies and interests to facilitate interacting with their online social networks. The Club Nexus community thus provided very rich profiles for its users to allow for detailed social network analysis, including identifying activities and preferences that determine the formation of friendship [22]. Figure 27.5 displays the Club Nexus visualization with a snippet of a Web community of over 2,000 Stanford students. In Fig. 27.5, the Club Nexus social network reflects only a subset of each person's contacts – the potential friends, since many students listed few or even no friends on the website.

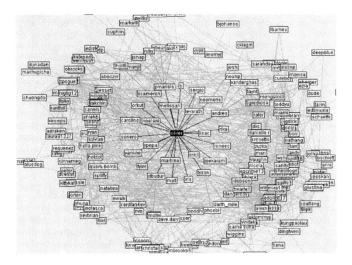

Fig. 27.5 Club Nexus: visualization of a Web community of Stanford students [21]

In addition to listing actors with their profiles for social network analysis, a modern visualization of social networks, Vizster, was contributed with customized techniques to visualize social relationships and community structures in 2005. Vizster was developed based on node-edge network layouts for exploring connectivity in large graph structures, supporting visual search and analysis, and automatically identifying and visualizing community structures [23]. Figure 27.6a shows the visualization of social relationships, and Fig. 27.6b further demonstrates the linkage view of Vizster visualization. Form the visualization design of Vizster, many advanced search and interactive navigation techniques are developed on Vizster to facilitate the analysis of social networks, such as highlighting, panning, zooming, and distortion techniques. Moreover, visual community analysis is provided to help users construct and explore higher-level structures of their online communities [23]. In Fig. 27.6c, the visualization of community structures is presented.

From the previous visualization of Web communities, the visualization techniques are mainly introduced to deal with the complex social relationships based on human-centric or user-centric views. As the development of Semantic Web, a project called FOAF (Friend-of-a-friend) was proposed to visualize such human-centric social relationships based on Semantic Web social metadata. With XML/RDF format, the FOAF relations can be explicitly defined for further social network analysis and visualization. Figure 27.7 shows Semantic Web social networks with FOAF [24].

Recently, Microsoft Research Asia proposed a novel object-level search service, called EntityCube[2], to help people discover real-world entities, such as people, locations, and organizations, and explore their social relationships. In the

---

[2] People EntityCube, http://entitycube.research.microsoft.com/

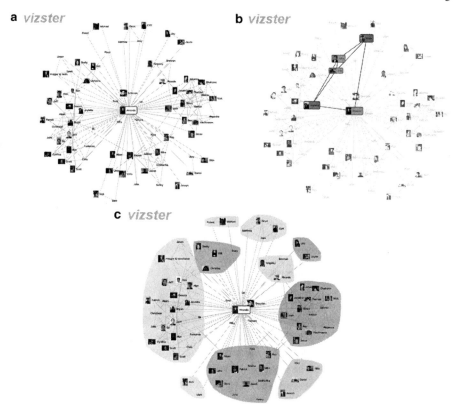

Fig. 27.6 Vizster: visualization of the Friendster service [23]. (**a**) Visualization of social relations.
(**b**) The linkage view of Vizster. (**c**) Visualization of community structures

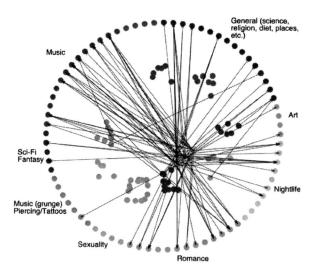

Fig. 27.7 FOAF: groups of actors with shared interests and social relations [24]

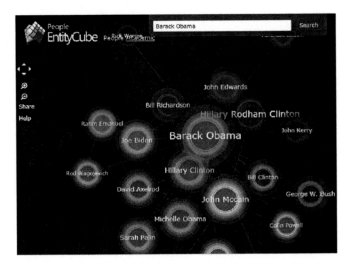

Fig. 27.8 People EntityCube: visualizing human social relationships[2]

EntityCube interface, Web entities are summarized from billions of Web pages with a modest presence. Therefore, users can intuitively browse and determine the social relationships among the returned entities. Figure 27.8 demonstrates People Entity-Cube with querying the American president "Barack Obama". From the visualized objects and relationships connected to Barrack Obama, users can immediately identify people with higher interactions, such as Hillary Clinton and John Mccain.

27.4.2 Email Groups

Email service is one of the most popular applications that people often use to connect each other and deliver messages in their daily lives. Personal online social networks are thus constructed through people's daily social interactions. For analyzing the social structures of the daily email activities, visualization techniques are employed to explore different patterns. In 2004, Soylent was developed to study the social patterns and the temporal rhythms of daily email activities [25]. Through the Soylent visualization, mutual interactions between different users and groups, and their everyday collaboration activities can be clearly displayed. Some recurrent patterns discovered in the social networks, such as the onion pattern, the nexus pattern, and the butterfly pattern, can thus suggest regular ways of understanding their interactions [25]. For example, the butterfly pattern, named for its two large "wings" surrounding a single center, can be interpreted as a member of a design team also involving in a research team. Figure 27.9 shows the full network view of Soylent [25].

In addition to the network view of email visualization, different aspects of social networks can be visualized for analysis. In 2005, two visual metaphors, Social

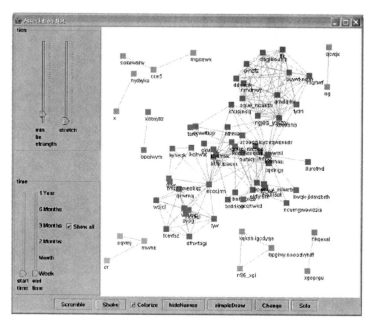

Fig. 27.9 Soylent: visualizing social relationships among email groups [25]

Network Fragments (SNF) and PostHistory, were employed to visualize the major two dimensions of email activities: people and time [26, 27]. In contrast to the integrated visualization of Soylent, the social relationships derived from the TO and CC lists in email archives are highlighted in SNF, and the temporal rhythms of interactions between ego and individual contacts over time are illustrated with a calendar metaphor in PostHistory, respectively. Figure 27.10a displays a complex cluster of contacts in SNF, where different colors are utilized to indicate people from different contexts of ego's social life.

In Fig. 27.10b, PostHistory presents social network visualization with a calendar panel on the left and a contacts panel on the right. The email exchange activities with time progress can thus be visualized in an interactive calendar-like interface. Moreover, both interfaces can work interoperably with each other to facilitate accessing email-based social network. For example, when users spot an interesting cluster of contacts in SNF, they can turn to PostHistory to locate the patterns of intensive email exchange that made those people's names coalesce into a single cluster [27]. More detailed explanations about how both visualizations work can be found in [26].

In 2006, an improved calendar-like visualization interface, called The mail, was developed to help analyze email-based social networks with a chronological sequence and the corresponding topics [28]. Through the analysis of email content, the social relations and mutual interactions between a user and her contacts can be clear presented in Themail. In advance, topic changes over time progress can be substantially traced with the chronological bar. Figure 27.10c displays the screenshot of Themail showing a user's email exchange with a friend during 18 months.

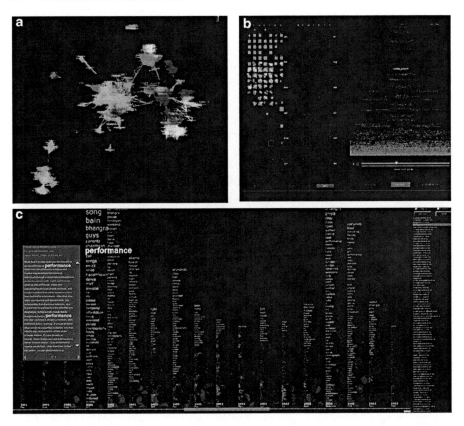

Fig. 27.10 Visualization of email groups and their social relations. (**a**) SNF: visualization of a complex cluster of contacts [27]. (**b**) PostHistory: visualization interface with calendar and contacts [27]. (**c**) Themail: visualization of email exchange with a friend during 18 months [28]

27.4.3 Digital Libraries

With the speedy publishing of digital contents on the Web, social networks are fast shaped among these electronic publications, particularly among the academic publications. In digital libraries, social networks can be mainly analyzed from two aspects: authors and writings.

27.4.3.1 Co-Authorship Networks

On the aspect of authors, co-authorships can be mined from the existing publications and organize the co-authorship networks. With the visualization of co-authorships, some characteristics, such as clustering coefficient and average path length, can be hence analyzed in co-authorship networks. Figure 27.11a shows the visualization

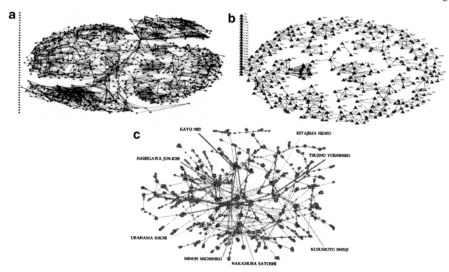

Fig. 27.11 Visualization of co-authorships in academic digital libraries. (**a**) The co-authorship network of JODL and D-lib community [29]. (**b**) The collaboration network of CiteSeer [30]. (**c**) Eight of the top co-authors from IEICE Transactions D (1993–2005) [31]

of co-authorship networks in the joint community of JODL and D-lib [29], and Fig. 27.11b illustrates the collaboration network of CiteSeer, respectively [30]. In 2007, a node-edge representation was also employed in visualizing the co-authorship network in a large Japanese academic society, IEICE, to show the similar characteristics of co-authorship networks in a specific domain [31]. Figure 27.11c demonstrates eight of the top co-authors with about four thousand nodes from IEICE Transactions D during 1993 and 2005. Beside the co-authorship network, the collaboration network of journal editors can be visualized for network analysis. Figure 27.12 displays the editorial board network of top 56 journals in the field of digital libraries [29].

From the visualization of the co-authorship networks illustrated above, a small world graph can be drawn with the connections of authors from different places in the world. In 2005, social network analysis for co-authorship was in-depth studied in digital libraries. Figure 27.13a illustrates the concept of a small world with calculating the largest component in the Joint Conference on Digital Libraries (JCDL) co-authorship network [32]. Other characteristics of social network analysis, such as higher clustering coefficient and longer path length, also indicate that co-authors of one author are more likely to publish together in the JCDL community, and authors from different groups are not as well connected as those in other co-authorship communities. In addition to the node-edge representation, a matrix representation was used in the co-authorship network to help analyze different co-authorship patterns. With the matrix representation, the interlaced problem of the node-edge representation caused by a large amount of nodes and complex relations can be effectively improved. Figure 27.13b shows the visualization of co-authorship network with a matrix representation [33].

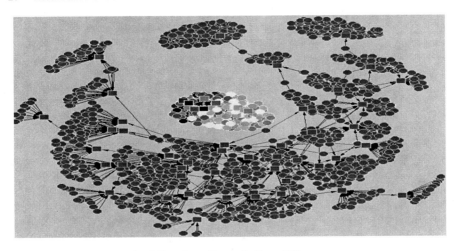

Fig. 27.12 Visualization of collaboration of journal editors [29]

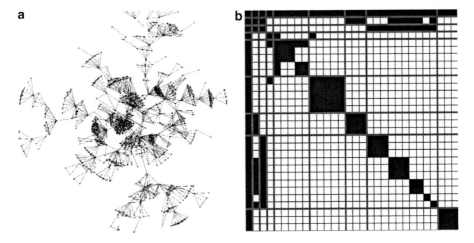

Fig. 27.13 Visual analysis of co-authorship in academic papers. (**a**) Visualization of co-authorship in JCDL [32]. (**b**) Visualization of co-authorship with the Matrix representation [33]

27.4.3.2 Co-Citation Relations

On contrary to the authorship view, social networks in digital libraries can be discovered from the citations and co-citations among writings themselves [34]. Since references are a crucial part of a document for readers to obtain information source, co-citation social networks can be formed through the continuously accumulated publications. With proper visualization of co-citation networks, documents with high impacts or similar citation patterns can be immediately identified, and the co-citation relationships can be intuitively observed as well. In 2006, a novel visualization tool, called CircleView, was proposed to visualize academic citation relations

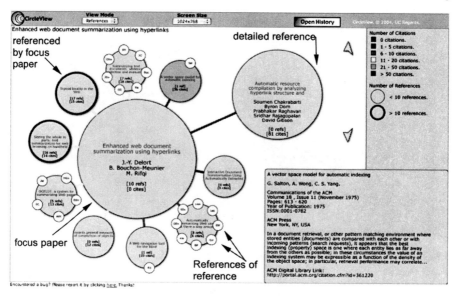

Fig. 27.14 CircleView: visualization of paper citation relations [35]

with interactive design and highlighted color [35]. In CircleView, the summarized contents of the focus papers, such as references, detail reference, and references of reference, are marked with different colors and highlighted circles. Figure 27.14 displays the CircleView user interface with scalable visualization and navigation of citation networks.

In 2007, an interactive visualization tool was developed to present large co-citation networks with latent visual cues and allows direct interaction with the visualized graphs. In [36], an interaction-based citation visualization system was proposed to visualize larger datasets with scalable functionalities and complemented the citation visualization of domain content analysis. Figure 27.15a displays the full view of network visualization with the interactive control panel in the right. In Fig. 27.15b, a closer look is presented by click at on of the cluster of Fig. 27.15a.

In co-citation networks, paper-reference matrices are generally transformed into reference-reference matrices to obtain co-citation relationships. Then these co-citation relationships can be visualized in different representations, typically as node-edge networks, to represent the intellectual structures of scientific domains [37]. However, the reference-reference visualization will bring about tightly knit components and make visual analysis of the intellectual structure a challenging task. In 2009, an innovative visualization technique, called FP-tree, was developed to present co-citation network from a new perspective, namely, visualizing social networks based on a paper-reference matrix instead of using a reference-reference matrix.

In [37], the paper-reference matrix was transformed into an FP-tree visualization to analyze the intellectual structure of two domains: Information Visualization

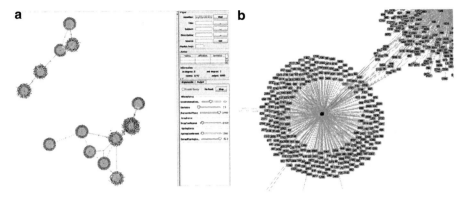

Fig. 27.15 Interactive visualization of co-citation networks by querying "knowledge management" in CiteSeer [36]. (**a**) Two sub graphs emerged from the co-citation graph. (**b**) A closer look at one of the cluster of (**a**)

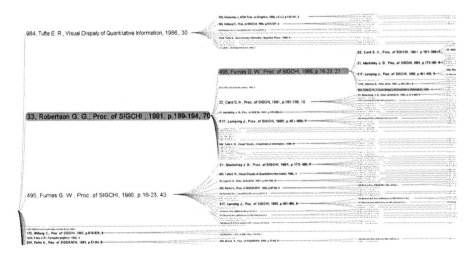

Fig. 27.16 The FP-tree visualization of the Infovis 2004 contest data [37]

and Sloan Digital Sky Survey (SDSS). The two real-world case studies further reveal that the FP-tree visualization can retain the important information in the intellectual structure of a domain and facilitate domain analysts to reveal fine-grained sub-structure when tightly knit clusters occurred in co-citation networks. Although the FP-tree visualization is friendly to help users analyze the intellectual structure, it will also cause multiple distributions of the same reference and make the tree structure larger than the co-citation network in several magnitude levels. Figure 27.16 shows the FP-tree visualization of co-citation relationships among three key documents.

27.4.4   Web 2.0 Services

Since the concept of Web 2.0 was proposed in 2004, online social activities are becoming more prosperous than before. Many Web 2.0 applications are popularly accessed by users to connect their social networks, such as Twitter and Facebook. For example, Twitter provides users convenient functionalities to share the up-to-date status with their followers. Since the following and the followed relationships can be quickly constructed, large social networks are created over the Twitter service, and many visualization applications are developed to analyze Twitter social networks. In 2007, a visualization interface was built to explore the community structure and properties of Twitter social networks. Figure 27.17a visualizes the Twitter social network of at least one-way acquaintanceship, and Fig. 27.17b displays the Twitter social network of mutual acquaintances[3]. From analyzing the community structure and properties of the two graphs, users can intuitively recognize the features and differences of two social groups over Twitter.

Another example of Web 2.0 services that forms large social networks is Facebook. As Facebook was proposed at Harvard in 2004, its social community grows explosively from U.S. to the rest of the world. Until today, Facebook has over 400 million active users worldwide, and large and complex social networks come along with the explosive growth of Facebook communities. Therefore, many interactive visualization applications and tools are developed to assist users to access and analyze such complicated social networks. Nexus[4] is a visualization application on Facebook communities to illustrate their large network graphs. With the Nexus visualization, user relationships can be properly displayed, and user names will pop

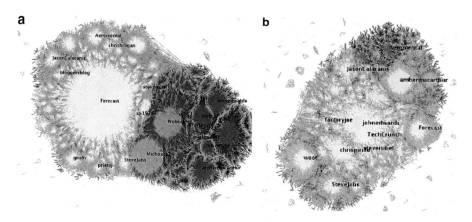

Fig. 27.17 Visual analysis of Twitter social network[3]. (**a**) Twitter social network of at least one-way acquaintance. (**b**) Twitter social network of mutual acquaintances

---

[3] Twitter social network, http://ebiquity.umbc.edu/blogger/2007/04/19/twitter-social-network-analysis/

[4] Nexus, http://nexus.ludios.net/

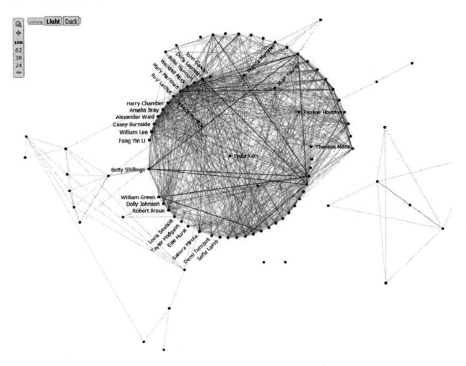

Fig. 27.18 Visualizing social relationships of Facebook with Nexus[4]

up when mouse is moved over the nodes. However, when user relationships are complicated, the social relationships in the Nexus visualization may become difficult to be recognized. Figure 27.18 shows the screenshot of Nexus.

To improve the interlaced visualization problem caused by the node-edge representation, visual icons and user photos are further employed in the Facebook visualization. TouchGraph[5] is a modern Facebook visualization that provides users with interactive functionalities to help access social networks. Figure 27.19 shows the TouchGraph visualization for Facebook. In Fig. 27.19, the user profiles, relations, and related photos are clearly displayed with the TouchGraph visualization interface, and thus, users can friendly interact with their social networks. However, the panorama of the community structure cannot be browse in a glance since Touch-Graph takes many clicks to obtain other attributes of the social network.

In 2010, an advanced interactive visualization interface, called IRNet, was proposed to further improve the shortcomings of Nexus and TouchGraph on visualizing Facebook communities. IRNet visualizes interpersonal relationships in social networks with focus + context techniques to present both local and global views [38]. To present a clear visualization of social networks, IRNet employs a hyperbolic view instead of using a force-directed model used in Vizster, and thus IRNet

---

[5] Touchgraph, http://www.touchgraph.com

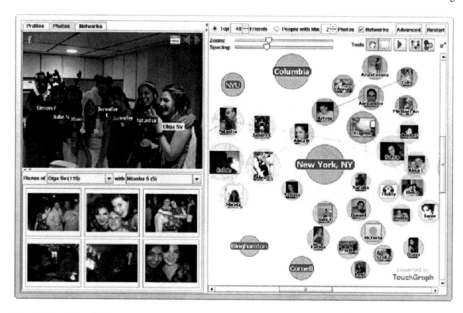

Fig. 27.19 Visualizing social relationships of Facebook with TouchGraph[5]

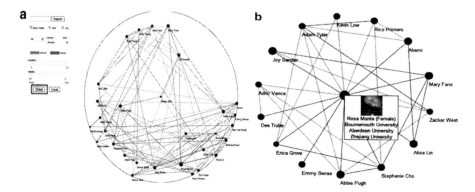

Fig. 27.20 The IRNet visualization for Facebook communities [38]. (**a**) A hyperbolic view for exploring the global social networks. (**b**) A local view with focus zooming from a single user perspective

can effectively improve the identification of social relationships. Many interactive operations, such as focus change zooming, color highlighting, attribute filtering, searching, and photo showing, are also designed in IRNet to facilitate accessing personal social networks. In Fig. 27.20a, a hyperbolic plane is displayed for browsing the global social network. Figure 27.20b shows the local view of the personal social relationships with a focus zooming view.

In addition to visualizations mentioned above, there are still versatile visualization applications developed to help people access social networks over Web 2.0

services. With the progress of visualization technologies, we can foresee that the immense information on the Web can be friendlier presented to people. Social network analysis on Web 2.0 communities can benefit from these advances as well.

27.4.5 Summary

According to the visualized subjects and relationships, many kinds of visualization techniques can be utilized to present social networks. From the categorized examples illustrated above, we have described and analyzed the online social network visualization by their nature of sociality. In addition, visualization of online social networks can be further categorized into three types by their social relationships: user-centric visualization, content-centric visualization, and hybrid visualization.

- User-centric visualization:

From the perspective of actors, visualizing user-centric social relationships can present various characteristics of actors and helps explore different subjects and relationships of interests. For example, visualizing user-centric social relationships can help people discover individuals and communities that meet the following expectations:

1. actors or groups with similar/complementary features,
2. key actors or those with high social impacts, and
3. actors with popular interpersonal relationships or active social interactions.

A great variety of online social networks are created and visualized according to the above user-centric social relationships, such as Club Nexus, Vizster, People Entity Cube, FOAF, SNF, and co-authorship networks. Such user-centric visualizations are widely utilized to help people access their social networks and discover the social networks of their interests.

- Content-centric visualization:

As the boosted development and evolution of Internet applications, particularly in the era of Web 2.0, an explosive amount of Web information was rapidly produced via various social network communities. Therefore, from the view of visualizing content-centric social relationships, various kinds of contents can be properly presented to facilitate people analyzing social networks. For example, at least the following three sorts of social network contents can displayed with content-centric visualization:

1. the distribution of user opinions, including key opinions and controversial comments,
2. user opinions with high impacts toward their social communities, especially the effective-impact period of time, and
3. the relations among different content groups.

In according with content-centric social relationships, several visual applications for online social networks are developed, such as visualizations for citation and co-citation social networks.

- Hybrid visualization:

Social activities among actors are generally more than one form and thus may consist of different kinds of relationships and interactions. Therefore, besides the user-centric visualization and content-centric visualization interfaces, still many visualization interfaces are designed according to hybrid relationships. Hybrid visualization is to visualize social networks from different aspects of attributes, e.g. people and contents. Particularly, online social activities, such as email and dating services, usually include such elements. Therefore, these online social networks are displayed with hybrid visualization techniques, such as PostHistory, Themail, TouchGraph, and IRNet.

27.5 Conclusions

The amount of Web information is much larger than that produced in the past decades. Particularly in the recent 10 years, the immense growth of Web information has caused at least two pressing problems to be solved: how to effectively and efficiently find the required information; how to properly display such a large amount of Web information. For the former problem, many state-of-the-art search algorithms and up-to-date Web frameworks, e.g. Semantic Web, have been in-depth studied to improve the retrieval performance. No matter how accurately these algorithms can facilitate searching, ranking, and filtering information, connecting people and the obtained information is still the most challenging issue. In a small-world network, social relationships between each individual are more tightly connected by the fast development of Internet technologies. When the connection between people and such large online social networks is concerned, information visualization shall play a more significant role to bridge human and network information.

In this chapter, we have reviewed the background of social network analysis and introduced the corresponding visualization technologies for social network analysis. In particular, many emphases have been focused on the description and analysis of the state-of-the-art visualizations for online social networks. From the developments and experiences of the state of the arts, we also see that there are still many challenges for social network visualization. Currently, the toughest challenges for visualizing online social network are from the immense amount of Web information and the immediate change of network status.

To properly solve these problems, we consider the following two aspects to be the most crucial fundamentals for breakthrough, namely, a systematic management framework for social networks and a friendly human-computer-interaction (HCI) design. For the future development of social network visualization, the two challenges will affect the manners of how people access their social networks and how people connect each other. For more practical use of online social network visualization in the future, development of visualization also demands profound considerations of aesthetics and physiology since visualizing online social networks is by nature related to the issues of how people communicate with each other and how people interact with information.

References

1. L. C. Freeman, "Visualizing Social Groups", In American Statistical Association 1999 Proceedings of the Section on Statistical Graphics, 2000, 47–54.
2. M. Sköld, "Social Network Visualization", Master Thesis, Royal Institute of Technology, Sweden, 2008.
3. M. Gurevich, "The Social Structure of Acquaintanceship Networks", PhD Thesis, MIT Press, Cambridge, 1961.
4. S. Brin and L. Page, "The Anatomy of Large-Scale Hypertextual Web Search Engine", Computer Networks and ISDN Systems, 30(1–7), 1998, 107–117.
5. J. Kleinberg, "Authoritative Sources in a Hyperlinked Environment", Journal of the ACM, 46(5), 1999, 604–632.
6. L. C. Freeman, "Visualizing Social Networks", Journal of Social Structure, 1, 2000, 1.
7. B. Bollobas, "Graph Theory: An Introductory Course", Springer, Verlag, 1979.
8. S. Wasserman and K. Faust, "Social Networks Analysis: Methods and Applications", Cambridge University Press, Cambridge, UK, 1994.
9. D. J. Watts and S. Strogatz, "Collective Dynamics of 'Small-world' Networks", Nature 393, 1998, 440–442.
10. N. Gershon, S. G. Eick, and S. Card, "Design: Information Visualization", ACM Interactions, 5(2), 1998, 9–15.
11. J. -D. Fekete, J. J. van Wijk, J. T. Stasko, and C. North, "The Value of Information Visualization". In: A. Kerren, J. T. Stasko, J. -D. Fekete, and C. North (Eds), Information Visualization – Human-Centered Issues and Perspectives. LNCS 4950, Springer, Verlag, 2008, 1–18.
12. R. Spence, "Information Visualization", Addison-Wesley, Reading, 2nd ed, 2006.
13. C. Ware, "Information Visualization: Perception for Design", Morgan Kaufmann, San Francisco, 2000.
14. J. Díaz, J. Petit, and M. Serna, "A Survey of Graph Layout Problems", ACM Computing Surveys (CSUR), 34(3), 2002, 313–356.
15. S. Mukherjea, J. Foley, and S. Hudson, "Visualizing Complex Hypermedia Networks through Multiple Hierarchical Views", In Proceedings of the ACM SIGCHI Conference on Human Factors in Computing Systems (CHI'95), Denver, 1995, 331–337.
16. J. Lamping, R. Rao, and P. Pirolli, "A Focus + Context Technique Based on Hyperbolic Geometry for Visualizing Large Hierarchies", In Proceedings of the ACM SIGCHI Conference on Human Factors in Computing Systems (CHI'95), Denver, 1995, 401–408.
17. K. -P. Yee, D. Fisher, R. Dhamija, and M. Hearst, "Animated Exploration of Dynamic Graphs with Radial Layout", In Proceedings of the 2001 IEEE Symposium on Information Visualization (InfoViz'01), 2001, 43.
18. T. Munzner, "H3: Laying Out Large Directed Graphs in 3D Hyperbolic Space", In Proceedings of the 1997 IEEE Symposium on Information Visualization (InfoViz'97), 1997, 2–10.
19. M. Ghoniem, J. D. Fekete, and P. Castagliola, "A Comparison of the Readability of Graphs Using Node-Link and Matrix-Based Representations", In Proceedings of 2004 IEEE Symposium on Information Visualization (InfoVis'04), Texas, 2004, 17–24.
20. N. Henry and J. -D. Fekete, "MatrixExplorer: a Dual-Representation System to Explore Social Networks", IEEE Transactions on Visualization and Computer Graphics, 12(5), 2006, 677–684.

21. L. A. Adamic, O. Buyukkokten, and E. Adar, "A Social Network Caught in the Web," First Monday, 8(6), 2003.
22. L. A. Adamic and E. Adar, "How to Search a Social Network", Social Networks, 27(3), 2005, 187–203.
23. J. Heer and D. Boyd, "Vizster: Visualizing Online Social Networks", In Proceedings of the 2005 IEEE Information Visualization Conference (InfoVis'05), 2005.
24. J. C. Paolillo and E. Wright, "Social Network Analysis on the Semantic Web: Techniques and Challenges for Visualizing FOAF", Visualizing the Semantic Web: XML-Based Internet and Information Visualization, Chapter 14, V. Geroimenko and C. Chen (Eds), Springer, Verlag, 2nd ed, 2006, 229–241.
25. D. Fisher and P. Dourish, "Social and Temporal Structures in Everyday Collaboration", In Proceedings of the SIGCHI Conference on Human Factors in Computing Systems (CHI'04), Vienna, Austria, 2004, 551–558.
26. F. B. Viégas, D. Boyd, D. Nguyen, J. Potter, and J. Donath, "Digital Artifacts for Remembering and Storytelling: PostHistory and Social Network Fragments", In Proceedings of the 37th Annual Hawaii International Conference on System Sciences (HICSS'04), 2004.
27. F. B. Viégas and J. Donath, "Social Network Visualization: Can We Go Beyond the Graph?", In Workshop on Social Networks (CSCW'04), Chicago, 2004, 6–10.
28. F. B. Viegas, S. Golder, and J. Donath, "Visualizing Email Content: Portraying Relationships from Conversational Histories", In Proceedings of the SIGCHI Conference on Human Factors in Computing Systems (CHI'06), 2006, 979–988.
29. M. Sharma and S. R. Urs, "Network Dynamics of Scholarship: A Social Network Analysis of Digital Library Community", In Proceedings of Workshop for Ph.D. Students in Information and Knowledge Management (PIKM'08), 2008, 101–104.
30. M. Sharma and S. R. Urs, "Network of Scholarship: Unconvering the structure of Digital Library Author Community", In Proceedings of the 11th International Conference on Asia-Pacific Digital Libraries (ICADL'08), 2008, 363–366.
31. G. La Rowe, R. Ichise, and B. Katy, "Visualizing Japanese Co-Authorship Data", In Proceedings of the 11th Annual Information Visualization International Conference (IV'07), 2007, 459–464.
32. X. Liu, J. Bollenb, M. L. Nelsonb, and H. V. de Sompel, "Co-authorship Networks in the Digital Library Research Community", Information Processing and Management, 41(6), 2005, 1462–1480.
33. Y. H. Said, E. J. Wegman, W. K. Sharabati, and J. T. Rigsby, "Social Networks of Author–Coauthor Relationships", Computational Statistics and Data Analysis, 52(4), 2008, 2177–2184.
34. C. Chen, "Information Visualization Research: Citation and Co-Citation Highlights", In Proceedings of the 2004 IEEE Symposium on Information Visualization (InfoViz'04), 2004, 216.
35. P. Bergstrom and J. E. Whitehead, "CircleView: Scalable Visualization and Navigation of Citation Networks", In Proceedings of the 2006 Symposium on Interactive Visual Information Collections and Activity (IVICA'06), College Station, Texas, 2006.
36. T. T. Chen and L. C. Hsieh, "On Visualization of Cocitation Networks", In Proceedings of the 11th International Conference Information Visualization, 2007, 470–475.
37. J. Zhang, C. Chen, and J. Li, "Visualizing the Intellectual Structure with Paper-Reference Matrices", IEEE Transactions on Visualization and Computer Graphics, 15(6), 2009, 1153–1160.
38. Y.-L. Ho, "Information Visualization on Interpersonal Relationships in Social Networks", Master Thesis, Yuan Ze University, Taiwan, 2009.
39. Y. Jia, J. Hoberock, M. Garland, and J. C. Hart, "On the Visualization of Social and other Scale-Free Networks", IEEE Transactions on Visualization and Computer Graphics, 14(6), 2008, 1285–1292.
40. B. Zhu and H. Chen, "Information Visualization", Annual Review of Information Science and Technology, 39, 2005, 139–177.

Chapter 28
Novel Visualizations and Interactions for Social Networks Exploration

Nathalie Henry Riche and Jean-Daniel Fekete

28.1 Introduction

In the last decade, the popularity of social networking applications has dramatically increased. Social networks are collection of persons or organizations connected by relations. Members of Facebook listed as friends or persons connected by family ties in genealogical trees are examples of social networks. Today's web surfers are often part of many online social networks: they communicate in groups or forums on topics of interests, exchange emails with their friends and colleagues, express their ideas on public blogs, share videos on YouTube, exchange and comment photos on Flickr, participate to the edition of the online encyclopedia Wikipedia or contribute to daily news by collaborating to Wikinews or Agoravox.

Recent online networking systems with a racing popularity such as Friendster, LinkedIn or Facebook are even exclusively dedicated to manage and extend one's own social network. Registered users voluntarily enter their contacts (family, friends or colleagues) and the nature or their relationships. Contacts not already registered on the website are personally invited to join the community. Thanks to this snowball effect, these online communities grow almost exponentially each day. Before this era of online social networking sites, large social networks were already available such as telephone networks listings, postal communication or bank transactions. However, the fact that these systems store all their data digitally and make it available online tremendously simplifies their collection and analysis processes. Compared to data collected through polls and interviews, collected networks are far larger and often contain much richer information. This avalanche of vast new datasets raises new challenges for their analysis: tools need to support a very large amount of data often evolving through time.

Analyzing how people communicate, collaborate, what information they exchange, what role they play in the social group is becoming a point of interest of a large variety of organizations, out passing the personal use. The stakes of social

N.H. Riche (✉)
Microsoft Research, Redmond, USA
e-mail: Nathalie.Henry@microsoft.com

B. Furht (ed.), *Handbook of Social Network Technologies and Applications*,
DOI 10.1007/978-1-4419-7142-5_28, © Springer Science+Business Media, LLC 2010

networks analysis are becoming very high. Since September 11, research has been led to help intelligence agencies monitor closely terrorist networks, attempting to discover when they will act. After epidemic diseases such as SARS or the bird flu, the need for effective analysis tools to study transmission networks and to seek and contain new outbreaks is becoming pressing. The needs to perform detailed social network analysis is also important, for company managers and research institutes, who aim at studying the flow of communication between employees or the strength of collaboration between scientific to evaluate them and improve their productivity. While a large part of research in social network analysis is dedicated to develop models of such social networks to predict their evolution or better study their structure, there is a clear need for tools supporting the exploratory analysis of real social networks.

In the last 5 years, an increasing part of the research in information visualization focused on graph exploration, tackling the problem from novel angles using alternative representations to traditional node-link diagrams, as well as novel interaction techniques, scaling to explore larger graphs. In this article, we review these novel techniques in the context of social network analysis.

28.2   Node-Link Diagrams

Jacob Moreno was the first pioneer of social network visualization [1]. More than 70 years ago, he published visual depictions of social friendship in schools, using these visualizations to support his findings. Figure 28.1 presents an example of node-link diagram depicting friendship between girls and boys. The principle of node-link diagrams is to graphically represent actors of the network by nodes and connections by links. In Fig. 28.1, different shapes are used for the nodes, marking males and females; arrows connect them, indicating the directionality of the friendship relation.

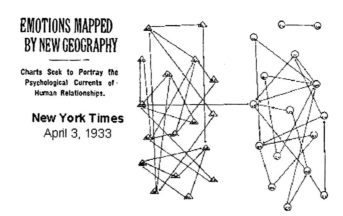

Fig. 28.1 Social network representing the friendship between boys (*triangles*) and girls (*circles*) by J. Moreno. A single actor connects both groups (*triangle* on the middle *left* part of the figure)

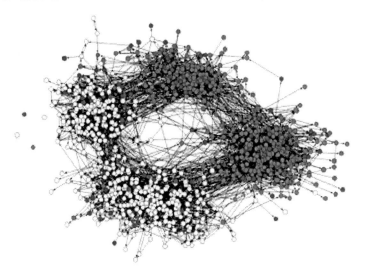

Fig. 28.2 Social network representing the friendship amongst high school students by J. Moody. The shades of *grey mark* the ethnicity of the students. Four groups emerge after running a clustering algorithm on age and ethnicity. These groups show that friendship is strongly correlated with age and ethnicity

Node-link diagrams are the most commonly used representation of graphs and networks. It is well illustrated by Freeman in his survey and history of social network visualization [2]. In this article, Freeman presents a wide variety of social networks and demonstrates that visual representations are a powerful tool to illustrate social network analysis concepts such as central actors or communities. Figure 28.1 demonstrates how a visual representation can highlight central actors, representing communities by two dense groups of nodes and links and placing the actor bridging them in the center of the representation. Figure 28.2 presents an example from Moody, in which four distinct communities emerge.

Node-link representations are widely used and familiar to a very large audience, making them a powerful communication tool. However, their readability and the message they convey greatly depends on the positions of their nodes. Whether they are manually drawn as in Fig. 28.1 or automatically generated as in Fig. 28.2, determining what makes a node-link diagram aesthetically pleasing, easy to read or conveying given findings is a difficult challenge. Since the 90s, an entire field of research is devoted to the problem of graph drawing, i.e. generating algorithms to place nodes in the space according to certain criteria such as minimizing the number of link crossing each other. A good introduction to graph drawing can be found in the book of Di Battista et al. [3] including more than 300 algorithms to layout graphs in 2D space. Additional state-of-the-art techniques to draw and navigate in node-link diagrams can be found in Herman et al. [4]. Researchers performed a number of studies [5,6] to identify which criteria are the most important to improve human understanding. However, the number of these criteria and their interaction with each other is so large that it is difficult to identify a core set and thus create the ideal layout algorithm.

Information visualization has a slightly different perspective on the topic [7]. This field of research focuses on visual exploration and the discovery or communication of insights about the data. For example, representations in Figs. 28.1 and 28.2 do not provide the best possible layout (and certainly do not minimize the number of link crossings) but they convey important information about the network highlighting central actors and social groups. Different representations may help discover different insights in the data. Thus, information visualization does not aim at the ideal representation but advocates for the use of multiple representations and multiple perspectives on the data, supported by interactions to quickly explore them. Following this philosophy, we present in this article a set of techniques to complement the use of traditional node-link diagrams for analyzing social networks.

28.3 Scaling to Larger Networks

While many systems exists for analyzing small and medium sized networks, up to a few hundred nodes, scaling to large networks with several thousand or even millions of nodes remains a challenge. Node-link diagrams with more than a few hundred nodes often become an undistinguishable hairball of nodes and links, difficult to transform either automatically or manually into a readable representation. In this case, analysts have to resort to one or more of these solutions:

1. Reducing the quantity of information by filtering or aggregating data
2. Representing a subset of the network and exploring it incrementally
3. Providing more visual space to represent the graph
4. Using an alternative representation.

28.3.1 Reducing the Quantity of Information

An obvious technique to reduce the size of a graph is to remove some of its vertices and edges. Two approaches exist to filter networks: (1) filtering out elements while preserving a representative sample or (2) filtering data that is not of current interest to the analyst.

1. There are multiple ways to sample a network [8]. However, this approach is particularly challenging for social networks as they often exhibit small-world networks properties [9]: globally sparse and locally dense networks. In these cases, preserving a representative topological structure is difficult as filtering links can result in disconnecting the network or losing the power-law distribution of the connections. Recent advances in graph drawing compute a hierarchical decomposition of graphs [10], each level being a coarsened version of the previous one. This decomposition is useful both to speed-up the layout computation and to

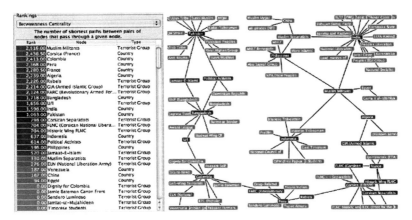

Fig. 28.3 Screenshot of Social Action, the panel on the *left* show an ordered list of actors sorted by betweeness centrality. The nodes are colored according to this measure and users can filter the network to show the top most central actors

visualize a meaningful structure at several zooming level. However, due to the small-world property, coarsening a locally dense graph still produces a locally dense graph albeit smaller.

2. The second approach is to filter nodes and edges according to the value of a given measure. This measure can be computed according to structural properties of the graph (e.g. filter by connected components), or based on data properties of the network (e.g. filter data by year). SocialAction [11] is a good example of social network analysis system based on filtering (Fig. 28.3). In this system, nodes and edges are ranked according to specific features or metrics such as centrality or betweenness selected by the user. This ranking controls the sections of the network displayed as well as visual encodings such as color and size.

A different approach to reduce the quantity of information displayed without filtering is to aggregate nodes and edges together. Many techniques exist to compute cluster data [12]. Ideally, the output of graph clustering techniques is a set of clusters regrouping similar vertices (according to some similarity metrics computed from topology or data attributes). Then, to gain space, vertices appearing in the same cluster can be aggregated into a single representative super-node (Fig. 28.4). This aggregation can be done iteratively, aggregating the network at multiple levels of details. Ask-GraphView [13] is a good example of such systems.

Reducing the quantity of information displayed lead to multiple issues. When filtering nodes and links, the topological structure of the network may be damaged and specific properties lost. When aggregating nodes together, detailed information on the connectivity inside the super-node is lost and data attributes of individual nodes have to be averaged or summarized in some ways. Other attributes can be created as well, such as the count of elements in the cluster, averages, min values, etc.

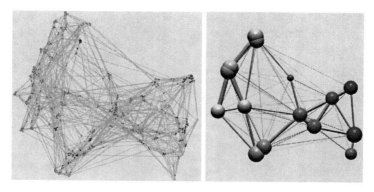

Fig. 28.4 Initial network on the *left*, resulting aggregated network on the *right*

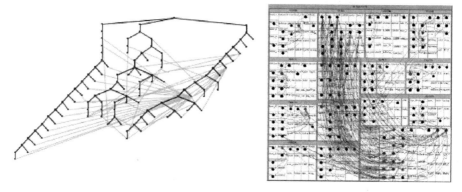

Fig. 28.5 A network represented as tree plus additional links on the *left*. A network represented as a Treemap plus additional links on the *right*

28.3.2 Incremental Exploration

When dealing with large networks, the main challenge is to obtain a readable layout in a reasonable time. Algorithms exist to handle special cases of networks such as large trees, able to draw trees without crossings, in a time linear with the number of nodes. Thus, researchers explored the possibilities to draw networks as trees and "fix" them by adding additional links [14] (Fig. 28.5). Unfortunately as the network gets further away of the tree structure, the visual representations become less readable. In this case, the remaining solution is used to show only a subset of the network and to provide interaction to explore the remaining parts. TreePlus [15] is a good example of such system, exploiting the readability of tree layout algorithms and combining it with fast interaction techniques (Fig. 28.6). The disadvantage of systems based on incremental exploration is the lack of overview provided to the user making it difficult to guide the analysis and therefore necessary to explore the whole network.

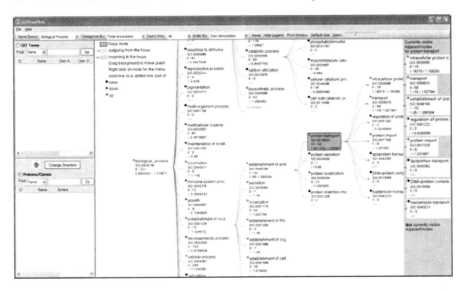

Fig. 28.6 A screenshot of TreePlus, representing a small part of a network as a tree and providing interaction to explore the remaining parts

28.3.3 Using More Visual Space

To augment the available visual space, a number of researcher work investigated the third dimension. One more dimension theoretically offers more display space and also provides an additional freedom to optimize aesthetic criteria such as minimizing the number of link crossings. A number of systems draw graphs in 3D [16, 17], examples are provided in Fig. 28.7. The main drawback of 3D representations is the occlusion and the difficulty for users to create a mental map of the whole network [18]. To solve these issues, some systems attempt to provide multiple views to users; others offer them navigation and interaction techniques to visualize the network under multiple angles. However, in most cases, these techniques disorient users, making visual exploration fruitless. Several studies show that if 3D visualizations may appear attractive, they do not improve performances, even decreasing them for several tasks [19].

Another approach to increase the visual space is to use alternate geometries such as hyperbolic geometry instead of Euclidian geometry. In the hyperbolic space, the parallelism axiom is rejected (i.e. two parallel lines in Euclidian space diverge from each other in hyperbolic space). Thus, considering a disk in hyperbolic space, the space increases exponentially as one gets further from its center. A network drawn on such a disk benefits from an infinite space on its borders. The principle applies to 2D [20] and 3D [21] (see Fig. 28.7). Unfortunately, to be displayed, hyperbolic spaces have to be projected in a Euclidian space and, similarly to 3D representations, navigating in hyperbolic space is disorienting for users, requires extensive navigation and makes it more difficult to build and maintain a mental map of the whole network.

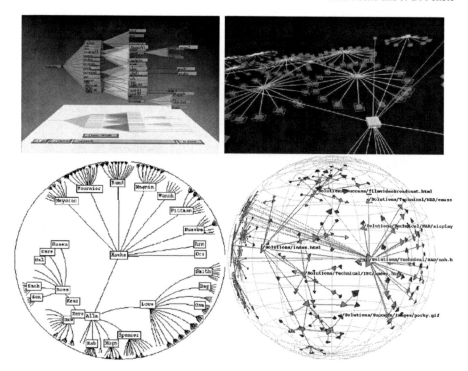

Fig. 28.7 *Top* images show networks drawn in 3D: ConeTrees on the left and visualization generated with the Tulip toolkit on the *right*. *Bottom* images show networks represented in hyperbolic space: 2D on the *left* and 3D on the *right*

28.3.4 Alternative Representations

The last solution to visualize large diagrams is to resort to a different representation than node-link diagrams. An obvious choice is to use the adjacency matrix representation. We dedicate the remaining of this chapter to its variations. Other alternative representations are Treemaps, a tree visualization similar to Venn Diagrams where sub-trees are depicted with inclusion [22]. Exploiting the earlier approach of visualizing networks as trees with additional links, researchers have attempted to use Treemaps + links [23] to represent networks (Fig. 28.5). Similarly to the attempts described earlier, these representations decrease in readability as the network get denser. Finally, a few systems use simple charts such as bar charts and scatter plots to analyze networks such as PaperLens [24] and NetLens [25] (Fig. 28.8). These charts represent different attributes of the actors of the network. While they do not provide any overview or visual depiction of the actual actors and connections, they allow users to answer questions by querying the charts back and forth.

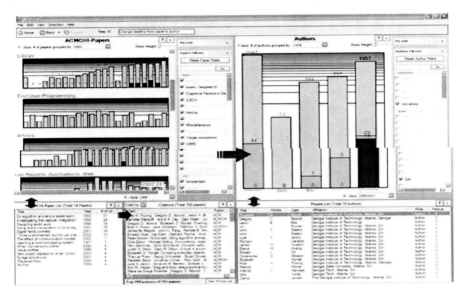

Fig. 28.8 A screenshot of NetLens, an interactive system to explore networks using simple bar charts. Users filter different attributes of the network by clicking on corresponding bars. NetLens provide the textual result on the lower windows

28.4 Adjacency Matrix Representations

An adjacency matrix is a table in which vertices of the graph are placed both in rows and columns. If vertex A is connected to vertex B, the cell at the intersection of the line of A and the column of B is marked. Since vertices are represented both in rows and columns, there are two cells corresponding to a pair of vertices, making it possible to represent directed edges. In the case of non-directed graphs, the mark is generally duplicated in both cells. Traditionally, a numerical value marks the connection (0 if no connection, 1 if there is one, n if the edge is weighted). Figure 28.9 shows an example.

Contrary to node-link diagrams, which suffer from link crossings when the network is dense and from the high complexity of the layout algorithm when the number of nodes of the network is large, adjacency matrices scale very well. Indeed, the cells representing the links do not cross of overlap each other and the time to draw the representation is low since the whole list of actors is placed linearly. However, two main factors have to be considered when using adjacency matrices to represent large graphs:

1. While always readable, matrices require reordering of their rows and columns to reveal insights about the data.
2. Matrices use an amount of space quadratic in the number of nodes, requiring effective navigation techniques to explore them.

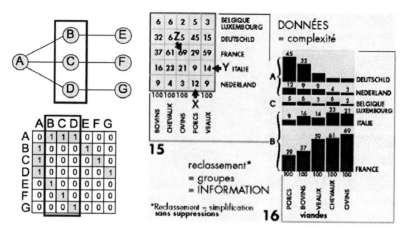

Fig. 28.9 Node-link diagram and its corresponding adjacency matrix on the *left*. Bertin's reordorable matrix [26] on the *right*

28.4.1 Reordering

In his "Semiology of graphics" [26], Jaques Bertin shows that replacing numerical values by visual indicators and reordering rows and columns dramatically improves the readability of tables and matrices. Figure 28.9 shows an example of the reorderable matrix. This matrix contains only five rows and five columns, representing the consumption of five types of meat in five countries. While the numerical table makes it possible to read any cell, it remains difficult to grasp higher-level organization of the data. However, once values are transformed into graphical indicators and rows and columns are manually reordered, one can discover a number of insights.

First, one can identify at a glance that France is the country producing the most meat overall, while Belgium is the country producing the least. One can also identify three profiles of production (marked as A, B and C on the Figure). To go a step further in interpreting this matrix, imagine that a law must be voted to limit the production of porcs (first column). According to the production profiles, this law would upset the two countries in group A. This representation shows that the country to convince is Belgium, since its profile of production is neutral. This example illustrates the importance of reordering the rows and columns of a matrix. While non-reordered matrices are readable, reordered matrices may help discover more insights about the data.

A large variety of techniques exists to reorder rows and columns of an adjacency matrix. Performing a survey of these techniques is a challenge since they come from a variety of domains and serve a variety of purposes. For example, techniques to linearize a graph (i.e. placing all the vertices linearly and ordering them to maximize an aesthetic criterion such as minimizing the number of edge crossing) or techniques to minimize the bandwidth of a table to optimize computation can be used to reorder adjacency matrices. These techniques vary in their complexity and the quality of

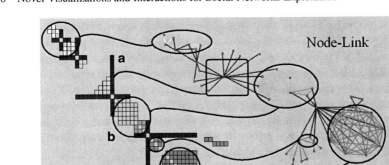

Fig. 28.10 Visual patterns in matrices and node-link diagrams: (**a**) central actor, (**b**) community, (**c**) clique

their results varies according to the context. Mueller et al. [27] attempted to compare the quality of eight algorithms. However, evaluating which order leads to better analysis results is challenging [28] since it depends on the data and tasks to be completed. A good measure of quality remains to be found.

Visual patterns can emerge from "well ordered" matrices, compare to "well placed" node-link diagrams. Figure 28.10 shows examples of relevant pattern for social network analysis. In this case, both representations were arranged manually. Several tools such as PermutMatrix [29] or VisuLab [30] offers visual representations of matrices and allows to experiment with multiple reordering techniques and their associated parameters. While we will not detail the categories of reordering techniques in this chapter, it is important to understand that a given ordering may have a strong impact on the readability and interpretation of matrices, similarly to the effect of the graph layout on node-link diagrams.

28.4.2 Navigation

Considering a given level of details, matrices require more space than node-link diagrams. For example, on a 17-inch monitor, matrices are limited to approximately a hundred of rows and columns if the analyst desires to read each label comfortably. Scaling to larger graph therefore requires extensive navigation.

In the field of Human-Computer Interaction, many techniques exist to navigate in large spaces, possibly at different levels of details. Most common techniques are Focus + Context [31] such as bird's eye views and fisheyes. Bird's eye views consist in miniature overviews of the whole representation in which users may move the position of their current view. This technique results in faster navigation than with standard scrollbars. Fisheyes allow visualizing multiple levels of details in a single view. Fisheyes act as magnifying lenses increasing details on regions of interest. TableLens [32] is a good example of the use of fisheyes in tables and matrices.

When navigating in large matrices it is essential to be able to read labels of rows and columns. For this reason, splitting the screen is a good solution. More sophisticated techniques exist, folding the space in 1D or 2D such as Melange [33] to provide both readable labels and context. A few navigation techniques have been specifically designed for navigating in adjacency matrices: MatrixZoom [34] or ZAME [35] provide navigation in aggregated matrices.

28.5 Visualizing Social Networks with Matrix-Based Representations

Matrices or node-link diagrams both have advantages and drawbacks for visualizing social networks. In this section, we present the pros and cons of each representation and propose a set of visualizations combining the best of both worlds.

28.5.1 Matrix or Node-Link Diagram?

Matrix and node-link diagrams have different properties making them suitable representations for different tasks and datasets. Ghoniem et al. [36] performed a user study to quantify the performance of both representations for several low-level readability tasks. To summarize their results, the study showed that node-link diagrams are more effective for very small (under 20 vertices) and sparse networks whereas matrices outperform them otherwise except when the task is to follow paths in the network. Building from these results and our experience, we attempt to list the main advantages of each representation in the following paragraph.

The advantages of matrices:

1. Matrices provide powerful overview visualization since the time to create them is low and since they are always readable. They constitute a good representation to initiate an exploration.
2. Matrices do not suffer from node overlapping, if the task requires to always read the actors' labels, this representation is more appropriate.
3. Matrices do not suffer from link crossing each other; therefore they are a viable alternative for dense networks.
4. Matrices show all possible pairs of vertices, they can highlight the lack of connections and also the directedness of the connections. They are particularly appropriate for directed and dense networks.

The advantages of node-link diagrams:

1. These representations are familiar to a wide audience; they constitute a powerful communication tool. In contrast, matrices require training and help decoding their meaning for novice users.
2. For small or sparse networks, Ghoniem et al. [36] proved that node-link diagrams were more effective than matrices.
3. For a similar level of details, the space used by matrices is larger than the space to display node-link diagrams. Therefore, for a compact representation, node-link diagrams are a better choice.
4. When the analysis requires to perform a number of path-related tasks (e.g. find the shortest path from John to Mary), node-link diagrams are more appropriate. Ghoniem et al. [36] showed that such tasks were difficult to perform with matrices.

28.5.2   Matrix + Node-Link Diagrams

To combine advantages of both representations and to support the visual exploration of social networks, we designed MatrixExplorer [37] (Fig. 28.11). To conceive this system, we observed and discussed with a small group of social scientists. We divided their analysis process in four main stages. For each, we describe how matrices and node-link diagrams can be combined to achieve the best of both worlds.

1. Initiate the exploration
2. Explore interactively and iteratively
3. Find a consensus in the data or validate an hypothesis
4. Present the findings

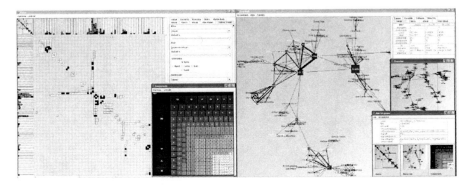

Fig. 28.11 A screenshot of MatrixExplorer. This system combines matrices (*left large window*) and node-link diagrams (*right large window*). The smaller window on the *left* shows a treemap view of the macrostructure of the network (connected components). The windows in the *lower right* corner show miniature bird's eye views of the visualizations. Queries and textual data are shown in *top* windows

28.5.2.1 Initiate Exploration

The main advantage of matrices is to always provide a readable representation of a network even when it is very large. Associated to their low rendering time, these two properties make them suitable representations to initiate the exploration. To illustrate this idea, we study the following example.

Figure 28.12 shows a matrix and a node-link representation of a social network containing the email exchange of more than 450 persons during a year. Persons are nodes or rows/columns, email exchanges between two persons are represented by a link or a cell filled with black in the matrix. The node-link representation, using a traditional force-directed layout, makes it difficult to identify specific nodes or links. After studying this diagram, an analyst may retain that the network is very dense and form the hypothesis that almost everyone have been exchanging emails with each other. One may also identify a few nodes on the periphery, indicating that a few persons did not communicate with the rest.

Studying the matrix representation conveys far more information. Each black dot represents a connection between a row and a column (i.e. an email exchange between two persons); the gray background shows the lack of connection. From the matrix presented in Fig. 28.12, an analyst can quickly assess that the network represented is, in fact, not very dense. Indeed, there is a majority of gray in the matrix showing that many actors did not exchange email with each other.

Studying further the representation, the analyst can observe clusters of black dots in the matrix. These blocks are groups of persons, exchanging a lot of email with each other. Since this data shows the email communication of a large research organization, glancing at the names of these actors reveals that these groups are in fact research teams. In addition to the clusters, the analyst can observe a cross pattern: vertical and horizontal lines constituted of black dots with an approximate length

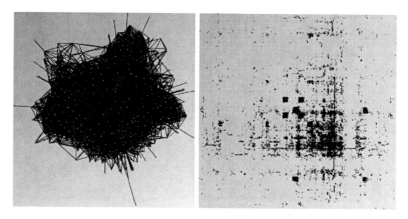

Fig. 28.12 Social network representing the email communication of more than 450 persons in a research institution over a year. The *left* image is a node-link diagram; the right image is a matrix (*black* shows connection, *grey* is no connection)

of half the matrix. Glancing at the names of the actors reveal that this patterns is associated with the administrative service, dealing with travels of the whole institutions and thus, communicating with many persons in the network.

This simple example shows that matrices have a strong potential to convey the overview of a network and initiate its exploration. We showed that, when correctly reordered, matrices highlight salient patterns of a network such as clusters or central actors. However, since they are far less familiar than node-link diagrams, some time is required to learn to decode and interpret these visual patterns.

28.5.2.2 Explore Interactively

After interviewing and observing multiple social network analysts, we realized that the exploration process itself is iterative and requires the creation of multiple visualizations. Interaction on these representations includes the configuration of the visualization (adjust its layout and its graphical attributes), the filtering as well as the grouping and possible aggregation of some of its elements.

Both the matrix and node-link representations support the analysis of the network at different levels of details. For instance, if an analyst is looking for an overview of the network to identify its main communities, the matrix is the best option. Then, when a more detailed analysis is required, to identify actors bridging two communities for example, node-link diagrams constitute a better alternative. With MatrixExplorer, we provide multiple views of the network and provide a number of tools to interactively manipulate matrix and node-link representations (Fig. 28.11).

Initially, the matrix and node-link representations are synchronized to combine their advantages and ease the identification of visual patterns. Selecting a row or column in the matrix highlights the corresponding node in the other representation.

In addition, visual variables such as size or color can be shared by both visualizations. Thus, it is possible to use matrices for some tasks and node-link diagrams for other. Selecting a visual pattern in the matrix and visualizing its equivalent in the node-link diagram also ease the understanding and learning of matrix representations, making them accessible to less expert users.

To interactively manipulate matrix and node-link representations, we provide the following set of tools:

1. *Interactive specification of visual attributes.* The user controls the mapping data-visual encoding by entering values in a text field or selecting a value in a list. Visual attributes of nodes, rows or columns such as label, color, transparency or size as well as attributes of links or cells such as thickness, color or texture may be associated to a data attribute.
2. *Interactive layout and reordering.* Users may directly move a node or a row/column in both representations to change its position or order.
3. *Automatic layout and reordering techniques.* Since laying out node-link diagrams or reordering large matrices by hand may be extremely tedious, we provide algorithms to automate layouts and reorderings. These techniques vary in their

computation time and quality. As we mentioned earlier, it is difficult to identify the appropriate techniques *a priori*, thus we provide users with several.

4. *Computer-assisted layout and reordering techniques.* We developed tools to support reordering, allowing users to apply layout and reordering algorithms to specific subsets of the network.

5. *Interactive filtering.* This functionality allows filtering actors or connections according to a selection or by selecting a specific value of a data attribute from a list (such as age or sex for example). Using the principle of dynamic queries [ref], the system provides dynamic feedback when the user modifies the parameters of the filter.

6. *Interactive clustering.* Once groups of actors are identified, we provide a simple mechanism to mark them and associate them to a visual attributed such as the color or shape of the nodes.

7. *Overview + Detail techniques to navigate in both representations.* To support navigation in large visual spaces, we propose two techniques providing focus + detail. We provide a brid's eye view to nagivate and a fisheye lens to magnify regions of interest for details. We also provide a Treemap to represent the macrostructure of the network (Fig. 28.11) and providing a fast filtering mechanism to isolate each connected component of the network.

By combining both representations of a network and by interacting with them, MatrixExplorer supports an iterative and interactive exploration process. Users can create multiple views on a network, compare them and explore them at different levels of details.

28.5.2.3   Find a Consensus in the Data

Each visualization may lead to the discovery of different insights. While in many cases, these insights may be confirmed by searching them using different representations, layouts or order during the analysis. It is possible that they differ slightly or even contradict each other when observed under different conditions. This may happen when attempting to identify clusters for example. In this case, different techniques to reorder the matrix may lead to different cluster sets. To help analysts find a consensus and validate hypotheses, some support is needed.

MatrixExplorer allows analysts to find consensus in the data through simple interactions. For example, by associating visual variables such as colors to different cluster sets and by reordering the matrix several times, analysts can identify clusters appearing clearly in multiple orders as more valid. In addition, to mark the uncertainty of attribution of an actor to a given cluster, MatrixExplorer also provides a technique to indicate the degree of membership of the element to a given cluster. Analysts can mark elements less likely to belong to a cluster with a lighter color. Finally, we support overlapping clusters and multiple sets of clusters: elements may belong to multiple clusters at the same time.

28.5.2.4   Present Findings

While matrix representations may prove effective when exploring large networks, node-link diagrams are essential to communicate findings to a wide audience. Many node-link diagrams may be created for presenting results with different filters and possibly different aggregations. To ease this process. MatrixExplorer allows users to generate pictures while performing the exploration.

28.5.3   Hybrid Representations

Providing both matrix and node-link diagrams to the user has a number of advantages but also drawbacks. First, it requires a large amount of display space. At least two display monitors are required to comfortably use MatrixExplorer; a third one is strongly recommended to display textual and detailed views. Secondly, we observed that switching from one representation to the other may induce high cognitive load to the user and split attention is always tiresome. Indeed, a single node on the node-link diagram becomes both a row and column in the matrix and a link, visually represented by a line, becomes a cell, i.e. a rectangle, in the matrix. Switching representations between tasks require a few seconds of adjustment, disorienting momentarily users. To minimize the display space required and limit the cognitive cost when switching representations, we developed two hybrid representations: MatLink [38] and NodeTrix [39]. The goal of these hybrids is to augment one representation to overcome its drawbacks and enrich it with the advantages of the other one.

28.5.3.1   Augmenting Matrices

As Ghoniem et al. demonstrated in their study, matrices do not support well path-following tasks. For example, finding the shortest path between two given actors is far easier in a node-link diagram, in which users can quickly investigate the multiple paths and assess what the shortest path is. These tasks being very common in social network analysis, we proposed to create a hybrid representation to overcome the problem in matrices: MatLink (Fig. 28.13).

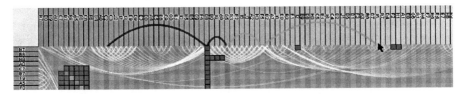

Fig. 28.13 Matlink support path-following tasks in standard matrices by adding links of their borders. *White* links are static and always shown. Links with a darker shades are interactive and follow the mouse pointer or selection

The principle of MatLink is to augment a standard matrix representation with links on its borders. These links provides a dual encoding of the connections between actors and ease path-following tasks since they use the visual representations of node-link diagrams. Two types of links are added to the representations: static links (in white on the figure) and interactive links (in a darker shade). The interactive links appear when the mouse cursor is moving over a specific row or column. When a row or column is selected, these links show a shortest path to any other row or column placed under the cursor.

Assessing the Readability of MatLink

To assess the performance of MatLink compare to traditional matrices, we performed a user study, borrowing the study design, low-level readability tasks and procedure from Ghoniem et al. [36]. In addition, we introduced specific tasks of social network analysis: find a cut point, find a clique and find communities (strongly connected groups). Our results show that MatLink significantly improve standard matrix representations. In particular, MatLink ease path-following tasks and performs even better than node-link diagrams for densely connected networks. The only task for which node-link diagrams still perform better is the identification of cut points. With MatLink, this task requires to identify specific visual patterns of the links. We believe this is possibly with more training, our participants having had only a few minutes of training with each technique for each task.

Using MatLink for Navigating in the Matrix

In addition to improving the readability of matrices, MatLink also supports navigation in large ones. Since matrices display actors in rows and columns, they require far more space than node-link diagrams to represent a network. Thus, it often happens that the neighbors of a given actor are placed outside of the current view; the reordering algorithm rarely offering strong guaranties regarding distances between connected nodes in the matrix. In standard matrices, visiting all neighbors of an actor placed in a row requires to review the whole set of columns, an extremely tedious task for large networks. In MatLink, all links connected to a given actor are displayed when this actor is selected. Thus, a direct visual feedback is provided on the number of neighbors and the curvature of the links provides an indication of their distance in the matrix as shown in Fig. 28.14.

In addition, to ease the navigation in very large matrix, we developed techniques helping users to navigate on these links and reach elements out of the view. The first technique Mélange [33] folds the space between two far away nodes as if it was a piece of paper (Fig. 28.15). Thus, users may see side by side parts of the matrix that are far away, the intervening folded space providing context. Mélange also offers the possibility to specify a different zoom factor for each non-folded region. The two other techniques use links as navigation support [40]. Bring-and-Go, brings

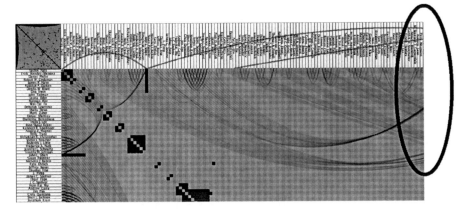

Fig. 28.14 Links in MatLink provide a visual cue that an actor on a path is outside the view. These links also provide a mean to quickly navigate to the neighbours by using Link Sliding [ref] for example

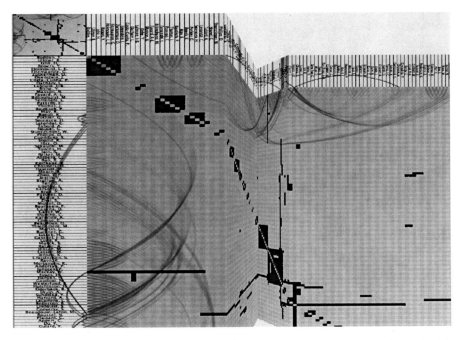

Fig. 28.15 Melange is a space folding technique designed to show far away parts of a matrix side by side while preserving the intermediate context

neighbors of an actor closer as if their links were elastic, by moving the cursor over one of the neighbor and releasing the mouse, the view and the node travel to its previous location. Link Sliding allows users to locks their cursor to a given link and travel very fast to its destination. These three techniques provide users with effective tools to navigate in large matrices with MatLink.

28.5.3.2 Merging Matrix and Node-Link Diagram

Node-link diagrams or matrices perform differently according to the types of visualized networks. For example, node-link diagrams or hybrids Treemap + links are well suited to represent tree-like networks. Conversely, for dense networks or bipartite networks, matrices are better suited, maximizing the use of space and remove any link crossing. For small-world networks, however, the choice of representation is not so clear. When visualizing such network with a node-link diagram, the dense regions (e.g. communities) suffer from link crossing and become difficult to read. However, when using a matrix representation, the visualization is very sparse and requires a lot of navigation for exploration.

To solve this problem, we created NodeTrix [39]: a hybrid visualization merging node-link diagrams and matrices. The principle of NodeTrix is to represent the global network as a node-link diagram and the locally dense subparts as matrices (Fig. 28.16).

Interactive Exploration

To ease creation, exploration and edition of matrices in NodeTrix, we developed a number of interactions based on traditional drag-and-drop of objects with the mouse cursor. The matrices may be generated automatically or created interactively. Performing a lasso selection on a group of nodes in the node-link diagrams transforms these nodes into a matrix representation. This representation on dense subparts of the networks allows identifying information such as the lack of connections between two actors. In the node-link representation, such information is difficult to read due to the high number of links and their crossings. It may also be useful to extract a set of communities from a standard matrix and place them in a NodeTrix view to better understand how they are connected.

Matrix representations have the advantage of placing actors of the network linearly (in rows and in columns), thus it becomes easy to identify the community members connected to external actors. To add or remove actors from the matrix,

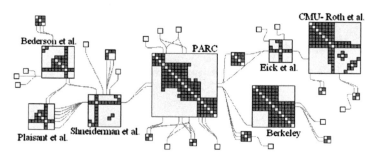

Fig. 28.16 NodeTrix representation of the collaboration network of researchers in information visualization, filtered down to a hundred actors

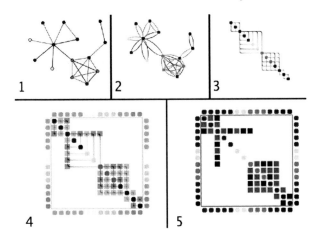

Fig. 28.17 Animation to transform a node-link diagram (1) into a matrix (5)

users simply select the node or row/column representing an actor and drag it in or out of the matrix. Other interactions include the possibility to merge two matrices or split them to get back to the original node-link representation. Finally, to help users understand the change of representation, we animate the transformation (see the steps of the animation in Fig. 28.17).

The main drawback of NodeTrix is the concrete representation of communities, making it impossible to place an actor in two different communities. To solve this problem, we provide users with the possibility to duplicate an actor and place it in two or more communities [41]. Preliminary results of a user study suggest that duplications improve readability by providing non-biased view of each community. It becomes easier to identify actors acting as bridge between communities and understand the inter-community connections. Our results also show that confusion can be minimized by visually representing links between duplicates.

Presenting Findings

Because matrices can be expanded showing detailed information on actors and connections or compacted (their rows and columns headers retracted and their size minimized) showing higher-level connection patterns, NodeTrix can be used for both exploration and communication. Figure 28.16 shows an example of the compact representation of a network with more than a hundred actors. Figure 28.18 shows the same network with more details.

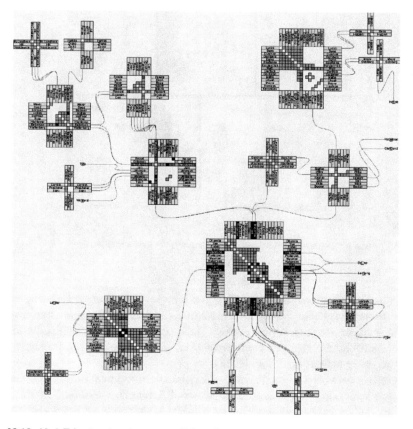

Fig. 28.18 NodeTrix showing the same collaboration network than Fig. 28.16 at a more detailed stage: including all labels of researchers and using shades of grey to indicate the number of publications

28.6 Conclusion

Given the vast amount of data available online, the visual analysis of social networks has become exciting but also challenging. Tools are required to scale to handle very large networks whereas traditional node-link representations do not scale very well. Without such visualization tools, statistical tools remain the most reliable approach to analyze large social networks. While statistical tools help answering a vast number of questions and validate hypotheses, they do not support the exploration process very well. Supporting this exploration process and helping analysts discover insights about the data and answering questions they did not even know they had is the goal of information visualization [42].

In this chapter, we presented a number of recent works to visually explore social networks. These novel information visualization techniques open a new era for the exploratory analysis of social networks. They allow scaling to larger networks and provide powerful communication means.

We initiated this chapter by presenting a number of techniques to help node-link diagrams scale to larger networks. We highlighted the familiarity of these representations and attempted to describe when these representations are more appropriate. However, node-link diagrams suffer from important readability problems [36]. For this reason, we presented a set of novel techniques based on adjacency matrix representations [43]. We showed that matrix-based representations can scale to larger networks and provide insightful overviews. Through the chapter, we stressed the necessity to reorder their rows and columns and learn to decode their visual patterns.

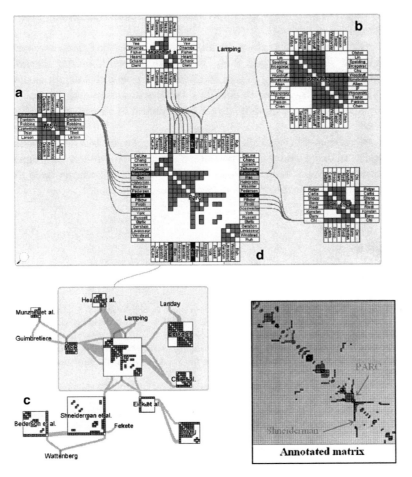

Fig. 28.19 Matrix-based representations depicting the collaboration network of researchers in information visualization. The matrix shows a central actor (Shneiderman) as well as a group of researchers collaborating strongly with each other (PARC). The NodeTrix view shows different patterns of collaboration. (**a**) shows a clique, (**b**) shows two cliques with three actors bridging them. Both (**a**) and (**b**) tend to be collaboration patterns of research companies, (**c**) shows a standard collaboration pattern for university professors (they collaborate with many students who rarely collaborate with each other) and (**d**) shows a hybrid version of these two patterns. The same patterns are visible in Fig. 28.16

Information visualization advocates for the use of multiple representations; providing analysts with multiple perspectives on their datasets and interactive tools to manipulate them. Following this philosophy, we combined both node-link diagrams and matrix representations with MatrixExplorer [37] and presented a number of techniques to interact with these representations. To go a step further, we presented novel representations merging node-link diagrams and matrices: MatLink [38], overcoming the problem of paths finding in matrices, and NodeTrix [39], improving the readability of dense clusters in node-link diagrams. This set of visualization techniques presented in this chapter aims at helping analysts explore social networks, raising novel questions about a particular dataset and discovering new insights.

A concrete example of exploratory analysis using matrix-based representations is presented in [44]. In this case study, we reported insights on the scientific collaboration in the field of HCI. Figure 28.19 presents a few visualizations extracted from this case study. Learning to decode specific patterns in matrices can lead to interesting discoveries and quickly attract the attention of an analyst on salient part of a network.

While we addressed the challenge of visualizing larger and denser social networks, other challenges remain. In particular, merging exploratory techniques with model-based techniques remains to be done to validate hypothesis once they are found visually or explore discrepancies from an expected model.

References

1. J. Moreno, "Who shall survive?", Nervous and Mental Disease Publishing Company, Washington, DC, 1934.
2. L. Freeman, "Visualizing social networks", Journal of Social Structure, 1, 2000, 1.
3. G. Di Battista, P. Eades, R. Tamassia, and I. G. Tollis, "Graph drawing: Algorithms for the visualization of graphs", Prentice Hall PTR, NJ, 1998.
4. I. Herman, G. Melancon, and S. Marshall, "Graph visualization and navigation in information visualization: A survey", IEEE Transactions on Visualization and Computer Graphics, 6(1), 2000, 24–43.
5. H. Purchase, "Which aesthetic has the greatest effect on human understanding?", Proceedings of Graph Drawing, 97, 1997, 248–261.
6. C. Ware, H. Purchase, L. Colpoys, and M. McGill, "Cognitive measurements of graph aesthetics", Journal of Information Visualization, 1(2), 2002, 248–261.
7. S. K. Card, J. D. Mackinlay, and B. Shneiderman, "Readings in information visualization: Using vision to think", Morgan Kaufmann Publishers, San Francisco, 1999.
8. O. Frank, "Sampling and estimation in large social networks", Social networks, 1, 1978, 91–101.
9. D. J. Watts and S. H. Strogatz, "Collective dynamics of 'small-world' networks", Nature, 393, 1998, 440–442.
10. Y. Koren, L. Carmel, and D. Harel, "Drawing huge graphs by algebraic multigrid optimization", Multiscale Modeling and Simulation, 1(4), 2003, 645–673.
11. A. Perer and B. Shneiderman, "Balancing systematic and flexible exploration of social networks", IEEE Transactions on Visualization and Computer Graphics, 12(5), 2006, 693–700.
12. A. K. Jain, M. N. Murty, and P. J. Flynn, "Data clustering: A review", ACM Computing Surveys, 31(3), 1999, 264–323.

13. J. Abello, F. van Ham, and N. Krishnan, "Ask-graphview: A large scale graph visualization system", IEEE Transactions on Visualization and Computer Graphics journal, 12(5), 2006, 669–676.
14. I. Herman, G. Melancon, M. M. de Ruiter, and M. Delest, "Latour: A tree visualisation system", Proceedings of the Graph Drawing symposium (GD' 99), LNCS, 1731, 1999, 392–399.
15. B. Lee, C. S. Parr, C. Plaisant, B. B. Bederson, V. D. Veksler, W. D. Gray, and C. Kotfila, "TreePlus: interactive exploration of networks with enhanced tree layouts", IEEE Transactions on Visualization and Computer Graphics, Special Issue on Visual Analytics, 12(6), 2006, 1414–1426.
16. G. G. Robertson, J. D. Mackinlay, and S. K. Card, "Cone trees: Animated 3D visualizations of hierarchical information", In Proceedings of the ACM CHI'91 Conference on Human Factors in Computing Systems, ACM Press, New York, 1991, 189–194.
17. D. Auber, "Tulip: A huge graph visualisation framework". In P. Mutzel and M. Jünger (Eds), Graph drawing software, mathematics and visualization, Springer, Verlag, 2003, 105–126.
18. A. G. Sutcliffe and U. Pater, "3D or not 3D: is it nobler to the mind?", In British Human Computer Interaction Conference, Cambridge University Press, Cambridge, 1996, 79–94.
19. A. Cockburn and B. McKenzie, "An evaluation of cone trees", People and Computers XV (Proceedings of the 2000 British Computer Society Conference on Human Computer Interaction., 2000.
20. J. Lamping and R. Rao, "The hyperbolic browser: A focus + context technique for visualizing large hierarchies", Journal of Visual Languages and Computing, 7(1), 1996, 33–35.
21. T. Munzner, "H3: Laying out large directed graphs in 3d hyperbolic space", Symposium on Information Visualization (InfoVis' 97), 1997, 2–10.
22. B. Shneiderman, "Tree visualization with tree-maps: 2-d space-filling approach", ACM Transactions on Graphics 11(1), 1992, 92–99.
23. J. -D. Fekete, D. Wang, N. Dang, and C. Plaisant, "Overlaying graph links on treemaps", IEEE Symposium on Information Visualization Conference Compendium (Demonstration), October 2003.
24. B. Lee, M. Czerwinski, G. Robertson, and B. B. Bederson, "Understanding eight years of infovis conferences using paperlens", In INFOVIS'04: Proceedings of the IEEE Symposium on Information Visualization (INFOVIS'04), Washington, DC, USA, 2004, 216.
25. H. Kang, C. Plaisant, B. Lee, and B. B. Bederson, "Netlens: Iterative exploration of content-actor network data", Proceedings of IEEE VAST, 2006, 91–98.
26. J. Bertin, "Semiology of graphics", University of Wisconsin Press, Madison, 1983.
27. C. Mueller, B. Martin, and A. Lumsdaine, "A comparison of vertex ordering algorithms for large graph visualization", In Asia-Pacific Symposium on Visualization (APVIS'07), February 2007.
28. N. Henry and J. -D. Fekete, "Evaluating visual table data understanding", In BEyond time and errors: novel evaLuation methods for Information Visualization (BELIV'06), ACM Press, Venice, Italy, 2006.
29. G. Caraux and S. Pinloche, "Permutmatrix: A graphical environment to arrange gene expression profiles in optimal linear order", Bioinformatics, 21, 2005, 1280–1281.
30. VisuLab, http://www.inf.ethz.ch/personal/hinterbe/Visulab
31. M. S. T. Carpendale, "Framework for elastic presentation space", Ph. D. thesis, Simon Fraser University, Canada, 1999.
32. R. Rao and S. K. Card, "The table lens: merging graphical and symbolic representations in an interactive focus + context visualization for tabular information", In CHI'94: Proceedings of the SIGCHI Conference on Human Factors in Computing Systems, New York, 1994, 318–322.
33. N. Elmqvist, N. Henry, Y. Riche, and J. -D. Fekete, "Melange: space-folding for multi-focus interaction", In CHI'08: Proceedings of the SIGCHI conference on Human Factors in computing systems, New York, 2008.
34. F. van Ham, "Using multilevel call matrices in large software projects", In Proceedings of the 2003 IEEE Symposium on Information Visualization, IEEE Press, Seattle, 2003, 227–232.

35. N. Elmqvist, T. -N. Do, H. Goodell, N. Henry, and J. -D. Fekete, "Navigating wikipedia with the zoomable adjacency matrix explorer", Proceedings of Pacific Visualization Conference, 2008.
36. M. Ghoniem, J. -D. Fekete, and P. Castagliola, "On the readability of graphs using node-link and matrix-based representations: a controlled experiment and statistical analysis", Information Visualization, 4(2), 2005, 114–135.
37. N. Henry and J. -D. Fekete, "MatrixExplorer: A dual-representation system to explore social networks", IEEE Transactions on Visualization and Computer Graphics (Infovis'06 proceedings), 12(5), 2006, 677–684.
38. N. Henry and J. -D. Fekete, "Matlink: Enhanced matrix visualization for analyzing social networks", In Lecture Notes in Computer Science (Proceedings of the 13th IFIP TC13 International Conference on Human-Computer Interaction, INTERACT'07), 4663, 2007, 288–302.
39. N. Henry, J. -D. Fekete, and M. McGuffin, "Nodetrix: Hybrid representation for analyzing social networks", TVCG (Proceedings of IEEE Information Visualization conference), 13(6), 2007, 1302–1309.
40. T. Moscovich, F. Chevalier, N. Henry, E. Pietriga, and J. -D. Fekete, "Topology-aware navigation in large networks", In Proceedings of the 27th international Conference on Human Factors in Computing Systems, Boston, 2009, 2319–2328.
41. N. Henry, A. Bezerianos, and J. -D. Fekete, "Improving the readability of clustered social networks by node duplication", IEEE Transactions on Visualization and Computer Graphics (Proceedings of Visualization/Information Visualization 2008), 14, 2008, 6.
42. J. -D. Fekete, J. J. van Wijk, J. T. Stasko, and C. North, "The value of information visualization". In: A. Kerren, J. T. Stasko, J. -D. Fekete, C. North (Eds), Information Visualization – Human-Centered Issues and Perspectives, LNCS, 4950, Springer, Verlag, 2008, 1–18.
43. N. Henry, "Exploring large social networks with matrix-based representations", Ph.D. Thesis, Cotutelle Université Paris-Sud (France) and University of Sydney (Australia), July 2008.
44. N. Henry, H. Goodell, N. Elmqvist, and J. -D. Fekete, "20 years of 4 HCI conferences: a visual exploration", In International Journal of Human Computer Interaction – Reflections on Human-Computer Interaction, A Special Issue in Honor of Ben Shneiderman's 60th Birthday, 23(3), 2007, 239–285.

Chapter 29
Applications of Social Network Analysis

P. Santhi Thilagam

29.1 Introduction

A social network [2] is a description of the social structure between actors, mostly persons, groups or organizations. It indicates the ways in which they are connected with each other by some relationship such as friendship, kinship, finance exchange etc. In a nutshell, when the person uses already known/unknown people to create new contacts, it forms social networking. The social network is not a new concept rather it can be formed when similar people interact with each other directly or indirectly to perform particular task. Examples of social networks include a friendship networks, collaboration networks, co-authorship networks, and co-employees networks which depict the direct interaction among the people. There are also other forms of social networks, such as entertainment networks, business Networks, citation networks, and hyperlink networks, in which interaction among the people is indirect. Generally, social networks operate on many levels, from families up to the level of nations and assists in improving interactive knowledge sharing, interoperability and collaboration.

Social networks create a social life in a smart way by linking persons around you. Primarily social networks are used to increase contacts, clients and also to gain popularity. Various online social networks such as profile-based social networks, content-based social networks, mobile social networks, micro-blogging, social search and Local Forums are useful to keep in touch with friends scattered all over country or world. These sites also allow users to create and publish or share their profile, search for interested persons, music, blogs, and research topics. Social networking sites can be considered as a talent search tool for organizations. Even social networks are useful for spreading the information about epidemic diseases etc. by the Government.

P.S. Thilagam (✉)
Department of Computer Engineering, National Institute of Technology Karnataka,
Surathkal, Mangalore 575025, India
e-mail: santhisocrates@gmail.com; santhi@nitk.ac.in

B. Furht (ed.), *Handbook of Social Network Technologies and Applications*,
DOI 10.1007/978-1-4419-7142-5_29, © Springer Science+Business Media, LLC 2010

The major strength of social networks lies in its analysis. From late 1970s, Social Network Analysis (SNA) have gained wide attentions, considerable developments, and successful applications in broad fields [12]. Hence, SNA is a thriving research area. The key research issues in social network analysis include modeling of social networks, handling the dynamic nature of networks, and the identification and application of suitable techniques for computational analysis of networks. Social Network Analysis techniques [6] are primarily applied to study structures of any types of interactions between any kinds of entities. In this chapter, we focus on the various applications of Social Network Analysis.

29.2 Social Network Analysis

Social Network Analysis [11] is vital technique in modern sociology. It is the study patterns of relations, not just relations between pairs. SNA differs from traditional data analysis in a way that its primary aspect of analysis are attributes of links between objects rather than only object attributes. Hence, it provides quantitative measures to study the qualitative nature of relationships among individuals within a social group. Social networks are generally modeled as a graph of linked individuals called as a social diagram or social network diagram as shown in Fig. 29.1. SNA involves applying various analytical graph algorithms to extract interested patterns of interaction and knowledge from the given instance of social diagrams.

The social networks are analyzed in three different ways. Firstly, Analyze all objects of population under consideration and connections among them. Secondly, Analyze ego-centric networks which are created by extracting only interested objects and interactions among them. In this case, it is required to understand personal community network and its effect on involved personals. Thirdly, Analyze

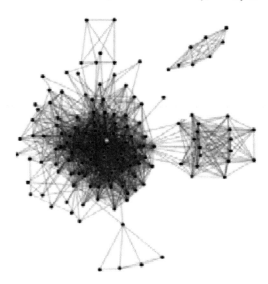

Fig. 29.1 Example of social network diagram

hybrid networks which are formed by extracting interested objects and links from a given social network and understand the interactions using links to external related players which are not formally available in the given network. Analysts uses two different tools to model social networks mathematically: Graphs and matrices. Sociologists uses one kind of representation borrowed from graph theory which includes nodes representing actors of social network and lines or edges to represent relation between actors. This model is called as sociogram or social diagram. Further the fundamental property of any social structures is power. Generally the power is mathematically measured in terms of centrality [10]. Centrality defines how popular or central particular actor is in given social network by computing quantity of other actors reachable in various ways. Sociologists measures Centrality in different ways i.e. degree centrality, betweenness centrality, closeness centrality etc.

One of the vital aspect of network analysis is their sub-structure in terms of groupings or cliques [16]. The interactions amongst these sub-structures are observed to understand likely behavior of the network as a whole, information flow etc. The location of actors is also measured in terms of cliques and sub-groups. Some actors are isolated, some act as a "bridge" between two kinds of gorpus, some represents their sub-group etc. Hence, the way these actors are connected in network indicates their role in the network.

Some analysts use the concept of equivalence or similarity to identify the similar actors of network. The mostly used measures of similarity and structural equivalence are Pearson correlation coefficients, Euclidean distances, Percent of Exact Matches, Jaccard coefficients [4]. It helps for network's positional analysis and their role in network analysis. Equivalence is also mathematically assessed with the notion of graph automorphism which search for multiple substitutable sub-structures in graphs.

Link prediction [4] is also one of the link analysis technique used in social network analysis. Link prediction seeks to predict the availability of link or edge between the actors. Various Link prediction approached differ in fact that some discovers hidden links using inference rules while some models such as probabilistic models, predicts possibility of presence of link in future. Further these techniques are classified as those based on node attributes and those based on network topology.

The SNA techniques have not been only applied to the network of individuals but also help to identify inter-community interactions and interdependence. SNA is not only applicable in area of information science but also has wide range of applications in areas including biology, economy and finance transaction studies, geographical analysis, social psychology etc.

29.3 Applications of Social Network Analysis

Graph representation and usage of graph theoretic algorithms to analyze the interdependency characteristics of involved entities allows analysts to use the SNA techniques to study any type of interactions between any types of entities. Hence, SNA has been utilized as relationship analysis tool for broad fields.

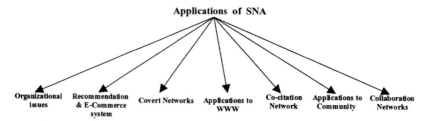

Fig. 29.2 Applications of SNA

The SNA has been used in organizations management to study employees interactions and their impact on project success in order to take corrective measures to improve the performance of organizations. SNA may also be used to increase productivity, employee satisfaction and motivation, overall organization well-being, and capitalizes on the most important asset in an organization of the people.

Another major application of SNA is to discover terrorists networks and to predict the terrorist activity. In various scientific research areas, SNA is used to understand the scope of any subject and to improve the research and innovation. Apart from human interactions, SNA is being successfully used in WWW and Information Sciences also.

We discuss the major applications of SNA in the following sections. We can categorize applications of social network analysis into broad categories as shown in Fig. 29.2.

29.3.1 Organizational Issues

Organizational Behavior is the study and application of knowledge about how people, individuals, and groups act within an organization. In any organization, cooperation and information sharing among the workers is very important for the success of an organization. SNA can also be used to identify the key or central persons of an organization which also helps to understand important to go people in an organization. Based on the knowledge obtained from SNA, corrective management strategies can be applied to improve the efficiency of an organization.

Team Formation

For the success of any project, right team formation is a very crucial issue which requires careful analysis of the available human resources of an organization. In larger organizations, it is obvious that two individuals work on similar projects without realizing it. It is possible to generate the teams of individuals having similar skills and interest using SNA. The trust factor is a central influencer on performance of project teams both tangibly and intangibly apart from skills of team members. The teams cohesiveness is also key factor which affects the projects success. In this context, various measures including centrality and closeness can be obtained from the social network of team members to study the networks cohesiveness. This knowledge aids the project leaders to build strategy to take proper actions to develop multi-agency team. Multi-disciplinary projects benefit from appropriate multi-agency team in terms of its better performance and results.

Improved information sharing

The SNA techniques have also been employed to understand the flow of knowledge or information. The exchange of information and ideas makes favorable conditions for innovation and introduction of new ways of working. Hence, the information sharing has become a important factor for the success of the project. SNA techniques are used to discover the sources of information, the structure of information sharing, and ways to access available knowledge. The above analysis identifies the right people in any project according to their area of expertise.

Identifying bottlenecks

Team may not function as expected even by having the right team and right information resources. The bottlenecks such as un-uniform distribution of workload and resources may have happened inadvertently but it affects the decision making and information sharing. Social network analysis can identify such bottlenecks in a team. The team can address these issues and plan ways to improve the efficiency and unlock the flow of resources in the network.

Hidden barriers

Since success of any company depends on efficiency of employees and their cooperation. Various hidden barriers to knowledge or resource sharing and co-operation affect the performance of multi-agency system. Hidden barriers arise because of different race, religion, cast, age, gender, professional or educational background, department etc. Other factors affecting co-operation may be unavailability of time, opportunity, physical presence to have relationship with other people having different corporate policies and cultures. Naturally, the interactions or bonds amongst similar people are more effective than dissimilar people. Social network analysis has been also used as a tool to identify such hidden barriers, to understand effect of these hidden barriers, and help people to plan for simple, targeted interventions. In this case, interactions amongst employees are modeled as a social network and various classification algorithms with cohesion [6] measure are used to find closely related groups to identify hidden barriers.

29.3.2 Recommendation and E-commerce Systems

Recommendation systems are web services that provide information about entertainment elements, scientific papers, books, fashion elements such as clothing etc. Typically recommendation systems allow users to select and rate items according their own interest and opinion, allowing users to create their own list of items according to their own likes, and allowing user to create their favorites. Hence, it reduces web browsing burden on users by presenting items that may be of their interest. Most of the e-commerce sites such as Amazon, ebay etc. have their own recommendation systems for recommending customized products to customers and also tries to improve targeted marketing of products. Various social network analysis techniques are applied on such information systems to retrieve user interest patterns and other users of same likes or dislikes. These recommendation systems collects database of users and items purchased for further analysis which is mostly done by using various data mining techniques.

One of the important requirements of the recommendation systems is to discover the users interaction patterns by searching users social network and similar likes and dislikes. The collaborative binding of persons in recommendation systems can be viewed as a social network. SNA in these systems is also useful to investigate the relationship between different individuals of system to predict users preference towards a set of items being published. Therefore, SNA can be used to discover relationships of users to aid in making recommendations.

Social Network analysis in recommendation systems helps to enhance selling by converting browsers into buyers. Also, these websites acts as recommender agents to learn customers, obtain their preference and provide items of their interest. Once a customer benefits from the recommendation services provided by a particular website then the customers trust factor increases and switching to other competing websites decreases over time. This will greatly improve customer loyalty to that service.

The SNA in e-learning recommendation systems is also proved to be useful to present learners with the proper documentation choice without having sufficient personal experience or knowledge of available informatics.

The performance of recommender systems has been evaluated by applying SNA techniques to measure the effectiveness of the system and to suggest the improvements required in the system. To facilitate this, the percentage of predictions given by system can be compared against that inferred from SNA of customers network.

The SNA makes use of various metrics such as centrality, cohesiveness, degree of vertex etc. each may reflect different meaning in recommendation system analysis. For instance, Node with high centrality means it has high impact on other nodes. The vertex similarity may be considered as metric to search the individuals having same interest or preference. In this case, system needs to be modelled as a network graph consisting of customers as nodes and each link represent the same purchase preference. The links can be weighted so that the extent of similarity can also be represented. A node with high vertex similarity with existing one is presented with the items of preference of existing customer.

Cohesiveness property of network defines a group of nodes of network bounded with each other by some relation and may have common characteristics. In the context of recommendation systems, a group in transaction network represents the customers having same interests or preferences. Apart from transactional network, customers personal social networks are also analyzed to predict the groups with similar interests. This type of analysis also infers customers preference and further improves personalized recommendation to the customer.

Generally, customers have a tendency to see and follow what other influential customers buy. Influential customers can be identified by using centrality measures such as betweenness centrality, closeness centrality and eigen vector centrality etc. SNA in this direction may require research attention.

29.3.3 Covert Networks

The covert networks are hidden, the actors of such network does not disclose their information to the external world. Covert groups have cellular networks structure which is different from hierarchical organizations. The terrorist and criminal networks are good examples of such networks. Generally, the information about actors, relationship among them and involvement in any external event is not easily available in terrorist networks. SNA has been successfully applied to such domains to understand covert cell operations and their organization. Intelligence analysis normally focused on the identification of network vulnerabilities within the different types and forms of criminal networks. Hence, combating terrorism is another field where SNA techniques have important and successful application.

SNA has been used to understand the communication and structure of terrorist cells. SNA is applied on terrorism database for predicting node and link, discovering interesting patterns and actors involved in an event. In this context, SNA discovers who is central within organizations, which individuals removal would most effectively disrupt the network, what roles individuals are playing, and which relationships are vital to monitor.

Another vital application of SNA for terrorist database is to predict terrorism activities. Terrorist organizations have special structures on recruitment, evolution, and ideas diffusion in network. SNA tools has been used to identify these organization structures and provide critical information for terrorist detection and terrorism prediction.

Studies have shown that these types of networks can be well understood by mapping them. The Valdis Krebs [9] has used social network analysis to map the terrorist network that attacked on 9/11. In spite of unavailability of complete and proper knowledge of all actors and connections in between them, his analysis has disclosed network which is almost near to real network.

Since terrorist groups and organizations are hidden networks which does not disclose their identity, generally the data to build and complete such networks is gathered from publicly available resources such as news papers. Sudhir Saxena [14] has analyzed such public data to discover the terrorist cells in Jammu and Kashmir and relations among them. Now a days Web resources such as blogs, emails etc. are also used for hidden communication. Hence, various data mining and social network analysis techniques are employed to extract necessary information to detect terror [16].

SNA techniques applied to terrorists network varies from basic measures to complex graph algorithms and data mining techniques. The basic measures includes betweenness and degree centrality measures, cohesion factors, closeness etc. Also, the network structure or topological measures are required in this type of analysis which may include node neighborhood search.

SNA considers terrorists networks analysis as a problem of connecting dots. Connecting multiple pairs of dots exposes the total network. Centrality is the most important and widely used measure in SNA used to identify key players in terrorist network and further the actors linked to these key players can be detected to reveals the whole network. To facilitate this, the regular day-to-day activities of the key players are monitored. The hidden actors are discovered by monitoring contact and the extend of contacts of known terrorists with other people. In order to measure the location of actors in the network, various measures such as centrality may give us insight into the details of connector actors, mavens, leaders, bridge actors, isolates, clusters, core actor, peripheral actors etc.

Structural cohesion is also used to find connectors among group of actors. This measure is used to identify sub-groups in an organization having similar features, skills and involvement in particular event.

With the advanced graph theoretic and link analysis techniques, SNA is applied to terrorists network to persecution of criminal activities.

29.3.4   Web Applications

From last two decades, the popularity of web has grown exponentially and web applications are becoming ubiquitous in nature. Web being a wealth of information, SNA finds a lot of applications in this domain.

Web is being used by different community for various purposes such academic improvement, knowledge sharing, interest sharing, communication and profiling, research, business etc. Hence, different techniques are required to improve and optimize the usability of web.

SNA has been used to solve various security problems in computer communication system. It has been successfully employed to detect insider threats and security violation of email systems. This is done by collecting and analyzing data from networks logs, network traffic, file shares and IM (Instant Messaging) logs. Individual's personal social network can be mapped and studied by tracing email flow. This helps to understand the person's comfortless and prestige.

Researches have been also employed to study the network of World Wide Web as a social network. It helps to understand how sociology evolves with respect to contents of the web. By analyzing the navigation and usage patterns of web, better improvements in web algorithms for gathering, searching and discovering information can be achieved. The evolution of web demands more computing power. SNA can be employed to infer the knowledge of web evolution in advance. By observing and analyzing current web usages, the evolution of web structure can be predicted. SNA has been also used for web to discover community. The web browsing or downloading patterns are analyzed to discover the individuals community and their interest in particular knowledge domain. SNA is also employed to predict the movie success and academy awards from IMDB network [8].

SNA models web as a graph where web pages are represented as nodes and hyperlinks as edges. Node similarity based SNA techniques are employed to classify the web based on its usage and contents in order to understand the scope of domain and density. Multi-mode network can be created by representing web resources, persons and community as nodes and web resources being used by community as edges to discover group of likely or similar persons by finding cliques with respect to each knowledge domain.

SNA is also used in search engines such as google to enhance keyword search quality. Google uses PageRank as a measure of popularity, which is obtained by simulating a random walk on network of web pages and computing prestige of web pages. Given a keyword query, matching documents are ordered by this score. Since this popularity score is precomputed independent of the query, Google can be as fast as any relevance-ranking search engine. Other type of search engines such as Alta Vista, are based on Hyperlink induced topic search does not crawl the web. Rather given a query it retrieves a subgraph of the Web whose nodes (pages) match the query. Pages citing or cited by these pages are also included.

29.3.5 Community Welfare

The SNA techniques are not limited to scientific and research areas, rather also used to improve the community welfare. SNA is used to analyze different types of relations such as communication patterns, physical contacts, sexual relationship etc. The SNA may reveal the patterns of human contact which may lead to spread of disease such as HIV in population. Considerable research has been done to analyze the spread of disease. It has been employed in epidemiology and has shown considerable results for community improvement. Another interesting application is to use SNA to examine and observe farm animal network to identify patterns of disease spread from one animal to another.

Mass surveillance is one of the modern practices undertaken by some organizations and governments to monitor the behavior of suspected people of population. This is done with the purpose of protecting people from criminals, terrorists or political subversives to maintain social control. In US, the Total Information Awareness program of the Information Awareness Office designed numerous technologies to be used to perform mass surveillance which made use of SNA tools.

The community of practices involves the people to share their information to improve their own knowledge. The SNA tools have also been used to assess the communities of practices. This information can further be used to improve knowledge sharing in community.

Social Networks which are made for strengthening community resilience against disasters (natural or human-made) can reveal vulnerabilities within a network [13]. These networks are analysed using SNA tools to study the changes that occur during disaster and further to improve disaster preparedness strategies.

29.3.6 Collaboration Networks

Collaboration network consists groups of persons working together to perform particular activity and studying human collaboration is an important topic in sociology. The widely studied collaboration network by researchers in context of SNs are science Co-authorship collaboration network and movie actor collaboration networks.

The co-authorship network is analyzed by various researchers to study dynamics in patterns of interactions between educational entities or communities. Further, these types of networks are analyzed to understand the influence of individual researchers. The structure of research collaboration in various scientific fields is disclosed by applying SNA methods to collaboration network of scientists or researchers which helps for strategic planning of research and development. SNA also identifies the most prominent actors in particular subject area and reveals their ego networks. The observations and results of time series and location based analysis captures the nature and characteristics of research subject over time and location. This helps to identify the scope of research discipline at particular location so that further new inventions in same can be promoted at respective region and using skills of subject experts.

The Co-authorship network analysis also helps to study and understand the interdisciplinary research which is key factor for innovation [1]. Better way to improve the interdisciplinary research is by identifying such current interactions and engaging involved institutions and researchers for future research.

The examples of co-authorship networks are Wikipedia article authors, network of the pacific Asia Conference on Information Systems [3], network of European Conference on Information Systems (ECIS) etc. SNA on these networks has been conducted to understand the research community which produces the research knowledge. Since, scope of research subject and persons subject interest may vary over time, these networks has been viewed as a dynamic social networks. So the development of such dynamic network is observed by using SNA techniques.

The required datasets for co-authorship network analysis is mostly extracted from sources including scientific journals, bibliographic records and digital libraries. The important SNA measures used for co-authorship network includes cohesion, network density and centrality. The cohesion is used to identify the subgroups within network with respect to each research subject. The node similarity measure in this context represents extend of similar subject skills. This will help to identify group of persons to engage in particular research knowing few expertise in that area. The identified hub in sub-network can represent the key researcher in that sub-network. The scope and popularity of particular subject in its evolution is measured by computing density over time and location. The various centrality measures are also used to analyze the impact of collaboration of researchers on research in particular discipline [5].

Movie actor network is analyzed to study the interaction amongst themselves, to discover closely related actors. It is built based on Internet movie database (www.imdb.com) consisting of all movies and their casts. In this network nodes represents and ties represent two connected nodes acted together in some movie. These networks are large scale consisting of millions of vertices and edges, so appropriate analysis techniques are required. The advanced techniques along with traditional analysis model such as random walk are also used on movie actor database for disambiguation of name in list.

Another type of collaboration network studied in this context is knowledge collaboration network [15]. The information about Open Source Software needs to be distributed amongst community or users because not all members have required knowledge or skills for such software usage and development. Hence, success of such software highly depends on distribution of knowledge using tools such as emails, discussion forums, web blogs etc. The extend and quality of such knowledge sharing is measured by applying SNA tools on knowledge collaboration networks.

Morel CM et al. [11] discusses methodologies and principles required to build programs on neglected diseases by understanding the current status of research in those areas through SNA.

29.3.7 Co-Citation Networks

In the area of analysis and computation, Co-citation is used as a measure of similarity between two objects. Co-citation analysis helps to understand the status and structure of scientific research. Basic two approaches of co-citation are author co-citation and document co-citation.

The Co-citation network can be viewed as a bipartite graph showing linkage between two different groups of documents. Basic application of co-citation analysis is to study the scientific communication.

There are different examples of co-citation analysis. In the field of methodological evaluation, co-citation analysis has been employed to search for invisible colleges [7]. This reveals the research network consisting of different institutions linked to each other informally by having indicators to each others documents/papers which can be used to get group of institutes having similar ongoing research. This may help to promote further research in respective area in those institutions.

SNA has been also studied as an approach to understand journals importance or prestige. It also helps to figure out how does any journal influence or get influenced by the other journals/papers in same or different discipline.

The node similarity measure is used to find similarity between two articles or publications. In this case, the nodes represent papers and existence of link shows that two articles were cited in other articles. As we have seen in above sections, the centrality measure can also be used for co-citation analysis. Centrality represents the scope or importance of paper or respective research subject. While analyzing the relation between different disciplines, the cohesion property is used to observe how close two subjects are.

29.4 Conclusion

Social Networks are useful at various levels and plays important role to understand relationship among people and groups, organization or other social entities. Social Network Analysis has became an important analytic tool for analyzing terrorist networks, friendly command and control structures, arms trade, biological warfare, the spread of diseases, among other applications. Detecting dynamic changes over time from an SNA perspective, may signal an underlying change within an organization, and may even predict significant events or behaviors. This chapter highlights the applications of SNA in various domains including organizational behavior, Social community, Recommendation and E-commerce system, Web applications, and collaboration and covert networks to enhance social welfare and security.

References

1. Bales, M., S. Johnson, and C. Weng, Social Network Analysis of Interdisciplinarity in Obesity Research, In Proc. of 2008 AMIA Fall Symp., 2008.
2. Bernardo A. Huberman, Daniel M. Romero and Fang Wu, Social networks that matter: Twitter under the microscope, Social Computing Laboratory, HP Labs, Volume 14, no. 1–5, Jan. 2009.
3. Cheong, France and Corbitt, Brian J., A Social Network Analysis of the Co-Authorship Network of the Pacific Asia Conference on Information Systems from 1993 to 2008. In proceedings of PACIS 2009, Paper 23, Indianapolis, IN, Nov. 2009.
4. David Liben-Nowell, Jon Kleinberg, The link-prediction problem for social networks, In Journal of the American Society for Information Science, Volume 58, Issue 7, pp: 1019–1031, 2007.
5. Erjia Yan, Ying Ding, Applying centrality measures to impact analysis: A coauthorship network analysis, In Journal of the American Society for Information Science and Technology, Volume 60, Issue 10, pp: 2107–2118, publisher Wiley, New York, NY, USA, Oct. 2009.
6. Gerhard Goos, Juris Hartmanis et al., Network Analysis Methodological Foundations, Lecture Notes in Computer Science, Commenced Publication in 1973.
7. Gmuer, Co-citation analysis and the search for invisible colleges: A methodological evaluation, In Scientometrics, Volume 57, Issue 1, pp: 27–57, May 2003.

8. Krauss, Jonas et al., Predicting Movie Success and Academy Awards Through Sentiment and Social Network Analysis, In Proc. of 16th European Conference on Information Systems (ECIS), Galway, Ireland, June 2008.
9. Krebs, Valdis, Mapping networks of terrorist cells, In Connections, Volume 24, Issue 3, pp: 43–52, 2002.
10. Mohsen Jamali and Hassan Abolhassani, Different Aspects of Social Network Analysis, In proceedings of IEEE/WIC/ACM conference on Web Intelligence, 2006.
11. Morel C.M., S.J. Serruya et al., Co-authorship network analysis: A powerful tool for strategic planning of research, development and capacity building programs on neglected diseases, In PLoS Neglected Tropical Disease, Volume 3, Issue 8, p: e501, 2009.
12. Panayiotis Zaphiris, Ulrike Pfeil, Introduction to Social Network Analysis, In Proceedings of the 21st BCS HCI Group Conference, Volume 2, 3–7 Sept. 2007.
13. Sammantha L. Magsino, Rapporteur, Applications of social network analysis for building community disaster resilience: Workshop summary 2009, Published on 21 Jul. 2009.
14. Sudhir Saxena, K. Santhanam et al., Application of Social Network Analysis (SNA) to terrorist networks in Jammu and Kashmir, Strategic Analysis, Volume 28, Issue 1, pp: 84 101, January 2004.
15. Takeshi Kakimoto, Yasutaka Kamei et al., Social Network Analysis on Communications for Knowledge Collaboration in OSS Communities, In Proc. of Second Intl. Workshop on Supporting Knowledge Collaboration in Software Development, Tokyo, Japan, Volume 1, pp: 123–126, Sept. 2006.
16. Y. Elovici, A. Kandel, M. Last et al., Using data mining techniques for detecting terror-related activities on the web, In Journal of Information Warfare, Volume 3, Issue 1, pp.:17–29, 2004.

Chapter 30
Online Advertising in Social Networks

Abraham Bagherjeiran, Rushi P. Bhatt, Rajesh Parekh, and Vineet Chaoji

30.1 Introduction

According to a study by Nielsen [3], two-thirds of the world's online population visits social networking and blogging websites. Moreover, the time spent on such websites is increasing three times faster than the time spent on the internet overall. This phenomenal growth in online social networking during the last decade has promoted a new class of social based applications like Flickr, Blogger, Youtube, Facebook, and Twitter. These applications have introduced new paradigms of online interaction and social sharing and have greatly influenced traditional methods. The plethora of information in the form of text articles, images, videos, and short messages generated by these applications yields rich insights about the users and their social connections.

Online marketing is one instance where social information has enriched the traditional approach. Traditional marketing media, such as print and television, take a broadcast approach to advertising with the focus on maximizing the *reach* – the number of unique users. They lack the ability to deliver customized marketing messages that consider user demographics, interests, and purchasing power. The growth of online communities is having a significant impact on online advertising. As users connect, communicate, and share through online media, they leave behind valuable information about their interests and preferences. This information has two important implications for advertisers and marketing agencies: (a) Interests of users with very little or no past history can be inferred from the interests of their immediate circle of friends. (b) Social networks induced by online communities provide a convenient channel for viral marketing.

Effective advertising requires predicting how a user will respond to an advertisement and then targeting the users who are most likely to respond favorably with appropriate messaging. In the case of online advertising, this involves constructing profiles for users based largely on passive observation. For example, one can observe

R. Parekh (✉)
Yahoo! Labs, Santa Clara, CA, USA
e-mail: rparekh@yahoo-inc.com

B. Furht (ed.), *Handbook of Social Network Technologies and Applications*,
DOI 10.1007/978-1-4419-7142-5_30, © Springer Science+Business Media, LLC 2010

which websites users have visited and what ads they have seen and responded to in the past. With social networking sites users can *declare* their interests through social interactions. For example, a user can add an application that displays sports scores, which tells us that he or she is interested in sports. If the user later recommends this application to friends, we can infer which friends are also interested in sports.

A key feature required of social networks to be useful for advertising is that people share interests with their friends and tend to be friends with people who share their interests. This feature, known as *homophily*, has been shown to exist in many social networks [24,26]. Homophily in the online community can also be effectively used for viral marketing [30] to spread the adoption of products. Social networks are therefore viewed as strategic resources that can be leveraged for effective online advertising.

30.1.1 Online Advertising

The growth of the internet and the increased share of time spent by users online have been a boon for online advertising. Advertisers are now spending significant portions of their overall advertising budgets on online advertising. Email marketing, display advertising, and sponsored search advertising are three popular forms of online advertising.

- **Email marketing** involves campaigning directly to the consumer via email without going through an intermediary. Email marketing is the online analog of telemarketing or door-to-door marketing that are popular offline direct marketing approaches. Email marketing is considerably cheaper compared to traditional print and television based marketing. Advertisers can use email lists from their own customer relationship management (CRM) systems or purchase them from data aggregators. Additionally, advertisers pay email marketing firms a small fixed amount per email delivered. Due to the relatively lower operational cost, even a modest response rate on email marketing ad campaigns is sufficient to break even.
- **Display advertising** involves showing graphical ads (banners) on webpages visited by a user. Display advertising has traditionally been used for brand advertising where advertisers reach out to vast and diverse online audiences to promote their brands. These ads are typically sold via guaranteed contracts wherein a website (also called the publisher) guarantees that a certain number of ad impressions will be served to visitors of the website over a fixed, pre-specified period of time. Guaranteed contracts are typically priced on a cost per thousand impressions (CPM) basis. Reach and frequency are the commonly used metrics associated with brand campaigns. Reach is the number of unique users who see the ad and frequency is the average number of times a single user sees the ad. Of late, display advertising is also used in performance marketing wherein the advertiser agrees to pay the publisher only if the user takes some action such as clicking or purchasing a product in response to the ad impression. These ads are sold

non-guaranteed in that the publisher makes a call on when to serve which ad and charges the advertiser using the cost per click (CPC) or cost per action (CPA) model.

- **Sponsored search advertising** involves presenting users with small text ads in response to a search query they issue on a search engine. Here the challenge is to find a ranked list of ads that best match the query made by the user. Like performance display advertising, sponsored search ads are typically charged on a CPC or CPA based pricing model.

Effective online advertising is based on three key factors: the *context* in which the ad appears; the *audience* to whom the ad is targeted; and the *creative* that specifies the message being delivered via the ad. A significant amount of research has been devoted to perfecting the science behind each of these three factors.

- **Advertising context** is critical to the success of an ad campaign. Advertisers in traditional media such as television have long known the importance of context. Television ads typically shown during an entertainment program are very different from ads typically shown during a financial news program. Context is used even in online advertising to influence the selection and delivery of contextually relevant ads. The context can be pre-specified by the advertiser by selecting certain webpages on which it is acceptable to show the ad or automatically inferred from the content of the web page and used by the ad serving optimization algorithm to decide which ads would be most appropriate to show alongside the given context [11].
- **Audience segmentation** is a widely adopted practice in marketing to improve the performance of ad campaigns [27]. It allows marketers to identify the right segments of users for marketing and to customize the advertising message to each segment. These segments are typically created using *demographic*, *geographic*, and *psychographic* attributes [1]. Recent advances in online advertising have popularized the use of *behavioral targeting* [12, 13, 39] which leverages online behavior to infer user interests and enables targeting the right ad to each user interest segment. With the growing popularity of online social networks, the notion of *social network ad targeting* is becoming prominent (see [28] for example). This form of targeting involves either seeding some users in the network with a viral marketing campaign or inferring a user's interests based on what is known about the user's social connections (friends). The natural question in the context of social networks is whether the rich social network information about users can be used either stand-alone or in conjunction with other targeting approaches to improve the overall effectiveness of ad campaigns.
- **Creative design and optimization** is critical to ensure that the right message is delivered to users to evoke the desired response. Brand advertisers carefully design their creatives to promote their brand image while performance advertisers focus on the call to action within the ad creative. Several online ad serving systems perform creative optimization on the fly thereby freeing the advertiser from having to decide which ad creative would be most appropriate for which user segment.

This chapter specifically focuses on the role of social network information in online display advertising. At a high level, this chapter addresses the following key questions related to social network advertising:

- Do friends in online social networks wield influence over one another? If so, how can this influence be measured?
- How can the social network information be used to effectively complement other known information about the users to improve the performance of ad campaigns?

The remainder of this chapter is organized as follows. Section 30.2 introduces some techniques for measuring the social network effect for a given marketing problem. Section 30.3 discusses techniques to identify potential marketing targets through use of various social and behavioral attributes available to the campaign designer. Section 30.4 discusses two applications that describe how the techniques for measuring the social network effect and for identifying potential marketing targets can be effectively deployed in practice. Finally, Sect. 30.5 provides a summary and directions for future work.

30.2 Identifying the Social Network Effect in Online Advertising

Social science literature has extensively studied the role of *homophily* [24, 26] and *influencers* [23,35] in social networks. Homophily is the tendency of friends to have similar interests. A recent analysis of the MSN Messenger network together with search results from Windows Live Search uncovered shared interests (captured in terms of common search terms) between people who are neighbors (friends) on the messenger network [32]. Influencers are typically characterized as thought leaders, critics, industry giants, or just plain interesting personalities who have the ability to influence potential buyers. In practice, these individuals may be identified as highly connected individuals or individuals that bridge (also called connectors [17]) two relatively large sub-communities. Both these concepts have a significant impact on the effectiveness of online advertising in social networks. This section explains how we can effectively measure the effect of homophily and influencers in online social networks.

30.2.1 Homophily

Online social networks are defined by users and their social connections (friends). Let u denote a given user, $N(u)$ denote the set of his or her friends, and $f \in N(u)$ denote a friend. The user u is characterized by a vector of features x_u. Examples of these features are demographic, geographic, and behavioral. The set of all users and their friends in the social network induces a social graph $G = \{V, E\}$ where

V is the set of nodes representing the users and E is the set of edges representing social connections between users and their friends. Homophily indicates that friends tend to have similar interests. Suppose that some concept X is true for n_X of u's friends. Homophily suggests that the concept X is likely to be true for u, and is more likely as n_X increases, that is $P(X \mid u, N(u)) \propto n_X$. In the context of online advertising, this would indicate that friends in a social network tend to see similar ads and conversely, users seeing similar ads tend to be friends.

30.2.1.1   Similarity Between Friends

Similarity between a pair of users may be defined based on the number of ads both the users have seen in a fixed time period t. Define A_u as the set of ads that the user u has seen and A_f as the set of ads some friend $f \in N(u)$ has seen. The Jaccard coefficient is one measure of similarity of the ads seen by a pair of users [21]. It is defined over the sets A_u and A_f as:

$$J(A_u, A_f) = \frac{|A_u \cap A_f|}{|A_u \cup A_f|}$$

Care must be taken in counting ad views, and one heuristic is to count multiple views of an ad as one. Although the relative timing of ad views between a user and his or her friends provides an important signal in assessing social influence, one may simplify computation of pairwise similarity of users greatly by ignoring this relative timing and instead relying only on the total views in a fixed time-period. We shall return to the relative timing aspect later in this section while investigating social influence in the social network.

   Although a high similarity in ads seen is important, it does not by itself indicate that this is due to the fact that the users are friends. One hypothesis that might explain the similarity is that because the set of possible ads to show is finite and far smaller than the number of opportunities to see an ad, there should be some overlap between any random pair of users. To control for this correlation, the Jaccard similarity of ads views between random pairs of users needs to be compared against that of connected friends. The exact details of this random sampling may vary based on domain knowledge of the social network, but sampling with uniform probability is a good first choice.

30.2.1.2   Are Similar Users Friends?

Consider the neighborhood of a user and his or her friends. Friends are expected to have similar interests and therefore see similar ads. However, in a large social network, there are likely to be many users who see similar ads. Some of these users will be friends but others will be completely unaware of each other. This leads to the question of whether users who are similar in behavior are also friends. A high degree of intersection between friends and pairs of similar users implies that a user's social network captures the relevant information to predict the user's interests. A low degree of intersection implies that information in the user's social network is insufficient to predict the user's interest.

The social network graph can be compared to a graph with the same degree distribution called a *similarity graph*. For each user u, let the degree of this user be d ($d = |N(u)|$). The similarity graph is defined as follows:

$$G_s = (V_s, E_s)$$
$$E_s = \{(u, f) \mid u, f \in U \wedge \theta(u, f) \geq \theta_d\}$$

where $\theta(\cdot, \cdot)$ is some similarity function and θ_d is the dth largest similarity. In the similarity graph, G_s, each user is connected to his or her d nearest neighbors. Given a pair of users u and f, similarity is measured as the cosine similarity between their respective features as follows:

$$\theta(u, f) = \frac{\langle x_u, x_f \rangle}{\|x_u\| \|x_f\|}$$

where x_u and x_f are the user feature vectors of the users and $\langle \cdot, \cdot \rangle$ is the inner product.

30.2.2 Influencers

Influencers are believed to be key to the success of viral marketing campaigns since they can leverage the power of their network to maximize the diffusion of a marketing message in the social network. Although the presence of influencers in online social communities is widely accepted, their ability to trigger large cascades of adoption of products and services has been questioned [35]. This section surveys the literature on the identification and extent of social influence. The following questions motivate the discussion. Answers to these questions about social behavior will help explain the role of influencers in online advertising.

- Do individuals wield influence over their friends in online social networks? If so, how do they influence the spread of information in the social network?
- Are highly connected users the same as social influencers?
- How far reaching is the influence in the graph? Is it limited to the local social neighborhood or is it global (i.e., network wide)?

30.2.2.1 Modeling the Spread of Influence

Many generative models have been proposed to explain the structure and dynamics of social networks. Watts and Strogatz formulated the small-world model, in which a social network starts as a random graph and is rewired to close small neighborhoods [36]. Several real-world networks were shown to fit this model. Large graphs such as the web graph are described as scale-free in which the degree of nodes is independent of the size of the graph [9]. The vast majority of nodes in such networks have very low degree but there is a heavy tail with some nodes having a degree in the hundreds or thousands. A recent development in statistical physics is non-extensive network analysis, in particular the social circles network model [37]. In this model, people form connections to people they know who, in turn, tend to establish links between friends-of-friends or people relatively near to them in terms of geodesic distance.

Analysis of the structure and dynamics of social networks leads to the topic of information diffusion in social networks. Granovetter's threshold model [18] is one of the simplest yet widely accepted diffusion models. It effectively states that each node v in the social network has a threshold θ_v representing the fraction of v's friends that must adopt the product before v would adopt the product. It has been observed that the probability of adoption of a user increases with the number of friends who have already adopted. Additional factors such as reputation and past similar activities, affect the adoption decision by a user.

Quantitative measures of *influence* can be studied relative to these diffusion models. For example, Watts and Dodds [35] ask whether highly influential nodes indeed are responsible for a *disproportionately higher* number of adoptions in their vicinity. Over a wide range of parameters, they show that, on an average, the *influencers* in social graphs are not responsible for more friends converting than average users. In their study of the Flickr social graph, Anagnostopoulos et al. [5] measure social influence using a shuffle test. They compare the correlation between co-tagging of images by friends to a temporally shuffled version of the same tagging. With social influence, the correlation between a user's tags and those of his or her friends should be expected to change when the tags are shuffled in time. The authors show that the correlation measures remain largely the same regardless of the temporal shuffling of tagging, implying little or no influence exists in the Flickr graph.

Cascades of information flowing within a social network are typically attributed to *influencers* [33]. Watts and Dodds [35] argue that over a large range of plausible network parameterizations, long cascades of adoptions are driven more by individuals that can be influenced easily rather than influencers.

In studies of viral marketing, a key conclusion is that adoption of a new product is not purely a social process. Factors other than the number of friends who have adopted affects whether a user will adopt, such as – in the case of recommender systems – reputation and previous similar activity [25]. Even assuming such influencers exist in a given social network, the immediate question then would be how to identify them for marketing. Kempe et al. [22] show that the general task of identifying such a set of individuals is NP-complete. They propose a greedy approximation for a range of network models (such as the threshold model), that are provably within 63% of the optimal solution. Richardson and Domingos apply a power method, similar to PageRank, to determine which users have most weight in influencing ultimate adoption. They suggest that users with highest influence over other users should be marketed to first [29].

30.2.2.2 Leveraging Rich Data for Social Network Based Marketing

With the availability of large real-world social graphs, new models have been proposed to describe external processes in terms of a social component and additional data. Agarwal et al. explore telephone call graphs and find that discrete attributes, such as a subscription to the same long-distance plan, influence the creation of edges between users [4]. Crandall et al. investigate whether adoption of a service (called an adoption process) can be purely described as a social activity [14]. A key conclusion is that some adoption processes, while clearly involving social communication, actually depend on similarity between users rather than any social component.

Backstrom et al. [6] identify important structural features of local graph structure and some behavioral features by interpreting decision trees trained to predict community membership. Domingos and Richardson [15] propose evaluating a user's *network value* in addition to their *intrinsic* value and its effectiveness in viral marketing. They compare the relative effectiveness of three marketing strategies: mass marketing, direct marketing, and network-based marketing. Hartline et al. [19] proposed an *influence-and-exploit* marketing strategy wherein a carefully chosen set of users is influenced with free distribution of the product and the remaining buyers are exploited for revenue maximization. Hill et al. [20] target audiences that are exposed to customers who have converted (adopted a product or service). Their argument, based on homophily, is that audience exposed to converted customers is more likely to sign-up for the product. Provost et al. [28] describe a privacy friendly method for extracting quasi-social networks from user generated content sites to identify good audiences for brand advertising. Bagherjeiran and Parekh [7] present an ensemble classifier based approach that combines user behavioral features along with social features to boost the probability that a user will click on a display ad.

While the presence of social influence in the causal sense can be debated, insights from the above studies can be combined to define practical marketing strategies which consider both the individual user's characteristics and the characteristics of his or her social neighborhood. Thus, knowledge of social neighborhoods that are ripe in adoption might drive the selection of the right set of *seed* users who may enable the spread of adoption through the network via the word-of-mouth effect. This aspect is discussed in more detail in Sect. 30.4.

30.3 Online Ad Targeting

This section surveys various methods for online ad targeting. For the purpose of this discussion, the ad targeting problem is posed as a classification problem, to determine whether the user will respond to an ad impression. The response to an ad impression can vary from a *click* to a *conversion* or *adoption*. For simplicity we focus on predicting ad clicks but the methodology described below is general enough to encompass other types of responses such as conversions.

Each targeting method is described in a common framework for ease of comparison. Denote the user by $u \in U$ and the neighborhood of the user by $N(u) \subseteq U$. At any moment in time τ, the user u is represented by a feature vector x_u that captures the entire user history until τ. The user features could include *demographic* elements such as age and gender; *geographic* information such as zip code, city, state, and country; and *behavioral* information such as number of views of a particular webpage, number of times a particular query was searched, etc. If there is an opportunity to serve an ad to the user u at time τ, the user feature vector x_u can be used to determine which ad to serve to the user. An ad targeting function $g^a(u) : x_u \to \mathbb{R}^+$ assigns a score denoting the propensity of the user u to click on an ad a. The ad view function $v^a(u) : x_u \to \{0, 1\}$ denotes whether the user u viewed the ad a and the ad click function $c^a(u) : x_u \to \{0, 1\}$ denotes whether the user u clicked on the ad a. Without loss of generality, the functions $g^a(u)$, $v^a(u)$, and $c^a(u)$ are represented as $g(u)$, $v(u)$, and $c(u)$ respectively in the context of a single ad a. Given an oracle, the perfect ad scoring function would be $g(u) = c(u)$. Here the users who would click on the ad are assigned a score of 1 and all other users are assigned a score of 0.

The ad targeting function g is evaluated with a Reach-CTR lift plot, similar to a Precision-Recall plot. Given a set of users $D \subseteq U$ let:

$$r(D) = \sum_{u \in D} v(u) \tag{30.1}$$

$$\beta(D) = \frac{\sum_{u \in D} c(u)}{\sum_{u \in D} v(u)} \tag{30.2}$$

where r is called the reach and β is called the *click through rate* (CTR). Each score value defines a subset of users as follows:

$$S(\delta) = \{u \mid u \in U \wedge g(u) \geq \delta\} \tag{30.3}$$

where δ is a threshold on the predicted CTR scores. Clearly, as the threshold δ decreases, the size of the set $S(\delta)$ increases, starting from $\{\}$ as $\delta \to \infty$ to U as $\delta \to 0$.

The list of users is sorted by $g(u)$ in decreasing order and the Reach-CTR lift plot, as shown in Fig. 30.1, is created by plotting the CTR lift versus the reach for decreasing values of the score. The CTR lift for any threshold δ is defined as the ratio $\beta(\delta)/\beta(U)$. The Reach-CTR lift plot should theoretically decrease monotonically because the scoring function $g(\cdot)$ should rank users with high true CTR higher in the order. The objective is to maximize the CTR for a given value of reach. Given a pre-determined threshold, $\delta^\star$, the point $(r(S(\delta^\star)), \beta(S(\delta^\star)))$ is called the operating point. All users $u \in S(\delta^\star)$ are said to *qualify* for the ad and may be shown the ad. An ad targeting function g' that results in a higher CTR than the ad targeting function g at the operating point $\delta^\star$ is said to be a better ad targeting function.

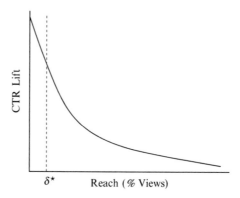

Fig. 30.1 Example of a click-through rate (CTR) lift, relative to overall average CTR, versus reach plot

30.3.1 Targeting Based on User Information

Most online ads today are targeted based solely on user information, independent of the social context. Generally, user information includes everything known about the user at the moment the ad is served. Specifically, this takes three forms: context, segments, and behavior.

30.3.1.1 Contextual Targeting

Contextual targeting is a simple, yet popular targeting mechanism. Advertisers specify the webpages on which their ads should be shown. Users visiting those webpages are targeted with the corresponding ads. For example, if the user is on Yahoo! Finance, a brokerage firm could show an ad for online stock trades. An advertiser who sells cars could show ads on websites about cars.

This form of contextual targeting is completely independent of the user's history or state, so one might argue that it is not really user targeting. However, the method exploits exactly one feature – the page the user is visiting at this moment. The contextual targeting function is defined as follows:

$$g(u) = \begin{cases} 1 & u \text{ is visiting } p \\ 0 & \text{otherwise} \end{cases}$$

where p is the current webpage. The effectiveness of this model assumes that there is a causal link between the page and the user's interest. If the user is visiting a page about cars, then the user has an interest in cars. Therefore, the user would likely be responsive to ads about cars.

30.3.1.2 User Segment Targeting

Marketing research and practice has a long history of profiling users. Users are grouped into homogeneous segments and different segments are targeted with appropriate ads. For example, a major beverage company wanting to increase demand of its low-calorie carbonated beverage might conduct market research and determine that the drink would appeal to the following segments:

- "youngsters": $s_{1,1} = age(u, (15, 25))$, $s_{1,2} = country(u, \text{"USA"})$
- "moms": $s_{2,1} = gender(u, F)$, $s_{2,2} = has\_children(u)$, $s_{2,3} = country(u, \text{"USA"})$

Segments are defined as logical predicates such as $age(u, (15, 25))$ which is true if the age of user u is between 15 and 25 years.

In the above example, the advertiser would define the targeting function as follows:

$$g(u) = \begin{cases} 1 & u \in S \\ 0 & u \notin S \end{cases}$$

$$S = \bigcup_{i=1}^{n} \bigcap_{j=1}^{m} s_{i,j}$$

where each $s_{i,j}$ is a segment as defined in the example.

Segment targeting is popular since it is easy to understand and implement and moreover provides advertisers transparency and control over the audience selected for targeting their ads. There are two main limitations. (a) The advertiser must match the ad to the pre-existing segments. (b) The segments may not be expressive enough to faithfully represent the user characteristics of interest to the advertiser.

30.3.1.3 Behavioral Targeting

In both contextual and segment targeting, the targeting function is determined via hand-crafted rules. In contrast, behavioral targeting (BT) provides an approach to learning the targeting function from historical data. A model is trained to predict for each user a score, indicating the probability that a user will click on the ad. The targeting function $g(u)$ predicts the CTR of the user u. Optionally, the model might output a confidence $\xi > 0$ in the score $g(u)$. An example of a learned targeting function is:

$$g(u) = \mathcal{F}(\langle w, x_u \rangle)$$

where x_u is the feature vector representing the user, w is a vector of learned coefficients with one coefficient per feature, $\langle ., . \rangle$ is the inner product, and the function $\mathcal{F}$ transforms the inner product to a real-valued score like the predicted CTR.

Behavioral targeting is becoming increasingly popular in online advertising. The predictive model can leverage a very rich set of user features and can be trained to directly optimize for the performance of the ad e.g., CTR, conversion rate, etc. More importantly, the framework of the behavioral targeting model is general enough to accommodate other information such as the current context – the webpage the user is visiting, membership in various user segments, etc.

30.3.2 Social Network Targeting

The rapid growth in online social networks has given rise to a whole new area of social network targeting. Social network targeting methods can be divided into two main groups: targeting individual users and targeting neighborhoods of users.

30.3.2.1 Using Peer-Pressure for Targeting

Social science literature has long studied adoption patterns in social networks. The primary objective was to explain current adoptions rather than predicting future adoptions. Granovetter's threshold model [18] is one of the simplest diffusion models. Using the notation of the generalized targeting model, the threshold model can be described as follows:

$$\theta(u) = \frac{|\{f \mid f \in N(u) \wedge c(f)\}|}{|N(u)|}$$

$$g(u) = \begin{cases} 1 & \theta(u) > \theta_u \\ 0 & \text{otherwise} \end{cases}$$

where $\theta(u)$ is the fraction of the users friends who have clicked in the past and θ_u is the threshold for user u which when exceeded would lead the user to click on the ad. This model is based on the peer-pressure effect within the network wherein users with a higher proportion of friends who have clicked earlier are more likely to click on the ad.

30.3.2.2 Using Friends for Targeting

Knowing the set of friends for a user provides a simple yet effective opportunity for social network based ad targeting. So given an initial set of users who have been identified for targeting (say using the behavioral targeting model g), the *socially aware* method simply augments the set by adding all the friends of these users. The argument used here is *homophily* – friends of users who have a high propensity to click on the ad share the same interests and hence are also likely to have a high propensity to click. The further advantage of this method is that it increases the reach of targeting by selecting friends of users. The social extension set, $S'(\delta)$, is created as follows:

$$S'(\delta) = S(\delta) \cup \{f \mid u \in S(\delta) \wedge f \in N(u)\}$$

which contains the set of users and their friends. The reach and CTR values are computed on this extended set $S'(\delta)$.

The set $S'(\delta)$ adds to the set $S(\delta)$ only those friends with lower scores. Friends with higher scores were already in some other set, $S(\delta')$ for $\delta' \geq \delta$. Essentially, a social connection between a user u and a friend f elevates the score of f to at least that of u. This is equivalent to replacing each user's score as follows:

$$g'(u) = \max \{\{g(u)\} \cup \{g(f) \mid f \in N(u)\}\}$$

This method of targeting friends of users is very easy to implement. However, simply targeting all friends of a user might not be a good idea. Users that are linked together as friends in online social networks might share very different relationships such as family, friends, colleagues, etc. Thus, depending on the context, friends might share some but not necessarily all of the interests. Knowing more information about the friends themselves and their interests based on their respective user profiles can help infer latent social connections within the online social network. These latent social connections highlight the friends that indeed share the same interests and would be more likely to respond if targeted along with the user. In situations, where the user features of the friends are not available or are very sparse, the simple approach of social reach extension can provide significant value.

30.3.2.3 Using Social Features for Targeting

The previous method simply involved including all of the user's friends for targeting. Another approach might be to construct a rich set of social features based on the user's network neighborhood. These network features denoted by the vector $s(u)$ could include the number of friends, the proportion of friends who have clicked on the ad, the strength of the relationship between the user and the friends, the number of friends of the user who are also friends with each other, similarity of the friends to the user, etc. [6]. Similar to the case of behavioral targeting, the social network targeting function could be defined as:

$$g(u) = \mathscr{G}(\langle w, s_u \rangle)$$

where s_u is the feature vector representing the user's social features, w is a vector of learned coefficients with one coefficient per feature, $\langle ., . \rangle$ is the inner product, and the function $\mathscr{G}$ transforms the inner product to a real-valued score like the predicted CTR. In fact, the model using the peer-pressure effect within the social network for targeting described above is a special case of this model.

30.3.2.4 Targeting in Social Neighborhoods

The social neighborhood targeting strategy leverages word-of-mouth marketing in the social network. Product adopters when suitably messaged can leverage the power of their network to promote the product among their friends. The key to effective social neighborhood marketing is identifying the right subset of product adopters who can maximize future adoptions. Domingos and Richardson [15] had posed the following problem: which set of individuals could be convinced to adopt the product so that they would in turn create a cascade of adoptions in future. The optimal solution for this problem is NP-hard [22]. The set of individuals for social neighborhood marketing can be identified by a variety of methods including simple heuristics such as picking from among the highest degree users, the earliest adopters, or most recent adopters. Define $\sigma(A)$ as the number of neighbors of a set of adopters A who adopt in a specified time period after A. Effective methods would identify the set A of adopters with the highest $\sigma(A)$. A model based approach for selecting the set A involves training a model to predict for any set A, the value of $\sigma(A)$.

A targeting function for social neighborhood targeting is defined as follows:

$$g(u) = \sigma(A)$$

A popular heuristic involves targeting high-degree adopters, as follows:

$$g(u) = |N(u)|$$

where $|N(u)|$ is the size of the neighborhood of user u who has already adopted the product. To see why this is a good heuristic, consider an independent adoption process for the neighborhood. Assume that the likelihood that a user's friend is influenced is p and that friends are influenced by the user u independent of other friends. Then the expected number of friends influenced is $|N(u)|\ p$. In order to maximize the number of influenced users, targeting users with highest degree is a good strategy.

30.3.3 Combining User Features and Social Network Features

Few works in the literature investigate how to combine user behavior features and social network features. This is often because researchers and practitioners do not have access to both sources of data. Effectively combining these two sources can be difficult because features from these sources might be correlated and further the information contained in one source of data might be weaker than the other. This section describes some methods that have been used to combine information from different sources.

30.3.3.1   Weighted Combination of Scores

Consider a user and his or her neighborhood. When the user first appears on the network, his or her historical profile contains little predictive data; however, the social connections link the user to other users who may have longer histories. In cases such as this, when there is insufficient data for the user's score to be trusted, the social network serves as a proxy for the historical profile. The general framework combines the user's original score, from the behavioral targeting model, with a default score, possibly from the social network, as follows:

$$g'(u) = \alpha(u)g_b(u) + (1 - \alpha(u))\, g_s(u)$$

where $g_b(u)$ is the user's score from the behavioral targeting model, $\alpha : U \rightarrow [0, 1]$ indicates the confidence in the user's behavioral score, and $g_s(u)$ is the score based on the user's social network features. The confidence function, $\alpha(u)$ is defined as follows:

$$\alpha(u) = \frac{\xi_u}{\xi_u + \varepsilon}$$

where ξ_u is the user's confidence score from the behavioral targeting model and ε is a constant capturing the default confidence in the behavioral targeting model. There are different approaches to computing the user's score based on the social network features.

A simple approach might be to use a global constant $g_s(u) = g_0$. Another approach computes a weighted average score over each of the friends' respective behavioral targeting scores.

$$g_s(u) = \frac{\sum_{f \in N(u)} \lambda_{u,f}\, g_u(f)}{\sum_{f \in N(u)} \lambda_{u,f}}$$

where $\lambda_{u,f} \geq 0$ indicates the strength of the relationship between the user u and the friend f.

A third approach involves building a predictive model using social features as described in Sect. 30.3.2.3.

$$g_s(u) = \mathscr{G}(\langle w, s_u \rangle)$$

30.3.3.2   Ensemble Classifier

A challenge with the weighted combination of behavioral and social scores as described above is that the combined score could potentially be worse than (say) the behavioral score alone. It would be beneficial to ensure that the combined model never degrades the performance compared to the behavioral targeting model alone. An ensemble learning approach, *boosting*, can be used to effectively combine the model scores from the behavioral and social models and ensure that the combined model would perform no worse than each individual model [31]. The ensemble learning approach works as follows:

First, a logistic regression classifier is used to transform the range of the user's behavioral targeting score. The targeting function of this classifier is expressed as:

$$g_b'(u) = \mathscr{L}(\mu_1 \log g_b(u) + \mu_2)$$

where μ_i are the parameters of the logistic model and $\mathscr{L}$ is the logistic function. A classifier $g_s(u)$ using social network information is then trained on a re-weighted set of training examples. The instances used to train the social classifier are re-weighted according to the following approach:

$$m_i = \frac{1}{1 + \exp[y_i h_i]}$$
$$h_i \in [-1, 1]$$

where y_i is the true label for the training instance i ($+1$ for click, -1 for not click) and h_i is the predicted score (<0 for not click) as output by the behavioral classifier $g_b'(u)$. This re-weighting assigns more weight to examples that are misclassified by transformed behavioral classifier $g_b'(u)$. Finally, a gating classifier is trained to select the most appropriate of the behavioral and social classifiers, as in the mixture of experts model, defined as follows:

$$g(g_b', g_s) = \mathscr{L}(\mu_1 \log g_b'(u) + \mu_2 \log g_s(u) + \mu_3)$$

Effectively, the gating classifier, g, decides which of the two classifiers to use for the final prediction. In standard boosting the resulting classifiers are added together to obtain the final result [31]. However this approach might not work on models that are trained using different data sources as is the case above with the behavioral and social features. In this case, it is better to train a gating classifier that would predict the per instance weight $w(u)$ to use for combining the individual classifiers in the ensemble.

$$g(u) = w(u)g_b'(u) + (1 - w(u))g_s(u)$$
$$w(u) = g(g_b', g_s)$$

where $g_b'(u)$ is the output of the transformed user behavior only model and $g_s(u)$ is the output of the social model.

30.4 Applications of Social Network Advertising

This section describes two practical applications of social network advertising studied at Yahoo! The first application leverages social network information to predict clicks on display advertisements while the second application models the spread of product adoption in online social networks. These applications demonstrate how the concepts described in Sects. 30.2 and 30.3 can be used in practice for effective social network advertising.

30.4.1   Yahoo! Instant Messenger Social Network

The two social network advertising studies described here are based on the Yahoo! Instant Messenger [38] (IM) social network. Instant Messaging is a popular form of communication where users who are connected to each other via *buddy* links can send instant messages to each other's computers. Users connected to each other on IM are called *friends*. The online social network graph is induced from IM users and their social connections (friends). The resulting social graph exhibits many of the characteristics of the large scale-free networks as described in [8].

30.4.1.1   Yahoo! IM Graph Statistics

The Yahoo! IM social graph is constructed from a snapshot of all active users in summer of 2008. Users are considered active if they have logged into the Yahoo! network at least once in the prior 6 months. Further, only users having at least one friend are retained. The resulting social graph contains approximately 100M nodes (users) and 1B edges (friendship connections). Two users are connected in the graph if they have communicated at least once during the observed period. Thus, this graph is a subset of the buddy list. The key statistics of the graph are summarized in Table 30.1. Note that actual numbers such as the number of nodes and edges of the social network graph are not provided for confidentiality reasons. Further, results in the following sections are normalized to preserve the underlying trends without disclosing confidential data.

Figure 30.2 shows the degree distribution and fits it to the power law and q-exponential distributions. The power law distribution is taken as $P(\lambda) \propto \lambda^{\gamma}$ where γ was fit via linear regression to $\gamma = -2.201$. The q-Exponential (Tsallis) distribution has been recently studied in the social circles model for social networks [37]. As shown in the figure, the q-Exponential distribution appears to be a better fit to the degree distribution. This suggests that people connect to others who

Table 30.1 Some basic statistics of the IM graph

Users	$O(10^8)$
Average degree	16.31
Power law exponent	−2.201
1st, 2nd Conn. components	95.20%, <0.1%
q Parameters	$q = 1.778$, $\kappa = 4.47$, shape = 1.28, scale = 5.73

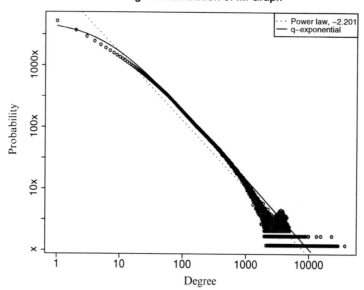

Fig. 30.2 IM graph degree distribution, showing a fit to the power law distribution (*dotted*) and the q-exponential distribution (*bold*)

are in their local neighborhoods, as opposed to arbitrary locations across the network. These local neighbors, the social circles, can be larger than the 1- or 2-level neighborhoods considered in the preferential attachment models [36]. The social circles model better explains the shape of the distribution than the power law, especially the curvature that starts at around ten friends. It suggests that users are highly connected within social circles, not just among a few isolated friends.

A *connected component* of a graph is defined as a subgraph in which any two vertices are connected together by at least one path. Figure 30.3 shows the distribution of the connected components of the IM graph with a single large connected component and a multitude of smaller components.

30.4.1.2 Conversations in the IM Social Network

Yahoo! IM users communicate with their friends by exchanging instant messages (IMs). The instant messaging conversations between friends are logged in the following format:

$$C = \{(u, f, t) \mid u, f \in U \land t \in \mathscr{T}\}$$

where u and f are two friends, t is the time of the start of the conversation, and $\mathscr{T}$ denotes the time range for data collection. Note that the actual contents of the conversations are not recorded, only the fact that there was a conversation between two users is available. Conversations are assumed to be bi-directional in that, for

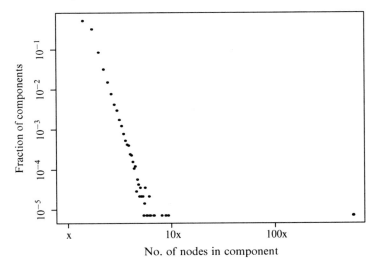

Fig. 30.3 Distribution of connected component size on a log–log scale

every conversation (u, f, t) a conversation (f, u, t) is assumed to occur. The number of conversations between two IM users can be used to determine the weight of the corresponding edge in the social graph. The weighted IM social graph is defined as follows:

$$G = (V, E, w)$$
$$V = U$$
$$E = \{(u, f) \mid u, f \in U \wedge \exists_{t \in \mathscr{T}} (u, f, t) \in C\}$$
$$w_{u,f} = |\{(u, f, t) \mid (u, f, t) \in C \wedge t \in \mathscr{T}\}|$$

where an edge implies that there was at least one conversation between the users during the time period T. The neighborhood $N(u)$ of a user u is defined as follows:

$$N(u) = \{f \mid u, f \in U \wedge \exists_{t \in \mathscr{T}} (u, f, t) \in C\}$$

where U is the set of all users. Here the concept of a user's neighborhood is limited to those users with whom he or she actually communicated during the data collection period.

30.4.2   Predicting Ad Clicks

Websites like Yahoo! are extremely popular among web users world-wide. This extensive user reach makes Yahoo! very attractive to advertisers who wish to promote their brand or enhance the adoption of their products or services via advertisements (ads) served to users on Yahoo! These ads typically appear alongside the web content. As described in Sect. 30.1, online advertising has three popular formats – email marketing, display advertising and sponsored search advertising. This discussion focuses on display advertising. Clicks on ads are a commonly used measure of the effectiveness of ad campaigns. Advertisers use *targeting* to improve the effectiveness of ad campaigns. Traditional methods involve targeting user segments based on *demographic, geographic,* and *psychographic* attributes [1]. Recent advances in online advertising have popularized the use of *behavioral targeting* [12, 13, 39] which leverages online user behavior to infer user interests and enables targeting the right ad to each user interest segment. With the growing popularity of online social networks, the notion of *social network ad targeting* is becoming prominent (see [28] for example). This form of targeting involves either seeding some users in the network with a viral marketing campaign or inferring a user's interests based on what is known about the user's social connections (friends). The natural question in the context of social networks is whether the rich social network information about users can be used either stand-alone or in conjunction with other targeting approaches to improve the overall effectiveness of ad campaigns. The following experiments are designed to study whether the users' social network information is predictive of ad clicks.

30.4.2.1 Dataset Description

The data for this analysis is derived from two main sources: historical user clickstream information comprising of URLs from Yahoo! web sites, web searches and clicks on search results and sponsored search ads, and views and clicks of display ads. This data is referred to as behavioral data as it summarizes the behavior of the user on the Yahoo! network. The social network data was derived from a snapshot of the Yahoo! IM social graph. The data contains for each user, a list of friends and the number of conversations between the user and each friend for a fixed time period. The behavioral data is collected over an N week time period that overlaps with the IM social graph snapshot. Further, the data is split by time into a train set (first k weeks) for building the models and a test set (the remaining $N - k$ weeks) for evaluating them.

30.4.2.2 Measuring the Social Network Effect in Ad Clicks

Section 30.2 presented several methods for studying the social network effect. This section describes the results of experiments performed to verify whether the social network effect exists in the ad click behavior of users.

The Jaccard similarity measure described in Sect. 30.2.1.1 can be used to measure the similarity between pairs of users based on the ads seen by the users in a fixed period of time. Specifically for this experiment, ads viewed by the user were counted only once even if the user saw the same ad multiple times. Further, the chronological order by time is ignored for this analysis. As a result, the similarity does not indicate which user saw the ad first. It is only important to determine that users see the same ads as their friends. The fact that the total number of unique ads to display is far smaller than the number of opportunities to display these ads, it is conceivable that there should be some overlap between ads viewed by any arbitrarily selected pair of users. Thus, the similarity of ads seen between randomly selected pairs of users is used as a baseline. For each user, a set of users matching the degree distribution of the IM graph, is randomly selected with uniform probability.

Figure 30.4 compares the distribution of similarity values for the IM graph and the randomly selected pairs of users. There are two interesting features to note. First, the large peak at similarity 0 for the randomly selected pairs of users suggests that most users see completely different ads. Secondly, the IM graph has a much longer tail than the random graph. This is evidence of homophily, that friends tend to see more similar ads than do randomly selected pairs of users. Users and their friends have similar enough behavior as to be targeted with similar ads.

Evidence of peer pressure within the social network is a further indication of the existence of the social network effect as discussed in Sect. 30.2.2. Figure 30.5 shows the average click-through rate on ads of users versus the number of the user's friends who have clicked on ads in the past. The results clearly indicate that having friends with past ad clicks increases the chance that a user will click in the future.

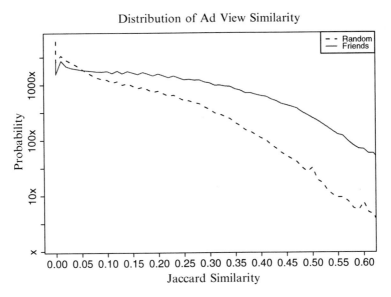

Fig. 30.4 The distribution of similarity between selected pairs of IM friends (*solid*) and randomly selected pairs of users (*black dashed*)

Friends vs. Click Probability

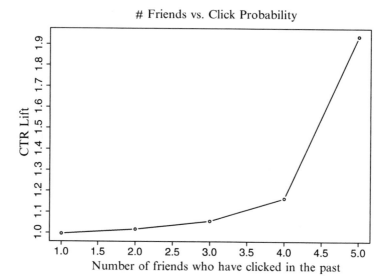

Fig. 30.5 CTR lift of users whose friends have clicked on the ads in the past. Increasing CTR lift shows that CTR of users increases with the number of friends who clicked on any ad in the past

30.4.2.3 Modeling Propensity to Click on Ads

The presence of the social network effect in ad click behavior is encouraging. This section shows how the user's social network information can be used to build a model for predicting future ad click propensity. More importantly, given that models to predict ad click propensity based on user behavior are prevalent as in behavioral targeting, it is important to identify the incremental benefit of adding the user's social network information. The following experiments depict the performance of social network based ad targeting.

Targeting to Friends

Homophily suggests that friends tend to have similar interests. The first simple experiment is based on homophily. It involves targeting users with high ad click propensity based on their behavioral features and all of their friends. Two other sets of users are selected for comparison. The first set includes only the users with high propensity to click while the second set combines users with high click propensity with randomly selected users. Figure 30.6 shows three reach-CTR plots for each of the three sets of users. The first plot (dotted line) shows the users rank ordered by their ad-click propensity based on their behavioral features alone. This represents the first comparison set. The second plot (solid line) shows the performance of the set of high click propensity users and all their friends. The set of friends of each user is assigned the same score as the user for the purpose of rank ordering. The third plot

Reach Vs. CTR of Targeting Friends

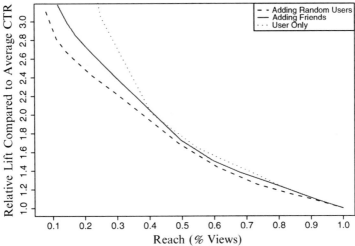

Fig. 30.6 Targeting users and all their friends compared to targeting only the high click propensity users and targeting high click propensity users along with randomly chosen users

(dashed line) depicts the performance where for each user, a randomly chosen set of users is added. The number of randomly chosen users is the same as the number of friends of the user. Further, just as in the above case, the randomly chosen users are given the same score as the user to determine the rank ordered set. The results show that both additions to the set of targeted users, either their friends or random users, have lower average CTR versus targeting users only for a given reach. However, adding the user's friends has higher average CTR for any given reach compared to adding randomly chosen users. This is further evidence that friends tend to have similar ad click patterns.

Weighted Combination of Scores

The next method involves combining scores from the model using behavioral model and the model using social network information as described in Sect. 30.3.3.1. Figure 30.7 shows the results of the experiments, comparing the new scores based on the weighted combination of models using behavioral and social information with the original scores from the model using behavioral information alone in one particular ad. The results show a marginal improvement using the weighted combination. Further, the improvement is not uniform across the entire reach-CTR plot. The results for other ads were observed to be similar.

Reach Vs. CTR of Targeting Friends

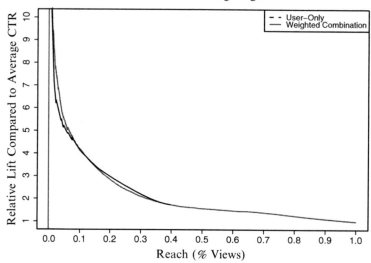

Fig. 30.7 Weighted combination of social network and behavioral scores

Ensemble Method

The ensemble method effectively combines the model based on the social information with the one based on behavioral information. The combination is structured
such that the social model boosts the performance of the behavioral model only
when the error from the user model is large. As discussed in Sect. 30.3.3.2, this
maximizes the contribution of the social model while preventing any adverse impact on the error. Figure 30.8 shows the result of the ensemble classifier. As can be
seen from the solid line, the performance of the ensemble method is strictly better
than or the same as the behavioral model alone. Overall, an average 5% improvement was obtained using the ensemble classifier.

30.4.3 Predicting Product Adoption in Social Networks

Advertising is commonly used to increase adoption of products and services. The
growing popularity of online social networks has engendered significant interest in
viral marketing which involves messaging to key individuals in the social network
who can in turn leverage the power of their social network to promote adoption. This
section describes the spread of product adoption in a large-scale online social network and its implications for advertising. The specific product discussed is the *PC
To Phone* calling available to users of Yahoo! IM. A popular feature of Yahoo! Instant Messenger is *PC to PC* calling wherein users can call their friends' computers

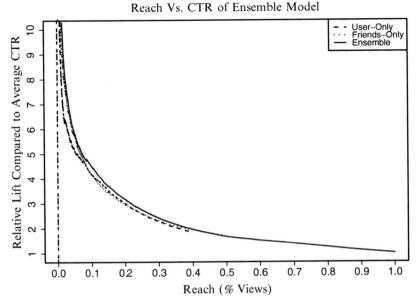

Fig. 30.8 Comparing the approach of targeting high click propensity users alone versus the ensemble classifier combining the social and behavioral models

and talk in person via VoIP (*voice over IP*). Users can optionally subscribe to a premium (paid) product called *PC To Phone* that enables them to call any traditional phone line (land or mobile) from their computers for a nominal charge. This section describes the adoption of the *PC To Phone* product among IM users and its implications for online advertising.

30.4.3.1 Dataset Description

The data for the study of the *PC To Phone* adoption in the Yahoo! IM social network was derived from three data sources. The Yahoo! IM social network graph data is described in Sect. 30.4.1.1. The behavioral, demographic, and geographic information corresponding to users in the Yahoo! IM graph is derived from the clickstream logs and from the information provided by users at the time of registration. These two datasets are combined to derive several *user* and *social* features described in Table 30.2. Social features such as *conn_bdy*, *reach_bdy* and *adj_bdy* are motivated from related work by Backstrom et al. [6]. The other features are chosen based on their availability and relevance to the prediction problem on hand. Information about the *PC To Phone* product adoption is obtained from the payment transaction logs. Adopters of this product together with their adoption date are identified over a 2 year period from summer 2006 – summer 2008. Analysis of the adoption trend over time and conversation with the business showed that this niche product is very important to Yahoo!

Table 30.2 User-level and network features of users of the Yahoo! IM social network

	Feature	Description
Network Features	*fringe*	Binary feature indicating if a node has at least one premium neighbor
	n_friends	Number of network neighbors
	n_friends_add	Number of network neighbors added during T
	n_friends_del	Number of network neighbors deleted during T
	prem_bdy	Number of network neighbors who have adopted premium product
	pc2pc	Number of PC to PC calls made during the given time period
	adj_bdy	Number of neighbors that are adjacent to each other
	conn_bdy	Number of neighbors that are within one hop
	reach_bdy	Number of users in the network a user can reach Essentially the size of the connected component
	buddy_countries	Number of unique countries to which neighbors belong, based on the IP address
User-level Features	*premium*	Binary feature indicating if the user has adopted the premium product. (**Target variable**)
	n_logins	Number of logins during a given period
	total_ims_sent	Total number of instant messages sent during time a given period
	country	Country decoded from IP of user
	active	Binary variable indicating whether the user was active during the given period
	gender	0 male, 1 female, −1 unknown
	age_cat	Categorical feature constructed from binning user age
	ten_cat	Categorical feature constructed from binning user tenure
	country_code	Country declared by the user
	i_entertainment	Binary variables indicating interest categories declared by the user
	i_music	
	i_small_business	
	i_business	
	i_personal_finance	
	i_travel	
	i_computers	
	i_shopping	
	i_home_family	
	i_sports	
	i_health	

30.4.3.2   Measuring the Social Network Effect in Product Adoption

Social Science literature often associates highly connected individual users with influencers based on the assumption that the adoption of a product by these individuals followed by subsequent word-of-mouth promotion among their friends would lead to a cascade of adoptions. The following results study the role of the highly connected individuals and the presence of the social network effect in promoting the adoption of the *PC To Phone* product in the IM social network.

High-Degree Users as Influencers

Figure 30.9a shows the adoption patterns over time of friends of high-degree individuals in the IM network. The figure shows the average number of successors (friends who have adopted the product after the individual) as a function of the number of predecessors (friends who adopted the product before the individual). The figure has four different plots by user degree quartiles. High-degree individuals have a higher average number of successors compared to lower-degree individuals. This is expected since by definition higher-degree individuals have more friends and hence the number of friends adopting just by chance will be higher for higher-degree individuals. However, Fig. 30.9b shows that the fraction of successors is much lower for high-degree individuals than for lower-degree users. In fact, the trend is completely reversed for all degree quartiles in Fig. 30.9b compared to Fig. 30.9a. This shows that high-degree users do not influence a disproportionately large fraction of their immediate friends to adopt after them.

   Figure 30.10 plots the fraction of successors of an adopter as a function of the number of predecessors. This relationship is the reverse of what was presented in Fig. 30.9a but still shows a nearly identical relationship as in Fig. 30.9a. If indeed high-degree individuals are influencers, one would not expect users with a high number of successors to also have a high average number of predecessors. These results are similar to those observed in Anagnostopoulos et al. [5] and they collectively indicate that adoption is less likely to be due to the influence of high-degree users but more related to the number of prior adoptions (predecessors) in the user's social neighborhood.

Cascades in Product Adoptions

Figure 30.11a shows a cumulative distribution of the total path length of adoption cascades. An adoption cascade is one where the first adopter has no predecessors, i.e., none of the user's friends have adopted before the user and continues a sequence of adoptions over time from the first adopter to one of his/her friends, then to one of their friends, and so on until the end of the cascade. All successive adoptions are limited to a period of 6 months from the original adoption. More than 60% of the adoption cascades are of length one, indicating that the original adopter was

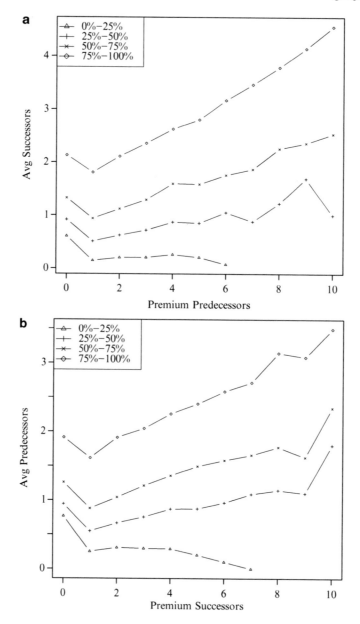

Fig. 30.9 (a) Number of friends who follow an adopting user as a function of premium predecessors. (b) Number of friends who precede an adopting user as a function of premium successors

followed by just one of his/her friends within 6 months. Similarly, nearly 80% of adoption cascades are of length two or lower. This indicates that most adoption cascades are local. The longer cascades were generally triggered by high-degree users (see plot with triangles in Fig. 30.11b). Further analysis showed that average

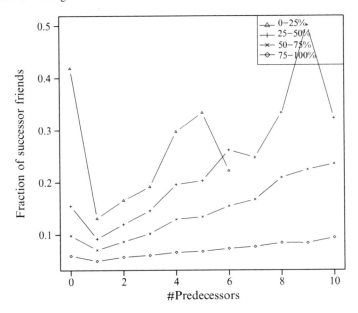

Fig. 30.10 Fraction of friends who follow an adopting user as a function of premium predecessors

degree of the users along the longer cascades (internal nodes) was in fact higher than that of users triggering these cascades (plot with circles in Fig. 30.11b). This observation indicates that while degree is correlated with longer cascades it is mostly not the cause for these cascades. The longer cascades are created simply by virtue of the users in the cascade being better connected. Users at the end of cascades generally have the lowest average degree (plot with plus sign in Fig. 30.11b).

This analysis of the Yahoo! IM graph shows that *influencers* as traditionally defined are rare. This is inline with the recent observations made by Watts and Dodds [35] that contradict the conventional wisdom in marketing where the role of the individual influencers is emphasized. Specifically, treating degree-central users as proxies for influencers, shows that degree-central users do not have a disproportionately higher fraction of their friends adopting after them compared to other users. Further, the cascades of adoptions triggered by the degree-central users are very short indicating that the influence (if any) is limited to the local neighborhood.

Network Effect and Threshold Model

While the above analysis shows that adoption patterns are not correlated with degree, there is evidence of the network effect in the adoption of the *PC To Phone* product in the data wherein adoption of a product by an individual is more likely if the product has been widely adopted in the individual's social neighborhood. This is evidence of the threshold model [18] which suggests that each individual has a

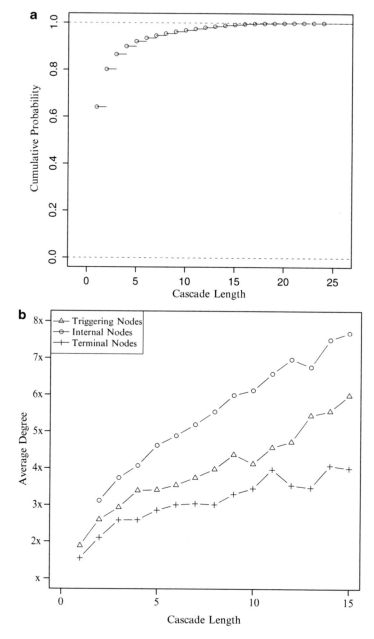

Fig. 30.11 (a) Cumulative distribution of cascade length distribution in premium subgraph. (b) Average degree of nodes that trigger cascades (*triangle*), are in the cascade but neither trigger nor terminate cascades (*circle*), and are last adopters (*terminal*) in cascades (*plus*)

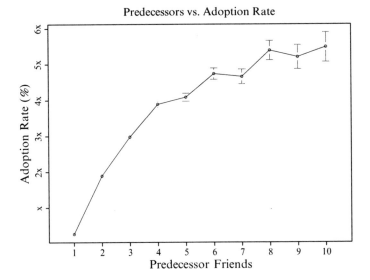

Fig. 30.12 Probability of a user's adoption as a function of friends adopting before the user

threshold representing the proportion of a user's friends who must adopt the product before the user decides to do so. Over one-half of all adopters had at least one predecessor (friend who adopted before them). Figure 30.12 shows that the probability of adoption of an individual user increases as the number of friends who have adopted prior to them increases. It also demonstrates diminishing returns where the presence of each additional predecessor beyond 5 does not increase the user's probability of adoption by much. Note though that the error bars are larger for users with a larger number of predecessor friends. This effect is consistent with the observations made in the studies of the LiveJournal and the DBLP datasets [6].

The spread of adoptions in the IM social network appears to follow the threshold model with each user v having a threshold θ_v indicating the fraction of the user's friends who must first adopt for the user to adopt. Figure 30.13 shows the probability of adoption as a function of number of friends (degree). Each plot is for a specific number of predecessors (friends adopting before). While users with higher number of predecessors have a higher probability of adoption regardless of degree, the probability of adoption decreases with higher degree.

Figure 30.14 shows that the probability of a user adopting the product increases, to an extent, as the fraction of their friends who adopted before them increases. The data where the fraction of friends adopting before is greater than 0.1 is sparse with at least one outlier (in the top right of the chart) with large error bars.

Adoption Rate with Number of Friends

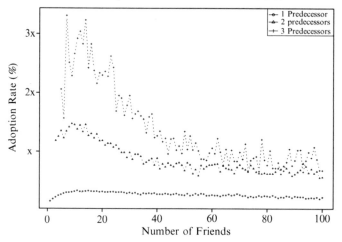

Fig. 30.13 Probability of a user's adoption as a function of number of friends. Each curve is for a specific number of friends adopting before the user's adoption

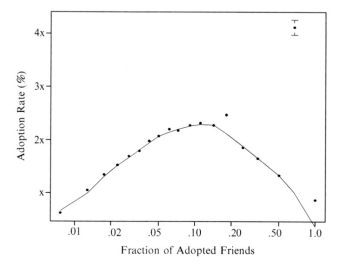

Fig. 30.14 Probability of a user's adoption increases with increasing fraction of immediate friends

Effect of Rich Neighborhoods

Local neighborhoods in the social network that are already rich in adoption tend to see further growth in adoptions. Figure 30.9 which shows the average number of successors as a function of the number of predecessors for each of the 4 degree quartiles highlights the growth of the rich neighborhoods with the upward sloping plots. This is attributed to the local connectedness of small-world graphs [10, 36] wherein new adoptions in neighborhoods that are already dense in adoptions trigger a percolating effect [34] and lead to higher number of new adoptions. This insight is the basis of the social neighborhood marketing strategy discussed below.

30.4.3.3   Modeling the Propensity to Adopt the PC to Phone Product

This section describes how the *PC To Phone* product can be effectively promoted using two different marketing strategies – direct marketing and social neighborhood marketing and analyzes the relationship between them.

Direct Marketing

Direct marketing involves targeting ads to users who have a high propensity to adopt the product in the future. Identifying the right set of users is a key challenge in direct marketing. The rich *user* and *social* features, described in Table 30.2, are used to build a classifier to reliably predict future adoptions. For training the classifier, user and social features are constructed for users who have not adopted the product during month M_i. Each user record is assigned a binary target indicating whether the user adopted in month M_{i+1} or not. Table 30.3 shows the relative importance score of the top features (see [16] for a description on how the relative importance is computed). Features with higher importance score are most predictive of the target (adoption). All other features (not shown in the table) have a relative importance score below 1.0.

The most predictive feature of user adoption is the *demographic* feature – user *country*. Non-US users are more likely to adopt the *PC To Phone* product since it offers a lower cost alternative to international calling. The next most important feature is a behavioral feature which denotes the number of *PC to PC* calls made by

Table 30.3 Relative importance of user and social features in predicting product adoption

Rank	Feature	Relative importance score
1	*country*	44.76
2	*pc2pc*	25.81
3	*prem_bdy*	6.32
4	*fringe*	6.03
5	*ten_cat*	4.51
6	*gender*	2.25
7	*age_cat*	2.20
8	*n_logins*	1.92
9	*n_friends*	1.51
10	*buddy_countries*	1.27
11	*reach_bdy*	1.00

the user. Presumably, users making *PC to PC* calls already have all the prerequisites in terms of the microphone and PC speakers set up to take the step towards making the online transaction to activate *PC To Phone* product. The third most predictive feature is the social feature *prem_bdy* which is the number of friends of the user who have already adopted the product. This is not surprising given the analysis in Fig. 30.12.

Although for the purposes of this experiment, the classifiers were built using the C5.0 [1] decision tree software, other supervised learning algorithms could have given similar results. The classifier was evaluated on a test set comprising of users (who had not already adopted the product) whose features were constructed based on their activity from month M_{i+1}. A binary target was assigned to each user record in the test set based on whether or not they adopted the product in month M_{i+2}. The model assigns a score for the user's propensity to adopt in the following month. Users can be rank ordered by their model score and the top $k\%$ can be targeted with ads where k is determined based on the available marketing campaign budget. A *cumulative gains chart* is used to calibrate the performance of the classifier. It shows the fraction of adopters in the following month within the top-$k\%$ users ranked by the probability score. A higher percentage of adopters for the same $k\%$ is desirable. Figure 30.15 shows the cumulative gains charts on the test dataset for the *user* features alone, the *social* features alone, and for the combined set of *user* and *social* features. Although the performance of both the *user* and *social* features is very similar, their combination shows a significant improvement which emphasizes the point that models leveraging as much pertinent information about the users as possible yield superior results. Selecting users by the number of premium friends

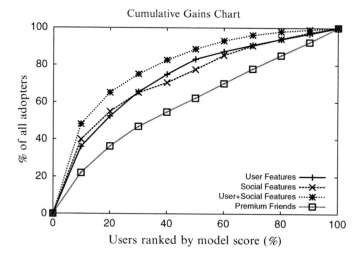

Fig. 30.15 Cumulative gains for adoption based on the model ranking

---

[1] C5.0 is a commercial version of C4.5. For enhancements in C5.0 see [2].

alone, a powerful predictor of social adoption, does not perform well. Note that the above results are based on retrospective analysis of data that is divided by time into train and test sets. The predictive ability of the model can be effectively tested in an online test where actual ads are served to users and their response rates are measured.

Social Neighborhood Marketing

As described in Sect. 30.3.2.4, the key problem in social neighborhood marketing is to identify a set of adopters A such that number of friends of the users in set A who adopt in a fixed time period after them, denoted by $\sigma(A)$, is maximized. Effective methods would identify the set of adopters A that maximizes $\sigma(A)$. As described earlier, the set A can be identified using simple heuristics such as picking the highest degree users, the earliest adopters, or the most recent adopters. Alternatively, a model based approach would involve training a regression model that would predict for any given set A, the value of $\sigma(A)$. The training and test datasets for training such a model were generated in the same way as described in the section on direct marketing above. The experiments involved training a regression model using the stochastic gradient boosted decision trees algorithm [16] though any suitable regression based model could be used. This model used the rich set of *user* and *social* features shown in Table 30.2. Figure 30.16 presents the test set results of the different methods for picking the set A for social neighborhood marketing. The heuristic that selects early adopters performs worse than random while the heuristic that selects the most recent adopters performs slightly better than random. The heuristic that selects highest degree adopters first performs quite well and provides a significant lift over random. The figure shows that the model using the combination of *user* and *social* features for predicting $\sigma(A)$ performs the best.

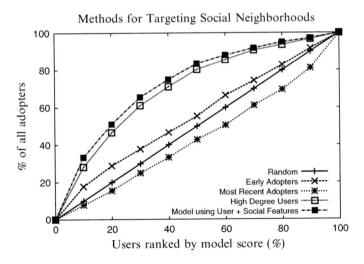

Fig. 30.16 Relative performance of various methods for identifying the set of users A for targeting

30.5 Conclusion

Advertising in social networks has recently become an important business due to the popularity of various online social networks. This chapter has provided a detailed review of the different online advertising methods that can be used in the social network setting. The methodology outlined in this chapter first describes how to measure the presence of the social network effect and secondly how the social network information can be suitably used to power successful advertising campaigns. The two applications of social network advertising – modeling click propensity on online ads and predicting product adoption in the social network – show how these methods can be applied in practice. The results show that not only does there exist a strong correlation between social connections and the users' response potential but the social network can be effectively leveraged to complement other known information about users, such as online user behavior, to build effective models that can predict the users' response propensity. This chapter also raises several interesting questions that merit further research as discussed below.

Social network targeting has focused quite extensively on leveraging the social features including the structural features of the social graph. However, as is true in multiple social settings, the level of influence wielded by specific friends on a given user depends on the expertise and interests of the friends themselves. Thus, the problem of social network targeting should really be viewed as that of identifying *subgraphs* of users with similar interests that may be receptive to the product being advertised. Identification of such subgraphs of users with common interests and high receptivity to niche products remains to be carefully studied.

A user's set of friends constitutes a very small proportion of his or her nearest neighbors in terms of behavior. While in general a user's behavior is the best predictor of the user's interests, correlation within local social neighborhoods can be used as a first approximation when no other information is available. As the user profile becomes richer, however, one may benefit by expanding the scope of social targeting models to include the local neighborhood in terms of behavior in addition to *social* neighborhoods. This chapter has presented a couple of approaches including a weighted combination of the behavioral scores and the social network scores and a method of learning an ensemble model to effectively combine information from the two sources. A more formal model of seamlessly combining information from multiple disparate data sources for more accurate targeting needs to be researched.

Section 30.4.3 studied predicting product adoption in online social networks. In contrast with other studies that analyzed growth of online communities or where conversion probabilities are assumed to be high [22, 34], the *PC To Phone* product adoption studied the spread of adoption of a niche but important product with a very low baseline adoption rate. Analysis showed that the spread of product adoption is unlikely to be due to the presence of *influencers* but a more a result of *peer-pressure* in the social network where users with more friends who adopted the product are more likely to adopt themselves. The results further showed that effectively combining *user* and *social* features can reliably predict future adoption and these models perform better than several commonly used heuristics in offline evaluations.

Quantifying influence in the online social network setting is challenging. It depends on a variety of factors including personal traits, individual's knowledge of the subject matter, and the ability to convince friends to adopt products they recommend. A formal model of influence propagation that is generally applicable to a wide array of social networks would be extremely valuable.

Direct marketing and social neighborhood marketing are complementary advertising strategies. An advertiser would like to target users with an appropriate message while simultaneously getting one (or more) of their friends to influence them via word-of-mouth marketing. The return on investment on the campaign depends on the response rate of the targeted users in the case of a direct marketing campaign and the ability of the targeted users to promote the adoption of the product among their friends in the case of social neighborhood marketing campaign. Determining how much budget to allocate between the two marketing strategies is based on the cost-benefit analysis of each strategy. The cost of the marketing campaign includes the cost of delivering the marketing message to the selected users and the cost of offering the right reward (or incentive) to users to adopt and possibly promote the product in their social network. Some of the incentives might be monetary or may involve recognition as in the case of reputation scores at Amazon.com or Yahoo! Answers. Selecting the right incentive that would motivate users to respond favorably to marketing campaigns or promote products among their friends is an interesting question that merits further research. Domingos and Richardson [15] used a tunable payoff parameter in their simulations. In practice, an accurate estimate of the payoff can only be determined by running actual advertising campaigns. The relationship between the relative effectiveness of direct marketing and social neighborhood marketing strategies is an interesting research question with very significant practical implications.

In summary, social network based advertising is a ripe young field replete with substantial challenges and significant opportunities. The explosive growth in online social networks will create many new areas in social network advertising with potential to completely change the landscape of online advertising itself. The methods presented in this chapter can be used as a toolkit in analyzing and evaluating new opportunities and the lessons learned from these opportunities can in turn be fed back to improve upon these methods.

Acknowledgments   We thank Duncan Watts, Sharad Goel, Jignashu Parikh, Narayan Bhamidipati, and Sergei Matsuevich for numerous enlightening discussions and help with data.

References

1. Nielsen Claritas PRIZM. http://en-us.nielsen.com/tab/product_families/nielsen_claritas/prizm
2. RuleQuest Research. Website. http://www.rulequest.com/see5-comparison.html
3. Nielsen Wire. Website (2009). http://blog.nielsen.com/nielsenwire/nielsen-news/social-networking-new-global-footprint/
4. Agarwal, D., Pregibon, D.: Enhancing communities of interest using bayesian stochastic block-models. In: Proc. 4th SIAM Int'l Conf. on Data Mining, pp. 291–299 (2004)

5. Anagnostopoulos, A., Kumar, R., Mahdian, M.: Influence and correlation in social networks. In: KDD '08: Proceeding of the 14th ACM SIGKDD International Conference on Knowledge Discovery and Data Mining, pp. 7–15. ACM, New York, NY, USA (2008)

6. Backstrom, L., Huttenlocher, D., Kleinberg, J., Lan, X.: Group formation in large social networks: Membership, growth, and evolution. In: KDD '06: Proceedings of the 12th ACM SIGKDD International Conference on Knowledge Discovery and Data Mining, pp. 44–54. ACM, New York, NY, USA (2006)

7. Bagherjeiran, A., Parekh, R.: Combining behavioral and social network data for online advertising. In: ICDMW '08: Proceedings of the 2008 IEEE International Conference on Data Mining Workshops, pp. 837–846. IEEE Computer Society, Washington, DC, USA (2008)

8. Barabási, A.L.: Linked: How Everything Is Connected to Everything Else and What It Means for Business, Science, and Everyday Life. Plume Books, New York (2003)

9. Barabási, A.L., Albert, R.: Emergence of scaling in random networks. Science **286**, 509–512 (1999)

10. Barabási, A.L., Oltvai, Z.N.: Network biology: Understanding the cell's functional organization. Nature Reviews Genetics **5**(2), 101–113 (2004)

11. Broder, A., Fontoura, M., Josifovski, V., Riedel, L.: A semantic approach to contextual advertising. In: SIGIR '07: Proceeding of the 30th International SIGIR Conference, pp. 559–566. ACM, New York, NY, USA (2007)

12. Chen, Y., Pavlov, D., Canny, J.: Large-scale behavioral targeting. In: Proceedings of the 15th ACM SIGKDD International Conference on Knowledge Discovery and Data Mining, pp. 209–218. ACM, New York, USA (2009)

13. Chung, C., Koran, J., Lin, L.J., Yin, H.: Model for generating user profiles in a behavioral targeting system. U. S. Patent Application (11/394,374) (2006)

14. Crandall, D., Cosley, D., Huttenlocher, D., Kleinberg, J., Suri, S.: Feedback effects between similarity and social influence in online communities. In: Proc. 14th Conf. on Knowledge Discovery & Data Mining, pp. 160–168. ACM, New York, NY, USA (2008)

15. Domingos, P., Richardson, M.: Mining the network value of customers. In: KDD '01: Proceedings of the Seventh ACM SIGKDD International Conference on Knowledge Discovery and Data Mining, pp. 57–66. ACM, New York, NY, USA (2001)

16. Friedman, J.H.: Greedy function approximation: A gradient boosting machine. Annals of Statistics **29**, 1189–1232 (1999)

17. Gladwell, M.: The Tipping Point: How Little Things Can Make a Big Difference, 1st edn. Little Brown, Boston (2000)

18. Granovetter, M.: Threshold models of collective behavior. American Journal of Sociology (83), 1420–1443 (1978)

19. Hartline, J., Mirrokni, V., Sundararajan, M.: Optimal marketing strategies over social networks. In: WWW '08: Proceeding of the 17th International Conference on World Wide Web, pp. 189–198. ACM, New York, NY, USA (2008)

20. Hill, S., Provost, F., Volinsky, C.: Network-based marketing: Identifying likely adopters via consumer networks. Statistical Science **22**(2), 256–275 (2006)

21. Jaccard, P.: Étude comparative de la distribution florale dans une portion des alpes et des jura. Bulletin del la Société Vaudoise des Sciences Naturelles **37**, 547–579 (1901)

22. Kempe, D., Kleinberg, J., Tardos, E.: Maximizing the spread of influence through a social network. In: KDD '03: Proceedings of the Ninth ACM SIGKDD International Conference on Knowledge Discovery and Data Mining, pp. 137–146. ACM, New York, NY, USA (2003)

23. Kempe, D., Kleinberg, J., Tardos, E.: Influential nodes in a diffusion model for social networks. In: ICALP (2005)

24. Lazarsfeld, P., Merton, R.K.: Friendship as a social process: A substantive and methodological analysis. In: M. Berger, T. Abel, C.H. Page (eds.) Freedom and Control in Modern Society, pp. 18–66. Van Nostrand, New York (1954)

25. Leskovec, J., Adamic, L.A., Huberman, B.A.: The dynamics of viral marketing. ACM Transactions on the Web **1**, (2007)

26. Mcpherson, M., Lovin, L.S., Cook, J.M.: Birds of a feather: Homophily in social networks. Annual Review of Sociology **27**(1), 415–444 (2001)

27. Pine, J.: Mass customizing products and services. Planning Review **July–August**, (1993)
28. Provost, F., Dalessandro, B., Hook, R., Zhang, X., Murray, A.: Audience selection for on-line brand advertising: Privacy-friendly social network targeting. In: KDD '09: Proceedings of the 15th ACM SIGKDD International Conference on Knowledge Discovery and Data Mining, pp. 707–716. ACM, New York, NY, USA (2009)
29. Richardson, M., Domingos, P.: The intelligent surfer: Probabilistic combination of link and content information in pageRank. In: Advances in Neural Information Processing Systems 14. MIT Press, Cambridge (2002)
30. Richardson, M., Domingos, P.: Mining knowledge-sharing sites for viral marketing. In: KDD '02: Proceedings of the Seventh ACM SIGKDD International Conference on Knowledge Discovery and Data Mining, pp. 51–70. ACM, New York, NY, USA (2002)
31. Schapire, R.E.: The boosting approach to machine learning: An overview. In: MSRI Workshop on Nonlinear Estimation and Classification. Berkeley, CA (2001)
32. Singla, P., Richardson, M.: Yes, there is a correlation: From social networks to personal behavior on the web. In: WWW '08: Proceeding of the 17th International Conference on World Wide Web, pp. 655–664. ACM, New York, NY, USA (2008)
33. Walkeri, R.: The hidden (in plain sight) persuaders. The New York Times Magazine, 69–75 (Dec. 5, 2004)
34. Watts, D.J.: A simple model of global cascades on random networks. Proceedings of the National Academy of Sciences of the United States of America **99**(9), 5766–5771 (2002)
35. Watts, D.J., Dodds, P.S.: Influentials, networks, and public opinion formation. Journal of Consumer Research **34**(4), 441–458 (2007)
36. Watts, D.J., Strogatz, S.H.: Collective dynamics of 'small-world' networks. Nature **393**, 440–442 (1998)
37. White, D.R., Kejzar, N., Tsallis, C., Farmer, J.D.: Generative model for feedback networks. Physical Review E **73** (2006)
38. Yahoo!: Messenger. http://messenger.yahoo.com
39. Yan, J., Liu, N., Wang, G., Zhang, W., Jiang, Y., Chen, Z.: How much can behavioral targeting help online advertising? In: WWW '09: Proceedings of the 18th International Conference on World Wide Web, pp. 261–270. ACM, New York, NY, USA (2009)

Chapter 31
Social Bookmarking on a Company's Intranet: A Study of Technology Adoption and Diffusion

Nina D. Ziv and Kerry-Ann White

31.1 Introduction

Until recent developments in digital-based innovation, companies were defined by how they made use of resources which were tangible things such as equipment, land, raw materials and human talent for the purpose of supplying goods and services to the economy [37]. Such companies had a clearly defined central management structure which was responsible for the general policies under which the company's hierarchy operated with well delineated reporting relationships and job responsibilities [47]. Within this rigid hierarchical organizational structure, decision making was bureaucratic and an anti-innovation bias was prevalent [55]. Even with the development of electronic communications and computing systems, innovation was relegated to the purview of professional R&D departments [22] within a highly structured corporate environment [51]. Indeed, in 1992, when managers were surveyed about the structure of their companies, most answered that their companies were still structured in a very traditional way, that is, with standardized jobs, procedures and policies and a hierarchical organization which emphasized a top-down chain of command [6].

With the emergence of the Internet, a robust technological platform on which new products and services are rapidly being created and new digital-based entrants have challenged the dominance of traditional physically-based companies, the nature of innovation is of necessity undergoing change. Indeed, as technology has evolved and become more strategic and key to a company's ability to maintain a competitive advantage, value creation has become more than just the production of physical goods; a company's core competency resides in the ability to bundle various technologies creatively and develop products and services that will be attractive to the customer [40].

N.D. Ziv (✉)
Department of Technology Management, Polytechnic Institute of New York University,
Brooklyn, NY, USA
e-mail: nziv123@gmail.com

B. Furht (ed.), *Handbook of Social Network Technologies and Applications*,
DOI 10.1007/978-1-4419-7142-5_31, © Springer Science+Business Media, LLC 2010

Moreover, in this post-industrial business environment, which is characterized by the availability of large amounts of information, increasing complexity, and increasing turbulence, organizational decision making is faster and more complex and therefore organizational structures have had to change accordingly [7]. Innovation in companies is now characterized by uncertainty, interrelatedness between various subsystems, and often relies on tacit knowledge accumulated by various members of the organization who may reside in different structures [51]. These structures may be internal, that is, part of the indigenous corporate structure or they may be found outside of this structure in the larger networked environment. In many companies, there is a recognition that informal networks of employees at all levels of the internal organization play an important role in gathering information and getting work done in the corporation [17]. Recent research has indicated that intra-firm connections among employees and sharing of knowledge through these networks are essential for fostering an environment where creativity and innovation can flourish. Moreover, the development of such an environment is an important managerial challenge [12, 26].

Many of these informal networks of employees use a variety of technological tools to aid them in knowledge gathering and sharing. One such tool is social bookmarking which enables users to store their bookmarks on websites which they would like to revisit. Several browsers allow users to store and name websites as a "Favorite" or "Bookmark"; however, the data is organized hierarchically in a tree-like structure of folders within folders and the links remain static on a particular user's browser. Social bookmarking, which serves as alternative to the hierarchical and static structure, creates an environment for interdependent and cooperative relationships and bookmark sharing that is better managed through pointers to links. The tool allows users to retrieve their browser-independent bookmarks, annotate their bookmarks with descriptions and comments, share resources with other users, discover their naming conventions, and discover communities through retrieving the bookmarks of others.

While on the surface, such technological innovations as social bookmarking are important for facilitating knowledge sharing, it is still unclear as to how such technologies are actually used by members of an organization and how they are incorporated into the daily activities of employees. There is considerable research on the notion of technology acceptance in various settings. One research stream uses the Technology Acceptance Model (TAM) [18, 52] which posits that "two beliefs, perceived usefulness and perceived ease of use, determine an individual's behavioral intention to use a system" [25]. Much of this research has been based on measuring the interaction between these two beliefs from a quantitative perspective. While this model and its variations have been successfully applied (see Sect. 31.2 – Review of Literature), there is another stream of research based on the constructs of Everett Rogers who developed a model which focuses on the process by which an innovation is diffused throughout an organization among members of a social system [44]. In his work on innovation-diffusion, Rogers describes various types of adopters as well as the attributes of innovation that determine the rate of adoption. Rogers' approach has been applied to more qualitative studies of organizations and their members [32, 45].

This paper will focus on a study of how employees in a research-oriented organization based in the United States adopted a social bookmarking tool in order to facilitate better sharing of knowledge among the members of the organization. The tool was developed by an in-house group of application developers in response to a need for such a tool that was specifically designed for this organization. Over the last 3 years, the leaders and developers of the team have developed the tool, had their pilot group populate the tool with relevant bookmarks, and recently fully implemented the tool for corporate-wide use. Using Rogers' constructs regarding types of adopters and attributes of the adoption of an innovation, the study will investigate how this tool was adopted by different kinds of users in the organization. In addition, the study will go beyond the technology acceptance issues and provide some insights as to the technology management challenges inherent in developing and implementing such technologies in organizations.

This paper is divided into three sections. The first section will provide some literature background on technology adoption and diffusion. The second section will describe the study that was conducted and provide an interpretation of the data that was gathered. The third section will offer a discussion and some conclusions based on the research that was conducted.

31.2   Review of Literature

As previously mentioned, TAM has been studied in various settings. However, before discussing TAM, two other models are worth noting. Previous researchers in many different fields have used the Theory of Planned Behavior (TPB), and the Theory of Reasoned Action (TRA) to explain particular behaviors with regard to adoption.

The TRA model as defined by Ajzen [21], is comprised of attitude and subjective norms as the independent variables, and intention to share as the dependent variable. A key construct is behavioral intention, that is, how hard a person will try and how much effort the person is planning to exert in order to perform the behavior. The TRA has also been combined with other models and extended to discover more about technology acceptance. In studying whether behavioral beliefs about Information Technology (IT) and normative beliefs about IT differentially influence pre-adoption and post-adoption behaviors, Karahanna [29] combined Innovation Diffusion Theory (IDT) and TRA because IDT lacks the element of how attitude is formed, and how it leads to the adoption or rejection of a technology. The combined model has two dependent variables: behavioral intention about adopting the IT, and behavioral intention about using the IT. Using these combined theories, the researchers found that attitude dominates behavioral intention with regard to the continuing use of a particular technology.

TPB, proposed by Mathieson [33], provides a framework for studying attitudes toward behavior. Intention, the most important determinant of one's behavior (the dependent variable) is a combination of attitude toward the behavior, subjective norms, and Perceived Behavior Control (PBC). These constructs are defined as:

- *Attitude* – the degree to which the person has a favorable or unfavorable evaluation of the behavior in question. Attitude stems from individual positive and negative evaluations of the particular behavior.
- *Subjective Norms* – the influence of social pressure that is perceived by the individual (normative beliefs) to perform or refrain from performing a certain behavior.
- *PBC* – the individual's confidence about the particular behavior. PBC is determined by control beliefs and perceived power, and means that a person's motivation is influenced by how difficult the behaviors are perceived to be, as well as the perception of how successfully the person can, or cannot, perform the activity. A person will have high PBC over a behavior if they hold strong beliefs about the existence of factors that will facilitate the behavior. A person will have low PBC if they hold strong beliefs that impede the behavior. The perception may reflect past experiences or obstructions, the attitude of influential norms, or anticipation of upcoming circumstances.

Like any other theory, The Theory of Planned Behavior has assumptions. With the Theory of Reasoned Action as its root, TPB assumes that humans are rational and use information systematically, and that people consider the outcome and implications of their actions before they decide to perform that action or to refrain from performing the said action.

TPB has been applied to tax compliance [10], investment behavior [13], heart health [35], and health promotion [46]. It has also been applied to politics [27] and sales [30]. While Chang [14] relied on both the TRA and the TPB to aid the research, other researchers have focused on one theory or the other. Christensen and Eining [15] and Woolley and Eining [56] relied on the Theory of Reasoned Action while Parthasarathy and Mittelstaedt [36] and D'Astous, Colbert and Montpetit [18] relied on the Theory of Planned Behavior (TPB). Both theories have been heavily used in studying Information Systems adoption, for example, Bock et al. [11].

Just as Fishbein and Ajzen's TRA [21] serves as the root of TPB, it also serves as the root of TAM which was proposed by Davis et al. [19] and widely applied in IT literature. The theory builds on acceptance theory [41, 54] and efficacy theory [8, 9]. The main variables of TAM are perceived usefulness, that is, how the technology is expected to improve performance of the user and perceived ease-of-use, the degree of effortlessness in adopting the technology. TAM has received much attention and some researchers have extended the model. Mathieson [33] proposed two additional constructs on Fishbein and Ajzen's model; Szajana [49] tried to develop a systems acceptance model; Compeau and Higgins [16] tried to incorporate self-efficacy antecedents; Taylor and Todd [50] tried to incorporate the role of prior experience. Yarbrough and Smith [57], Hong et al. [28], and Shih [48] are others who have extended the model. TAM has been accepted despite its limitations and in moving away from limited testing towards experimental and field-based settings may be more applicable and generalizable to a variety of situations.

A competing theory to TAM is the theory of Perceived Characteristics of Innovating (PCI), which has received its share of popularity. PCI was developed by Moore and Benbasat [34] and further investigated by Agarwal and Prasad [1], Gagliardi and Compeau [23], and Moore and Benbasat [34]. Plouffe et al. [34] compared both the TAM and the PCI model and found that PCI constructs were better able to predict intention to adopt a technology. PCI incorporates:

- *Relative advantage* – the degree of perceived superiority of one technology over its precursor
- *Compatibility* – the degree to which an innovation is perceived as being consistent with the existing values, needs, and past experiences of the potential adopters
- *Trialability* – the degree to which technology may be experimented with before adoption
- *Voluntariness* – the degree to which adoption is under users' control
- *Visibility* – the degree to which the technology is involved in diffusion
- *Result Demonstrability* – the obvious presence of the benefits to the users

While the main models mentioned above, and four other technology adoption models, i.e., Motivational Model (MM), Model of PC Utilization (TMCU), Social Cognitive Theory (SCT), and Combined technology acceptance and planned behavior model (C-TAM-TBP) all serve their purpose, they have been mostly applied in quantitative studies. After two decades of studying technology acceptance (TA) and diffusion, the lack of a unified model indicates that there is still work to be done in the field or it could stem from the fact that diffusion theory is not one theory but a group of theories stemming from a wide variety of disciplines with each theory focusing on a different element of the innovation process.

The present qualitative study relies on the theories of Everett Rogers [43], who is known for the development and synthesis of diffusion theory. Rogers defines diffusion as, "the process by which an innovation is communicated through certain channels over time among members of a social system" [43]. Rogers delineated the product-based factors of innovation diffusion as relative advantage, compatibility, trialability, complexity and observability. The first three variables are defined above as part of the theory of PCI; the fourth variable is complexity, that is, the degree to which an innovation is perceived as being difficult to use; and the fifth variable is observability which is the degree to which the result of an innovation are observable to others and therefore leads to adoption of the innovation.

Another theory of Rogers, that of Individual Innovativeness, is also of importance to this study. This theory views the S-curve as a series of bell-curves, each representing a part of the population which adopts an innovation. According to Rogers there are five categories. The first bell-curve represents "Innovators" who are the first to adopt an innovation. "Early Adopters" is the second bell-curve representing those who adopt an innovation close to its introduction; these are the opinion leaders. The next category is the "Early Majority" who adopt an innovation after some time. The "Early Majority" adoption time is significantly longer than that of the previous two categories. These people show some opinion leadership and generally have contact with the "Early Adopters". Following "Early Majority" is the "Late Majority" bell-curve. These "Late Majority" individuals approach the innovation with a high degree of skepticism and adopt only after the majority of society has already done so. However, they are in contact with the individuals in their own category as well as individuals in the "Early Majority" category. Finally, the "Laggards" represents the last bell-curve, representing individuals who show little to no opinion leadership, and focus on "traditions." While the other groups of adopters are in contact with other category of adopters, "Laggards" are only in contact with their family and close friends [42]. In a later work, Rogers modified his series of bell curves and created one bell curve which incorporated all five categories [44].

The research cited above focuses on the users of technologies and their adoption of technologies. As noted in the Introduction (Sect. 31.1), an important managerial challenge is fostering an environment where creativity and innovation can occur and lead to experimentation and adoption of new technological innovations. However, few studies focus on the crucial role of management in developing the appropriate organization and culture for example, in order for such adoption to take place. While Rogers' constructs will be used as the theoretical framework for this study, the role of management in the diffusion and adoption of innovation at the research company will be highlighted and addressed as an important aspect of technology adoption and diffusion.

31.3   The Study

31.3.1   Overview of the Research Center

The Research Company X (hereby referred to as RCX) operates as an FFRDC (Federally Funded Research Development Center). The company has several government agencies as sponsors. RCX thrives on its ability to initiate and continue meaningful long-term relationships with its sponsors by providing research to these sponsors which enables them in turn to understand their evolving roles, challenges and issues in today's globalized economy.

RCX's R&D centers operate as self-contained divisions, but collaboration across centers is encouraged. Employees are hired for their specializations which helps to increase the effectiveness of the organization. Technical experts are essential to RCX's overall vision and its functional structure. RCX's culture facilitates collaboration and fosters ease of access to necessary information to perform the tasks as assigned by the sponsors, whether the project is long term, short term, or in between. Employees can easily coordinate schedules to exchange non-sensitive information and develop communities of practice. These practices are a direct result of the open door culture, and the interconnectivity of the buildings at the headquarters location which includes many dining facilities, and over 30 high-tech conference rooms with a Collaborative Virtual Workspace.

With the exclusion of certain mandatory project tools, RCX employees have the freedom to select and adopt the most fitting tools to enhance their work practices and maximize their efforts from the company's available resources. Employees can choose these optional technologies and adopt the ones which are most fitting to their work practices. Currently, collaborative tools have minimized the need for closed communication and have enabled users to put information in such collaborative tools, which facilitate knowledge transfer and supplement basic communication vehicles such as the telephone, face-to-face meetings, and the Internet.

RCX's culture fosters coordination through the promotion of certain cultural values which are based on the overarching vision of the company. Even though the company is large and security is a high priority, there are extensive interactions among technical and domain employee experts throughout both headquarters and the sponsors' sites. For example, an Intranet People Finder was created to enable RCX to more easily find its diverse and disbursed experts in their varied fields throughout all domestic and international locations.

31.3.2 Overview of the Social Bookmarking Tool (SBT)

A few years ago, RCX began using a Social Bookmarking Tool, hereby designated as SBT, to fulfill the need for a in-house tool for knowledge gathering and information sharing. SBT is a web-based tool with a central repository which users can access from any location, browser, or machine. Since SBT stores references and pointers to resources, not a copy of the actual resource, it does not require a lot of space and thus the technical team did not expect performance issues to occur with the tool.

The SBT project is a clear example of collaboration across centers within RCX. SBT was promoted by targeting select user communities, such as librarian researchers, who pre-populated the system with resources. Other methods of promotion used included word-of-mouth solicitation by users of the system; advertisement banners on the Intranet; tool demonstrations in coffee shops and other small retailers; demonstrations to groups of people (departments, administrations, projects, etc); physical paper Bookmarks which were distributed to people advertising what SBT was and how to access it; and emails which were sent to each Center. An important group of users in the company is the Fast-track group which is comprised of employees who generally want to keep abreast of the latest technology offered inside the company, and may be more willing to try such technologies. Although there was no marketing explicitly directed toward Fast-track, they did serve as another group which helped to attract users and thus were an additional marketing vehicle.

During the prototype of SBT, librarians were asked to bookmark resources using the tool because it was compatible with their work practices and would allow them to easily disseminate their research efforts. SBT users were able to provide feedback, e.g., questions, bugs, comments, or requests using the feedback link and could also call the Help Desk. The development team then made releases of the product on an arranged schedule when they had received enough change suggestions to make a release worthwhile.

SBT is a feature-rich application. One feature of the SBT website enables users to view top 15 bookmarks from "delicious", a public social bookmarking tool, and to decipher who the top information providers are by several categories: bookmarks, department, division, and Center. SBT's website provides a central location for gathering and tagging links while exploring what others have linked and tagged and provides the users with useful information such as a list of the last bookmarks posted, top bookmarkers, tip of the day, and new users.

The Sharing and Storing Bookmarks and Knowledge features allow users the unique ability to share internal bookmarks, internal resources, and external resources internally, regardless of browser or machine. SBT is integrated with email and allows the user to email and bookmark at the same time, including simultaneous posting to "delicious" and SBT. Users can also import bookmarks from their browsers which are stored hierarchically and import their "delicious" bookmarks into the tool. SBT allows users to retrieve the top 15 "delicious" bookmarks on any given topic so that they can see those bookmarks side by side with the SBT bookmarks. Users can also click on a tag and see all the links for that tag. An integral part of sharing is the ability to search bookmarks whether by user or throughout the collection. Users can quickly search tags using Boolean operations. The developers have also enabled users to compare tags from two different people and see what bookmarks they have in common.

Another feature that is unique to SBT is the feed to the Finding Experts feature on the Intranet. SBT feeds the corporate expertise finder and enables users to utilize the tool as a way to find experts on particular topics. This can save time for employees seeking a specialist in a particular area and serves as a social, professional networking aide. SBT also has a built-in comment field which enables users to comment on the bookmarks of another user. Once a comment is made on a bookmark, the tool sends an email to the owner of the bookmark stating that another user has commented on their bookmark. This feature could stimulate conversation around a particular area of interest.

SBT also allows users the ability to set up Really Simply Syndication or Rich Site Summary (RSS) feeds of SBT bookmarks or related tags. Users can add feeds as filtered content to their personal website pages or have them directed to their Outlook inboxes. They can then retrieve the email links from their Inbox or search SBT for updates on the particular tags of interest. The RSS feed will automatically pull information on the tag or related tags selected by the users, which enables them to leverage all the other resources of users who have tagged their keyword of interest. Prior to the advent of SBT, the RSS capability was not available to users at RCX.

SBT also enables users to establish newsletters, maintain active links, access collections and create and maintain a visual repository space. Information stewards at RCX are using SBT for lightweight newsletter distribution. Users can subscribe to the feed based on a specific tag or they can set up the feed as a streaming newsletter to their SharePoint personal sites. Some users have access to special tags which are used to denote special RCX collections of bookmarks. This feature gives such users access to particular collections such as digital libraries, case studies, or technical reports. Lastly, some project groups have decided to use SBT as their virtual repository for all their pertinent bookmarks. They create special project-specific tags which they use to point to resources on the Internet or deliverables on their SharePoint site, in transfer folders, and on wikis. One particular project which heavily uses SBT has seven pages of bookmarks with bookmarks dating from the initial incorporation of SBT through 2009.

31.3.3 Data Collection and Analysis

In order to get a better understanding of the diffusion of SBT in RCX, a qualitative study was conducted at the company. The study consisted of in-depth interviews conducted by one of the authors of the study with 23 users of SBT. During the interviews, a series of semi-structured questions were asked concerning the motivation for the adoption of SBT, what users viewed as the benefits of adoption and the negative aspects of SBT, how they used the technology and their contributions to the process of development of the software, such as feedback they offered to the development team. Twenty of the users were either engineering/technical users or librarian/information managers users. The remaining three users were two managers who oversaw the project and a software development manager who is overseeing the full implementation of SBT. Using Rogers' categories for types of adopters and attributes of innovation (here designated as product-based factors of innovation diffusion – see Sect. 31.2 – Review of Literature), the interviews were coded and mapped against the categories in an effort to understand the trajectory of technology diffusion of SBT within RCX (See Table 31.1 – Exhibit A: Types of adopters and Table 31.2 – Exhibit B: Rogers' five factors of innovation diffusion). The three managers' responses were not categorized or coded. However, their remarks will be analyzed with respect to the managerial challenges they identified in implementing SBT within RCX.

As described in Sect. 31.2, Rogers plotted the types of users on a bell curve with most of the users falling into the "Early Adopter", i.e., those who adopt an innovation early on in its inception and "Late Majority" adopters, i.e., those who have contact with "Early Adopters" but are slower to accept the innovation and

Table 31.1 Exhibit A: Types of adopters (by user #)

	Technical/Engineer	Librarian/Information Manager
Innovator	2, 3, 18	1, 16, 20
Early Adopter	4, 6, 7, 10, 17, 18, 9, 5	8, 12, 14, 15, 19, 22
Early Majority		
Late Majority		
Laggard		

Table 31.2 Exhibit B: Rogers's five factors of innovation diffusion

	Relative advantage	Compatibility	Complexity	Trialability	Observability
Innovator – user 1	High				Low
Innovator – user 2	High		Low		Low
Innovator – user 3	High	Medium			
Innovator – user 16	High		Low		High
Innovator – user 18	Low			Low	
Innovator – user 20	High			Low	
Early ad – user 4	Medium		Low		
Early ad – user 5	Low		High		
Early ad – user 6	Medium		High	High	Low (negative)
Early ad – user 7	Medium				Low (negative)
Early ad – user 8	High		Medium	High	Low (negative)
Early ad – user 9	Medium		High		Low (negative)
Early ad – user 10	High		High	High	Medium
Early ad – user 12	Medium		Low		High
Early ad – user 14	High				
Early ad – user 15	High		Low		High
Early ad – user 17	Medium				Low (negative)
Early ad – user 19	High			High	High
Early ad – user 20	High				Low
Early ad – user 22			High		

essentially wait until the innovation has begun to proliferate in the organization. In contrast, the 20 non-managerial users who were interviewed, i.e., those who were either engineer/technical types or librarian/information manager types, the majority appeared to be either "Innovators" or "Early Adopters". The "Innovators" were those who were very early users of the technology and participated in pilots of SBT or were engaged in prototyping of the SBT. Of the six "Innovators", three were engineers while the other three were librarian/information manager users. Several of these users suggested that trying out this new technology was part of what they did, i.e., they were researchers who were constantly on the lookout for new technologies or ways of doing things or their job entailed working on developing new systems or applications for RCX. Thus for example, one user said:

> I went to a fast-track meeting, which is an internal RCX group that tries to do cross RCX identification of leading technologies that could be used in novel ways. So, I have belonged to it since it has started.... Someone talked about it in one of the meetings, I thought I should go be a user; I should go try the stuff. So I did and got started.

This group of "Innovators" were the pioneers in the initial use of SBT. They were joined by another group of users who fell into the category of "Early Adopters" but also exhibited characteristics of "Innovators" in that they became aware of the pilot project apparently long before many of their peers did and decided to adopt it. Thus one user indicated that he had been familiar with SBT for a number of years but was not one of the "Innovators" who initially developed the product. He was one of those who used it once it was up on a beta site. Another user in this group found out about SBT through a discussion with a colleague who pointed out that RCX was using a social bookmarking tool similar to "delicious". Another user in this group was aware of the product because she worked in the same division as some of the "Innovators". These users then did not necessarily consult with the "Innovators" in order to adopt the SBT but did adopt it before many others in the organization.

While the "Early Adopters" described above were in a sense self-motivated to try out SBT and began to use it because it was part of the general cadre of tools which were available, there were a number of "Early Adopters" who were explicitly directed by their management to use SBT in their work. Thus, many of these users were told to use the system or in one case, a user was hired to work on the technology. For example, one user who was a female librarian/information manager stated:

> I guess there was an announcement or it was asked of my group to use it and test it out. We are often to test out new technology; so I started to test it out and I've been using it... Initially, I was doing it because we were asked to do it.

It is interesting to note that the "Early Adopters" who were identified fell equally among the engineering types and the librarian users. Thus, it appears that early adoption had little to do with a person's training or job description.

Though the analysis of categories of adopters was initially useful, what seems more compelling given the type of data gleaned from these interviews, were the comments that mapped to the product-based factors that govern the rate of innovation diffusions, i.e., those factors that are intrinsic to the good or service being offered. These factors as described above include relative advantage, compatibility, complexity, trialability, and observability (See Sect. 31.2). Responses were coded on a spectrum of low, medium and high for each of the factors (See Table 31.2 – Exhibit B). Each one of the factors will be discussed below with respect to the innovator and the early adopter type of user. Based on this analysis, some conclusions will be drawn.

1. *Relative advantage* – This factor is often perceived as viewed as an economic benefit, that is, the innovation that replaces the older version leads to reduced costs, or other monetary benefits for the organization. However, relative advantage can also be viewed more abstractly, i.e., in terms of benefits such as greater productivity or efficiency [24]. For the "Innovators", the relative advantages of SBT were high with one exception. Most of the "Innovators" stated that the new product had provided more features or was more useful than the previous products used at RCX. For example, one of the librarian/information managers stated:

> I adopted it because it was much easier to use than the content management system. And it was, for me, a much quicker way of putting in, and managing the materials that I want to send out – particularly being able to use the feature to get into SharePoint using the RSS feature, which we do a lot of. We put various tags and feed them into various community share sites that I deal with. It was a no-brainer for me. In terms of the mechanics of it, it was just a one-stop shop to put the things in and to get it out to various areas that we need to.

Another innovator who was an engineer stated that SBT gave her a jump start on her research because she could see what others had posted and thus she could get a better understanding of what was going on in the community. Indeed, the aspect most cited by the "Innovators" was the ability of SBT to offer users at RCX a way of sharing information with each other internally. The 'reach' of the product was significant. Moreover, SBT was viewed by these users as a time saver, that is, they saw it as an efficient way to provide information company-wide through the generation of emails to everyone. In addition, all users had access to the public information being posted by everyone. While overwhelmingly, the "Innovators" viewed the relative advantage of SBT over other previous products, one of the "Innovators", an engineer, rated SBT as a poor substitute for external products which she found to be more useful:

> I've looked at "popular" bookmarks at RCX occasionally, but it really hasn't been providing that much value because most of the other popular bookmarks at RCX are ones that I already use. So, I've looked at things from a tagging perspective. I haven't found it a tremendous utility for SBT, to tell you the truth....The external public social bookmarking is helpful because I've got one place to put all my bookmarks and to categorize all of my reference information. And, I like that because I can go to any computer and pull up my bookmarks, and get to things ...and other people can find mine. But, from within RCX's perspective, I do not find the same utility.

With the "Early Adopters", the degree of relative advantage was medium or high. For those who viewed SBT with a high degree of relative advantage, the reasons cited were the same as the innovator group, that is ease of use, and features that made the product more useful than previous products they had tried out such as "delicious". Four out of the "Early Adopters" viewed SBT with a medium degree of relative advantage. These users all used other tools such as "delicious" for their bookmarking needs and did not use SBT very actively. Like the innovator who viewed the relative advantage of SBT as low, these users thought that SBT lacked the public accessibility that was necessary for making the product an optimal one.

2. *Compatibility* – This factor posits the degree to which a user views the innovation as compatible with his or her beliefs or previously adopted ideas. The factor of compatibility was only apparent in an interview with one of the "Innovators" who thought that SBT was more compatible with the need for the users in the company to have privacy regarding the information they amassed. This factor appeared to have the least influence on whether this sample of users at RCX was ready to adopt SBT into their business practices.

3. Complexity – This factor deals with the degree to which an innovation is perceived as being difficult or complex to use and therefore not easily adopted by users. Among the population of users interviewed, both "Innovators" and "Early Adopters", there was an even division between those who viewed SBT as having a low degree of complexity with those who viewed it with a high degree of complexity. Users who viewed SBT as having a low degree of complexity commented on how easy it was to use the product and also remarked on its convenience. These users were also the ones who perceived the relative advantage of

SBT over other products that were available. Users who viewed SBT as having a high degree of complexity cited the fact that SBT was a difficult product to understand and lacked features that would make it useful to a majority of the people at RCX. A key point brought up by an "Early Adopter" was that most people at RCX do not understand how to use the SBT or what bookmarking is. Thus, this user stated:

> I think most people when they first start using SBT, they don't really understand why they are tagging things; I don't think they understand that other people might be interested in the same thing they're interested in. They just look at it as a tool for themselves... I'm not sure they are really thinking that their bookmarks are going to be useful to somebody else. So the whole idea of tagging is new to lots of people. Maybe they even don't understand why they should be tagging. I don't think it's that they are being selfish; some of them just don't know.

4. *Trialability* – This factor posits the degree to which users experiment with the innovation. Clearly, the "Innovators" and "Early Adopters" who comprised the users who were interviewed were at the forefront of experimenting and using SBT. However, there were mixed views as to whether the general population at RCX was actually experimenting with the product. At least two of the "Innovators" suggested that the degree of trialability was low and accounted for the reason why SBT had not been adopted throughout the organization. One of the "Innovators" suggested that there were multiple tools used at RCX instead of people using just one set of tools. She stated that the adoption of SBT had been slow because people were simply not using the product in their jobs. Another innovator echoed these concerns:

> I don't know if there are any downfalls. Maybe not enough people know about it and actually use it. That could be a downfall. I don't know if that's just because they're just not aware of it or they don't see the applicability to the work they are doing. It's another place to put stuff. So, you have to go through the effort to put it there. And if you're not seeing value, if you're not saving time on the other end, you might not use it. So, it probably depends on what people's needs are.

On the other hand, many of the "Early Adopters" thought that users were experimenting with the product in the organization. One suggested that SBT was filling a need and observed that people were using SBT from time to time or at least trying it out. Another early adopter contended that some of SBT's features such as newsletters containing bookmarks have led to the adoption of SBT by many people because they subscribe to the newsletters and viewed them as a good source of information.

5. *Observability* – This factor is concerned with the degree to which people observe others using an innovation which in turn leads to them adopting the innovation. While one of the "Innovators" thought that there was a high degree of observability in the organization and several of the "Early Adopters" also thought that there was a high degree of observability, many of the "Early Adopters" thought that there was a low degree of observability and that this contributed significantly to the lack of diffusion of SBT throughout RCX. Thus, one user stated that SBT

would not be successful because there was not a critical mass using it which would get others in the organization to adopt the innovation:

> I suspect there's kind of a minimum mass that you need in order for these things to become successful-to be really successful. One of the reasons why "delicious" or Flickr is successful is that they have huge communities using them.

Another "Early Adopter" suggested that people simply did not know the tool existed who could benefit from adopting it:

> I'm not sure how many other people you've talked to, but I think you'll find that the tool, even though it's been around for quite a while now, it's still not known as widely as it could be in the company. So, therefore, I don't think it's been adopted nearly as much as it should be. I don't know that they are going to do to try to change that. But, I think that it's a good challenge for anyone who wants to undertake it because I think it's a really good tool and I think it's being under-utilized. I know that at the beginning they were not trying to roll it out too widely because they were still making changes on it, and they wanted to do it right. But, I think it's at a point now where it should be much more used, frankly.

Finally, and perhaps most significantly, the low degree of observability was tied by at least one "Early Adopter" to the fact that there are corporate stewards designated within the organization who were tasked with essentially populating SBT with links in order to spur people to use the tool. In effect, these corporate stewards conducted research for other people and then posted the bookmarks for others to use. Such a practice led many in RCX to have a negative view of SBT:

> While I see the reason they are doing it because it is a service to have people researching certain technologies and aggregating that somewhere where we can all get it, I feel that it kind of gets in the way and shows kind of like a false positive. Because, it tells me that this person is interested in a topic but they're really not. They are just researching it for other people. So there's no personal value to them.

The three managers who were responsible for the implementation of SBT within RCX provided some insights into the motivation for implementing SBT within the company and some of the obstacles that they saw which stood in the way of the adoption of the tool company-wide. According to these managers, the motivation for deploying the tool was to "displace SBT inside the firewall as a prototype to see if it had value." The managers knew that people were using tools such as "delicious" to bookmark information on the public Internet. Indeed, they viewed SBT as a complementary tool to other tools being used by employees such as wikis and other information gathering tools and thought that having a social bookmarking tool within the company's firewall would facilitate better sharing of information among company employees. However, as one manager pointed out, there are several optional tools in the company and there was clearly a need to find a way to integrate the tools so that they truly complemented each other in terms of functionality.

While the idea of implementing the tool seemed admirable, the managers recognized that there were many obstacles they would have to overcome. Despite all of the methods used for communicating the value of the product to the employees as described earlier in this paper and the assertion by one of the managers that "at least 48% of the company had at least looked at SBT", it was unclear to the project leader if "we've penetrated half of the corporation." This manager believed that communicating the value of SBT was the biggest obstacle to its penetration:

> I would say that the biggest obstacle has been trying to communicate with our end users in RCX what this product is because even today there are many, many people in RCX who don't...even say we have a social bookmarking capability. They don't know what social bookmarking is. It is such a new concept that even the word... to say the word has no meaning to people. And you could say... we tried saying things like "Oh, it's like delicious." Well, a large percent of people at RCX have never used or seen "delicious". So you can't assume everybody even knows the concept of some of these Web 2.0 tools. They don't. And, as you probably know just from being an RCX person, it's hard to know every IT tool and capability that's available.

A second obstacle according to this manager, was getting people to change their work practices and the culture of the company so that people would begin to use SBT rather than to email bookmarks around which has been the primary method of communication at RCX for several decades and is ingrained in the culture:

> One of the features we added to SBT was the ability to... when you're tagging something, we added a little checkbox that say "email this too." So, we were trying to make it so that at the same time you are bookmarking, you could also do your email because you know people breeze through email. So it was still a change; you had to bookmark first, open the bookmark form and email from there, and there's still lots and lots of people who don't think to do that.

Another manager echoed the notion that there was a cultural issue or perhaps a generational bias against using a social bookmarking tool within RCX.

In addition to these obstacles, one of the managers indicated that they did not hold managers accountable for having their staff use SBT since it is not a compulsory tool. Instead she suggested that it was more of a grass roots tool so that if people within the organization experimented with it and found that it worked for them, then such people would adopt the tool. Finally, two of the managers indicated that little thought had been given as to how to measure the success of the deployment of SBT. They had looked at some benchmarks for adoption but overall the management recognized that "it's very hard to measure the Return On Investment of knowledge management tools."

31.4 Discussion

This study used a subset of Rogers' theories of innovation diffusion to identify types of adopters as well as to gauge the factors that would influence the adoption of the innovation within RCX. The researchers recognize that the sample population, i.e., 23 interviewed users was small in comparison to the overall 6,000 potential users at the company and that this constitutes a significant limitation of the present study.

Nevertheless, there are some conclusions that can be drawn from this study which may be a starting point for further analysis in the area of technology adoption and diffusion.

After collecting the data in the form of interviews, the researchers attempted to categorize the respondents into the five types of adopters posited by Rogers and to plot them against the bell curve he developed. In fact, as was discussed in the previous section, the 20 users (excluding management) all fell into the "Innovator" or "Early Adopter" categories. This was unlike Rogers' categorization where the majority of users fell into the "Early Majority" and "Late Majority" categories. This result could have been because of the type of users who were interviewed who were not representative of the general population of users. However, more significantly, many of these users exhibited characteristics of both types of adopter. For example, some "Early Adopters" could be categorized as hybrid "Innovators/Early Adopters". This hybrid type of categorization led the researchers to conclude that these categories were not distinctive enough or applicable in this study and that another way to view the adopter categories was to plot them on a continuum where there could be overlap between the various types of adopters.

In trying to use Rogers' criteria for categorizing adopters into types, it was impossible to ignore the role that management had played in shaping the adoption of the product even by the so-called "Innovators". Thus, while the "Innovators" by their very nature wanted to try things out, they were not self-motivated, i.e., all of them had been invited to try out the pilot software in the context of their jobs. Clearly, from an early stage, management was involved in the diffusion process and had a hand in directing the Innovators to try out the new product even though these users suggested that they were all 'invited' rather than directed by management to use the product. For some of the "Early Adopters", the role of management was even more pronounced. Many of them admitted to using SBT not because of their own interest or motivation but because they were told by their management to adopt the technology. It is unclear from the interviews whether these "Early Adopters" would have tried out the technology on their own like their colleagues who were more self-motivated.

In analyzing the product-based factors influencing the adoption of the innovation in the company, there were also other factors that were identified which influenced the adoption and diffusion of SBT in RCX and extended the five suggested by Rogers. For example, the one factor that appeared to be significant among the users was relative advantage. Thus, SBT was perceived to have a high degree of relative advantage over previous content management products and clearly this would contribute to the diffusion of the innovation throughout RCX, especially since it provided a way to bookmark company resources without compromising the sensitivity of the information. However, the fact that some users, albeit a minority, viewed other products in the marketplace as being more 'user-friendly' indicates that a high degree of relative advantage is necessary but not the only factor in assuring diffusion of such an innovation in the organization. This is in keeping with the widely held view that relative advantage is a necessary but not sufficient product-based driver of innovation [24].

Indeed, with respect to relative advantage, it appears that management contributed to the perception that SBT did not have a high degree of relative advantage over previous products. For one thing, managers admitted to the monumental task of marketing SBT within the company and getting buy-in for its use among the employees. At RCX, managers employ various strategies for educating their subordinates about the plethora of available tool options. Some managers frequently discuss these tools at their group meetings, or email their team about the capabilities on the Intranet. Other managers are more committed to using the top tools used by the people in their teams and will utilize these tools in their projects as a way to promote them in their teams. But overall, there was no particular commitment to SBT versus another tool and thus the marketing of a tool such as SBT would be a fragmented effort which would compete with other tools used in the company.

The complexity of a product conceivably should play a role in the diffusion of an innovation in an organization. However, in this case, it is unclear whether the complexity (low or high) of the product as discussed above really influenced its diffusion through the organization. Indeed, one user remarked that the diffusion of SBT was linked in part to how the people in RCX were educated about SBT's value to them. While this is only one user, here too, one of Rogers' product-based factors appeared to be linked to a managerial issue, that of taking into account the need to educate the users about the value of the product for their work practices.

As described above, the trialability of SBT appeared to be low with the respondents indicating that they were unsure as to whether people were actually trying out the product. Aside from the users not knowing about it, the trialability factor could have been influenced by the lack of commitment by management to SBT. Indeed, the project team leader suggested that a commercial replacement was being considered for the company which would replace SBT. When the project prototype proposal was created, there were no existing commercial tool available for enterprise social bookmarking. However, since then, IBM has developed a social bookmarking tool named Dogear and the research team at RCX has had discussions with IBM about the use of the product. SBT may also lose one of its primary users, the newsletter creator, who may be switching to a commercial application for handling RSS feeds. In the commercial product, feeds and articles from other sources are automatically brought into one portal which then allows the users to select which ones they want to tag to create a feed. Once the Librarians set up a feed using the other commercial application, users would not have to go out to different resources to tag since everything would be in one central location thus obviating the use of SBT. Finally, the corporate intranet, where SBT is accessed, may undergo restructuring in the near future and allow users to access other kinds of social bookmarking tools along with SBT which would give users other options for information posting and gathering.

Along with the other factors that need to be taken into consideration when analyzing data with Rogers' constructs is the fact that Rogers conducted the majority of his research on technology adoption and diffusion in the years before the Internet was fully available to users. In his seminal work on the diffusion of innovations, Rogers briefly discusses communication within virtual organizations and computer literacy [44]. But he does not discuss the effect that the Internet would have on the diffusion of innovation and indeed, it might have been hard for him in 1995 to anticipate the evolution of this vast network which would link millions of users together and provide a platform for diffusing innovations on a global scale.

Three points bear thinking about with respect to the relationship of technology adoption and diffusion to the development of the Internet. One concerns the notion of network effect which suggests that the more users who use a product, the more valuable it becomes [39]. In the online environment where SBT was implemented, it is important to consider whether the network effect would influence the proliferation of an innovation such as social bookmarking as much as or more than a high degree of relative advantage or a low degree of complexity. In fact, one of the "Early Adopters" pointed out that SBT "has become more valuable as more people use it," an indication that the adoption of the tool gained credence as more people used it in the internal networked environment.

A second point is that while the managers who implemented SBT saw it as a tool that could fulfill the users' needs within the confines of the company firewall, many users had already been exposed to other tools such as "delicious" in the general online environment outside of the company. In fact, users at RCX were able to access public innovations from anywhere because of the Internet. This suggests that it is no longer possible to consider technology adoption and diffusion solely within the confines of a 'brick and mortar' company environment; rather the ability of users to tap into a global network of innovations is important to take into account when studying the diffusion of an innovation within a particular company. Finally, in their desire to make sure that SBT was being used in the company, managers endorsed the deliberate posting of bookmarks by research analysts/corporate stewards and claimed it was a useful way to get information out to people. Yet in this new networked environment, users are seen as an important source of innovation and creativity and therefore for an innovation to be successfully diffused, managers need to be in-sync with their employees and co-create with them rather than try to impose a particular tool and expect people to adopt it as the managers at RCX attempted to do.

Although limited in scope, the study at RCX provided some insights into the adoption and diffusion of a new kind of innovation, social bookmarking, in a research-based organization. Clearly, Rogers' constructs on types of adopters and factors of innovation diffusion are useful in analyzing how diffusion occurred in the organization. However, in light of the data that was generated, it is also clear that the role of management needs to be considered as a significant factor in studying technology adoption and diffusion. Further, the technological infrastructure, i.e., the Internet, which has been developed since Rogers' set forth his constructs, also needs to be considered in studying adoption of technologies within organizations. One area which was not addressed in the study concerns the role that users play in the diffusion process, that is, their role in providing valuable feedback and also using a technology such as SBT as a platform on which to innovate and create new products and services. The interviewees were asked about their contributions to the project but because of the scope of this study, such data was not considered and can be the basis of a further study about the development of SBT within RCX. Finally, it would be useful to conduct a follow-up study with a larger population at RCX in order to more fully understand the proliferation or lack of proliferation of SBT within the company.

References

1. R. Agarwal and J. Prasad, "The Role of Innovation Characteristics and Perceived Voluntariness in the Acceptance of Information Technologies," Decision Science, Vol. 28, No. 3, 1997, pp. 557–582.
2. I. Ajzen, "Attitude, Personality and Behavior," Milton Keynes, UK: Open University Press, 1988.
3. I. Ajzen, "The Theory of Planned Behavior," Organizational Behavior and Human Decision Processes, Vol. 50, 1991, pp. 179–211.
4. I. Ajzen, "Perceived Behavioral Control, Self-efficacy, Locus of Control, and the Theory of Planned Behavior," Journal of Applied Social Psychology, Vol. 32, No. 4, 2002, pp. 665–683.
5. I. Ajzen, "Constructing a TPB Questionnaire: Conceptual and Methodological Consideration," Retrieved April 1, 2009 from http://people.umass.edu/aizen/pdf/tpb.measurement.pdf, January 2006.
6. L. M. Applegate, "Business Transformation Self-assessment: Summary of Findings – 1992–93," Harvard Business School, Note 194–013, Cambridge, MA: Harvard Business School Press, 1995.
7. L. M. Applegate, "Managing in an Information Age: Organizational Challenges and Opportunities," Harvard Business School, Case #9–196–002, Cambridge, MA: Harvard Business School Press, 1995.
8. A. Bandura, "Self-efficacy: Toward a Unifying Theory of Behavioral Change," Psychological Review, Vol. 84, No. 2, 1977, pp. 191–215.
9. A. Bandura, "Self-Efficacy Mechanism in Human Agency," American Psychologist, Vol. 37, No. 2, 1982, pp. 122–147.
10. D. Bobek and R. Hatfield, "An Investigation of the Theory of Planned Behavior and the Role of Moral Obligation in Tax Compliance," Behavioral Research in Accounting, Vol. 15, 2003, pp. 13–38.
11. G. W. Bock, R. W. Zmud, Y. Kim, and J. Lee, "Behavioral Intention Formation in Knowledge Sharing: Examining the Roles of Extrinsic Motivators, Social-Psychological Forces, and Organizational Climate," MIS Quarterly, Vol. 29, No. 1, 2005, pp. 87–111.
12. T. Boone and R. Ganeshan, "Knowledge Acquisition and Transfer Among Engineers: Effects of Network Structure," Managerial and Decision Economics, Vol. 29, 2008, pp. 459–468.
13. M. G. Borrello, M. Morricone, A. Pedon, and P. Benevene, "Ethical Finance Between Saving and Investment," Paper presented at the 29th Annual Colloquium of the International Association for Economic Psychology/SABE-IAREP Conference, Philadelphia, USA, 2004.
14. K. M. Chang, "Predicting Unethical Behavior: A Comparison of the Theory of Reasoned Action and the Theory of Planned Behavior," Journal of Business Ethics, Vol. 17, No. 16, 1998, pp. 1825–1834.
15. A. L. Christensen and M. M. Eining, "Factors Influencing Software Piracy: Implications for Accountants," Journal of Information Systems, Vol. 5, No. 1, 1991, pp. 67–80.
16. D. R. Compeau and C. Higgins, "Computer Self-Efficacy: Development of a Measure and Initial Test," MIS Quarterly, Vol. 19, No. 2, 1995, pp. 189–211.
17. R. Cross and L. Prusak, "The People Who Make Organizations Go-Or Stop," Harvard Business Review, Cambridge, MA: Harvard Business School Press, 2002.
18. A. D'Astous, F. Colbert, and D. Montpetit, "Music Piracy on the Web – How Effective Are Anti-Piracy Arguments? Evidence from the Theory of Planned Behavior," Journal of Consumer Policy, Vol. 28, 2005, pp. 289–310.
19. F. D. Davis, "Perceived Usefulness, Perceived Ease of Use, and User Acceptance of Information Technology," MIS Quarterly, Vol. 13, No. 3, 1989, pp. 319–340.
20. M. Eisend and P. Schuchert-Guller, "Explaining Counterfeit Purchase," Academy of Marketing Science, Vol. 12, 2006, pp. 1–22.
21. M. Fishbein and I. Ajzen, "Belief, Attitude, Intention and Behavior: An Introduction to Theory and Research," Reading, MA: Addison-Wesley, 1975.

22. C. Freeman and L. Soete, "The Economics of Industrial Innovation," Cambridge, MA: MIT Press, 1999.
23. R. Gagliardi and D. Compeau, "The Effect of Group Presentations on Intentions to Adopt Smart Card Technology: A diffusion of Innovations Approach," Proceedings of the Administrative Sciences Association of Canada 23rd Conference ASAC, Vol. 16, No. 4, 1995.
24. J. T. Gourville, "Note on Innovation Diffusion: Rogers' Five Factors," Case #9–505–075, Cambridge, MA: Harvard Business School Press, 2006.
25. G. Greenfield and F. Rohde, "Technology Acceptance: Not all Organizations or Workers May Be the Same," International Journal of Accounting Information Systems, Vol. 10, No. 4, December 2009, pp. 263–272.
26. S. Hemlin, "Creative Knowledge Environments: An Interview Study with Group Members and Group Leaders of University and Industry R&D Groups in Biotechnology," Creativity and Innovation Management, Vol. 18, No. 4, 2009, pp. 278–285.
27. S. Hinkle, "Grassroots Political Action as an Inter-group Phenomenon," Journal of Social Issues, Vol. 52, No. 1, 1996, pp. 39–52.
28. W. Hong, J. Thong, W. Wong, and K. Tam, "Determinants of User Acceptance of Digital Libraries: An Empirical Examination of Individual Differences and Systems Characteristics," Journal of Management Information Systems, Vol. 18, No. 3, Winter 2001–2002, pp. 97–124.
29. E. Karahanna, D. W. Straub, and N. L. Chervany, "Information Technology Adoption Across Time: A Cross-Sectional Comparison of Pre-Adoption and Post-Adoption Beliefs," MIS Quarterly, Vol. 23, No. 2, 1999, pp. 183–213.
30. N. B. Kurland, "Ethical Intentions and the Theories of Reasoned Action and Planned Behavior," Journal of Applied Social Psychology, Vol. 25, No. 4, 1995, pp. 297–313.
31. N. B. Kurland, "Sale Agents and Clients: Ethics, Incentives, and a Modified Theory of Planned Behavior," Human Relations, Vol. 49, No. 1, 1996, pp. 51–75.
32. T. Lee, "Nurses' Adoption of Technology: Application of Rogers' Innovation-Diffusion Model" Applied Nursing Research, Vol. 17, No. 4, 2004, pp. 231–238.
33. K. Mathieson, "Predicting User Intentions: Comparing the Technology Acceptance Model with the Theory of Planned Behavior," Information Systems Research, Vol. 2, No. 3, September 1991, pp. 173–192.
34. G. C. Moore and I. Benbasat, "Development of an Instrument to Measure the Perceptions of Adopting an Information Technology Innovation," Information Systems Research, Vol. 2, No. 3, 1991, pp. 192–222.
35. M. N. Nguyen, "Regular Exercise in 30-to-60 Year Old Men: Combining the Stages-of-Change Model and the Theory of Planned Behavior to Identify Determinants for Targeting Heart Health Interventions," Journal of Community Health, Vol. 22, No. 4, 1997, pp. 233–247.
36. M. Parthasarathy and R. A. Mittelstaedt, "Illegal Adoption of a New Product: A Model of Software Piracy Behavior," in Advances in Consumer Research 22, Eds., F. R. Kardes and M. S. Provo, Provo, UT: Association for Consumer Research, 1995, pp. 693–698.
37. E. Penrose, "The Theory of the Growth of the Firm," New York: Oxford University Press, 1959.
38. C. R. Plouffe, J. S. Hulland, and M. Vandenbosch, "Richness Versus Parsimony in Modeling Technology Adoption Decisions – Understanding Merchant Adoption of a Smart Card-Based Payment System," Information Systems Research, Vol. 12, No. 2, 2001, pp. 208–222.
39. M. Porter, "Strategy and the Internet," Harvard Business Review, Cambridge, MA: Harvard Business School Press, 2001, pp. 63–78.
40. C. K. Prahalad, "The Role of Core Competencies in the Corporation" in Managing Strategic Innovation and Change, M. Tushman and P. Anderson, Eds., New York: Oxford University Press, 1997.
41. D. Robey, "User Attitudes and Management Information Systems Use," Academy of Management Journal, Vol. 22, No. 3, 1979, pp. 527–538.
42. E. Rogers, "Diffusion of Innovations," New York: The Free Press, 1962.
43. E. Rogers, "Diffusion of Innovations (3rd Edition)," New York: The Free Press, 1983.
44. E. Rogers, "Diffusion of Innovations, (4th Edition)," New York: The Free Press, 1995.

45. E. Rogers, "Diffusion of Preventive Innovations," Addictive Behaviors, Vol. 27, 2002, pp. 989–993.
46. D. B. Schifter and I. Ajzen, "Intention, Perceived Control and Weight Loss: An Application of the Theory of Planned Behavior," Journal of Personality and Social Psychology, Vol. 49, 1985, pp. 843–851.
47. C. B. Schoonhoven and M. Jelinek, "Dynamic Tension in Innovative, High Technology Companies: Managing Rapid Technological Change Through Organizational Structure," in "Managing Strategic Innovation and Change," M. Tushman and P. Anderson, Eds., New York: Oxford University Press, 1997.
48. H. Shih, "Extended Technology Acceptance Model of Internet Utilization Behavior," Information & Management, Vol. 41, No. 6, 2004, pp. 719–725.
49. B. Szajna, "Empirical Evaluation of the Revised Technology Acceptance Model," Management Science, Vol. 42, No. 1, 1996, pp. 85–92.
50. S. Taylor and P. A. Todd, "Assessing IT Usage: The Role of Prior Experience," MIS Quarterly, Vol. 19, No. 2, 1995, pp. 561–570.
51. D. J. Teece, "Design Issues for Innovative Companies: Bureaucracy, Incentives and Industrial Structure," in "The Dynamic Company: The Role of Technology, Strategy, Organization and Regions," A. Chandler, Jr., P. Hagstrom, and O. Solvell, Eds., New York: Oxford University Press, 1998.
52. V. Venkatesh, "Creation of Favorable User Perceptions Exploring the Role of Intrinsic Motivations," MIS Quarterly, Vol. 23, No. 2, 1999, pp. 239–260.
53. V. Venkatesh, M. G. Morris, G. B. Davis, and F. D. Davis, "User Acceptance of Information Technology: Toward a Unified View," MIS Quarterly, Vol. 27, No. 3, 2003, pp. 425–478.
54. V. H. Vroom, "Work and Motivation," New York: Wiley, 1964.
55. O.E. Williamson, "Markets and Hierarchies," New York: The Free Press, 1975.
56. D. J. Woolley and M. M. Eining, "Software Piracy Among Accounting Students: A Longitudinal Comparison of Changes and Sensitivity," Journal of Information Systems, Vol. 20, No. 1, 2006, pp. 49–63.
57. A. K. Yarbrough and T. B. Smith, "Technology Acceptance Among Physicians: A New Take on TAM," Medical Care Research and Review, Vol. 64, No. 6, 2007, pp. 650–672.

Index

A

Accessible software, 410
Actor, 3–6, 9, 10, 12–16, 18, 19, 117, 155, 165, 169, 170, 227, 228, 296, 384, 520, 523, 528, 529, 542, 575, 585–587, 595, 596, 612–615, 618, 619, 621, 622, 624–631, 633, 643, 644, 646, 647
Agglomerative hierarchical clustering, 125–126
Authority ranking, 45–51, 53, 55, 56
Average path length, 588, 599

B

Betweenness centrality, 14, 139, 140, 523, 531, 553–554, 588, 589, 639, 643
Blind people, 411
Blog, 4, 59, 101, 130, 205, 241, 281, 303, 350, 379, 412, 442, 474, 501, 576, 585, 611, 637, 651

C

Cellular phone service, 24, 25, 38
Centrality, 12, 45, 128, 156, 169, 186, 273, 332, 429, 452, 523, 551, 579, 588, 615, 639
Clique, 12, 15, 17, 129, 169, 270, 274, 335, 337, 454, 455, 621, 628, 633, 639, 645
Closed-caption news,
Closeness centrality, 14, 15, 139, 531, 553, 588, 589, 639, 643
Cluster analysis, 121, 122
Clustering, 117, 154, 201, 229, 271, 282, 304, 331, 388, 429, 589, 613
Clustering coefficient, 117, 118, 154–156, 209, 336, 589, 599, 600
Collaborative filtering, 236, 269, 317–329, 367, 471, 472

Commercial, 19, 95–112, 119, 120, 213, 246, 265, 295, 296, 318, 356, 358, 423, 440, 498–500, 520, 571, 707
Community discovery, 380–384, 391, 398, 400, 406
Community dynamics, 390, 405
Community mining, 171, 331–338, 340, 342
Complete/whole network, 5, 14–16, 208, 272, 369, 480, 538, 542, 564, 616, 617, 644
Component size, 206, 588, 590, 669
Content-centric visualization, 607, 608
Context-awareness, 429–431

D

Deaf people, 411
Degree centrality, 14, 138, 139, 523, 538, 551–552, 588–589, 639, 644
Density, 12, 13, 36, 38, 87, 88, 117, 152, 156, 159, 333, 439, 458, 487, 588, 589, 645–647
Diffusion, 17, 59, 186, 269, 643, 691
Digital library, 245
Directed graph, 6, 7, 38, 81, 127, 133, 170, 172, 174, 175, 385, 449, 454, 457, 462–463, 482, 588, 619
Disability, 409
Distance, 13–14, 71, 72, 75, 117, 123, 127, 130, 132, 150, 154, 162, 213, 229, 232, 252, 270, 308, 310, 317, 320, 321, 362, 374, 382, 387, 388, 390, 405, 435–437, 450, 455, 456, 523, 525–527, 531, 553, 554, 586, 588, 628, 639, 657, 658
Dynamic networks, 343–344, 381, 391, 396, 405, 646

E

Efficiency, 14, 50, 67, 201, 202, 209, 245, 334, 361, 371, 411, 526, 528, 640, 641, 701

B. Furht (ed.), *Handbook of Social Network Technologies and Applications*,
DOI 10.1007/978-1-4419-7142-5, © Springer Science+Business Media, LLC 2010

Ego network, 5–7, 13, 15–17, 153, 646
Elderly people, 410, 411
Entertainment, 91, 96, 110, 281, 300, 409,
        423, 427, 430, 637, 642, 653, 676
Everett Rogers, 692, 695

F
FACEBOOK, 45, 55, 59, 63–65, 80, 81, 102,
        107, 130, 251, 253, 255, 259, 260, 263,
        281, 349, 350, 357, 362, 379–381, 406,
        409, 411–415, 418, 420–423, 438, 441,
        447, 471, 473, 475, 476, 498, 499, 571,
        572, 575, 585, 604–606, 611, 651
Face name association,
FacetNet, 382, 383, 391, 393, 395, 396, 405
Factorization, contact recommendations, 46
Film, 16, 95, 98–99, 103, 158, 295, 298
Focus context, 45
Force-directed, 590, 591, 605, 624
FP-tree, 602, 603

G
Graph mining, 209, 381
Graph theory, 3, 13, 19, 116, 117, 171, 332,
        335, 448, 450, 523, 587–588, 639
Guideline, 410, 411, 415–417, 419–422, 570,
        580

H
Handicapped user, 410
Hearing impaired people, 411
Heuristics, 53, 57, 95, 96, 103, 108, 109, 111,
        166, 235, 237, 352, 664, 685, 686
Hierarchical clustering, 125–128, 236, 271,
        273
Human behavior, 4, 12, 91, 132, 427–444
Human-computer-interaction (HCI), 586, 608,
        621
Hybrid visualization, 607, 608, 630
Hyperbolic tree, 592
Hyperlink-induced topic search (HITS),
        47–51, 55, 56, 102, 133, 134, 211, 332,
        335, 336, 381, 391, 396, 585, 588, 645

I
Influence, 3, 54, 102, 117, 150, 170, 186, 224,
        244, 294, 352, 379, 429, 471, 519, 526,
        550, 640, 651, 693
Information and communication technologies
        (ICTs), 17, 18, 117

Information sharing, 12, 250, 261, 269, 640,
        641, 697
Innovation, 17, 55, 60, 64, 79, 81, 351, 428,
        434–435, 640, 641, 646, 691–693, 695,
        696, 699–708

K
Knowledge inference, 429, 435

L
Latent semantics, 202, 304, 306, 309, 404
Length, 6, 13, 18, 180, 182, 199, 209, 255,
        256, 291, 367, 380, 387, 388, 401–403,
        450, 452, 453, 462, 465, 530, 556, 588,
        599, 600, 624, 677, 678
Links, 3, 24, 48, 64, 98, 116, 169, 185, 227,
        247, 286, 331, 352, 381, 411, 438, 452,
        498, 528, 552, 569, 589, 612, 638, 657,
        692,
Log file analysis, 116, 119–121

M
Mainstream users, 411, 420
Managerial, 692, 696, 699, 700, 707
Marketing, 11, 24, 30, 37, 102, 122, 185, 203,
        204, 206, 207, 237, 415, 429, 440, 447,
        499, 500, 516, 527, 642, 651–654,
        656–658, 661, 664, 670, 674, 679,
        683–685, 697, 707
Memorability, 411
Memory-based methods, 317–321
MetaFac, 382, 383, 404, 406
Multidimensional scaling (MDS), 124, 586
Multi-relational mining, 382
Music, 55, 65, 80, 96, 98, 102–104, 108, 109,
        130, 236, 262, 281, 282, 284, 289,
        294–296, 299, 300, 355, 412, 505, 637,
        676
Mutual awareness, 382–387, 390, 392
MySpace, 63, 79, 96, 97, 102, 106, 130, 251,
        255, 263, 282, 411–413, 418–423, 471,
        473, 475, 476, 499

N
Nearest neighborhood algorithm, 318
NETMINER, 18, 19, 116, 275
Network, 3, 23, 45, 59, 95, 115, 147, 169, 185,
        223, 241, 269, 281, 303, 317, 331, 349,
        379, 409, 427, 447, 471, 497, 523, 549,
        569, 585, 611, 637, 651, 692

News video face,
Node, 3, 24, 47, 59, 100, 116, 150, 170, 202,
    227, 255, 331, 352, 385, 429, 448, 478,
    506, 523, 551, 585, 612, 639, 655
Node degree, 28, 30, 36, 38, 39, 551, 587–588
Node density, 588
Node-edge diagram, 590–593

O
One mode network, 16, 148, 164
Operability, 247, 411, 509
Operable, 416, 421
Organizational, 19, 80–82, 91, 131, 132, 242,
    264, 265, 397, 506, 529, 640–641, 691,
    692

P
PageRank, 47, 55, 56, 133, 134, 211, 381, 391,
    396, 477, 478, 529, 585, 588, 645, 657
PAJEK, 18, 19, 116, 275
PARAFAC, 49–51, 53, 54, 408
Partitional clustering, 123, 124
Path, 6, 56, 117, 170, 205, 249, 273, 336, 351,
    388, 412, 437, 449, 479, 523, 553, 588,
    622, 668
Path length, 13–14, 180, 182, 209, 388, 588,
    599, 600, 677
People with cognitive problems, 411
People with mobility and movement problems,
    411
Perceivable, 416, 420, 421
Perceptibility, 411
Personalization, 56, 226, 236, 237, 428, 434,
    435
Power law, 23, 24, 26, 27, 31, 32, 40, 343, 551,
    614, 667, 668
Principal component analysis, 10, 124, 125,
    130
Privacy, 54, 199, 242, 350, 428, 478, 497, 556,
    570, 658, 702

R
Radial tree, 592
Reality mining, 237, 428
Recommender system, 188, 317–321, 324,
    326, 327, 329, 471, 642, 657
Robust, 50, 61, 82, 147, 148, 155, 164, 202,
    237, 265, 352, 354, 369, 372–374, 411,
    417, 422, 493, 691

S
Scale-free network, 31, 667
Semantic web, 45, 227, 229, 340, 342, 362,
    478, 595, 608
Similarity, 56, 123, 154, 204, 228, 270, 300,
    317, 366, 389, 429, 493, 513, 615, 639,
    655
Singular value decomposition, 49, 124
Six degree of separation, 585
Small-world network, 608, 614, 630
Social actor, 3–6, 10, 12, 15, 16, 18
Social bookmarking, 65, 130, 368, 691–708
Social capital, 11, 18, 185, 189
Sociality, 587, 594, 607
Social media, 54, 55, 59, 62, 63, 65, 68,
    79–81, 285, 300, 379–381, 383,
    396–400, 403, 405, 406, 443
Social network, 3, 23, 45, 59, 95, 115, 147,
    169, 185, 223, 241, 269, 281, 303, 331,
    349, 379, 409, 427, 447, 471, 497, 523,
    549, 569, 585, 611, 637, 651
Social network analysis (SNA), 3–20, 59, 83,
    116–123, 129–134, 147–166, 169, 171,
    182, 186, 201, 203–204, 209, 216, 275,
    331, 337, 342, 381, 391, 429, 448, 451,
    526–531, 587–589, 594, 595, 600, 608,
    612, 613, 615, 621, 627, 628, 637–648
Social networking service (SNS), 4, 24, 32–37,
    212, 213, 349, 350, 352, 353, 357, 360,
    362, 374, 498, 499, 507, 520, 646
Social networks, quantitative analysis, 9, 96,
    100–111
Social structure, 3, 4, 9, 11, 15, 18, 117, 129,
    132, 153, 164, 169, 173, 594, 597, 637,
    639
Social tagging, 285, 353, 657
SocialWeb, 48, 56, 410
Sociogram, 586, 587, 639
Special needs user, 420
Spectral clustering, 127, 135, 136, 138, 140
STOCNET, 18
Structural hole, 11, 18
STRUCTURE, 18, 19

T
Technical robustness, 411
Technology Acceptance Model (TAM),
    692–695
Technology adoption, 691–708
Tensor, 45–57, 382, 383, 397–404, 406

Tie, 3–5, 8, 11–14, 16–18, 59, 61, 65, 100,
     110, 117, 135, 188, 190, 206, 208, 209,
     227, 283, 353, 384, 396, 405, 473, 589,
     611, 647
Traffic, 23–32, 38, 42, 102, 131, 261, 412, 443,
     510, 549, 550, 555, 556, 558, 566, 644
Twitter, 45–48, 52, 54, 55, 59, 64, 80–84, 87,
     90, 350, 368, 369, 379, 380, 475, 572,
     579, 585, 604, 651
Two mode network, 5, 15, 16

U
UCINET, 18
Understandability, 411
Understandable, 121, 229, 235, 265, 416, 421,
     451, 455, 458

Undirected graph, 6, 127, 449, 454, 457, 462,
     463, 588
Usability standard, 410
User-centric, 249, 250, 258, 260, 283, 428,
     434, 595, 607
User-centric visualization, 607, 608

V
Visually impaired people, 411

W
Web 2.0 service, 594, 604–607
Web Content Accessibility Guidelines, 415